N.Y. 2008.

Julia.
enjoy the range
of DINERS...
much love
Richard

ZIPPY ANNUAL 4

THE ZIPPY ANNUAL

October 2002 – October 2003

Bill Griffith • Fantagraphics Books

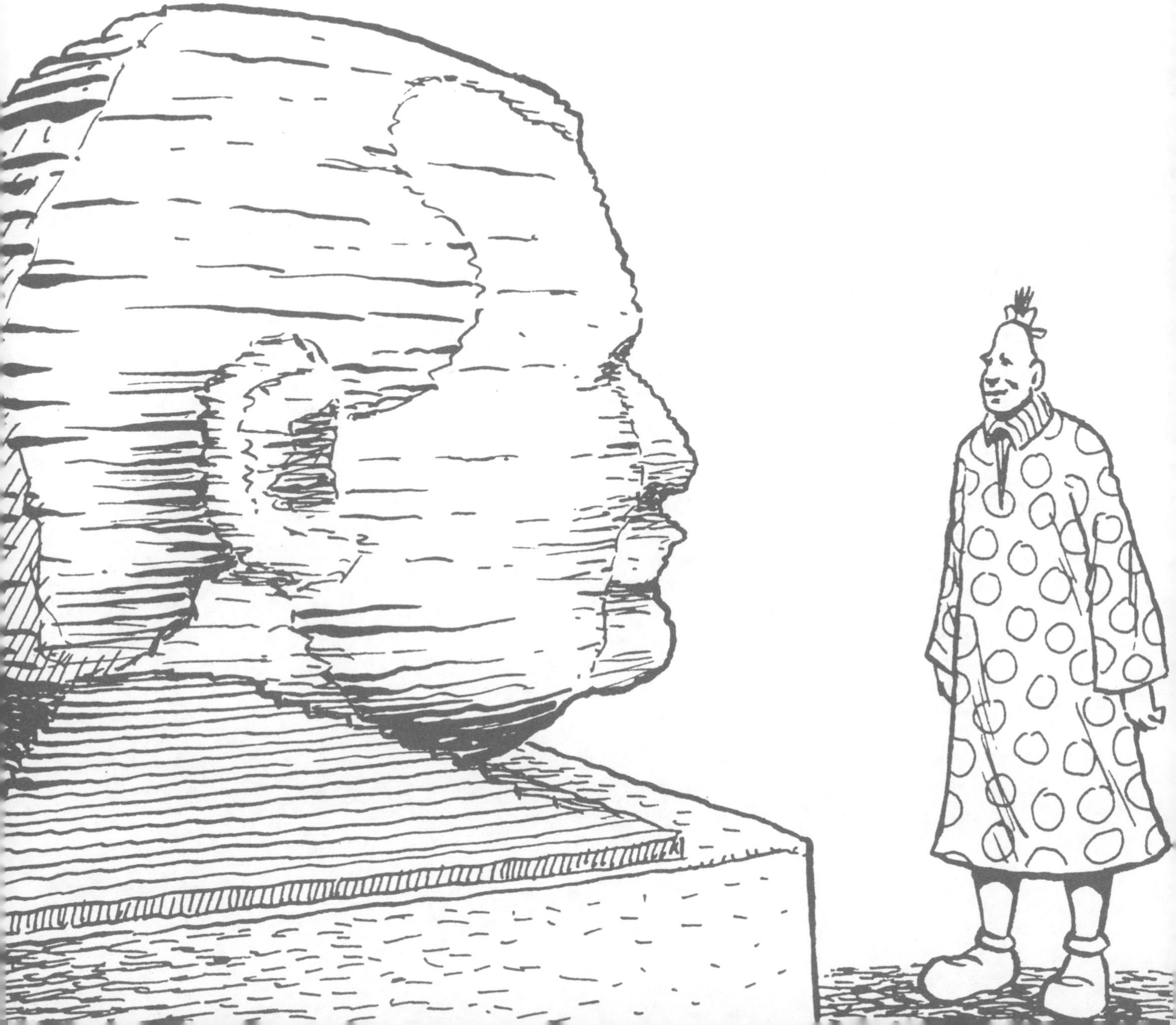

ZIPPY ANNUAL 2003
Volume 4

FANTAGRAPHICS BOOKS

7563 Lake City Way NE, Seattle WA 98115
www.fantagraphics.com
Call 1-800-657-1100 for a full color catalog of fine comics publications.

First Edition: November 2003
Designed by Bill Griffith
Production managed by Kim Thompson
Production by Paul Baresh
Cover Production by Carrie Whitney
Published by Gary Groth and Kim Thompson

Printed in Canada
ISBN: 1-56097-563-6

The comic strips in this book have appeared in newspapers in the United States and abroad, distributed by King Features Syndicate, 888 7th Avenue, NY NY 10019 : www.kingfeatures.com

For more on Zippy (and lots of added features, including the new "Zippy Storefront"), visit: www.zippythepinhead.com

Thanks and a tip o' th' pin to: Diane Noomin, Jay Kennedy, American Color, Gary Groth, Kim Thompson, intern Kristin Griffin and all the roadside field researchers who sent in so many great photos. Special thanks again to Georgiana Goodwin (www.ggdllc.com).

Books by Bill Griffith:
Zippy Stories • Nation of Pinheads • Pointed Behavior
Pindemonium • Are We Having Fun Yet? • Kingpin
Pinhead's Progress • Get Me A Table Without Flies, Harry
From A To Zippy • Zippy's House of Fun • Zippy Quarterly
Griffith Observatory • Zippy Annual #1 • Zippy Annual 2001
Zippy Annual 2002

To contact Bill Griffith:
Pinhead Productions, LLC
P.O. Box 88, Hadlyme CT 06439
Griffy@zippythepinhead.com

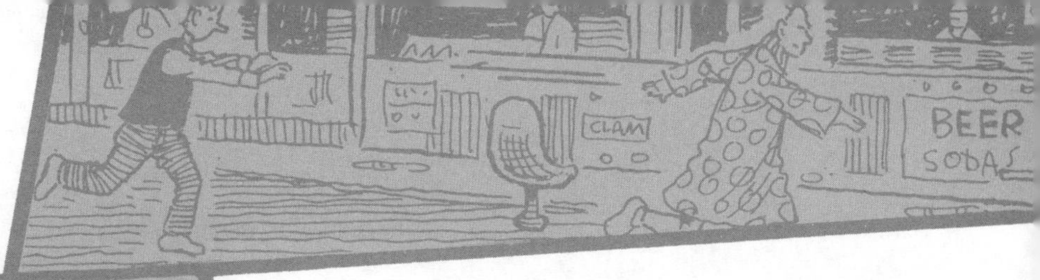

CLAM
BEER
SODAS

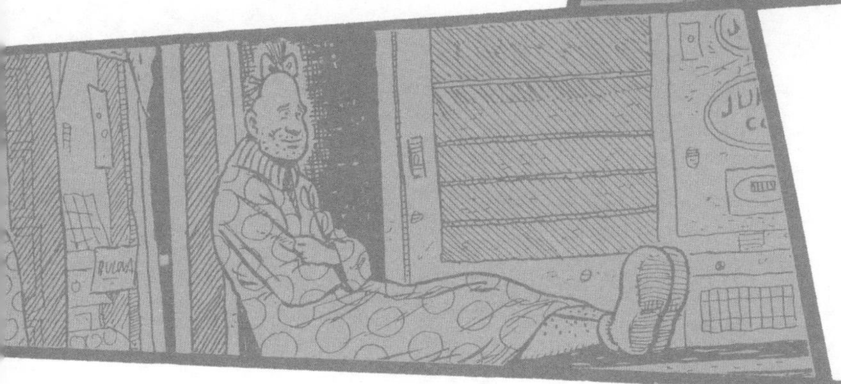

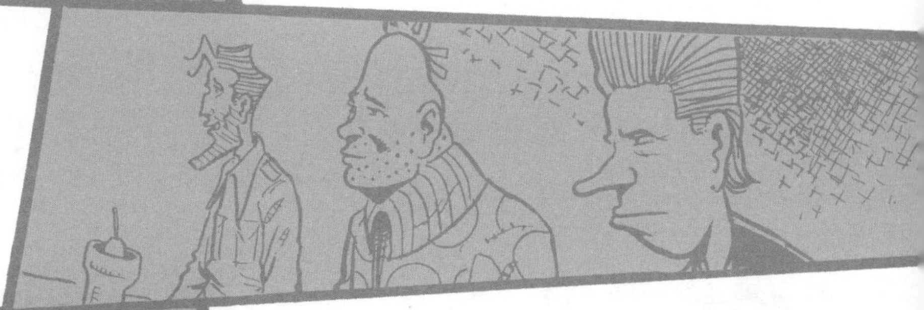

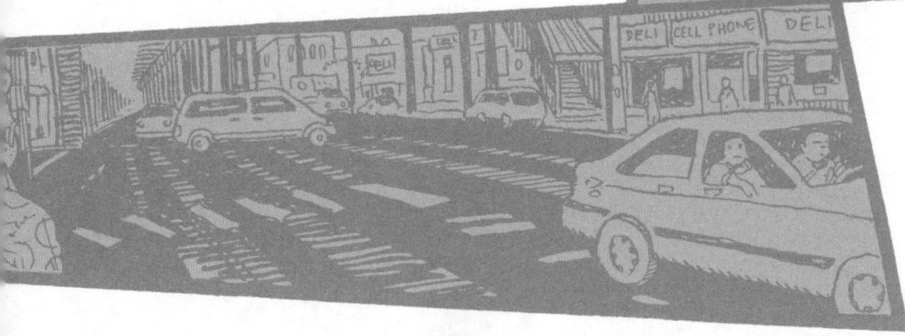

DELI
CELL PHONE
DELI

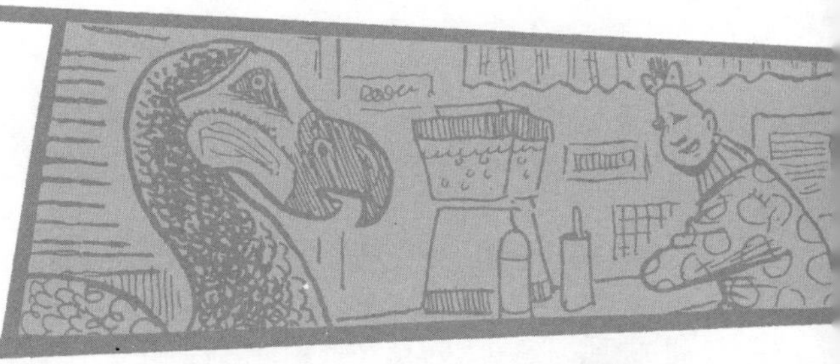

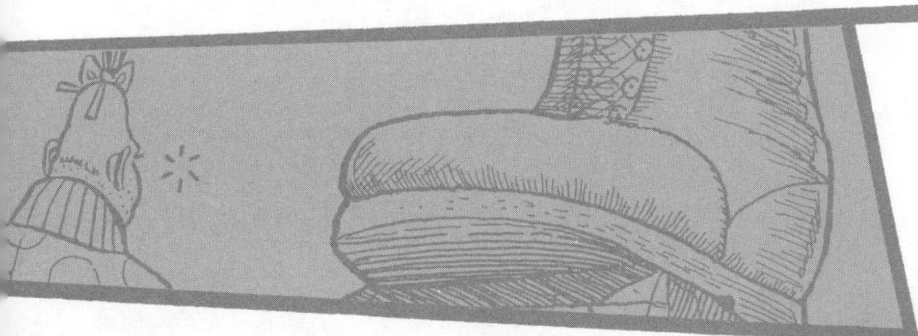

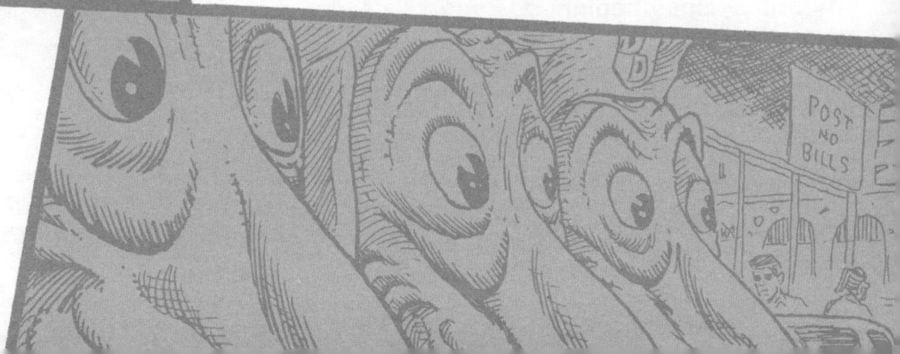

POST NO BILLS

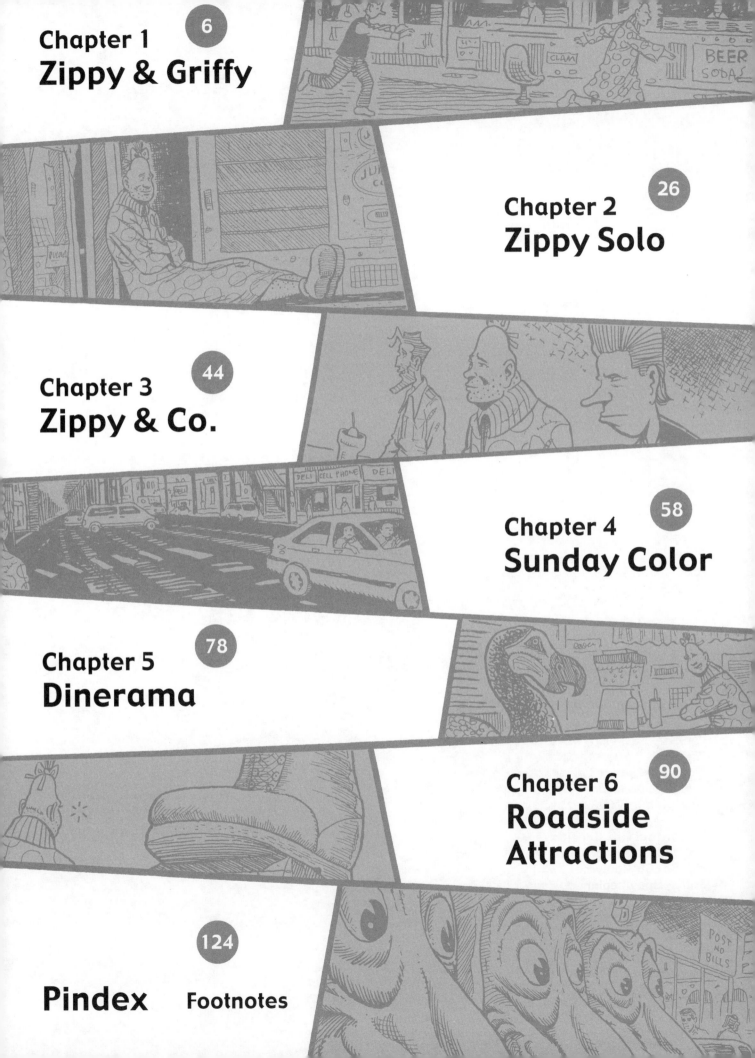

Zippy & Griffy

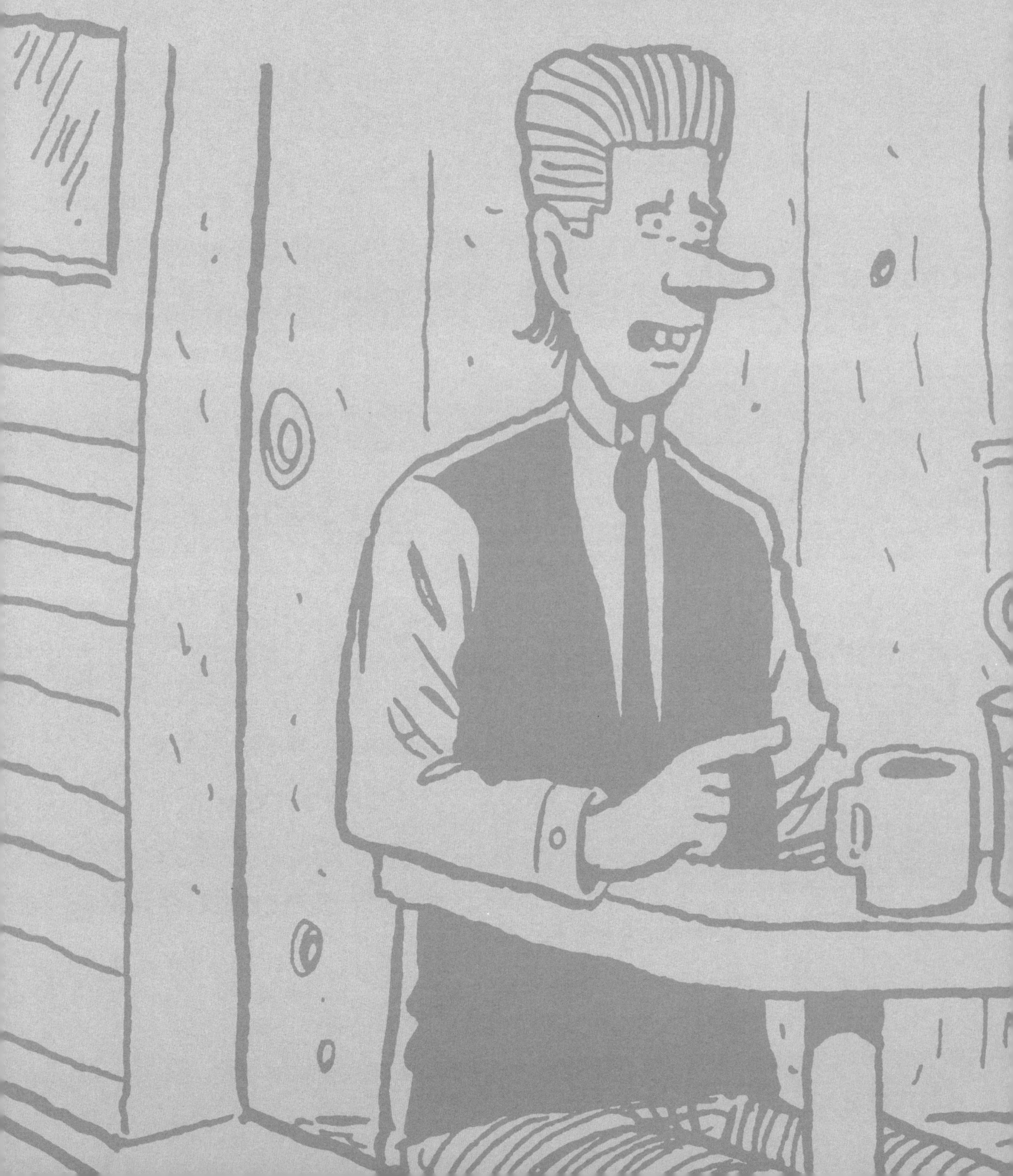

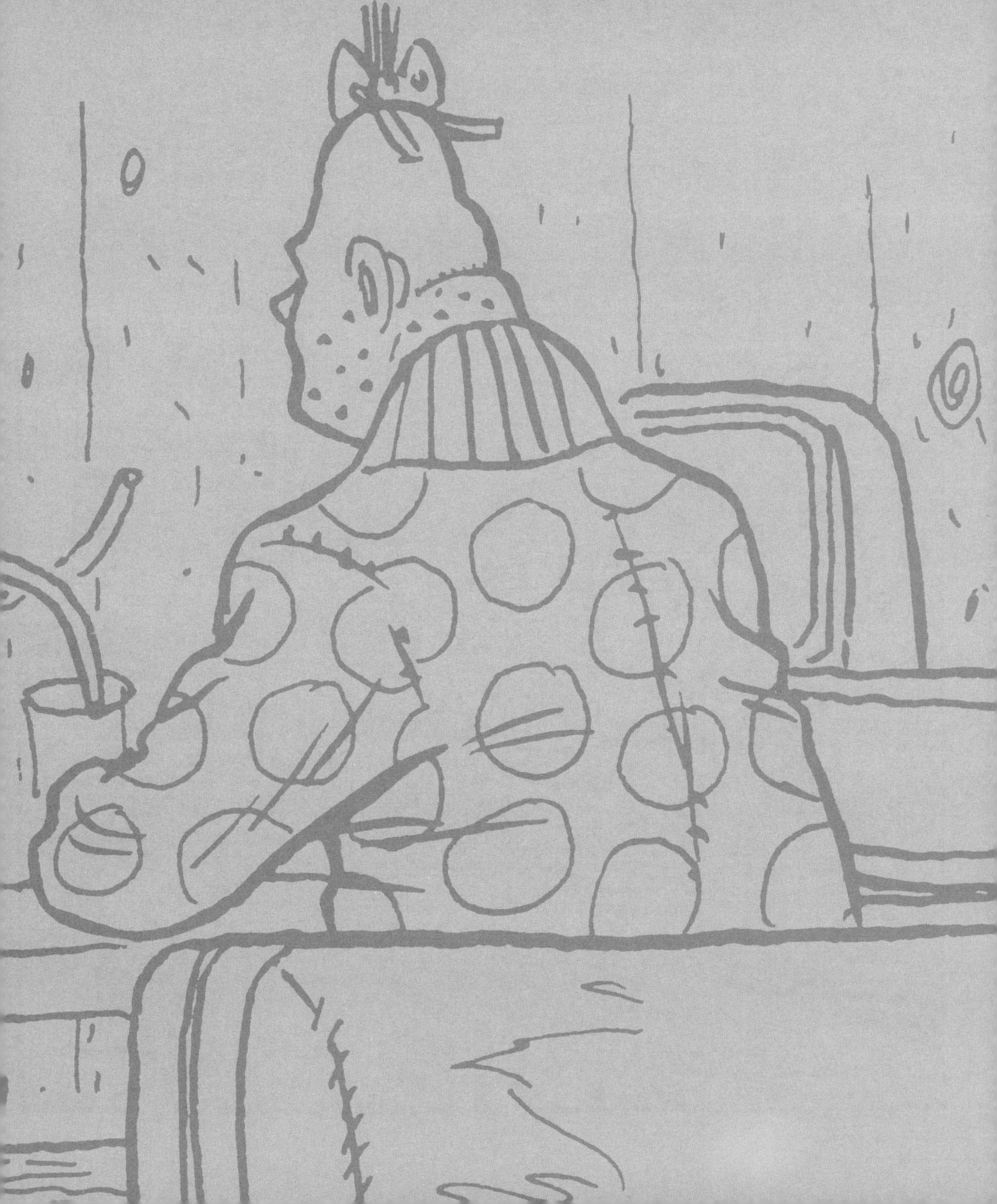

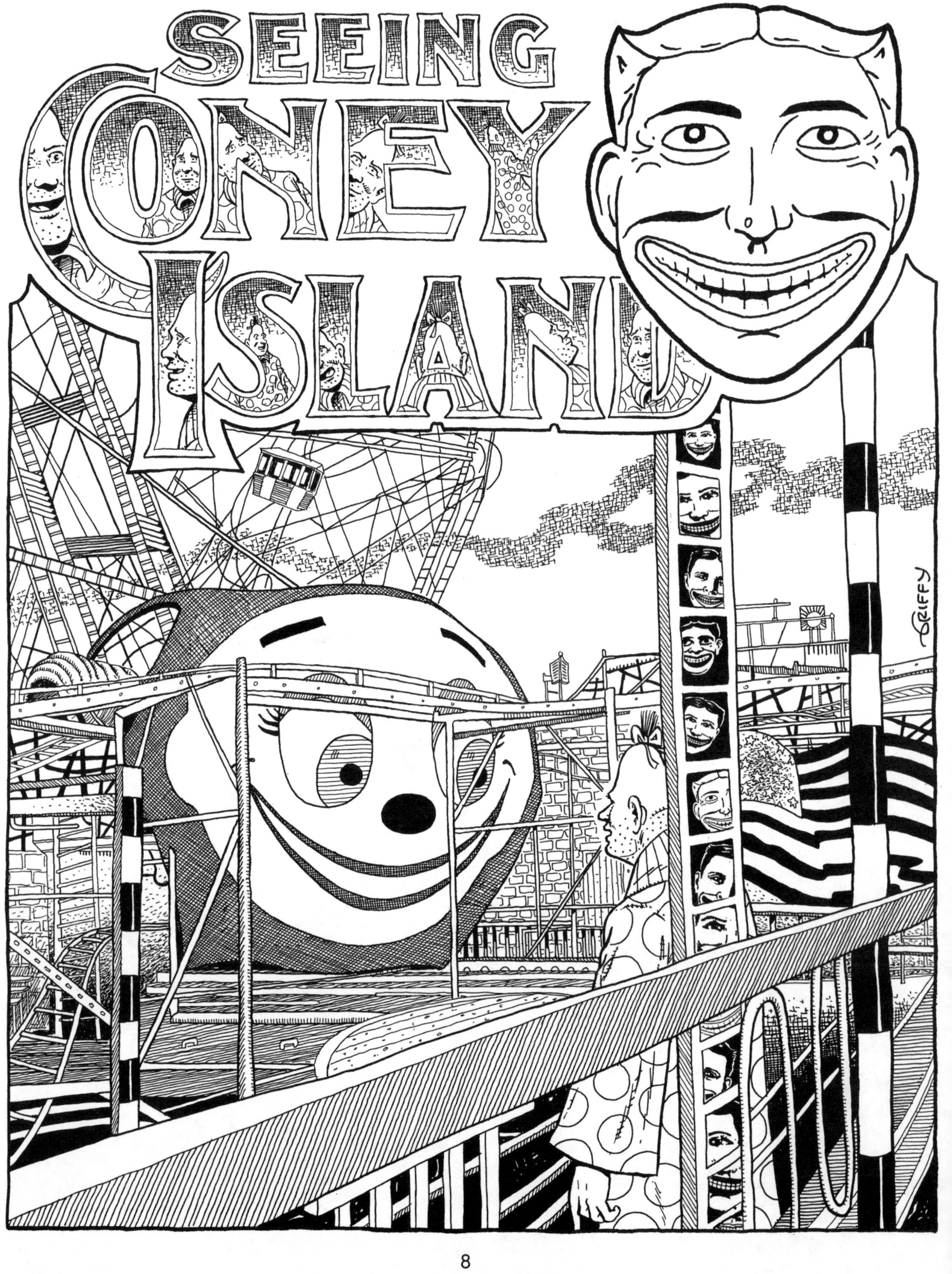
SEEING CONEY ISLAND
GRIFFY

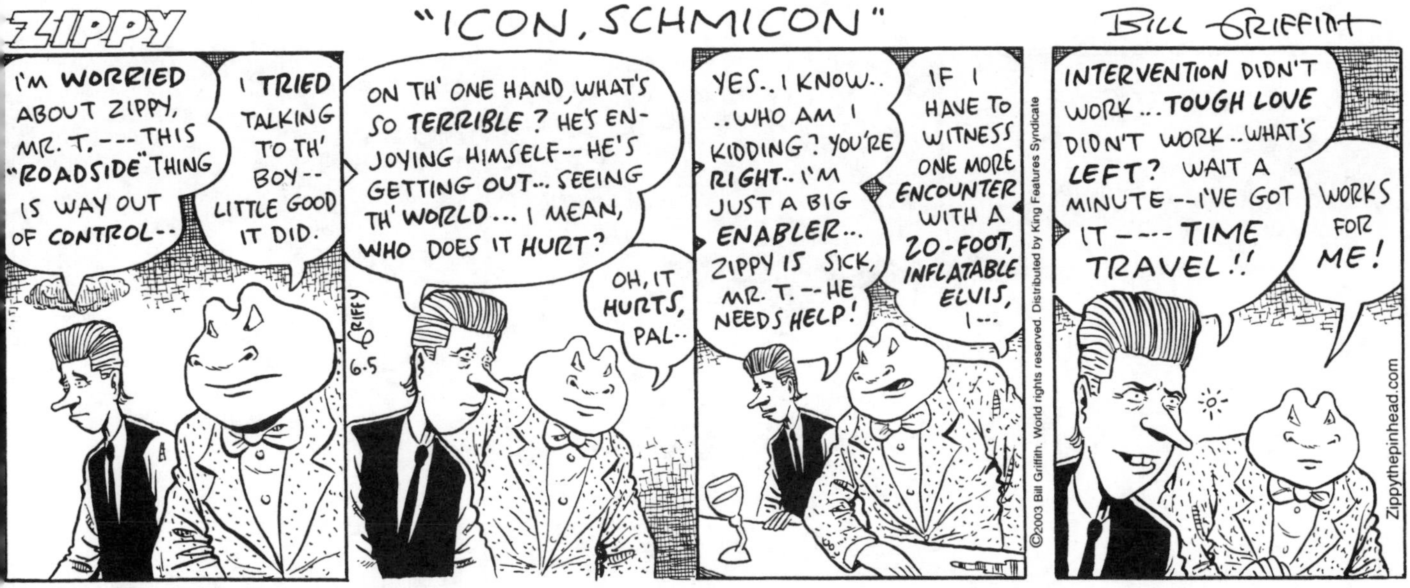
ZIPPY
"ICON, SCHMICON"
BILL GRIFFITH
I'M WORRIED ABOUT ZIPPY, MR. T. --- THIS "ROADSIDE" THING IS WAY OUT OF CONTROL--
I TRIED TALKING TO TH' BOY -- LITTLE GOOD IT DID.
ON TH' ONE HAND, WHAT'S SO TERRIBLE? HE'S ENJOYING HIMSELF--HE'S GETTING OUT... SEEING TH' WORLD... I MEAN, WHO DOES IT HURT?
OH, IT HURTS, PAL..
GRIFFY 6-5
YES..I KNOW.. ..WHO AM I KIDDING? YOU'RE RIGHT.. I'M JUST A BIG ENABLER... ZIPPY IS SICK, MR. T. --HE NEEDS HELP!
IF I HAVE TO WITNESS ONE MORE ENCOUNTER WITH A 20-FOOT, INFLATABLE ELVIS, I---
©2003 Bill Griffith. World rights reserved. Distributed by King Features Syndicate
INTERVENTION DIDN'T WORK... TOUGH LOVE DIDN'T WORK.. WHAT'S LEFT? WAIT A MINUTE --I'VE GOT IT ---- TIME TRAVEL!!
WORKS FOR ME!
Zippythepinhead.com

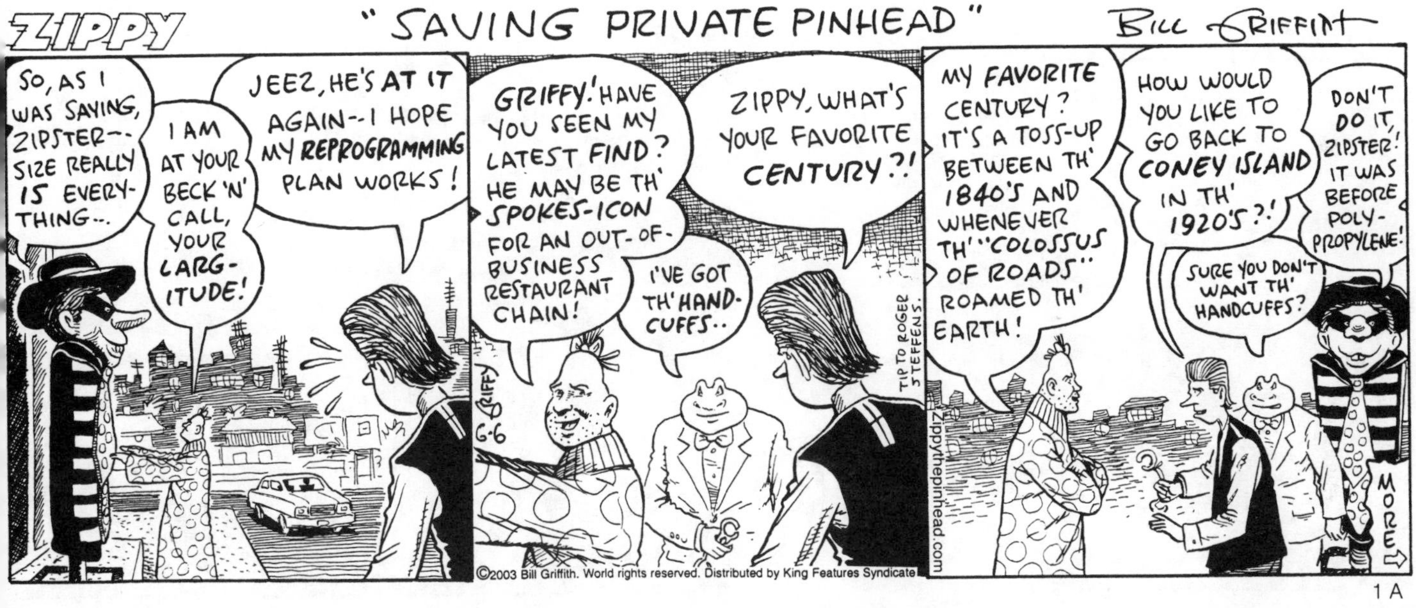
ZIPPY
"SAVING PRIVATE PINHEAD"
BILL GRIFFITH
SO, AS I WAS SAYING, ZIPSTER-- SIZE REALLY IS EVERYTHING..
I AM AT YOUR BECK 'N' CALL, YOUR LARGITUDE!
JEEZ, HE'S AT IT AGAIN--I HOPE MY REPROGRAMMING PLAN WORKS!
GRIFFY! HAVE YOU SEEN MY LATEST FIND? HE MAY BE TH' SPOKES-ICON FOR AN OUT-OF-BUSINESS RESTAURANT CHAIN!
I'VE GOT TH' HANDCUFFS..
ZIPPY, WHAT'S YOUR FAVORITE CENTURY?!
GRIFFY 6-6
TIP TO ROGER STEFFENS.
©2003 Bill Griffith. World rights reserved. Distributed by King Features Syndicate
MY FAVORITE CENTURY? IT'S A TOSS-UP BETWEEN TH' 1840'S AND WHENEVER TH' "COLOSSUS OF ROADS" ROAMED TH' EARTH!
HOW WOULD YOU LIKE TO GO BACK TO CONEY ISLAND IN TH' 1920'S?!
DON'T DO IT, ZIPSTER! IT WAS BEFORE POLYPROPYLENE!
SURE YOU DON'T WANT TH' HANDCUFFS?
Zippythepinhead.com
MORE

1 A

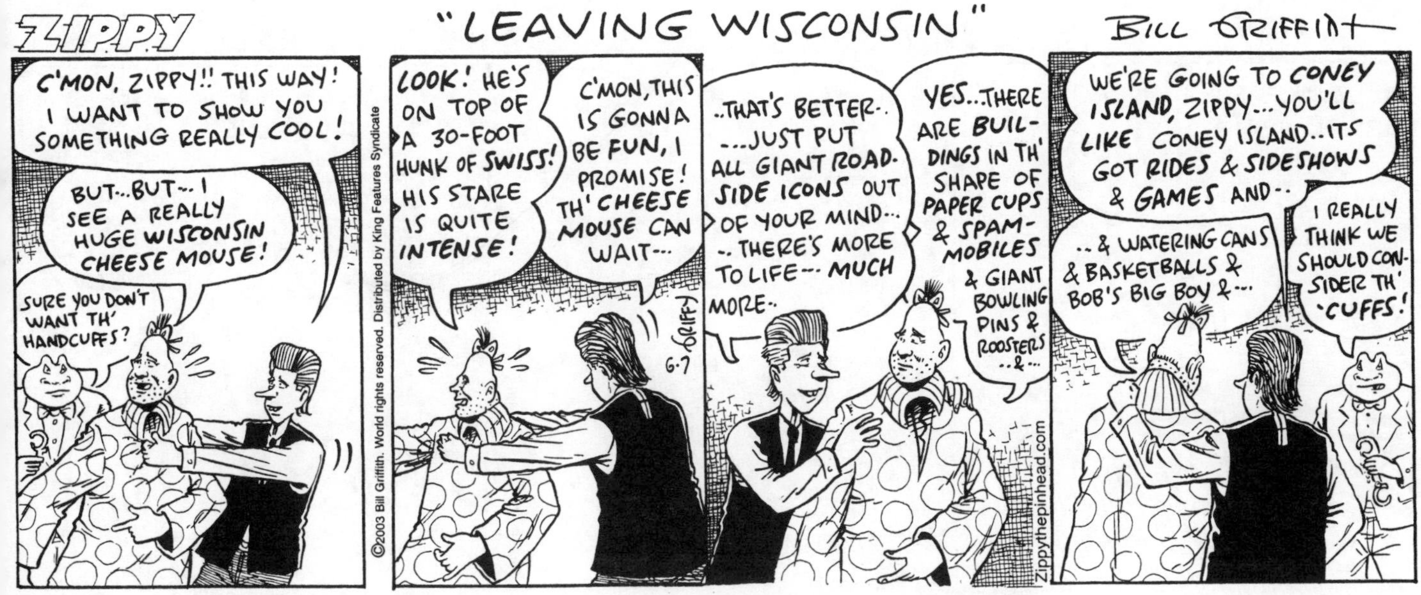
ZIPPY
"LEAVING WISCONSIN"
BILL GRIFFITH
C'MON, ZIPPY!! THIS WAY! I WANT TO SHOW YOU SOMETHING REALLY COOL!
BUT...BUT--I SEE A REALLY HUGE WISCONSIN CHEESE MOUSE!
SURE YOU DON'T WANT TH' HANDCUFFS?
©2003 Bill Griffith. World rights reserved. Distributed by King Features Syndicate
LOOK! HE'S ON TOP OF A 30-FOOT HUNK OF SWISS! HIS STARE IS QUITE INTENSE!
C'MON, THIS IS GONNA BE FUN, I PROMISE! TH' CHEESE MOUSE CAN WAIT--
GRIFFY 6-7
..THAT'S BETTER.. ...JUST PUT ALL GIANT ROADSIDE ICONS OUT OF YOUR MIND... ..THERE'S MORE TO LIFE-- MUCH MORE..
YES...THERE ARE BUILDINGS IN TH' SHAPE OF PAPER CUPS & SPAM-MOBILES & GIANT BOWLING PINS & ROOSTERS ..&..
Zippythepinhead.com
WE'RE GOING TO CONEY ISLAND, ZIPPY... YOU'LL LIKE CONEY ISLAND.. ITS GOT RIDES & SIDESHOWS & GAMES AND-.
..& WATERING CANS & BASKETBALLS & BOB'S BIG BOY &--.
I REALLY THINK WE SHOULD CONSIDER TH' 'CUFFS!

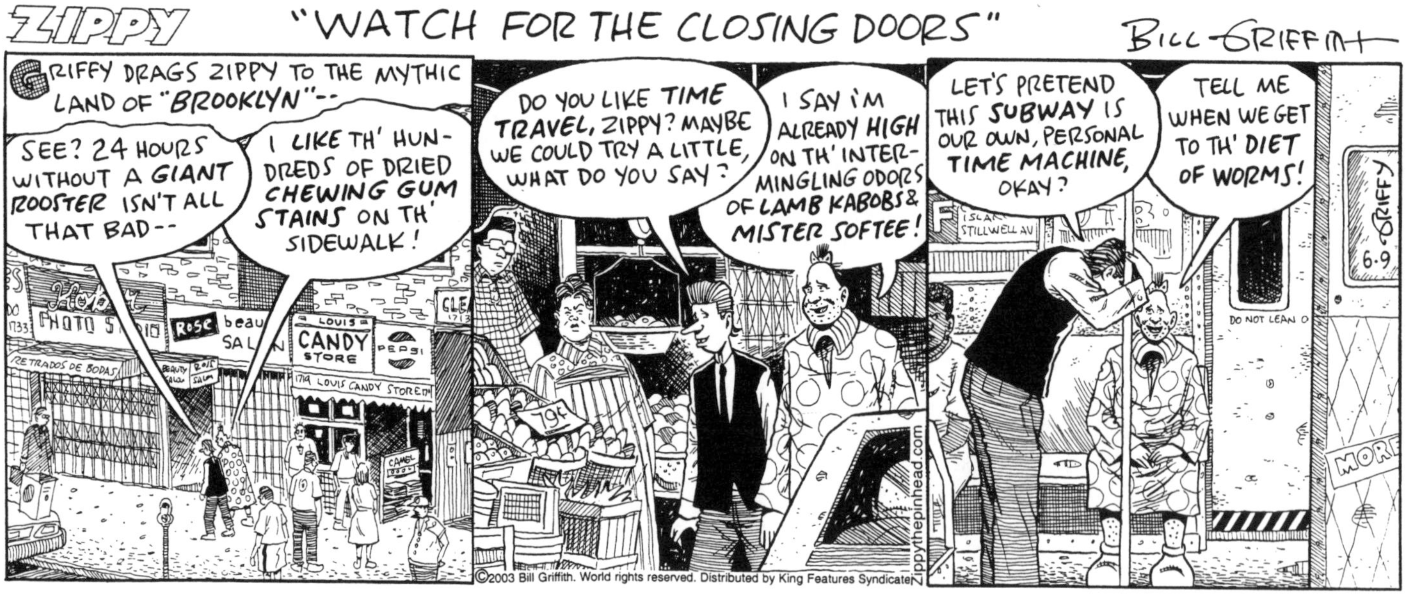
ZIPPY
"WATCH FOR THE CLOSING DOORS"
BILL GRIFFITH
GRIFFY DRAGS ZIPPY TO THE MYTHIC LAND OF "BROOKLYN"--
SEE? 24 HOURS WITHOUT A GIANT ROOSTER ISN'T ALL THAT BAD--
I LIKE TH' HUNDREDS OF DRIED CHEWING GUM STAINS ON TH' SIDEWALK!
PHOTO
ROSE beau SALON
LOUIS CANDY STORE
PEPSI
RETRATOS DE BODAS
1714 LOUIS CANDY STORE INC
CAMEL
DO YOU LIKE TIME TRAVEL, ZIPPY? MAYBE WE COULD TRY A LITTLE, WHAT DO YOU SAY?
I SAY I'M ALREADY HIGH ON TH' INTERMINGLING ODORS OF LAMB KABOBS & MISTER SOFTEE!
79¢
zippythepinhead.com
©2003 Bill Griffith. World rights reserved. Distributed by King Features Syndicate
LET'S PRETEND THIS SUBWAY IS OUR OWN, PERSONAL TIME MACHINE, OKAY?
TELL ME WHEN WE GET TO TH' DIET OF WORMS!
STILLWELL AV
DO NOT LEAN
MORE
6·9 GRIFFY

1 B

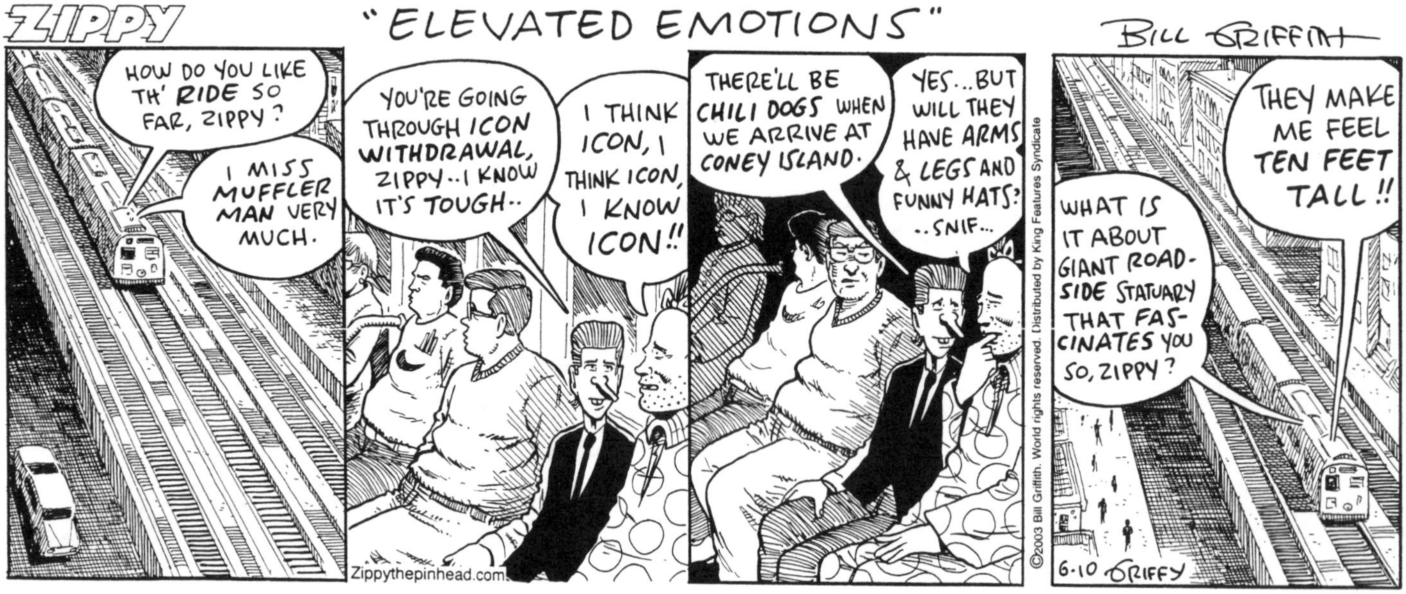
ZIPPY
"ELEVATED EMOTIONS"
BILL GRIFFITH
HOW DO YOU LIKE TH' RIDE SO FAR, ZIPPY?
I MISS MUFFLER MAN VERY MUCH.
YOU'RE GOING THROUGH ICON WITHDRAWAL, ZIPPY..I KNOW IT'S TOUGH..
I THINK ICON, I THINK ICON, I KNOW ICON!!
Zippythepinhead.com
THERE'LL BE CHILI DOGS WHEN WE ARRIVE AT CONEY ISLAND.
YES...BUT WILL THEY HAVE ARMS & LEGS AND FUNNY HATS? ..SNIF...
©2003 Bill Griffith. World rights reserved. Distributed by King Features Syndicate
WHAT IS IT ABOUT GIANT ROADSIDE STATUARY THAT FASCINATES YOU SO, ZIPPY?
THEY MAKE ME FEEL TEN FEET TALL!!
6·10 GRIFFY

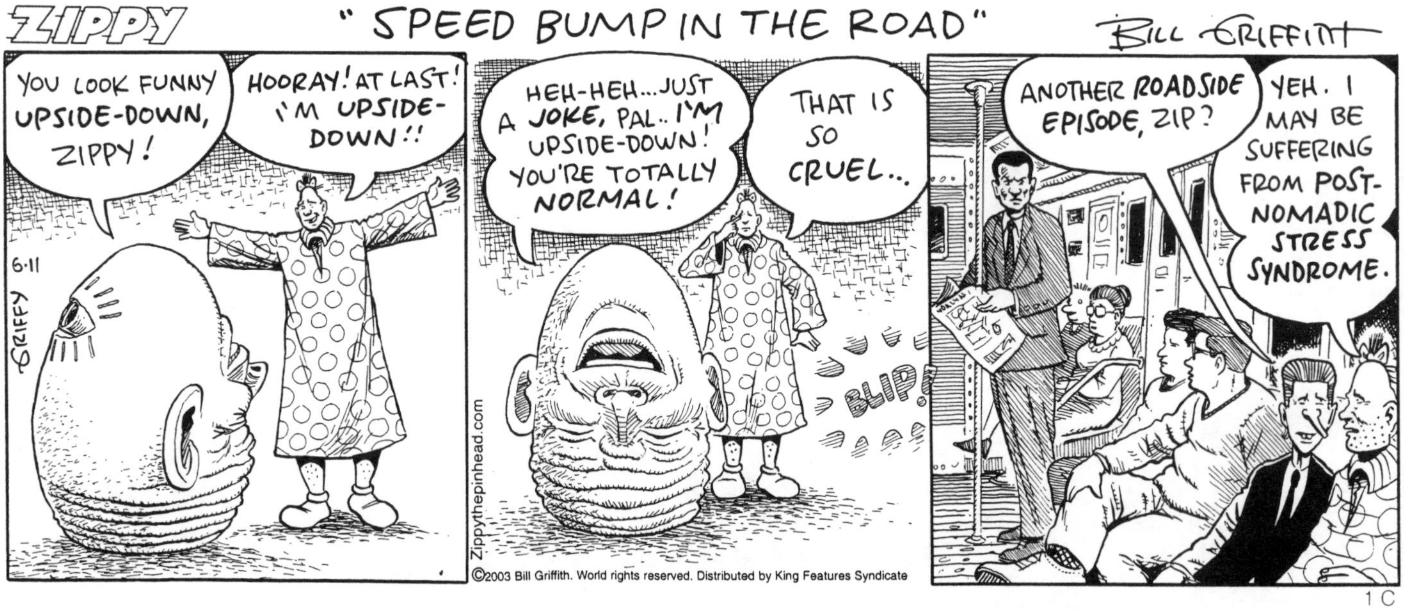
ZIPPY
"SPEED BUMP IN THE ROAD"
BILL GRIFFITH
YOU LOOK FUNNY UPSIDE-DOWN, ZIPPY!
HOORAY! AT LAST! I'M UPSIDE-DOWN!!
6·11 GRIFFY
HEH-HEH...JUST A JOKE, PAL..I'M UPSIDE-DOWN! YOU'RE TOTALLY NORMAL!
THAT IS SO CRUEL...
BLIP!
Zippythepinhead.com
©2003 Bill Griffith. World rights reserved. Distributed by King Features Syndicate
ANOTHER ROADSIDE EPISODE, ZIP?
YEH. I MAY BE SUFFERING FROM POST-NOMADIC STRESS SYNDROME.

1 C

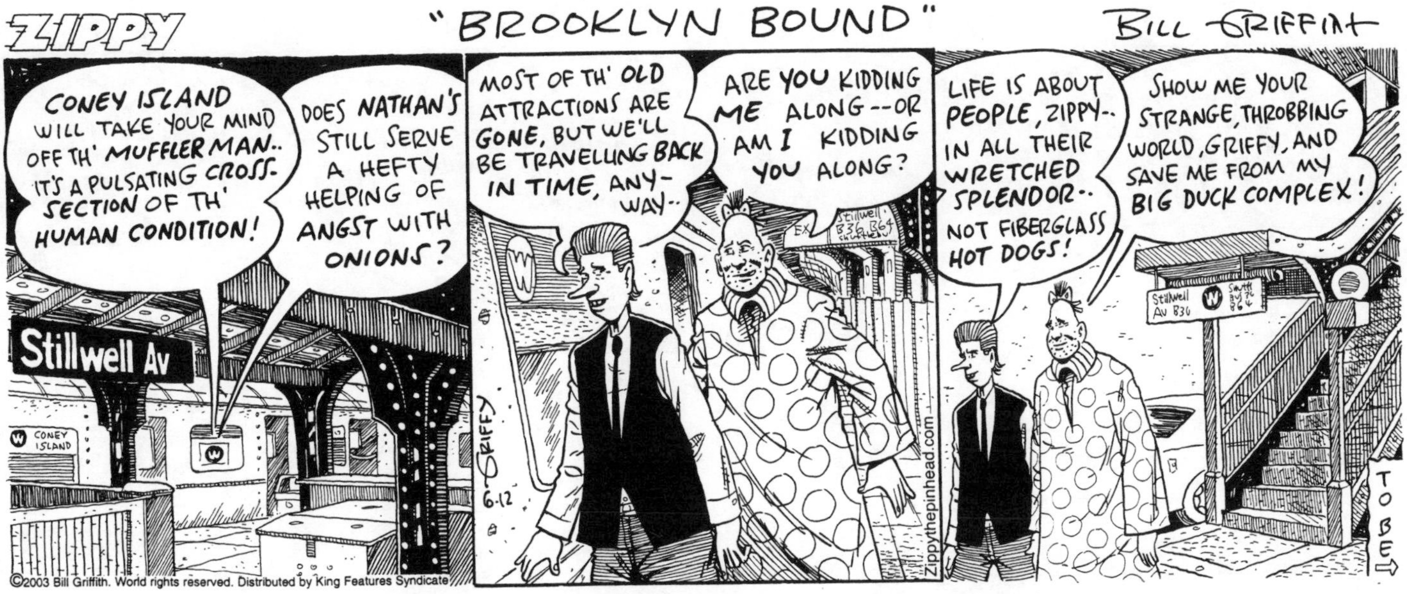
ZIPPY
"BROOKLYN BOUND"
BILL GRIFFITH
CONEY ISLAND WILL TAKE YOUR MIND OFF TH' MUFFLER MAN.. IT'S A PULSATING CROSS-SECTION OF TH' HUMAN CONDITION!
DOES NATHAN'S STILL SERVE A HEFTY HELPING OF ANGST WITH ONIONS?
Stillwell Av
CONEY ISLAND
MOST OF TH' OLD ATTRACTIONS ARE GONE, BUT WE'LL BE TRAVELLING BACK IN TIME, ANY-WAY..
ARE YOU KIDDING ME ALONG--OR AM I KIDDING YOU ALONG?
GRIFFY 6-12
Zippythepinhead.com
LIFE IS ABOUT PEOPLE, ZIPPY.. IN ALL THEIR WRETCHED SPLENDOR.. NOT FIBERGLASS HOT DOGS!
SHOW ME YOUR STRANGE, THROBBING WORLD, GRIFFY, AND SAVE ME FROM MY BIG DUCK COMPLEX!
TO BE ⇨
©2003 Bill Griffith. World rights reserved. Distributed by King Features Syndicate

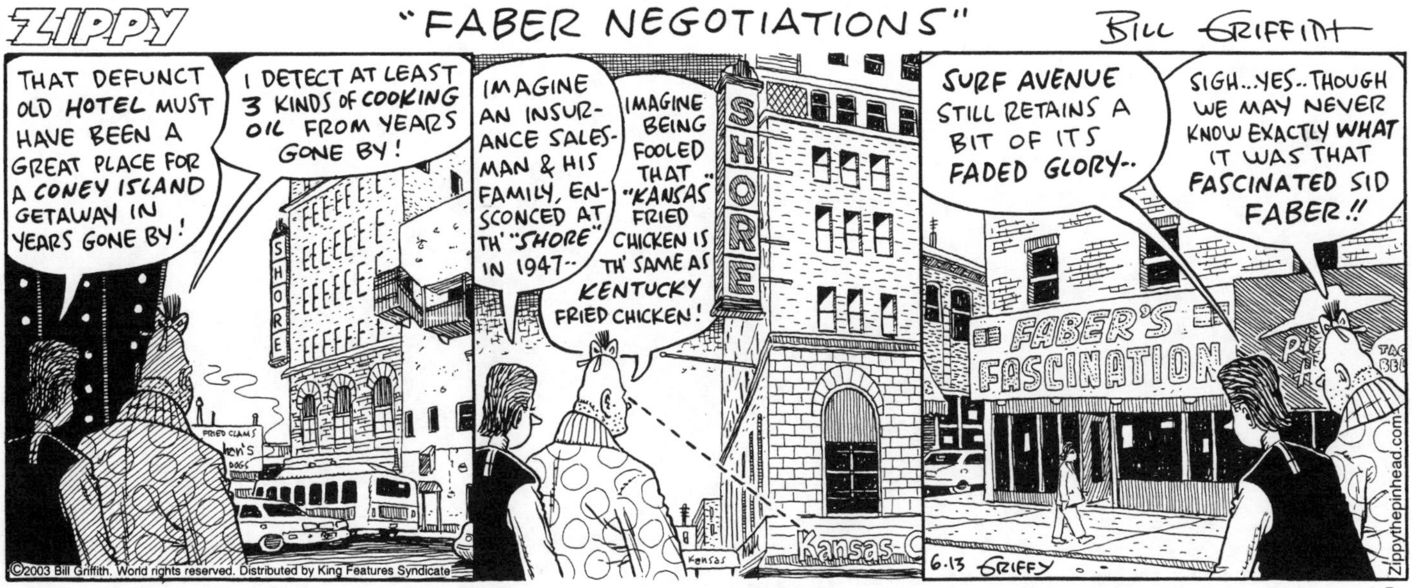
ZIPPY
"FABER NEGOTIATIONS"
BILL GRIFFITH
THAT DEFUNCT OLD HOTEL MUST HAVE BEEN A GREAT PLACE FOR A CONEY ISLAND GETAWAY IN YEARS GONE BY!
I DETECT AT LEAST 3 KINDS OF COOKING OIL FROM YEARS GONE BY!
SHORE
FRIED CLAMS
IMAGINE AN INSURANCE SALESMAN & HIS FAMILY, ENSCONCED AT TH' "SHORE" IN 1947..
IMAGINE BEING FOOLED THAT "KANSAS" FRIED CHICKEN IS TH' SAME AS KENTUCKY FRIED CHICKEN!
SHORE
Kansas
SURF AVENUE STILL RETAINS A BIT OF ITS FADED GLORY..
SIGH..YES..THOUGH WE MAY NEVER KNOW EXACTLY WHAT IT WAS THAT FASCINATED SID FABER!!
FABER'S FASCINATION
6.13 GRIFFY
Zippythepinhead.com
©2003 Bill Griffith. World rights reserved. Distributed by King Features Syndicate

1 D

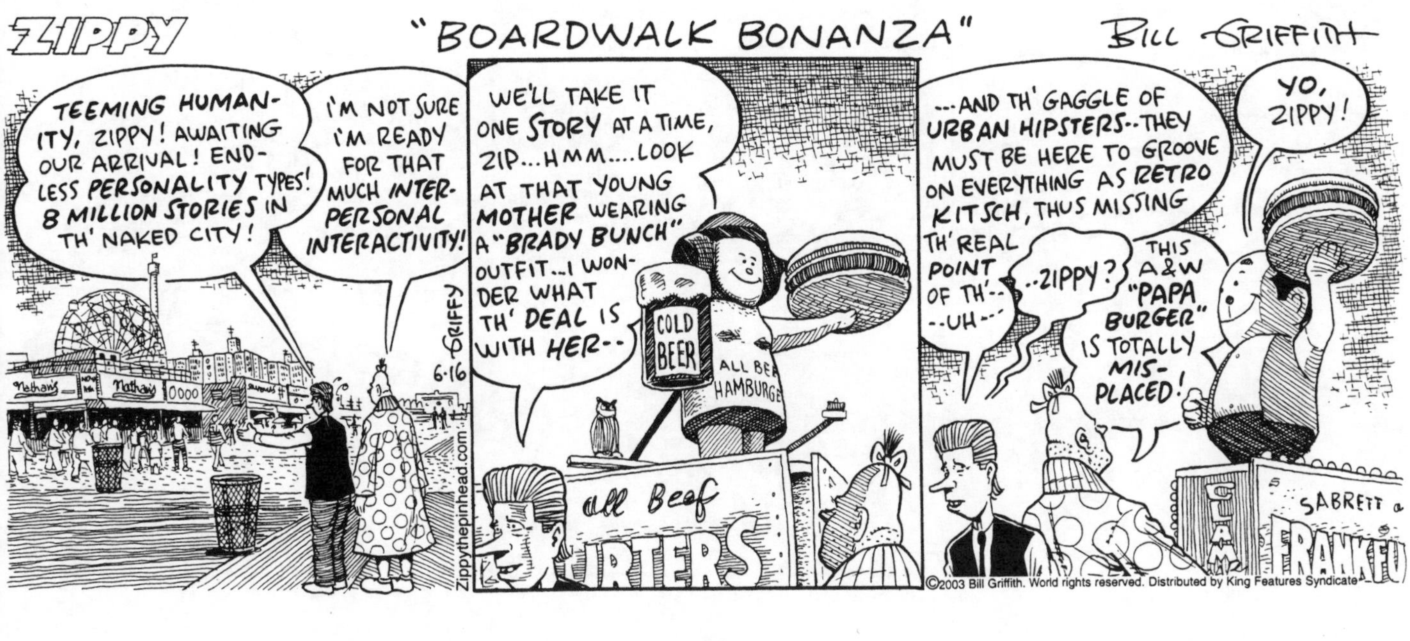
ZIPPY
"BOARDWALK BONANZA"
BILL GRIFFITH
TEEMING HUMANITY, ZIPPY! AWAITING OUR ARRIVAL! ENDLESS PERSONALITY TYPES! 8 MILLION STORIES IN TH' NAKED CITY!
I'M NOT SURE I'M READY FOR THAT MUCH INTERPERSONAL INTERACTIVITY!
Nathan's
GRIFFY 6-16
Zippythepinhead.com
WE'LL TAKE IT ONE STORY AT A TIME, ZIP...HMM....LOOK AT THAT YOUNG MOTHER WEARING A "BRADY BUNCH" OUTFIT...I WONDER WHAT TH' DEAL IS WITH HER--
COLD BEER
ALL BEEF HAMBURGERS
All Beef
RTERS
...AND TH' GAGGLE OF URBAN HIPSTERS--THEY MUST BE HERE TO GROOVE ON EVERYTHING AS RETRO KITSCH, THUS MISSING TH' REAL POINT OF TH'-- --UH--
..ZIPPY?
THIS A&W "PAPA BURGER" IS TOTALLY MISPLACED!
YO, ZIPPY!
SABRETT
FRANKFU
©2003 Bill Griffith. World rights reserved. Distributed by King Features Syndicate

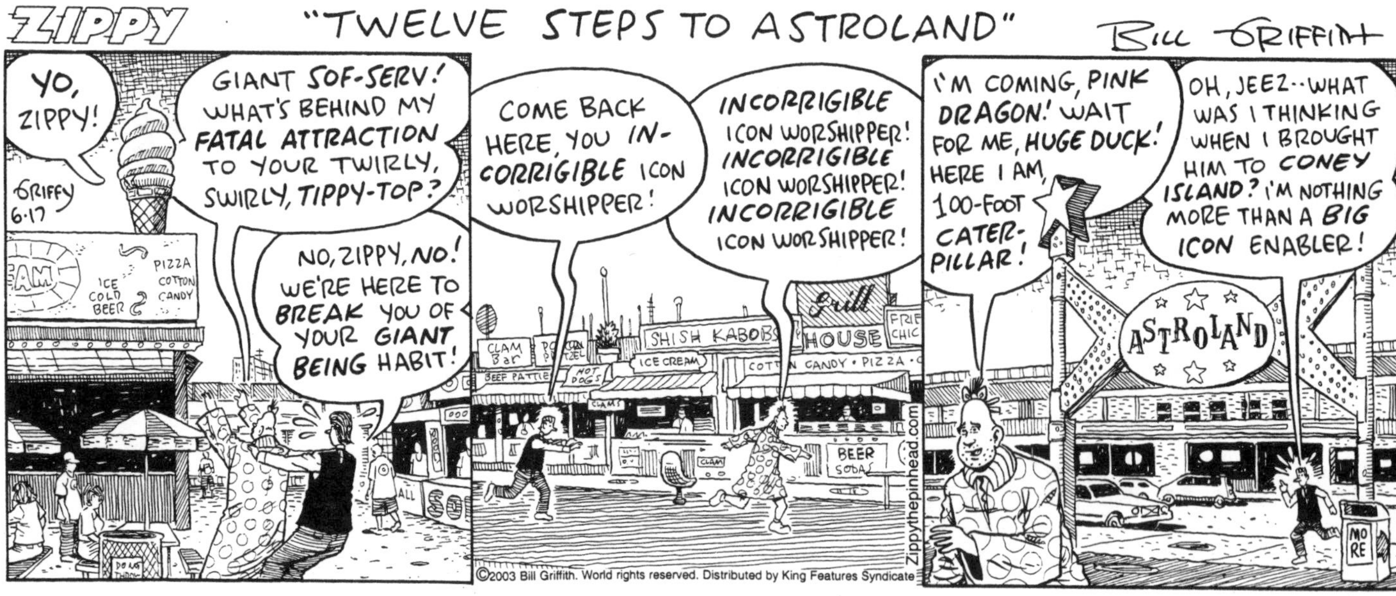
ZIPPY
"TWELVE STEPS TO ASTROLAND"
BILL GRIFFITH
YO, ZIPPY!
GIANT SOF-SERV! WHAT'S BEHIND MY FATAL ATTRACTION TO YOUR TWIRLY, SWIRLY, TIPPY-TOP?
GRIFFY 6-17
PIZZA
ICE COLD BEER
COTTON CANDY
NO, ZIPPY, NO! WE'RE HERE TO BREAK YOU OF YOUR GIANT BEING HABIT!
COME BACK HERE, YOU INCORRIGIBLE ICON WORSHIPPER!
INCORRIGIBLE ICON WORSHIPPER! INCORRIGIBLE ICON WORSHIPPER! INCORRIGIBLE ICON WORSHIPPER!
CLAM BAR
SHISH KABOBS
Grill HOUSE
ICE CREAM
BEEF PATTIES
HOT DOGS
BEER SODA
I'M COMING, PINK DRAGON! WAIT FOR ME, HUGE DUCK! HERE I AM, 100-FOOT CATERPILLAR!
OH, JEEZ.. WHAT WAS I THINKING WHEN I BROUGHT HIM TO CONEY ISLAND? I'M NOTHING MORE THAN A BIG ICON ENABLER!
ASTROLAND
MORE
©2003 Bill Griffith. World rights reserved. Distributed by King Features Syndicate
Zippythepinhead.com

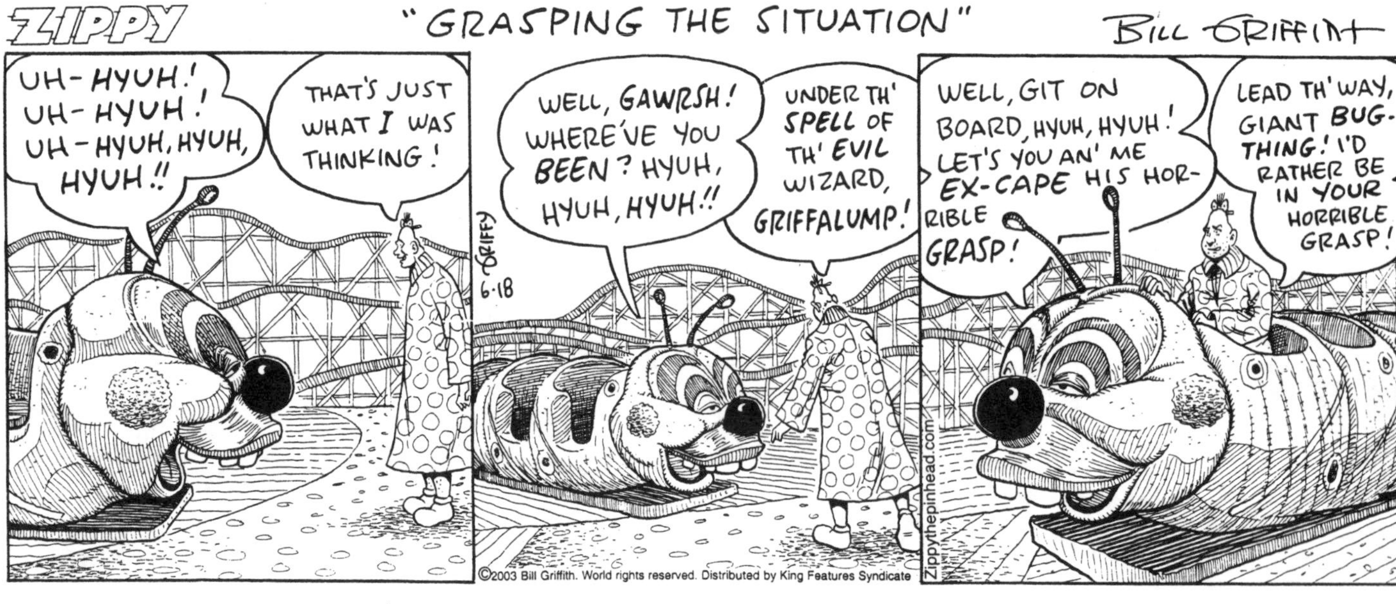
ZIPPY
"GRASPING THE SITUATION"
BILL GRIFFITH
UH-HYUH! UH-HYUH! UH-HYUH, HYUH, HYUH!!
THAT'S JUST WHAT I WAS THINKING!
GRIFFY 6-18
WELL, GAWRSH! WHERE'VE YOU BEEN? HYUH, HYUH, HYUH!!
UNDER TH' SPELL OF TH' EVIL WIZARD, GRIFFALUMP!
WELL, GIT ON BOARD, HYUH, HYUH! LET'S YOU AN' ME EX-CAPE HIS HORRIBLE GRASP!
LEAD TH' WAY, GIANT BUG-THING! I'D RATHER BE IN YOUR HORRIBLE GRASP!
©2003 Bill Griffith. World rights reserved. Distributed by King Features Syndicate
Zippythepinhead.com

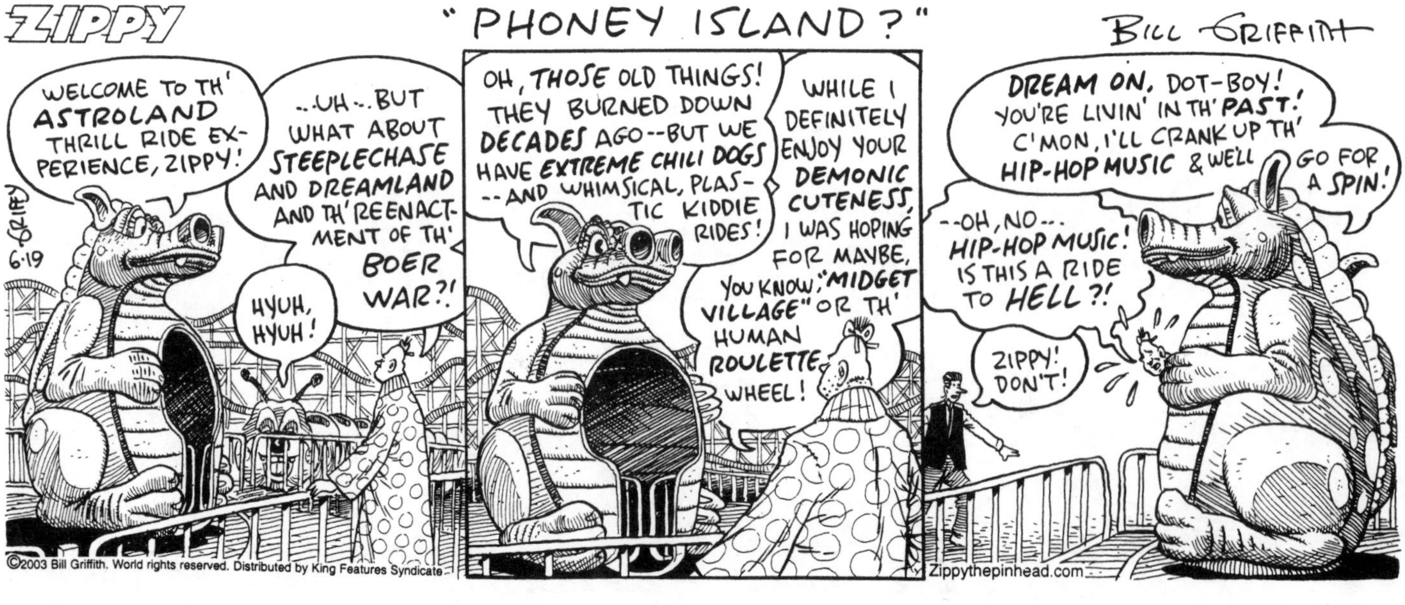
ZIPPY
"PHONEY ISLAND?"
BILL GRIFFITH
WELCOME TO TH' ASTROLAND THRILL RIDE EXPERIENCE, ZIPPY!
..UH..BUT WHAT ABOUT STEEPLECHASE AND DREAMLAND AND TH' REENACTMENT OF TH' BOER WAR?!
GRIFFY 6-19
HYUH, HYUH!
OH, THOSE OLD THINGS! THEY BURNED DOWN DECADES AGO--BUT WE HAVE EXTREME CHILI DOGS --AND WHIMSICAL, PLASTIC KIDDIE RIDES!
WHILE I DEFINITELY ENJOY YOUR DEMONIC CUTENESS, I WAS HOPING FOR MAYBE, YOU KNOW, "MIDGET VILLAGE" OR TH' HUMAN ROULETTE WHEEL!
DREAM ON, DOT-BOY! YOU'RE LIVIN' IN TH' PAST! C'MON, I'LL CRANK UP TH' HIP-HOP MUSIC & WE'LL GO FOR A SPIN!
--OH, NO--. HIP-HOP MUSIC! IS THIS A RIDE TO HELL?!
ZIPPY! DON'T!
©2003 Bill Griffith. World rights reserved. Distributed by King Features Syndicate
Zippythepinhead.com

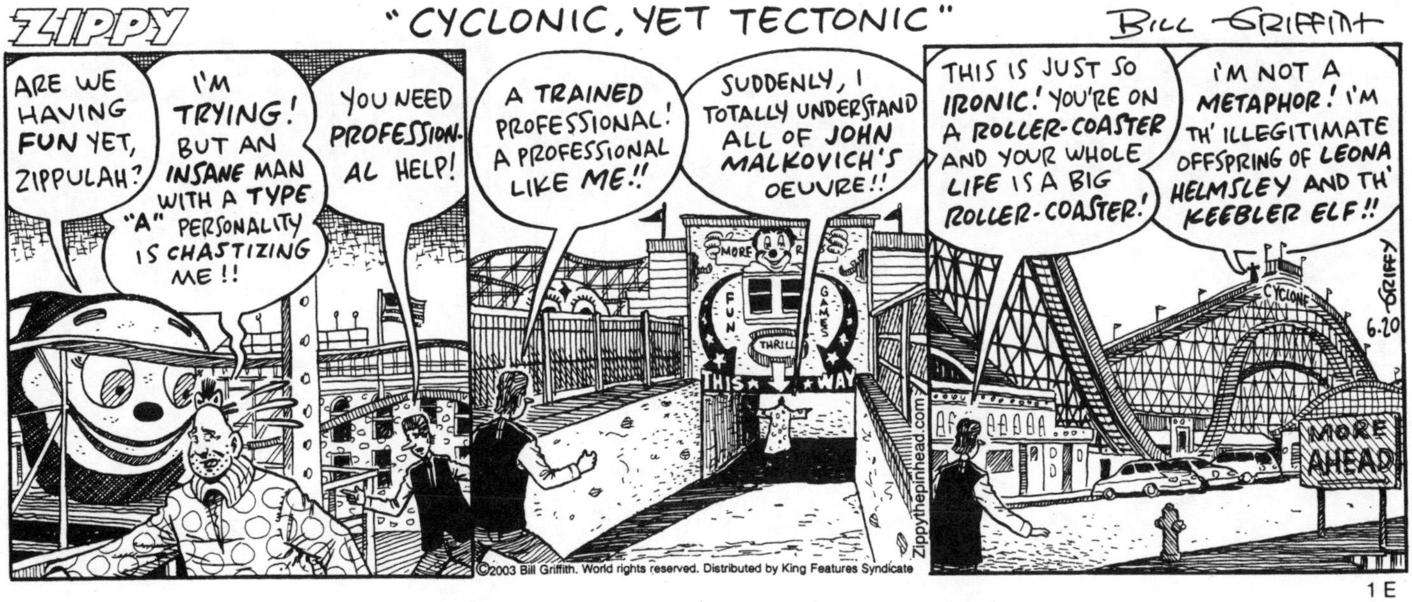
ZIPPY
"CYCLONIC, YET TECTONIC"
BILL GRIFFITH
ARE WE HAVING FUN YET, ZIPPULAH?
I'M TRYING! BUT AN INSANE MAN WITH A TYPE "A" PERSONALITY IS CHASTIZING ME!!
YOU NEED PROFESSIONAL HELP!
A TRAINED PROFESSIONAL! A PROFESSIONAL LIKE ME!!
SUDDENLY, I TOTALLY UNDERSTAND ALL OF JOHN MALKOVICH'S OEUVRE!!
THIS IS JUST SO IRONIC! YOU'RE ON A ROLLER-COASTER AND YOUR WHOLE LIFE IS A BIG ROLLER-COASTER!
I'M NOT A METAPHOR! I'M TH' ILLEGITIMATE OFFSPRING OF LEONA HELMSLEY AND TH' KEEBLER ELF!!
MORE
FUN
GAMES
THRILLS
THIS WAY
CYCLONE
MORE AHEAD
GRIFFY 6·20
Zippythepinhead.com
©2003 Bill Griffith. World rights reserved. Distributed by King Features Syndicate

1 E

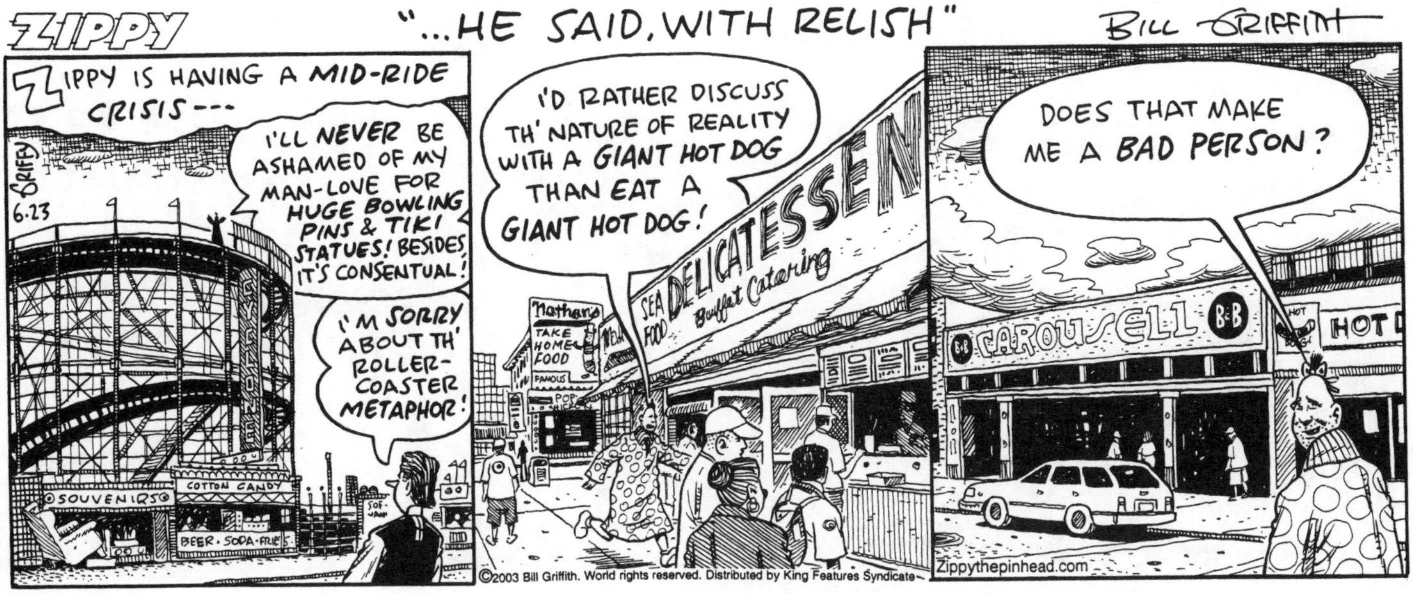
ZIPPY
"...HE SAID, WITH RELISH"
BILL GRIFFITH
ZIPPY IS HAVING A MID-RIDE CRISIS---
I'LL NEVER BE ASHAMED OF MY MAN-LOVE FOR HUGE BOWLING PINS & TIKI STATUES! BESIDES, IT'S CONSENTUAL!
I'M SORRY ABOUT TH' ROLLER-COASTER METAPHOR!
I'D RATHER DISCUSS TH' NATURE OF REALITY WITH A GIANT HOT DOG THAN EAT A GIANT HOT DOG!
DOES THAT MAKE ME A BAD PERSON?
GRIFFY 6·23
SOUVENIRS
COTTON CANDY
BEER · SODA · FRIES
Nathan's
TAKE HOME FOOD
FAMOUS
SEA FOOD
DELICATESSEN
Buffet Catering
CAROUSELL
B&B
HOT
Zippythepinhead.com
©2003 Bill Griffith. World rights reserved. Distributed by King Features Syndicate

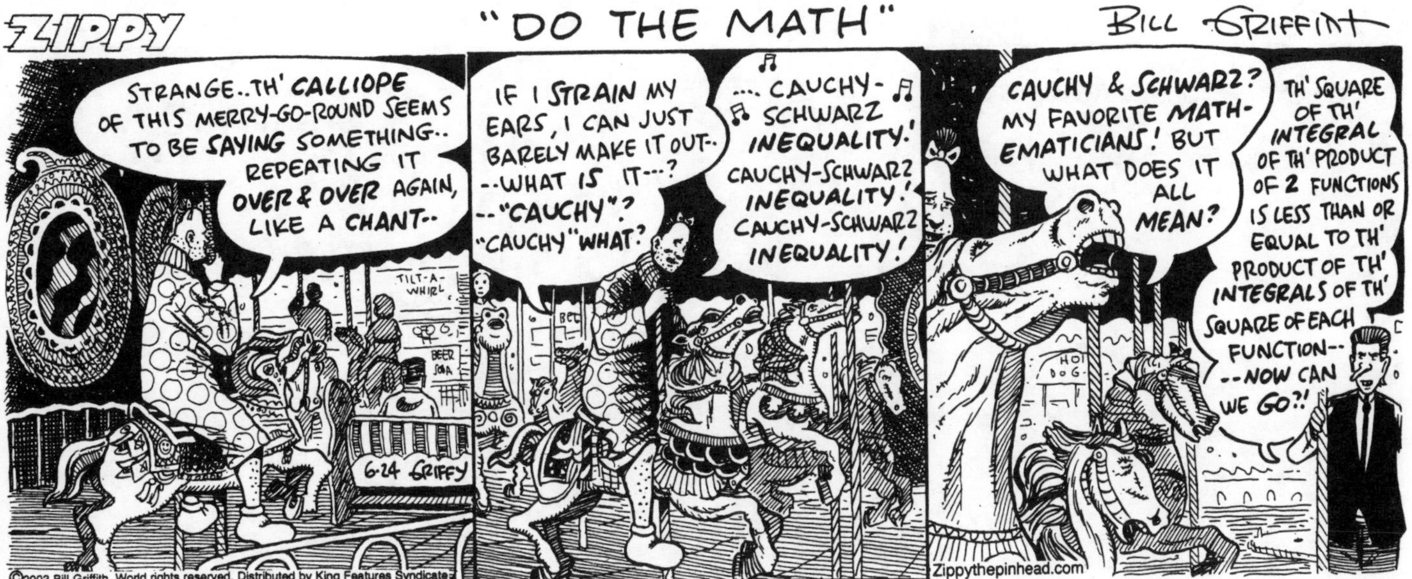
ZIPPY
"DO THE MATH"
BILL GRIFFITH
STRANGE..TH' CALLIOPE OF THIS MERRY-GO-ROUND SEEMS TO BE SAYING SOMETHING.. REPEATING IT OVER & OVER AGAIN, LIKE A CHANT--
IF I STRAIN MY EARS, I CAN JUST BARELY MAKE IT OUT-- --WHAT IS IT--? --"CAUCHY"? "CAUCHY" WHAT?
.... CAUCHY-SCHWARZ INEQUALITY! CAUCHY-SCHWARZ INEQUALITY! CAUCHY-SCHWARZ INEQUALITY!
CAUCHY & SCHWARZ? MY FAVORITE MATHEMATICIANS! BUT WHAT DOES IT ALL MEAN?
TH' SQUARE OF TH' INTEGRAL OF TH' PRODUCT OF 2 FUNCTIONS IS LESS THAN OR EQUAL TO TH' PRODUCT OF TH' INTEGRALS OF TH' SQUARE OF EACH FUNCTION-- --NOW CAN WE GO?!
TILT-A-WHIRL
BEER SODA
HOT DOG
6·24 GRIFFY
Zippythepinhead.com
©2003 Bill Griffith. World rights reserved. Distributed by King Features Syndicate

1 F

ZIPPY "FUN HOUSE FROLICS" BILL GRIFFITH

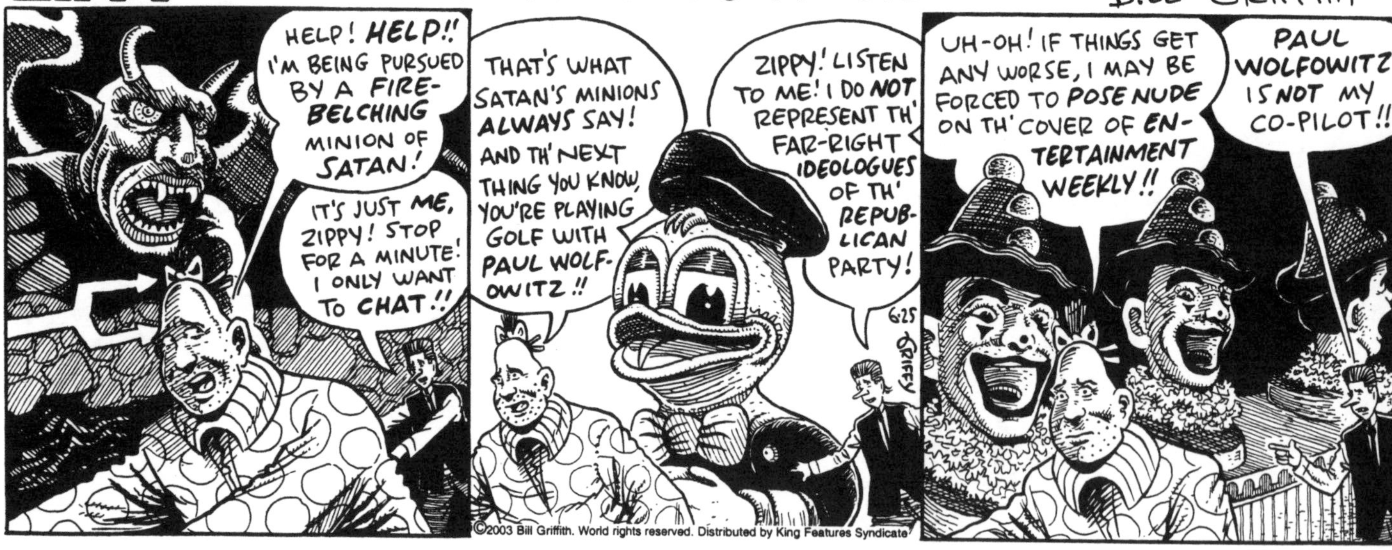

HELP! HELP!! I'M BEING PURSUED BY A FIRE-BELCHING MINION OF SATAN!
IT'S JUST ME, ZIPPY! STOP FOR A MINUTE! I ONLY WANT TO CHAT!!
THAT'S WHAT SATAN'S MINIONS ALWAYS SAY! AND TH' NEXT THING YOU KNOW, YOU'RE PLAYING GOLF WITH PAUL WOLF-OWITZ!!
ZIPPY! LISTEN TO ME! I DO NOT REPRESENT TH' FAR-RIGHT IDEOLOGUES OF TH' REPUB-LICAN PARTY!
6.25
GRIFFY
©2003 Bill Griffith. World rights reserved. Distributed by King Features Syndicate
UH-OH! IF THINGS GET ANY WORSE, I MAY BE FORCED TO POSE NUDE ON TH' COVER OF EN-TERTAINMENT WEEKLY!!
PAUL WOLFOWITZ IS NOT MY CO-PILOT!!

1 G

ZIPPY "ROOM SERVICE IN THE TWILIGHT ZONE" BILL GRIFFITH

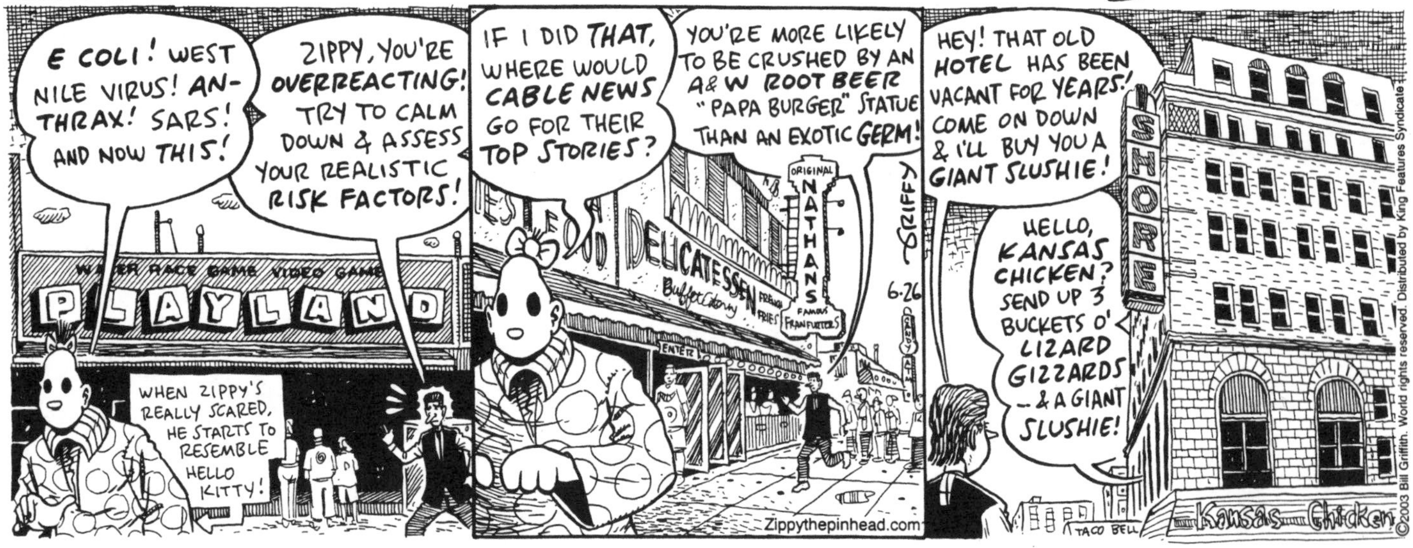

E COLI! WEST NILE VIRUS! AN-THRAX! SARS! AND NOW THIS!
ZIPPY, YOU'RE OVERREACTING! TRY TO CALM DOWN & ASSESS YOUR REALISTIC RISK FACTORS!
PLAYLAND
WHEN ZIPPY'S REALLY SCARED, HE STARTS TO RESEMBLE HELLO KITTY!
IF I DID THAT, WHERE WOULD CABLE NEWS GO FOR THEIR TOP STORIES?
YOU'RE MORE LIKELY TO BE CRUSHED BY AN A&W ROOT BEER "PAPA BURGER" STATUE THAN AN EXOTIC GERM!
DELICATESSEN
ORIGINAL NATHANS FAMOUS FRANKFURTERS
GRIFFY
6.26
Zippythepinhead.com
HEY! THAT OLD HOTEL HAS BEEN VACANT FOR YEARS! COME ON DOWN & I'LL BUY YOU A GIANT SLUSHIE!
SHORE
HELLO, KANSAS CHICKEN? SEND UP 3 BUCKETS O' LIZARD GIZZARDS .. & A GIANT SLUSHIE!
TACO BELL
Kansas Chicken
©2003 Bill Griffith. World rights reserved. Distributed by King Features Syndicate

ZIPPY "CHECK-OUT TIME" BILL GRIFFITH

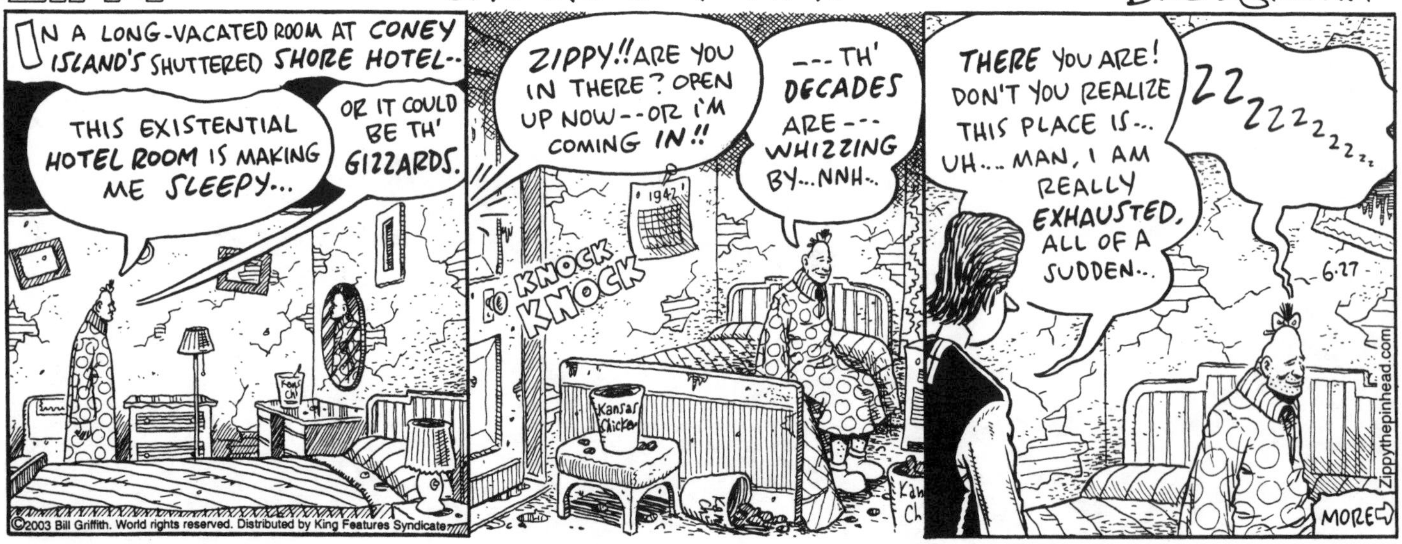

IN A LONG-VACATED ROOM AT CONEY ISLAND'S SHUTTERED SHORE HOTEL--
THIS EXISTENTIAL HOTEL ROOM IS MAKING ME SLEEPY...
OR IT COULD BE TH' GIZZARDS.
©2003 Bill Griffith. World rights reserved. Distributed by King Features Syndicate
ZIPPY!! ARE YOU IN THERE? OPEN UP NOW--OR I'M COMING IN!!
---TH' DECADES ARE--- WHIZZING BY...NNH..
1942
KNOCK KNOCK
Kansas Chicken
THERE YOU ARE! DON'T YOU REALIZE THIS PLACE IS... UH... MAN, I AM REALLY EXHAUSTED, ALL OF A SUDDEN...
ZZZZZZZZZ
6.27
Zippythepinhead.com
MORE

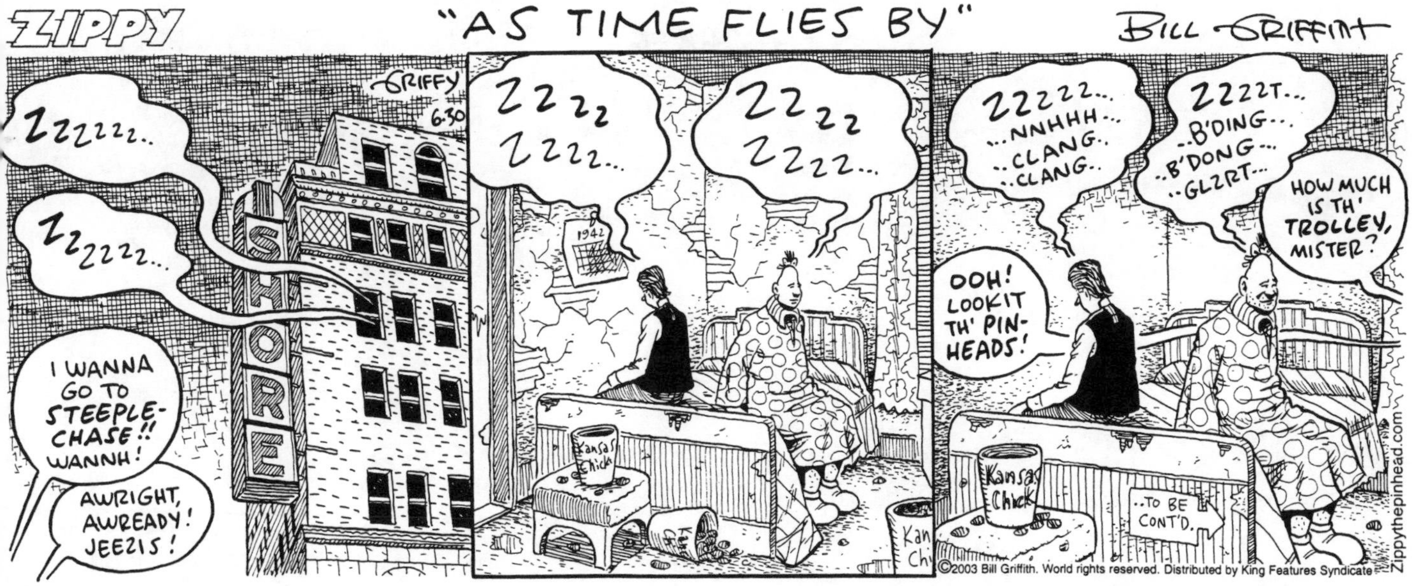
ZIPPY
"AS TIME FLIES BY"
BILL GRIFFITH
GRIFFY 6-30
Zzzzzz..
Zzzzzz...
SHORE
I WANNA GO TO STEEPLE-CHASE!! WANNH!
AWRIGHT, AWREADY! JEEZIS!
Zzzz Zzzz...
1942
Zzzz Zzzz...
Kansas Chick
ZZZZZ... ...NNHHH... ..CLANG.. ..CLANG..
ZZZZT... ..B'DING.. ..B'DONG... ..GLZRT...
HOW MUCH IS TH' TROLLEY, MISTER?
OOH! LOOKIT TH' PIN-HEADS!
Kansas Chick
..TO BE CONT'D.
Zippythepinhead.com

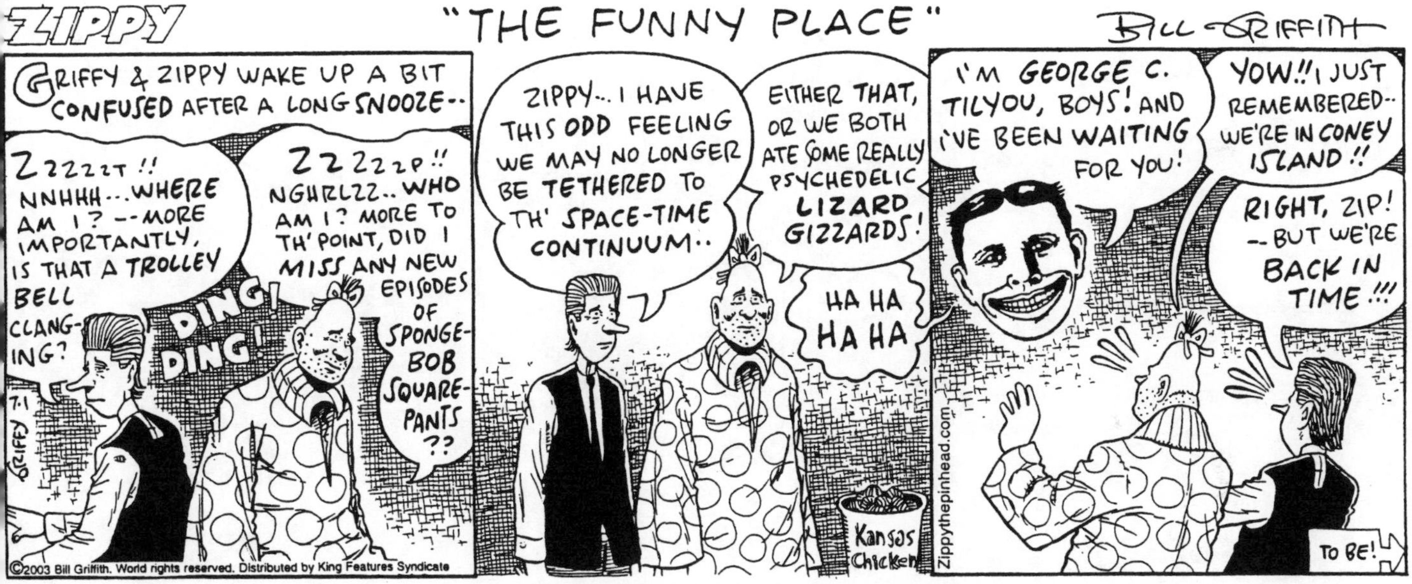
ZIPPY
"THE FUNNY PLACE"
BILL GRIFFITH
GRIFFY & ZIPPY WAKE UP A BIT CONFUSED AFTER A LONG SNOOZE--
Zzzzzt!! NNHHH...WHERE AM I? --MORE IMPORTANTLY, IS THAT A TROLLEY BELL CLANG-ING?
ZZZZZP!! NGHRLZZ.. WHO AM I? MORE TO TH' POINT, DID I MISS ANY NEW EPISODES OF SPONGE-BOB SQUARE-PANTS??
DING! DING!
GRIFFY 7-1
ZIPPY... I HAVE THIS ODD FEELING WE MAY NO LONGER BE TETHERED TO TH' SPACE-TIME CONTINUUM..
EITHER THAT, OR WE BOTH ATE SOME REALLY PSYCHEDELIC LIZARD GIZZARDS!
HA HA HA HA
Kansas Chicken
I'M GEORGE C. TILYOU, BOYS! AND I'VE BEEN WAITING FOR YOU!
YOW!! I JUST REMEMBERED-- WE'RE IN CONEY ISLAND!!
RIGHT, ZIP! --BUT WE'RE BACK IN TIME!!!
TO BE!
Zippythepinhead.com

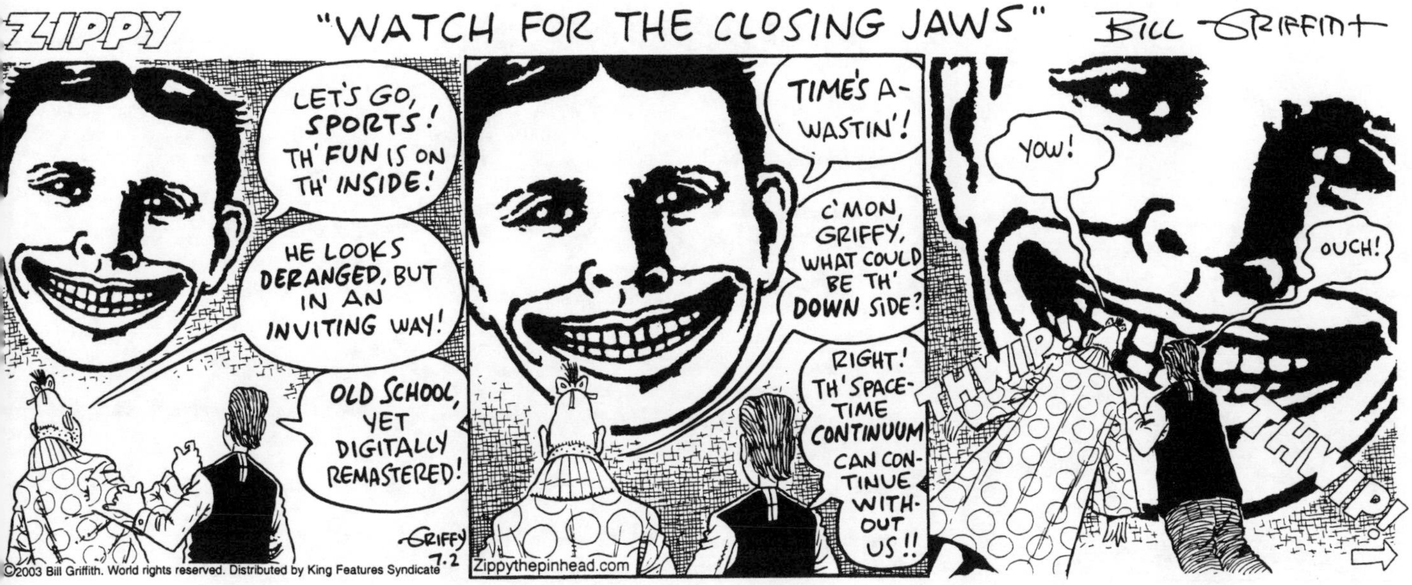
ZIPPY
"WATCH FOR THE CLOSING JAWS"
BILL GRIFFITH
LET'S GO, SPORTS! TH' FUN IS ON TH' INSIDE!
HE LOOKS DERANGED, BUT IN AN INVITING WAY!
OLD SCHOOL, YET DIGITALLY REMASTERED!
GRIFFY 7-2
TIME'S A-WASTIN'!
C'MON, GRIFFY, WHAT COULD BE TH' DOWN SIDE?
RIGHT! TH' SPACE-TIME CONTINUUM CAN CON-TINUE WITH-OUT US!!
Zippythepinhead.com
YOW!
OUCH!
THWIP!
THWIP!

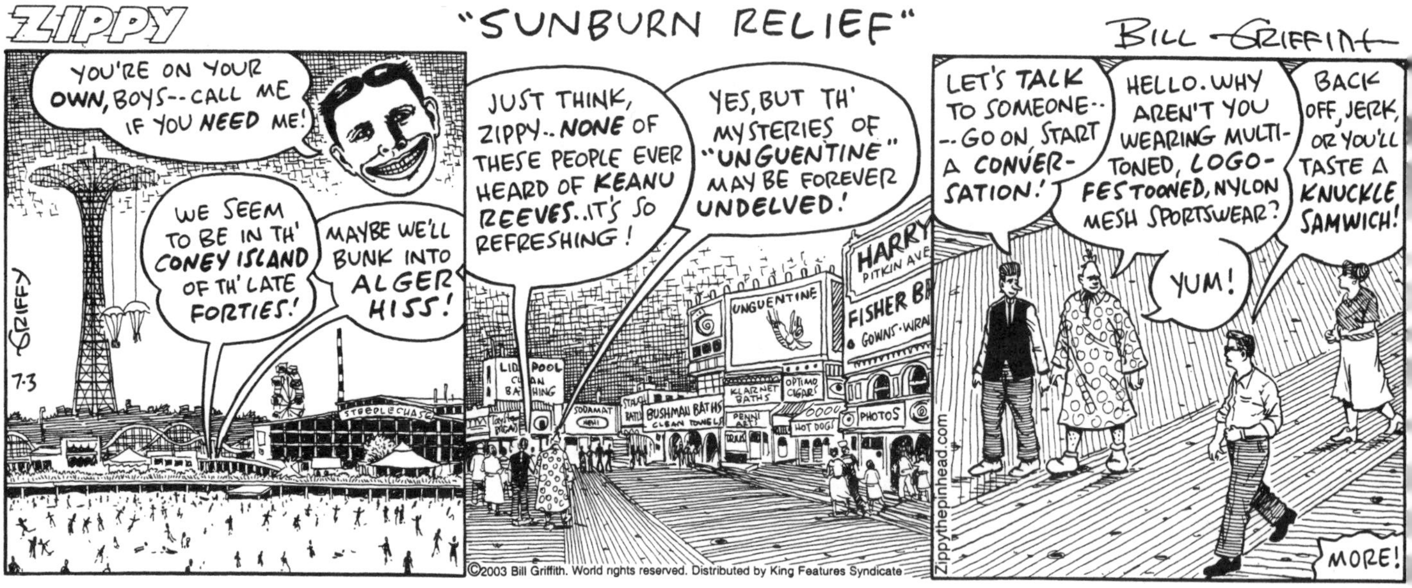
ZIPPY
"SUNBURN RELIEF"
BILL GRIFFITH
YOU'RE ON YOUR OWN, BOYS--CALL ME IF YOU NEED ME!
WE SEEM TO BE IN TH' CONEY ISLAND OF TH' LATE FORTIES!
MAYBE WE'LL BUNK INTO ALGER HISS!
GRIFFY 7-3
STEEPLECHASE
JUST THINK, ZIPPY.. NONE OF THESE PEOPLE EVER HEARD OF KEANU REEVES.. IT'S SO REFRESHING!
YES, BUT TH' MYSTERIES OF "UNGUENTINE" MAY BE FOREVER UNDELVED!
HARRY PITKIN AVE
FISHER BR
GOWNS·WRA
UNGUENTINE
LIDO POOL CLEAN BATHING
BUSHMAN BATHS CLEAN TOWELS
KLARNET BATHS
OPTIMO CIGARS
HOT DOGS
PHOTOS
©2003 Bill Griffith. World rights reserved. Distributed by King Features Syndicate
LET'S TALK TO SOMEONE-- --GO ON, START A CONVERSATION!
HELLO. WHY AREN'T YOU WEARING MULTI-TONED, LOGO-FESTOONED, NYLON MESH SPORTSWEAR?
BACK OFF, JERK, OR YOU'LL TASTE A KNUCKLE SAMWICH!
YUM!
Zippythepinhead.com
MORE!

1 H

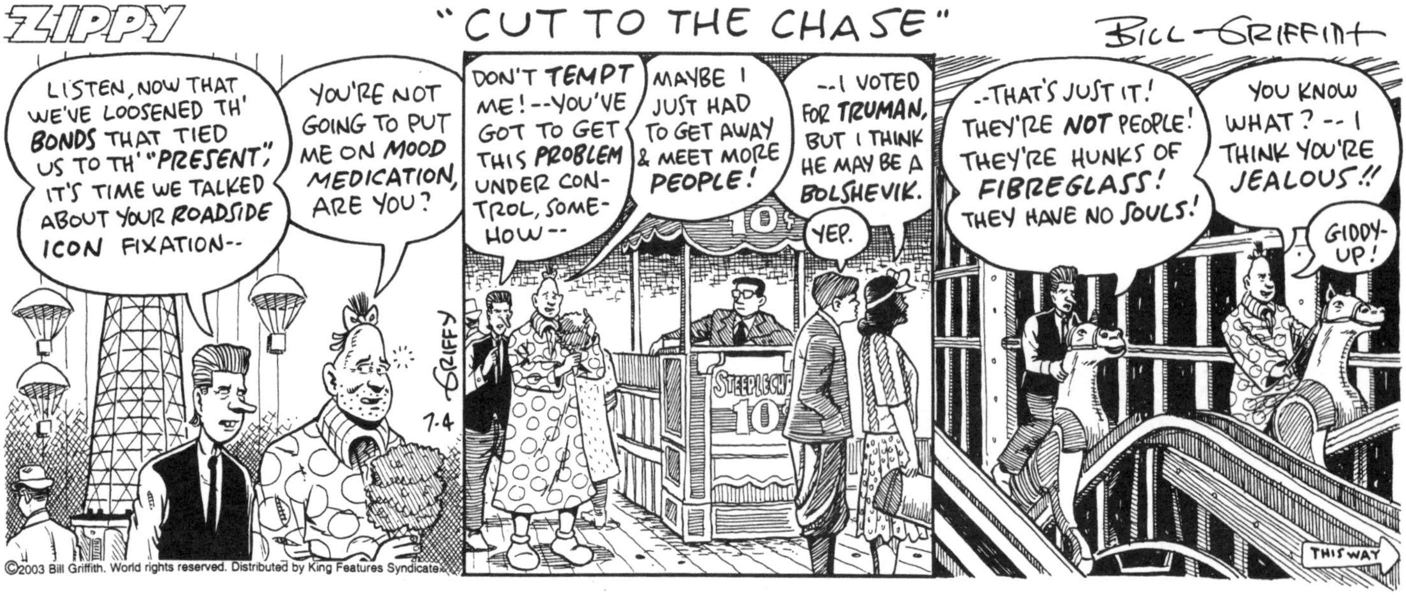
ZIPPY
"CUT TO THE CHASE"
BILL GRIFFITH
LISTEN, NOW THAT WE'VE LOOSENED TH' BONDS THAT TIED US TO TH' "PRESENT", IT'S TIME WE TALKED ABOUT YOUR ROADSIDE ICON FIXATION--
YOU'RE NOT GOING TO PUT ME ON MOOD MEDICATION, ARE YOU?
GRIFFY 7-4
©2003 Bill Griffith. World rights reserved. Distributed by King Features Syndicate
DON'T TEMPT ME! --YOU'VE GOT TO GET THIS PROBLEM UNDER CONTROL, SOMEHOW--
MAYBE I JUST HAD TO GET AWAY & MEET MORE PEOPLE!
--I VOTED FOR TRUMAN, BUT I THINK HE MAY BE A BOLSHEVIK.
YEP.
10¢
STEEPLECHASE 10¢
--THAT'S JUST IT! THEY'RE NOT PEOPLE! THEY'RE HUNKS OF FIBREGLASS! THEY HAVE NO SOULS!
YOU KNOW WHAT? --I THINK YOU'RE JEALOUS!!
GIDDY-UP!
THIS WAY

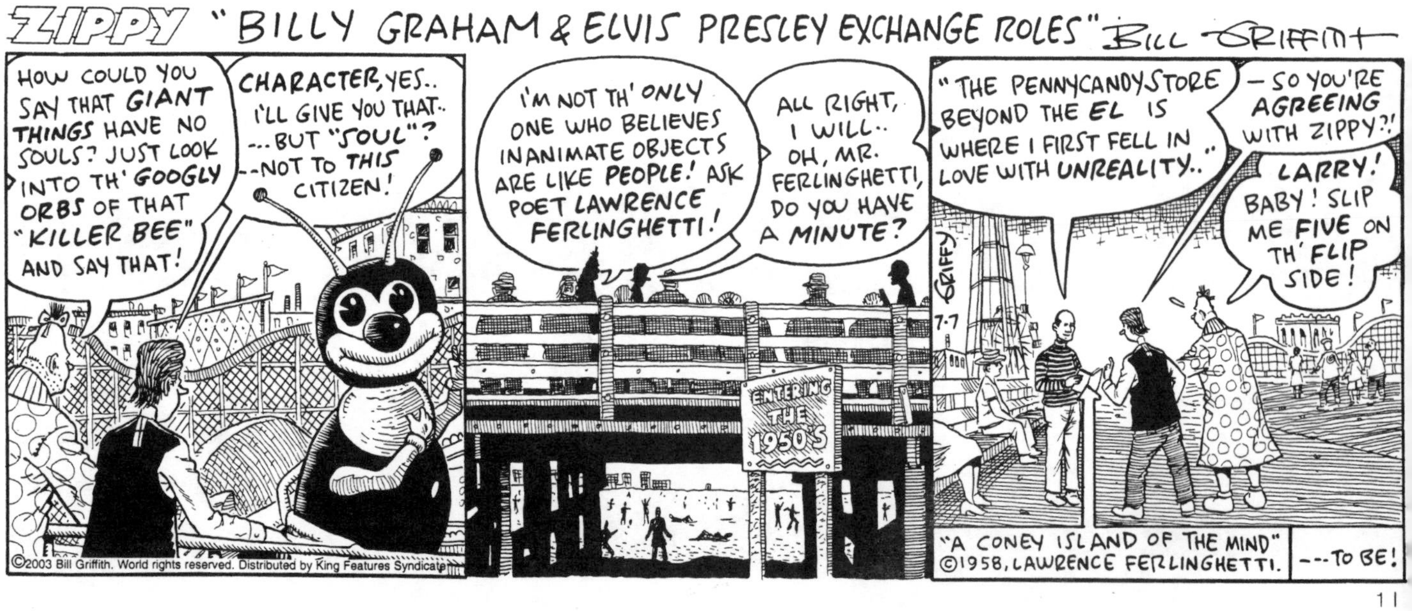
ZIPPY
"BILLY GRAHAM & ELVIS PRESLEY EXCHANGE ROLES"
BILL GRIFFITH
HOW COULD YOU SAY THAT GIANT THINGS HAVE NO SOULS? JUST LOOK INTO TH' GOOGLY ORBS OF THAT "KILLER BEE" AND SAY THAT!
CHARACTER, YES.. I'LL GIVE YOU THAT.. --BUT "SOUL"? --NOT TO THIS CITIZEN!
©2003 Bill Griffith. World rights reserved. Distributed by King Features Syndicate
I'M NOT TH' ONLY ONE WHO BELIEVES INANIMATE OBJECTS ARE LIKE PEOPLE! ASK POET LAWRENCE FERLINGHETTI!
ALL RIGHT, I WILL.. OH, MR. FERLINGHETTI, DO YOU HAVE A MINUTE?
ENTERING THE 1950'S
"THE PENNYCANDYSTORE BEYOND THE EL IS WHERE I FIRST FELL IN LOVE WITH UNREALITY.."
--SO YOU'RE AGREEING WITH ZIPPY?!
LARRY! BABY! SLIP ME FIVE ON TH' FLIP SIDE!
GRIFFY 7-7
"A CONEY ISLAND OF THE MIND" ©1958, LAWRENCE FERLINGHETTI.
---TO BE!

1 I

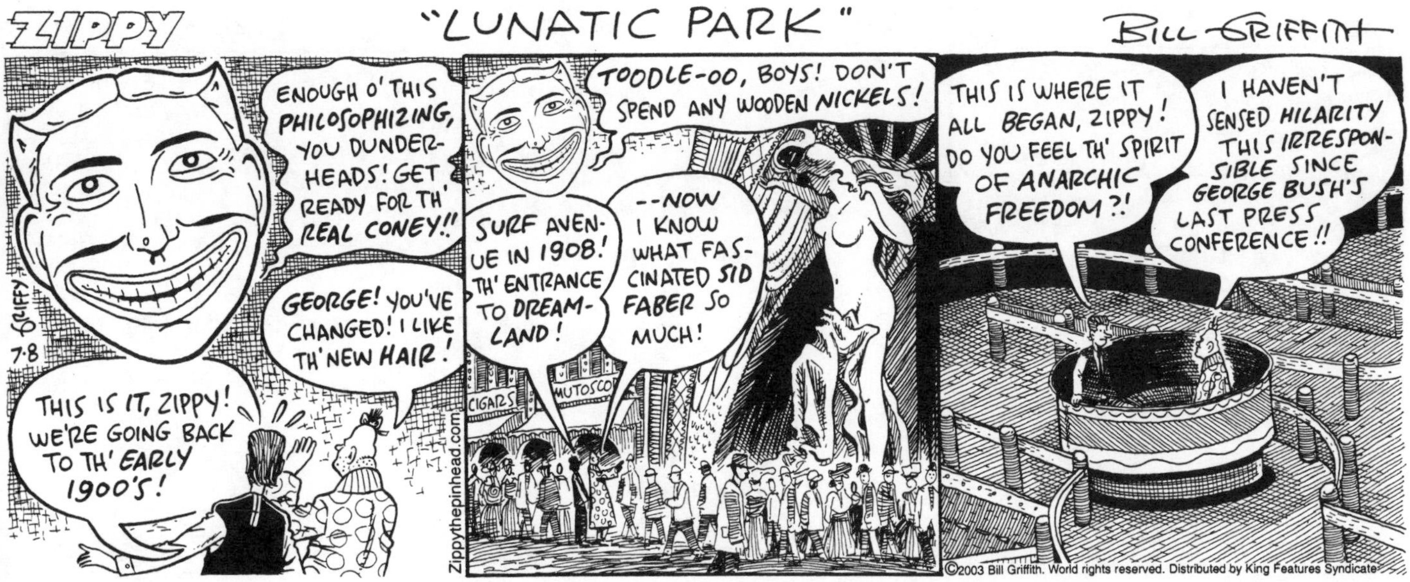
ZIPPY
"LUNATIC PARK"
BILL GRIFFITH
ENOUGH O' THIS PHILOSOPHIZING, YOU DUNDERHEADS! GET READY FOR TH' REAL CONEY!!
GEORGE! YOU'VE CHANGED! I LIKE TH' NEW HAIR!
THIS IS IT, ZIPPY! WE'RE GOING BACK TO TH' EARLY 1900'S!
GRIFFY 7·8
Zippythepinhead.com
TOODLE-OO, BOYS! DON'T SPEND ANY WOODEN NICKELS!
SURF AVENUE IN 1908! TH' ENTRANCE TO DREAMLAND!
--NOW I KNOW WHAT FASCINATED SID FABER SO MUCH!
CIGARS
MUTOSCO
THIS IS WHERE IT ALL BEGAN, ZIPPY! DO YOU FEEL TH' SPIRIT OF ANARCHIC FREEDOM?!
I HAVEN'T SENSED HILARITY THIS IRRESPONSIBLE SINCE GEORGE BUSH'S LAST PRESS CONFERENCE!!
©2003 Bill Griffith. World rights reserved. Distributed by King Features Syndicate

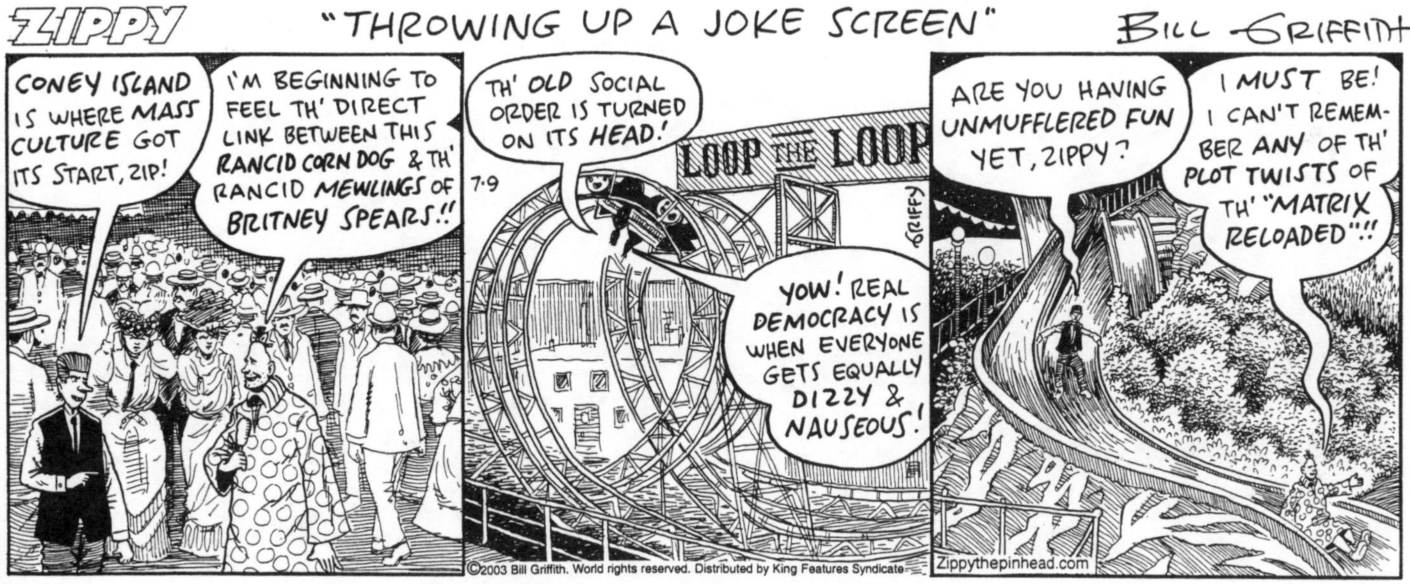
ZIPPY
"THROWING UP A JOKE SCREEN"
BILL GRIFFITH
CONEY ISLAND IS WHERE MASS CULTURE GOT ITS START, ZIP!
I'M BEGINNING TO FEEL TH' DIRECT LINK BETWEEN THIS RANCID CORN DOG & TH' RANCID MEWLINGS OF BRITNEY SPEARS!!
TH' OLD SOCIAL ORDER IS TURNED ON ITS HEAD!
LOOP THE LOOP
7·9
GRIFFY
YOW! REAL DEMOCRACY IS WHEN EVERYONE GETS EQUALLY DIZZY & NAUSEOUS!
©2003 Bill Griffith. World rights reserved. Distributed by King Features Syndicate
ARE YOU HAVING UNMUFFLERED FUN YET, ZIPPY?
I MUST BE! I CAN'T REMEMBER ANY OF TH' PLOT TWISTS OF TH' "MATRIX RELOADED"!!
Zippythepinhead.com

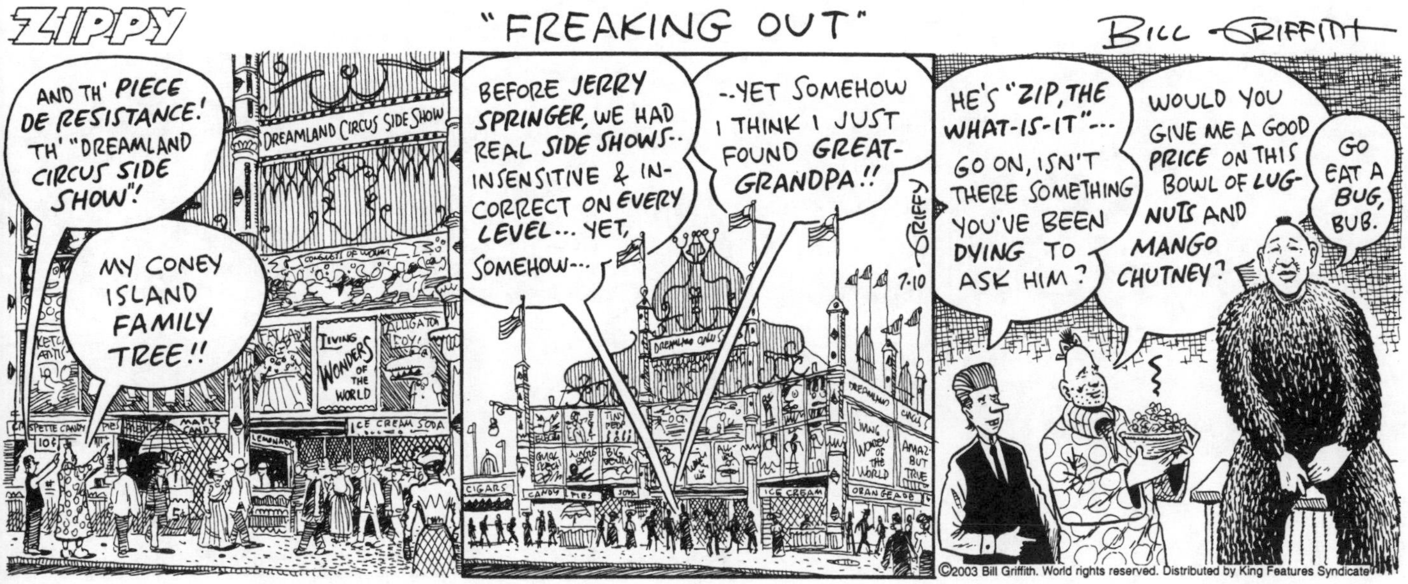
ZIPPY
"FREAKING OUT"
BILL GRIFFITH
AND TH' PIECE DE RESISTANCE! TH' "DREAMLAND CIRCUS SIDE SHOW"!
DREAMLAND CIRCUS SIDE SHOW
MY CONEY ISLAND FAMILY TREE!!
LIVING WONDERS OF THE WORLD
ICE CREAM SODA
BEFORE JERRY SPRINGER, WE HAD REAL SIDE SHOWS.. INSENSITIVE & INCORRECT ON EVERY LEVEL... YET, SOMEHOW...
--YET SOMEHOW I THINK I JUST FOUND GREAT-GRANDPA!!
GRIFFY 7·10
CIGARS
ICE CREAM
HE'S "ZIP, THE WHAT-IS-IT"... GO ON, ISN'T THERE SOMETHING YOU'VE BEEN DYING TO ASK HIM?
WOULD YOU GIVE ME A GOOD PRICE ON THIS BOWL OF LUG-NUTS AND MANGO CHUTNEY?
GO EAT A BUG, BUB.
©2003 Bill Griffith. World rights reserved. Distributed by King Features Syndicate

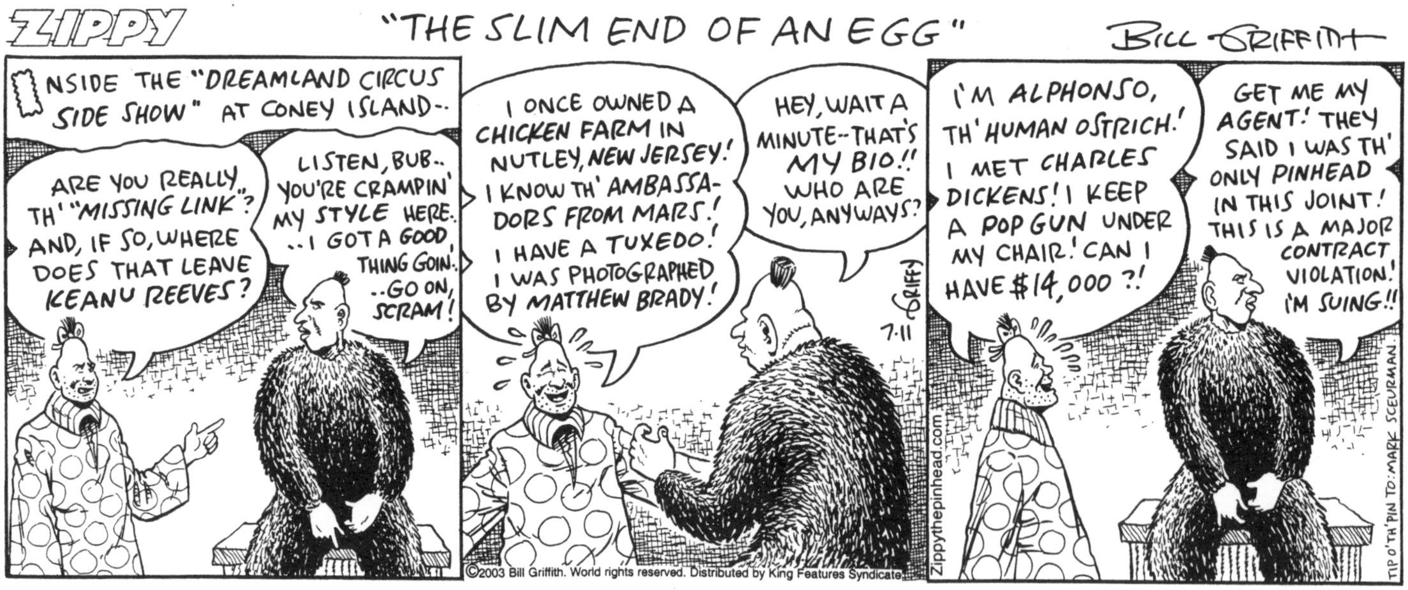
ZIPPY
"THE SLIM END OF AN EGG"
BILL GRIFFITH
INSIDE THE "DREAMLAND CIRCUS SIDE SHOW" AT CONEY ISLAND--
ARE YOU REALLY TH' "MISSING LINK"? AND, IF SO, WHERE DOES THAT LEAVE KEANU REEVES?
LISTEN, BUB.. YOU'RE CRAMPIN' MY STYLE HERE.. ..I GOT A GOOD THING GOIN'.. ..GO ON, SCRAM!
I ONCE OWNED A CHICKEN FARM IN NUTLEY, NEW JERSEY! I KNOW TH' AMBASSADORS FROM MARS! I HAVE A TUXEDO! I WAS PHOTOGRAPHED BY MATTHEW BRADY!
HEY, WAIT A MINUTE--THAT'S MY BIO!! WHO ARE YOU, ANYWAYS?
GRIFFY
7-11
©2003 Bill Griffith. World rights reserved. Distributed by King Features Syndicate
Zippythepinhead.com
I'M ALPHONSO, TH' HUMAN OSTRICH! I MET CHARLES DICKENS! I KEEP A POP GUN UNDER MY CHAIR! CAN I HAVE $14,000?!
GET ME MY AGENT! THEY SAID I WAS TH' ONLY PINHEAD IN THIS JOINT! THIS IS A MAJOR CONTRACT VIOLATION! I'M SUING!!
TIP O' TH' PIN TO: MARK SCEURMAN

1 J

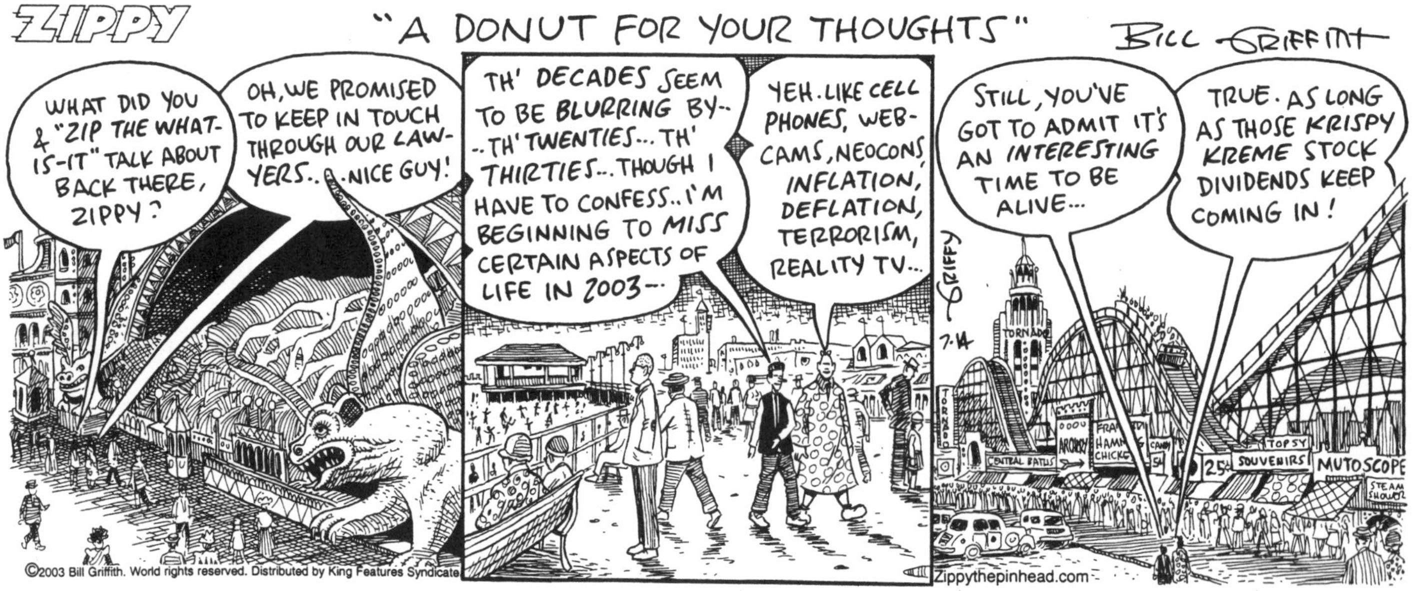
ZIPPY
"A DONUT FOR YOUR THOUGHTS"
BILL GRIFFITH
WHAT DID YOU & "ZIP THE WHAT-IS-IT" TALK ABOUT BACK THERE, ZIPPY?
OH, WE PROMISED TO KEEP IN TOUCH THROUGH OUR LAWYERS.. ..NICE GUY!
©2003 Bill Griffith. World rights reserved. Distributed by King Features Syndicate
TH' DECADES SEEM TO BE BLURRING BY-- --TH' TWENTIES... TH' THIRTIES... THOUGH I HAVE TO CONFESS.. I'M BEGINNING TO MISS CERTAIN ASPECTS OF LIFE IN 2003--
YEH. LIKE CELL PHONES, WEBCAMS, NEOCONS, INFLATION, DEFLATION, TERRORISM, REALITY TV...
GRIFFY
7-14
STILL, YOU'VE GOT TO ADMIT IT'S AN INTERESTING TIME TO BE ALIVE...
TRUE. AS LONG AS THOSE KRISPY KREME STOCK DIVIDENDS KEEP COMING IN!
TORNADO
SOUVENIRS
MUTOSCOPE
Zippythepinhead.com

1 K

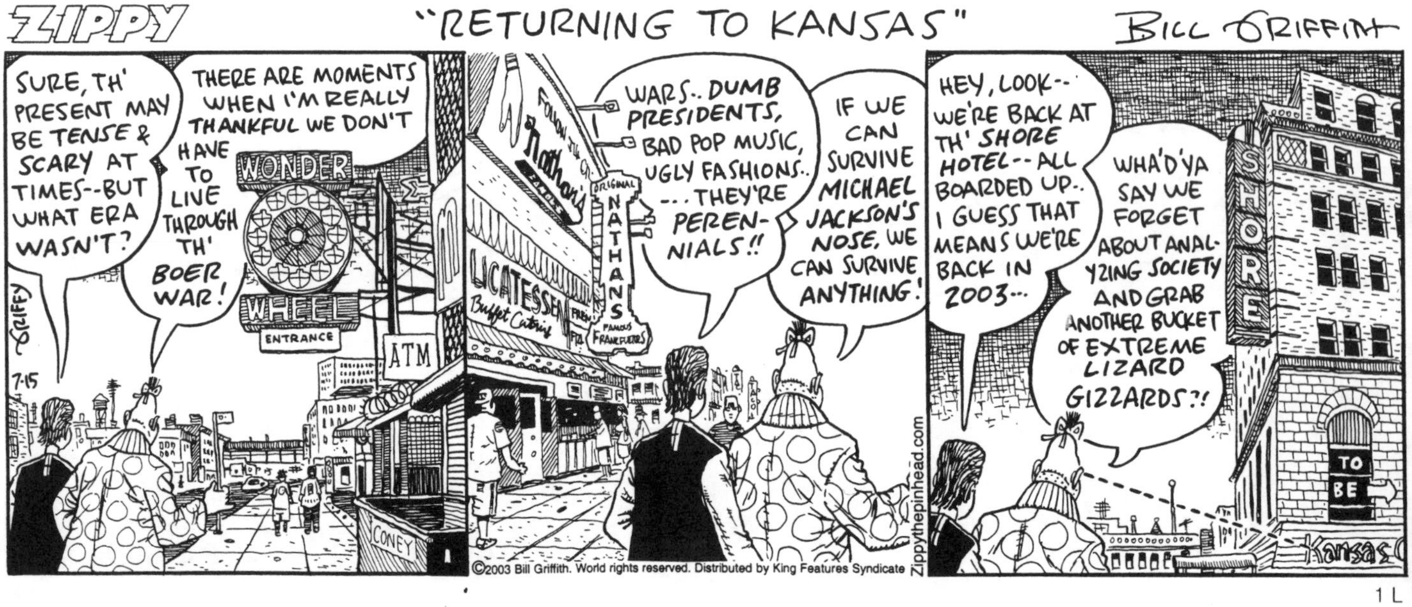
ZIPPY
"RETURNING TO KANSAS"
BILL GRIFFITH
SURE, TH' PRESENT MAY BE TENSE & SCARY AT TIMES--BUT WHAT ERA WASN'T?
THERE ARE MOMENTS WHEN I'M REALLY THANKFUL WE DON'T HAVE TO LIVE THROUGH TH' BOER WAR!
WONDER WHEEL
ENTRANCE
ATM
GRIFFY
7-15
WARS.. DUMB PRESIDENTS, BAD POP MUSIC, UGLY FASHIONS.. ...THEY'RE PERENNIALS!!
IF WE CAN SURVIVE MICHAEL JACKSON'S NOSE, WE CAN SURVIVE ANYTHING!
NATHAN'S
©2003 Bill Griffith. World rights reserved. Distributed by King Features Syndicate
Zippythepinhead.com
HEY, LOOK-- WE'RE BACK AT TH' SHORE HOTEL--ALL BOARDED UP.. I GUESS THAT MEANS WE'RE BACK IN 2003--
WHA'D'YA SAY WE FORGET ABOUT ANALYZING SOCIETY AND GRAB ANOTHER BUCKET OF EXTREME LIZARD GIZZARDS?!
SHORE
TO BE
KANSAS

1 L

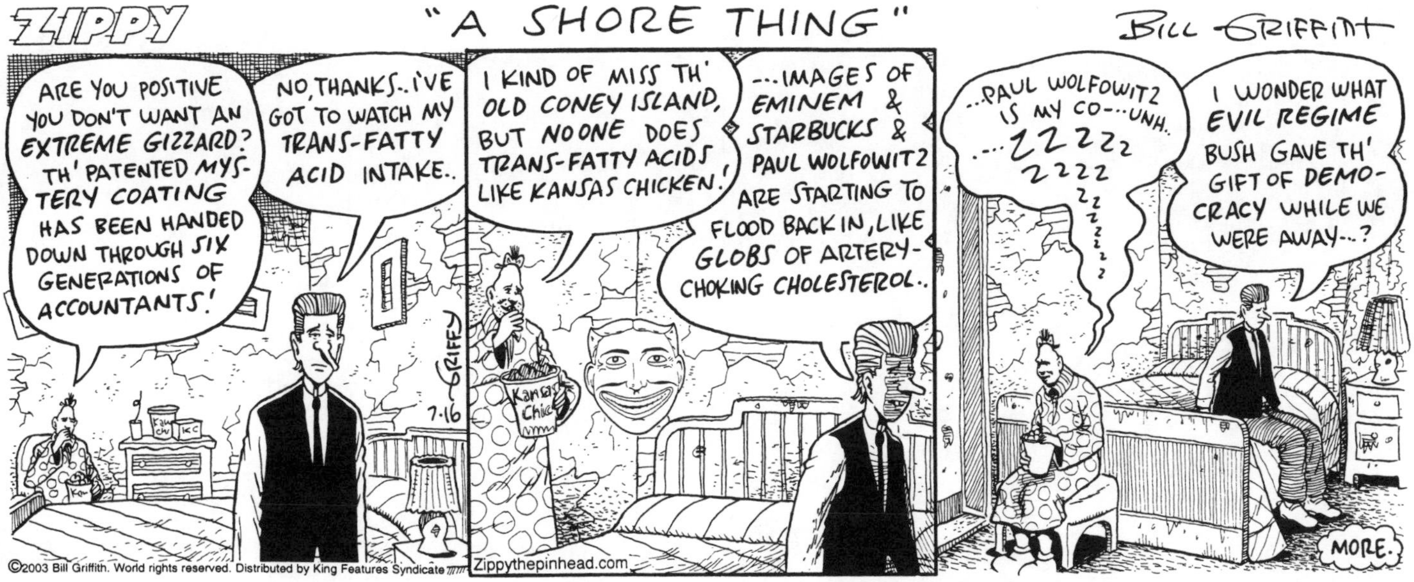
ZIPPY
"A SHORE THING"
BILL GRIFFITH
ARE YOU POSITIVE YOU DON'T WANT AN EXTREME GIZZARD? TH' PATENTED MYSTERY COATING HAS BEEN HANDED DOWN THROUGH SIX GENERATIONS OF ACCOUNTANTS!
NO, THANKS.. I'VE GOT TO WATCH MY TRANS-FATTY ACID INTAKE..
GRIFFY 7·16
I KIND OF MISS TH' OLD CONEY ISLAND, BUT NOONE DOES TRANS-FATTY ACIDS LIKE KANSAS CHICKEN!
...IMAGES OF EMINEM & STARBUCKS & PAUL WOLFOWITZ ARE STARTING TO FLOOD BACK IN, LIKE GLOBS OF ARTERY-CHOKING CHOLESTEROL..
...PAUL WOLFOWITZ IS MY CO---UNH.. ...ZZZZZ ZZZZ
I WONDER WHAT EVIL REGIME BUSH GAVE TH' GIFT OF DEMOCRACY WHILE WE WERE AWAY...?
MORE.
©2003 Bill Griffith. World rights reserved. Distributed by King Features Syndicate
Zippythepinhead.com

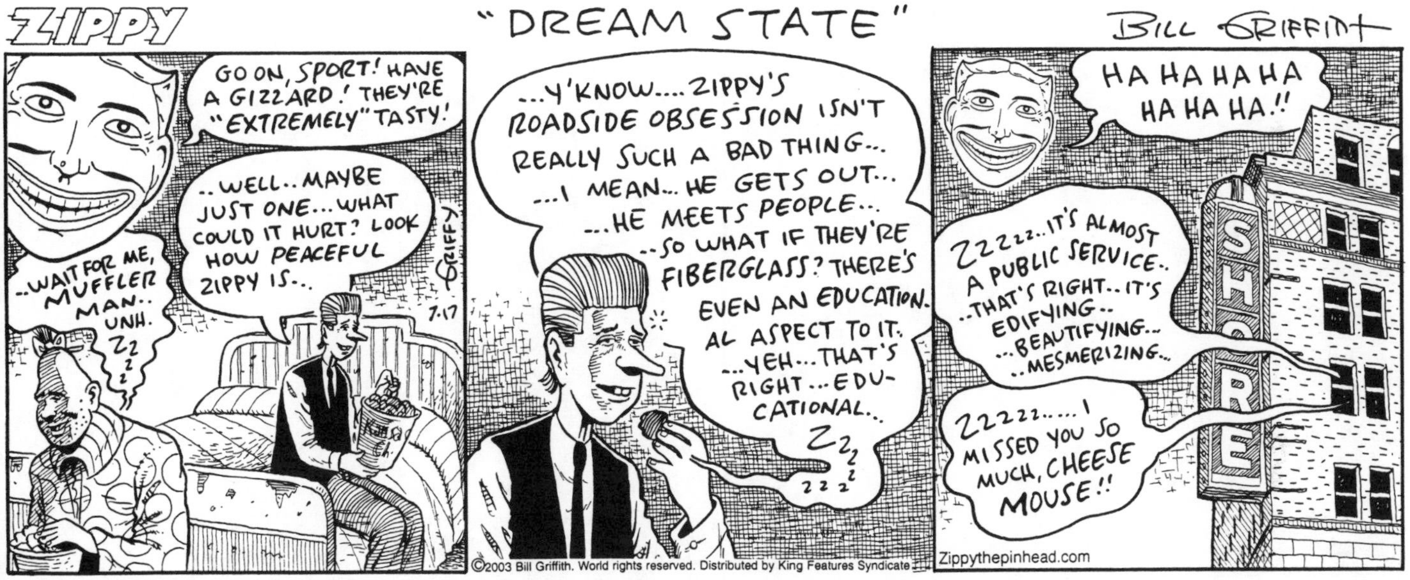
ZIPPY
"DREAM STATE"
BILL GRIFFITH
GO ON, SPORT! HAVE A GIZZARD! THEY'RE "EXTREMELY" TASTY!
..WELL.. MAYBE JUST ONE... WHAT COULD IT HURT? LOOK HOW PEACEFUL ZIPPY IS...
..WAIT FOR ME, MUFFLER MAN.. UNH. ZZZ
GRIFFY 7·17
...Y'KNOW.... ZIPPY'S ROADSIDE OBSESSION ISN'T REALLY SUCH A BAD THING... ...I MEAN... HE GETS OUT... ...HE MEETS PEOPLE... ..SO WHAT IF THEY'RE FIBERGLASS? THERE'S EVEN AN EDUCATIONAL ASPECT TO IT. ...YEH...THAT'S RIGHT...EDUCATIONAL... ZZZZZ
HA HA HA HA HA HA HA!!
ZZZZZ.. IT'S ALMOST A PUBLIC SERVICE.. ..THAT'S RIGHT.. IT'S EDIFYING.. ..BEAUTIFYING.. ..MESMERIZING..
ZZZZZ.... I MISSED YOU SO MUCH, CHEESE MOUSE!!
SHORE
©2003 Bill Griffith. World rights reserved. Distributed by King Features Syndicate
Zippythepinhead.com

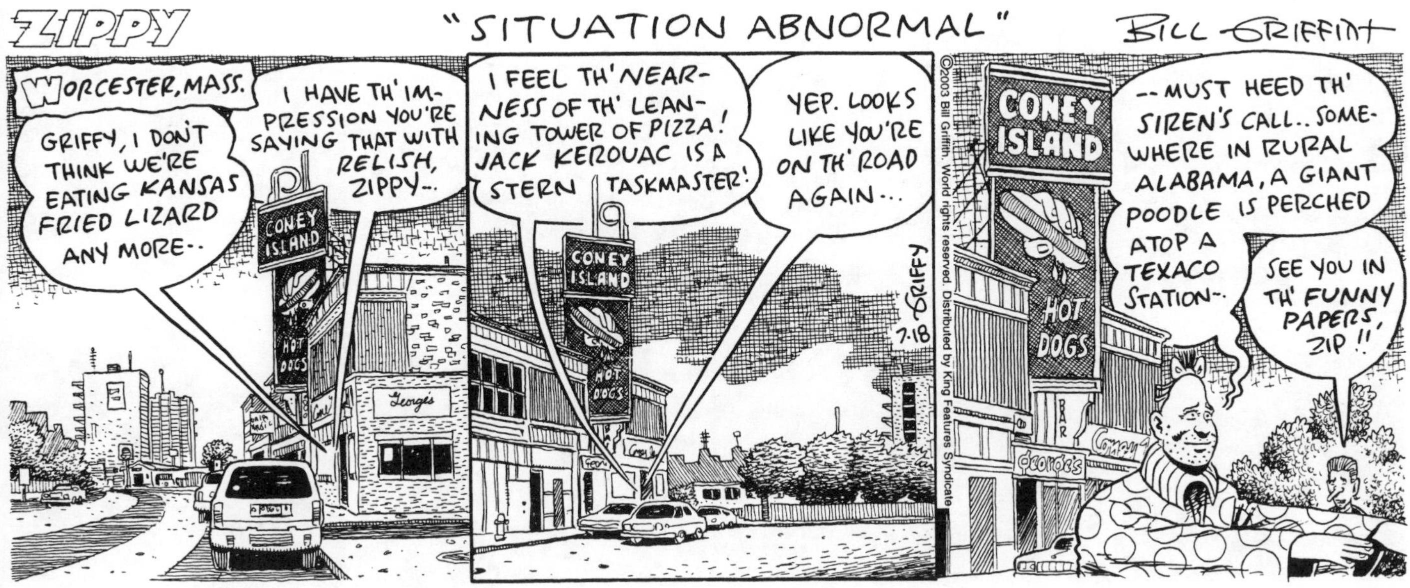
ZIPPY
"SITUATION ABNORMAL"
BILL GRIFFITH
WORCESTER, MASS.
GRIFFY, I DON'T THINK WE'RE EATING KANSAS FRIED LIZARD ANY MORE..
I HAVE TH' IMPRESSION YOU'RE SAYING THAT WITH RELISH, ZIPPY..
CONEY ISLAND
HOT DOGS
I FEEL TH' NEARNESS OF TH' LEANING TOWER OF PIZZA! JACK KEROUAC IS A STERN TASKMASTER!
YEP. LOOKS LIKE YOU'RE ON TH' ROAD AGAIN...
GRIFFY 7·18
©2003 Bill Griffith. World rights reserved. Distributed by King Features Syndicate
CONEY ISLAND
HOT DOGS
--MUST HEED TH' SIREN'S CALL.. SOMEWHERE IN RURAL ALABAMA, A GIANT POODLE IS PERCHED ATOP A TEXACO STATION..
SEE YOU IN TH' FUNNY PAPERS, ZIP!!

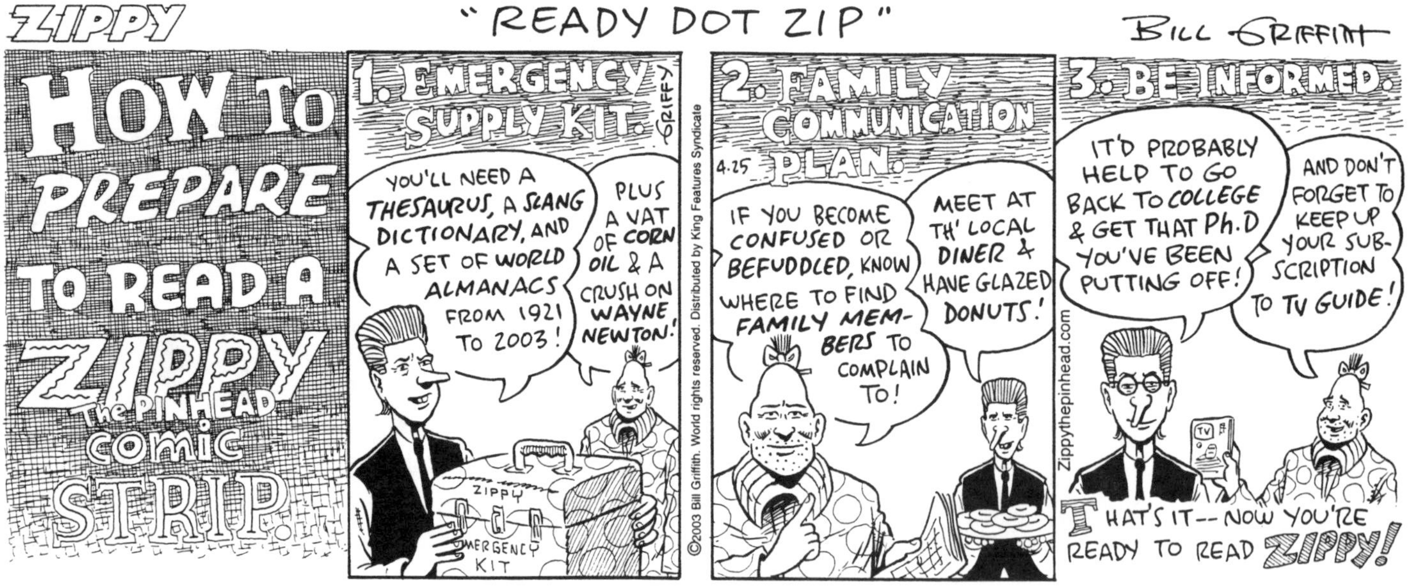
ZIPPY
"READY DOT ZIP"
BILL GRIFFITH
HOW TO PREPARE TO READ A ZIPPY The PINHEAD comic STRIP.
1. EMERGENCY SUPPLY KIT.
YOU'LL NEED A THESAURUS, A SLANG DICTIONARY, AND A SET OF WORLD ALMANACS FROM 1921 TO 2003!
PLUS A VAT OF CORN OIL & A CRUSH ON WAYNE NEWTON!
ZIPPY EMERGENCY KIT
GRIFFY
©2003 Bill Griffith. World rights reserved. Distributed by King Features Syndicate
2. FAMILY COMMUNICATION PLAN.
4.25
IF YOU BECOME CONFUSED OR BEFUDDLED, KNOW WHERE TO FIND FAMILY MEMBERS TO COMPLAIN TO!
MEET AT TH' LOCAL DINER & HAVE GLAZED DONUTS!
Zippythepinhead.com
3. BE INFORMED.
IT'D PROBABLY HELP TO GO BACK TO COLLEGE & GET THAT Ph.D YOU'VE BEEN PUTTING OFF!
AND DON'T FORGET TO KEEP UP YOUR SUBSCRIPTION TO TV GUIDE!
THAT'S IT -- NOW YOU'RE READY TO READ ZIPPY!

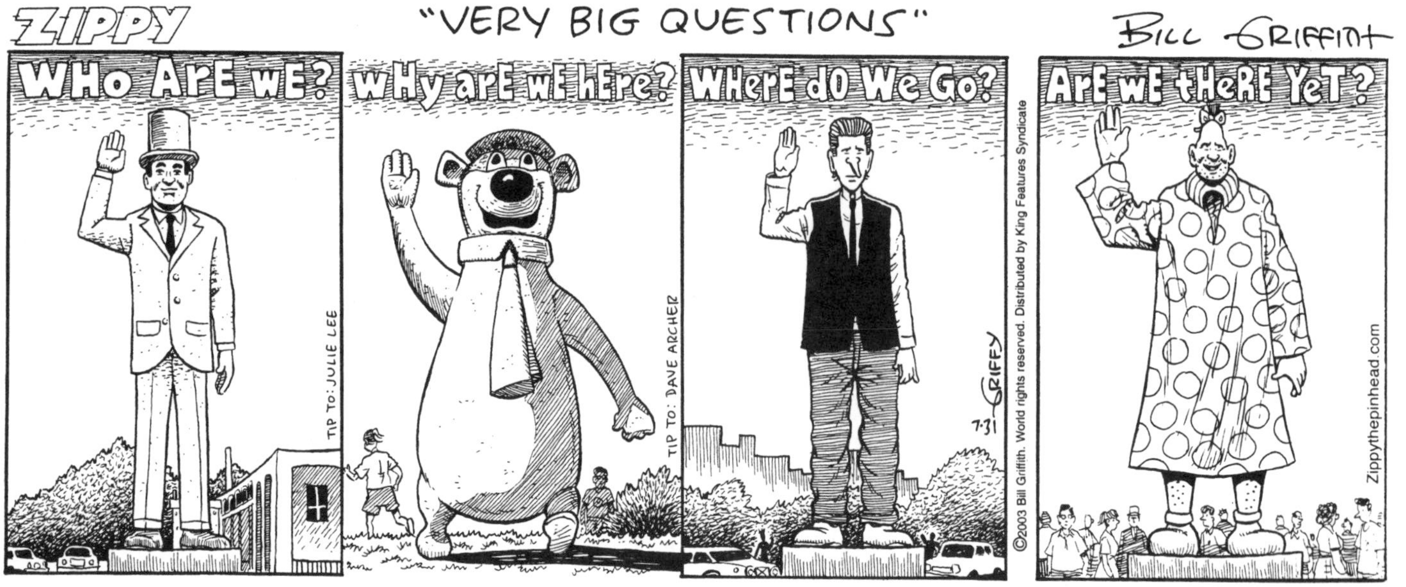
ZIPPY
"VERY BIG QUESTIONS"
BILL GRIFFITH
WHO ARE WE?
TIP TO: JULIE LEE
WHY ARE WE HERE?
TIP TO: DAVE ARCHER
WHERE DO WE GO?
GRIFFY
7.31
©2003 Bill Griffith. World rights reserved. Distributed by King Features Syndicate
ARE WE THERE YET?
Zippythepinhead.com

2

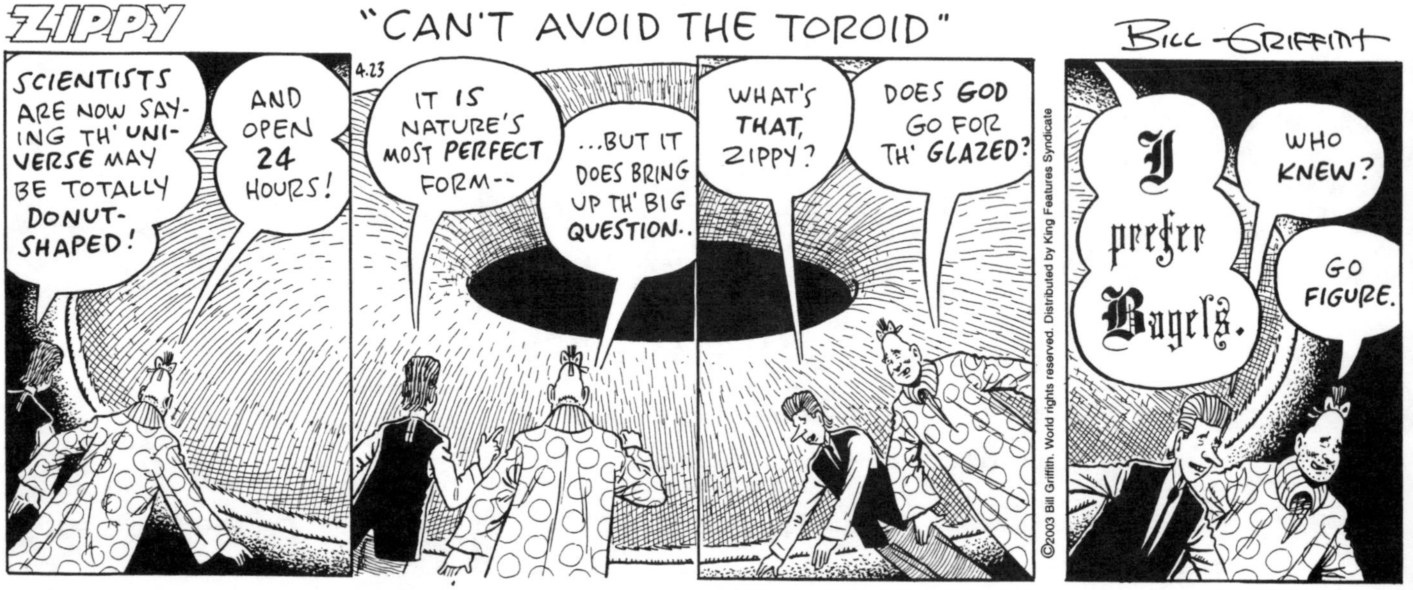
ZIPPY
"CAN'T AVOID THE TOROID"
BILL GRIFFITH
SCIENTISTS ARE NOW SAYING TH' UNIVERSE MAY BE TOTALLY DONUT-SHAPED!
AND OPEN 24 HOURS!
4.23
IT IS NATURE'S MOST PERFECT FORM--
...BUT IT DOES BRING UP TH' BIG QUESTION..
WHAT'S THAT, ZIPPY?
DOES GOD GO FOR TH' GLAZED?
©2003 Bill Griffith. World rights reserved. Distributed by King Features Syndicate
I prefer Bagels.
WHO KNEW?
GO FIGURE.

3

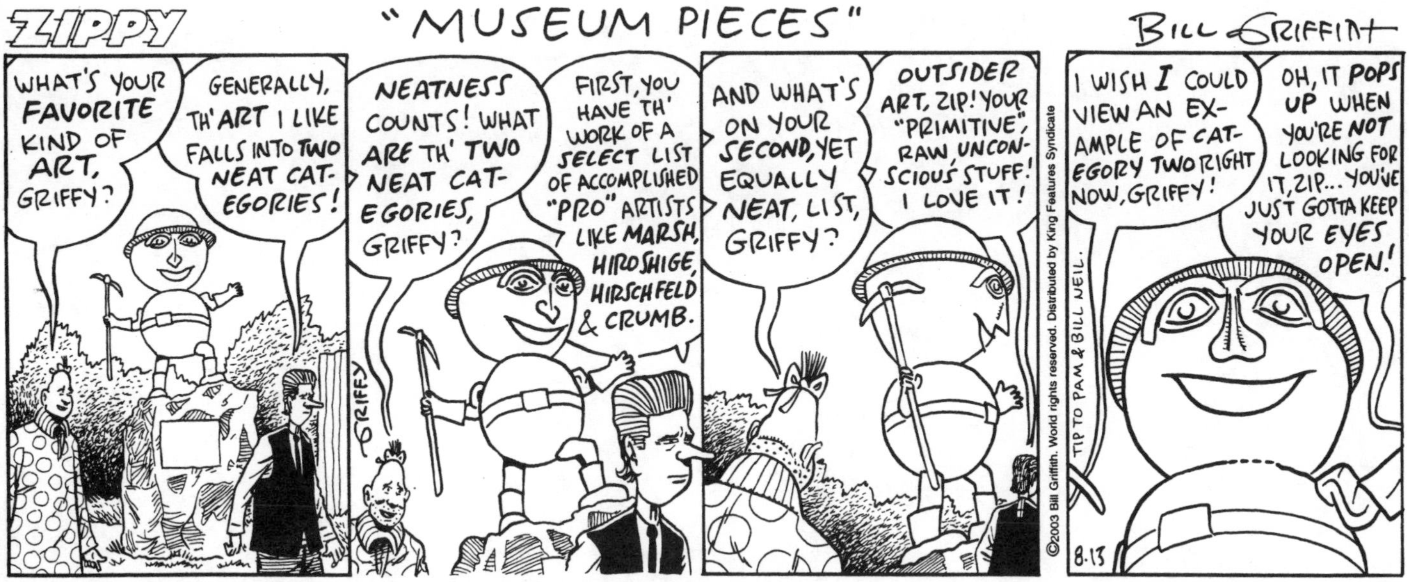
ZIPPY
"MUSEUM PIECES"
BILL GRIFFITH
WHAT'S YOUR FAVORITE KIND OF ART, GRIFFY?
GENERALLY, TH' ART I LIKE FALLS INTO TWO NEAT CATEGORIES!
NEATNESS COUNTS! WHAT ARE TH' TWO NEAT CATEGORIES, GRIFFY?
FIRST, YOU HAVE TH' WORK OF A SELECT LIST OF ACCOMPLISHED "PRO" ARTISTS LIKE MARSH, HIROSHIGE, HIRSCHFELD & CRUMB.
AND WHAT'S ON YOUR SECOND, YET EQUALLY NEAT, LIST, GRIFFY?
OUTSIDER ART, ZIP! YOUR "PRIMITIVE", RAW, UNCONSCIOUS STUFF! I LOVE IT!
I WISH I COULD VIEW AN EXAMPLE OF CATEGORY TWO RIGHT NOW, GRIFFY!
OH, IT POPS UP WHEN YOU'RE NOT LOOKING FOR IT, ZIP... YOU'VE JUST GOTTA KEEP YOUR EYES OPEN!
GRIFFY
TIP TO PAM & BILL NEIL.
©2003 Bill Griffith. World rights reserved. Distributed by King Features Syndicate
8.13

4

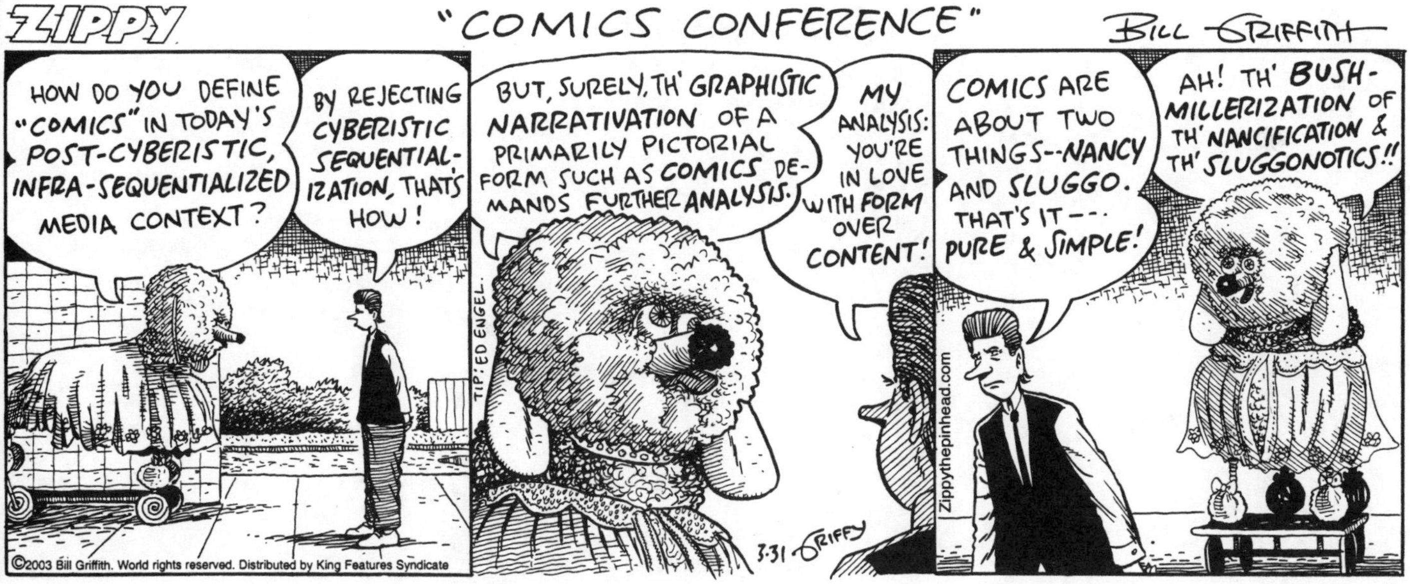
ZIPPY
"COMICS CONFERENCE"
BILL GRIFFITH
HOW DO YOU DEFINE "COMICS" IN TODAY'S POST-CYBERISTIC, INFRA-SEQUENTIALIZED MEDIA CONTEXT?
BY REJECTING CYBERISTIC SEQUENTIALIZATION, THAT'S HOW!
BUT, SURELY, TH' GRAPHISTIC NARRATIVATION OF A PRIMARILY PICTORIAL FORM SUCH AS COMICS DEMANDS FURTHER ANALYSIS.
MY ANALYSIS: YOU'RE IN LOVE WITH FORM OVER CONTENT!
COMICS ARE ABOUT TWO THINGS--NANCY AND SLUGGO. THAT'S IT---. PURE & SIMPLE!
AH! TH' BUSH-MILLERIZATION OF TH' NANCIFICATION & TH' SLUGGONOTICS!!
TIP: ED ENGEL.
3.31 GRIFFY
Zippythepinhead.com
©2003 Bill Griffith. World rights reserved. Distributed by King Features Syndicate

5

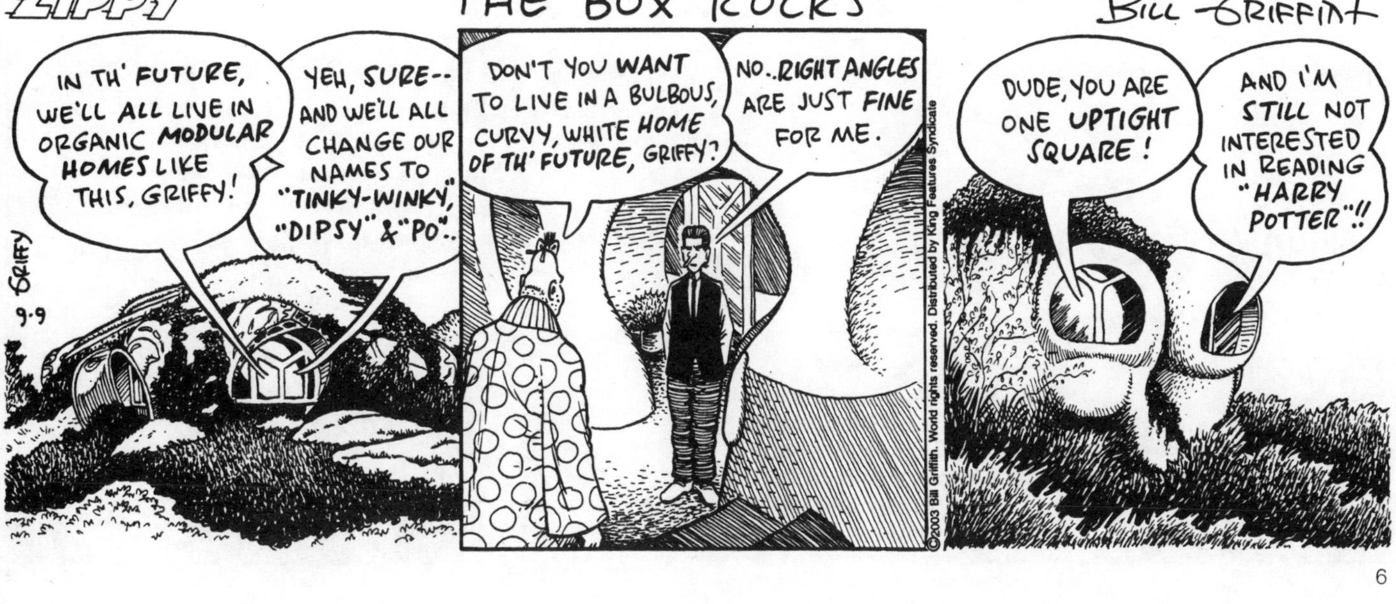
ZIPPY
"THE BOX ROCKS"
BILL GRIFFITH
IN TH' FUTURE, WE'LL ALL LIVE IN ORGANIC MODULAR HOMES LIKE THIS, GRIFFY!
YEH, SURE-- AND WE'LL ALL CHANGE OUR NAMES TO "TINKY-WINKY", "DIPSY" & "PO"..
DON'T YOU WANT TO LIVE IN A BULBOUS, CURVY, WHITE HOME OF TH' FUTURE, GRIFFY?
NO.. RIGHT ANGLES ARE JUST FINE FOR ME.
DUDE, YOU ARE ONE UPTIGHT SQUARE!
AND I'M STILL NOT INTERESTED IN READING "HARRY POTTER"!!
GRIFFY 9.9
©2003 Bill Griffith. World rights reserved. Distributed by King Features Syndicate

6

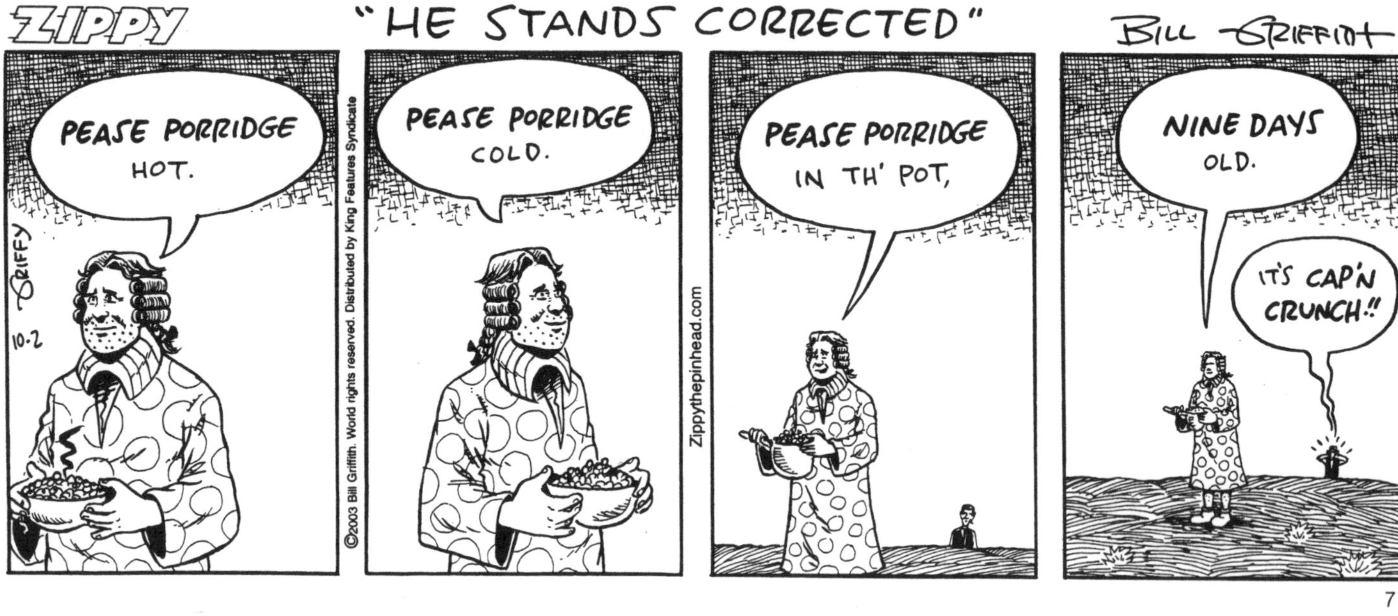
ZIPPY
"HE STANDS CORRECTED"
BILL GRIFFITH
PEASE PORRIDGE HOT.
GRIFFY 10-2
©2003 Bill Griffith. World rights reserved. Distributed by King Features Syndicate
PEASE PORRIDGE COLD.
Zippythepinhead.com
PEASE PORRIDGE IN TH' POT,
NINE DAYS OLD.
IT'S CAP'N CRUNCH!!
7

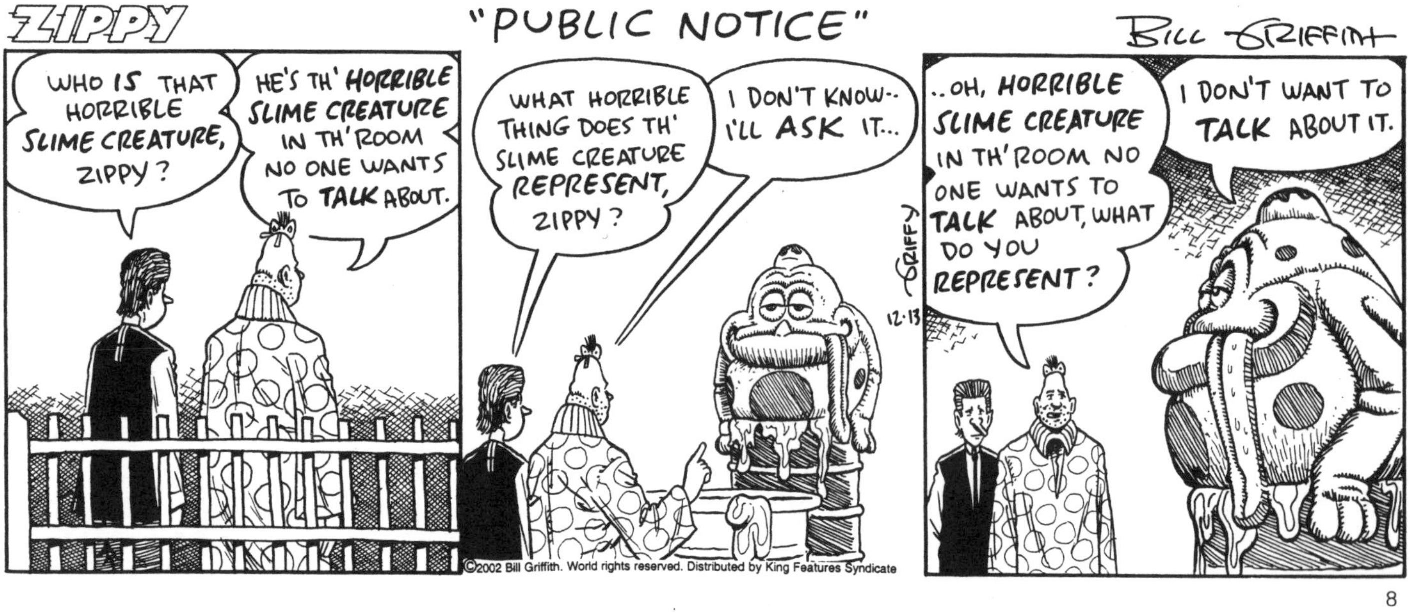
ZIPPY
"PUBLIC NOTICE"
BILL GRIFFITH
WHO IS THAT HORRIBLE SLIME CREATURE, ZIPPY?
HE'S TH' HORRIBLE SLIME CREATURE IN TH' ROOM NO ONE WANTS TO TALK ABOUT.
WHAT HORRIBLE THING DOES TH' SLIME CREATURE REPRESENT, ZIPPY?
I DON'T KNOW.. I'LL ASK IT...
©2002 Bill Griffith. World rights reserved. Distributed by King Features Syndicate
GRIFFY 12-13
..OH, HORRIBLE SLIME CREATURE IN TH' ROOM NO ONE WANTS TO TALK ABOUT, WHAT DO YOU REPRESENT?
I DON'T WANT TO TALK ABOUT IT.
8

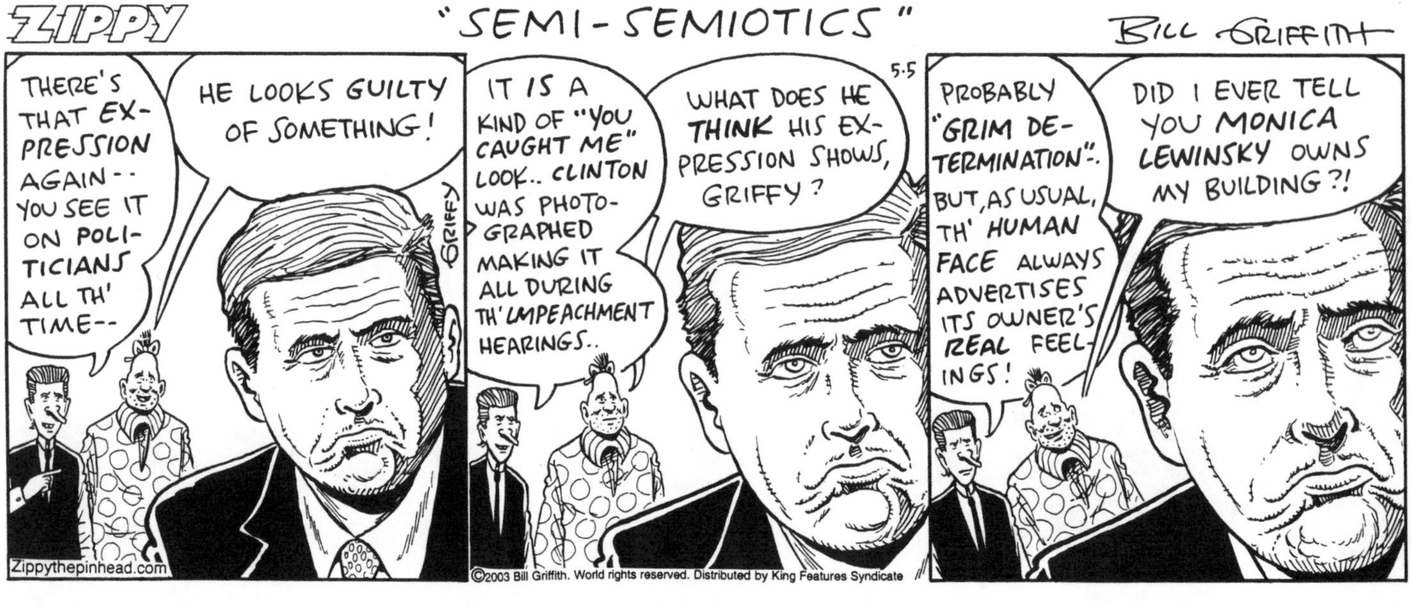
ZIPPY
"SEMI-SEMIOTICS"
BILL GRIFFITH
THERE'S THAT EXPRESSION AGAIN -- YOU SEE IT ON POLITICIANS ALL TH' TIME --
HE LOOKS GUILTY OF SOMETHING!
GRIFFY
Zippythepinhead.com
IT IS A KIND OF "YOU CAUGHT ME" LOOK.. CLINTON WAS PHOTOGRAPHED MAKING IT ALL DURING TH' IMPEACHMENT HEARINGS..
5-5
WHAT DOES HE THINK HIS EXPRESSION SHOWS, GRIFFY?
©2003 Bill Griffith. World rights reserved. Distributed by King Features Syndicate
PROBABLY "GRIM DETERMINATION".. BUT, AS USUAL, TH' HUMAN FACE ALWAYS ADVERTISES ITS OWNER'S REAL FEELINGS!
DID I EVER TELL YOU MONICA LEWINSKY OWNS MY BUILDING?!

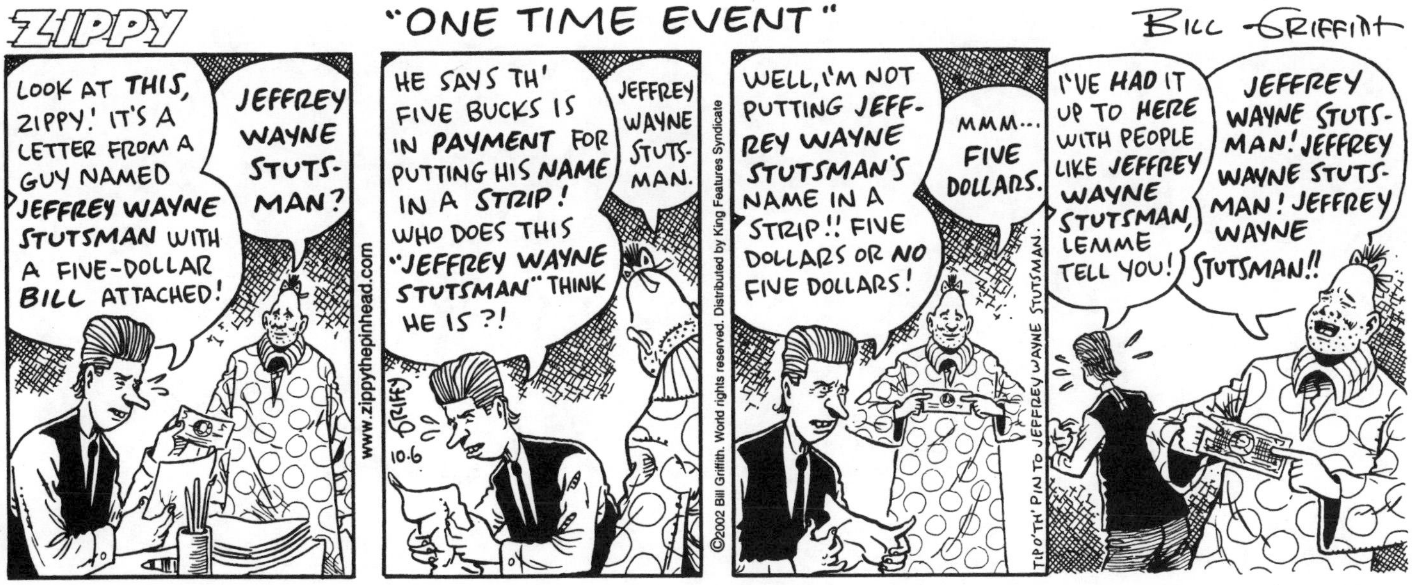
ZIPPY
"ONE TIME EVENT"
BILL GRIFFITH
LOOK AT THIS, ZIPPY! IT'S A LETTER FROM A GUY NAMED JEFFREY WAYNE STUTSMAN WITH A FIVE-DOLLAR BILL ATTACHED!
JEFFREY WAYNE STUTSMAN?
www.zippythepinhead.com
HE SAYS TH' FIVE BUCKS IS IN PAYMENT FOR PUTTING HIS NAME IN A STRIP! WHO DOES THIS "JEFFREY WAYNE STUTSMAN" THINK HE IS?!
JEFFREY WAYNE STUTSMAN.
GRIFFY 10-6
©2002 Bill Griffith. World rights reserved. Distributed by King Features Syndicate
WELL, I'M NOT PUTTING JEFFREY WAYNE STUTSMAN'S NAME IN A STRIP!! FIVE DOLLARS OR NO FIVE DOLLARS!
MMM... FIVE DOLLARS.
TIP O' TH' PIN TO JEFFREY WAYNE STUTSMAN.
I'VE HAD IT UP TO HERE WITH PEOPLE LIKE JEFFREY WAYNE STUTSMAN, LEMME TELL YOU!
JEFFREY WAYNE STUTSMAN! JEFFREY WAYNE STUTSMAN! JEFFREY WAYNE STUTSMAN!!

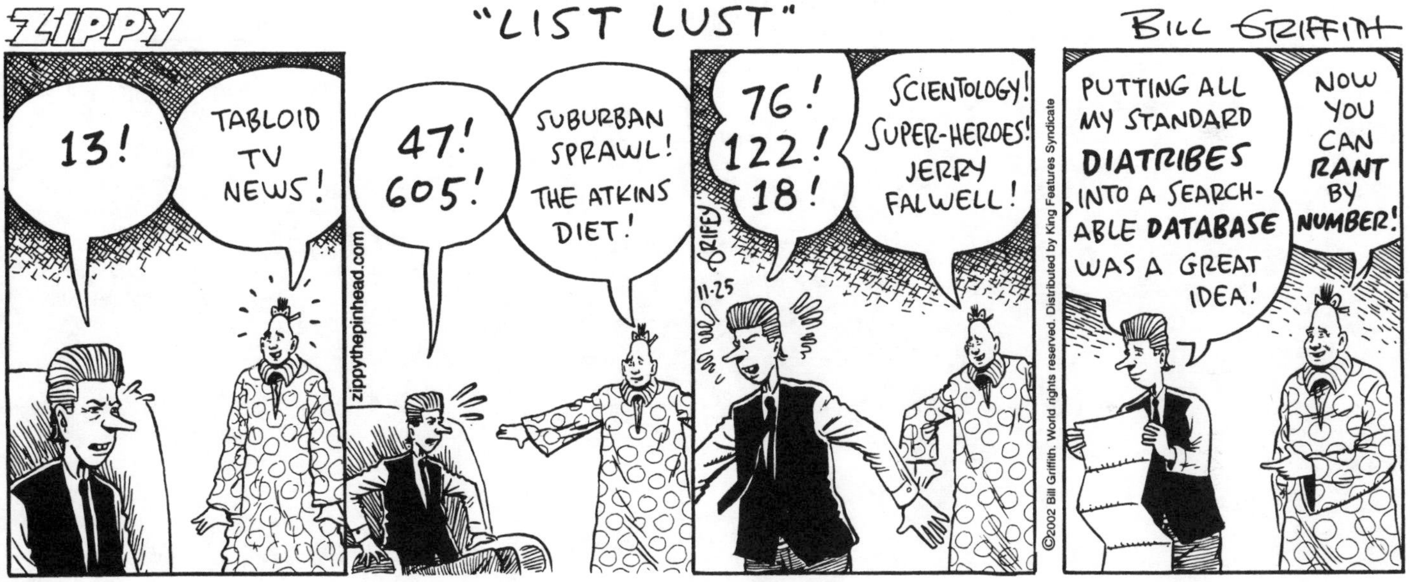
ZIPPY
"LIST LUST"
BILL GRIFFITH
13!
TABLOID TV NEWS!
zippythepinhead.com
47! 605!
SUBURBAN SPRAWL! THE ATKINS DIET!
GRIFFY 11-25
76! 122! 18!
SCIENTOLOGY! SUPER-HEROES! JERRY FALWELL!
©2002 Bill Griffith. World rights reserved. Distributed by King Features Syndicate
PUTTING ALL MY STANDARD DIATRIBES INTO A SEARCHABLE DATABASE WAS A GREAT IDEA!
NOW YOU CAN RANT BY NUMBER!

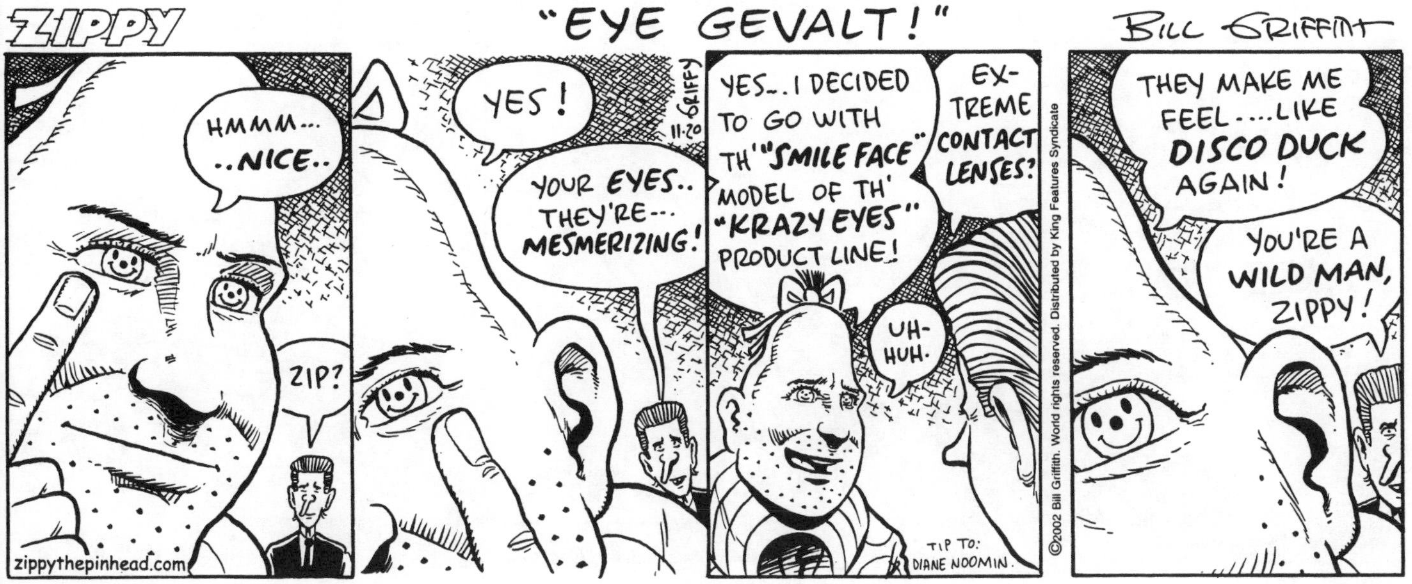
ZIPPY
"EYE GEVALT!"
BILL GRIFFITH
HMMM... ..NICE..
ZIP?
zippythepinhead.com
YES!
GRIFFY 11-20
YOUR EYES.. THEY'RE... MESMERIZING!
YES... I DECIDED TO GO WITH TH' "SMILE FACE" MODEL OF TH' "KRAZY EYES" PRODUCT LINE!
EXTREME CONTACT LENSES?
UH-HUH.
TIP TO: DIANE NOOMIN.
©2002 Bill Griffith. World rights reserved. Distributed by King Features Syndicate
THEY MAKE ME FEEL....LIKE DISCO DUCK AGAIN!
YOU'RE A WILD MAN, ZIPPY!

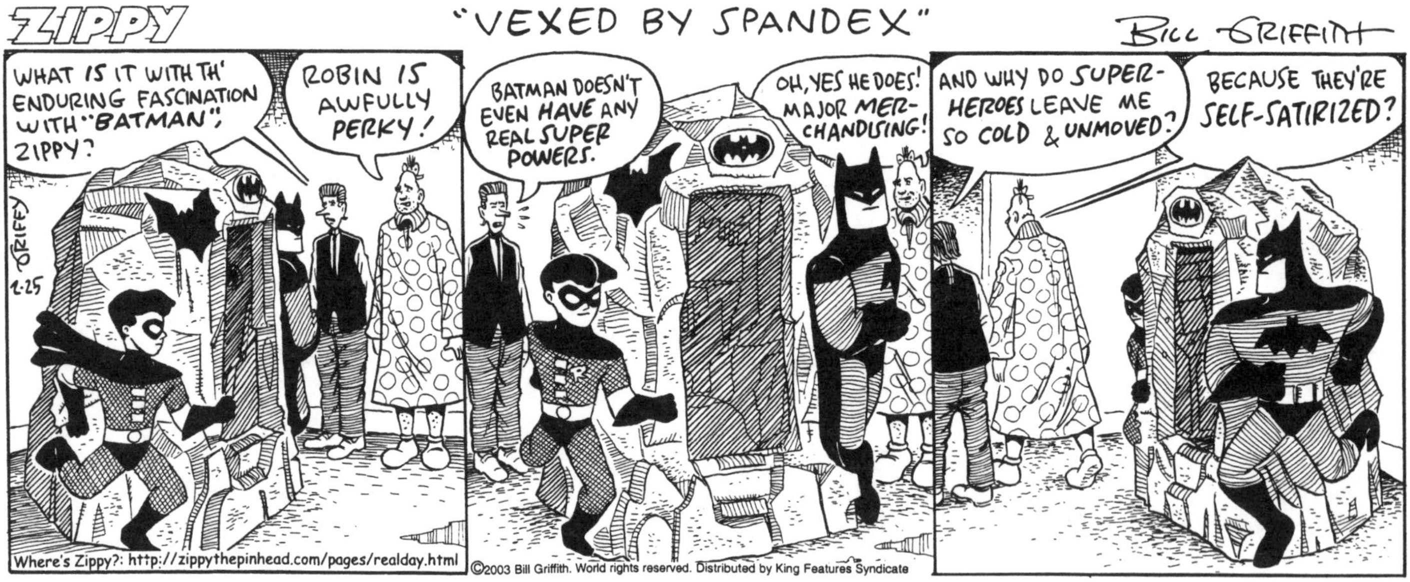
ZIPPY
"VEXED BY SPANDEX"
BILL GRIFFITH
WHAT IS IT WITH TH' ENDURING FASCINATION WITH "BATMAN", ZIPPY?
ROBIN IS AWFULLY PERKY!
GRIFFY 2·25
BATMAN DOESN'T EVEN HAVE ANY REAL SUPER POWERS.
OH, YES HE DOES! MAJOR MER-CHANDISING!
AND WHY DO SUPER-HEROES LEAVE ME SO COLD & UNMOVED?
BECAUSE THEY'RE SELF-SATIRIZED?
Where's Zippy?: http://zippythepinhead.com/pages/realday.html
©2003 Bill Griffith. World rights reserved. Distributed by King Features Syndicate

9

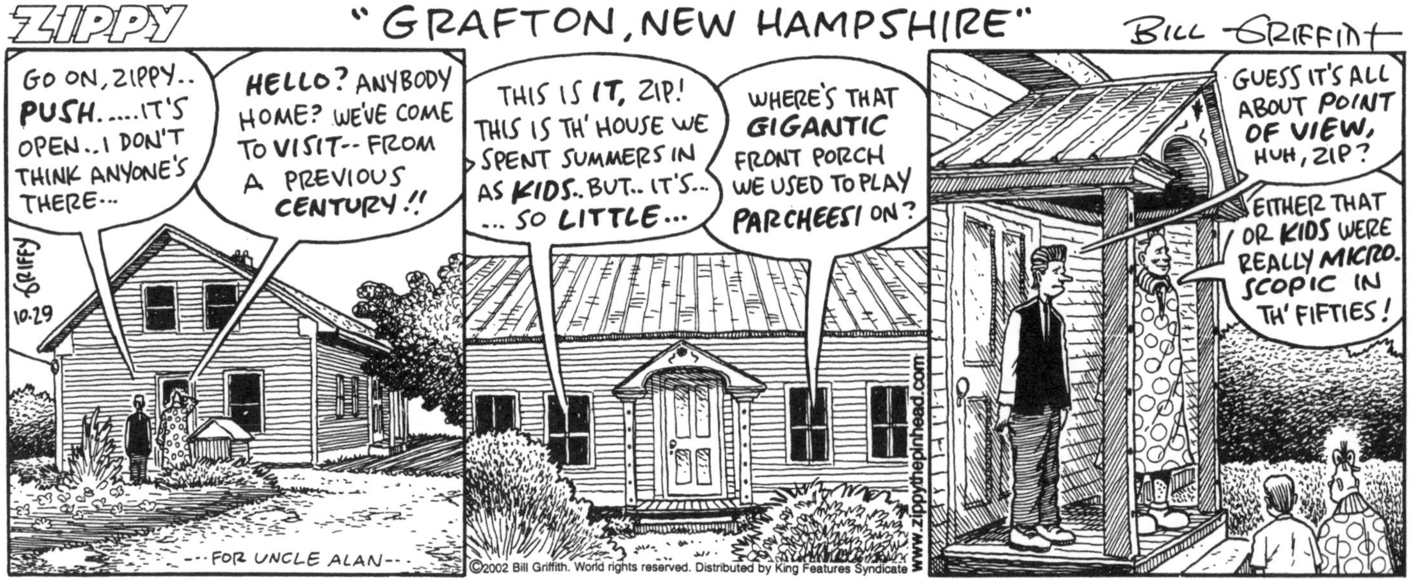
ZIPPY
"GRAFTON, NEW HAMPSHIRE"
BILL GRIFFITH
GO ON, ZIPPY.. PUSH.....IT'S OPEN..I DON'T THINK ANYONE'S THERE...
HELLO? ANYBODY HOME? WE'VE COME TO VISIT-- FROM A PREVIOUS CENTURY!!
GRIFFY 10·29
---FOR UNCLE ALAN---
THIS IS IT, ZIP! THIS IS TH' HOUSE WE SPENT SUMMERS IN AS KIDS..BUT.. IT'S... ...SO LITTLE...
WHERE'S THAT GIGANTIC FRONT PORCH WE USED TO PLAY PARCHEESI ON?
©2002 Bill Griffith. World rights reserved. Distributed by King Features Syndicate
www.zippythepinhead.com
GUESS IT'S ALL ABOUT POINT OF VIEW, HUH, ZIP?
EITHER THAT OR KIDS WERE REALLY MICRO-SCOPIC IN TH' FIFTIES!

10

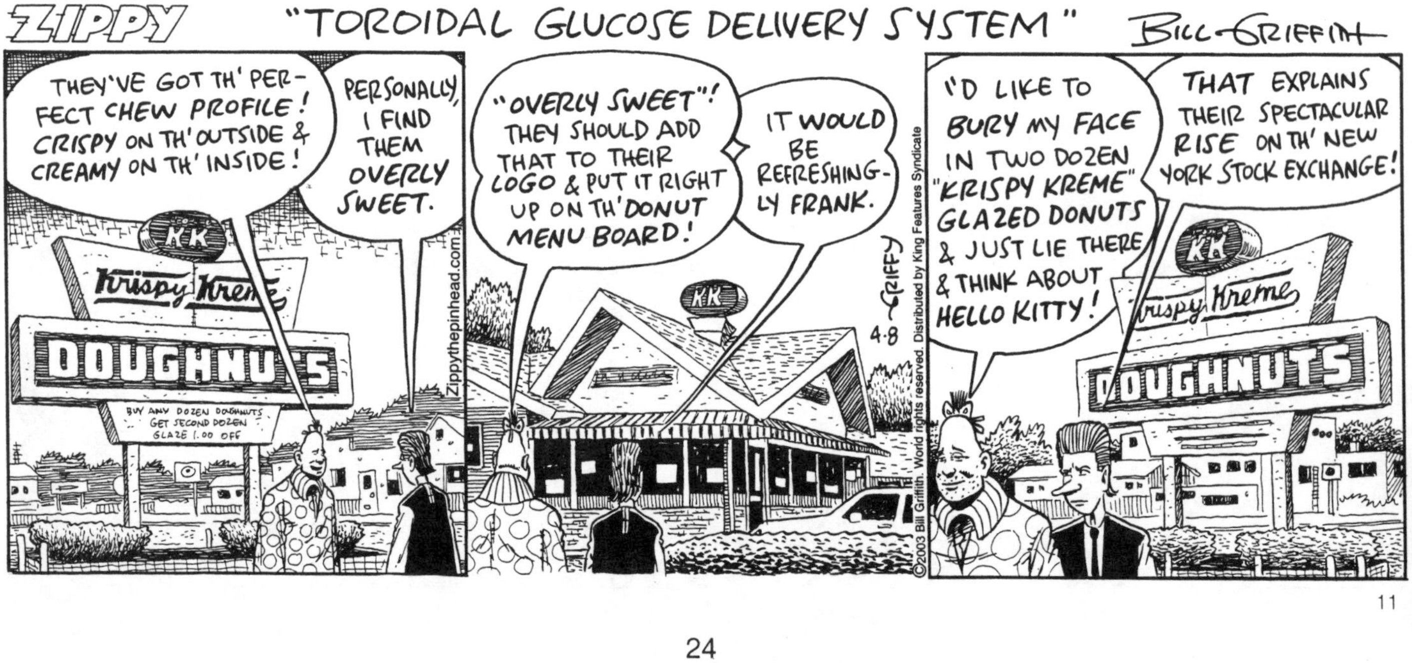
ZIPPY
"TOROIDAL GLUCOSE DELIVERY SYSTEM"
BILL GRIFFITH
THEY'VE GOT TH' PER-FECT CHEW PROFILE! CRISPY ON TH' OUTSIDE & CREAMY ON TH' INSIDE!
PERSONALLY, I FIND THEM OVERLY SWEET.
KK
Krispy Kreme
DOUGHNUTS
BUY ANY DOZEN DOUGHNUTS GET SECOND DOZEN GLAZE 1.00 OFF
Zippythepinhead.com
"OVERLY SWEET"! THEY SHOULD ADD THAT TO THEIR LOGO & PUT IT RIGHT UP ON TH' DONUT MENU BOARD!
IT WOULD BE REFRESHING-LY FRANK.
GRIFFY 4·8
©2003 Bill Griffith. World rights reserved. Distributed by King Features Syndicate
I'D LIKE TO BURY MY FACE IN TWO DOZEN "KRISPY KREME" GLAZED DONUTS & JUST LIE THERE & THINK ABOUT HELLO KITTY!
THAT EXPLAINS THEIR SPECTACULAR RISE ON TH' NEW YORK STOCK EXCHANGE!

11

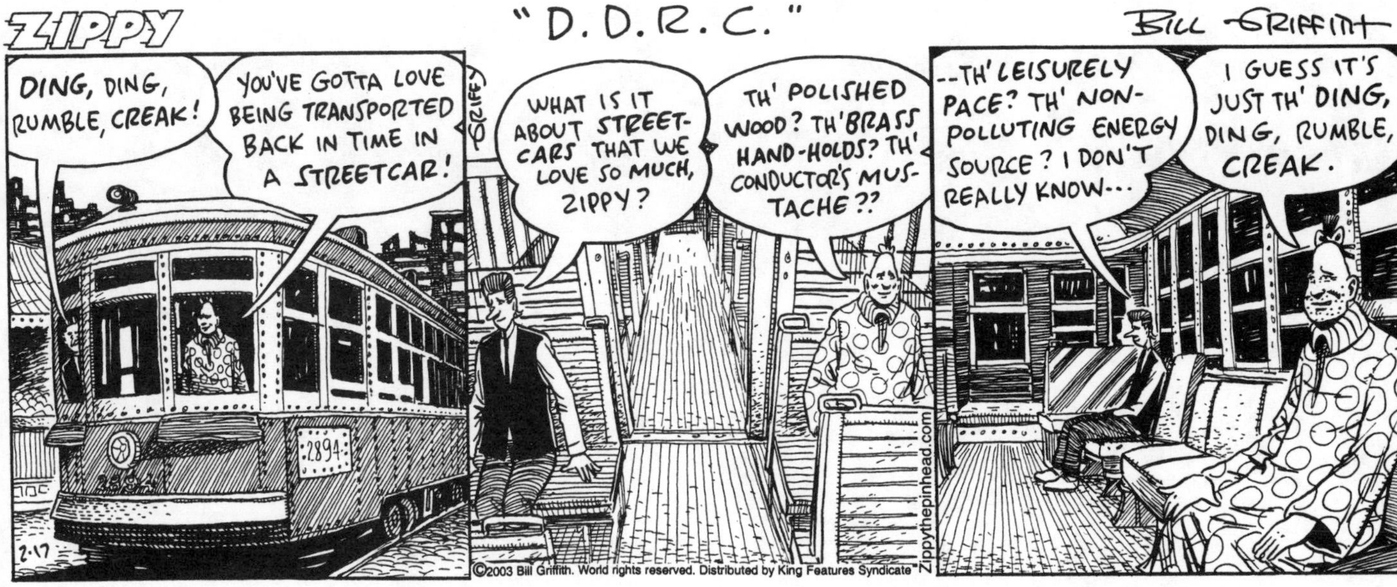
ZIPPY
"D.D.R.C."
BILL GRIFFITH
DING, DING, RUMBLE, CREAK!
YOU'VE GOTTA LOVE BEING TRANSPORTED BACK IN TIME IN A STREETCAR!
2894
2·17
GRIFFY
WHAT IS IT ABOUT STREET-CARS THAT WE LOVE SO MUCH, ZIPPY?
TH' POLISHED WOOD? TH' BRASS HAND-HOLDS? TH' CONDUCTOR'S MUS-TACHE??
©2003 Bill Griffith. World rights reserved. Distributed by King Features Syndicate
Zippythepinhead.com
--TH' LEISURELY PACE? TH' NON-POLLUTING ENERGY SOURCE? I DON'T REALLY KNOW...
I GUESS IT'S JUST TH' DING, DING, RUMBLE, CREAK.

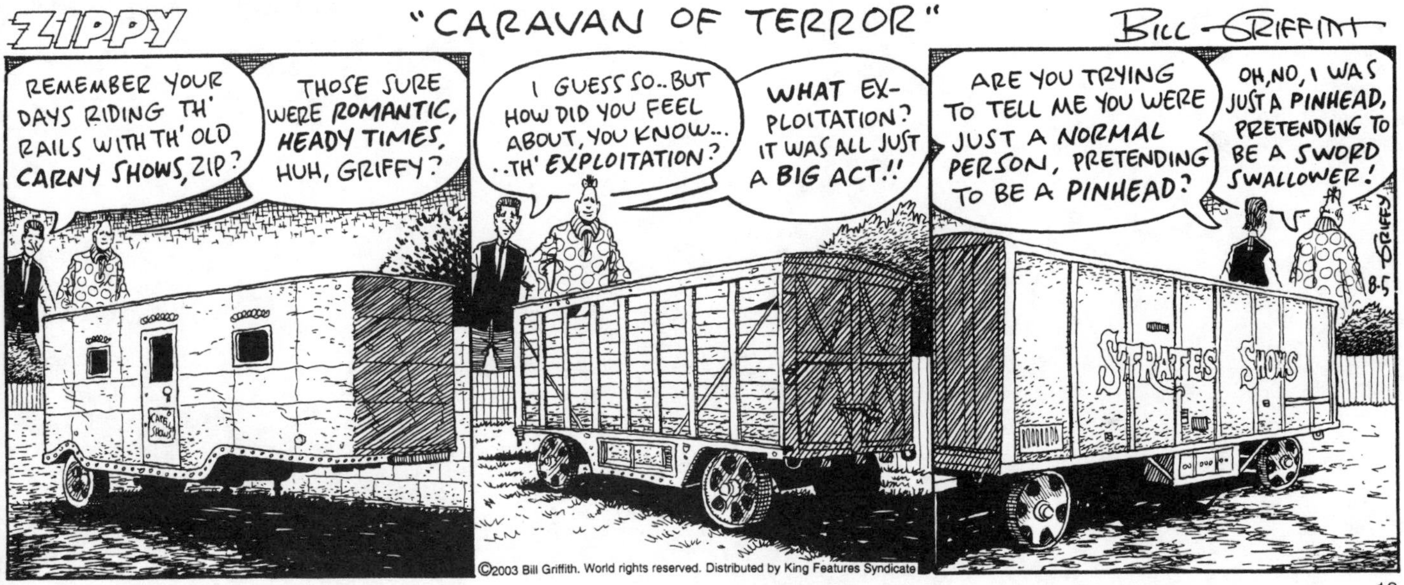
ZIPPY
"CARAVAN OF TERROR"
BILL GRIFFITH
REMEMBER YOUR DAYS RIDING TH' RAILS WITH TH' OLD CARNY SHOWS, ZIP?
THOSE SURE WERE ROMANTIC, HEADY TIMES, HUH, GRIFFY?
I GUESS SO.. BUT HOW DID YOU FEEL ABOUT, YOU KNOW... ..TH' EXPLOITATION?
WHAT EX-PLOITATION? IT WAS ALL JUST A BIG ACT!!
©2003 Bill Griffith. World rights reserved. Distributed by King Features Syndicate
ARE YOU TRYING TO TELL ME YOU WERE JUST A NORMAL PERSON, PRETENDING TO BE A PINHEAD?
OH, NO, I WAS JUST A PINHEAD, PRETENDING TO BE A SWORD SWALLOWER!
GRIFFY
8·5
STRATES SHOWS

12

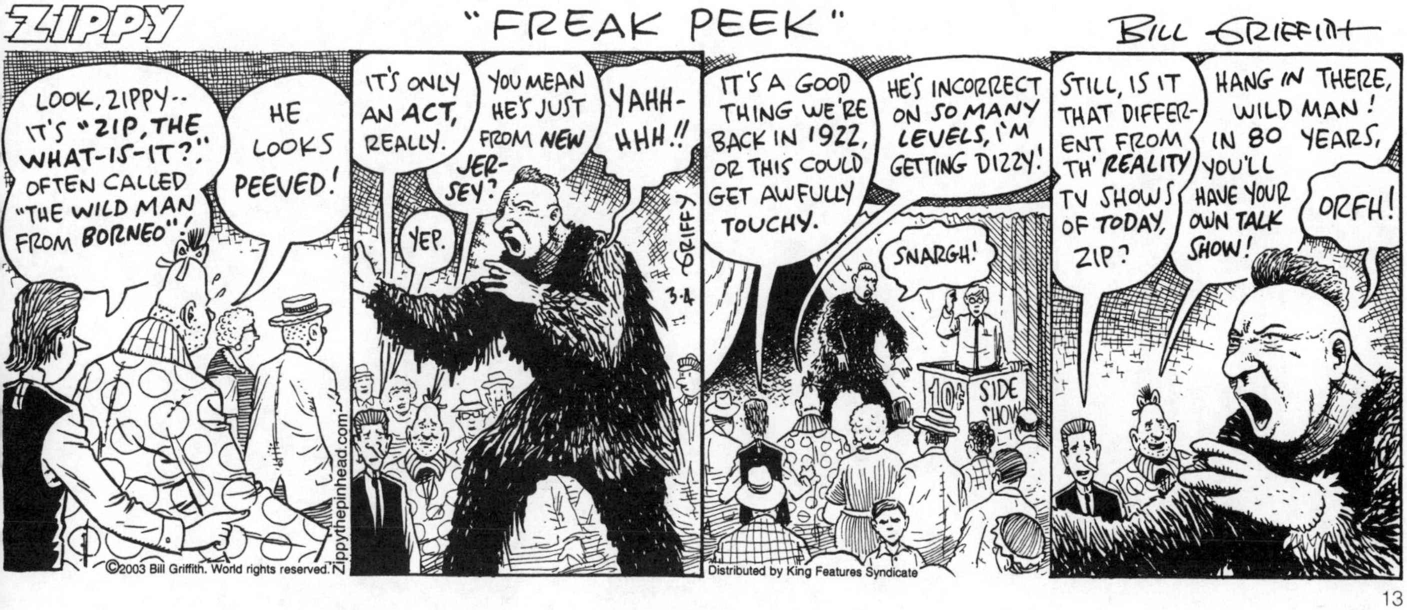
ZIPPY
"FREAK PEEK"
BILL GRIFFITH
LOOK, ZIPPY-- IT'S "ZIP, THE WHAT-IS-IT?", OFTEN CALLED "THE WILD MAN FROM BORNEO"!
HE LOOKS PEEVED!
©2003 Bill Griffith. World rights reserved.
Zippythepinhead.com
IT'S ONLY AN ACT, REALLY.
YOU MEAN HE'S JUST FROM NEW JER-SEY?
YAHH-HHH!!
YEP.
GRIFFY
3·4
IT'S A GOOD THING WE'RE BACK IN 1922, OR THIS COULD GET AWFULLY TOUCHY.
HE'S INCORRECT ON SO MANY LEVELS, I'M GETTING DIZZY!
SNARGH!
10¢
SIDE SHOW
Distributed by King Features Syndicate
STILL, IS IT THAT DIFFER-ENT FROM TH' REALITY TV SHOWS OF TODAY, ZIP?
HANG IN THERE, WILD MAN! IN 80 YEARS, YOU'LL HAVE YOUR OWN TALK SHOW!
ORFH!

13

Zippy Solo

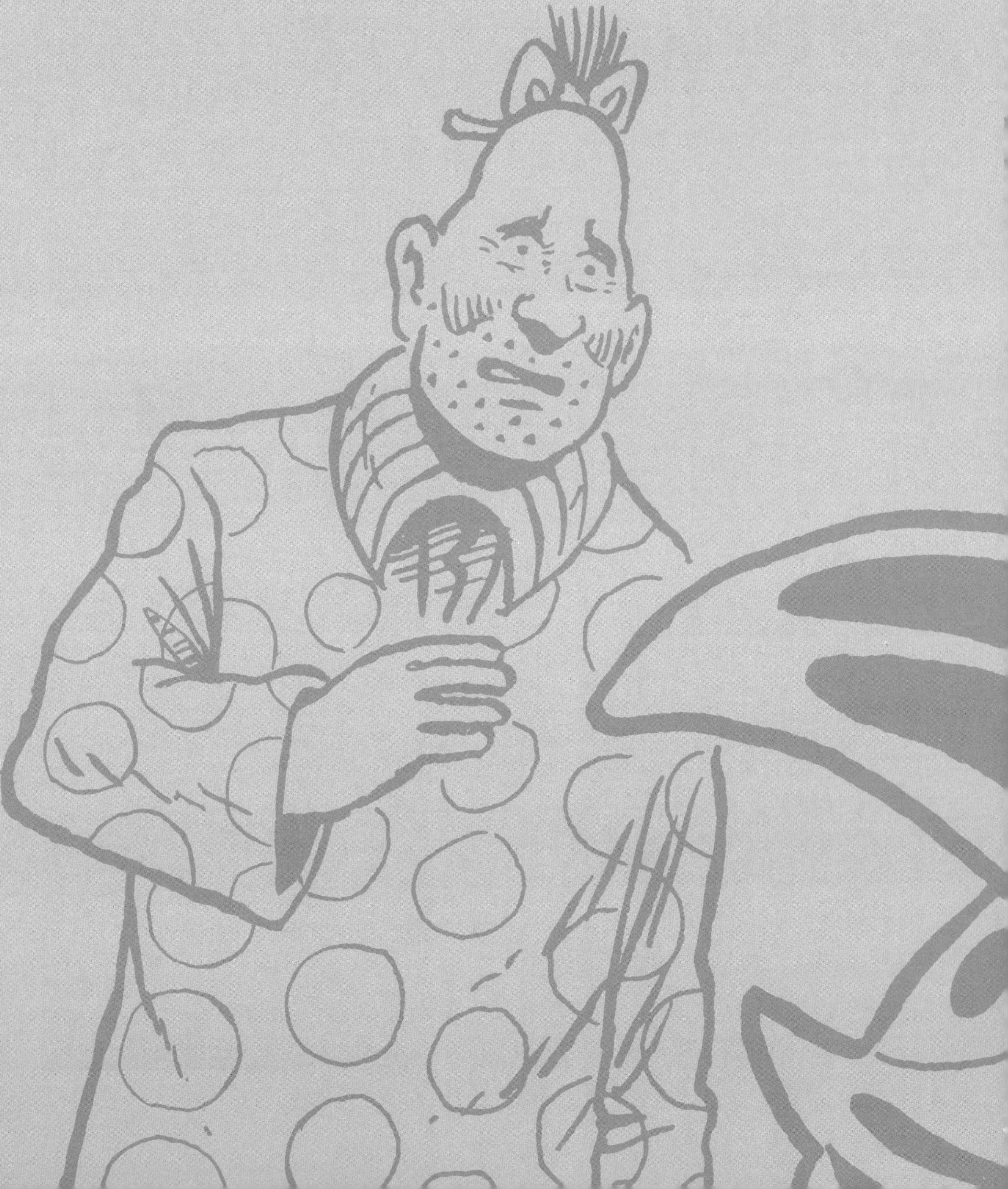

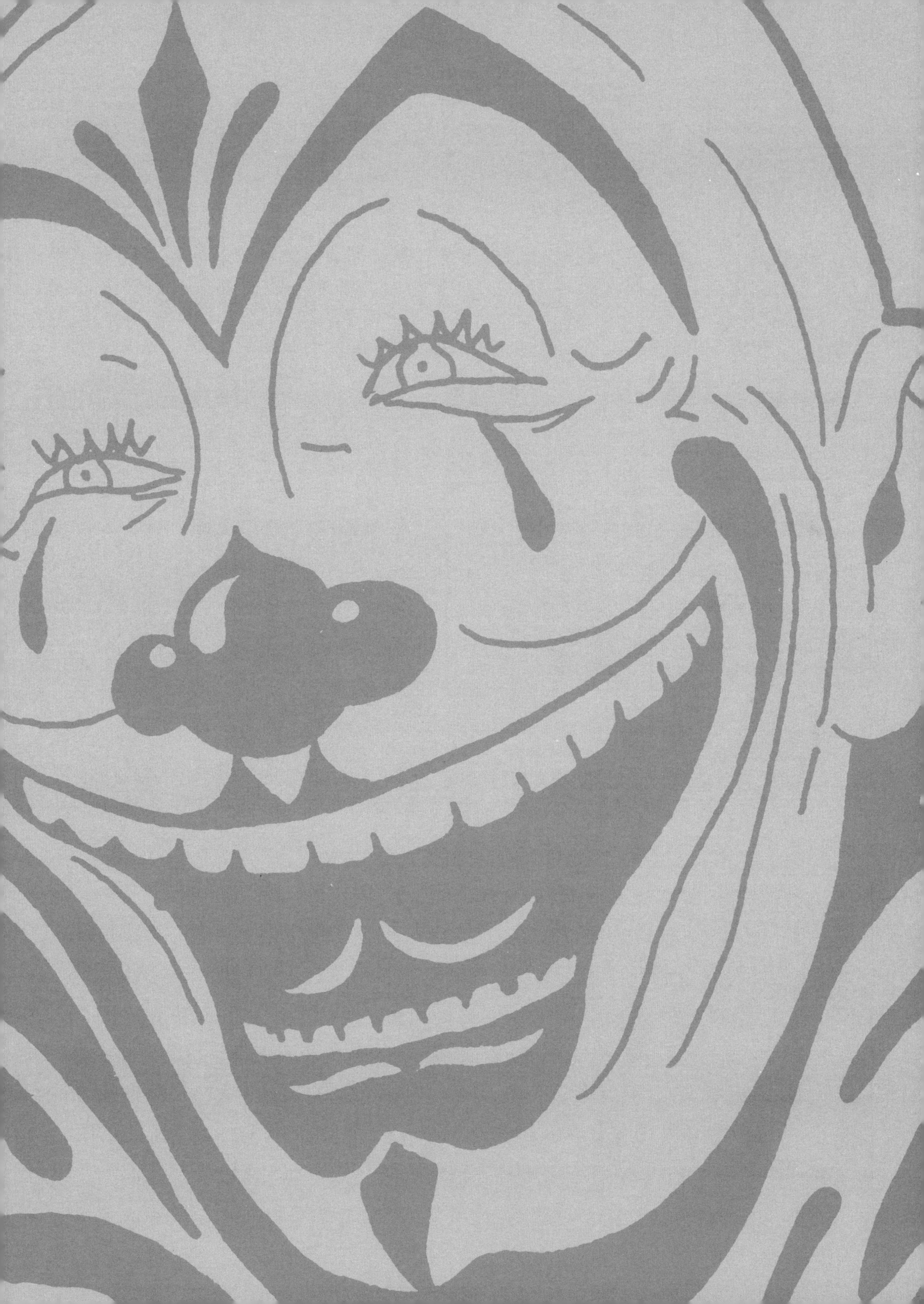

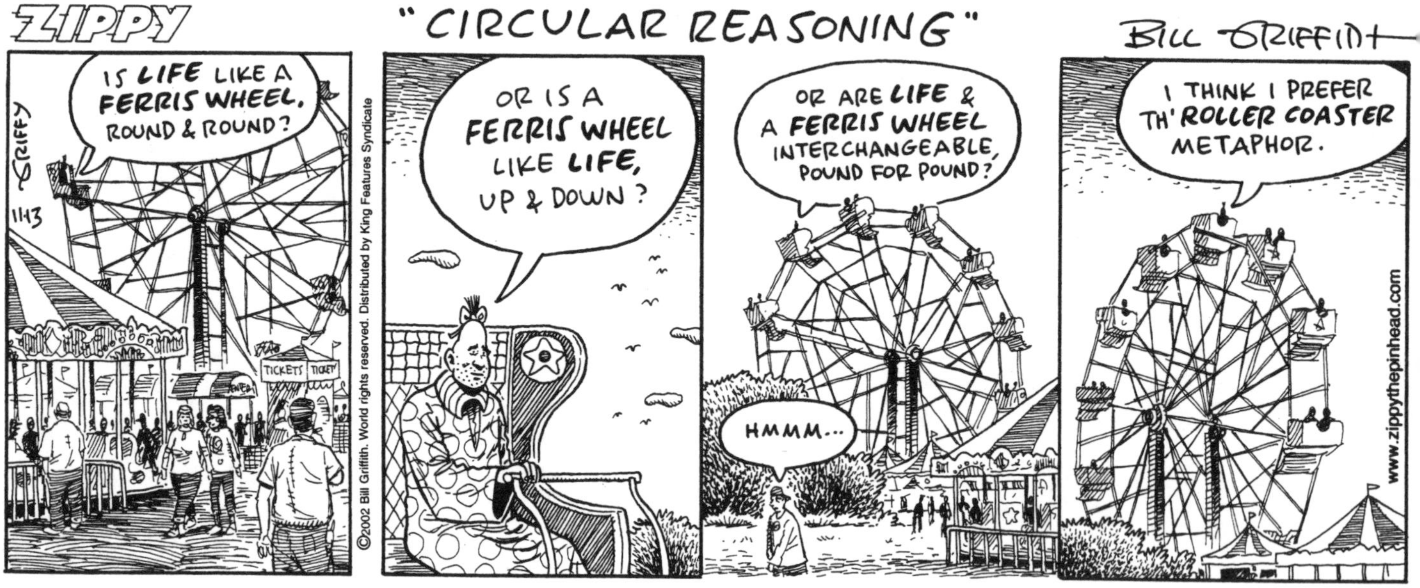
ZIPPY
"CIRCULAR REASONING"
BILL GRIFFITH
IS LIFE LIKE A FERRIS WHEEL, ROUND & ROUND?
OR IS A FERRIS WHEEL LIKE LIFE, UP & DOWN?
OR ARE LIFE & A FERRIS WHEEL INTERCHANGEABLE, POUND FOR POUND?
HMMM...
I THINK I PREFER TH' ROLLER COASTER METAPHOR.
TICKETS
©2002 Bill Griffith. World rights reserved. Distributed by King Features Syndicate
www.zippythepinhead.com

14 A

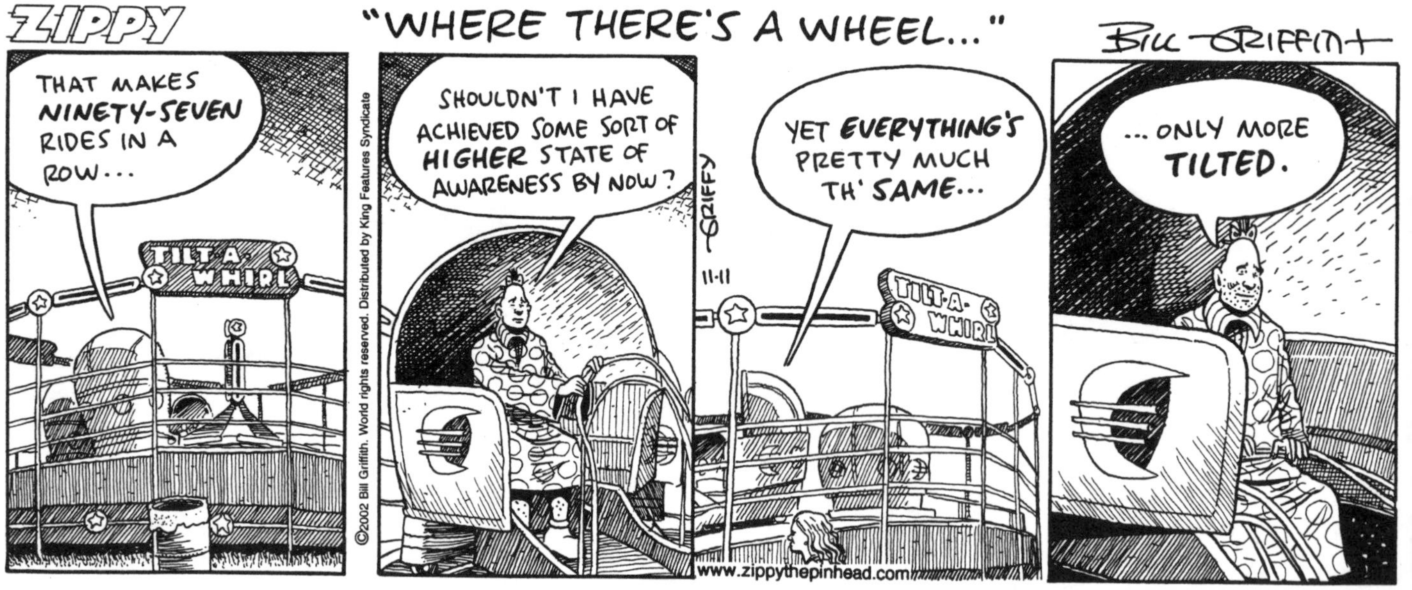
ZIPPY
"WHERE THERE'S A WHEEL..."
BILL GRIFFITH
THAT MAKES NINETY-SEVEN RIDES IN A ROW...
SHOULDN'T I HAVE ACHIEVED SOME SORT OF HIGHER STATE OF AWARENESS BY NOW?
YET EVERYTHING'S PRETTY MUCH TH' SAME...
...ONLY MORE TILTED.
TILT-A-WHIRL
©2002 Bill Griffith. World rights reserved. Distributed by King Features Syndicate
www.zippythepinhead.com

14 B

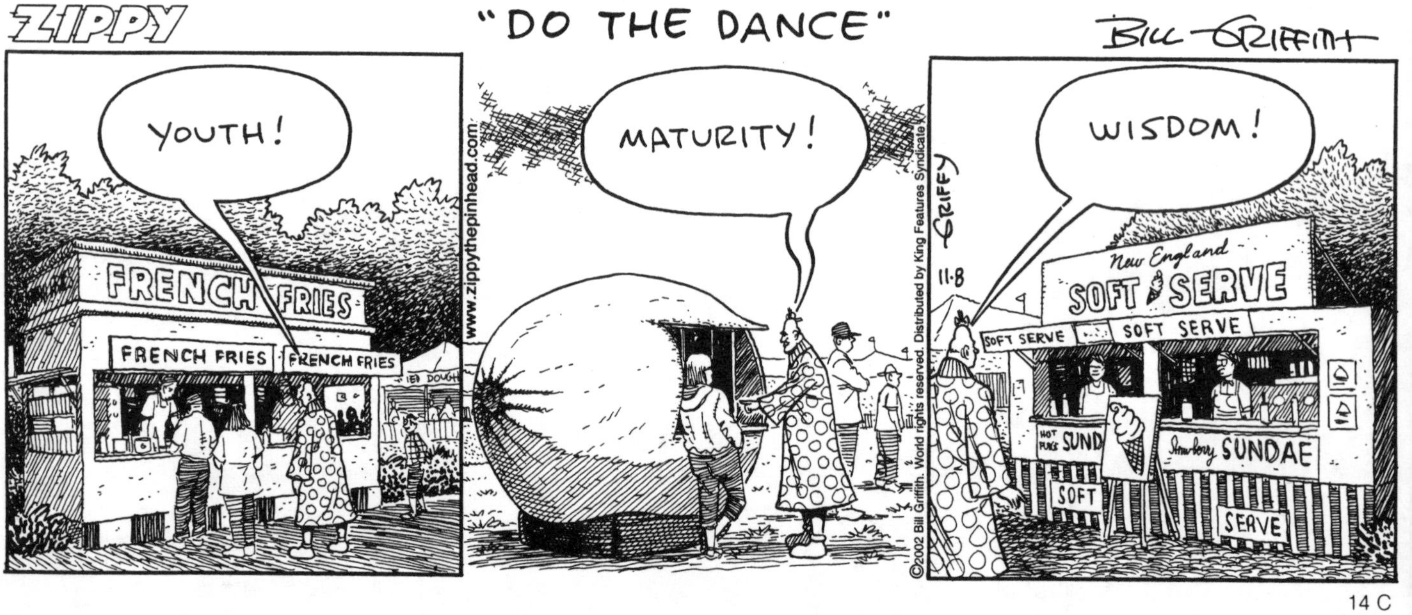
ZIPPY
"DO THE DANCE"
BILL GRIFFITH
YOUTH!
MATURITY!
WISDOM!
FRENCH FRIES
FRENCH FRIES
FRENCH FRIES
New England SOFT SERVE
SOFT SERVE
SOFT SERVE
SUNDAE
SOFT
SERVE
www.zippythepinhead.com
©2002 Bill Griffith. World rights reserved. Distributed by King Features Syndicate

14 C

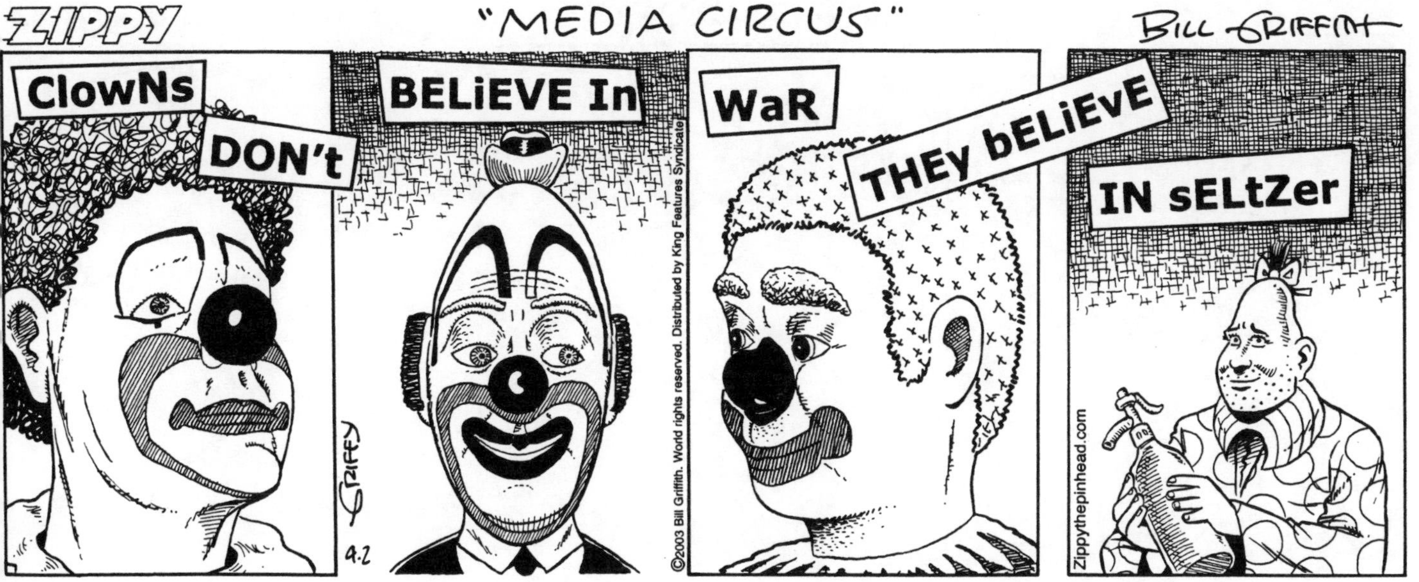
ZIPPY
"MEDIA CIRCUS"
BILL GRIFFITH
ClowNs
DON't
BELiEVE In
WaR
THEy bELiEvE
IN sELtZer
GRIFFY
9.2
©2003 Bill Griffith. World rights reserved. Distributed by King Features Syndicate
Zippythepinhead.com

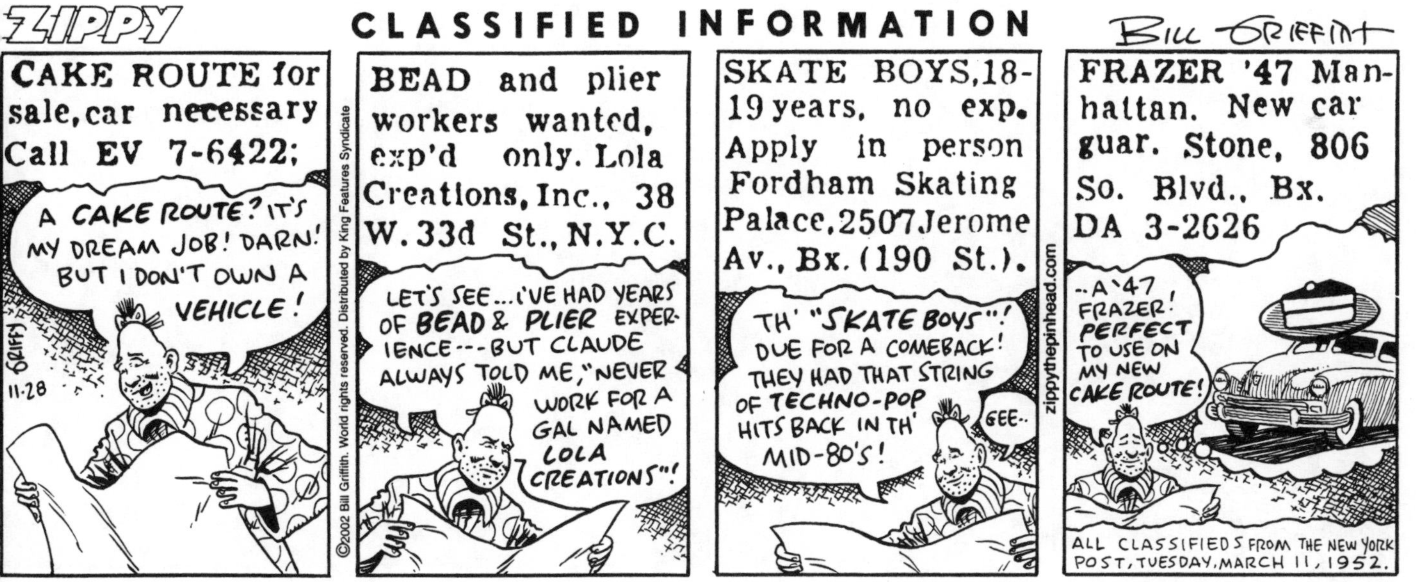
ZIPPY
CLASSIFIED INFORMATION
BILL GRIFFITH
CAKE ROUTE for sale, car necessary Call EV 7-6422;
A CAKE ROUTE? IT'S MY DREAM JOB! DARN! BUT I DON'T OWN A VEHICLE!
GRIFFY
11-28
©2002 Bill Griffith. World rights reserved. Distributed by King Features Syndicate
BEAD and plier workers wanted, exp'd only. Lola Creations, Inc., 38 W. 33d St., N.Y.C.
LET'S SEE... I'VE HAD YEARS OF BEAD & PLIER EXPERIENCE--- BUT CLAUDE ALWAYS TOLD ME, "NEVER WORK FOR A GAL NAMED LOLA CREATIONS"!
SKATE BOYS, 18-19 years, no exp. Apply in person Fordham Skating Palace, 2507 Jerome Av., Bx. (190 St.).
TH' "SKATE BOYS"! DUE FOR A COMEBACK! THEY HAD THAT STRING OF TECHNO-POP HITS BACK IN TH' MID-80'S!
GEE..
zippythepinhead.com
FRAZER '47 Manhattan. New car guar. Stone, 806 So. Blvd., Bx. DA 3-2626
--A '47 FRAZER! PERFECT TO USE ON MY NEW CAKE ROUTE!
ALL CLASSIFIEDS FROM THE NEW YORK POST, TUESDAY, MARCH 11, 1952.

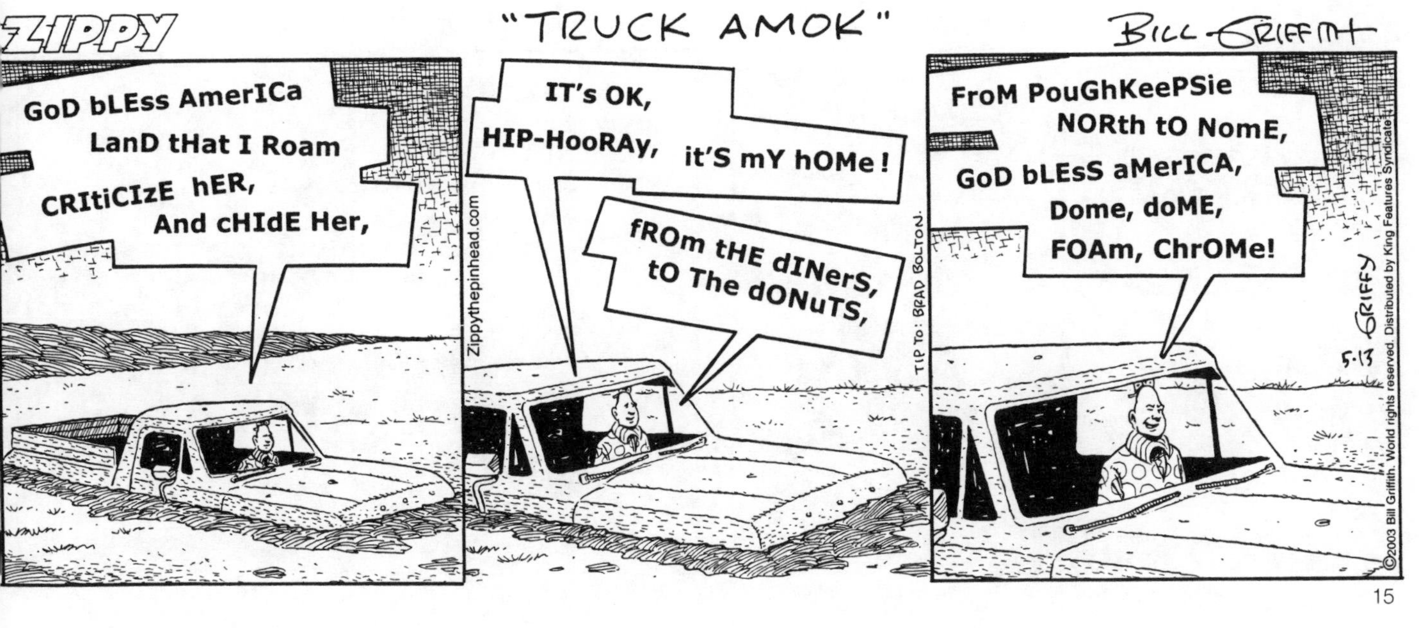
ZIPPY
"TRUCK AMOK"
BILL GRIFFITH
GoD bLEss AmerICa
LanD tHat I Roam
CRItiCIzE hER,
And cHIdE Her,
IT's OK,
HIP-HooRAy, it'S mY hOMe!
fROm tHE dINerS, tO The dONuTS,
Zippythepinhead.com
TIP TO: BRAD BOLTON.
FroM PouGhKeePSie
NORth tO NomE,
GoD bLEsS aMerICA,
Dome, doME,
FOAm, ChrOMe!
GRIFFY
5-13
©2003 Bill Griffith. World rights reserved. Distributed by King Features Syndicate

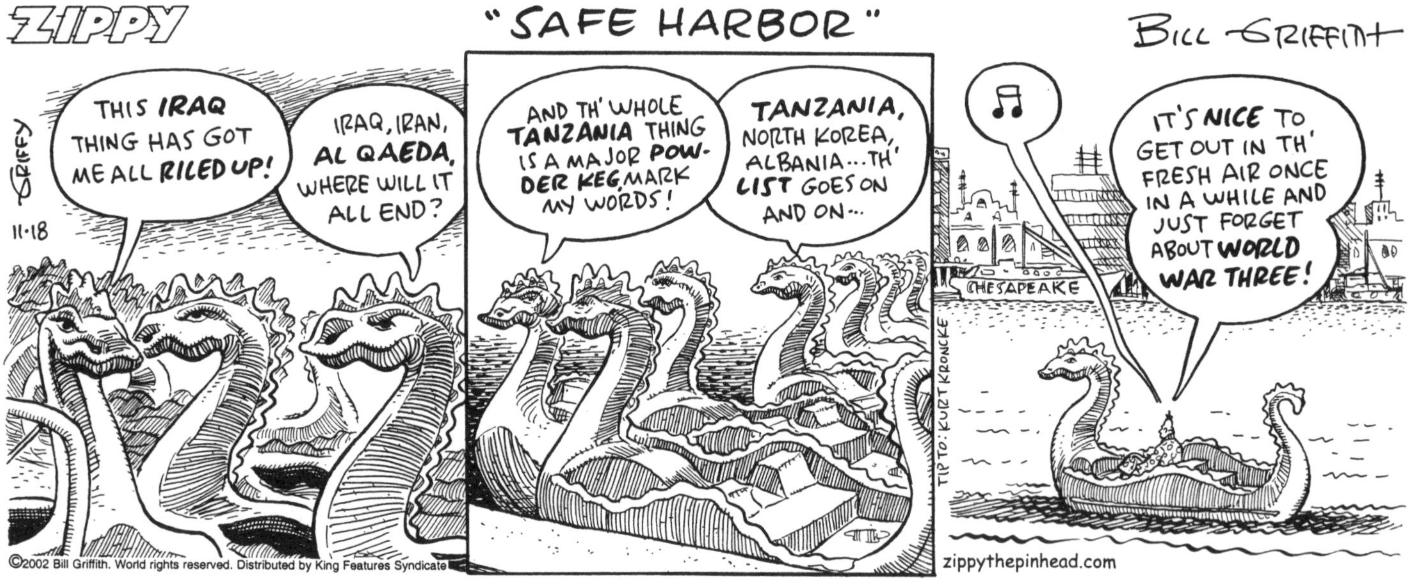
ZIPPY
"SAFE HARBOR"
BILL GRIFFITH
GRIFFY 11·18
THIS IRAQ THING HAS GOT ME ALL RILED UP!
IRAQ, IRAN, AL QAEDA, WHERE WILL IT ALL END?
AND TH' WHOLE TANZANIA THING IS A MAJOR POWDER KEG, MARK MY WORDS!
TANZANIA, NORTH KOREA, ALBANIA...TH' LIST GOES ON AND ON...
TIP TO: KURT KRONCKE
CHESAPEAKE
♫
IT'S NICE TO GET OUT IN TH' FRESH AIR ONCE IN A WHILE AND JUST FORGET ABOUT WORLD WAR THREE!
©2002 Bill Griffith. World rights reserved. Distributed by King Features Syndicate
zippythepinhead.com

16

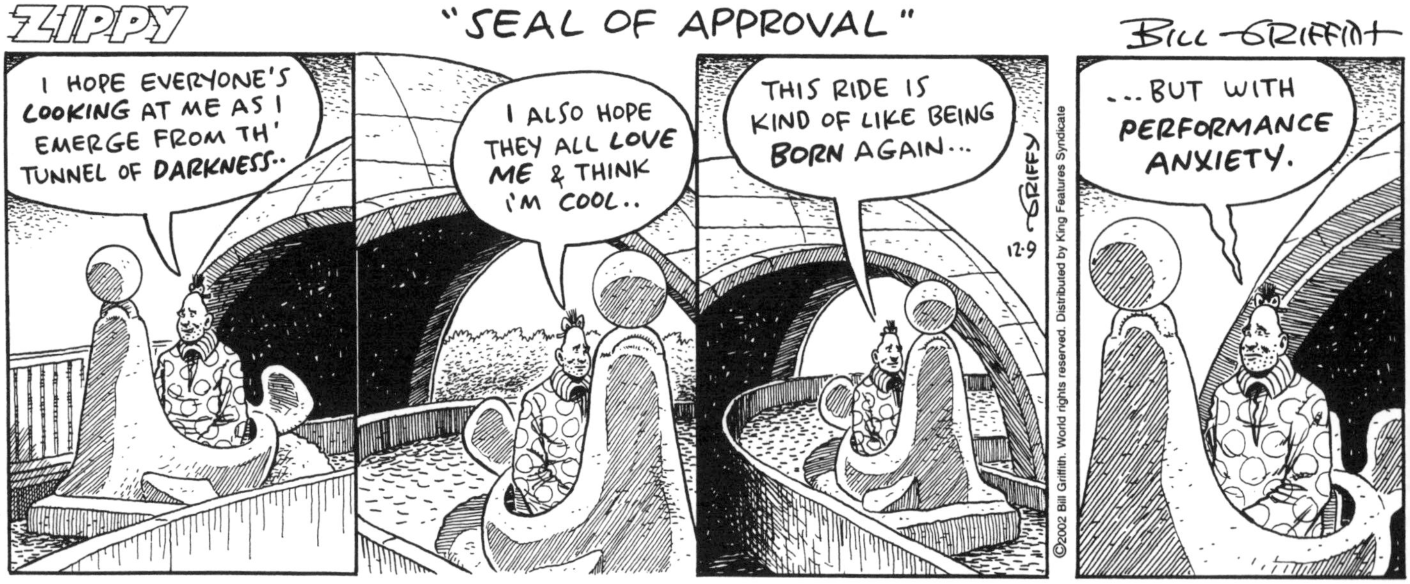
ZIPPY
"SEAL OF APPROVAL"
BILL GRIFFITH
I HOPE EVERYONE'S LOOKING AT ME AS I EMERGE FROM TH' TUNNEL OF DARKNESS..
I ALSO HOPE THEY ALL LOVE ME & THINK I'M COOL..
THIS RIDE IS KIND OF LIKE BEING BORN AGAIN...
GRIFFY 12·9
©2002 Bill Griffith. World rights reserved. Distributed by King Features Syndicate
...BUT WITH PERFORMANCE ANXIETY.

17

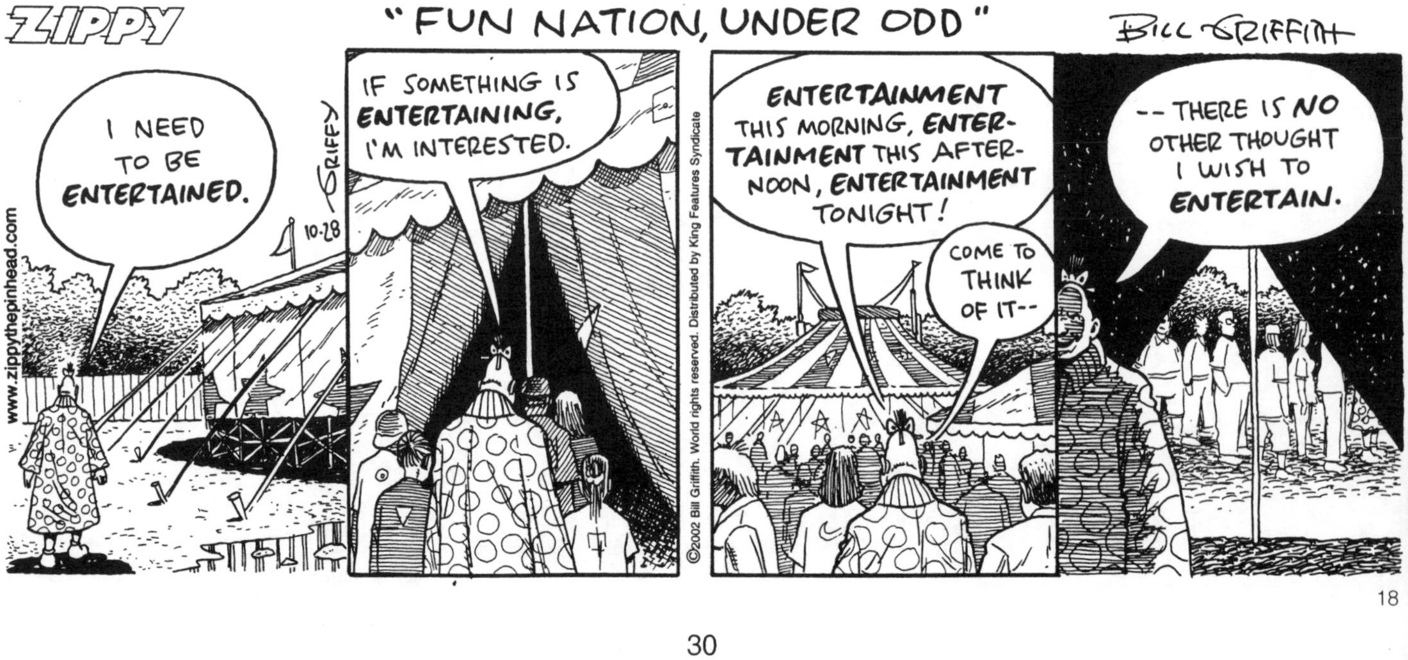
ZIPPY
"FUN NATION, UNDER ODD"
BILL GRIFFITH
www.zippythepinhead.com
I NEED TO BE ENTERTAINED.
GRIFFY 10·28
IF SOMETHING IS ENTERTAINING, I'M INTERESTED.
©2002 Bill Griffith. World rights reserved. Distributed by King Features Syndicate
ENTERTAINMENT THIS MORNING, ENTERTAINMENT THIS AFTERNOON, ENTERTAINMENT TONIGHT!
COME TO THINK OF IT--
-- THERE IS NO OTHER THOUGHT I WISH TO ENTERTAIN.

18

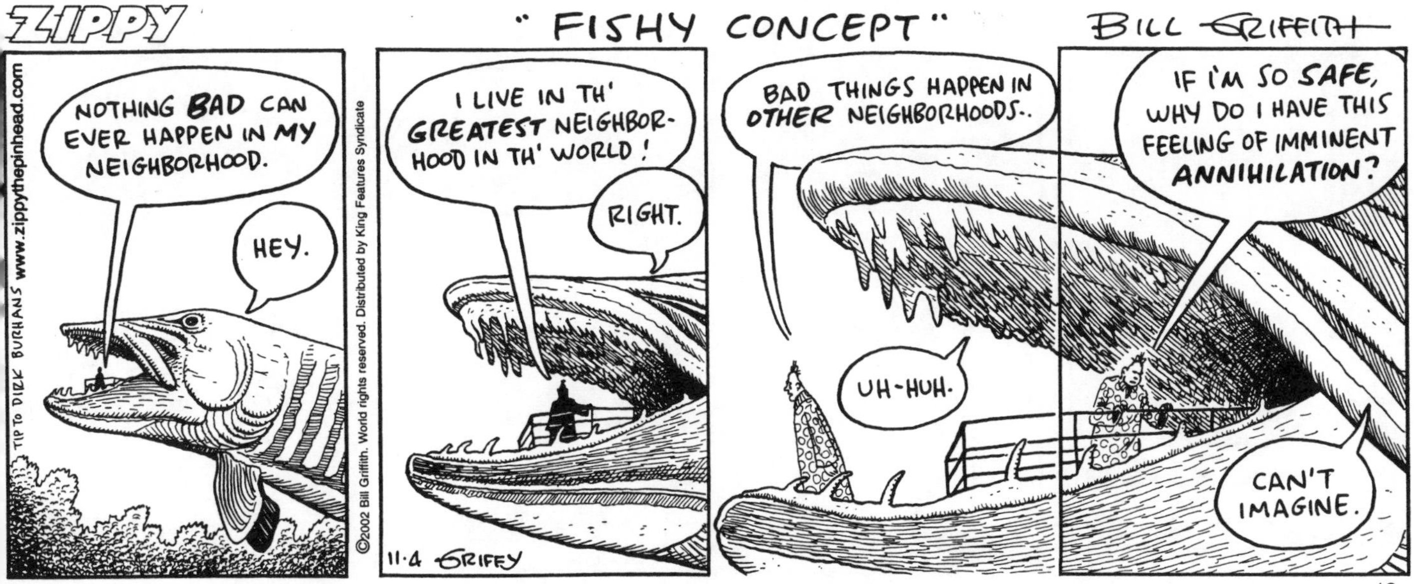
ZIPPY
"FISHY CONCEPT"
BILL GRIFFITH
NOTHING BAD CAN EVER HAPPEN IN MY NEIGHBORHOOD.
HEY.
I LIVE IN TH' GREATEST NEIGHBORHOOD IN TH' WORLD!
RIGHT.
BAD THINGS HAPPEN IN OTHER NEIGHBORHOODS..
UH-HUH.
IF I'M SO SAFE, WHY DO I HAVE THIS FEELING OF IMMINENT ANNIHILATION?
CAN'T IMAGINE.
TIP TO DIRK BURHANS www.zippythepinhead.com
©2002 Bill Griffith. World rights reserved. Distributed by King Features Syndicate
11·4 GRIFFY

19

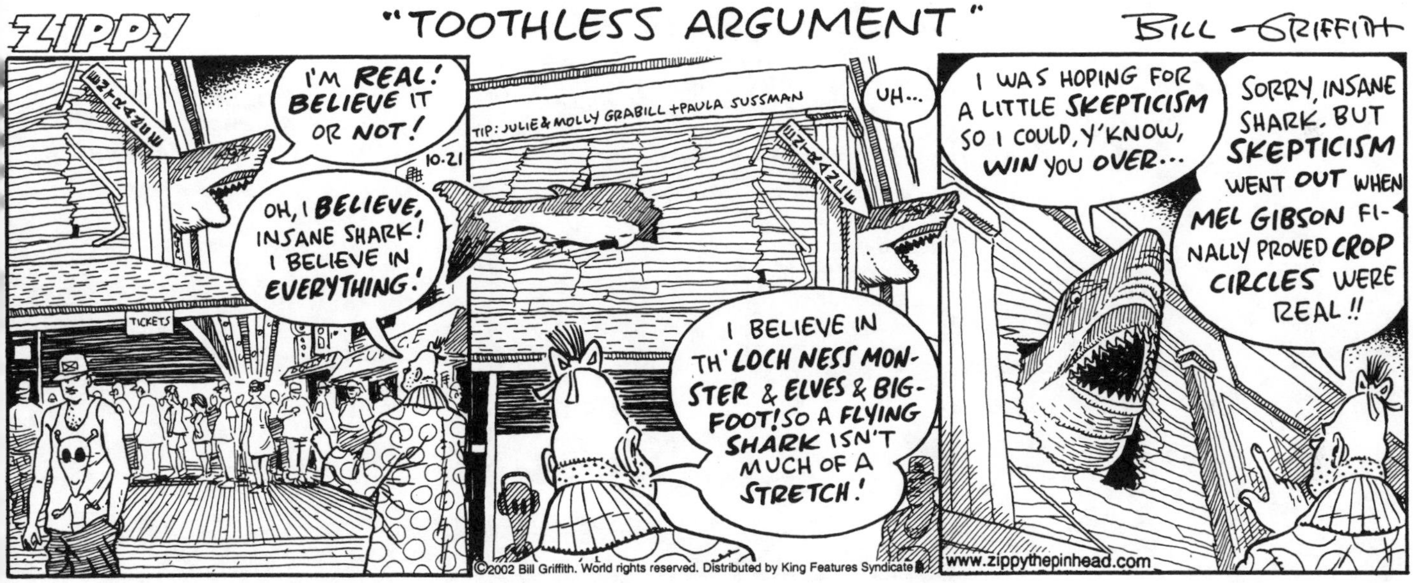
ZIPPY
"TOOTHLESS ARGUMENT"
BILL GRIFFITH
I'M REAL! BELIEVE IT OR NOT!
OH, I BELIEVE, INSANE SHARK! I BELIEVE IN EVERYTHING!
TICKETS
TIP: JULIE & MOLLY GRABILL + PAULA SUSSMAN
10.21
UH...
I BELIEVE IN TH' LOCH NESS MONSTER & ELVES & BIGFOOT! SO A FLYING SHARK ISN'T MUCH OF A STRETCH!
I WAS HOPING FOR A LITTLE SKEPTICISM SO I COULD, Y'KNOW, WIN YOU OVER...
SORRY, INSANE SHARK. BUT SKEPTICISM WENT OUT WHEN MEL GIBSON FINALLY PROVED CROP CIRCLES WERE REAL!!
©2002 Bill Griffith. World rights reserved. Distributed by King Features Syndicate
www.zippythepinhead.com

20

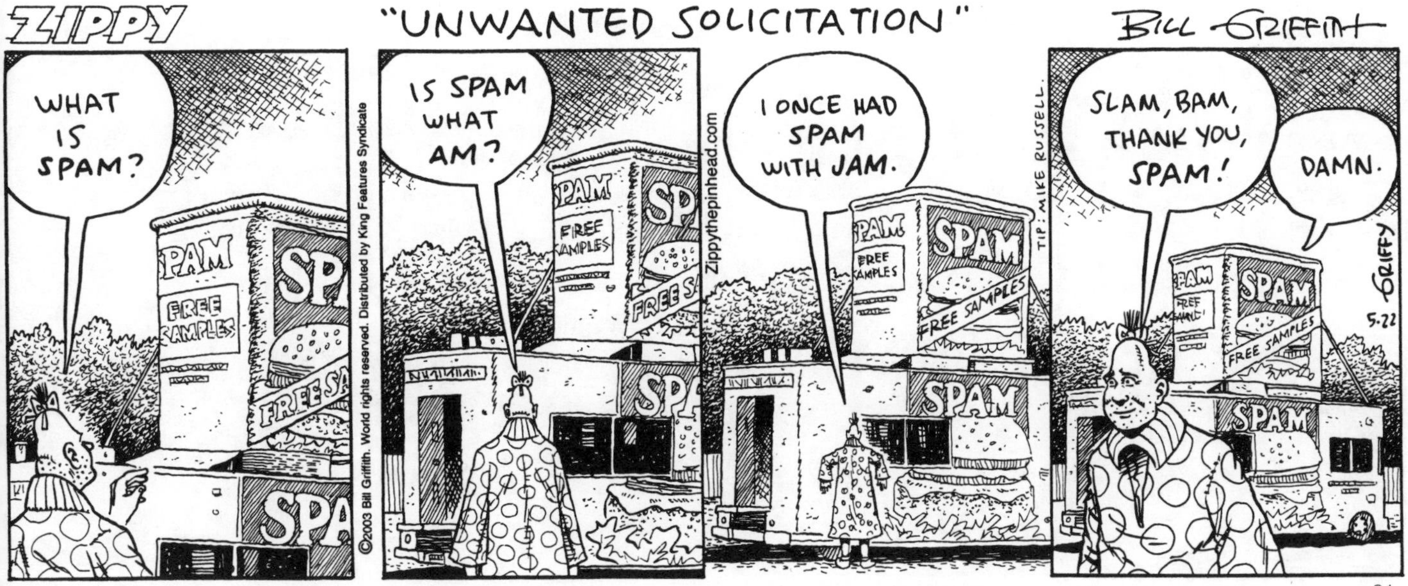
ZIPPY
"UNWANTED SOLICITATION"
BILL GRIFFITH
WHAT IS SPAM?
SPAM
FREE SAMPLES
©2003 Bill Griffith. World rights reserved. Distributed by King Features Syndicate
IS SPAM WHAT AM?
zippythepinhead.com
I ONCE HAD SPAM WITH JAM.
TIP: MIKE RUSSELL
SLAM, BAM, THANK YOU, SPAM!
DAMN.
GRIFFY 5-22

21

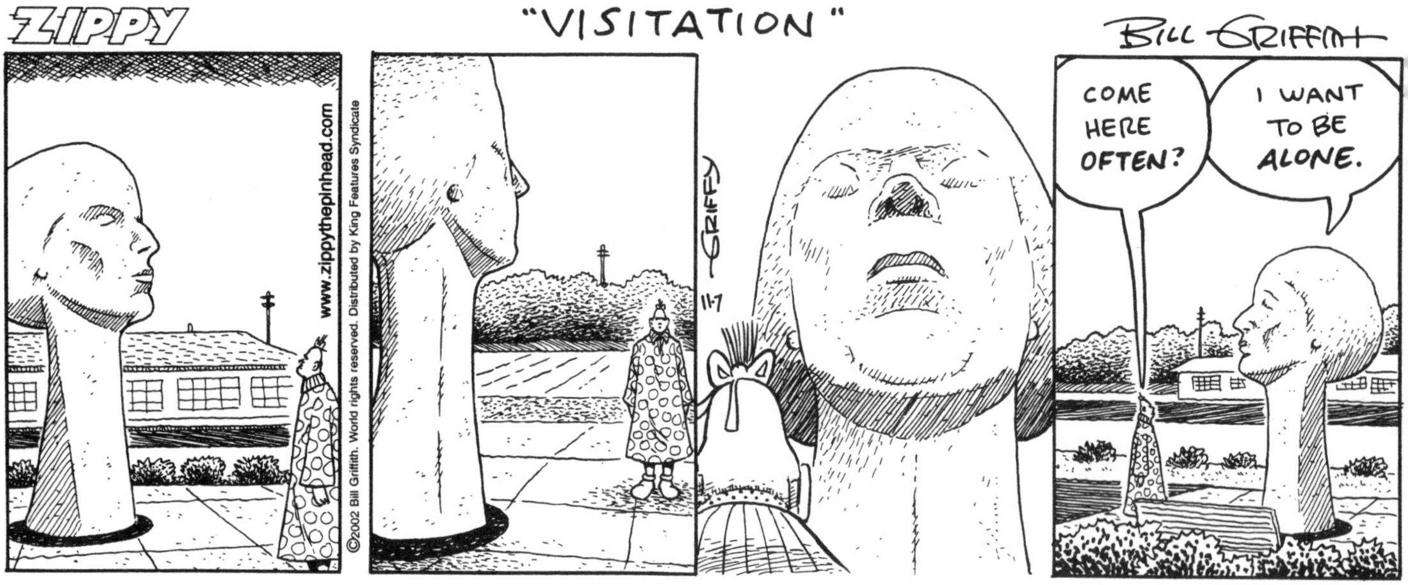
ZIPPY
"VISITATION"
BILL GRIFFITH
www.zippythepinhead.com
©2002 Bill Griffith. World rights reserved. Distributed by King Features Syndicate
GRIFFY 11-7
COME HERE OFTEN?
I WANT TO BE ALONE.

22 A

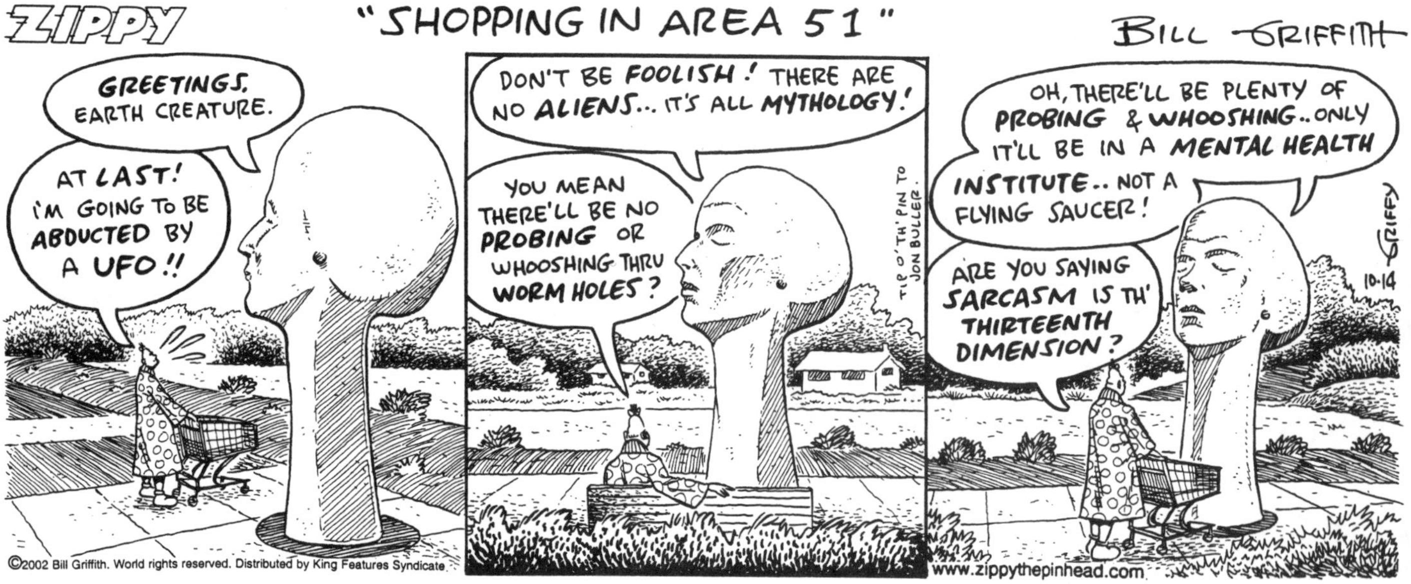
ZIPPY
"SHOPPING IN AREA 51"
BILL GRIFFITH
GREETINGS, EARTH CREATURE.
AT LAST! I'M GOING TO BE ABDUCTED BY A UFO!!
DON'T BE FOOLISH! THERE ARE NO ALIENS... IT'S ALL MYTHOLOGY!
YOU MEAN THERE'LL BE NO PROBING OR WHOOSHING THRU WORM HOLES?
TIP O' TH' PIN TO JON BULLER.
OH, THERE'LL BE PLENTY OF PROBING & WHOOSHING.. ONLY IT'LL BE IN A MENTAL HEALTH INSTITUTE.. NOT A FLYING SAUCER!
ARE YOU SAYING SARCASM IS TH' THIRTEENTH DIMENSION?
GRIFFY 10-14
©2002 Bill Griffith. World rights reserved. Distributed by King Features Syndicate
www.zippythepinhead.com

22 B

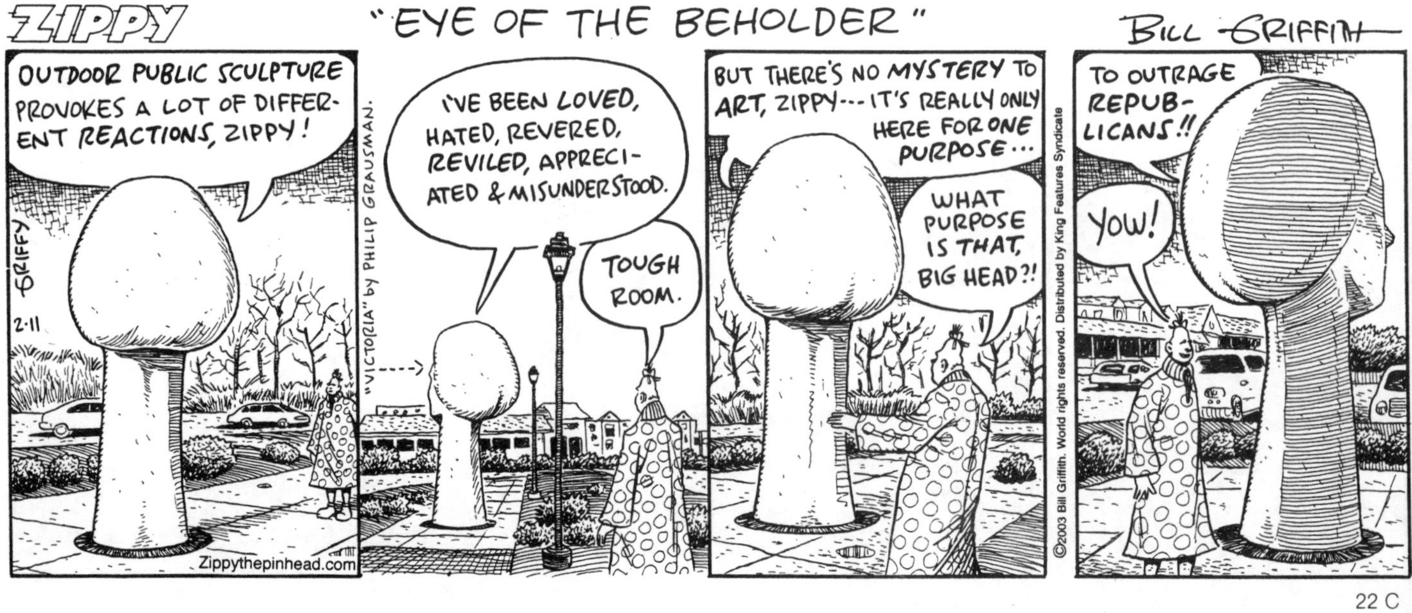
ZIPPY
"EYE OF THE BEHOLDER"
BILL GRIFFITH
OUTDOOR PUBLIC SCULPTURE PROVOKES A LOT OF DIFFERENT REACTIONS, ZIPPY!
GRIFFY 2-11
Zippythepinhead.com
"VICTORIA" by PHILIP GRAUSMAN.
I'VE BEEN LOVED, HATED, REVERED, REVILED, APPRECIATED & MISUNDERSTOOD.
TOUGH ROOM.
BUT THERE'S NO MYSTERY TO ART, ZIPPY--- IT'S REALLY ONLY HERE FOR ONE PURPOSE...
WHAT PURPOSE IS THAT, BIG HEAD?!
©2003 Bill Griffith. World rights reserved. Distributed by King Features Syndicate
TO OUTRAGE REPUBLICANS!!
YOW!

22 C

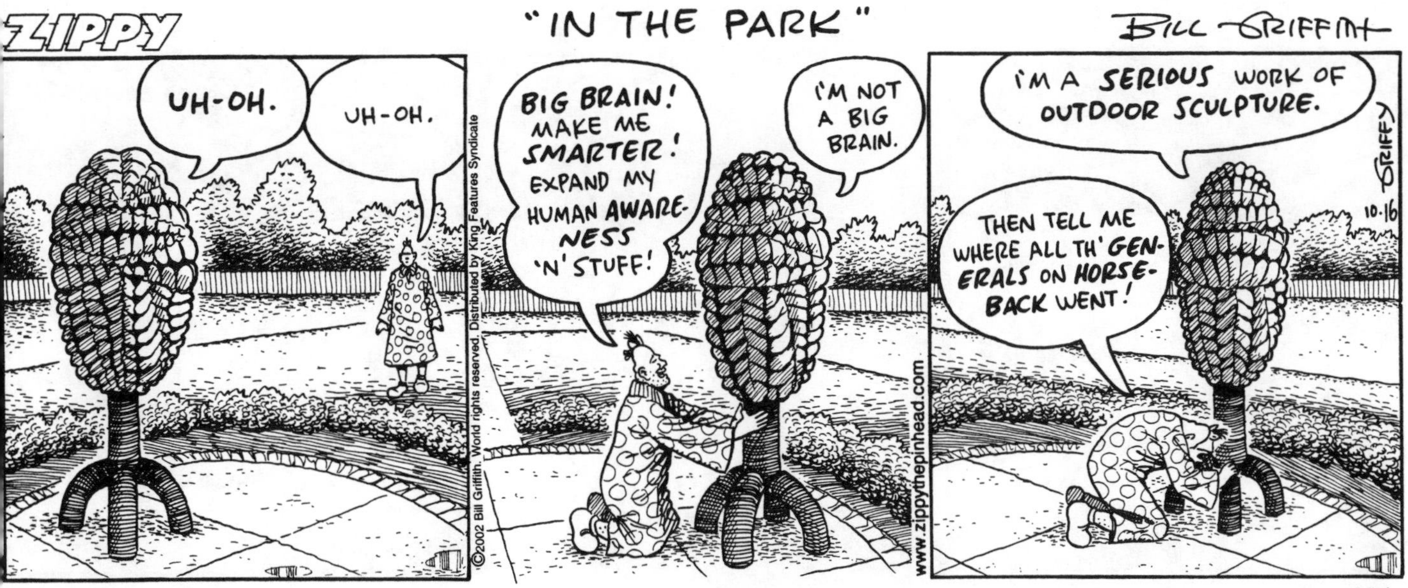

ZIPPY
"IN THE PARK"
BILL GRIFFITH
UH-OH.
UH-OH.
BIG BRAIN! MAKE ME SMARTER! EXPAND MY HUMAN AWARENESS 'N' STUFF!
I'M NOT A BIG BRAIN.
I'M A SERIOUS WORK OF OUTDOOR SCULPTURE.
THEN TELL ME WHERE ALL TH' GENERALS ON HORSEBACK WENT!
GRIFFY 10·16
©2002 Bill Griffith. World rights reserved. Distributed by King Features Syndicate
www.zippythepinhead.com

23 A

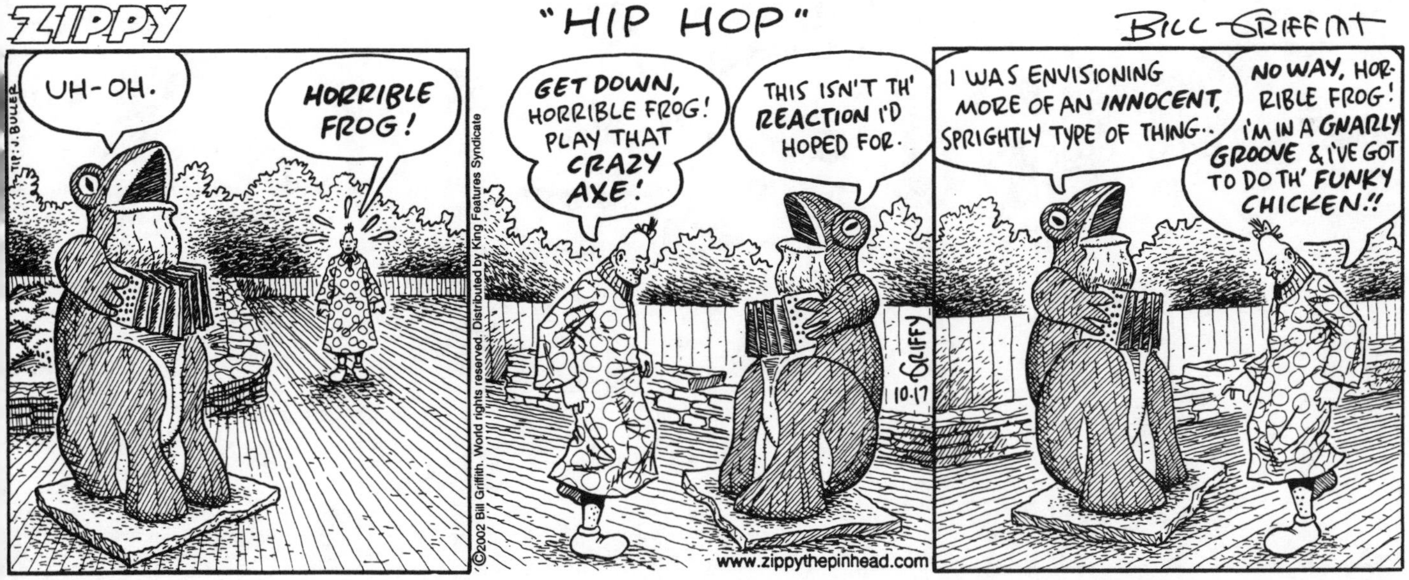

ZIPPY
"HIP HOP"
BILL GRIFFITH
TIP: J. BULLER
UH-OH.
HORRIBLE FROG!
GET DOWN, HORRIBLE FROG! PLAY THAT CRAZY AXE!
THIS ISN'T TH' REACTION I'D HOPED FOR.
I WAS ENVISIONING MORE OF AN INNOCENT, SPRIGHTLY TYPE OF THING..
NO WAY, HORRIBLE FROG! I'M IN A GNARLY GROOVE & I'VE GOT TO DO TH' FUNKY CHICKEN!!
GRIFFY 10·17
©2002 Bill Griffith. World rights reserved. Distributed by King Features Syndicate
www.zippythepinhead.com

23 B

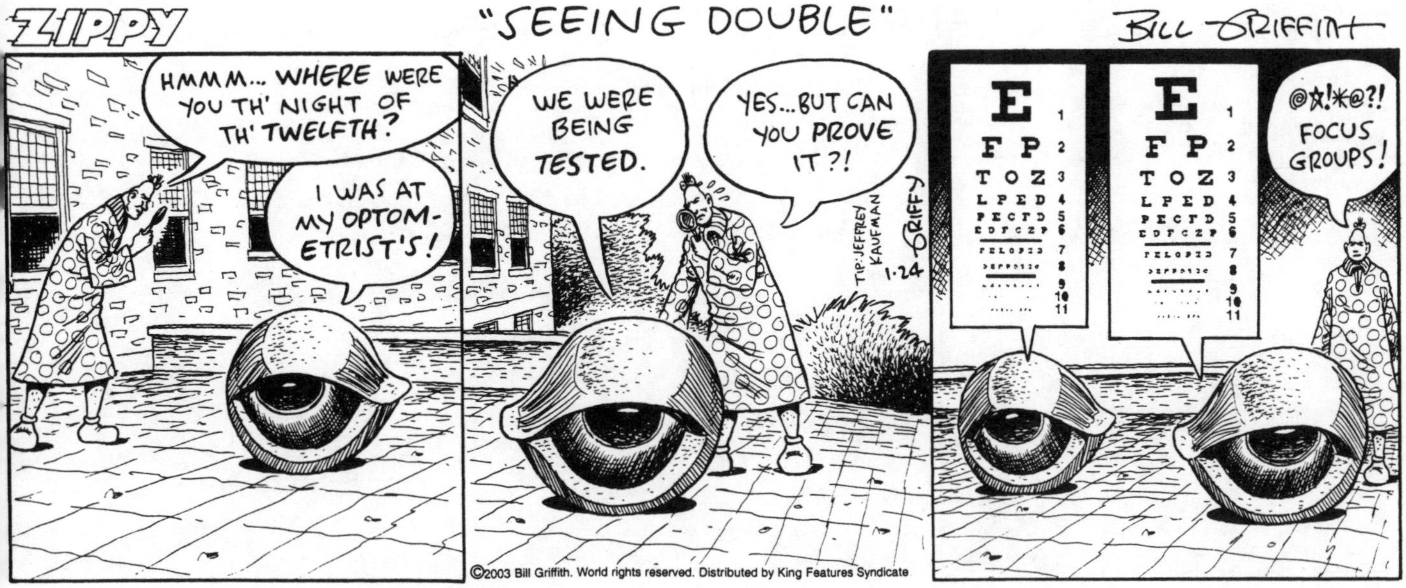

ZIPPY
"SEEING DOUBLE"
BILL GRIFFITH
HMMM... WHERE WERE YOU TH' NIGHT OF TH' TWELFTH?
I WAS AT MY OPTOMETRIST'S!
WE WERE BEING TESTED.
YES...BUT CAN YOU PROVE IT?!
TIP: JEFFREY KAUFMAN
GRIFFY 1·24
E
F P
T O Z
L P E D
@☆!✳@?! FOCUS GROUPS!
©2003 Bill Griffith. World rights reserved. Distributed by King Features Syndicate

24

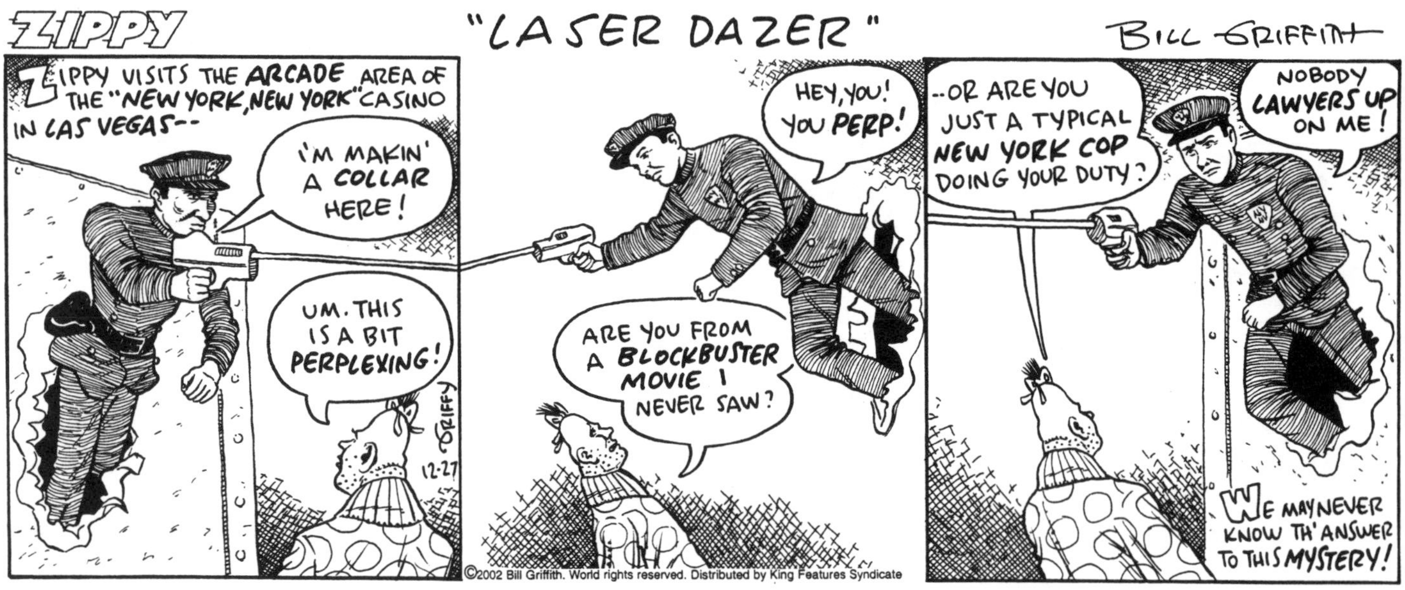
ZIPPY
"LASER DAZER"
BILL GRIFFITH
ZIPPY VISITS THE ARCADE AREA OF THE "NEW YORK, NEW YORK" CASINO IN LAS VEGAS--
I'M MAKIN' A COLLAR HERE!
UM. THIS IS A BIT PERPLEXING!
GRIFFY 12-27
HEY, YOU! YOU PERP!
ARE YOU FROM A BLOCKBUSTER MOVIE I NEVER SAW?
--OR ARE YOU JUST A TYPICAL NEW YORK COP DOING YOUR DUTY?
NOBODY LAWYERS UP ON ME!
WE MAY NEVER KNOW TH' ANSWER TO THIS MYSTERY!
©2002 Bill Griffith. World rights reserved. Distributed by King Features Syndicate

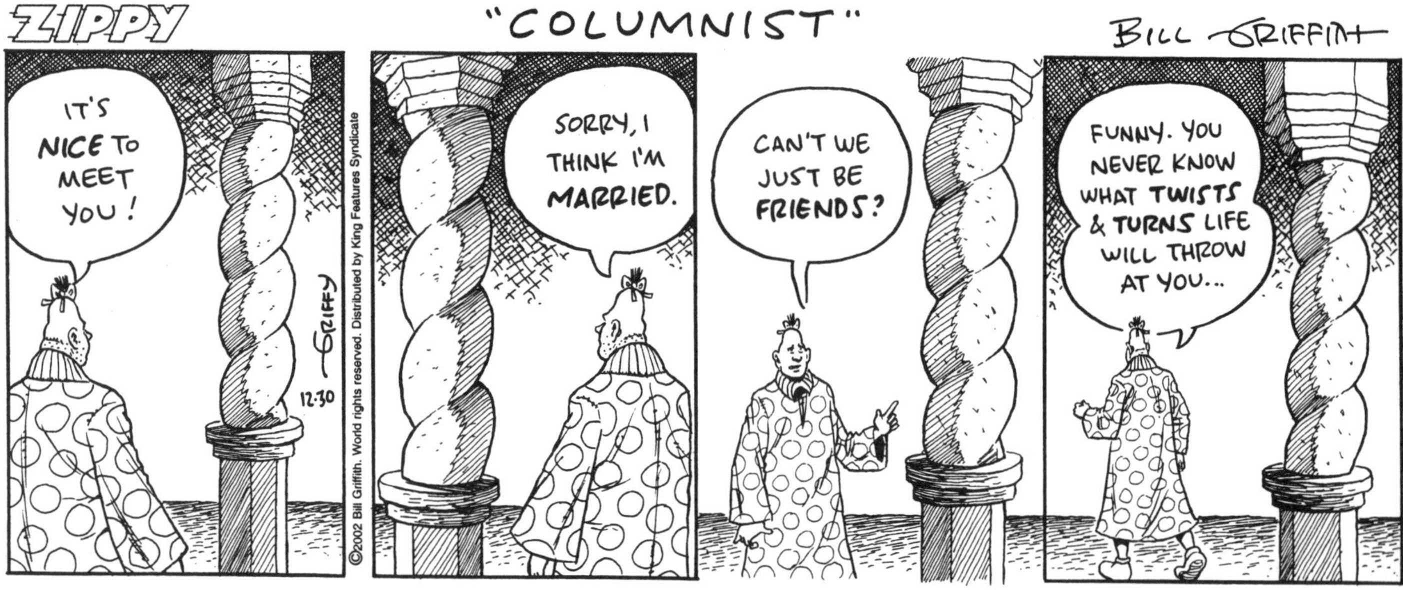
ZIPPY
"COLUMNIST"
BILL GRIFFITH
IT'S NICE TO MEET YOU!
GRIFFY 12-30
©2002 Bill Griffith. World rights reserved. Distributed by King Features Syndicate
SORRY, I THINK I'M MARRIED.
CAN'T WE JUST BE FRIENDS?
FUNNY. YOU NEVER KNOW WHAT TWISTS & TURNS LIFE WILL THROW AT YOU...

25 A

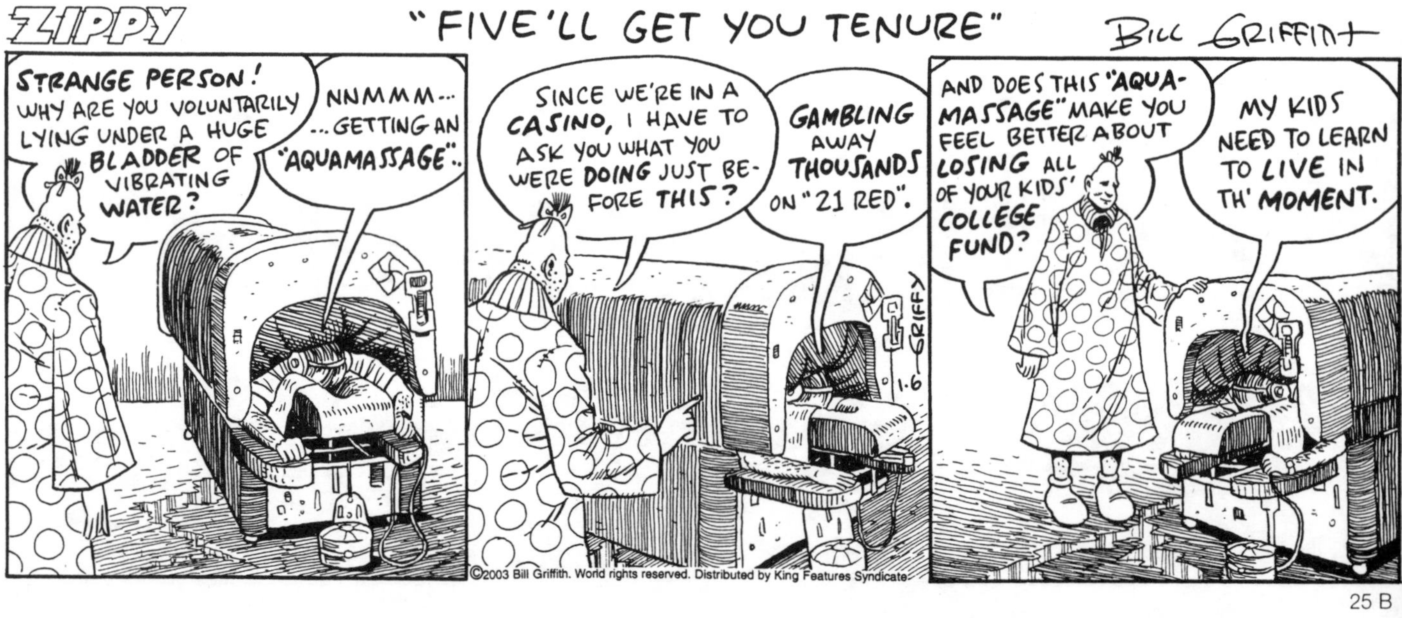
ZIPPY
"FIVE'LL GET YOU TENURE"
BILL GRIFFITH
STRANGE PERSON! WHY ARE YOU VOLUNTARILY LYING UNDER A HUGE BLADDER OF VIBRATING WATER?
NNMMM... ...GETTING AN "AQUAMASSAGE"..
SINCE WE'RE IN A CASINO, I HAVE TO ASK YOU WHAT YOU WERE DOING JUST BEFORE THIS?
GAMBLING AWAY THOUSANDS ON "21 RED".
GRIFFY 1-6
AND DOES THIS "AQUA-MASSAGE" MAKE YOU FEEL BETTER ABOUT LOSING ALL OF YOUR KIDS' COLLEGE FUND?
MY KIDS NEED TO LEARN TO LIVE IN TH' MOMENT.
©2003 Bill Griffith. World rights reserved. Distributed by King Features Syndicate

25 B

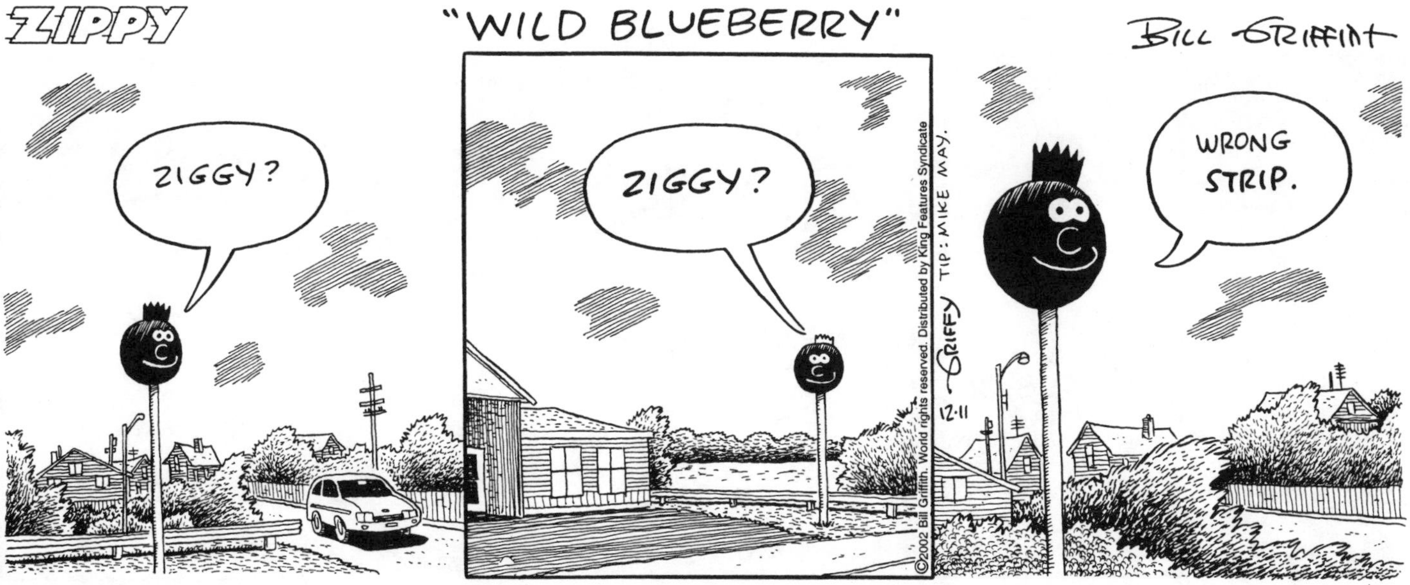

ZIPPY
"WILD BLUEBERRY"
BILL GRIFFITH
ZIGGY?
ZIGGY?
©2002 Bill Griffith. World rights reserved. Distributed by King Features Syndicate
TIP: MIKE MAY.
GRIFFY
12·11
WRONG STRIP.

26

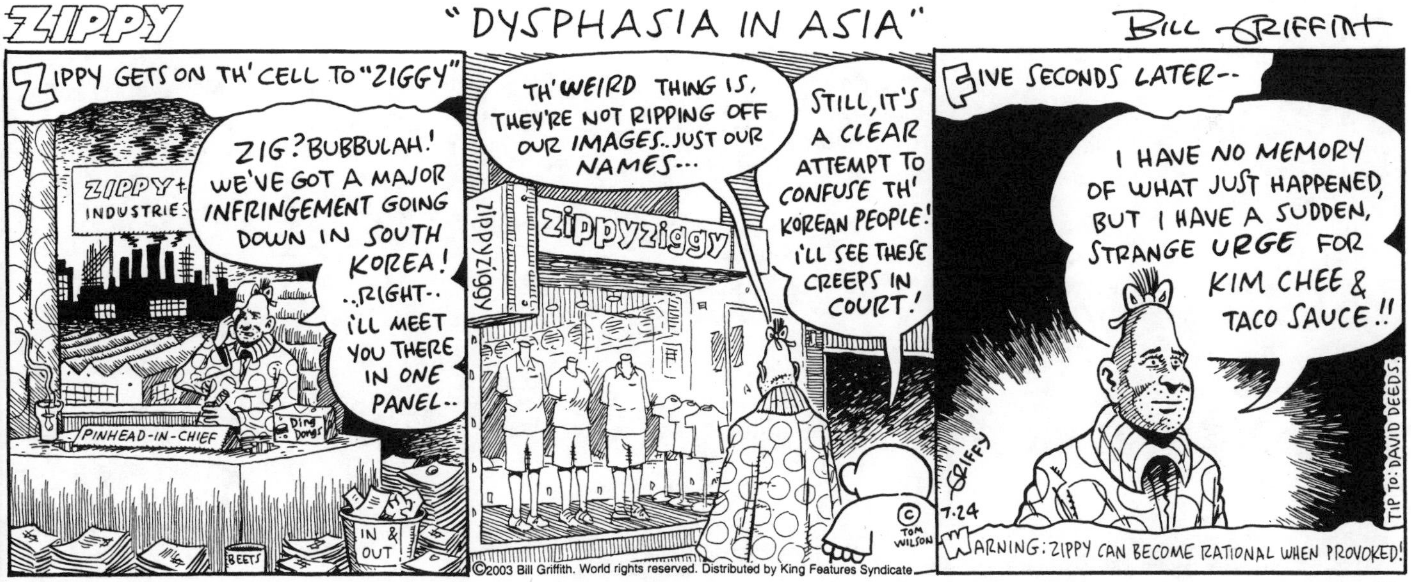

ZIPPY
"DYSPHASIA IN ASIA"
BILL GRIFFITH
ZIPPY GETS ON TH' CELL TO "ZIGGY"
ZIPPY INDUSTRIES
ZIG? BUBBULAH! WE'VE GOT A MAJOR INFRINGEMENT GOING DOWN IN SOUTH KOREA! ..RIGHT.. I'LL MEET YOU THERE IN ONE PANEL..
PINHEAD-IN-CHIEF
DING DONGS
IN & OUT
BEETS
TH' WEIRD THING IS, THEY'RE NOT RIPPING OFF OUR IMAGES.. JUST OUR NAMES...
STILL, IT'S A CLEAR ATTEMPT TO CONFUSE TH' KOREAN PEOPLE! I'LL SEE THESE CREEPS IN COURT!
zippyziggy
zippyziggy
© TOM WILSON
©2003 Bill Griffith. World rights reserved. Distributed by King Features Syndicate
FIVE SECONDS LATER--
I HAVE NO MEMORY OF WHAT JUST HAPPENED, BUT I HAVE A SUDDEN, STRANGE URGE FOR KIM CHEE & TACO SAUCE!!
GRIFFY
7·24
TIP TO: DAVID DEEDS.
WARNING: ZIPPY CAN BECOME RATIONAL WHEN PROVOKED!

27

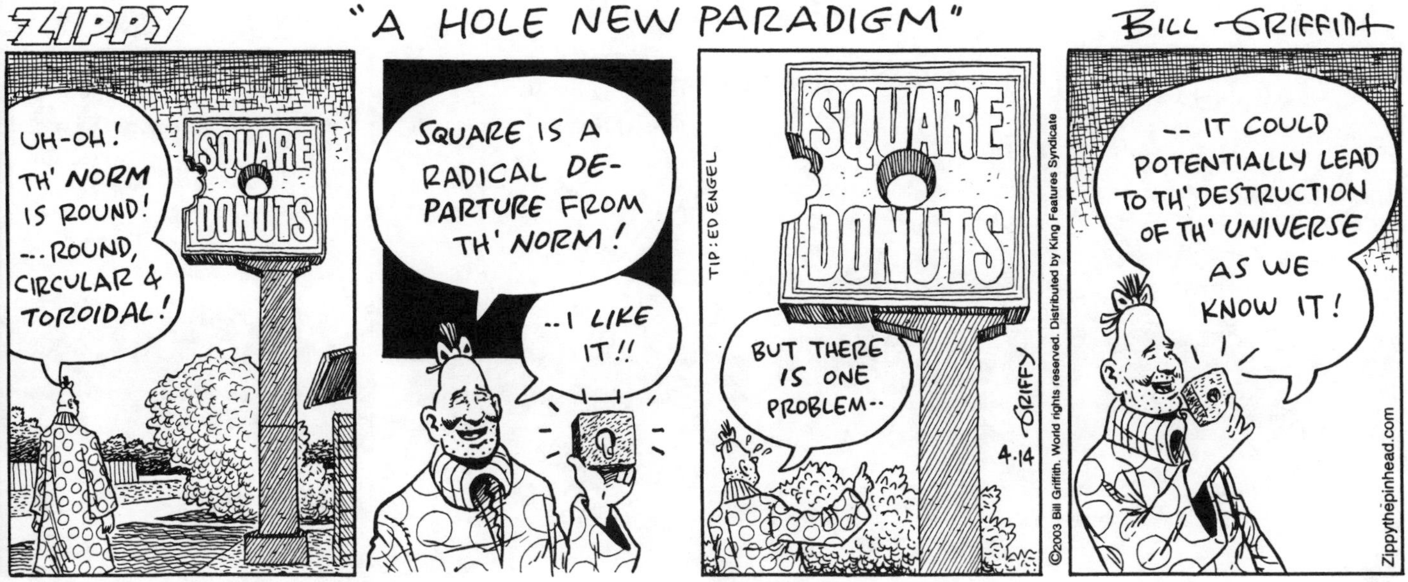

ZIPPY
"A HOLE NEW PARADIGM"
BILL GRIFFITH
UH-OH! TH' NORM IS ROUND! --. ROUND, CIRCULAR & TOROIDAL!
SQUARE DONUTS
SQUARE IS A RADICAL DE-PARTURE FROM TH' NORM!
..I LIKE IT!!
TIP: ED ENGEL
SQUARE DONUTS
BUT THERE IS ONE PROBLEM--
GRIFFY
4·14
©2003 Bill Griffith. World rights reserved. Distributed by King Features Syndicate
-- IT COULD POTENTIALLY LEAD TO TH' DESTRUCTION OF TH' UNIVERSE AS WE KNOW IT!
Zippythepinhead.com

28

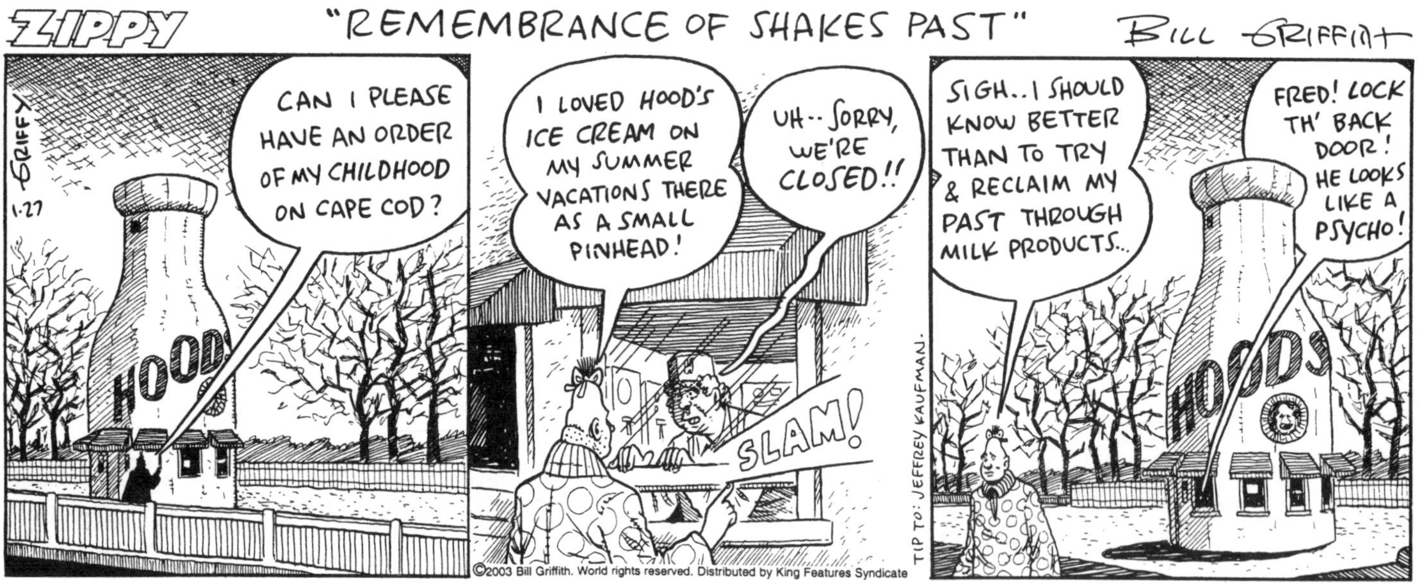
ZIPPY
"REMEMBRANCE OF SHAKES PAST"
BILL GRIFFITH
GRIFFY 1-27
CAN I PLEASE HAVE AN ORDER OF MY CHILDHOOD ON CAPE COD?
HOODS
I LOVED HOOD'S ICE CREAM ON MY SUMMER VACATIONS THERE AS A SMALL PINHEAD!
UH.. SORRY, WE'RE CLOSED!!
SLAM!
©2003 Bill Griffith. World rights reserved. Distributed by King Features Syndicate
SIGH.. I SHOULD KNOW BETTER THAN TO TRY & RECLAIM MY PAST THROUGH MILK PRODUCTS..
FRED! LOCK TH' BACK DOOR! HE LOOKS LIKE A PSYCHO!
TIP TO: JEFFREY KAUFMAN.

29

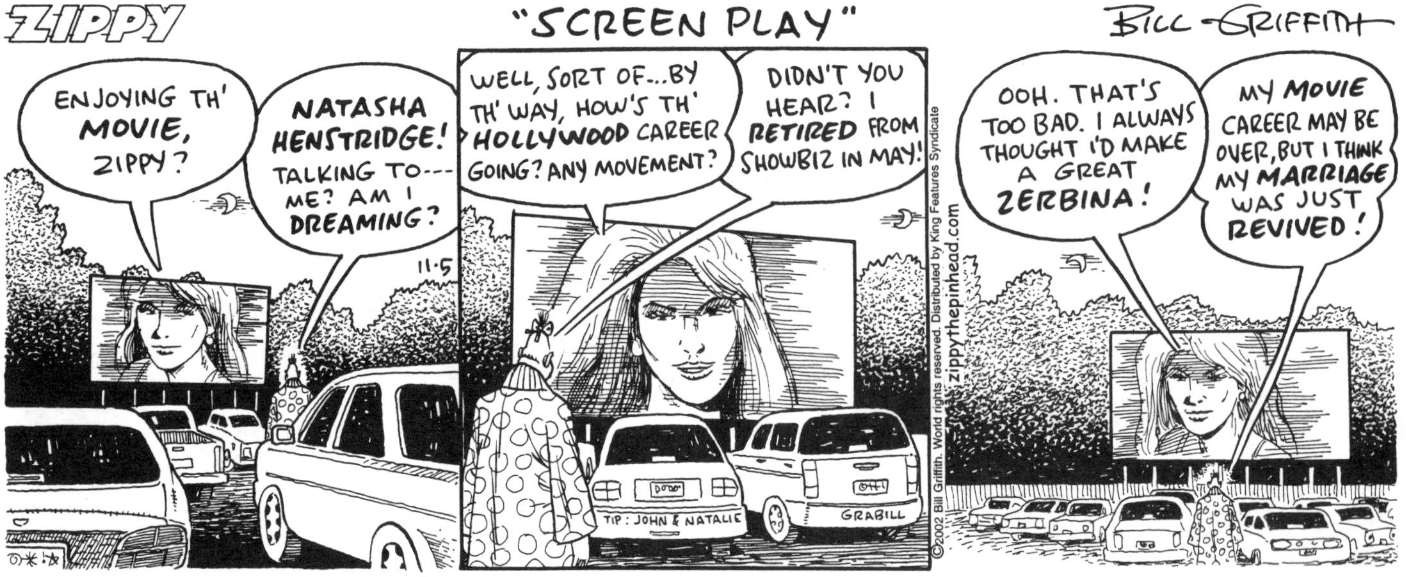
ZIPPY
"SCREEN PLAY"
BILL GRIFFITH
ENJOYING TH' MOVIE, ZIPPY?
NATASHA HENSTRIDGE! TALKING TO--- ME? AM I DREAMING?
11-5
WELL, SORT OF...BY TH' WAY, HOW'S TH' HOLLYWOOD CAREER GOING? ANY MOVEMENT?
DIDN'T YOU HEAR? I RETIRED FROM SHOWBIZ IN MAY!
TIP: JOHN & NATALIE
GRABILL
©2002 Bill Griffith. World rights reserved. Distributed by King Features Syndicate
zippythepinhead.com
OOH. THAT'S TOO BAD. I ALWAYS THOUGHT I'D MAKE A GREAT ZERBINA!
MY MOVIE CAREER MAY BE OVER, BUT I THINK MY MARRIAGE WAS JUST REVIVED!

30

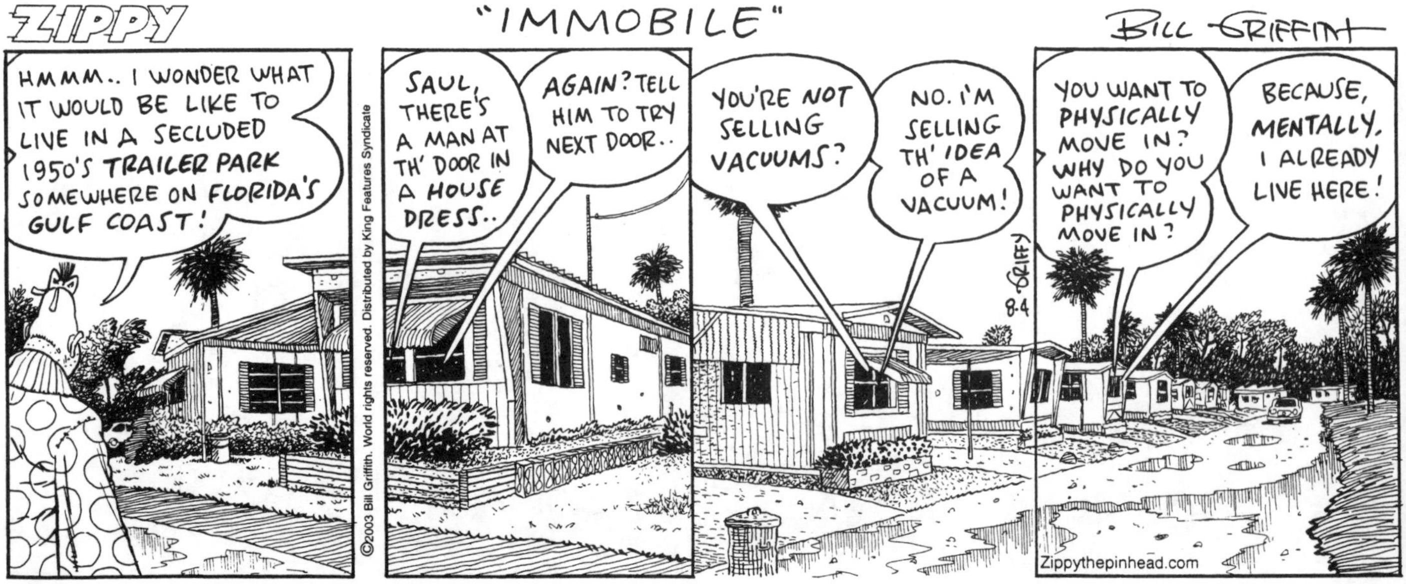
ZIPPY
"IMMOBILE"
BILL GRIFFITH
HMMM.. I WONDER WHAT IT WOULD BE LIKE TO LIVE IN A SECLUDED 1950'S TRAILER PARK SOMEWHERE ON FLORIDA'S GULF COAST!
©2003 Bill Griffith. World rights reserved. Distributed by King Features Syndicate
SAUL, THERE'S A MAN AT TH' DOOR IN A HOUSE DRESS..
AGAIN? TELL HIM TO TRY NEXT DOOR..
YOU'RE NOT SELLING VACUUMS?
NO. I'M SELLING TH' IDEA OF A VACUUM!
GRIFFY 8-4
YOU WANT TO PHYSICALLY MOVE IN? WHY DO YOU WANT TO PHYSICALLY MOVE IN?
BECAUSE, MENTALLY, I ALREADY LIVE HERE!
Zippythepinhead.com

31

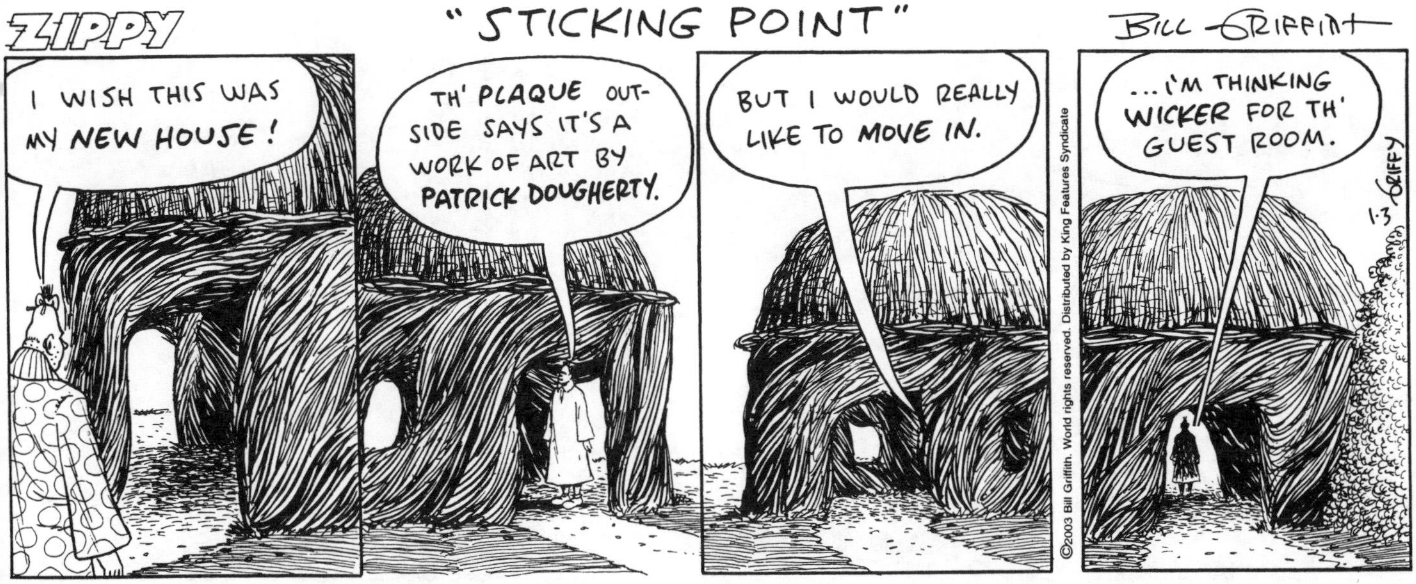
ZIPPY
"STICKING POINT"
BILL GRIFFITH
I WISH THIS WAS MY NEW HOUSE!
TH' PLAQUE OUTSIDE SAYS IT'S A WORK OF ART BY PATRICK DOUGHERTY.
BUT I WOULD REALLY LIKE TO MOVE IN.
...I'M THINKING WICKER FOR TH' GUEST ROOM.
GRIFFY 1·3
©2003 Bill Griffith. World rights reserved. Distributed by King Features Syndicate

32

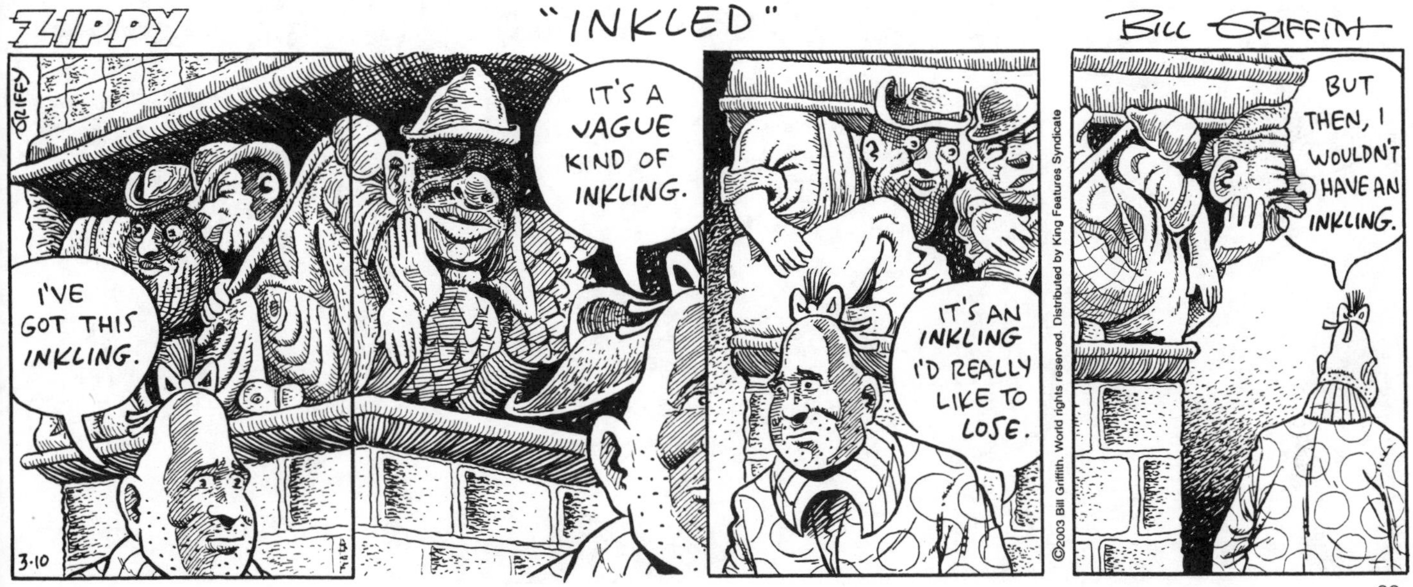
ZIPPY
"INKLED"
BILL GRIFFITH
GRIFFY 3·10
I'VE GOT THIS INKLING.
IT'S A VAGUE KIND OF INKLING.
IT'S AN INKLING I'D REALLY LIKE TO LOSE.
BUT THEN, I WOULDN'T HAVE AN INKLING.
©2003 Bill Griffith. World rights reserved. Distributed by King Features Syndicate

33

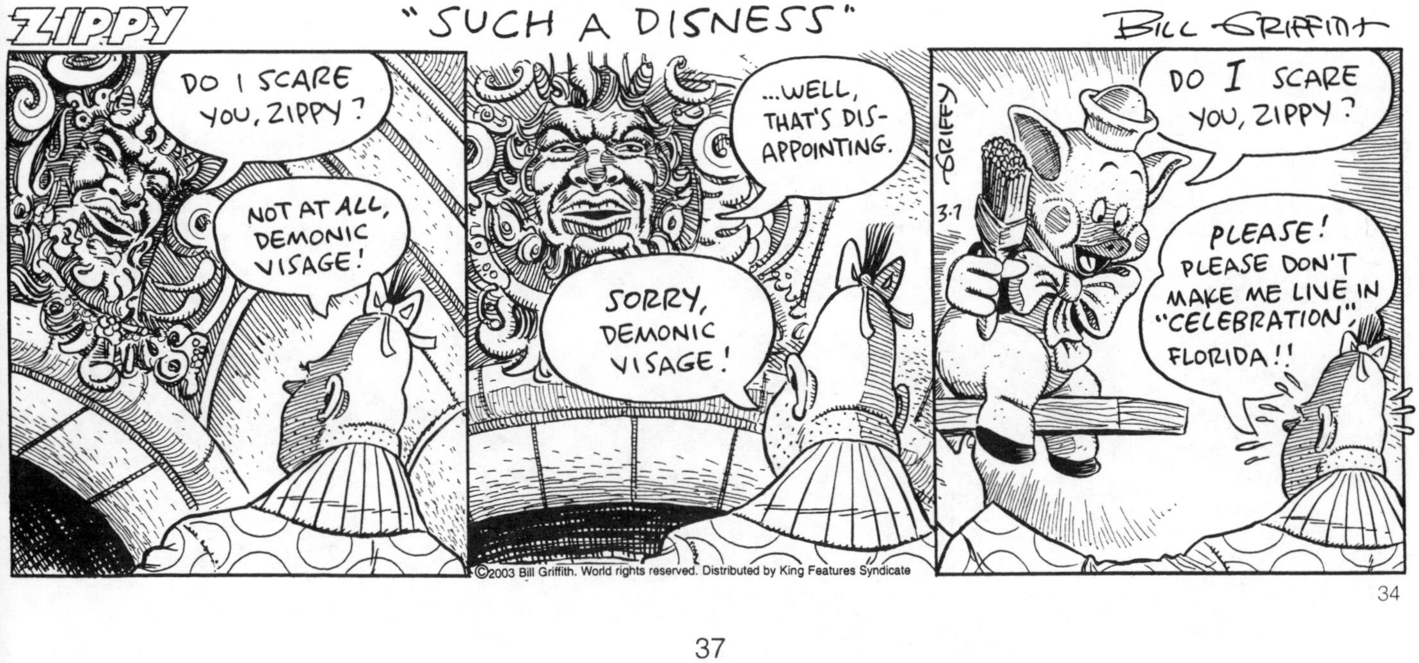
ZIPPY
"SUCH A DISNESS"
BILL GRIFFITH
DO I SCARE YOU, ZIPPY?
NOT AT ALL, DEMONIC VISAGE!
...WELL, THAT'S DISAPPOINTING.
SORRY, DEMONIC VISAGE!
GRIFFY 3·7
DO I SCARE YOU, ZIPPY?
PLEASE! PLEASE DON'T MAKE ME LIVE IN "CELEBRATION", FLORIDA!!
©2003 Bill Griffith. World rights reserved. Distributed by King Features Syndicate

34

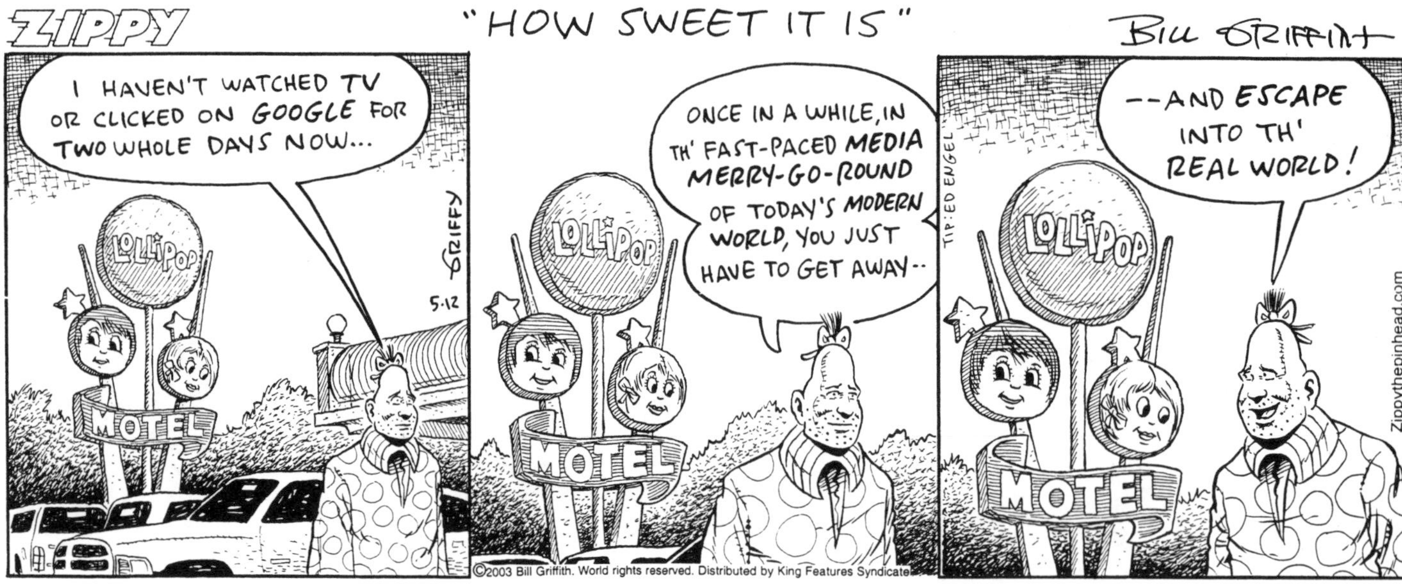
ZIPPY
"HOW SWEET IT IS"
BILL GRIFFITH
I HAVEN'T WATCHED TV OR CLICKED ON GOOGLE FOR TWO WHOLE DAYS NOW...
LOLLIPOP
MOTEL
GRIFFY
5.12
ONCE IN A WHILE, IN TH' FAST-PACED MEDIA MERRY-GO-ROUND OF TODAY'S MODERN WORLD, YOU JUST HAVE TO GET AWAY--
TIP: ED ENGEL
--AND ESCAPE INTO TH' REAL WORLD!
Zippythepinhead.com
©2003 Bill Griffith. World rights reserved. Distributed by King Features Syndicate

35

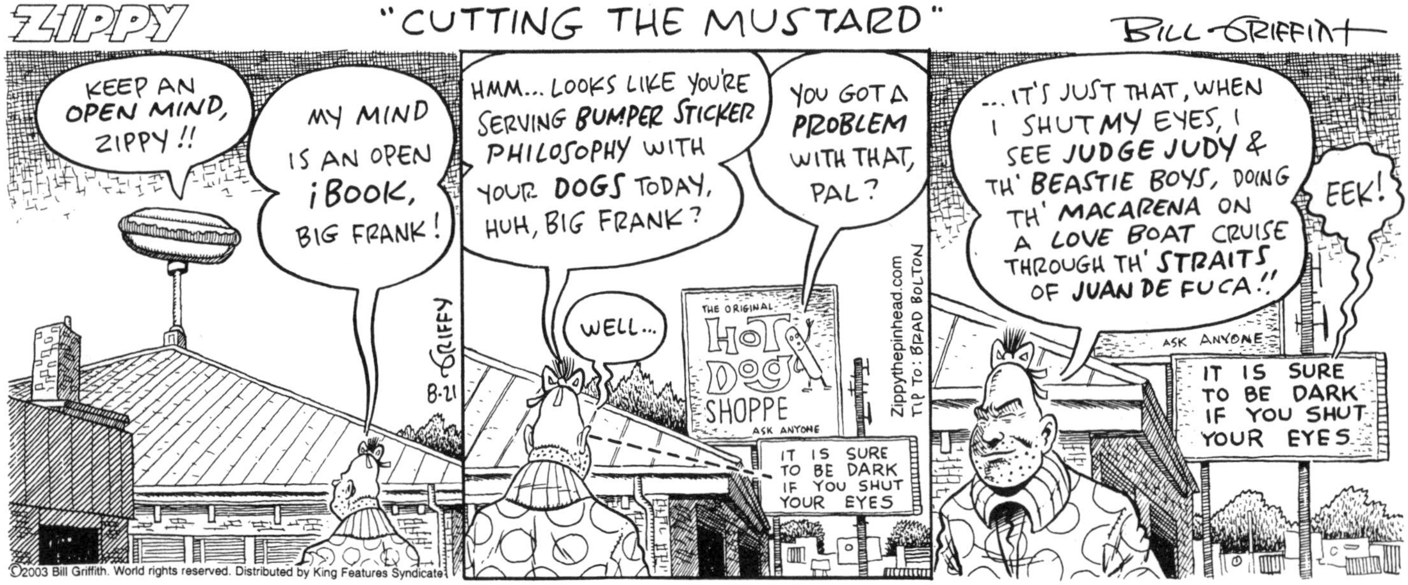
ZIPPY
"CUTTING THE MUSTARD"
BILL GRIFFITH
KEEP AN OPEN MIND, ZIPPY!!
MY MIND IS AN OPEN iBOOK, BIG FRANK!
GRIFFY
8.21
HMM... LOOKS LIKE YOU'RE SERVING BUMPER STICKER PHILOSOPHY WITH YOUR DOGS TODAY, HUH, BIG FRANK?
YOU GOT A PROBLEM WITH THAT, PAL?
WELL...
THE ORIGINAL HOT DOG SHOPPE
ASK ANYONE
IT IS SURE TO BE DARK IF YOU SHUT YOUR EYES
Zippythepinhead.com
TIP TO: BRAD BOLTON
...IT'S JUST THAT, WHEN I SHUT MY EYES, I SEE JUDGE JUDY & TH' BEASTIE BOYS, DOING TH' MACARENA ON A LOVE BOAT CRUISE THROUGH TH' STRAITS OF JUAN DE FUCA!!
EEK!
ASK ANYONE
IT IS SURE TO BE DARK IF YOU SHUT YOUR EYES
©2003 Bill Griffith. World rights reserved. Distributed by King Features Syndicate

36

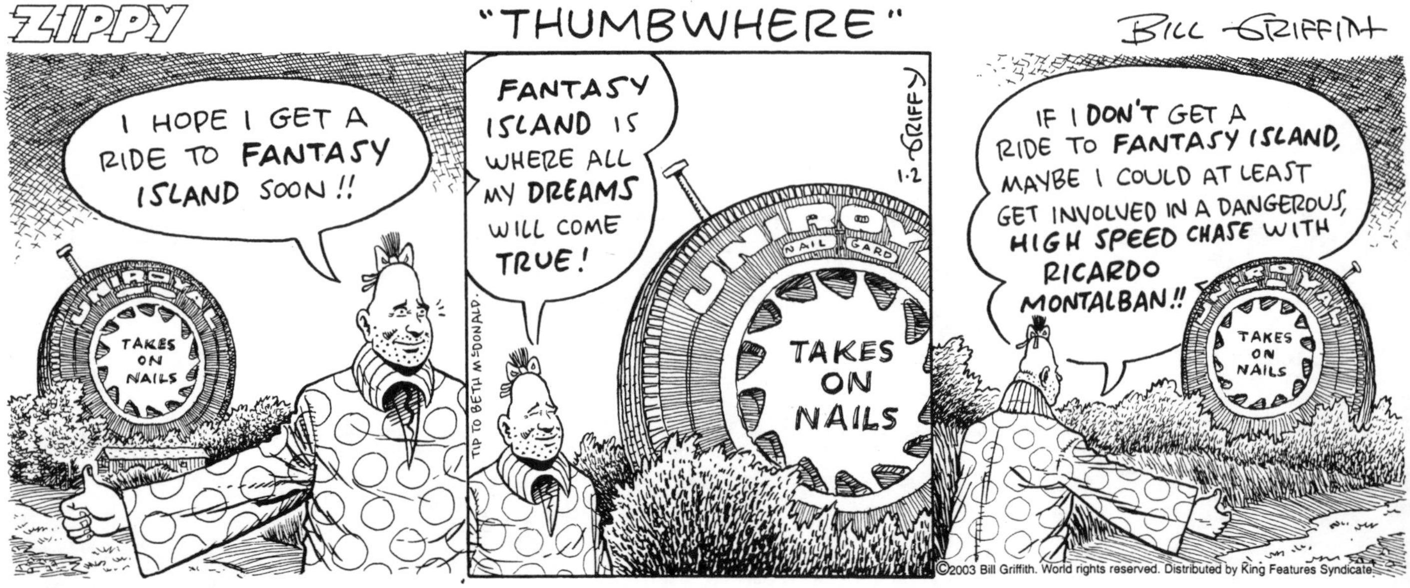
ZIPPY
"THUMBWHERE"
BILL GRIFFITH
I HOPE I GET A RIDE TO FANTASY ISLAND SOON!!
UNIROYAL
TAKES ON NAILS
FANTASY ISLAND IS WHERE ALL MY DREAMS WILL COME TRUE!
TIP TO BETH McDONALD.
GRIFFY
1.2
UNIROYAL
NAIL GARD
TAKES ON NAILS
IF I DON'T GET A RIDE TO FANTASY ISLAND, MAYBE I COULD AT LEAST GET INVOLVED IN A DANGEROUS, HIGH SPEED CHASE WITH RICARDO MONTALBAN!!
TAKES ON NAILS
©2003 Bill Griffith. World rights reserved. Distributed by King Features Syndicate

37

ZIPPY "SHOW ME, SHOW YOU" BILL GRIFFITH

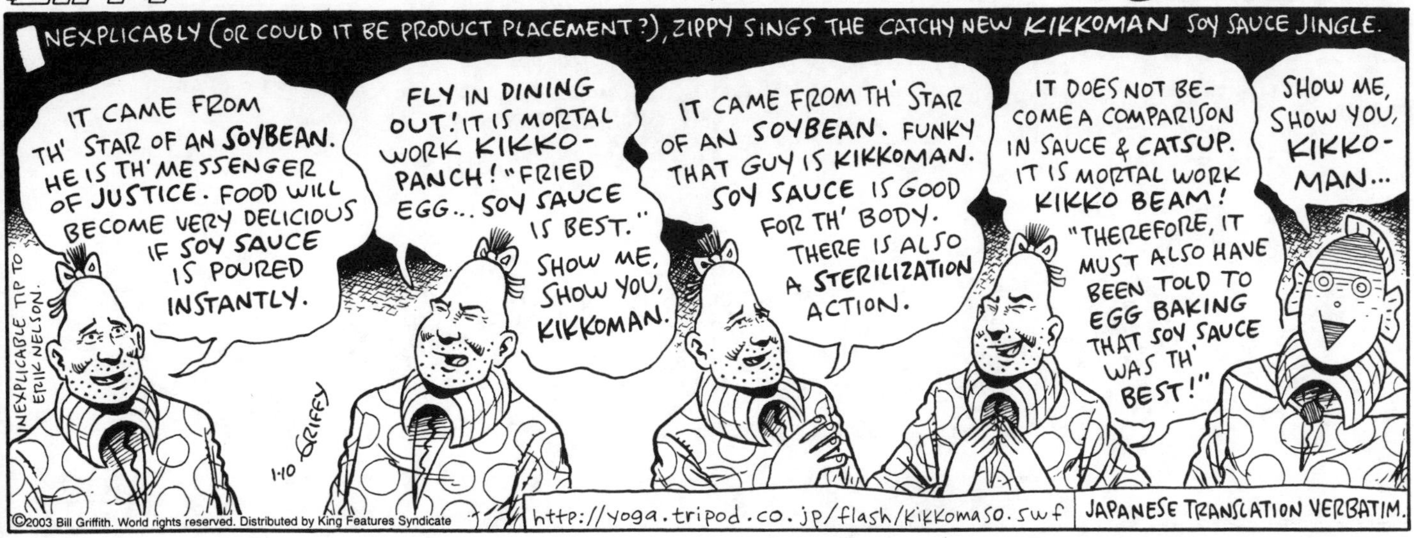

INEXPLICABLY (OR COULD IT BE PRODUCT PLACEMENT?), ZIPPY SINGS THE CATCHY NEW KIKKOMAN SOY SAUCE JINGLE.
IT CAME FROM TH' STAR OF AN SOYBEAN. HE IS TH' MESSENGER OF JUSTICE. FOOD WILL BECOME VERY DELICIOUS IF SOY SAUCE IS POURED INSTANTLY.
INEXPLICABLE TIP TO ERIK NELSON.
1-10 GRIFFY
FLY IN DINING OUT! IT IS MORTAL WORK KIKKO-PANCH! "FRIED EGG... SOY SAUCE IS BEST." SHOW ME, SHOW YOU, KIKKOMAN.
IT CAME FROM TH' STAR OF AN SOYBEAN. FUNKY THAT GUY IS KIKKOMAN. SOY SAUCE IS GOOD FOR TH' BODY. THERE IS ALSO A STERILIZATION ACTION.
IT DOES NOT BECOME A COMPARISON IN SAUCE & CATSUP. IT IS MORTAL WORK KIKKO BEAM! "THEREFORE, IT MUST ALSO HAVE BEEN TOLD TO EGG BAKING THAT SOY SAUCE WAS TH' BEST!"
SHOW ME, SHOW YOU, KIKKO-MAN...
©2003 Bill Griffith. World rights reserved. Distributed by King Features Syndicate
http://yoga.tripod.co.jp/flash/kikkomaso.swf
JAPANESE TRANSLATION VERBATIM.

ZIPPY "LONGING FOR LONG ISLAND" BILL GRIFFITH

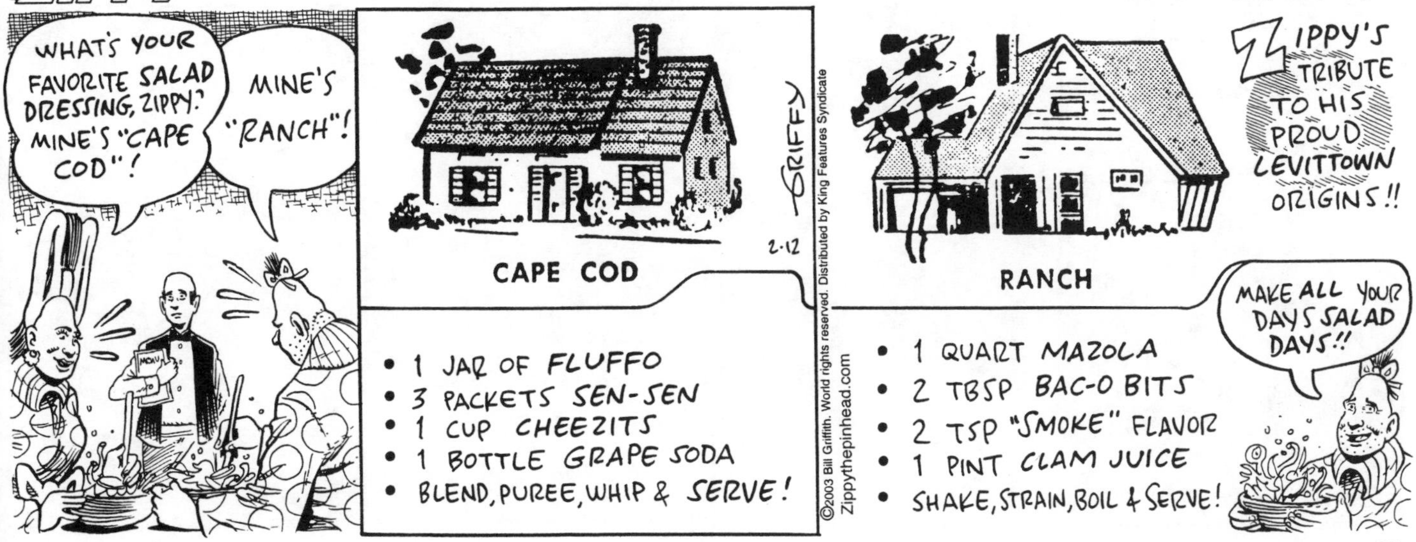

WHAT'S YOUR FAVORITE SALAD DRESSING, ZIPPY? MINE'S "CAPE COD"!
MINE'S "RANCH"!
MENU
CAPE COD
GRIFFY 2-12
• 1 JAR OF FLUFFO
• 3 PACKETS SEN-SEN
• 1 CUP CHEEZITS
• 1 BOTTLE GRAPE SODA
• BLEND, PUREE, WHIP & SERVE!
©2003 Bill Griffith. World rights reserved. Distributed by King Features Syndicate
Zippythepinhead.com
RANCH
ZIPPY'S TRIBUTE TO HIS PROUD LEVITTOWN ORIGINS!!
• 1 QUART MAZOLA
• 2 TBSP BAC-O BITS
• 2 TSP "SMOKE" FLAVOR
• 1 PINT CLAM JUICE
• SHAKE, STRAIN, BOIL & SERVE!
MAKE ALL YOUR DAYS SALAD DAYS!!

38

ZIPPY "THE HOLY TRIFECTA" BILL GRIFFITH

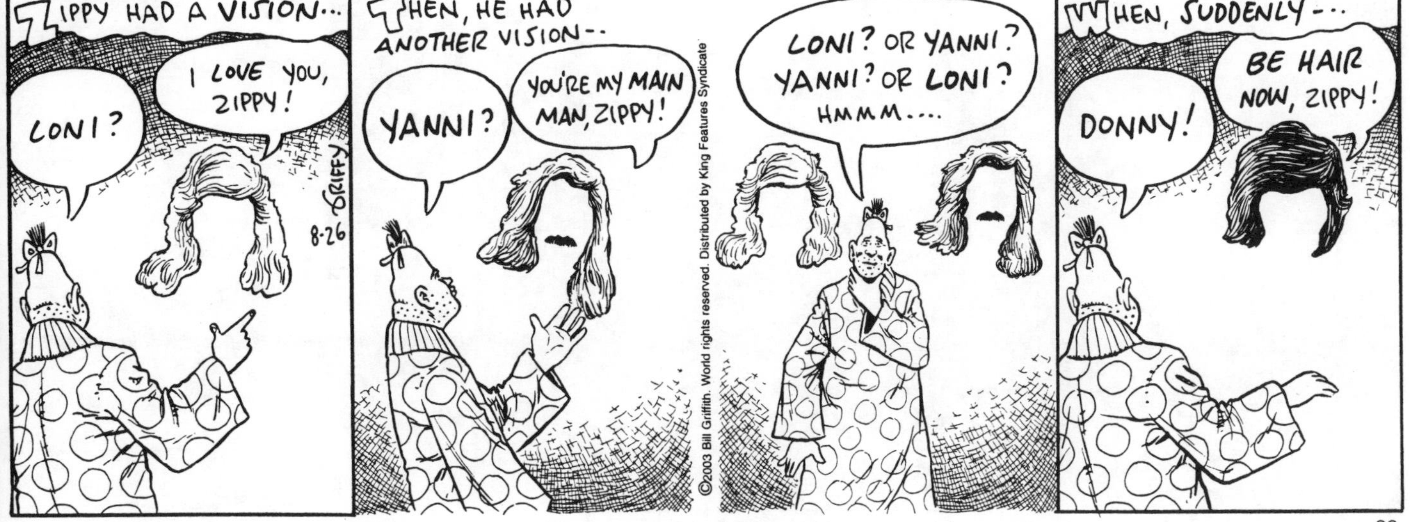

ZIPPY HAD A VISION...
LONI?
I LOVE YOU, ZIPPY!
GRIFFY 8-26
THEN, HE HAD ANOTHER VISION--
YANNI?
YOU'RE MY MAIN MAN, ZIPPY!
©2003 Bill Griffith. World rights reserved. Distributed by King Features Syndicate
LONI? OR YANNI? YANNI? OR LONI? HMMM....
WHEN, SUDDENLY--
DONNY!
BE HAIR NOW, ZIPPY!

39

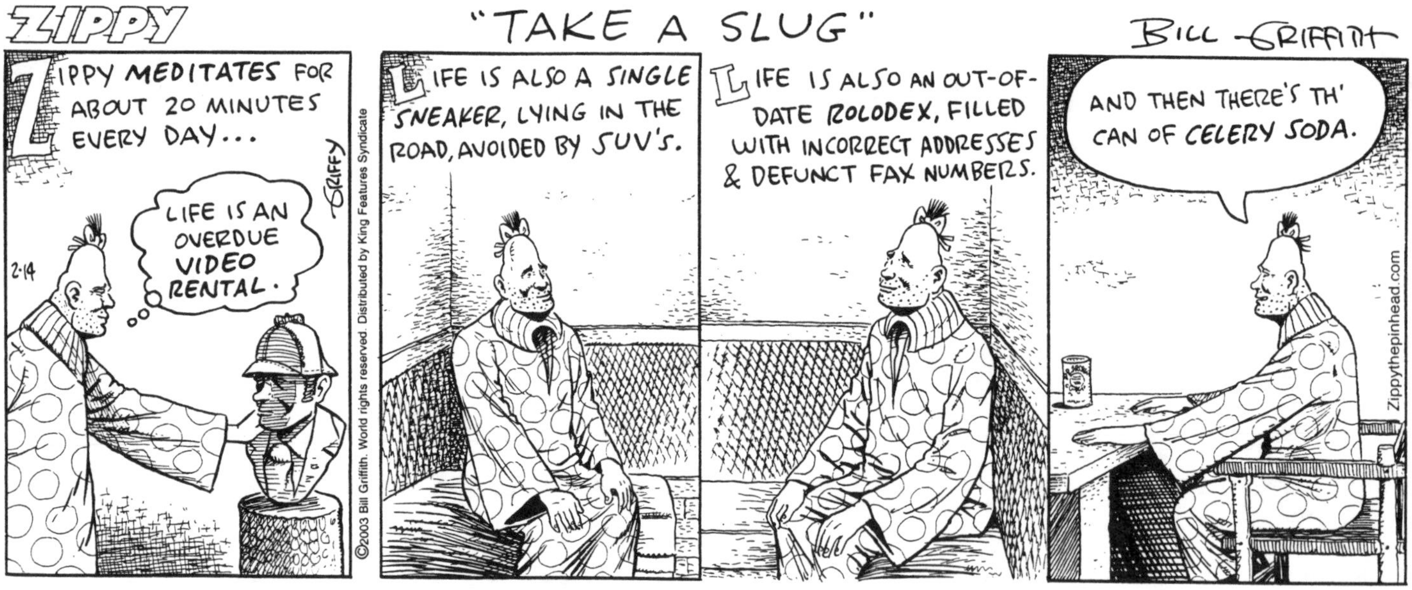
ZIPPY
"TAKE A SLUG"
BILL GRIFFITH
ZIPPY MEDITATES FOR ABOUT 20 MINUTES EVERY DAY...
LIFE IS AN OVERDUE VIDEO RENTAL.
LIFE IS ALSO A SINGLE SNEAKER, LYING IN THE ROAD, AVOIDED BY SUV'S.
LIFE IS ALSO AN OUT-OF-DATE ROLODEX, FILLED WITH INCORRECT ADDRESSES & DEFUNCT FAX NUMBERS.
AND THEN THERE'S TH' CAN OF CELERY SODA.
©2003 Bill Griffith. World rights reserved. Distributed by King Features Syndicate
Zippythepinhead.com

40 A

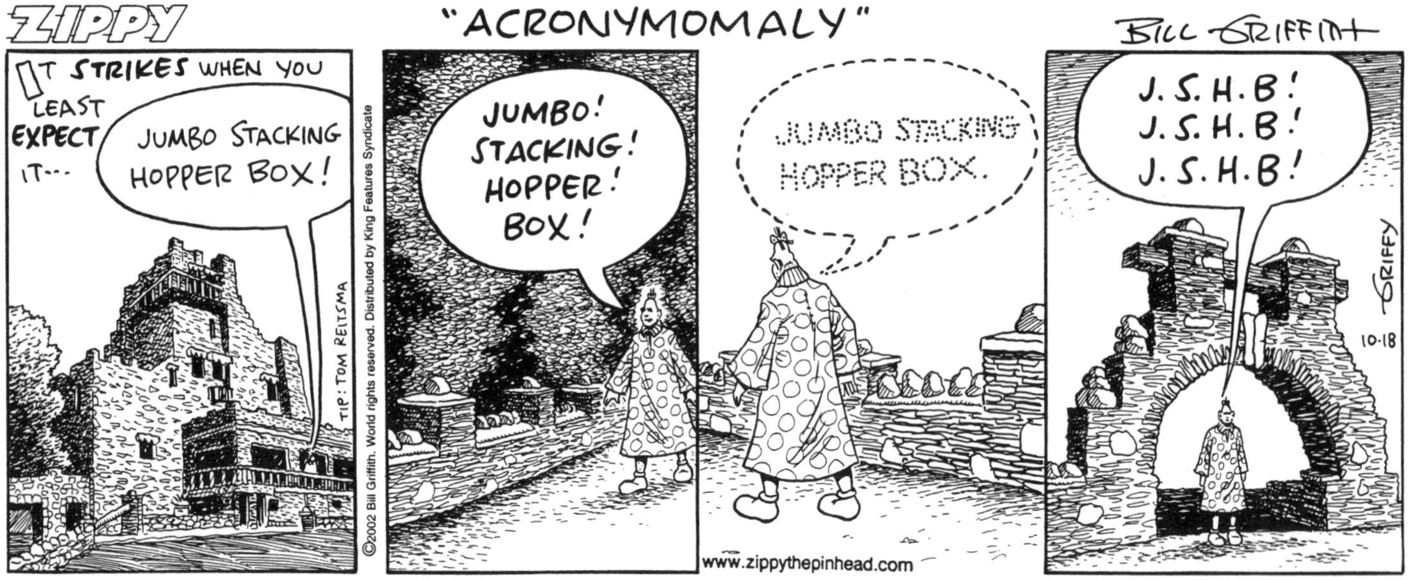
ZIPPY
"ACRONYMOMALY"
BILL GRIFFITH
IT STRIKES WHEN YOU LEAST EXPECT IT...
JUMBO STACKING HOPPER BOX!
TIP: TOM REITSMA
JUMBO! STACKING! HOPPER! BOX!
JUMBO STACKING HOPPER BOX.
J.S.H.B! J.S.H.B! J.S.H.B!
©2002 Bill Griffith. World rights reserved. Distributed by King Features Syndicate
www.zippythepinhead.com

40 B

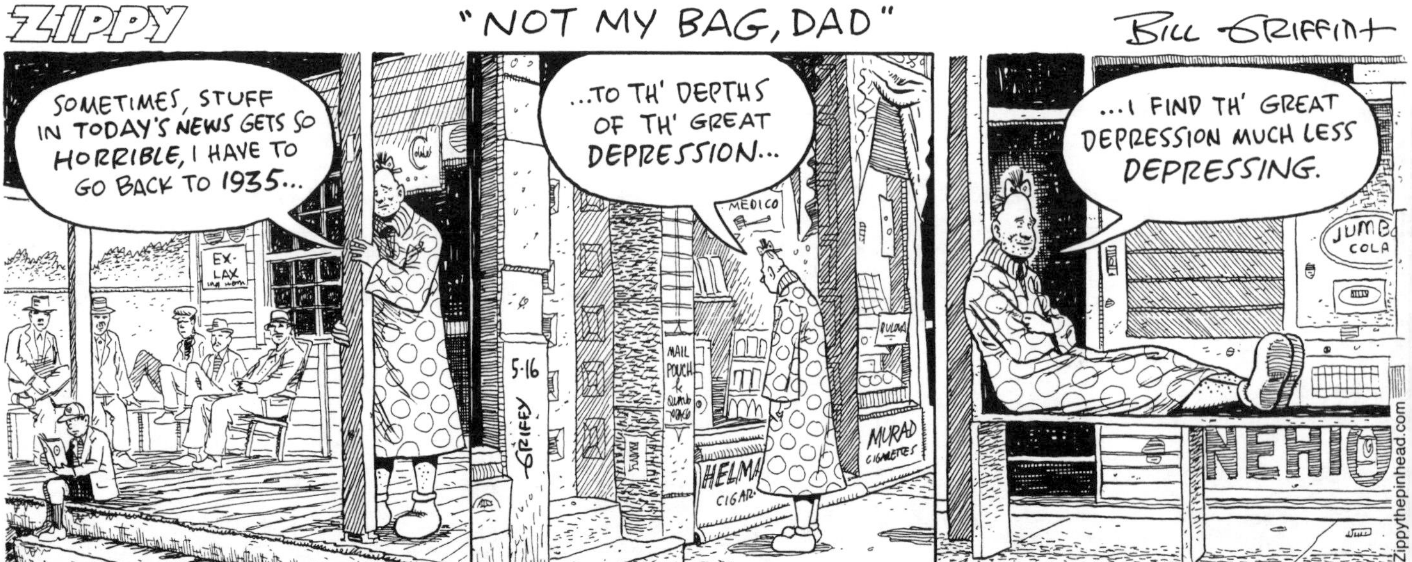
ZIPPY
"NOT MY BAG, DAD"
BILL GRIFFITH
SOMETIMES, STUFF IN TODAY'S NEWS GETS SO HORRIBLE, I HAVE TO GO BACK TO 1935...
EX-LAX
...TO TH' DEPTHS OF TH' GREAT DEPRESSION...
MEDICO
MAIL POUCH
HELMAR CIGAR
MURAD CIGARETTES
...I FIND TH' GREAT DEPRESSION MUCH LESS DEPRESSING.
JUMBO COLA
NEHI
©2003 Bill Griffith. World rights reserved. Distributed by King Features Syndicate
Zippythepinhead.com

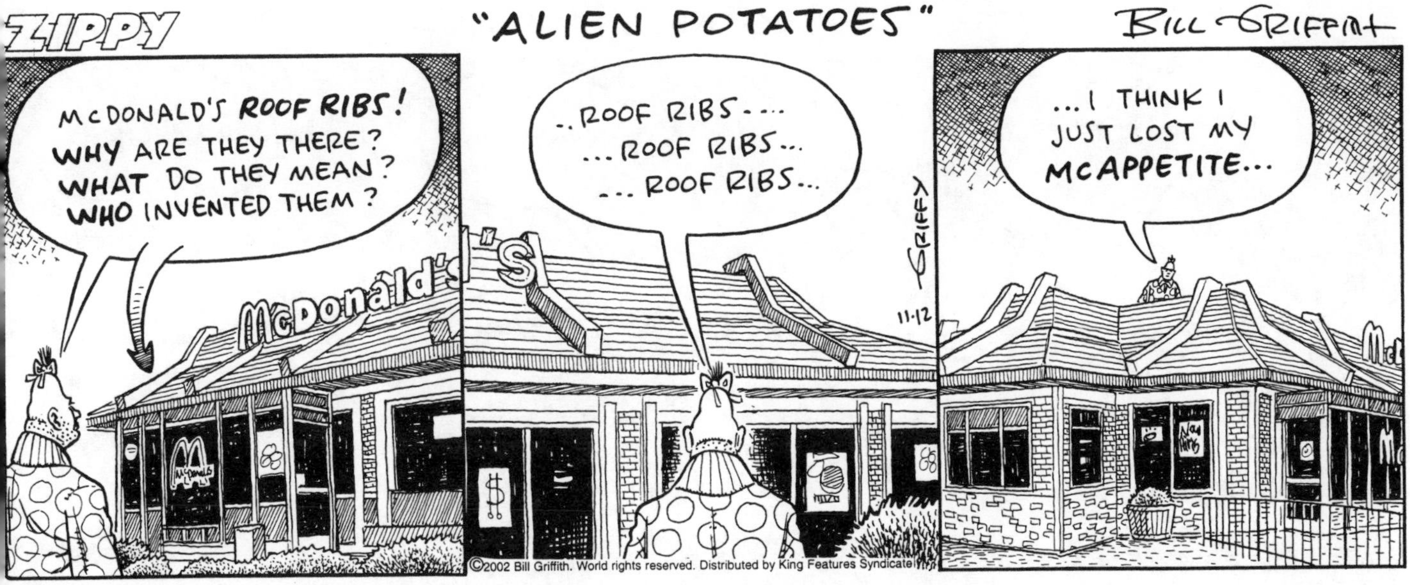
ZIPPY
"ALIEN POTATOES"
BILL GRIFFITH
McDONALD'S ROOF RIBS! WHY ARE THEY THERE? WHAT DO THEY MEAN? WHO INVENTED THEM?
McDonald's
..ROOF RIBS.... ...ROOF RIBS... ...ROOF RIBS...
GRIFFY 11-12
...I THINK I JUST LOST MY McAPPETITE...
©2002 Bill Griffith. World rights reserved. Distributed by King Features Syndicate

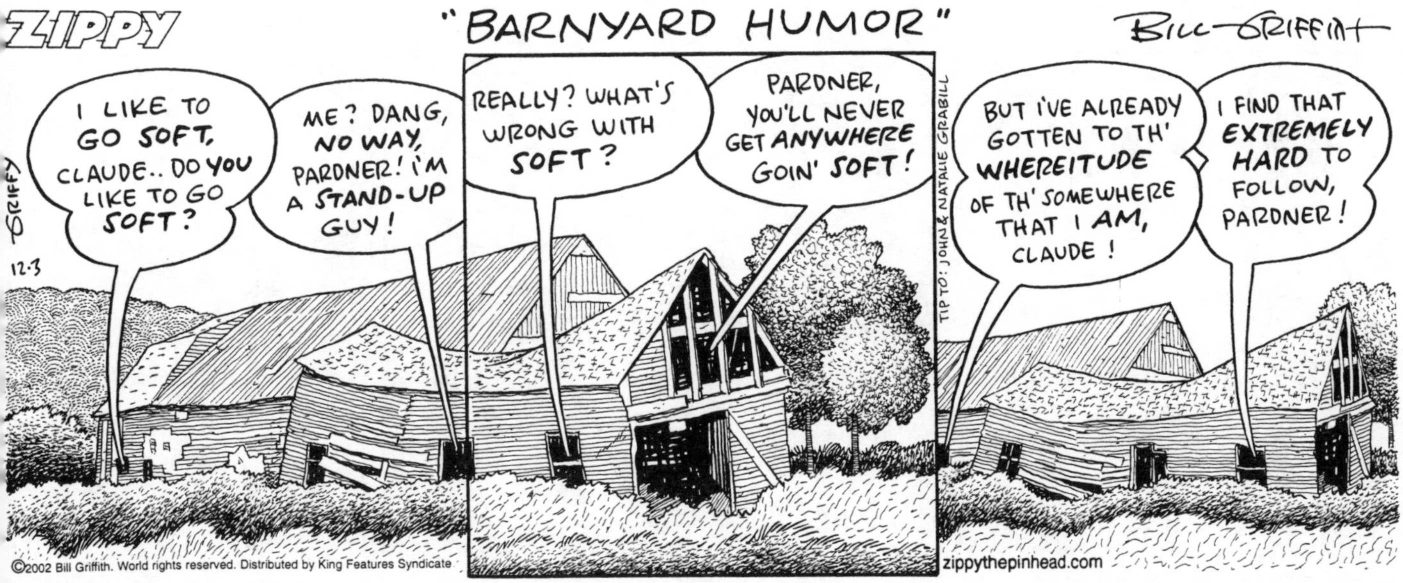
ZIPPY
"BARNYARD HUMOR"
BILL GRIFFITH
GRIFFY 12-3
I LIKE TO GO SOFT, CLAUDE.. DO YOU LIKE TO GO SOFT?
ME? DANG, NO WAY, PARDNER! I'M A STAND-UP GUY!
REALLY? WHAT'S WRONG WITH SOFT?
PARDNER, YOU'LL NEVER GET ANYWHERE GOIN' SOFT!
TIP TO: JOHN & NATALIE GRABILL
BUT I'VE ALREADY GOTTEN TO TH' WHEREITUDE OF TH' SOMEWHERE THAT I AM, CLAUDE!
I FIND THAT EXTREMELY HARD TO FOLLOW, PARDNER!
©2002 Bill Griffith. World rights reserved. Distributed by King Features Syndicate
zippythepinhead.com

41

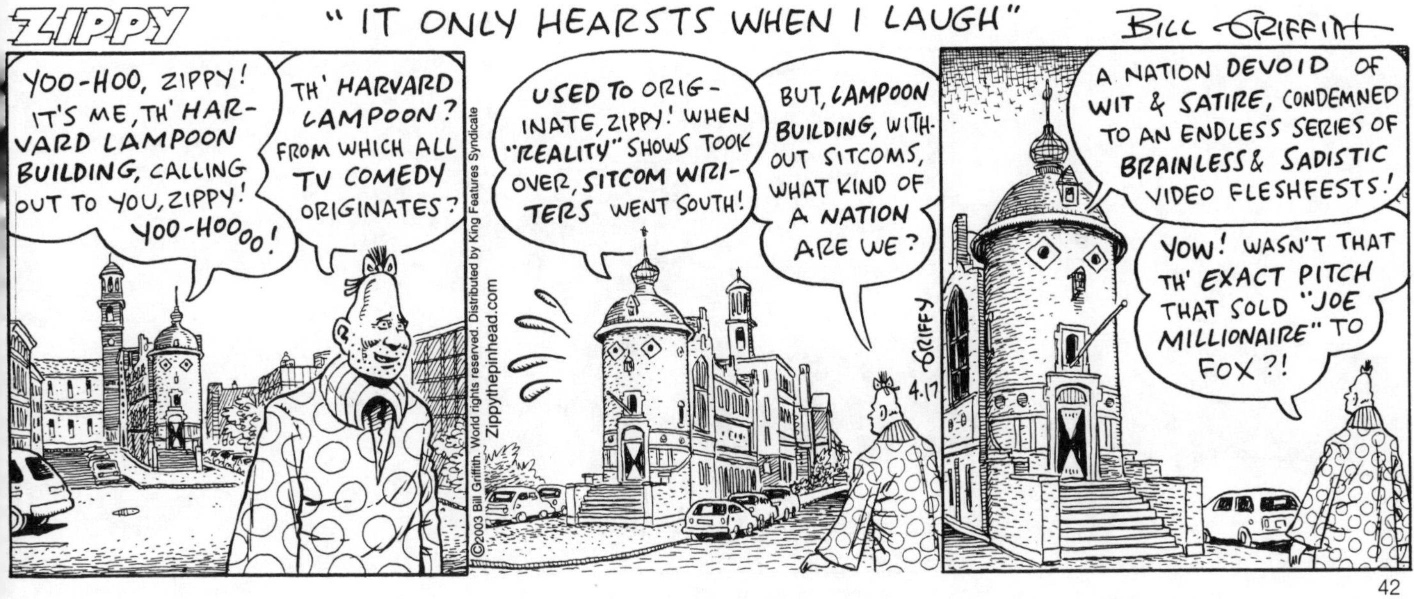
ZIPPY
"IT ONLY HEARSTS WHEN I LAUGH"
BILL GRIFFITH
YOO-HOO, ZIPPY! IT'S ME, TH' HARVARD LAMPOON BUILDING, CALLING OUT TO YOU, ZIPPY! YOO-HOOoo!
TH' HARVARD LAMPOON? FROM WHICH ALL TV COMEDY ORIGINATES?
©2003 Bill Griffith. World rights reserved. Distributed by King Features Syndicate
zippythepinhead.com
USED TO ORIGINATE, ZIPPY! WHEN "REALITY" SHOWS TOOK OVER, SITCOM WRITERS WENT SOUTH!
BUT, LAMPOON BUILDING, WITHOUT SITCOMS, WHAT KIND OF A NATION ARE WE?
GRIFFY 4-17
A NATION DEVOID OF WIT & SATIRE, CONDEMNED TO AN ENDLESS SERIES OF BRAINLESS & SADISTIC VIDEO FLESHFESTS!
YOW! WASN'T THAT TH' EXACT PITCH THAT SOLD "JOE MILLIONAIRE" TO FOX?!

42

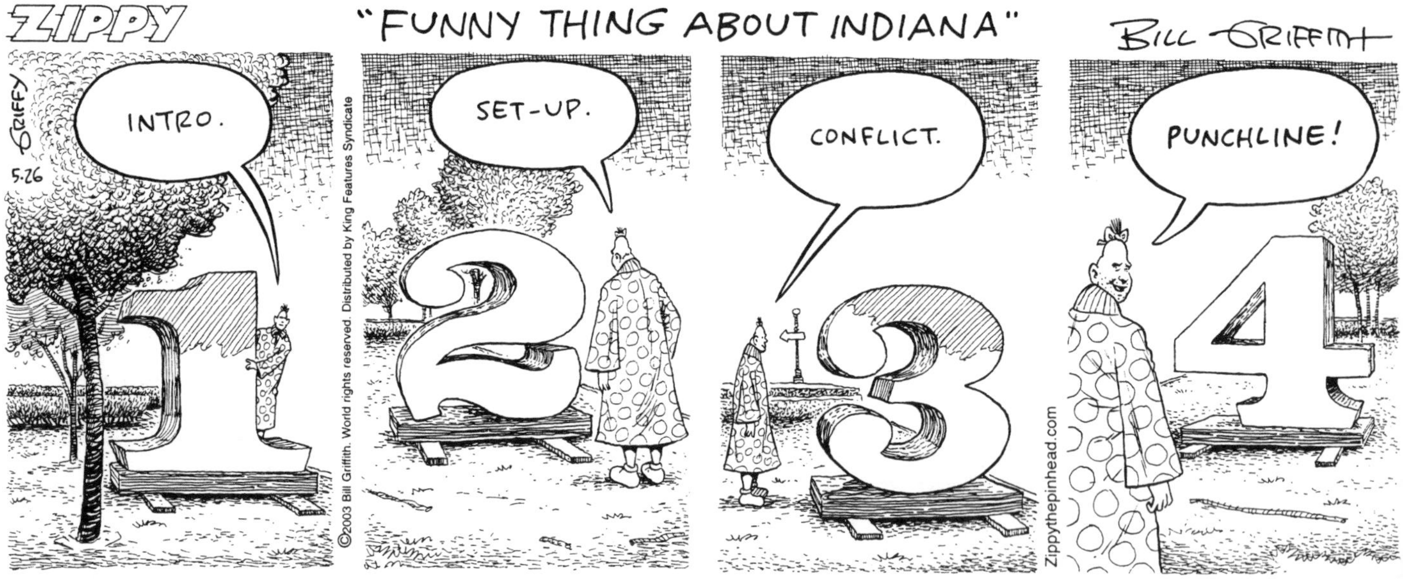
ZIPPY
"FUNNY THING ABOUT INDIANA"
BILL GRIFFITH
INTRO.
SET-UP.
CONFLICT.
PUNCHLINE!
GRIFFY
5·26
©2003 Bill Griffith. World rights reserved. Distributed by King Features Syndicate
Zippythepinhead.com

43

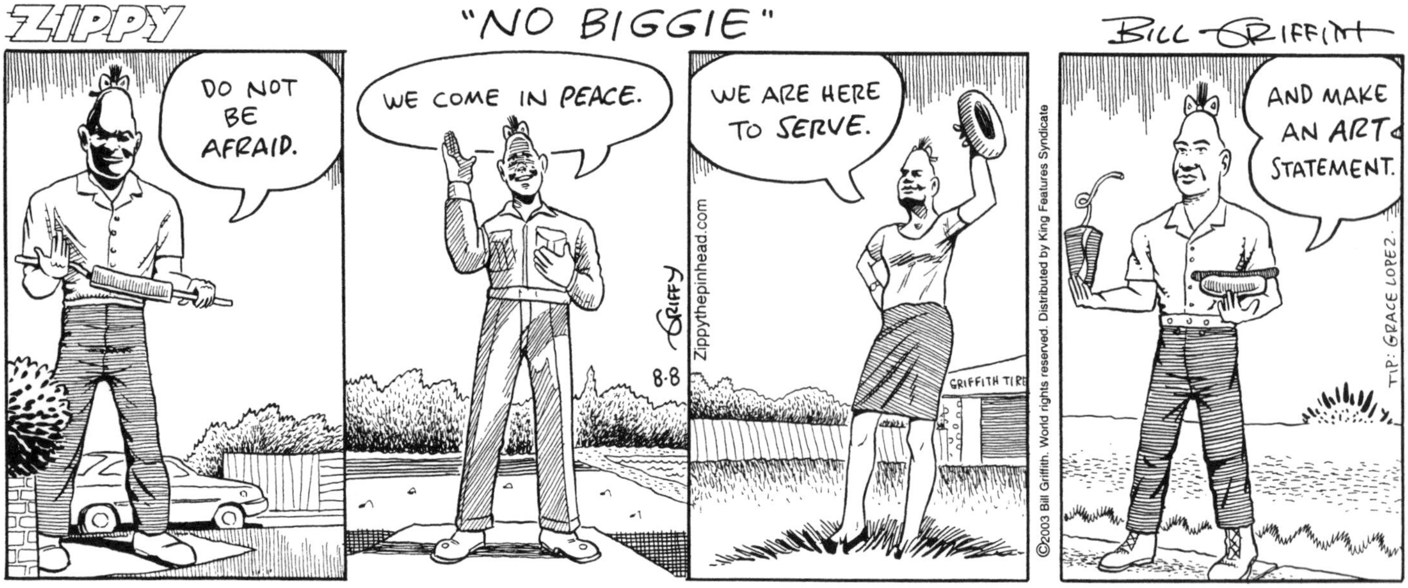
ZIPPY
"NO BIGGIE"
BILL GRIFFITH
DO NOT BE AFRAID.
WE COME IN PEACE.
WE ARE HERE TO SERVE.
AND MAKE AN ART STATEMENT.
GRIFFY
8·8
Zippythepinhead.com
GRIFFITH TIRE
©2003 Bill Griffith. World rights reserved. Distributed by King Features Syndicate
TIP: GRACE LOPEZ

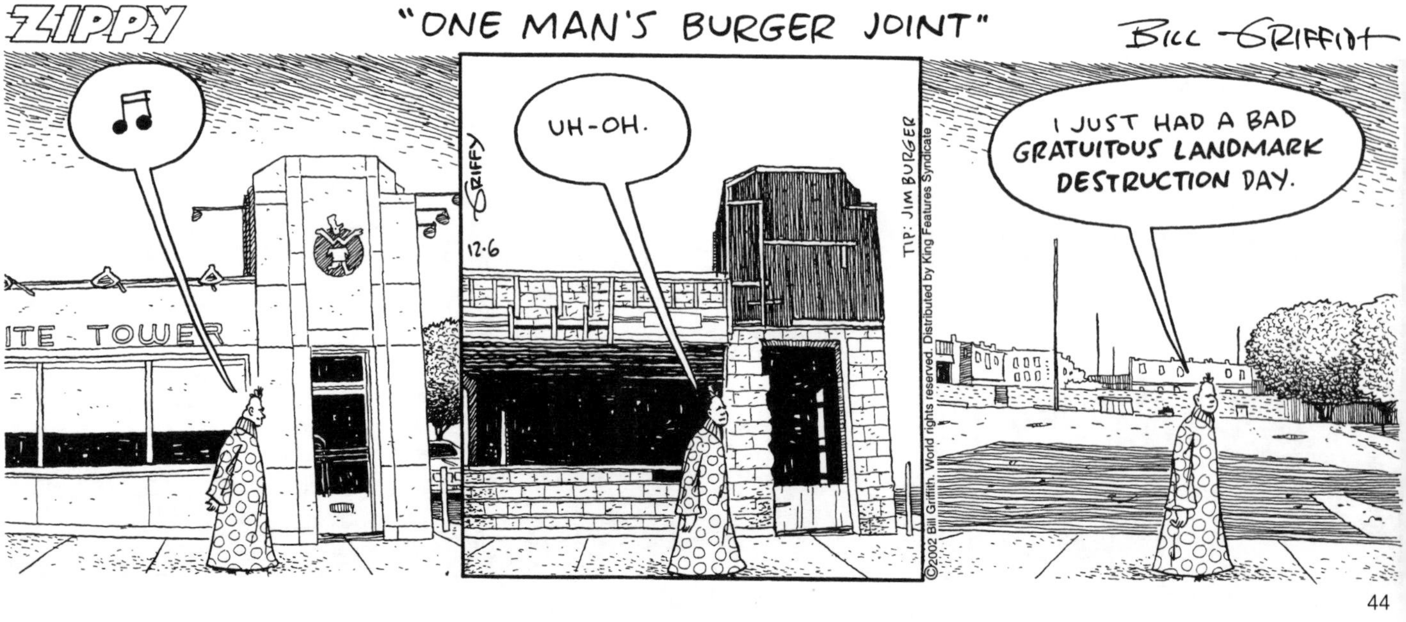
ZIPPY
"ONE MAN'S BURGER JOINT"
BILL GRIFFITH
♫
ITE TOWER
UH-OH.
GRIFFY
12·6
TIP: JIM BURGER
©2002 Bill Griffith. World rights reserved. Distributed by King Features Syndicate
I JUST HAD A BAD GRATUITOUS LANDMARK DESTRUCTION DAY.

44

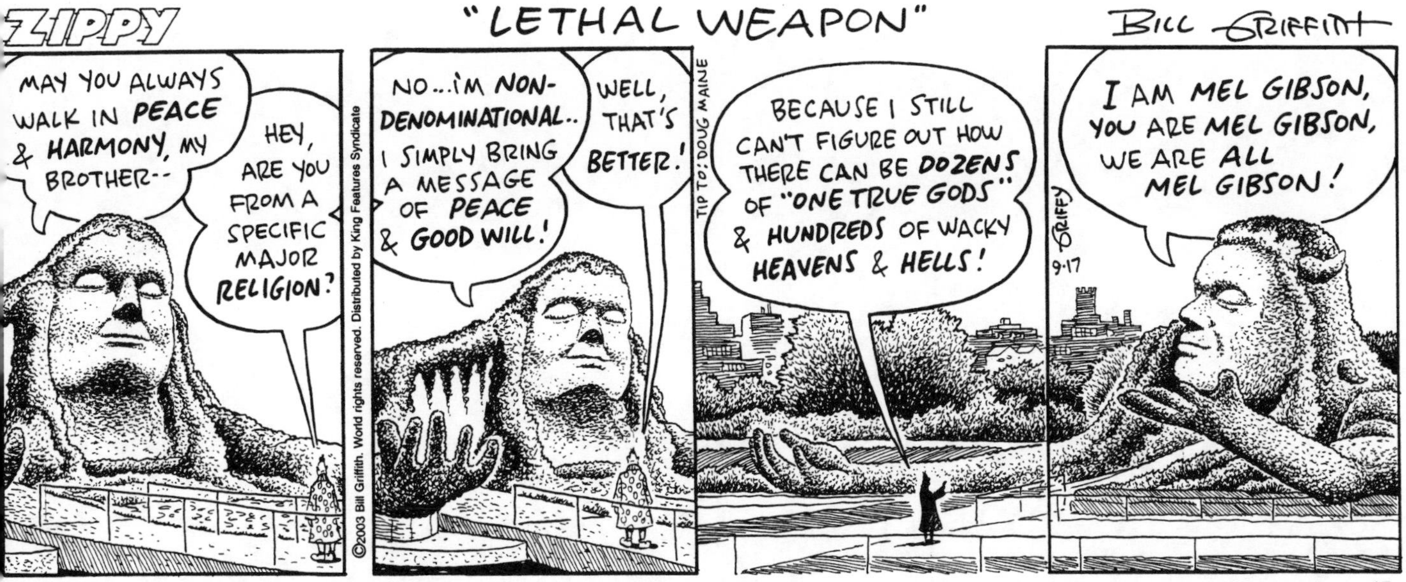
ZIPPY
"LETHAL WEAPON"
BILL GRIFFITH
MAY YOU ALWAYS WALK IN PEACE & HARMONY, MY BROTHER--
HEY, ARE YOU FROM A SPECIFIC MAJOR RELIGION?
©2003 Bill Griffith. World rights reserved. Distributed by King Features Syndicate
NO...I'M NON-DENOMINATIONAL.. I SIMPLY BRING A MESSAGE OF PEACE & GOOD WILL!
WELL, THAT'S BETTER!
TIP TO: DOUG MAINE
BECAUSE I STILL CAN'T FIGURE OUT HOW THERE CAN BE DOZENS OF "ONE TRUE GODS" & HUNDREDS OF WACKY HEAVENS & HELLS!
GRIFFY 9·17
I AM MEL GIBSON, YOU ARE MEL GIBSON, WE ARE ALL MEL GIBSON!

45

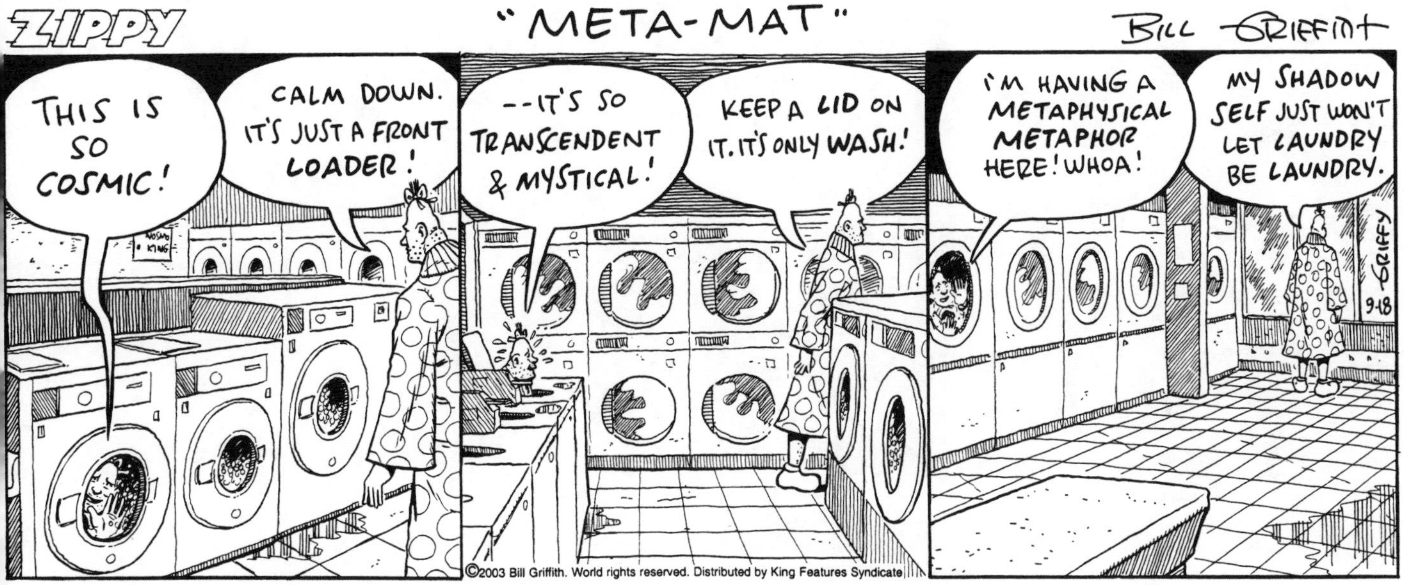
ZIPPY
"META-MAT"
BILL GRIFFITH
THIS IS SO COSMIC!
CALM DOWN. IT'S JUST A FRONT LOADER!
--IT'S SO TRANSCENDENT & MYSTICAL!
KEEP A LID ON IT. IT'S ONLY WASH!
I'M HAVING A METAPHYSICAL METAPHOR HERE! WHOA!
MY SHADOW SELF JUST WON'T LET LAUNDRY BE LAUNDRY.
GRIFFY 9·18
©2003 Bill Griffith. World rights reserved. Distributed by King Features Syndicate

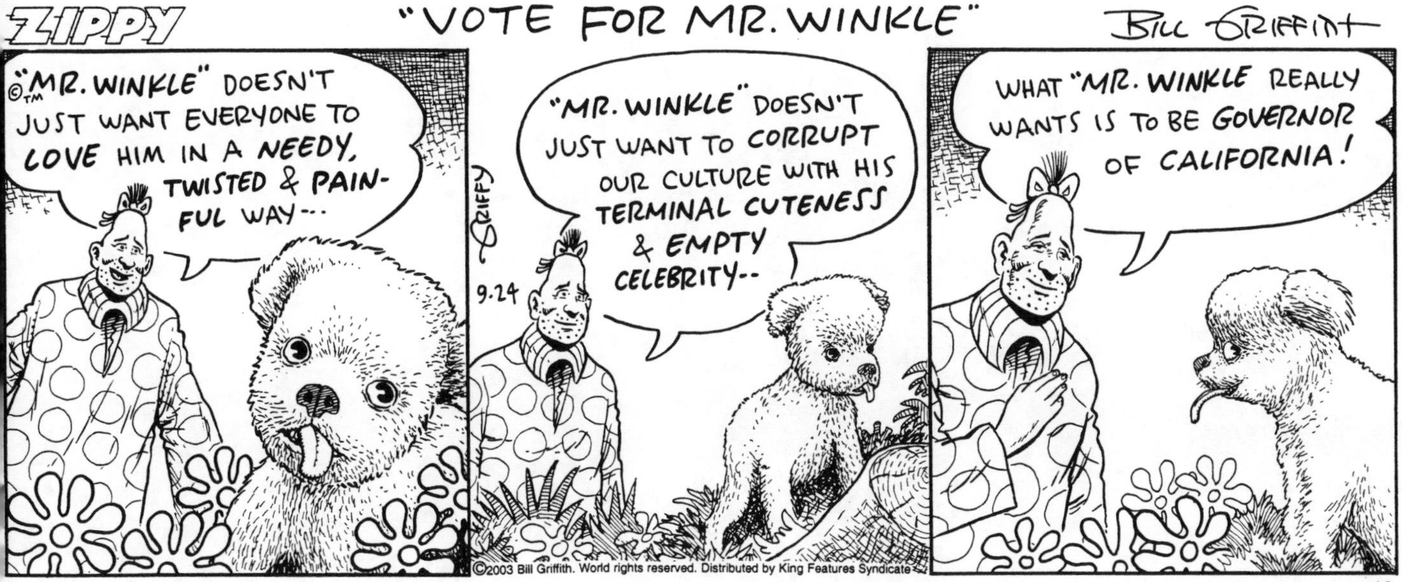
ZIPPY
"VOTE FOR MR. WINKLE"
BILL GRIFFITH
©TM "MR. WINKLE" DOESN'T JUST WANT EVERYONE TO LOVE HIM IN A NEEDY, TWISTED & PAIN-FUL WAY--
GRIFFY 9·24
"MR. WINKLE" DOESN'T JUST WANT TO CORRUPT OUR CULTURE WITH HIS TERMINAL CUTENESS & EMPTY CELEBRITY--
WHAT "MR. WINKLE REALLY WANTS IS TO BE GOVERNOR OF CALIFORNIA!
©2003 Bill Griffith. World rights reserved. Distributed by King Features Syndicate

46

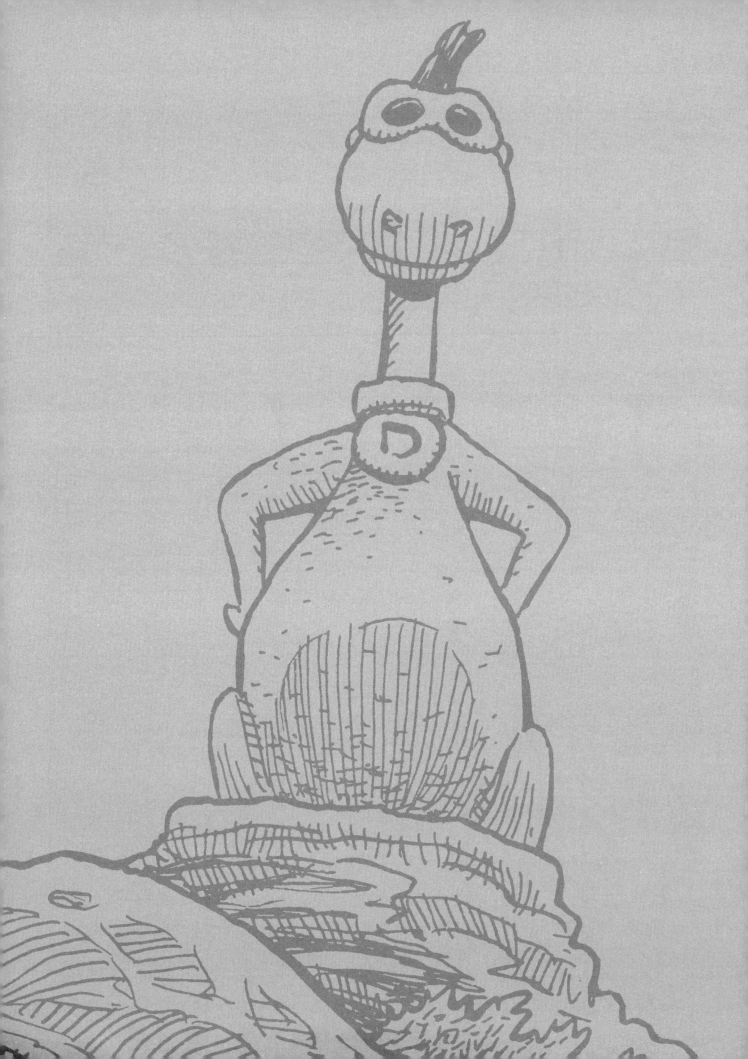

Zippy & Co.

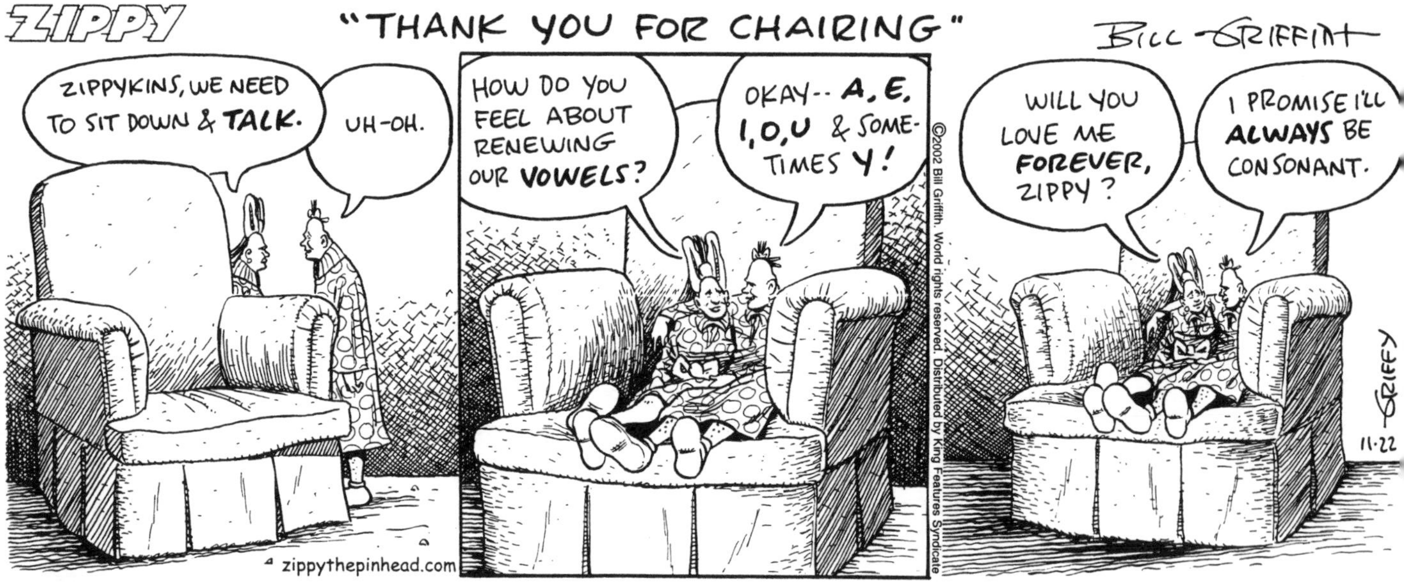
ZIPPY
"THANK YOU FOR CHAIRING"
BILL GRIFFITH
ZIPPYKINS, WE NEED TO SIT DOWN & TALK.
UH-OH.
HOW DO YOU FEEL ABOUT RENEWING OUR VOWELS?
OKAY-- A, E, I, O, U & SOMETIMES Y!
WILL YOU LOVE ME FOREVER, ZIPPY?
I PROMISE I'LL ALWAYS BE CONSONANT.
GRIFFY 11-22
zippythepinhead.com
©2002 Bill Griffith. World rights reserved. Distributed by King Features Syndicate

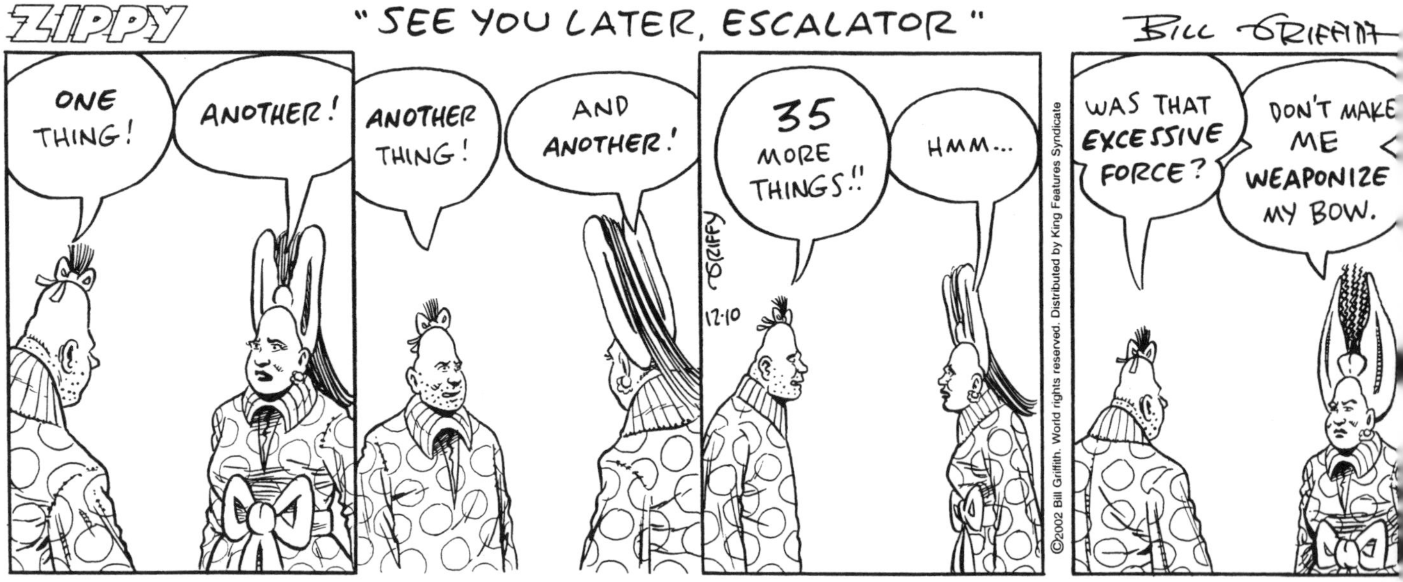
ZIPPY
"SEE YOU LATER, ESCALATOR"
BILL GRIFFITH
ONE THING!
ANOTHER!
ANOTHER THING!
AND ANOTHER!
GRIFFY 12-10
35 MORE THINGS!!
HMM...
WAS THAT EXCESSIVE FORCE?
DON'T MAKE ME WEAPONIZE MY BOW.
©2002 Bill Griffith. World rights reserved. Distributed by King Features Syndicate

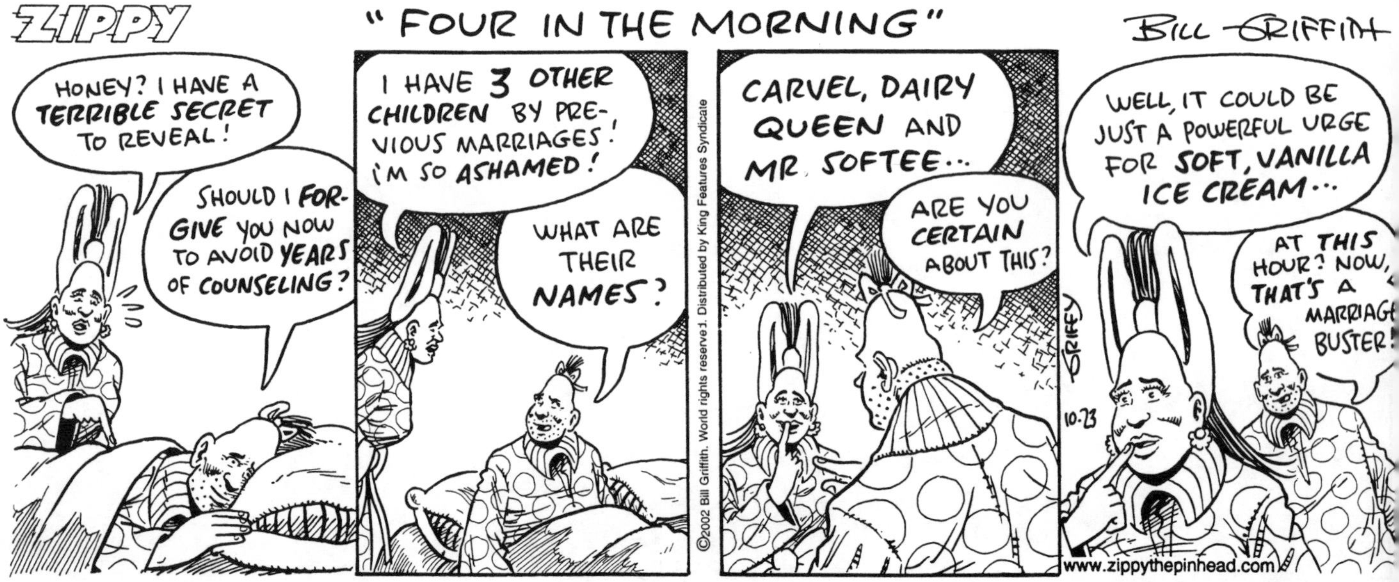
ZIPPY
"FOUR IN THE MORNING"
BILL GRIFFITH
HONEY? I HAVE A TERRIBLE SECRET TO REVEAL!
SHOULD I FORGIVE YOU NOW TO AVOID YEARS OF COUNSELING?
I HAVE 3 OTHER CHILDREN BY PREVIOUS MARRIAGES! I'M SO ASHAMED!
WHAT ARE THEIR NAMES?
©2002 Bill Griffith. World rights reserve1. Distributed by King Features Syndicate
CARVEL, DAIRY QUEEN AND MR. SOFTEE...
ARE YOU CERTAIN ABOUT THIS?
GRIFFY 10-23
WELL, IT COULD BE JUST A POWERFUL URGE FOR SOFT, VANILLA ICE CREAM...
AT THIS HOUR? NOW, THAT'S A MARRIAGE BUSTER!
www.zippythepinhead.com

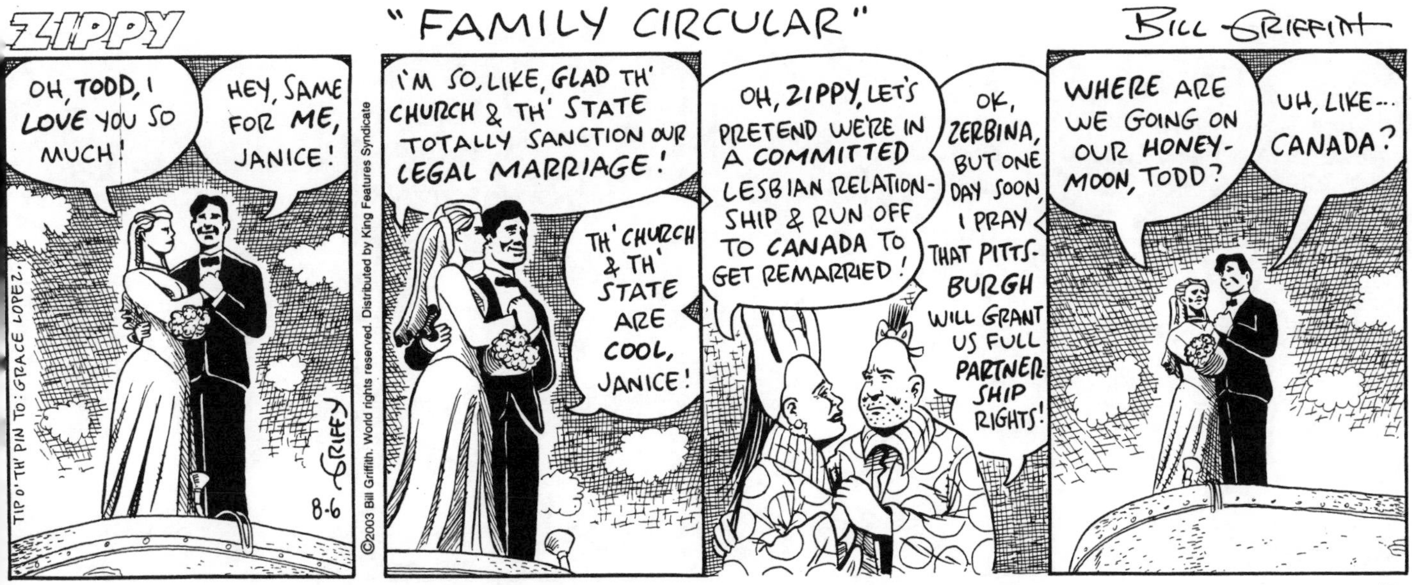
ZIPPY
"FAMILY CIRCULAR"
BILL GRIFFITH
OH, TODD, I LOVE YOU SO MUCH!
HEY, SAME FOR ME, JANICE!
TIP O' TH' PIN TO: GRACE LOPEZ.
GRIFFY 8-6
©2003 Bill Griffith. World rights reserved. Distributed by King Features Syndicate
I'M SO, LIKE, GLAD TH' CHURCH & TH' STATE TOTALLY SANCTION OUR LEGAL MARRIAGE!
TH' CHURCH & TH' STATE ARE COOL, JANICE!
OH, ZIPPY, LET'S PRETEND WE'RE IN A COMMITTED LESBIAN RELATION-SHIP & RUN OFF TO CANADA TO GET REMARRIED!
OK, ZERBINA, BUT ONE DAY SOON, I PRAY THAT PITTS-BURGH WILL GRANT US FULL PARTNER-SHIP RIGHTS!
WHERE ARE WE GOING ON OUR HONEY-MOON, TODD?
UH, LIKE... CANADA?

47

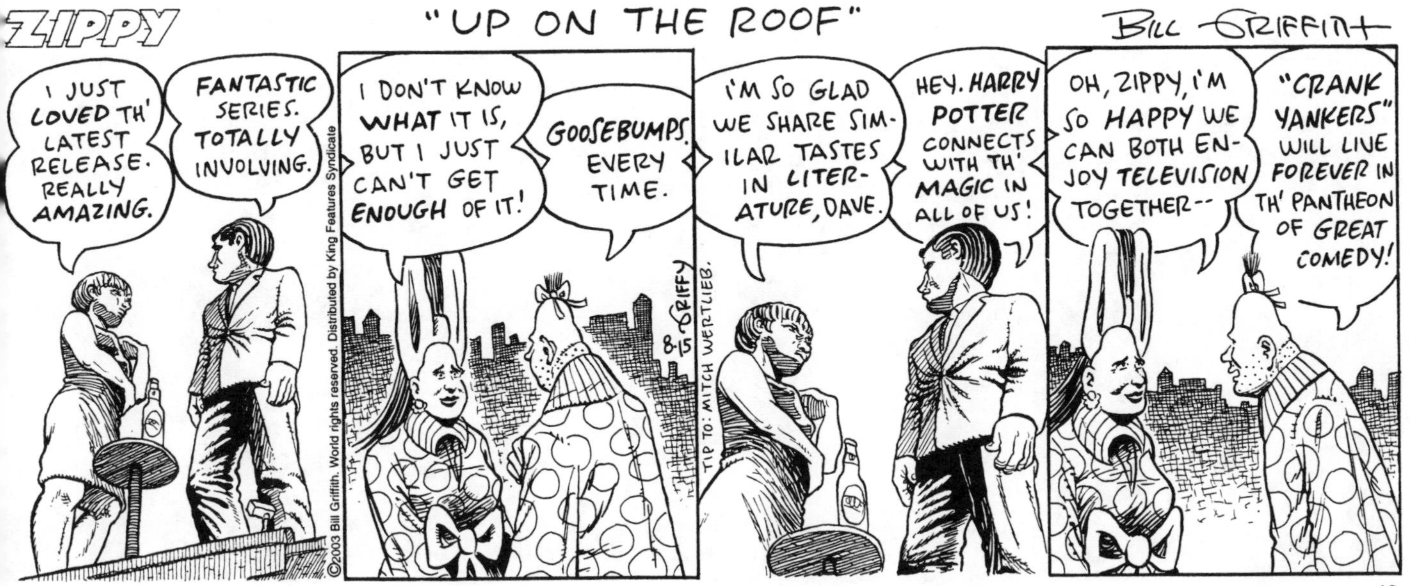
ZIPPY
"UP ON THE ROOF"
BILL GRIFFITH
I JUST LOVED TH' LATEST RELEASE. REALLY AMAZING.
FANTASTIC SERIES. TOTALLY INVOLVING.
©2003 Bill Griffith. World rights reserved. Distributed by King Features Syndicate
I DON'T KNOW WHAT IT IS, BUT I JUST CAN'T GET ENOUGH OF IT!
GOOSEBUMPS. EVERY TIME.
GRIFFY 8-15
TIP TO: MITCH WERTLIEB.
I'M SO GLAD WE SHARE SIM-ILAR TASTES IN LITER-ATURE, DAVE.
HEY. HARRY POTTER CONNECTS WITH TH' MAGIC IN ALL OF US!
OH, ZIPPY, I'M SO HAPPY WE CAN BOTH EN-JOY TELEVISION TOGETHER--
"CRANK YANKERS" WILL LIVE FOREVER IN TH' PANTHEON OF GREAT COMEDY!

48

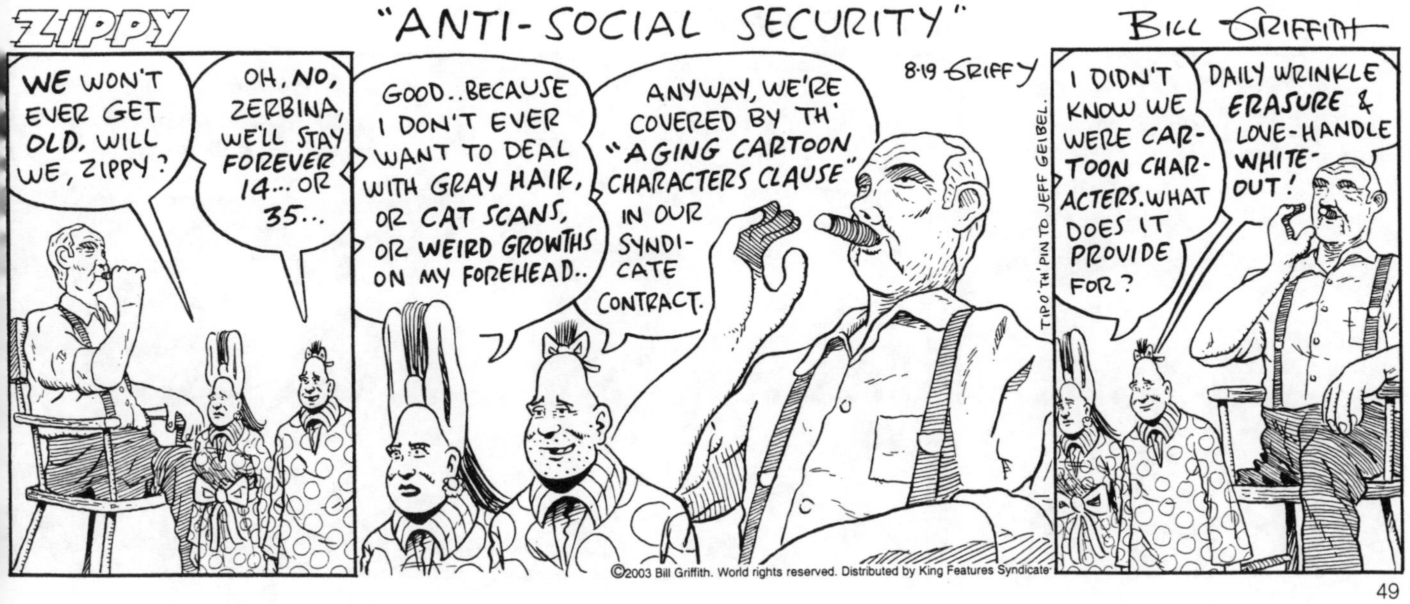
ZIPPY
"ANTI-SOCIAL SECURITY"
BILL GRIFFITH
WE WON'T EVER GET OLD, WILL WE, ZIPPY?
OH, NO, ZERBINA, WE'LL STAY FOREVER 14... OR 35...
GOOD.. BECAUSE I DON'T EVER WANT TO DEAL WITH GRAY HAIR, OR CAT SCANS, OR WEIRD GROWTHS ON MY FOREHEAD..
8-19 GRIFFY
ANYWAY, WE'RE COVERED BY TH' "AGING CARTOON CHARACTERS CLAUSE" IN OUR SYNDI-CATE CONTRACT.
TIP O' TH' PIN TO JEFF GEIBEL.
I DIDN'T KNOW WE WERE CAR-TOON CHAR-ACTERS. WHAT DOES IT PROVIDE FOR?
DAILY WRINKLE ERASURE & LOVE-HANDLE WHITE-OUT!
©2003 Bill Griffith. World rights reserved. Distributed by King Features Syndicate

49

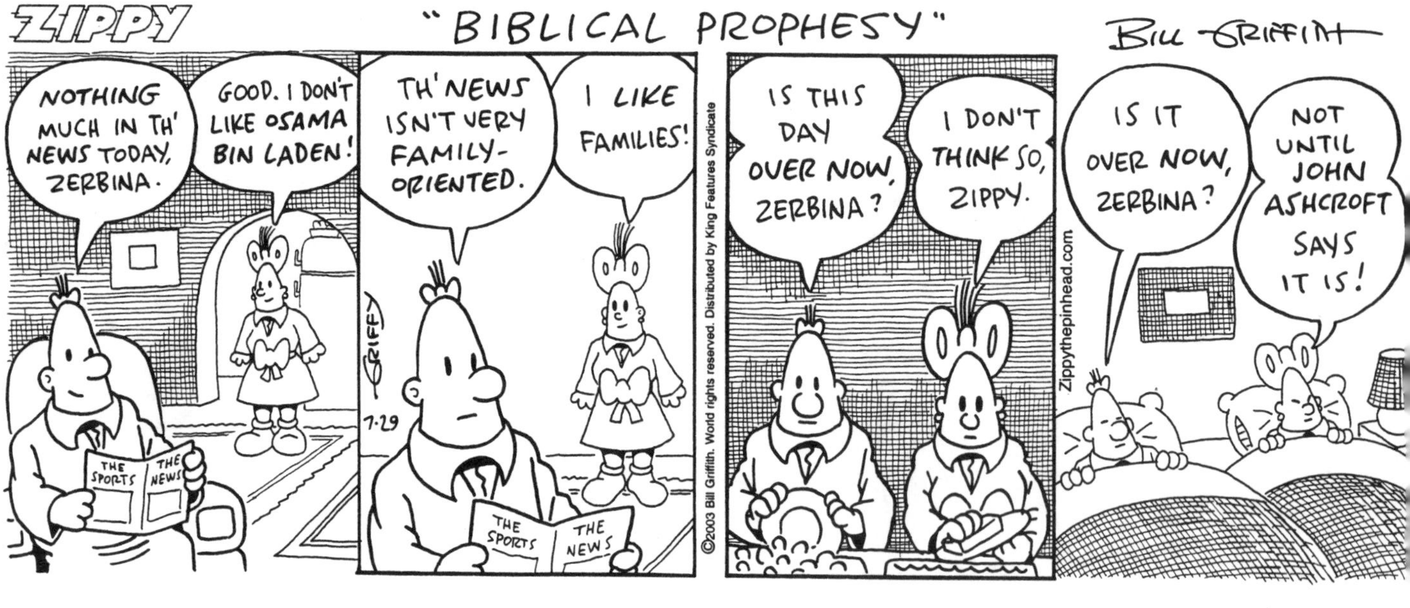
ZIPPY
"BIBLICAL PROPHESY"
BILL GRIFFITH
NOTHING MUCH IN TH' NEWS TODAY, ZERBINA.
GOOD. I DON'T LIKE OSAMA BIN LADEN!
THE SPORTS THE NEWS
GRIFFY 7·29
TH' NEWS ISN'T VERY FAMILY-ORIENTED.
I LIKE FAMILIES!
THE SPORTS THE NEWS
©2003 Bill Griffith. World rights reserved. Distributed by King Features Syndicate
IS THIS DAY OVER NOW, ZERBINA?
I DON'T THINK SO, ZIPPY.
Zippythepinhead.com
IS IT OVER NOW, ZERBINA?
NOT UNTIL JOHN ASHCROFT SAYS IT IS!

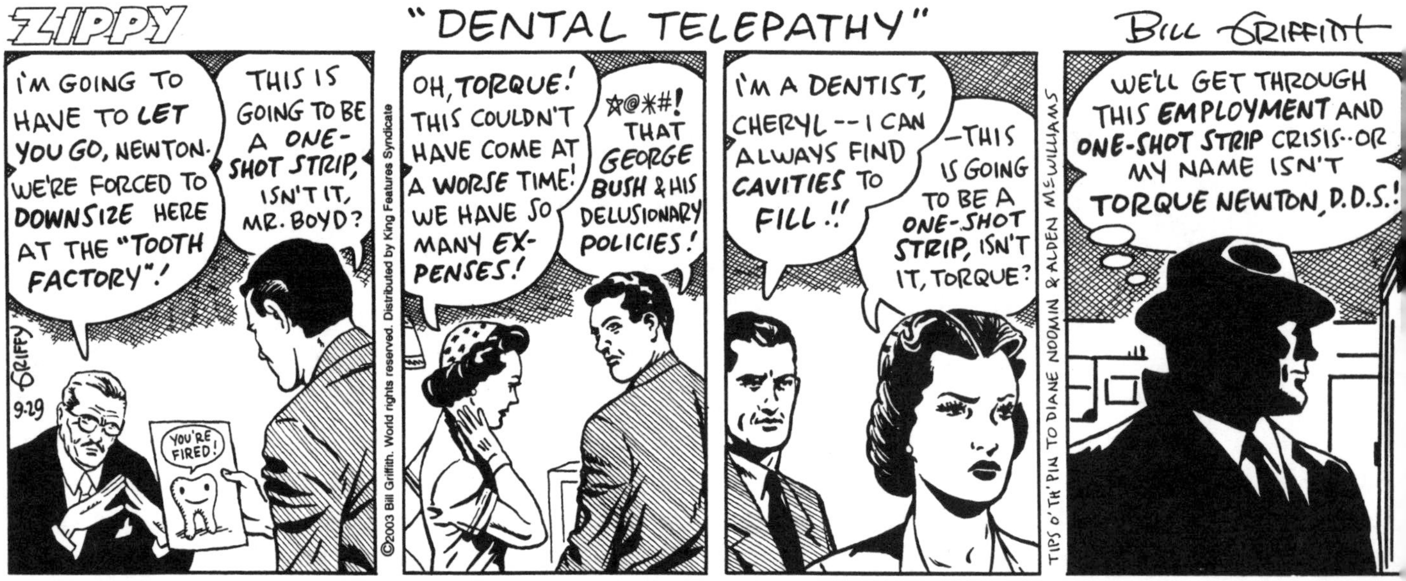
ZIPPY
"DENTAL TELEPATHY"
BILL GRIFFITH
I'M GOING TO HAVE TO LET YOU GO, NEWTON. WE'RE FORCED TO DOWNSIZE HERE AT THE "TOOTH FACTORY"!
THIS IS GOING TO BE A ONE-SHOT STRIP, ISN'T IT, MR. BOYD?
YOU'RE FIRED!
GRIFFY 9·29
©2003 Bill Griffith. World rights reserved. Distributed by King Features Syndicate
OH, TORQUE! THIS COULDN'T HAVE COME AT A WORSE TIME! WE HAVE SO MANY EX-PENSES!
☆@✱#! THAT GEORGE BUSH & HIS DELUSIONARY POLICIES!
I'M A DENTIST, CHERYL -- I CAN ALWAYS FIND CAVITIES TO FILL!!
—THIS IS GOING TO BE A ONE-SHOT STRIP, ISN'T IT, TORQUE?
TIPS O' TH' PIN TO DIANE NOOMIN & ALDEN McWILLIAMS
WE'LL GET THROUGH THIS EMPLOYMENT AND ONE-SHOT STRIP CRISIS.. OR MY NAME ISN'T TORQUE NEWTON, D.D.S.!

50 A

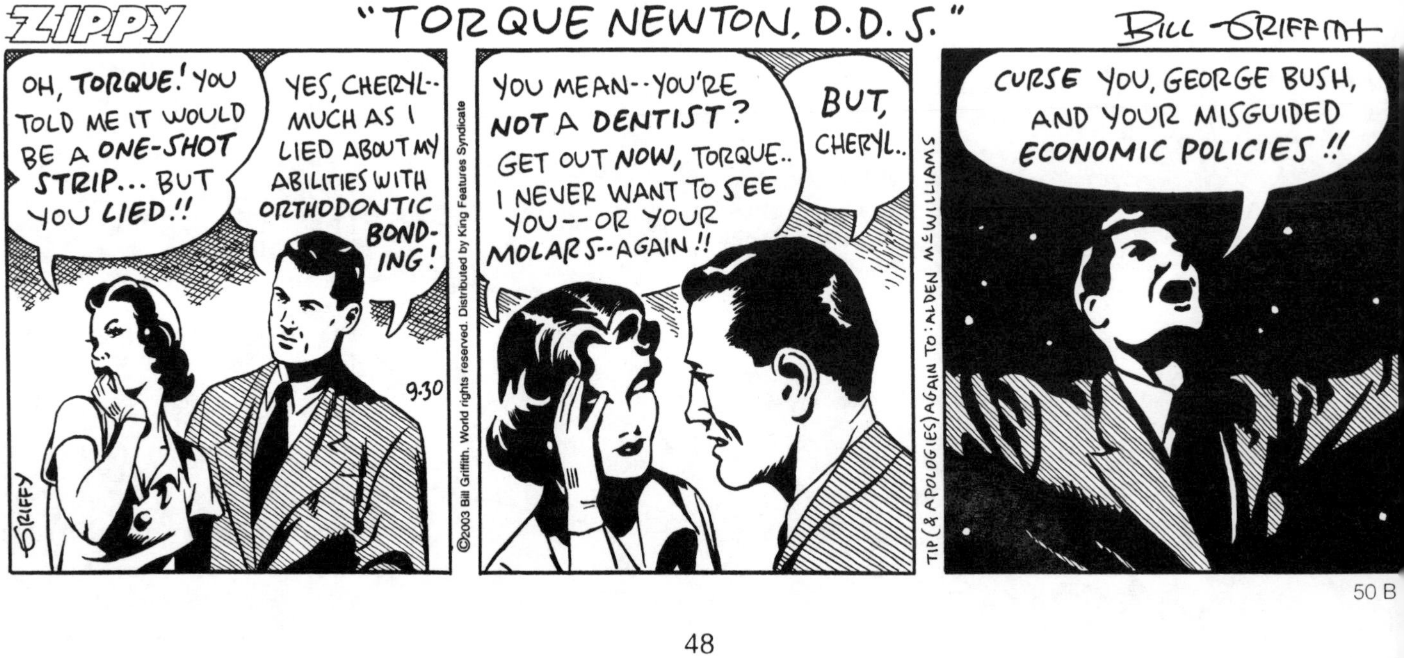
ZIPPY
"TORQUE NEWTON, D.D.S."
BILL GRIFFITH
OH, TORQUE! YOU TOLD ME IT WOULD BE A ONE-SHOT STRIP... BUT YOU LIED!!
YES, CHERYL-- MUCH AS I LIED ABOUT MY ABILITIES WITH ORTHODONTIC BONDING!
9·30
GRIFFY
©2003 Bill Griffith. World rights reserved. Distributed by King Features Syndicate
YOU MEAN--YOU'RE NOT A DENTIST? GET OUT NOW, TORQUE.. I NEVER WANT TO SEE YOU--OR YOUR MOLARS--AGAIN!!
BUT, CHERYL..
TIP (& APOLOGIES) AGAIN TO: ALDEN McWILLIAMS
CURSE YOU, GEORGE BUSH, AND YOUR MISGUIDED ECONOMIC POLICIES!!

50 B

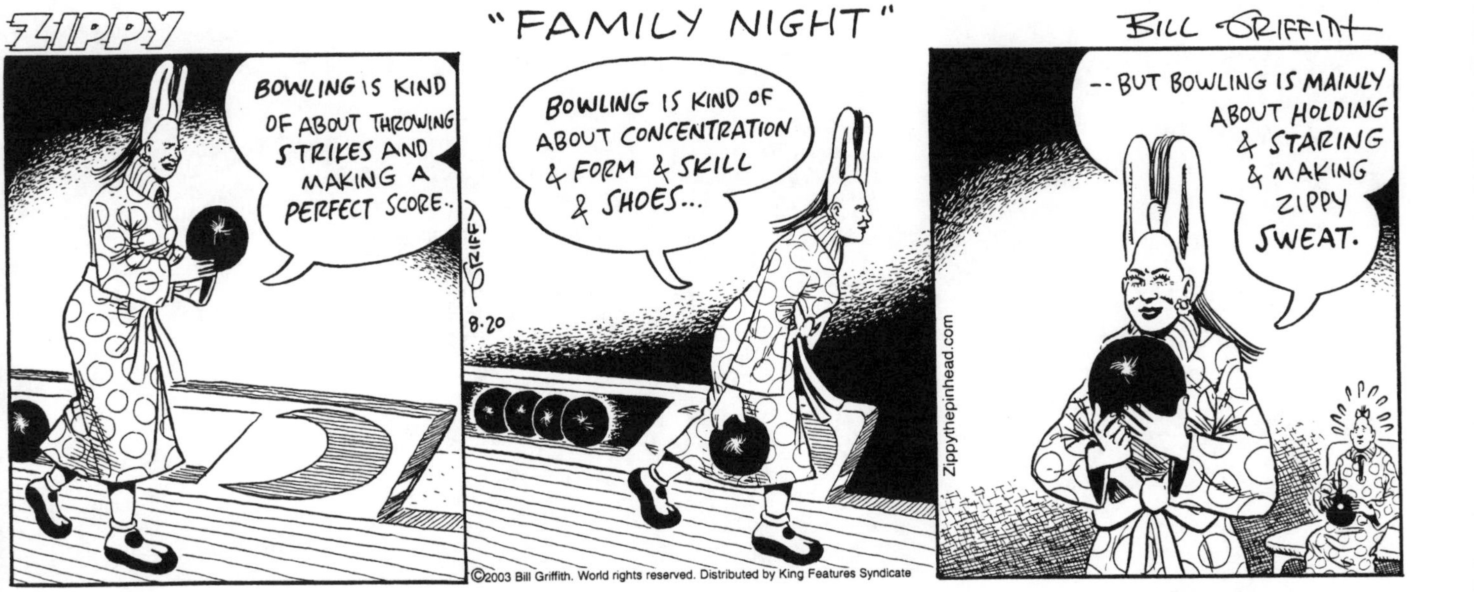
ZIPPY
"FAMILY NIGHT"
BILL GRIFFITH
BOWLING IS KIND OF ABOUT THROWING STRIKES AND MAKING A PERFECT SCORE..
GRIFFY
8-20
BOWLING IS KIND OF ABOUT CONCENTRATION & FORM & SKILL & SHOES...
Zippythepinhead.com
--BUT BOWLING IS MAINLY ABOUT HOLDING & STARING & MAKING ZIPPY SWEAT.
©2003 Bill Griffith. World rights reserved. Distributed by King Features Syndicate

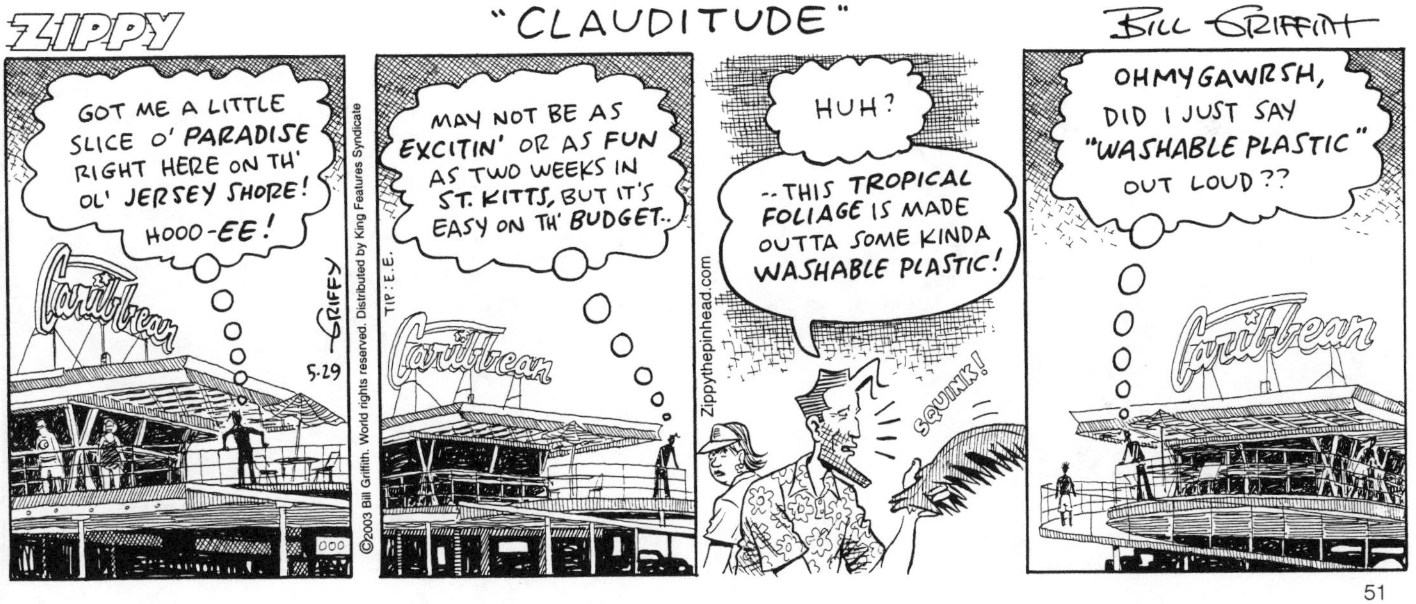
ZIPPY
"CLAUDITUDE"
BILL GRIFFITH
GOT ME A LITTLE SLICE O' PARADISE RIGHT HERE ON TH' OL' JERSEY SHORE! HOOO-EE!
GRIFFY
5-29
©2003 Bill Griffith. World rights reserved. Distributed by King Features Syndicate
TIP: E.E.
MAY NOT BE AS EXCITIN' OR AS FUN AS TWO WEEKS IN ST. KITTS, BUT IT'S EASY ON TH' BUDGET..
Zippythepinhead.com
HUH?
--THIS TROPICAL FOLIAGE IS MADE OUTTA SOME KINDA WASHABLE PLASTIC!
SQUINK!
OHMYGAWRSH, DID I JUST SAY "WASHABLE PLASTIC" OUT LOUD??

51

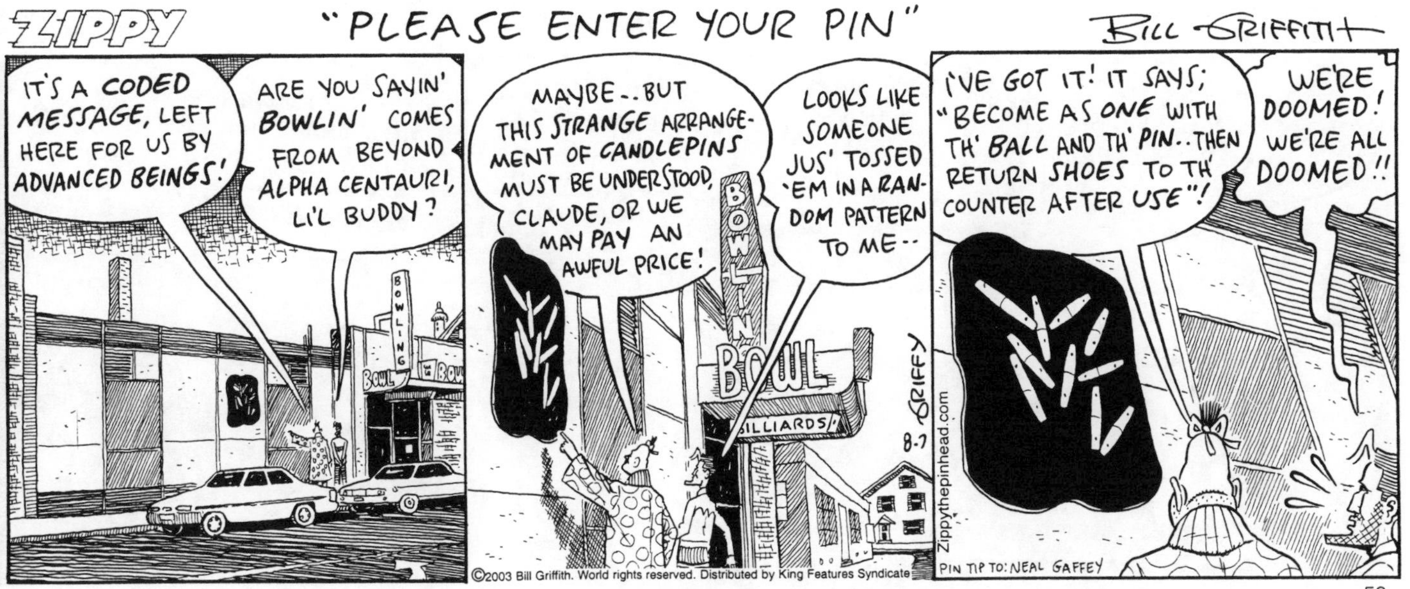
ZIPPY
"PLEASE ENTER YOUR PIN"
BILL GRIFFITH
IT'S A CODED MESSAGE, LEFT HERE FOR US BY ADVANCED BEINGS!
ARE YOU SAYIN' BOWLIN' COMES FROM BEYOND ALPHA CENTAURI, LI'L BUDDY?
BOWLING
MAYBE--BUT THIS STRANGE ARRANGEMENT OF CANDLEPINS MUST BE UNDERSTOOD, CLAUDE, OR WE MAY PAY AN AWFUL PRICE!
LOOKS LIKE SOMEONE JUS' TOSSED 'EM IN A RANDOM PATTERN TO ME--
BOWLING
BOWL
BILLIARDS
GRIFFY
8-7
Zippythepinhead.com
I'VE GOT IT! IT SAYS; "BECOME AS ONE WITH TH' BALL AND TH' PIN..THEN RETURN SHOES TO TH' COUNTER AFTER USE"!
WE'RE DOOMED! WE'RE ALL DOOMED!!
©2003 Bill Griffith. World rights reserved. Distributed by King Features Syndicate
PIN TIP TO: NEAL GAFFEY

52

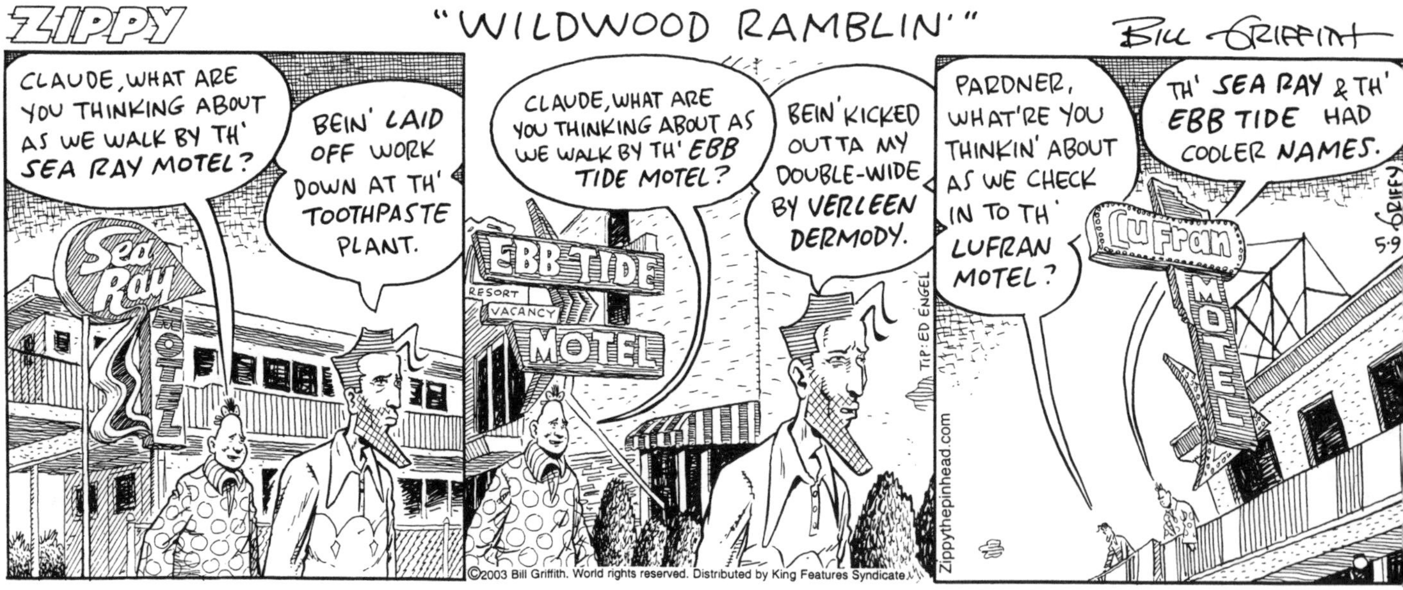
ZIPPY
"WILDWOOD RAMBLIN'"
BILL GRIFFITH
CLAUDE, WHAT ARE YOU THINKING ABOUT AS WE WALK BY TH' SEA RAY MOTEL?
BEIN' LAID OFF WORK DOWN AT TH' TOOTHPASTE PLANT.
Sea Ray
MOTEL
CLAUDE, WHAT ARE YOU THINKING ABOUT AS WE WALK BY TH' EBB TIDE MOTEL?
BEIN' KICKED OUTTA MY DOUBLE-WIDE BY VERLEEN DERMODY.
EBB TIDE
RESORT
VACANCY
MOTEL
TIP: ED ENGEL
Zippythepinhead.com
PARDNER, WHAT'RE YOU THINKIN' ABOUT AS WE CHECK IN TO TH' LUFRAN MOTEL?
TH' SEA RAY & TH' EBB TIDE HAD COOLER NAMES.
LuFran
MOTEL
GRIFFY
5-9
©2003 Bill Griffith. World rights reserved. Distributed by King Features Syndicate

53

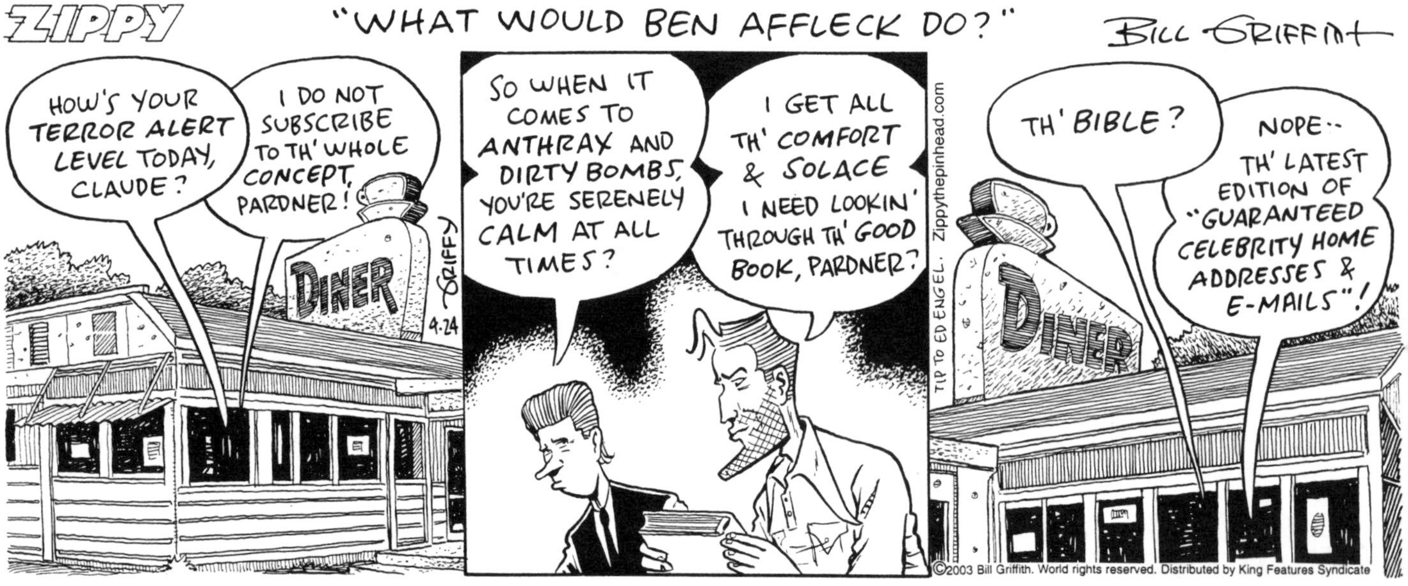
ZIPPY
"WHAT WOULD BEN AFFLECK DO?"
BILL GRIFFITH
HOW'S YOUR TERROR ALERT LEVEL TODAY, CLAUDE?
I DO NOT SUBSCRIBE TO TH' WHOLE CONCEPT, PARDNER!
DINER
GRIFFY
4-24
SO WHEN IT COMES TO ANTHRAX AND DIRTY BOMBS, YOU'RE SERENELY CALM AT ALL TIMES?
I GET ALL TH' COMFORT & SOLACE I NEED LOOKIN' THROUGH TH' GOOD BOOK, PARDNER.
Zippythepinhead.com
TIP TO ED ENGEL
TH' BIBLE?
NOPE-- TH' LATEST EDITION OF "GUARANTEED CELEBRITY HOME ADDRESSES & E-MAILS"!
DINER
©2003 Bill Griffith. World rights reserved. Distributed by King Features Syndicate

54

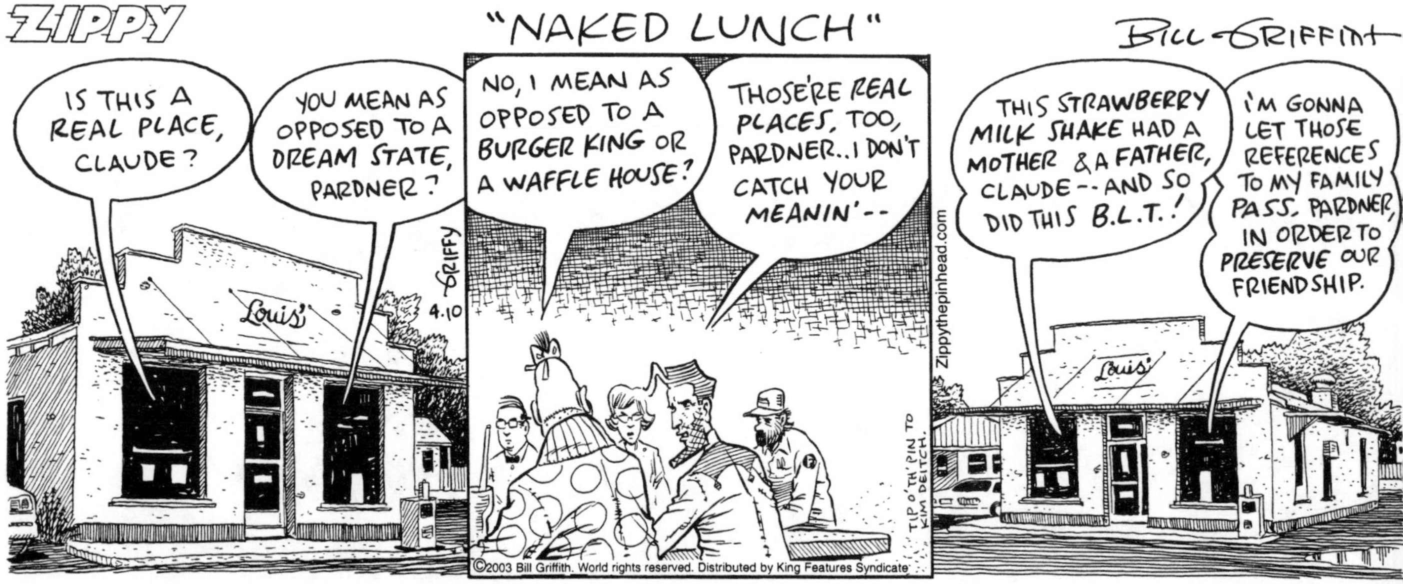
ZIPPY
"NAKED LUNCH"
BILL GRIFFITH
IS THIS A REAL PLACE, CLAUDE?
YOU MEAN AS OPPOSED TO A DREAM STATE, PARDNER?
Louis'
GRIFFY
4-10
NO, I MEAN AS OPPOSED TO A BURGER KING OR A WAFFLE HOUSE?
THOSE'RE REAL PLACES, TOO, PARDNER.. I DON'T CATCH YOUR MEANIN'--
Zippythepinhead.com
TIP O' TH' PIN TO KIM DEITCH.
THIS STRAWBERRY MILK SHAKE HAD A MOTHER & A FATHER, CLAUDE--AND SO DID THIS B.L.T.!
I'M GONNA LET THOSE REFERENCES TO MY FAMILY PASS, PARDNER, IN ORDER TO PRESERVE OUR FRIENDSHIP.
Louis'
©2003 Bill Griffith. World rights reserved. Distributed by King Features Syndicate

55

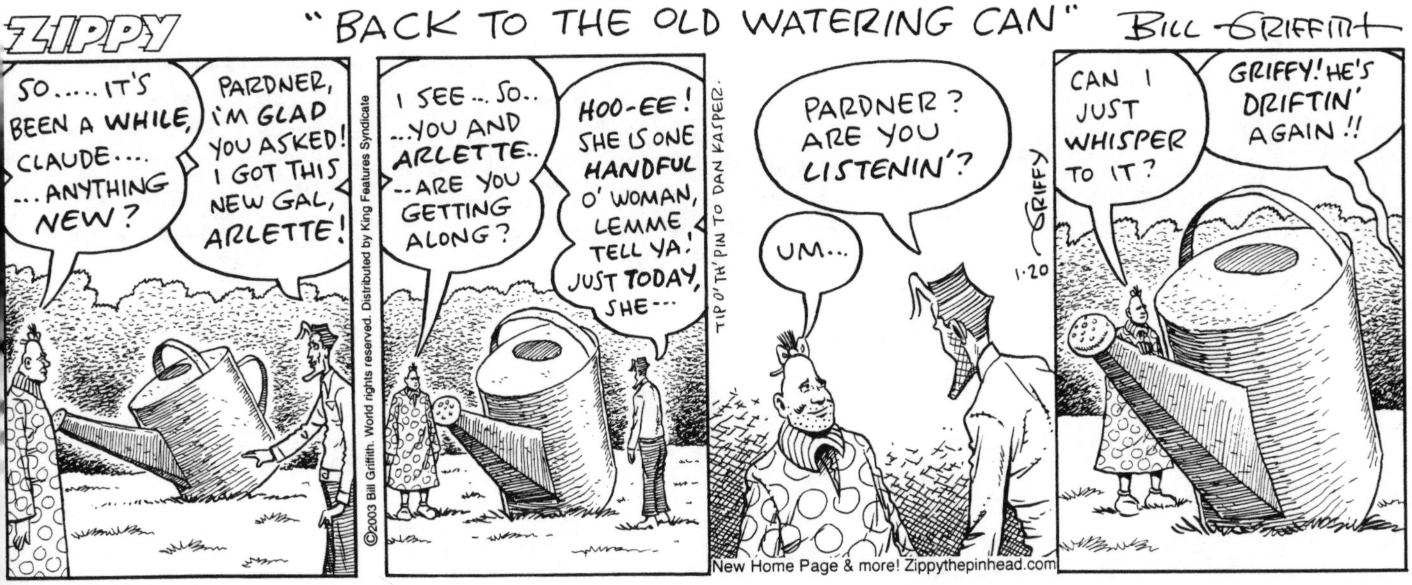
ZIPPY
"BACK TO THE OLD WATERING CAN"
BILL GRIFFITH
SO..... IT'S BEEN A WHILE, CLAUDE.... ...ANYTHING NEW?
PARDNER, I'M GLAD YOU ASKED! I GOT THIS NEW GAL, ARLETTE!
©2003 Bill Griffith. World rights reserved. Distributed by King Features Syndicate
I SEE... SO.. ...YOU AND ARLETTE.. --ARE YOU GETTING ALONG?
HOO-EE! SHE IS ONE HANDFUL O' WOMAN, LEMME TELL YA! JUST TODAY, SHE---
TIP O' TH' PIN TO DAN KASPER
PARDNER? ARE YOU LISTENIN'?
UM...
GRIFFY 1-20
New Home Page & more! Zippythepinhead.com
CAN I JUST WHISPER TO IT?
GRIFFY! HE'S DRIFTIN' AGAIN!!

56

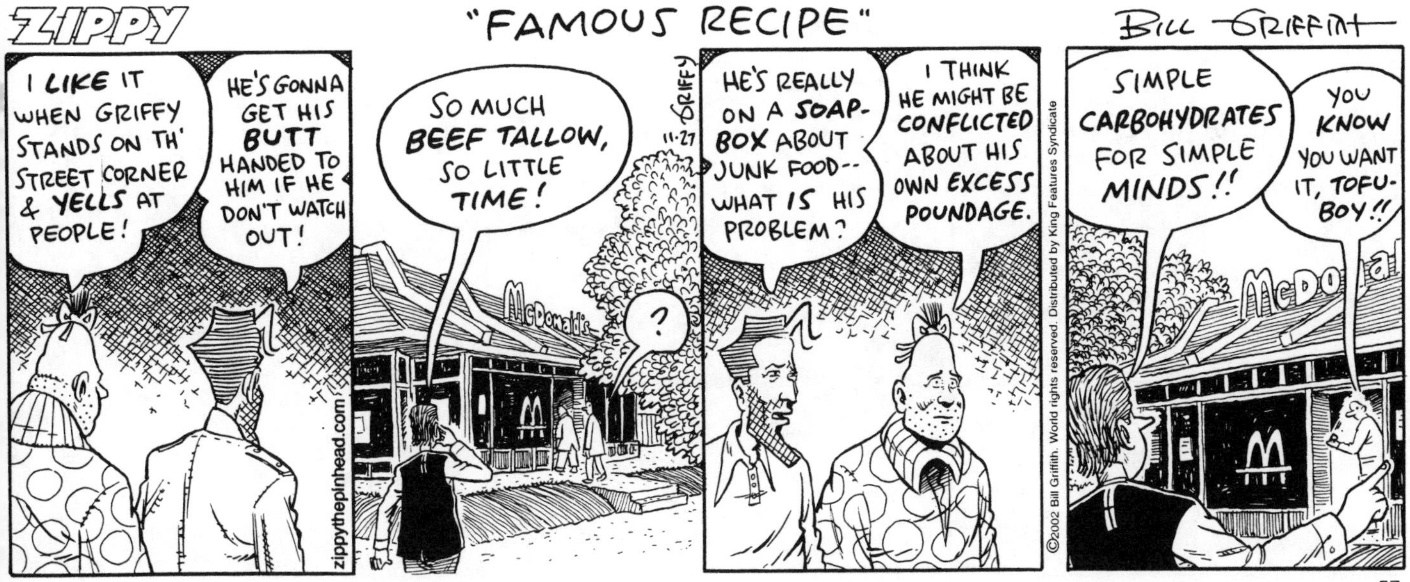
ZIPPY
"FAMOUS RECIPE"
BILL GRIFFITH
I LIKE IT WHEN GRIFFY STANDS ON TH' STREET CORNER & YELLS AT PEOPLE!
HE'S GONNA GET HIS BUTT HANDED TO HIM IF HE DON'T WATCH OUT!
zippythepinhead.com
SO MUCH BEEF TALLOW, SO LITTLE TIME!
GRIFFY 11-27
McDonald's
?
HE'S REALLY ON A SOAP-BOX ABOUT JUNK FOOD-- WHAT IS HIS PROBLEM?
I THINK HE MIGHT BE CONFLICTED ABOUT HIS OWN EXCESS POUNDAGE.
©2002 Bill Griffith. World rights reserved. Distributed by King Features Syndicate
SIMPLE CARBOHYDRATES FOR SIMPLE MINDS!!
YOU KNOW YOU WANT IT, TOFU-BOY!!
McDo

57

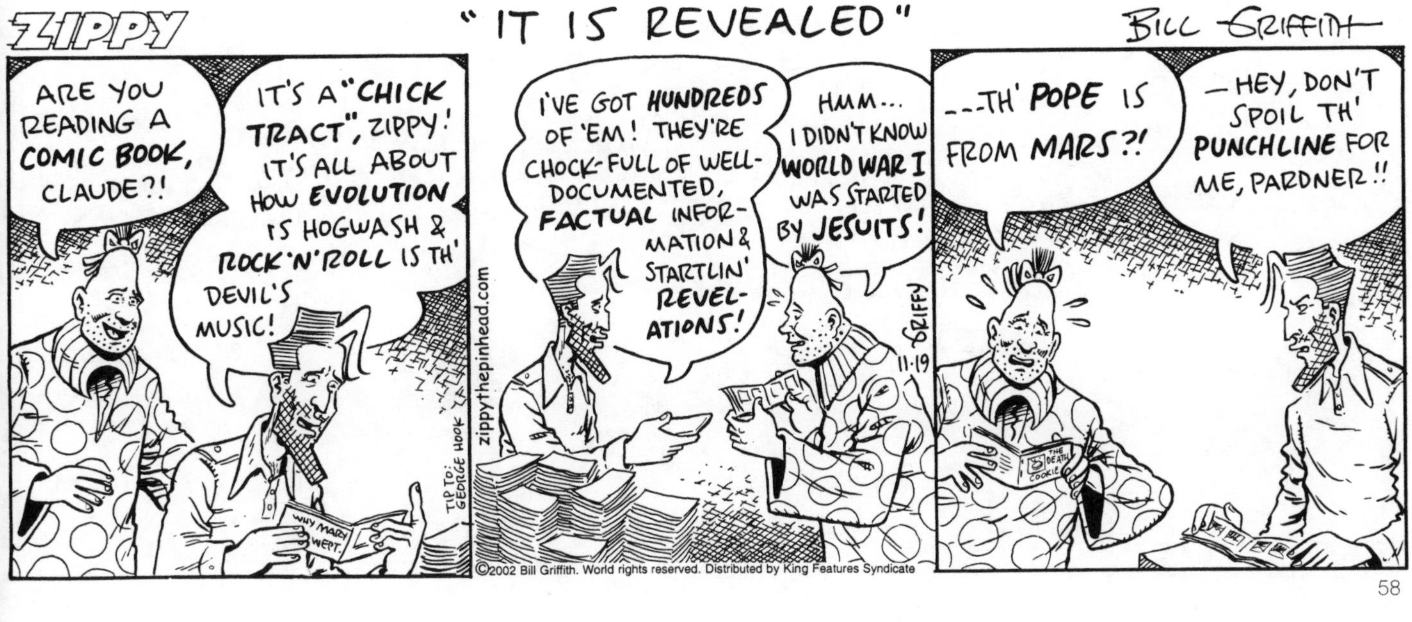
ZIPPY
"IT IS REVEALED"
BILL GRIFFITH
ARE YOU READING A COMIC BOOK, CLAUDE?!
IT'S A "CHICK TRACT", ZIPPY! IT'S ALL ABOUT HOW EVOLUTION IS HOGWASH & ROCK 'N' ROLL IS TH' DEVIL'S MUSIC!
WHY MARY WEPT
zippythepinhead.com
TIP TO: GEORGE HOOK
I'VE GOT HUNDREDS OF 'EM! THEY'RE CHOCK-FULL OF WELL-DOCUMENTED, FACTUAL INFOR-MATION & STARTLIN' REVEL-ATIONS!
HMM... I DIDN'T KNOW WORLD WAR I WAS STARTED BY JESUITS!
GRIFFY 11-19
©2002 Bill Griffith. World rights reserved. Distributed by King Features Syndicate
---TH' POPE IS FROM MARS?!
THE DEATH COOKIE
—HEY, DON'T SPOIL TH' PUNCHLINE FOR ME, PARDNER!!

58

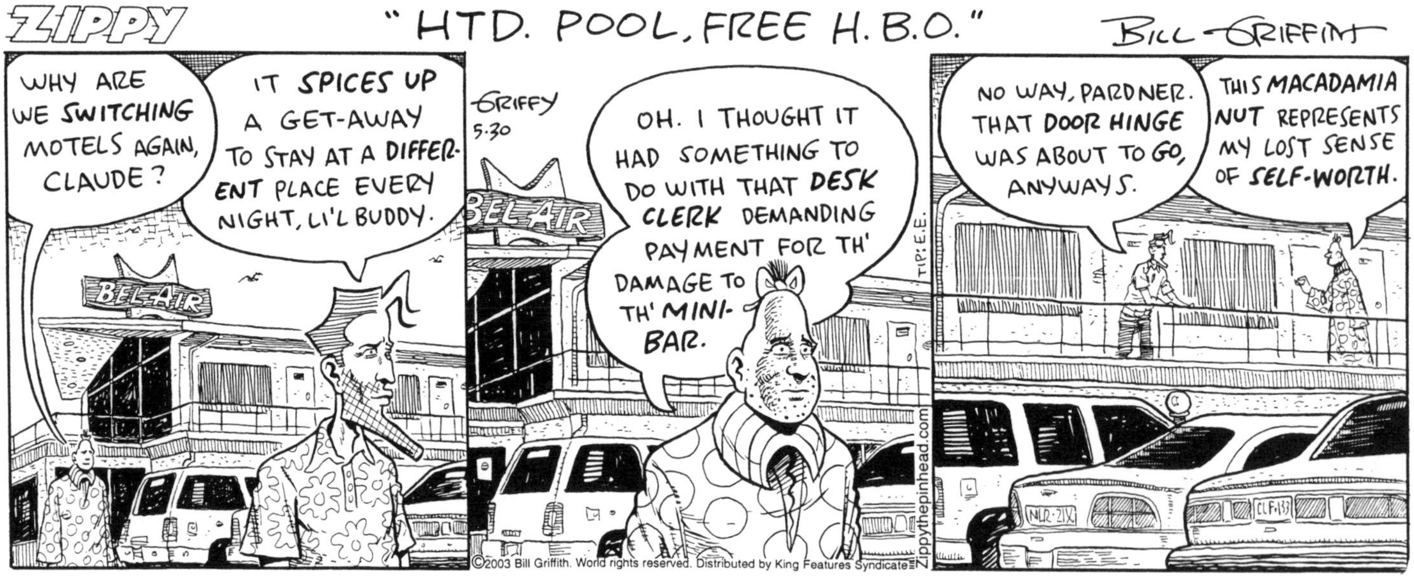
ZIPPY
"HTD. POOL, FREE H.B.O."
BILL GRIFFITH
WHY ARE WE SWITCHING MOTELS AGAIN, CLAUDE?
IT SPICES UP A GET-AWAY TO STAY AT A DIFFERENT PLACE EVERY NIGHT, LI'L BUDDY.
BEL-AIR
GRIFFY 5-30
OH. I THOUGHT IT HAD SOMETHING TO DO WITH THAT DESK CLERK DEMANDING PAYMENT FOR TH' DAMAGE TO TH' MINI-BAR.
TIP: E.E.
NO WAY, PARDNER. THAT DOOR HINGE WAS ABOUT TO GO, ANYWAYS.
THIS MACADAMIA NUT REPRESENTS MY LOST SENSE OF SELF-WORTH.
©2003 Bill Griffith. World rights reserved. Distributed by King Features Syndicate
Zippythepinhead.com

59

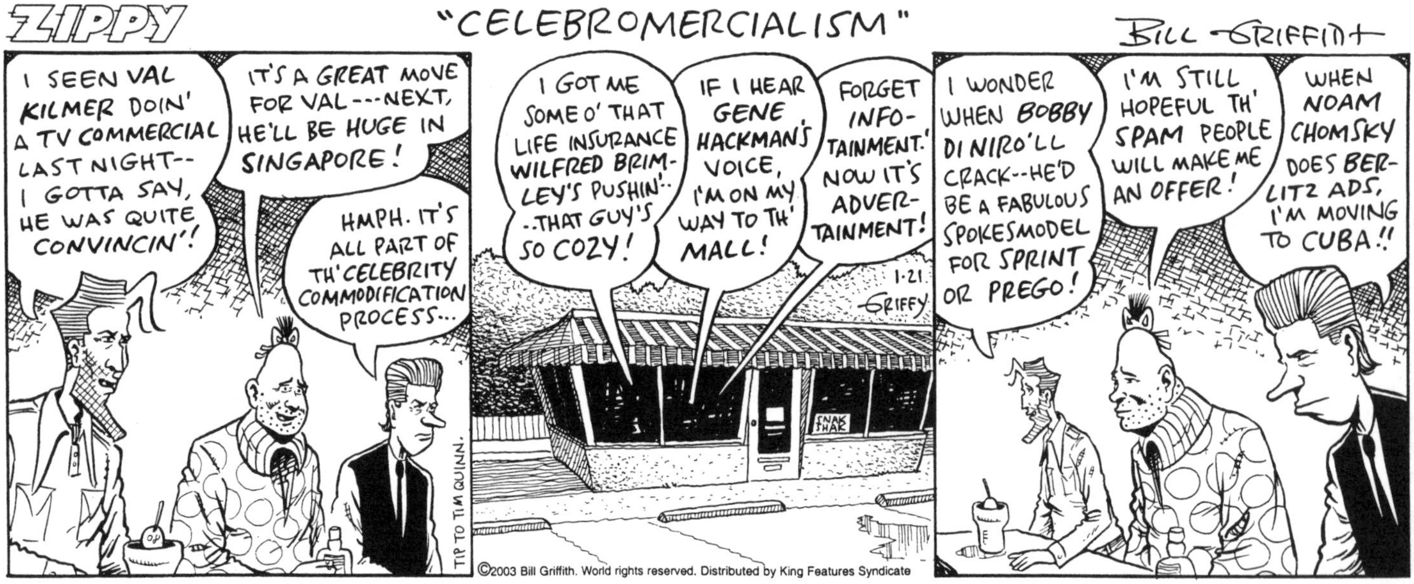
ZIPPY
"CELEBROMERCIALISM"
BILL GRIFFITH
I SEEN VAL KILMER DOIN' A TV COMMERCIAL LAST NIGHT-- I GOTTA SAY, HE WAS QUITE CONVINCIN'!
IT'S A GREAT MOVE FOR VAL---NEXT, HE'LL BE HUGE IN SINGAPORE!
HMPH. IT'S ALL PART OF TH' CELEBRITY COMMODIFICATION PROCESS...
TIP TO TIM QUINN.
I GOT ME SOME O' THAT LIFE INSURANCE WILFRED BRIMLEY'S PUSHIN'.. ..THAT GUY'S SO COZY!
IF I HEAR GENE HACKMAN'S VOICE, I'M ON MY WAY TO TH' MALL!
FORGET INFO-TAINMENT! NOW IT'S ADVER-TAINMENT!
1-21 GRIFFY
SNAK SHAK
I WONDER WHEN BOBBY DI NIRO'LL CRACK--HE'D BE A FABULOUS SPOKESMODEL FOR SPRINT OR PREGO!
I'M STILL HOPEFUL TH' SPAM PEOPLE WILL MAKE ME AN OFFER!
WHEN NOAM CHOMSKY DOES BERLITZ ADS, I'M MOVING TO CUBA!!
©2003 Bill Griffith. World rights reserved. Distributed by King Features Syndicate

60

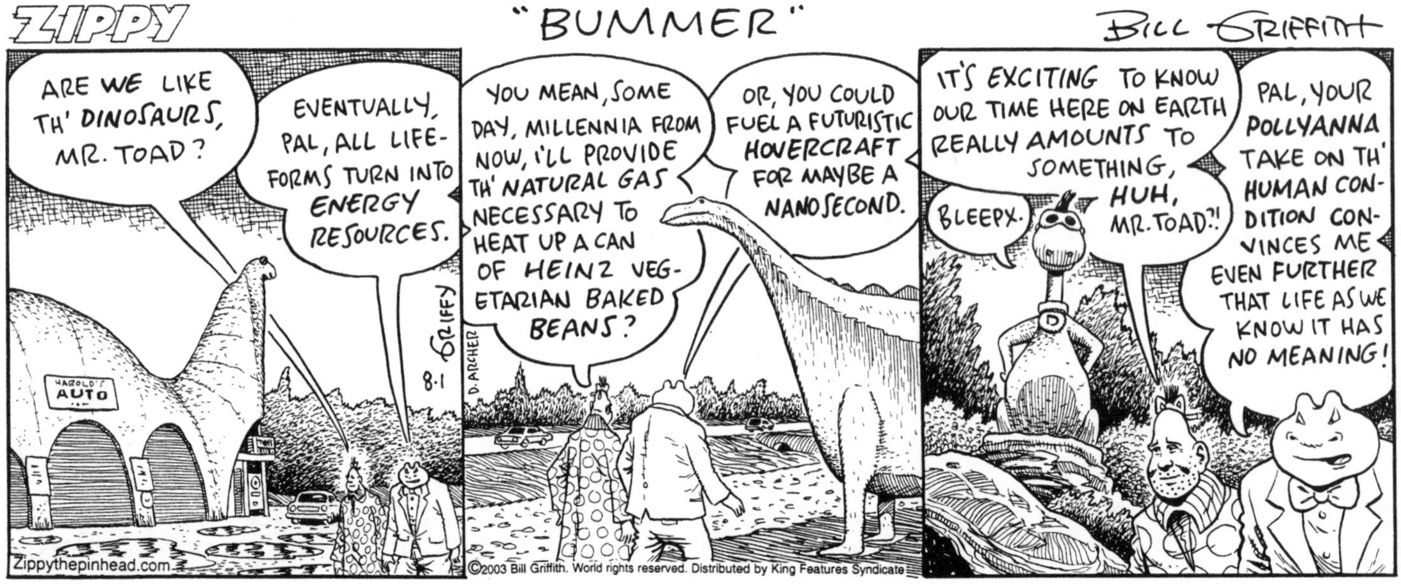
ZIPPY
"BUMMER"
BILL GRIFFITH
ARE WE LIKE TH' DINOSAURS, MR. TOAD?
EVENTUALLY, PAL, ALL LIFE-FORMS TURN INTO ENERGY RESOURCES.
HAROLD'S AUTO
GRIFFY 8-1
YOU MEAN, SOME DAY, MILLENNIA FROM NOW, I'LL PROVIDE TH' NATURAL GAS NECESSARY TO HEAT UP A CAN OF HEINZ VEGETARIAN BAKED BEANS?
OR, YOU COULD FUEL A FUTURISTIC HOVERCRAFT FOR MAYBE A NANOSECOND.
D. ARCHER
IT'S EXCITING TO KNOW OUR TIME HERE ON EARTH REALLY AMOUNTS TO SOMETHING, HUH, MR. TOAD?!
BLEEPX.
PAL, YOUR POLLYANNA TAKE ON TH' HUMAN CONDITION CONVINCES ME EVEN FURTHER THAT LIFE AS WE KNOW IT HAS NO MEANING!
Zippythepinhead.com
©2003 Bill Griffith. World rights reserved. Distributed by King Features Syndicate

61

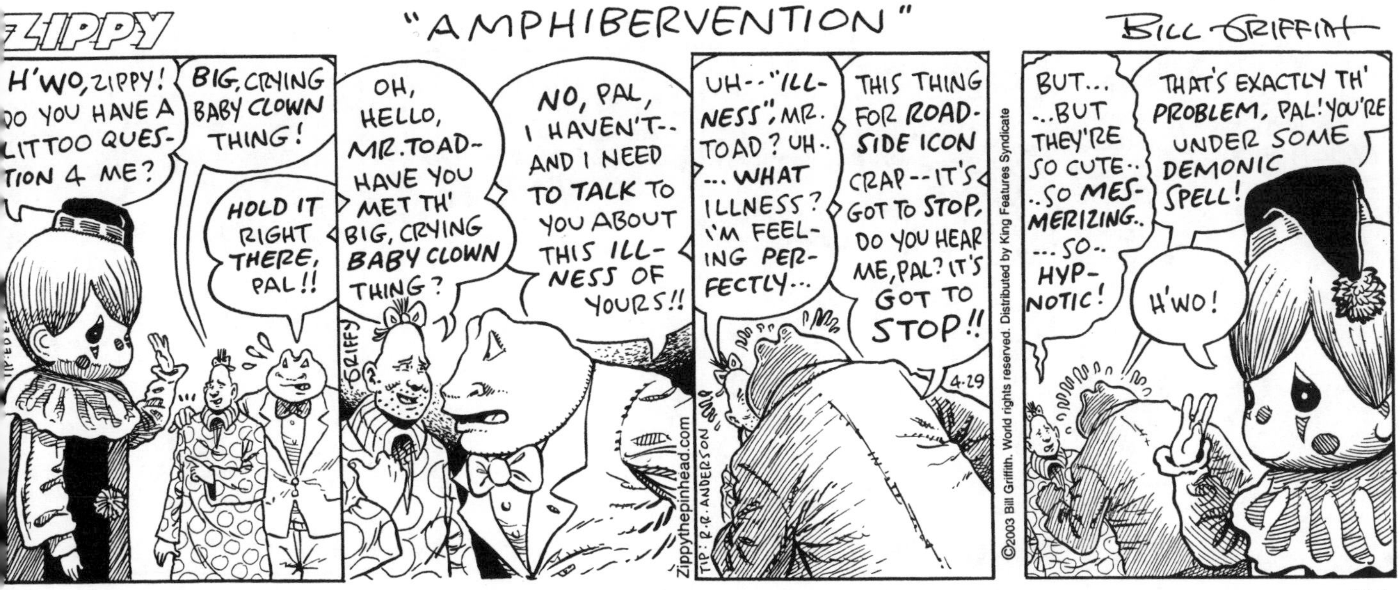
ZIPPY
"AMPHIBERVENTION"
BILL GRIFFITH
H'WO, ZIPPY! DO YOU HAVE A LITTOO QUESTION 4 ME?
BIG, CRYING BABY CLOWN THING!
HOLD IT RIGHT THERE, PAL!!
OH, HELLO, MR. TOAD- HAVE YOU MET TH' BIG, CRYING BABY CLOWN THING?
NO, PAL, I HAVEN'T-- AND I NEED TO TALK TO YOU ABOUT THIS ILLNESS OF YOURS!!
UH--"ILLNESS", MR. TOAD? UH.. ...WHAT ILLNESS? I'M FEELING PERFECTLY...
THIS THING FOR ROADSIDE ICON CRAP--IT'S GOT TO STOP, DO YOU HEAR ME, PAL? IT'S GOT TO STOP!!
BUT... ..BUT THEY'RE SO CUTE.. ..SO MESMERIZING.. ...SO.. HYPNOTIC!
THAT'S EXACTLY TH' PROBLEM, PAL! YOU'RE UNDER SOME DEMONIC SPELL!
H'WO!
TIP: R.R. ANDERSON
Zippythepinhead.com
©2003 Bill Griffith. World rights reserved. Distributed by King Features Syndicate
4-29

62 A

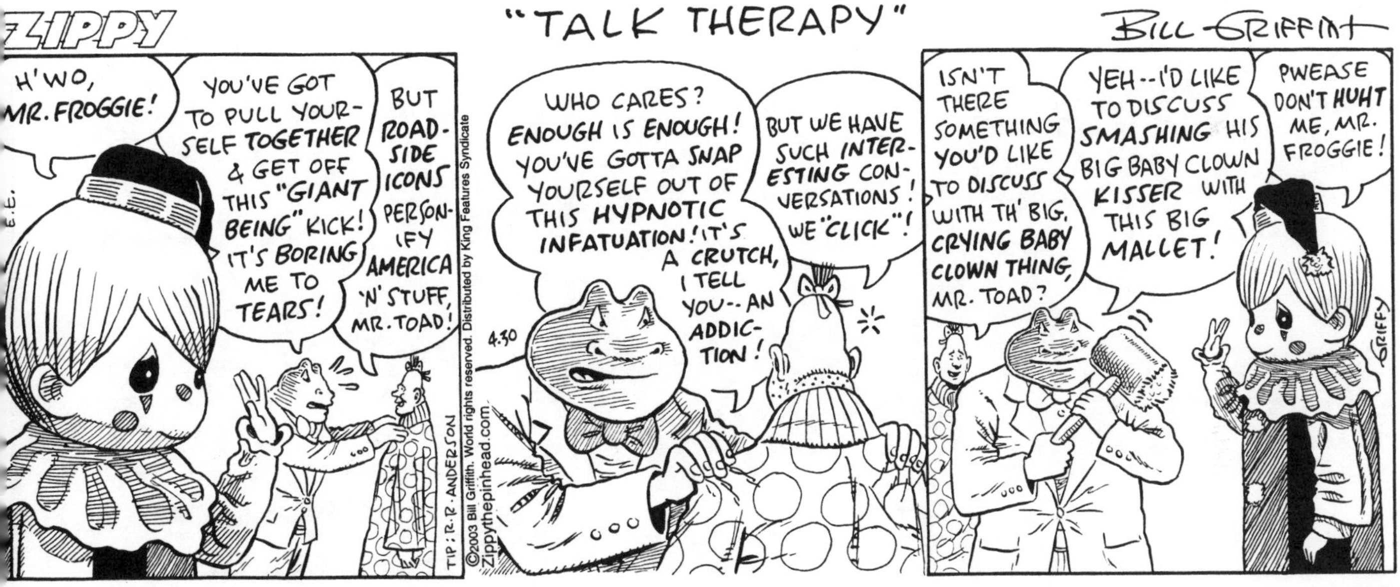
ZIPPY
"TALK THERAPY"
BILL GRIFFITH
H'WO, MR. FROGGIE!
YOU'VE GOT TO PULL YOURSELF TOGETHER & GET OFF THIS "GIANT BEING" KICK! IT'S BORING ME TO TEARS!
BUT ROADSIDE ICONS PERSONIFY AMERICA 'N' STUFF, MR. TOAD!
TIP: R.R. ANDERSON
©2003 Bill Griffith. World rights reserved. Distributed by King Features Syndicate
Zippythepinhead.com
4-30
WHO CARES? ENOUGH IS ENOUGH! YOU'VE GOTTA SNAP YOURSELF OUT OF THIS HYPNOTIC INFATUATION! IT'S A CRUTCH, I TELL YOU-- AN ADDICTION!
BUT WE HAVE SUCH INTERESTING CONVERSATIONS! WE "CLICK"!
ISN'T THERE SOMETHING YOU'D LIKE TO DISCUSS WITH TH' BIG, CRYING BABY CLOWN THING, MR. TOAD?
YEH--I'D LIKE TO DISCUSS SMASHING HIS BIG BABY CLOWN KISSER WITH THIS BIG MALLET!
PWEASE DON'T HUHT ME, MR. FROGGIE!

62 B

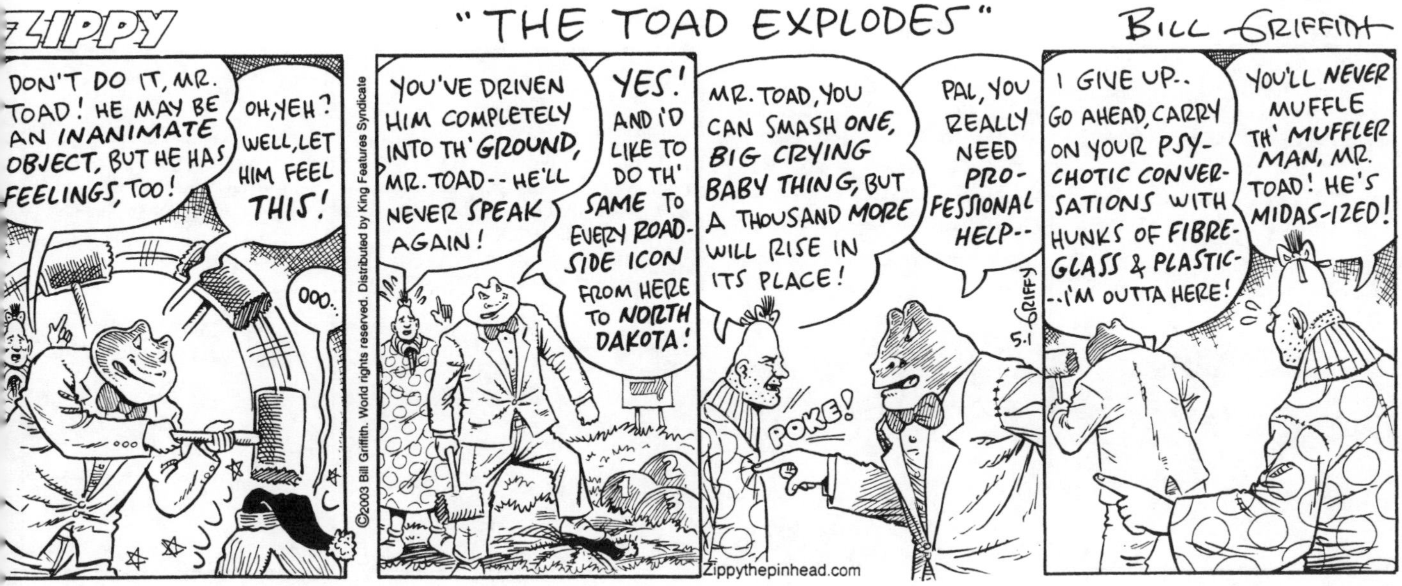
ZIPPY
"THE TOAD EXPLODES"
BILL GRIFFITH
DON'T DO IT, MR. TOAD! HE MAY BE AN INANIMATE OBJECT, BUT HE HAS FEELINGS, TOO!
OH, YEH? WELL, LET HIM FEEL THIS!
OOO..
©2003 Bill Griffith. World rights reserved. Distributed by King Features Syndicate
YOU'VE DRIVEN HIM COMPLETELY INTO TH' GROUND, MR. TOAD-- HE'LL NEVER SPEAK AGAIN!
YES! AND I'D LIKE TO DO TH' SAME TO EVERY ROADSIDE ICON FROM HERE TO NORTH DAKOTA!
MR. TOAD, YOU CAN SMASH ONE, BIG CRYING BABY THING, BUT A THOUSAND MORE WILL RISE IN ITS PLACE!
PAL, YOU REALLY NEED PROFESSIONAL HELP--
POKE!
5-1
I GIVE UP.. GO AHEAD, CARRY ON YOUR PSYCHOTIC CONVERSATIONS WITH HUNKS OF FIBREGLASS & PLASTIC- --I'M OUTTA HERE!
YOU'LL NEVER MUFFLE TH' MUFFLER MAN, MR. TOAD! HE'S MIDAS-IZED!
Zippythepinhead.com

62 C

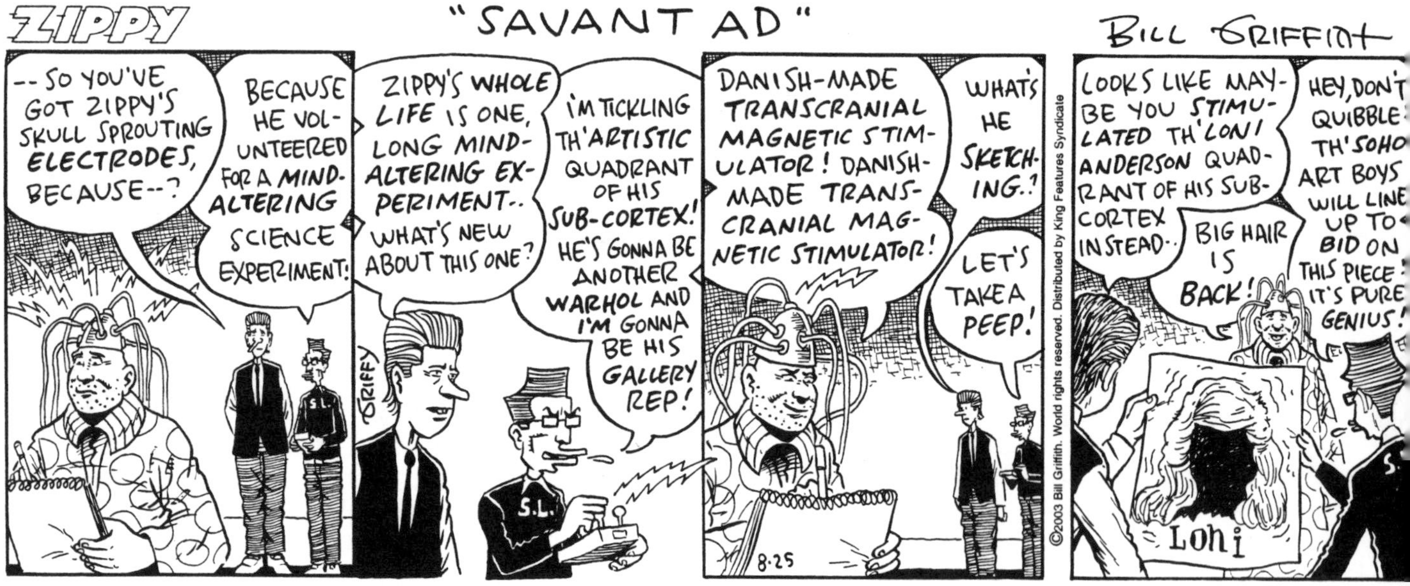
ZIPPY
"SAVANT AD"
BILL GRIFFITH
-- SO YOU'VE GOT ZIPPY'S SKULL SPROUTING ELECTRODES, BECAUSE--?
BECAUSE HE VOLUNTEERED FOR A MIND-ALTERING SCIENCE EXPERIMENT!
ZIPPY'S WHOLE LIFE IS ONE, LONG MIND-ALTERING EXPERIMENT.. WHAT'S NEW ABOUT THIS ONE?
I'M TICKLING TH' ARTISTIC QUADRANT OF HIS SUB-CORTEX! HE'S GONNA BE ANOTHER WARHOL AND I'M GONNA BE HIS GALLERY REP!
GRIFFY
DANISH-MADE TRANSCRANIAL MAGNETIC STIMULATOR! DANISH-MADE TRANSCRANIAL MAGNETIC STIMULATOR!
WHAT'S HE SKETCHING..?
LET'S TAKE A PEEP!
8-25
©2003 Bill Griffith. World rights reserved. Distributed by King Features Syndicate
LOOKS LIKE MAYBE YOU STIMULATED TH' LONI ANDERSON QUADRANT OF HIS SUB-CORTEX INSTEAD..
BIG HAIR IS BACK!
HEY, DON'T QUIBBLE! TH' SOHO ART BOYS WILL LINE UP TO BID ON THIS PIECE! IT'S PURE GENIUS!
Loni

63

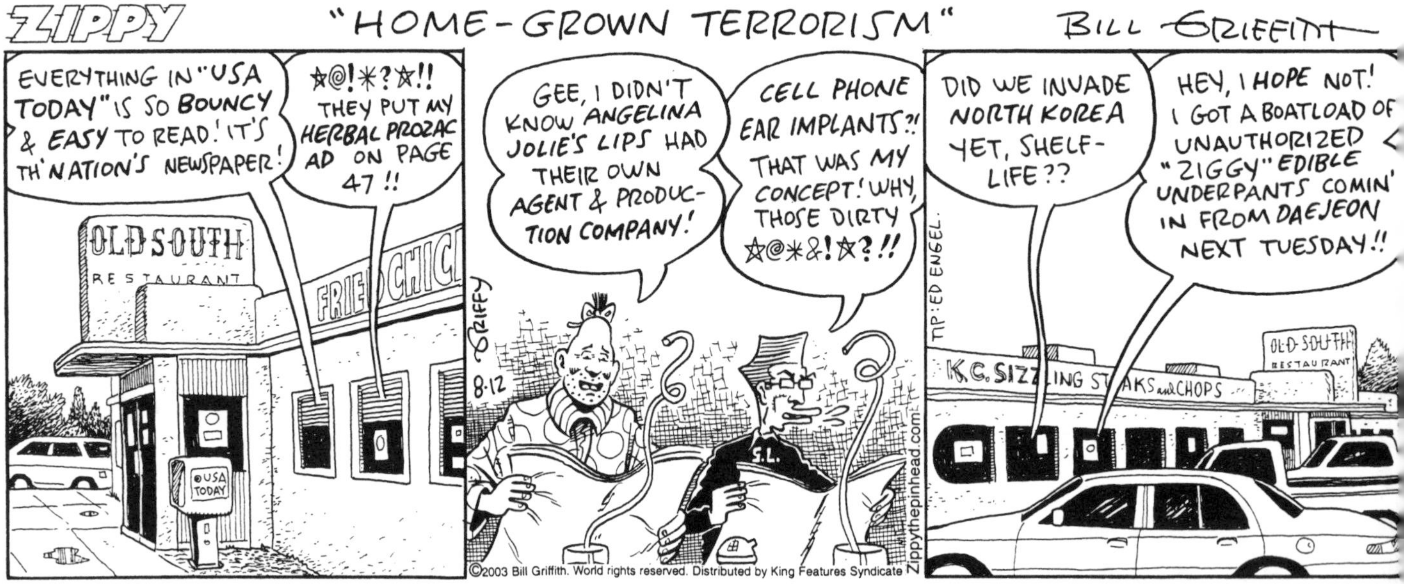
ZIPPY
"HOME-GROWN TERRORISM"
BILL GRIFFITH
EVERYTHING IN "USA TODAY" IS SO BOUNCY & EASY TO READ! IT'S TH' NATION'S NEWSPAPER!
☆@!✳?☆!! THEY PUT MY HERBAL PROZAC AD ON PAGE 47!!
OLD SOUTH RESTAURANT
FRIED CHIC
USA TODAY
GRIFFY
8-12
GEE, I DIDN'T KNOW ANGELINA JOLIE'S LIPS HAD THEIR OWN AGENT & PRODUCTION COMPANY!
CELL PHONE EAR IMPLANTS?! THAT WAS MY CONCEPT! WHY, THOSE DIRTY ☆@✳&!☆?!!
©2003 Bill Griffith. World rights reserved. Distributed by King Features Syndicate
Zippythepinhead.com
TIP: ED ENGEL.
DID WE INVADE NORTH KOREA YET, SHELF-LIFE??
HEY, I HOPE NOT! I GOT A BOATLOAD OF UNAUTHORIZED "ZIGGY" EDIBLE UNDERPANTS COMIN' IN FROM DAEJEON NEXT TUESDAY!!
K.C. SIZZ LING ST AKS and CHOPS
OLD SOUTH RESTAURANT

64

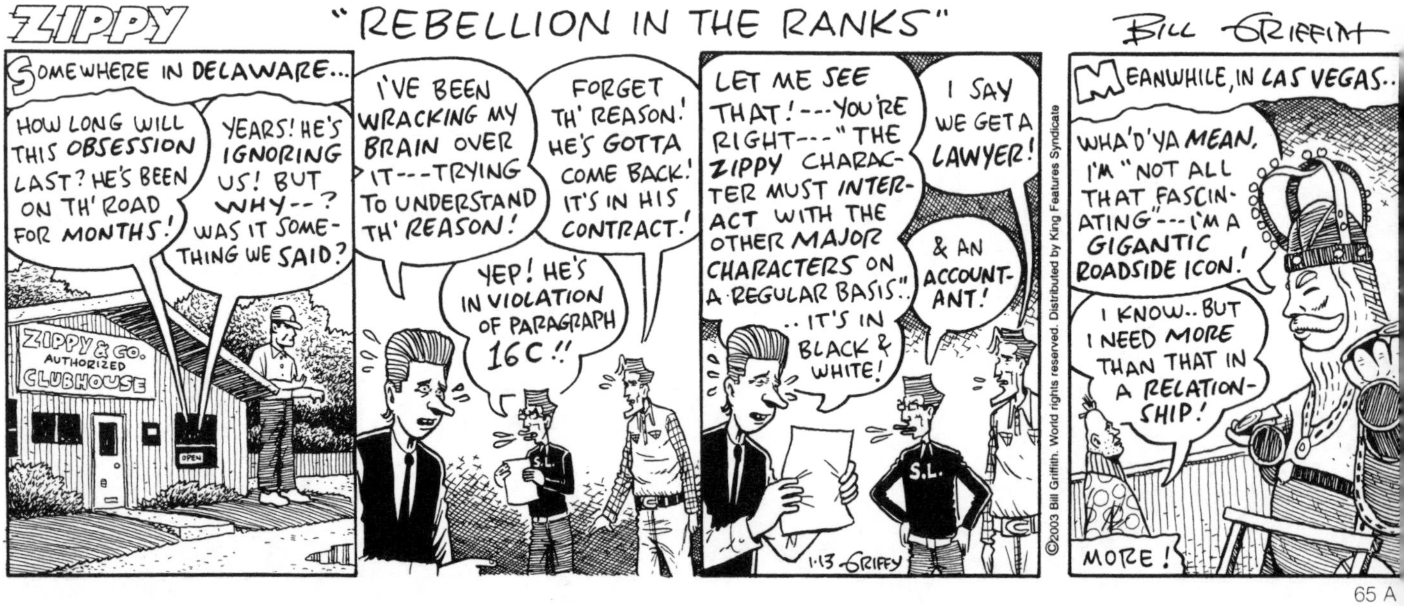
ZIPPY
"REBELLION IN THE RANKS"
BILL GRIFFITH
SOMEWHERE IN DELAWARE...
HOW LONG WILL THIS OBSESSION LAST? HE'S BEEN ON TH' ROAD FOR MONTHS!
YEARS! HE'S IGNORING US! BUT WHY--? WAS IT SOMETHING WE SAID?
ZIPPY & CO. AUTHORIZED CLUBHOUSE
OPEN
I'VE BEEN WRACKING MY BRAIN OVER IT---TRYING TO UNDERSTAND TH' REASON!
FORGET TH' REASON! HE'S GOTTA COME BACK! IT'S IN HIS CONTRACT!
YEP! HE'S IN VIOLATION OF PARAGRAPH 16C!!
LET ME SEE THAT!---YOU'RE RIGHT---"THE ZIPPY CHARACTER MUST INTERACT WITH THE OTHER MAJOR CHARACTERS ON A REGULAR BASIS".. ..IT'S IN BLACK & WHITE!
I SAY WE GET A LAWYER!
& AN ACCOUNTANT!
1-13 GRIFFY
©2003 Bill Griffith. World rights reserved. Distributed by King Features Syndicate
MEANWHILE, IN LAS VEGAS...
WHA'D'YA MEAN, I'M "NOT ALL THAT FASCINATING"---I'M A GIGANTIC ROADSIDE ICON!
I KNOW.. BUT I NEED MORE THAN THAT IN A RELATIONSHIP!
MORE!

65 A

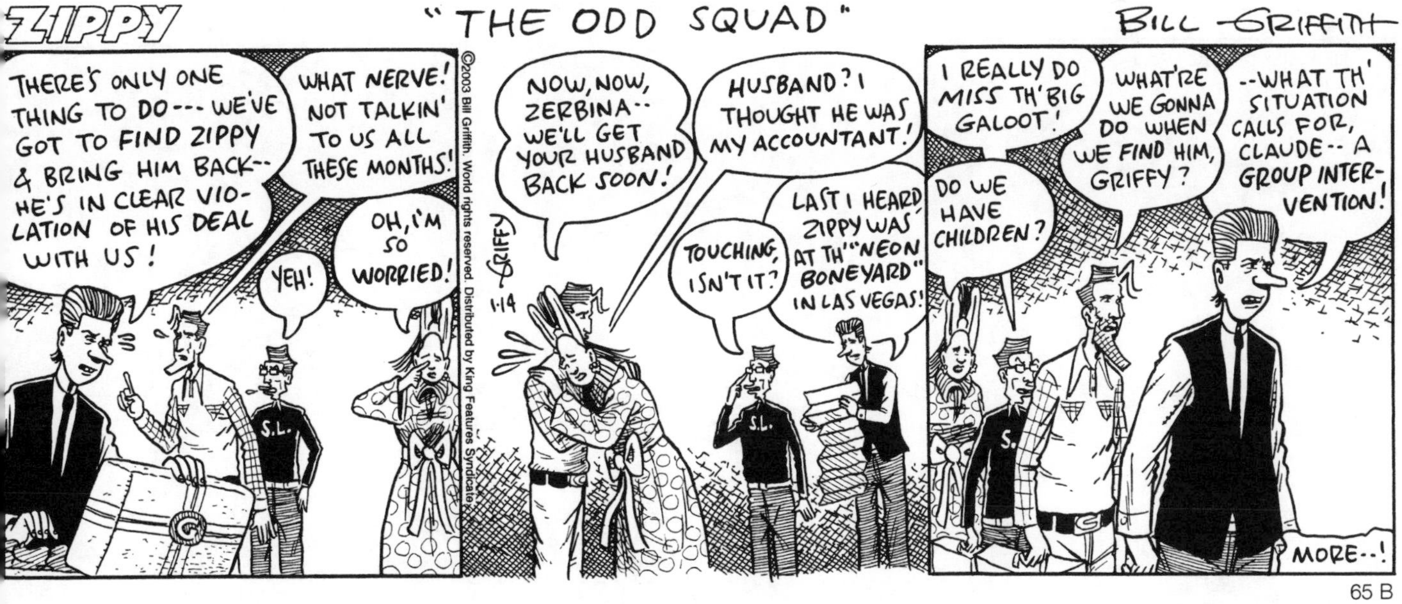
ZIPPY
"THE ODD SQUAD"
BILL GRIFFITH
THERE'S ONLY ONE THING TO DO--- WE'VE GOT TO FIND ZIPPY & BRING HIM BACK-- HE'S IN CLEAR VIOLATION OF HIS DEAL WITH US!
WHAT NERVE! NOT TALKIN' TO US ALL THESE MONTHS!
YEH!
OH, I'M SO WORRIED!
©2003 Bill Griffith. World rights reserved. Distributed by King Features Syndicate
GRIFFY 1·14
NOW, NOW, ZERBINA-- WE'LL GET YOUR HUSBAND BACK SOON!
HUSBAND? I THOUGHT HE WAS MY ACCOUNTANT!
TOUCHING, ISN'T IT?
LAST I HEARD ZIPPY WAS AT TH' "NEON BONEYARD" IN LAS VEGAS!
I REALLY DO MISS TH' BIG GALOOT!
DO WE HAVE CHILDREN?
WHAT'RE WE GONNA DO WHEN WE FIND HIM, GRIFFY?
--WHAT TH' SITUATION CALLS FOR, CLAUDE-- A GROUP INTERVENTION!
MORE--!

65 B

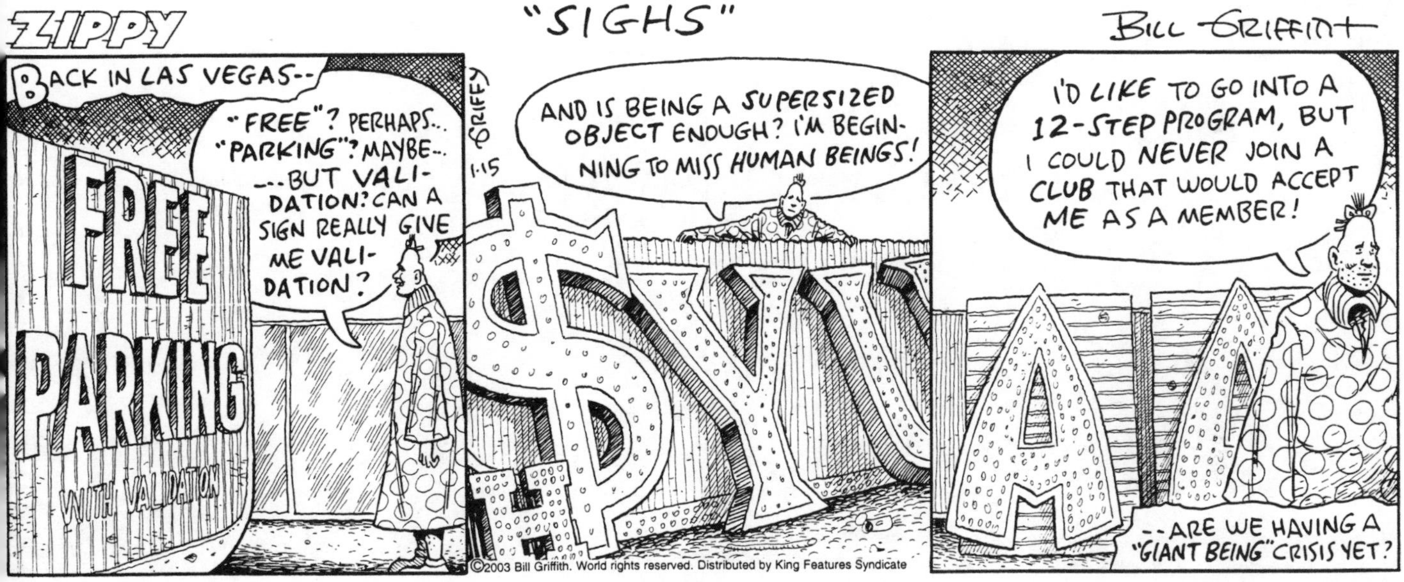
ZIPPY
"SIGHS"
BILL GRIFFITH
BACK IN LAS VEGAS--
"FREE"? PERHAPS.. "PARKING"? MAYBE.. --BUT VALIDATION? CAN A SIGN REALLY GIVE ME VALIDATION?
FREE PARKING
WITH VALIDATION
GRIFFY 1·15
AND IS BEING A SUPERSIZED OBJECT ENOUGH? I'M BEGINNING TO MISS HUMAN BEINGS!
I'D LIKE TO GO INTO A 12-STEP PROGRAM, BUT I COULD NEVER JOIN A CLUB THAT WOULD ACCEPT ME AS A MEMBER!
--ARE WE HAVING A "GIANT BEING" CRISIS YET?
©2003 Bill Griffith. World rights reserved. Distributed by King Features Syndicate

65 C

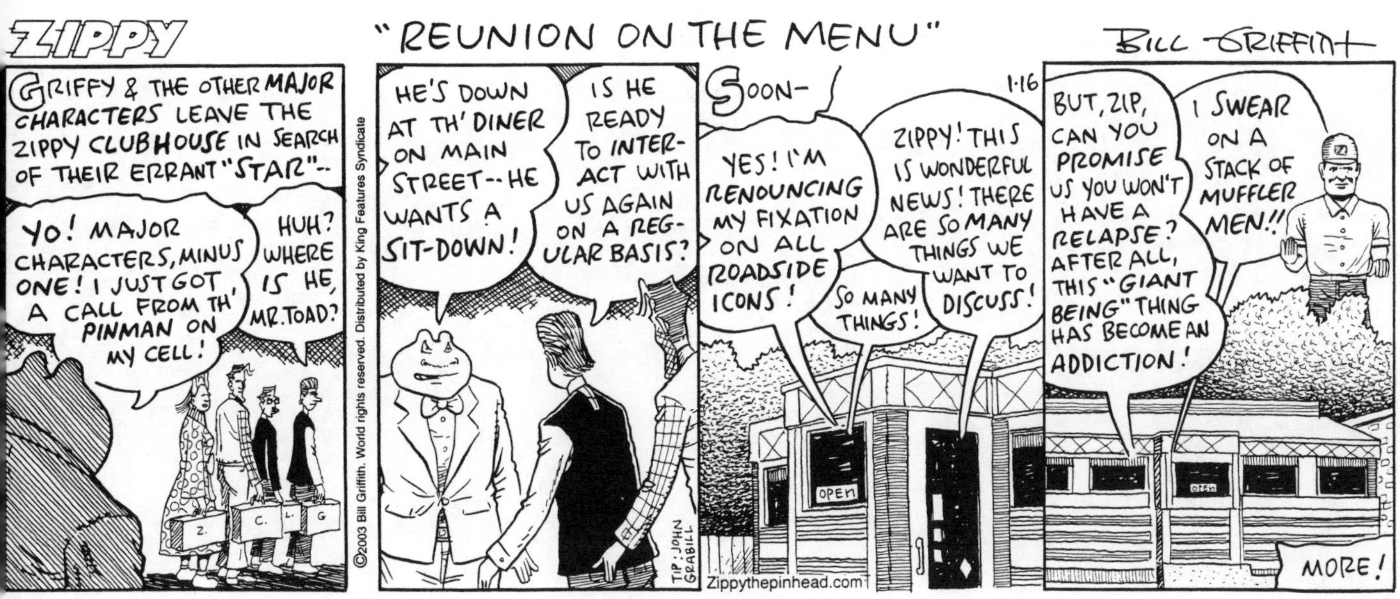
ZIPPY
"REUNION ON THE MENU"
BILL GRIFFITH
GRIFFY & THE OTHER MAJOR CHARACTERS LEAVE THE ZIPPY CLUBHOUSE IN SEARCH OF THEIR ERRANT "STAR"--
YO! MAJOR CHARACTERS, MINUS ONE! I JUST GOT A CALL FROM TH' PINMAN ON MY CELL!
HUH? WHERE IS HE, MR. TOAD?
Z.
C.
L.
G
©2003 Bill Griffith. World rights reserved. Distributed by King Features Syndicate
HE'S DOWN AT TH' DINER ON MAIN STREET--HE WANTS A SIT-DOWN!
IS HE READY TO INTERACT WITH US AGAIN ON A REGULAR BASIS?
TIP: JOHN GRABILL
SOON-
1·16
YES! I'M RENOUNCING MY FIXATION ON ALL ROADSIDE ICONS!
ZIPPY! THIS IS WONDERFUL NEWS! THERE ARE SO MANY THINGS WE WANT TO DISCUSS!
SO MANY THINGS!
OPEN
Zippythepinhead.com
BUT, ZIP, CAN YOU PROMISE US YOU WON'T HAVE A RELAPSE? AFTER ALL, THIS "GIANT BEING" THING HAS BECOME AN ADDICTION!
I SWEAR ON A STACK OF MUFFLER MEN!!
MORE!

65 D

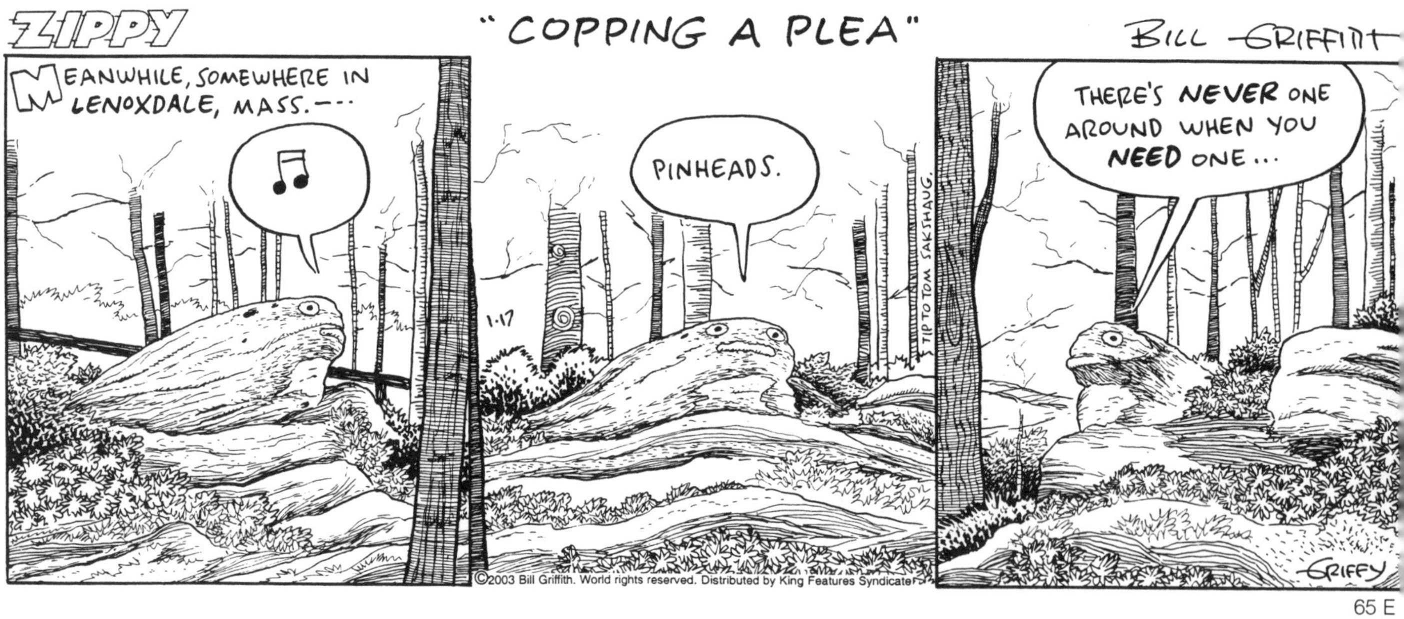
ZIPPY
"COPPING A PLEA"
BILL GRIFFITH
MEANWHILE, SOMEWHERE IN LENOXDALE, MASS.---
♫
1·17
PINHEADS.
TIP TO TOM SAKSHAUG.
THERE'S NEVER ONE AROUND WHEN YOU NEED ONE...
GRIFFY
©2003 Bill Griffith. World rights reserved. Distributed by King Features Syndicate

65 E

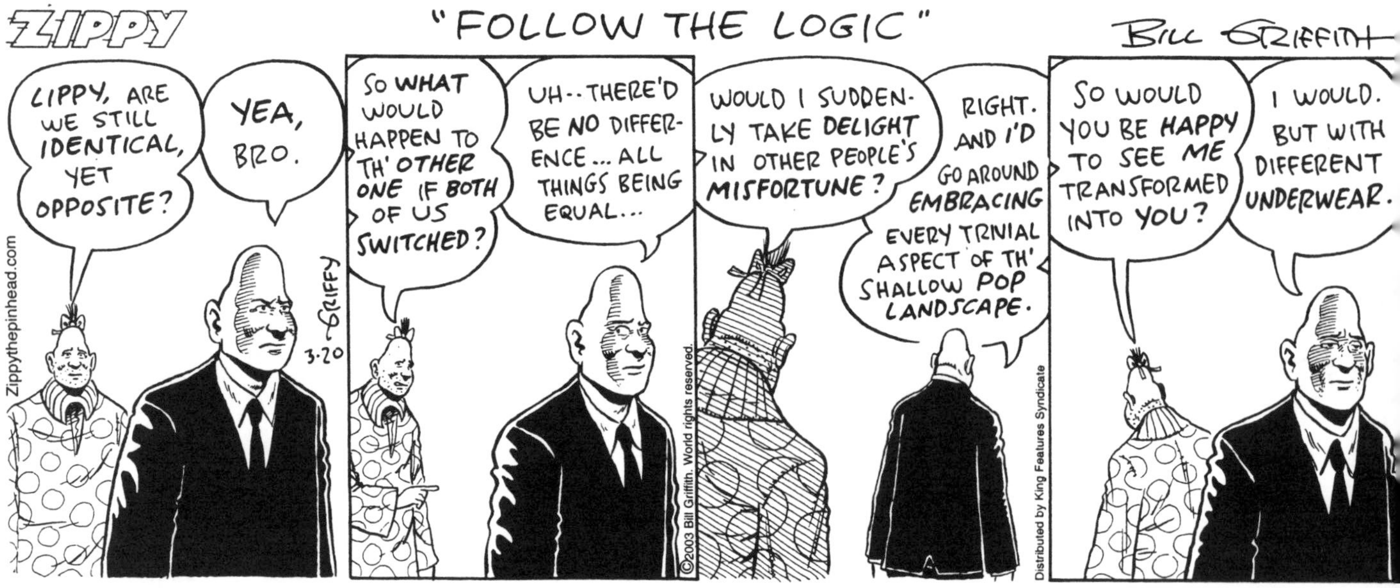
ZIPPY
"FOLLOW THE LOGIC"
BILL GRIFFITH
ZIPPY, ARE WE STILL IDENTICAL, YET OPPOSITE?
YEA, BRO.
Zippythepinhead.com
GRIFFY 3·20
SO WHAT WOULD HAPPEN TO TH' OTHER ONE IF BOTH OF US SWITCHED?
UH--THERE'D BE NO DIFFERENCE... ALL THINGS BEING EQUAL...
©2003 Bill Griffith. World rights reserved.
WOULD I SUDDENLY TAKE DELIGHT IN OTHER PEOPLE'S MISFORTUNE?
RIGHT. AND I'D GO AROUND EMBRACING EVERY TRIVIAL ASPECT OF TH' SHALLOW POP LANDSCAPE.
Distributed by King Features Syndicate
SO WOULD YOU BE HAPPY TO SEE ME TRANSFORMED INTO YOU?
I WOULD. BUT WITH DIFFERENT UNDERWEAR.

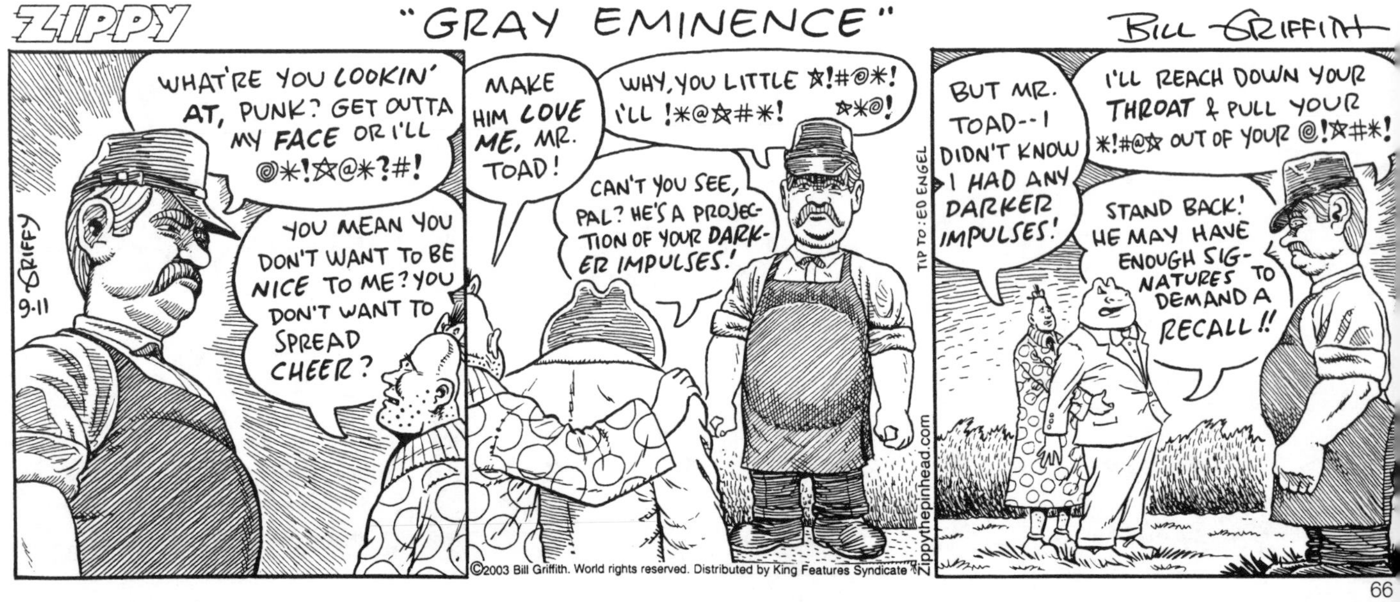
ZIPPY
"GRAY EMINENCE"
BILL GRIFFITH
WHAT'RE YOU LOOKIN' AT, PUNK? GET OUTTA MY FACE OR I'LL @*!☆@*?#!
GRIFFY 9·11
YOU MEAN YOU DON'T WANT TO BE NICE TO ME? YOU DON'T WANT TO SPREAD CHEER?
MAKE HIM LOVE ME, MR. TOAD!
WHY, YOU LITTLE ☆!#@*! I'LL !*@☆#*! ☆*@!
CAN'T YOU SEE, PAL? HE'S A PROJECTION OF YOUR DARKER IMPULSES!
TIP TO: ED ENGEL
BUT MR. TOAD--I DIDN'T KNOW I HAD ANY DARKER IMPULSES!
I'LL REACH DOWN YOUR THROAT & PULL YOUR *!#@☆ OUT OF YOUR @!☆#*!
STAND BACK! HE MAY HAVE ENOUGH SIGNATURES TO DEMAND A RECALL!!
©2003 Bill Griffith. World rights reserved. Distributed by King Features Syndicate
Zippythepinhead.com

66

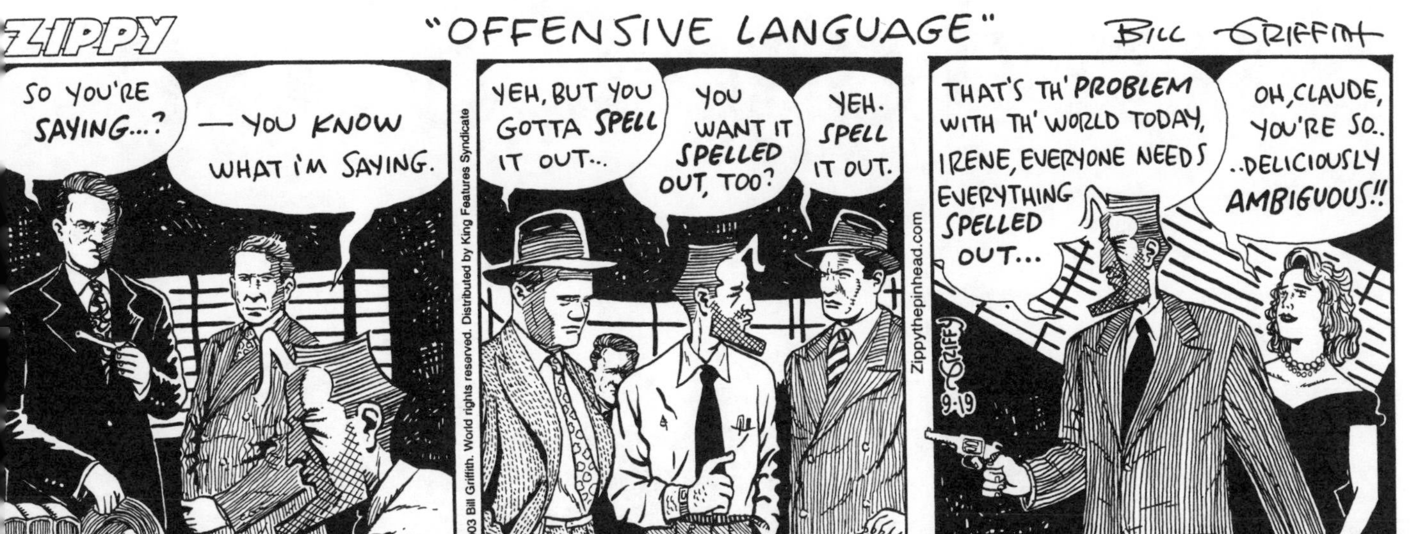
ZIPPY
"OFFENSIVE LANGUAGE"
BILL GRIFFITH
SO YOU'RE SAYING...?
— YOU KNOW WHAT I'M SAYING.
YEH, BUT YOU GOTTA SPELL IT OUT...
YOU WANT IT SPELLED OUT, TOO?
YEH. SPELL IT OUT.
©2003 Bill Griffith. World rights reserved. Distributed by King Features Syndicate
Zippythepinhead.com
THAT'S TH' PROBLEM WITH TH' WORLD TODAY, IRENE, EVERYONE NEEDS EVERYTHING SPELLED OUT...
OH, CLAUDE, YOU'RE SO.. ..DELICIOUSLY AMBIGUOUS!!
GRIFFY 9-19

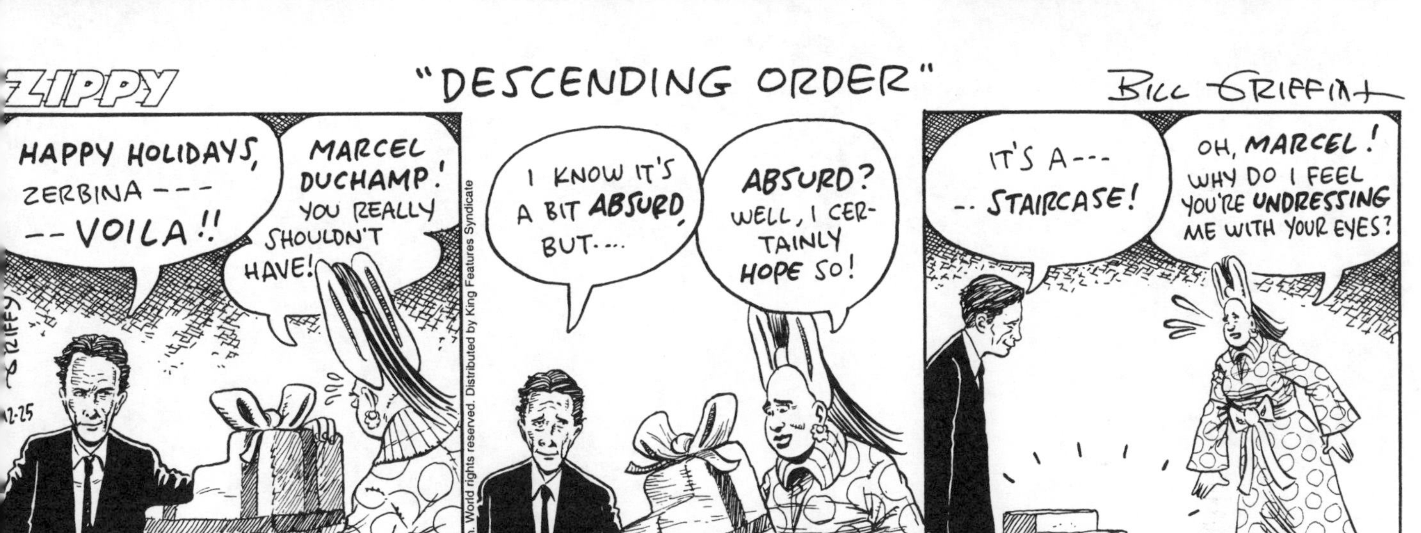
ZIPPY
"DESCENDING ORDER"
BILL GRIFFITH
HAPPY HOLIDAYS, ZERBINA --- --VOILA!!
MARCEL DUCHAMP! YOU REALLY SHOULDN'T HAVE!
GRIFFY 12-25
©2002 Bill Griffith. World rights reserved. Distributed by King Features Syndicate
I KNOW IT'S A BIT ABSURD, BUT....
ABSURD? WELL, I CERTAINLY HOPE SO!
IT'S A--- --STAIRCASE!
OH, MARCEL! WHY DO I FEEL YOU'RE UNDRESSING ME WITH YOUR EYES?

67

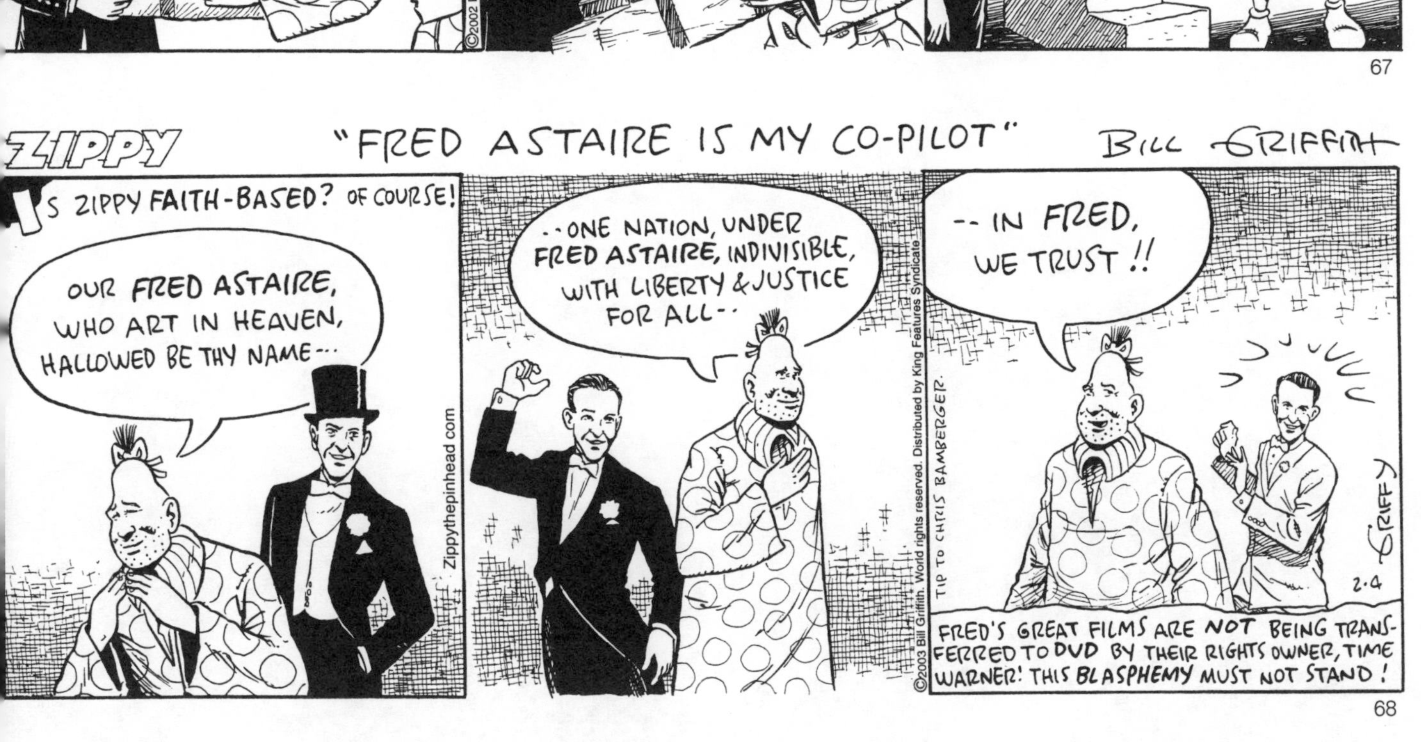
ZIPPY
"FRED ASTAIRE IS MY CO-PILOT"
BILL GRIFFITH
IS ZIPPY FAITH-BASED? OF COURSE!
OUR FRED ASTAIRE, WHO ART IN HEAVEN, HALLOWED BE THY NAME...
Zippythepinhead.com
..ONE NATION, UNDER FRED ASTAIRE, INDIVISIBLE, WITH LIBERTY & JUSTICE FOR ALL..
©2003 Bill Griffith. World rights reserved. Distributed by King Features Syndicate
TIP TO CHRIS BAMBERGER.
-- IN FRED, WE TRUST!!
GRIFFY 2·4
FRED'S GREAT FILMS ARE NOT BEING TRANSFERRED TO DVD BY THEIR RIGHTS OWNER, TIME WARNER! THIS BLASPHEMY MUST NOT STAND!

68

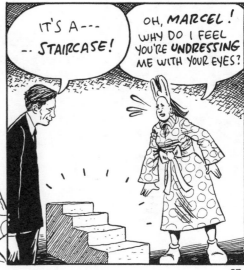

Sunday Color

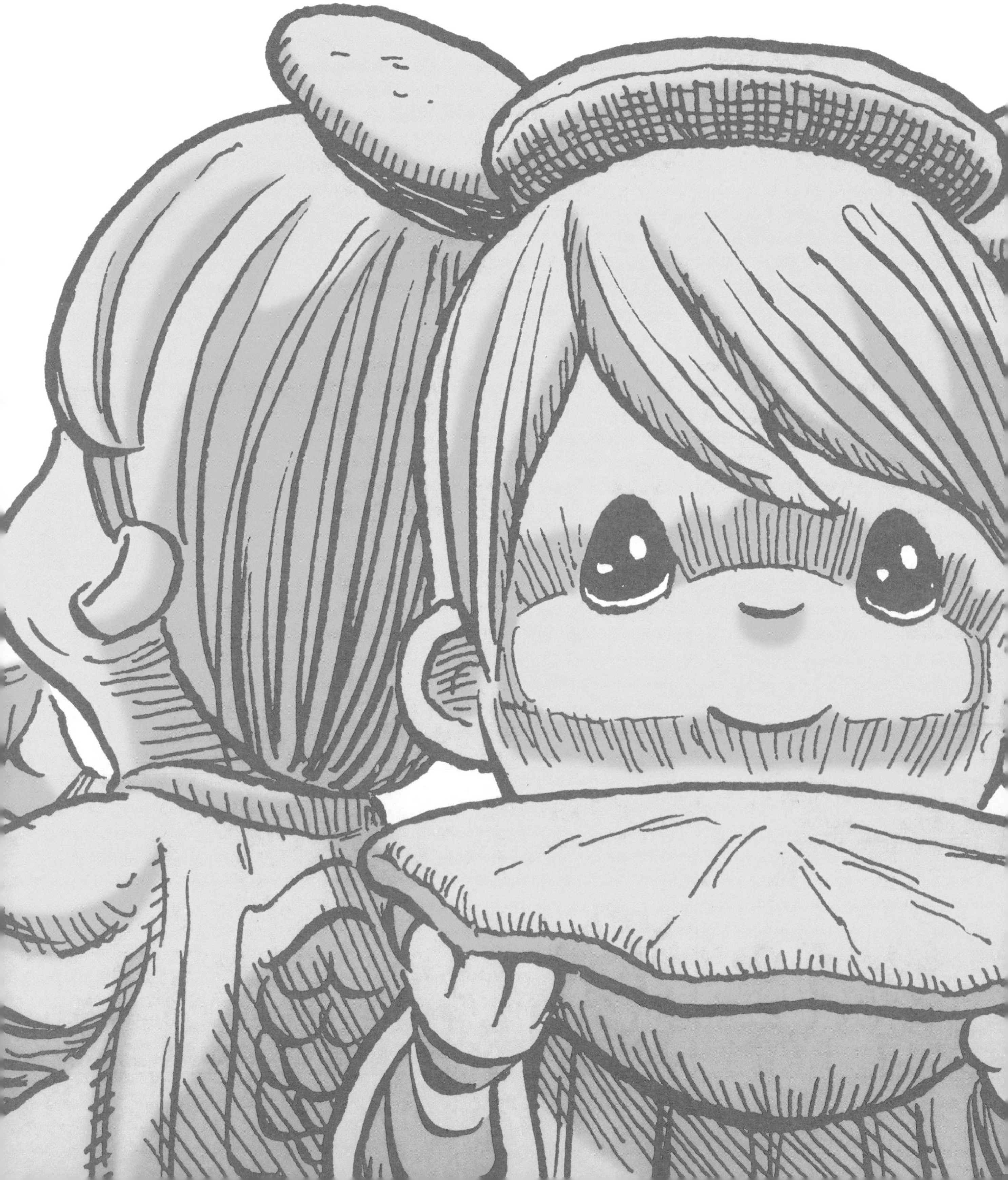

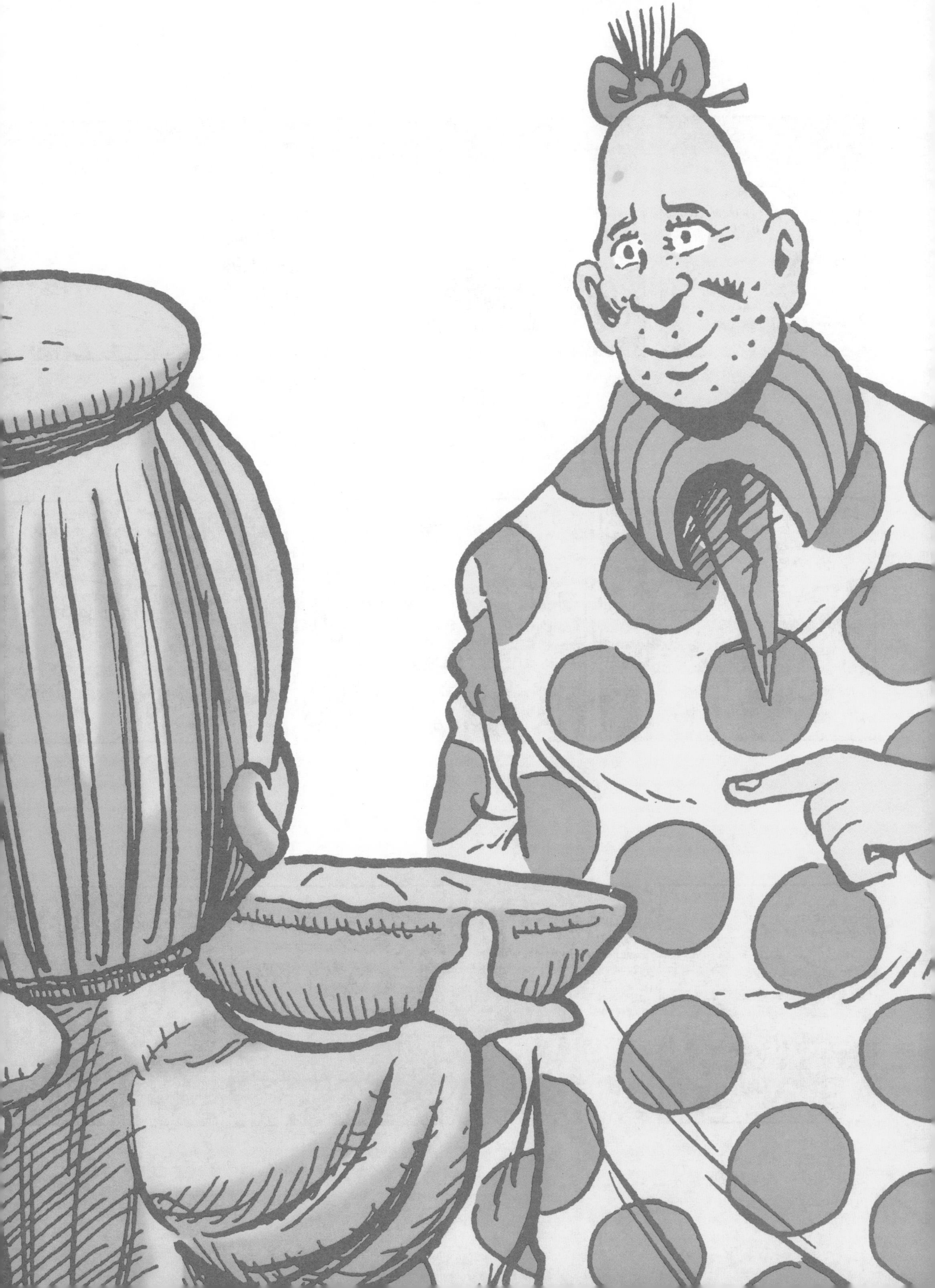

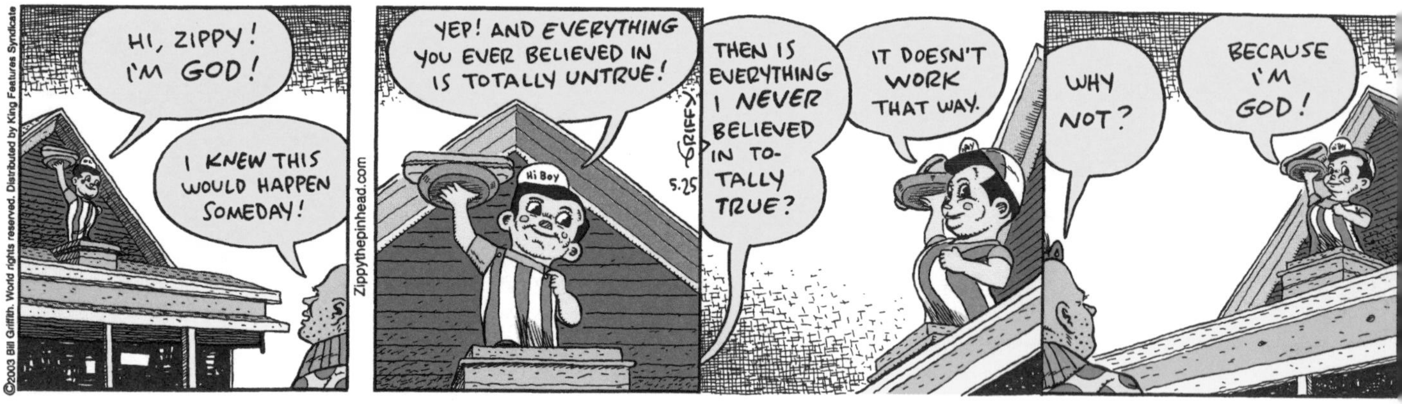
©2003 Bill Griffith. World rights reserved. Distributed by King Features Syndicate
HI, ZIPPY! I'M GOD!
I KNEW THIS WOULD HAPPEN SOMEDAY!
Zippythepinhead.com
YEP! AND EVERYTHING YOU EVER BELIEVED IN IS TOTALLY UNTRUE!
Hi Boy
GRIFFY 5.25
THEN IS EVERYTHING I NEVER BELIEVED IN TO-TALLY TRUE?
IT DOESN'T WORK THAT WAY.
WHY NOT?
BECAUSE I'M GOD!

69

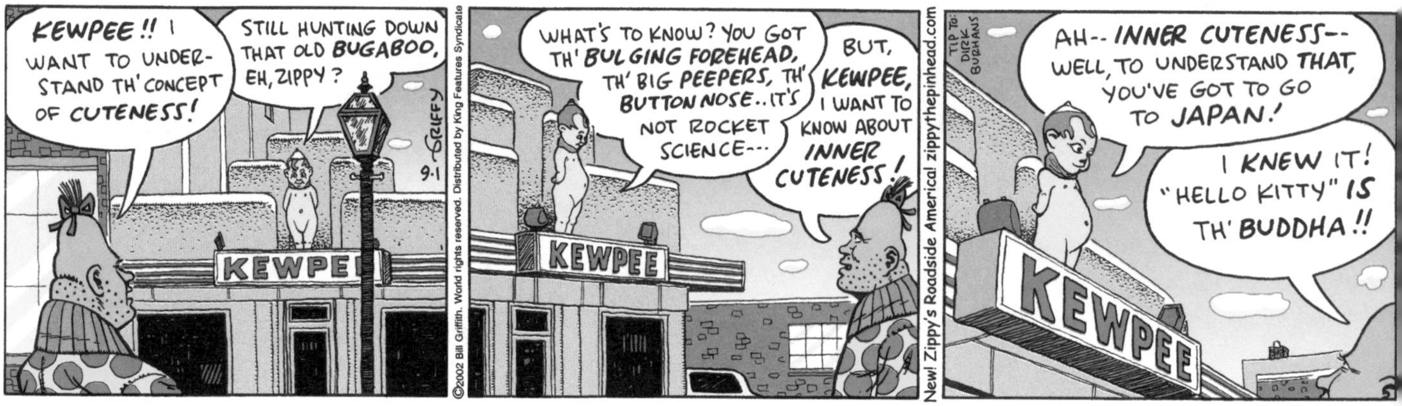
KEWPEE!! I WANT TO UNDER-STAND TH' CONCEPT OF CUTENESS!
STILL HUNTING DOWN THAT OLD BUGABOO, EH, ZIPPY?
GRIFFY 9.1
KEWPE
©2002 Bill Griffith. World rights reserved. Distributed by King Features Syndicate
WHAT'S TO KNOW? YOU GOT TH' BULGING FOREHEAD, TH' BIG PEEPERS, TH' BUTTON NOSE.. IT'S NOT ROCKET SCIENCE---
BUT, KEWPEE, I WANT TO KNOW ABOUT INNER CUTENESS!
KEWPEE
New! Zippy's Roadside America! zippythepinhead.com
TIP TO DIRK BURHANS
AH-- INNER CUTENESS-- WELL, TO UNDERSTAND THAT, YOU'VE GOT TO GO TO JAPAN!
I KNEW IT! "HELLO KITTY" IS TH' BUDDHA!!
KEWPEE

70

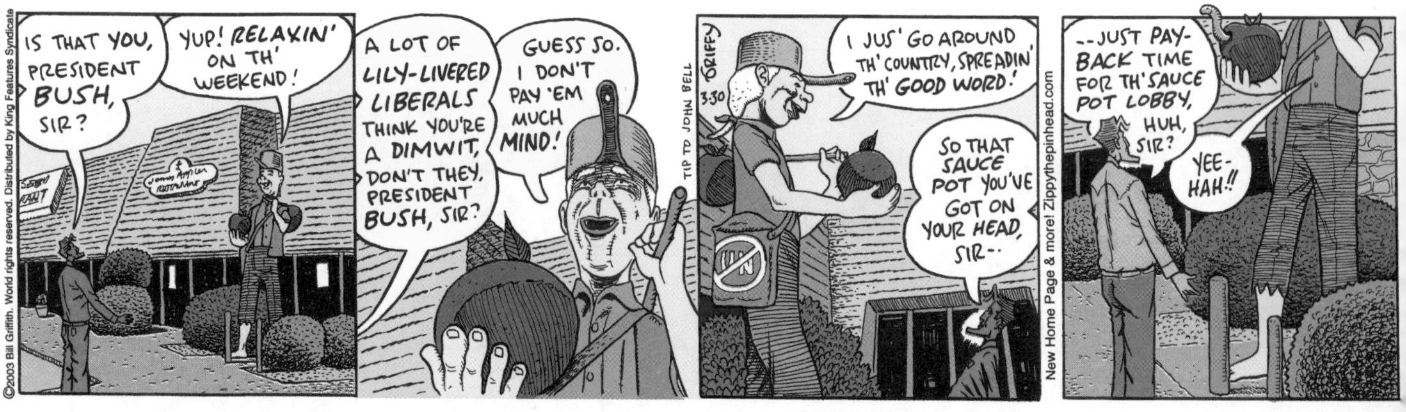
©2003 Bill Griffith. World rights reserved. Distributed by King Features Syndicate
IS THAT YOU, PRESIDENT BUSH, SIR?
YUP! RELAXIN' ON TH' WEEKEND!
A LOT OF LILY-LIVERED LIBERALS THINK YOU'RE A DIMWIT, DON'T THEY, PRESIDENT BUSH, SIR?
GUESS SO. I DON'T PAY 'EM MUCH MIND!
TIP TO JOHN BELL
GRIFFY 3.30
I JUS' GO AROUND TH' COUNTRY, SPREADIN' TH' GOOD WORD!
SO THAT SAUCE POT YOU'VE GOT ON YOUR HEAD, SIR--
New Home Page & more! Zippythepinhead.com
--JUST PAY-BACK TIME FOR TH' SAUCE POT LOBBY, HUH, SIR?
YEE-HAH!!

71

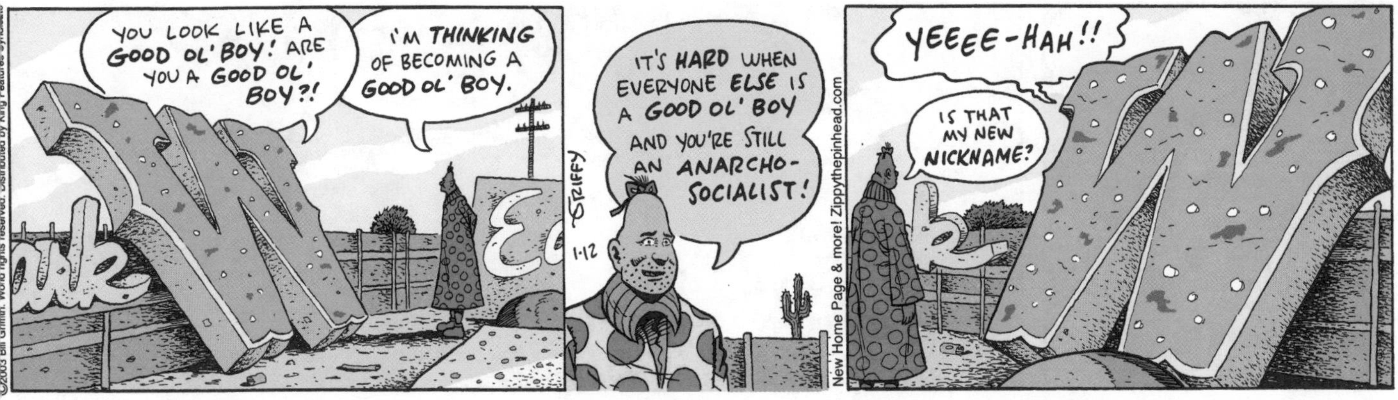

YOU LOOK LIKE A GOOD OL' BOY! ARE YOU A GOOD OL' BOY?!
I'M THINKING OF BECOMING A GOOD OL' BOY.
IT'S HARD WHEN EVERYONE ELSE IS A GOOD OL' BOY AND YOU'RE STILL AN ANARCHO-SOCIALIST!
GRIFFY 1-12
YEEEE-HAH!!
IS THAT MY NEW NICKNAME?
New Home Page & more! Zippythepinhead.com
©2003 Bill Griffith. World rights reserved. Distributed by King Features Syndicate

72 A

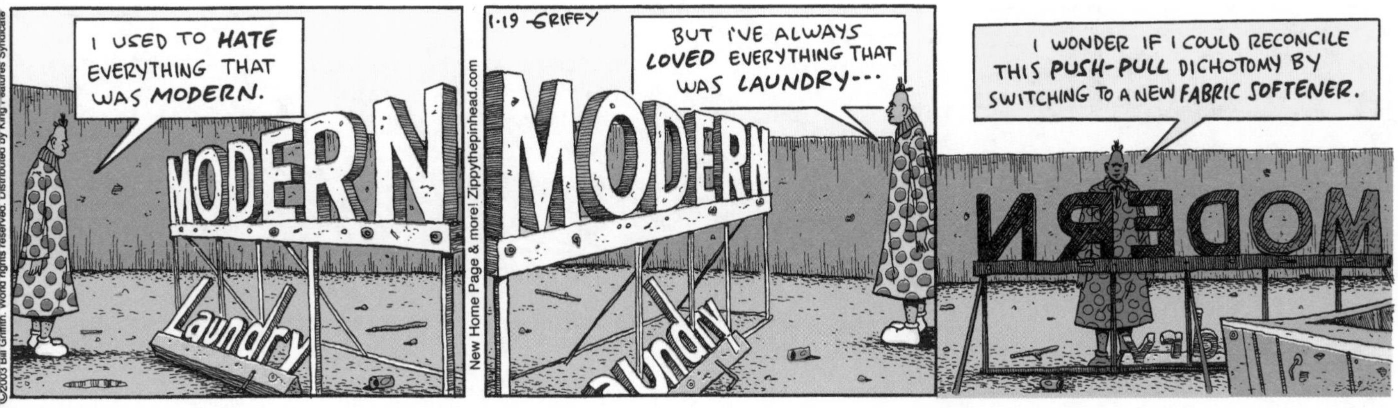

I USED TO HATE EVERYTHING THAT WAS MODERN.
MODERN
Laundry
1-19 GRIFFY
BUT I'VE ALWAYS LOVED EVERYTHING THAT WAS LAUNDRY---
I WONDER IF I COULD RECONCILE THIS PUSH-PULL DICHOTOMY BY SWITCHING TO A NEW FABRIC SOFTENER.
New Home Page & more! Zippythepinhead.com
©2003 Bill Griffith. World rights reserved. Distributed by King Features Syndicate

72 B

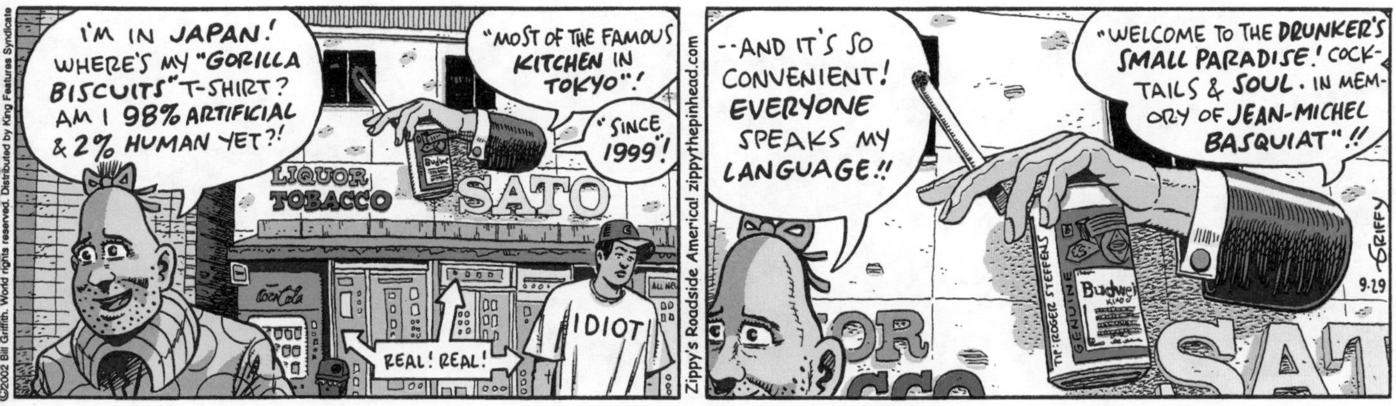

I'M IN JAPAN! WHERE'S MY "GORILLA BISCUITS" T-SHIRT? AM I 98% ARTIFICIAL & 2% HUMAN YET?!
"MOST OF THE FAMOUS KITCHEN IN TOKYO"!
"SINCE 1999"!
LIQUOR TOBACCO
SATO
IDIOT
REAL! REAL!
--AND IT'S SO CONVENIENT! EVERYONE SPEAKS MY LANGUAGE!!
"WELCOME TO THE DRUNKER'S SMALL PARADISE! COCKTAILS & SOUL. IN MEMORY OF JEAN-MICHEL BASQUIAT"!!
GRIFFY 9-29
Zippy's Roadside America! zippythepinhead.com
©2002 Bill Griffith. World rights reserved. Distributed by King Features Syndicate

73

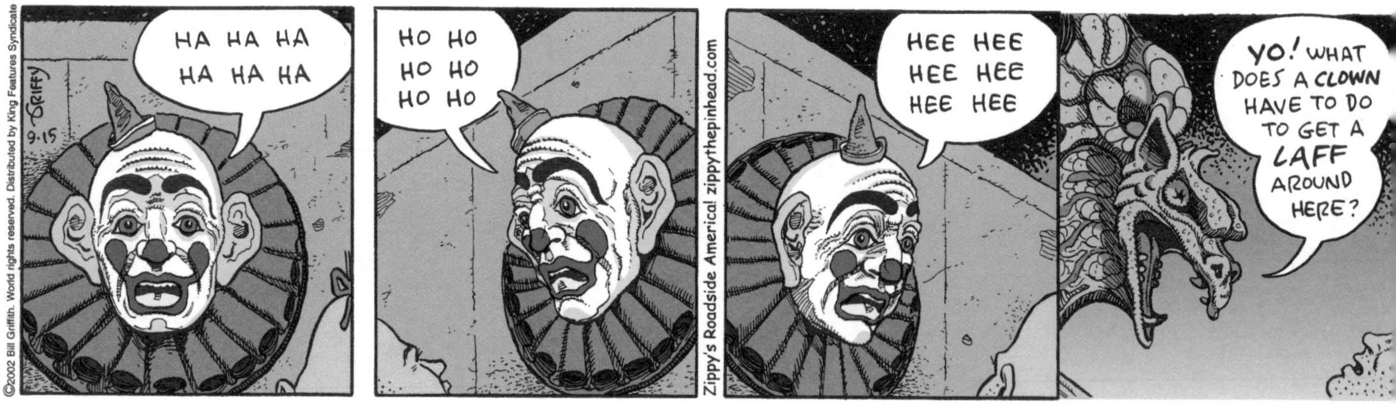
©2002 Bill Griffith. World rights reserved. Distributed by King Features Syndicate
GRIFFY 9.15
HA HA HA HA HA HA
HO HO HO HO HO HO
Zippy's Roadside America! zippythepinhead.com
HEE HEE HEE HEE HEE HEE
YO! WHAT DOES A CLOWN HAVE TO DO TO GET A LAFF AROUND HERE?

74

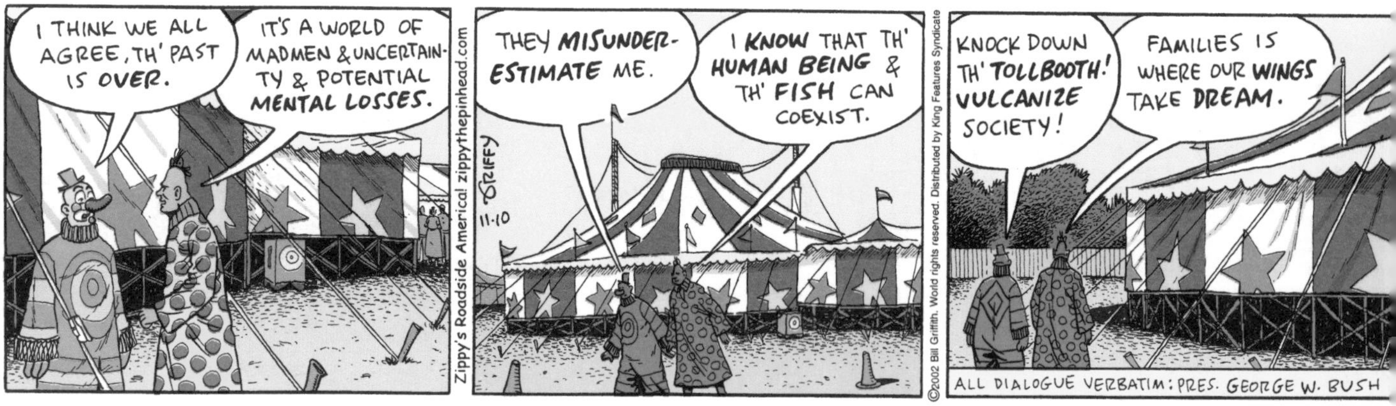
I THINK WE ALL AGREE, TH' PAST IS OVER.
IT'S A WORLD OF MADMEN & UNCERTAINTY & POTENTIAL MENTAL LOSSES.
zippythepinhead.com
THEY MISUNDERESTIMATE ME.
I KNOW THAT TH' HUMAN BEING & TH' FISH CAN COEXIST.
GRIFFY 11.10
Zippy's Roadside America! zippythepinhead.com
©2002 Bill Griffith. World rights reserved. Distributed by King Features Syndicate
KNOCK DOWN TH' TOLLBOOTH! VULCANIZE SOCIETY!
FAMILIES IS WHERE OUR WINGS TAKE DREAM.
ALL DIALOGUE VERBATIM: PRES. GEORGE W. BUSH

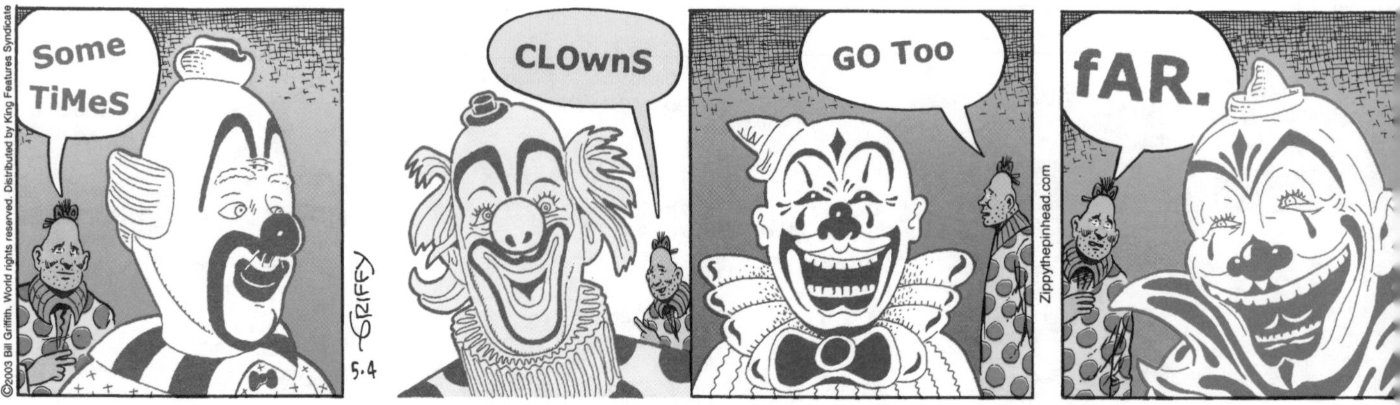
©2003 Bill Griffith. World rights reserved. Distributed by King Features Syndicate
Some TiMeS
GRIFFY 5.4
CLOwnS
GO Too
Zippythepinhead.com
fAR.

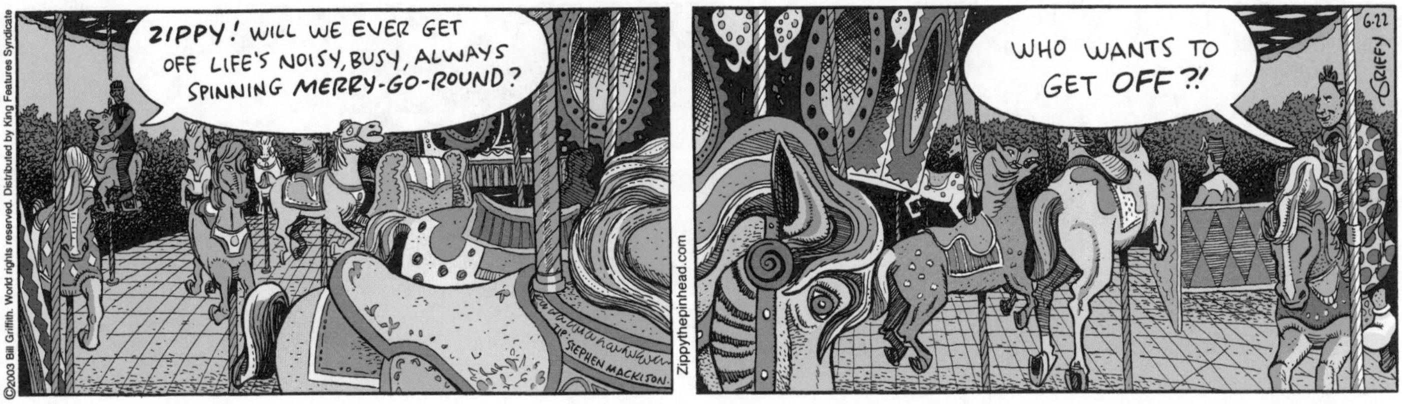
ZIPPY! WILL WE EVER GET OFF LIFE'S NOISY, BUSY, ALWAYS SPINNING MERRY-GO-ROUND?
TIP: STEPHEN MACKISON.
©2003 Bill Griffith. World rights reserved. Distributed by King Features Syndicate
Zippythepinhead.com
WHO WANTS TO GET OFF?!
6-22
GRIFFY

75

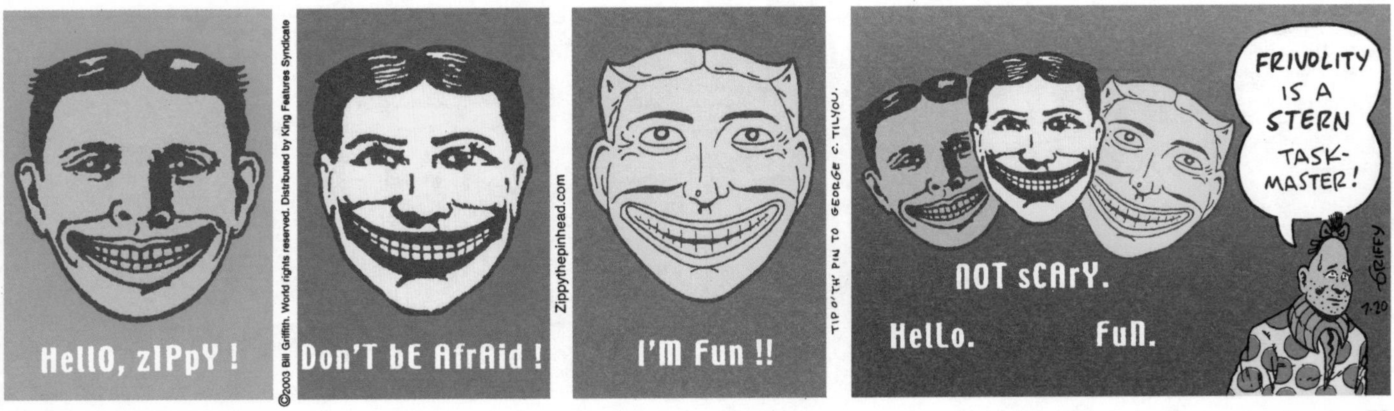
HellO, zIPpY!
Don'T bE AfrAid!
©2003 Bill Griffith. World rights reserved. Distributed by King Features Syndicate
I'M Fun!!
Zippythepinhead.com
TIP O' TH' PIN TO GEORGE C. TILYOU.
NOT sCArY.
HelLo.
FuN.
FRIVOLITY IS A STERN TASK-MASTER!
GRIFFY
7-20

76

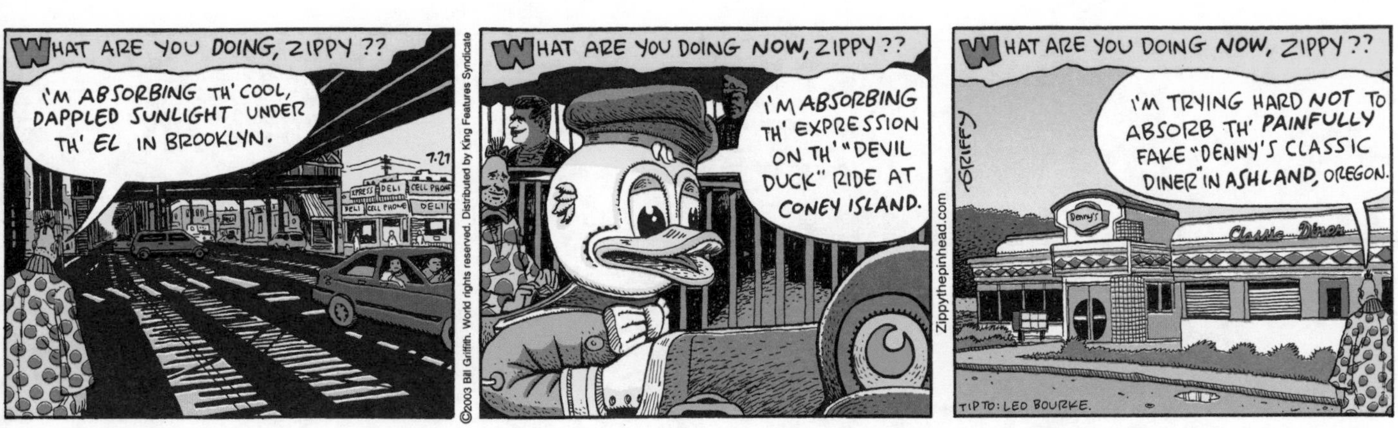
WHAT ARE YOU DOING, ZIPPY??
I'M ABSORBING TH' COOL, DAPPLED SUNLIGHT UNDER TH' EL IN BROOKLYN.
7-21
©2003 Bill Griffith. World rights reserved. Distributed by King Features Syndicate
WHAT ARE YOU DOING NOW, ZIPPY??
I'M ABSORBING TH' EXPRESSION ON TH' "DEVIL DUCK" RIDE AT CONEY ISLAND.
Zippythepinhead.com
WHAT ARE YOU DOING NOW, ZIPPY??
I'M TRYING HARD NOT TO ABSORB TH' PAINFULLY FAKE "DENNY'S CLASSIC DINER" IN ASHLAND, OREGON.
GRIFFY
Denny's
Classic Diner
TIP TO: LEO BOURKE.

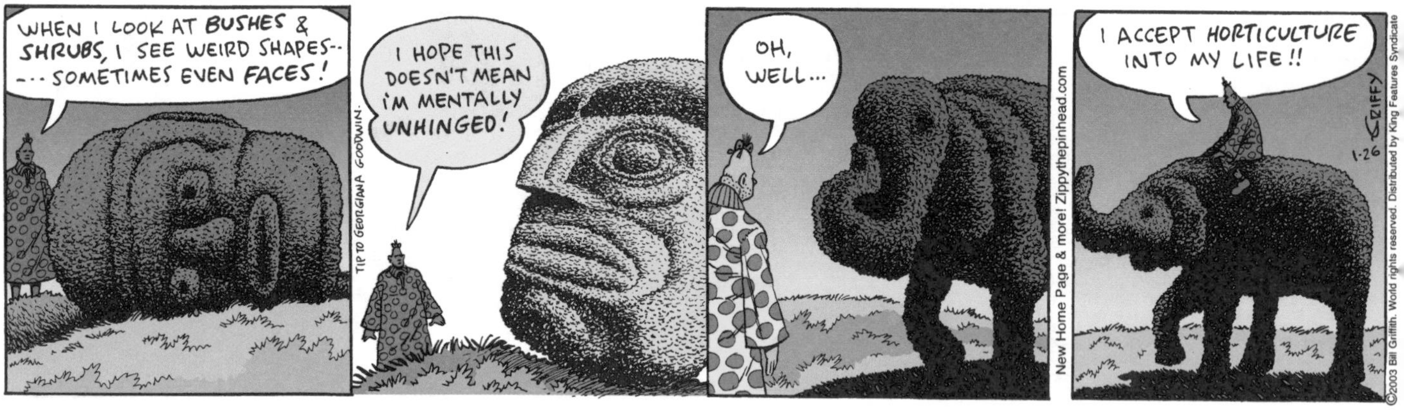
WHEN I LOOK AT BUSHES & SHRUBS, I SEE WEIRD SHAPES-- --- SOMETIMES EVEN FACES!
TIP TO GEORGIANA GOODWIN.
I HOPE THIS DOESN'T MEAN I'M MENTALLY UNHINGED!
OH, WELL...
New Home Page & more! Zippythepinhead.com
I ACCEPT HORTICULTURE INTO MY LIFE!!
GRIFFY
1-26
©2003 Bill Griffith. World rights reserved. Distributed by King Features Syndicate

77

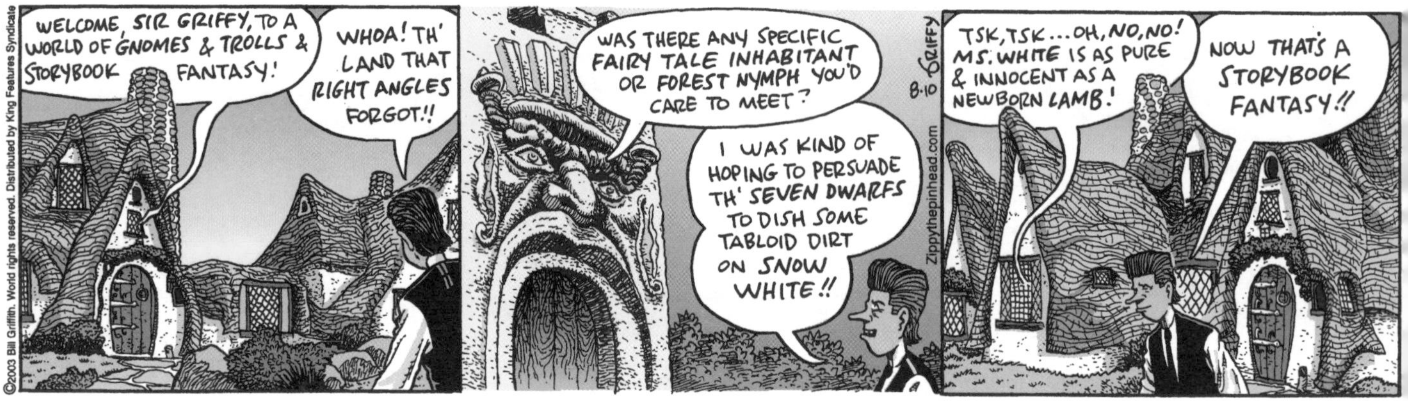
©2003 Bill Griffith. World rights reserved. Distributed by King Features Syndicate
WELCOME, SIR GRIFFY, TO A WORLD OF GNOMES & TROLLS & STORYBOOK FANTASY!
WHOA! TH' LAND THAT RIGHT ANGLES FORGOT!!
WAS THERE ANY SPECIFIC FAIRY TALE INHABITANT OR FOREST NYMPH YOU'D CARE TO MEET?
I WAS KIND OF HOPING TO PERSUADE TH' SEVEN DWARFS TO DISH SOME TABLOID DIRT ON SNOW WHITE!!
GRIFFY
8-10
Zippythepinhead.com
TSK, TSK... OH, NO, NO! MS. WHITE IS AS PURE & INNOCENT AS A NEWBORN LAMB!
NOW THAT'S A STORYBOOK FANTASY!!

78

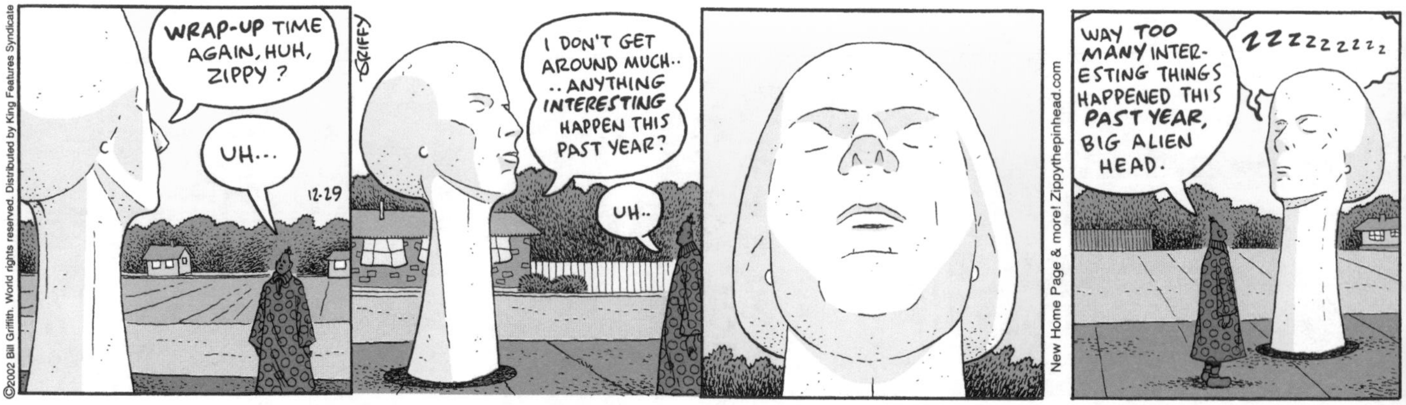
©2002 Bill Griffith. World rights reserved. Distributed by King Features Syndicate
WRAP-UP TIME AGAIN, HUH, ZIPPY?
UH...
12-29
GRIFFY
I DON'T GET AROUND MUCH.. ..ANYTHING INTERESTING HAPPEN THIS PAST YEAR?
UH..
New Home Page & more! Zippythepinhead.com
WAY TOO MANY INTERESTING THINGS HAPPENED THIS PAST YEAR, BIG ALIEN HEAD.
ZZZZZZZZZ

79

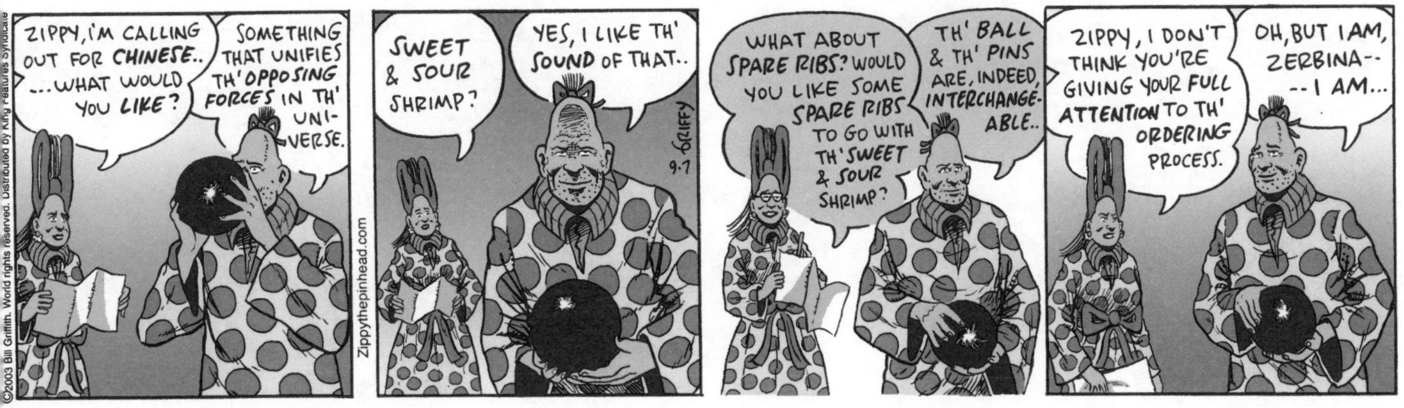

ZIPPY, I'M CALLING OUT FOR CHINESE.. ...WHAT WOULD YOU LIKE?
SOMETHING THAT UNIFIES TH' OPPOSING FORCES IN TH' UNI-VERSE.
SWEET & SOUR SHRIMP?
YES, I LIKE TH' SOUND OF THAT..
GRIFFY 9·7
Zippythepinhead.com
WHAT ABOUT SPARE RIBS? WOULD YOU LIKE SOME SPARE RIBS TO GO WITH TH' SWEET & SOUR SHRIMP?
TH' BALL & TH' PINS ARE, INDEED, INTERCHANGE-ABLE..
ZIPPY, I DON'T THINK YOU'RE GIVING YOUR FULL ATTENTION TO TH' ORDERING PROCESS.
OH, BUT I AM, ZERBINA-- --I AM...
©2003 Bill Griffith. World rights reserved. Distributed by King Features Syndicate

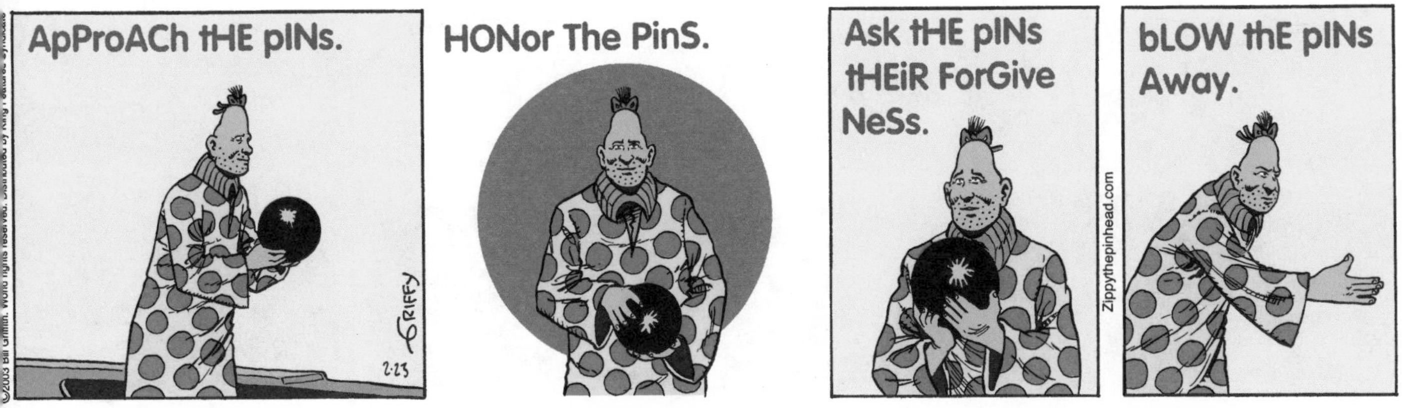

ApProACh tHE pINs.
GRIFFY 2·23
HONor The PinS.
Ask tHE pINs tHEiR ForGive NeSs.
bLOW thE pINs Away.
Zippythepinhead.com

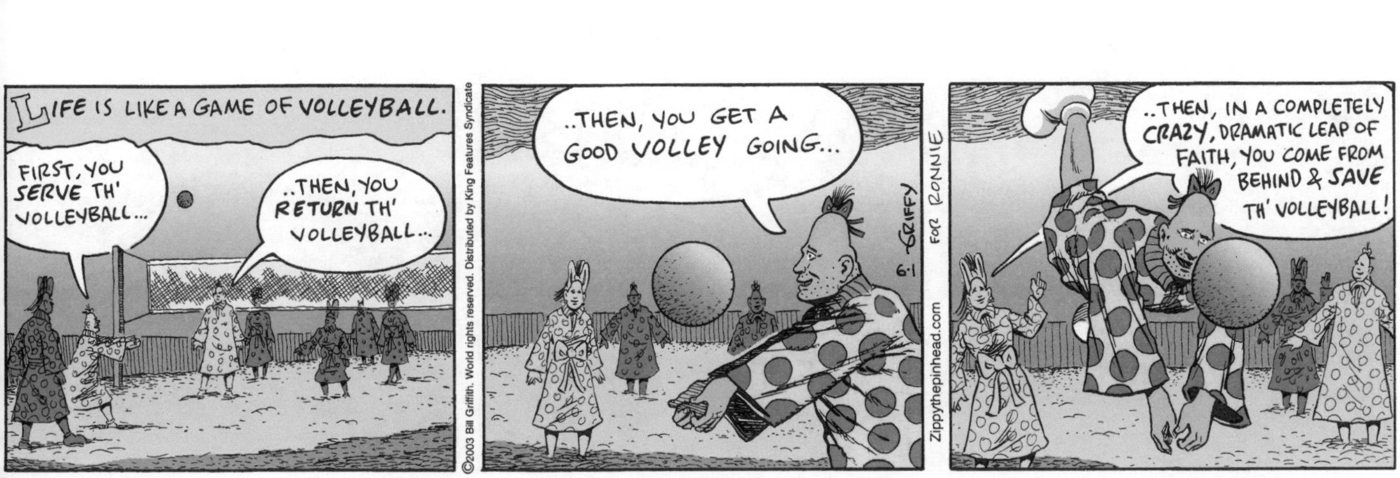

LIFE IS LIKE A GAME OF VOLLEYBALL.
FIRST, YOU SERVE TH' VOLLEYBALL...
..THEN, YOU RETURN TH' VOLLEYBALL...
..THEN, YOU GET A GOOD VOLLEY GOING...
GRIFFY 6·1 FOR RONNIE
©2003 Bill Griffith. World rights reserved. Distributed by King Features Syndicate
Zippythepinhead.com
..THEN, IN A COMPLETELY CRAZY, DRAMATIC LEAP OF FAITH, YOU COME FROM BEHIND & SAVE TH' VOLLEYBALL!

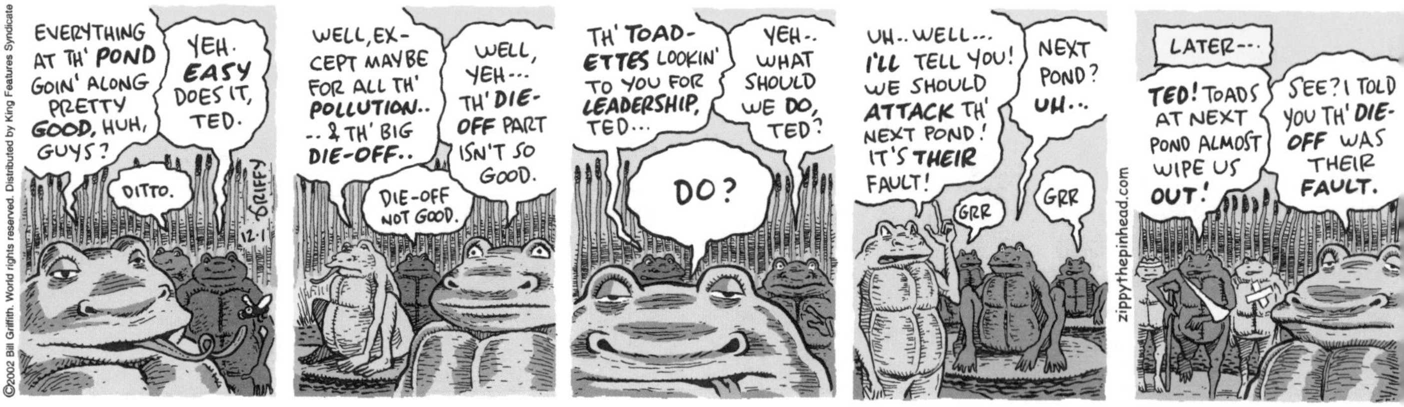
©2002 Bill Griffith. World rights reserved. Distributed by King Features Syndicate
EVERYTHING AT TH' **POND** GOIN' ALONG PRETTY **GOOD**, HUH, GUYS?
YEH. **EASY** DOES IT, TED.
DITTO.
GRIFFY 12·1
WELL, EX-CEPT MAYBE FOR ALL TH' **POLLUTION**.. -- & TH' BIG **DIE-OFF**..
WELL, YEH--- TH' **DIE-OFF** PART ISN'T SO GOOD.
DIE-OFF NOT GOOD.
TH' **TOAD-ETTES** LOOKIN' TO YOU FOR **LEADERSHIP**, TED...
YEH-- WHAT SHOULD WE **DO**, TED?
DO?
UH.. WELL--- **I'LL** TELL YOU! WE SHOULD **ATTACK** TH' NEXT POND! IT'S **THEIR** FAULT!
NEXT POND? **UH**...
GRR
GRR
zippythepinhead.com
LATER---
TED! TOADS AT NEXT POND ALMOST WIPE US **OUT!**
SEE? I TOLD YOU TH' **DIE-OFF** WAS THEIR **FAULT.**

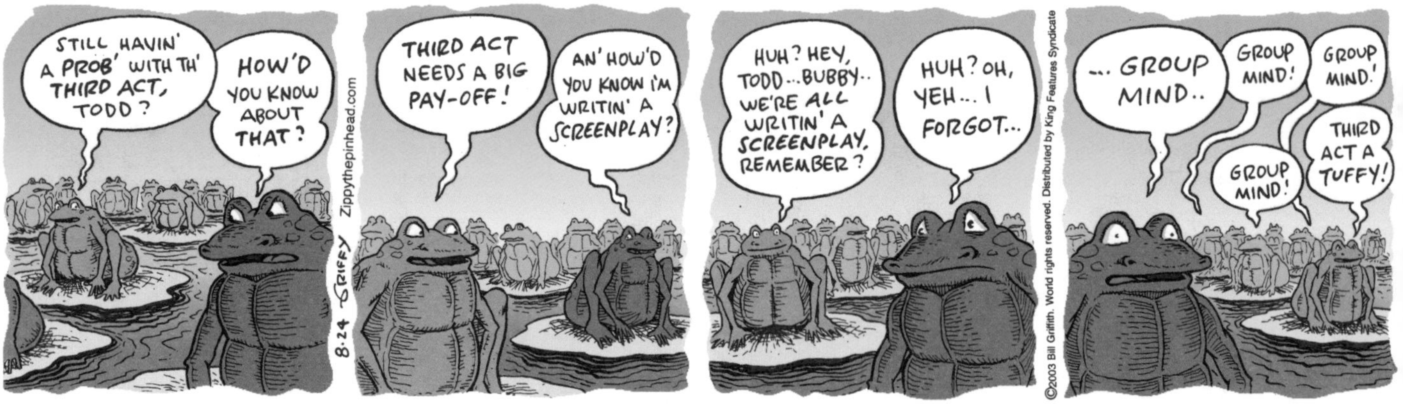
STILL HAVIN' A **PROB'** WITH TH' **THIRD ACT**, TODD?
HOW'D YOU KNOW ABOUT **THAT**?
Zippythepinhead.com
GRIFFY 8·24
THIRD ACT NEEDS A BIG PAY-OFF!
AN' HOW'D YOU KNOW I'M WRITIN' A SCREENPLAY?
HUH? HEY, TODD... BUBBY.. WE'RE **ALL** WRITIN' A **SCREENPLAY**, REMEMBER?
HUH? OH, YEH... I FORGOT...
©2003 Bill Griffith. World rights reserved. Distributed by King Features Syndicate
-- GROUP MIND..
GROUP MIND!
GROUP MIND!
GROUP MIND!
THIRD ACT A TUFFY!

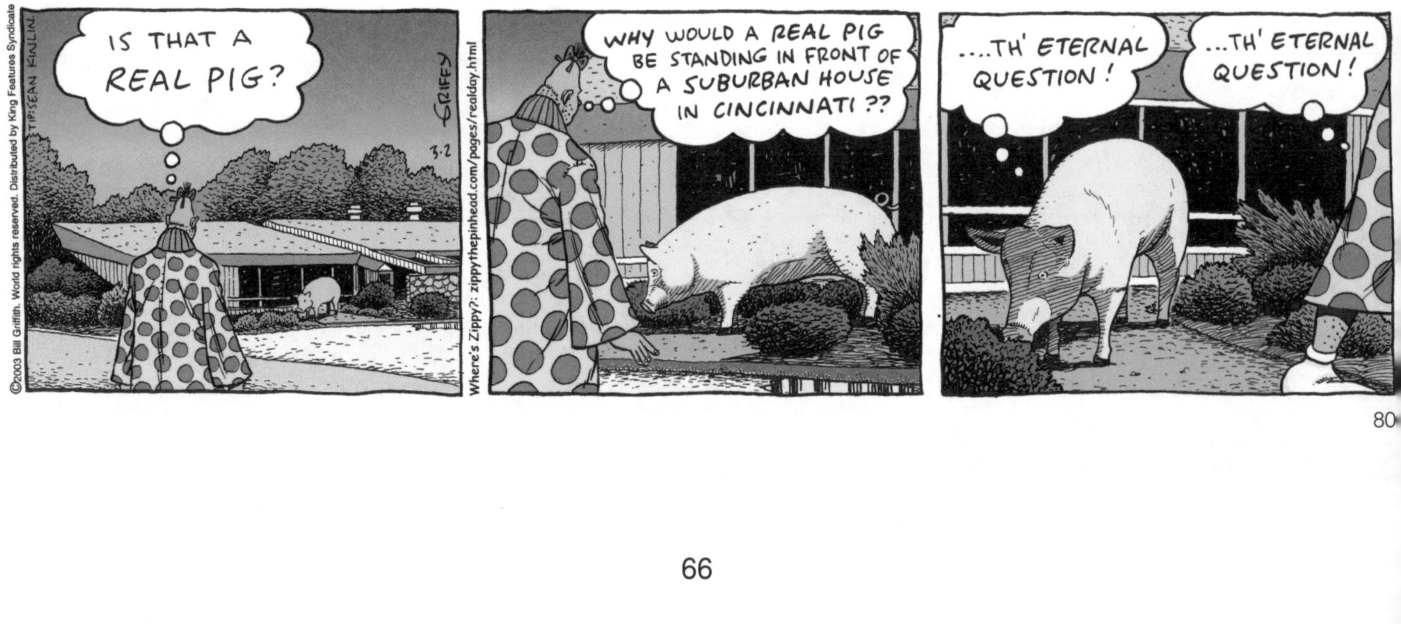
©2003 Bill Griffith. World rights reserved. Distributed by King Features Syndicate
TIP: SEAN KINLIN
IS THAT A REAL PIG?
GRIFFY 3·2
Where's Zippy?: zippythepinhead.com/pages/realday.html
WHY WOULD A **REAL PIG** BE STANDING IN FRONT OF A SUBURBAN HOUSE IN CINCINNATI ??
....TH' ETERNAL QUESTION!
...TH' ETERNAL QUESTION!

80

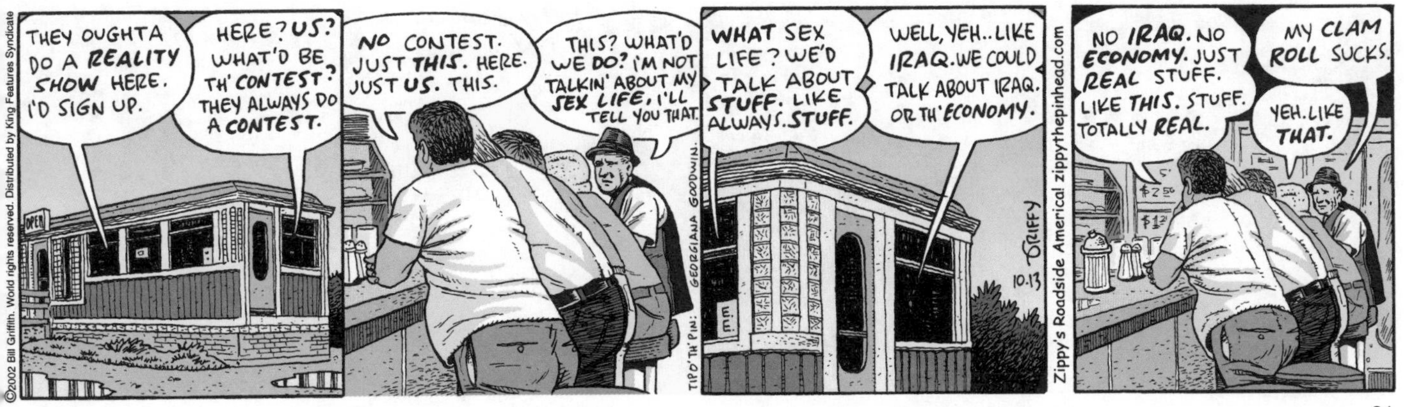
THEY OUGHTA DO A REALITY SHOW HERE. I'D SIGN UP.
HERE? US? WHAT'D BE TH' CONTEST? THEY ALWAYS DO A CONTEST.
NO CONTEST. JUST THIS. HERE. JUST US. THIS.
THIS? WHAT'D WE DO? I'M NOT TALKIN' ABOUT MY SEX LIFE, I'LL TELL YOU THAT.
WHAT SEX LIFE? WE'D TALK ABOUT STUFF. LIKE ALWAYS. STUFF.
WELL, YEH.. LIKE IRAQ. WE COULD TALK ABOUT IRAQ. OR TH' ECONOMY.
NO IRAQ. NO ECONOMY. JUST REAL STUFF. LIKE THIS. STUFF. TOTALLY REAL.
MY CLAM ROLL SUCKS.
YEH. LIKE THAT.
TIP O' TH' PIN: GEORGIANA GOODWIN
GRIFFY 10.13
©2002 Bill Griffith. World rights reserved. Distributed by King Features Syndicate
Zippy's Roadside America! zippythepinhead.com

81

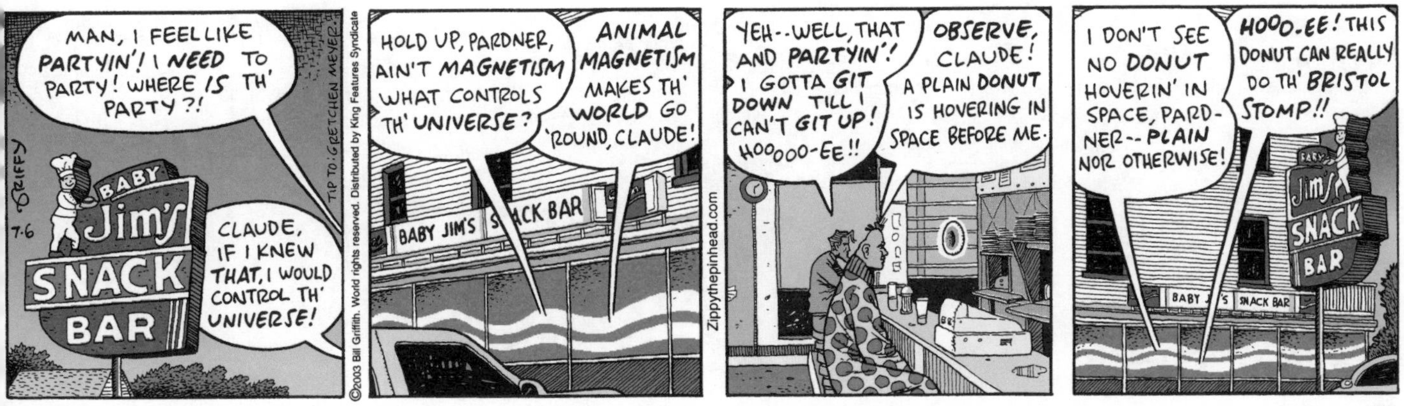
MAN, I FEEL LIKE PARTYIN'! I NEED TO PARTY! WHERE IS TH' PARTY?!
CLAUDE, IF I KNEW THAT, I WOULD CONTROL TH' UNIVERSE!
BABY Jim's SNACK BAR
GRIFFY 7.6
TIP TO: GRETCHEN MEYER
©2003 Bill Griffith. World rights reserved. Distributed by King Features Syndicate
HOLD UP, PARDNER, AIN'T MAGNETISM WHAT CONTROLS TH' UNIVERSE?
ANIMAL MAGNETISM MAKES TH' WORLD GO 'ROUND, CLAUDE!
BABY JIM'S SNACK BAR
zippythepinhead.com
YEH--WELL, THAT AND PARTYIN'! I GOTTA GIT DOWN TILL I CAN'T GIT UP! HOOOOOO-EE!!
OBSERVE, CLAUDE! A PLAIN DONUT IS HOVERING IN SPACE BEFORE ME.
I DON'T SEE NO DONUT HOVERIN' IN SPACE, PARDNER-- PLAIN NOR OTHERWISE!
HOOO-EE! THIS DONUT CAN REALLY DO TH' BRISTOL STOMP!!
BABY Jim's SNACK BAR

82

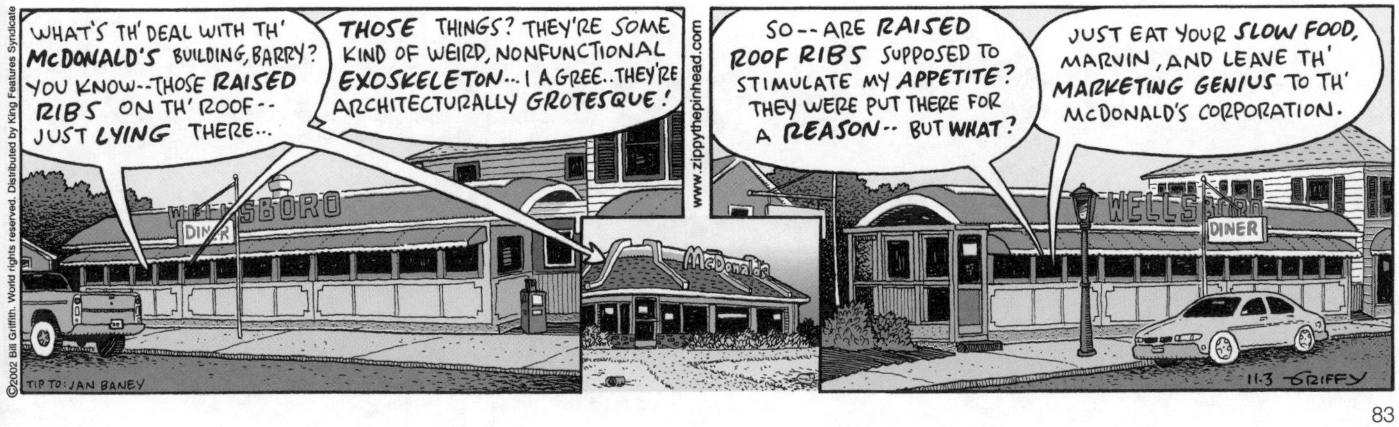
WHAT'S TH' DEAL WITH TH' McDONALD'S BUILDING, BARRY? YOU KNOW--THOSE RAISED RIBS ON TH' ROOF-- JUST LYING THERE...
THOSE THINGS? THEY'RE SOME KIND OF WEIRD, NONFUNCTIONAL EXOSKELETON... I AGREE.. THEY'RE ARCHITECTURALLY GROTESQUE!
WELLSBORO DINER
McDonald's
TIP TO: JAN BANEY
©2002 Bill Griffith. World rights reserved. Distributed by King Features Syndicate
www.zippythepinhead.com
SO-- ARE RAISED ROOF RIBS SUPPOSED TO STIMULATE MY APPETITE? THEY WERE PUT THERE FOR A REASON-- BUT WHAT?
JUST EAT YOUR SLOW FOOD, MARVIN, AND LEAVE TH' MARKETING GENIUS TO TH' McDONALD'S CORPORATION.
WELLSBORO DINER
11.3 GRIFFY

83

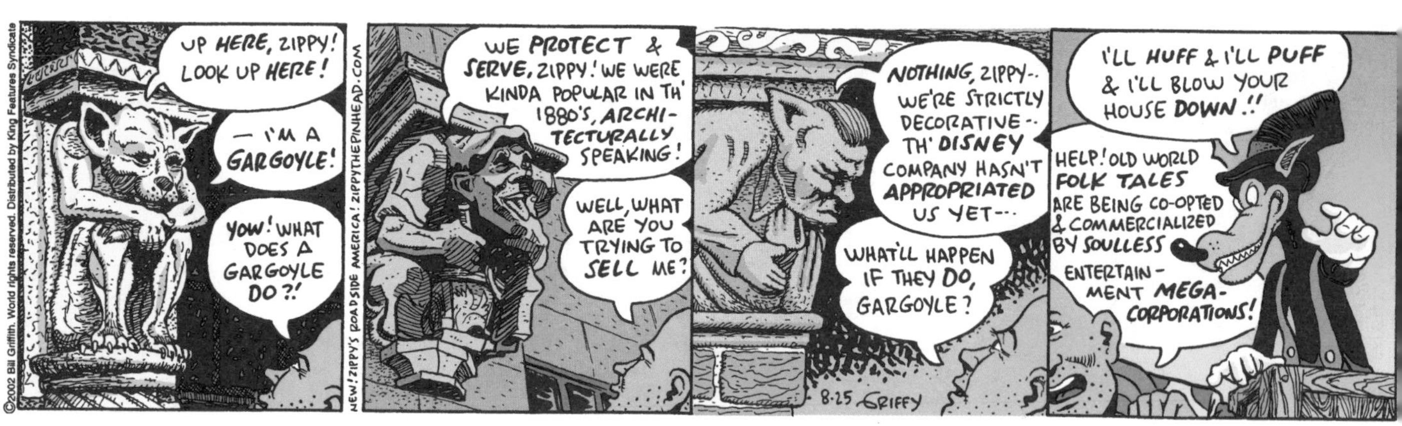
©2002 Bill Griffith. World rights reserved. Distributed by King Features Syndicate
UP HERE, ZIPPY! LOOK UP HERE!
— I'M A GARGOYLE!
YOW! WHAT DOES A GARGOYLE DO?!
NEW! ZIPPY'S ROADSIDE AMERICA! ZIPPYTHEPINHEAD.COM
WE PROTECT & SERVE, ZIPPY! WE WERE KINDA POPULAR IN TH' 1880'S, ARCHITECTURALLY SPEAKING!
WELL, WHAT ARE YOU TRYING TO SELL ME?
NOTHING, ZIPPY.. WE'RE STRICTLY DECORATIVE.. TH' DISNEY COMPANY HASN'T APPROPRIATED US YET...
WHAT'LL HAPPEN IF THEY DO, GARGOYLE?
8.25 GRIFFY
I'LL HUFF & I'LL PUFF & I'LL BLOW YOUR HOUSE DOWN!!
HELP! OLD WORLD FOLK TALES ARE BEING CO-OPTED & COMMERCIALIZED BY SOULLESS ENTERTAINMENT MEGA-CORPORATIONS!

84

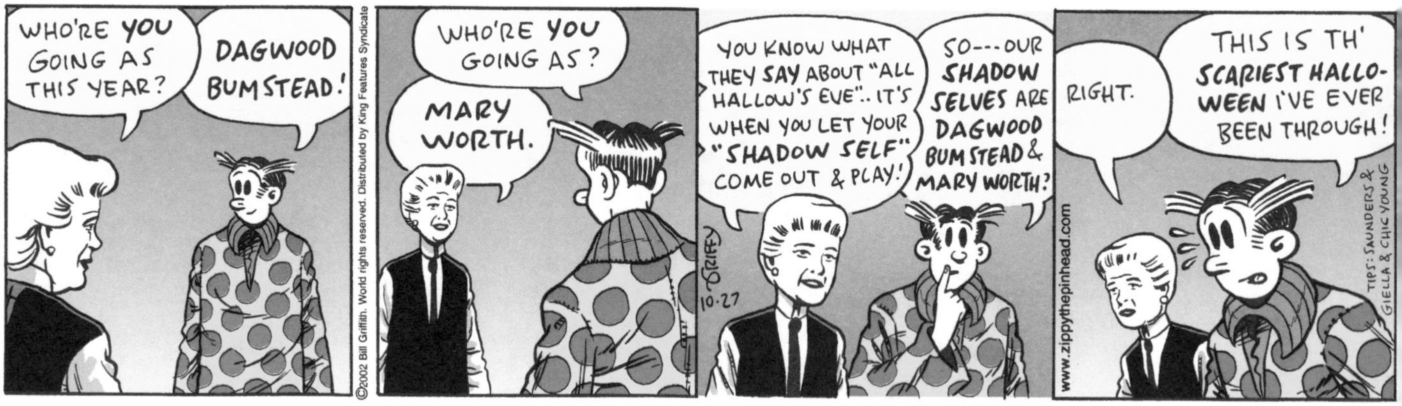
WHO'RE YOU GOING AS THIS YEAR?
DAGWOOD BUMSTEAD!
©2002 Bill Griffith. World rights reserved. Distributed by King Features Syndicate
WHO'RE YOU GOING AS?
MARY WORTH.
GRIFFY 10.27
YOU KNOW WHAT THEY SAY ABOUT "ALL HALLOW'S EVE".. IT'S WHEN YOU LET YOUR "SHADOW SELF" COME OUT & PLAY!
SO--- OUR SHADOW SELVES ARE DAGWOOD BUMSTEAD & MARY WORTH?
www.zippythepinhead.com
RIGHT.
THIS IS TH' SCARIEST HALLOWEEN I'VE EVER BEEN THROUGH!
TIPS: SAUNDERS & GIELLA & CHIC YOUNG

85

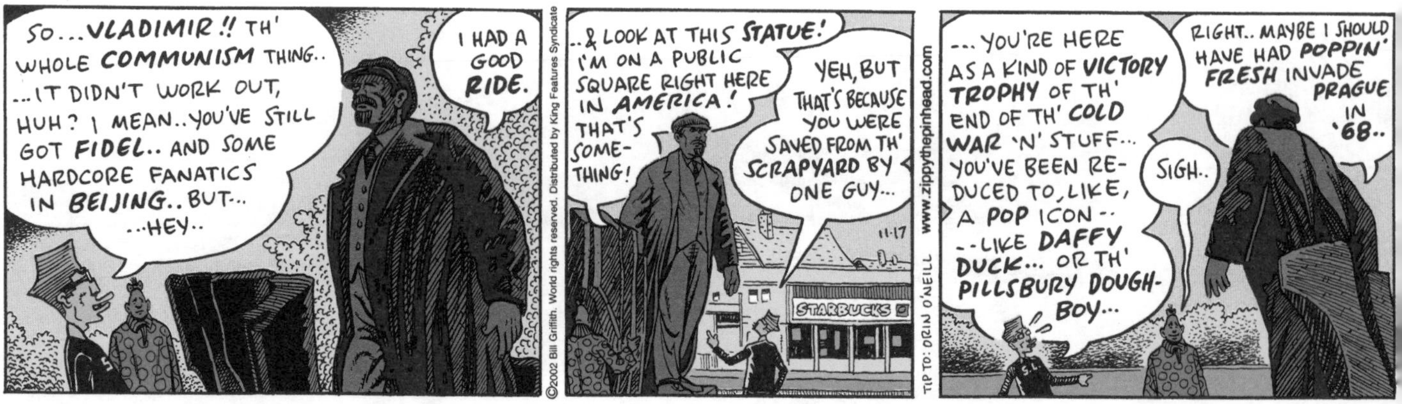
SO... VLADIMIR!! TH' WHOLE COMMUNISM THING.. ...IT DIDN'T WORK OUT, HUH? I MEAN.. YOU'VE STILL GOT FIDEL.. AND SOME HARDCORE FANATICS IN BEIJING.. BUT... ...HEY..
I HAD A GOOD RIDE.
©2002 Bill Griffith. World rights reserved. Distributed by King Features Syndicate
..& LOOK AT THIS STATUE! I'M ON A PUBLIC SQUARE RIGHT HERE IN AMERICA! THAT'S SOMETHING!
YEH, BUT THAT'S BECAUSE YOU WERE SAVED FROM TH' SCRAPYARD BY ONE GUY...
STARBUCKS
11.17
www.zippythepinhead.com
TIP TO: ORIN O'NEILL
... YOU'RE HERE AS A KIND OF VICTORY TROPHY OF TH' END OF TH' COLD WAR 'N' STUFF... YOU'VE BEEN REDUCED TO, LIKE, A POP ICON -- --LIKE DAFFY DUCK... OR TH' PILLSBURY DOUGH-BOY...
RIGHT.. MAYBE I SHOULD HAVE HAD POPPIN' FRESH INVADE PRAGUE IN '68..
SIGH..

86

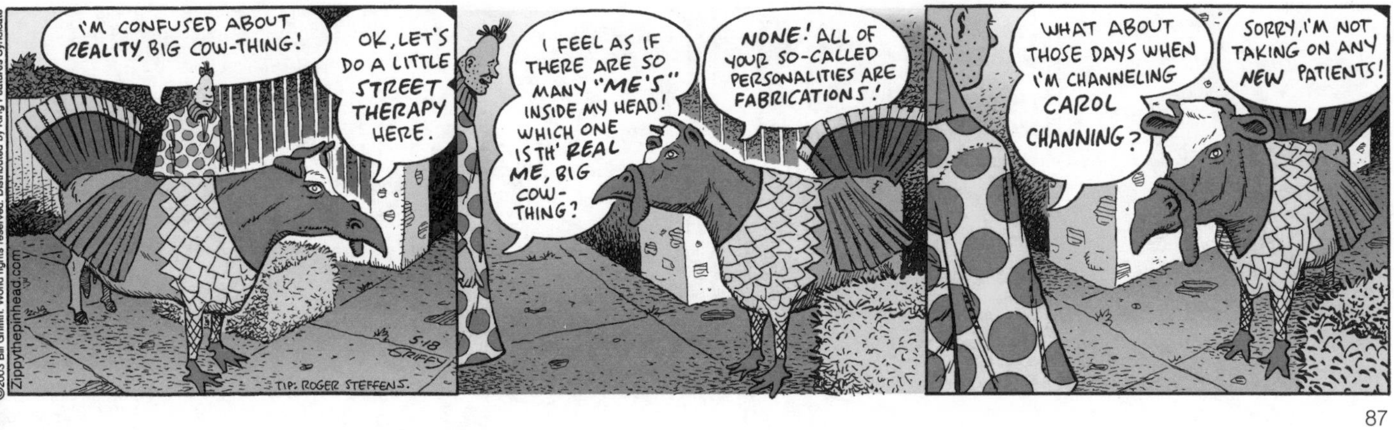

I'M CONFUSED ABOUT REALITY, BIG COW-THING!
OK, LET'S DO A LITTLE STREET THERAPY HERE.
I FEEL AS IF THERE ARE SO MANY "ME'S" INSIDE MY HEAD! WHICH ONE IS TH' REAL ME, BIG COW-THING?
NONE! ALL OF YOUR SO-CALLED PERSONALITIES ARE FABRICATIONS!
WHAT ABOUT THOSE DAYS WHEN I'M CHANNELING CAROL CHANNING?
SORRY, I'M NOT TAKING ON ANY NEW PATIENTS!
5·18 GRIFFY
TIP: ROGER STEFFENS.
©2003 Bill Griffith. World rights reserved. Distributed by King Features Syndicate
Zippythepinhead.com

87

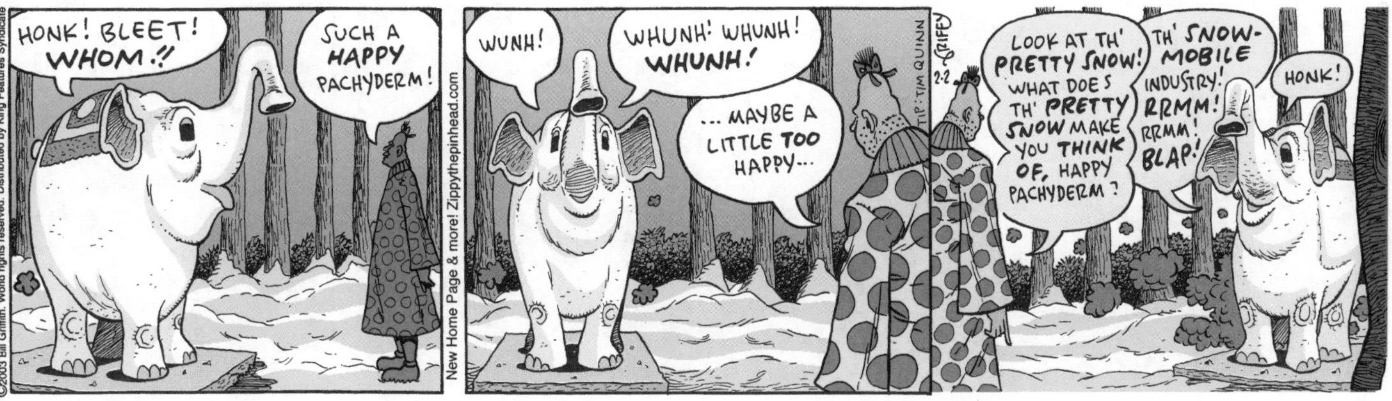

HONK! BLEET! WHOM!!
SUCH A HAPPY PACHYDERM!
WUNH!
WHUNH! WHUNH! WHUNH!
... MAYBE A LITTLE TOO HAPPY...
LOOK AT TH' PRETTY SNOW! WHAT DOES TH' PRETTY SNOW MAKE YOU THINK OF, HAPPY PACHYDERM?
TH' SNOW-MOBILE INDUSTRY! RRMM! RRMM! BLAP!
HONK!
2·2 GRIFFY
TIP: TIM QUINN
©2003 Bill Griffith. World rights reserved. Distributed by King Features Syndicate
New Home Page & more! Zippythepinhead.com

88

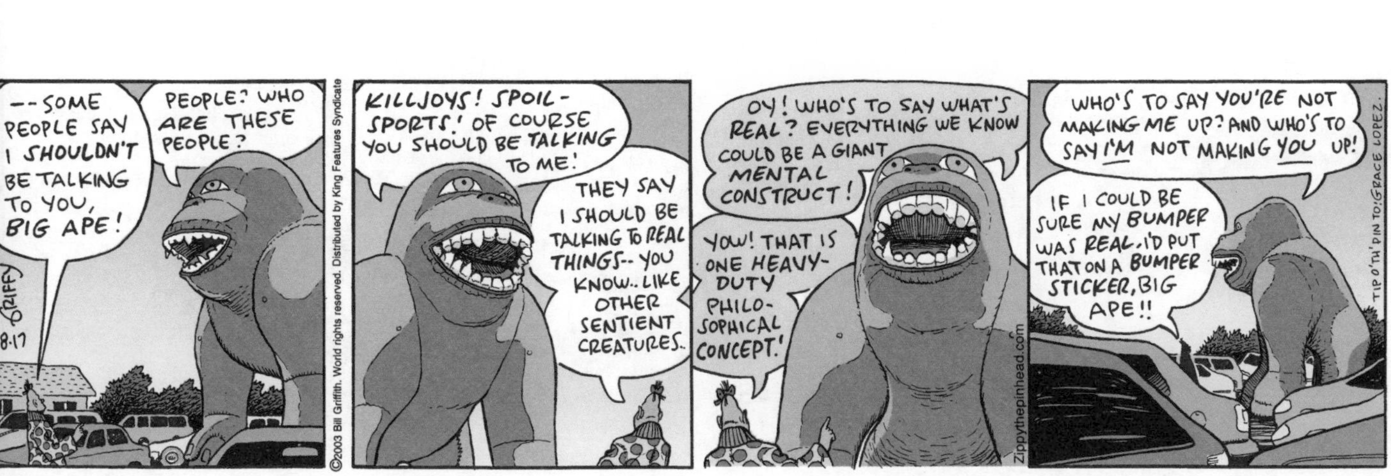

-- SOME PEOPLE SAY I SHOULDN'T BE TALKING TO YOU, BIG APE!
PEOPLE? WHO ARE THESE PEOPLE?
KILLJOYS! SPOIL-SPORTS! OF COURSE YOU SHOULD BE TALKING TO ME!
THEY SAY I SHOULD BE TALKING TO REAL THINGS-- YOU KNOW.. LIKE OTHER SENTIENT CREATURES..
OY! WHO'S TO SAY WHAT'S REAL? EVERYTHING WE KNOW COULD BE A GIANT MENTAL CONSTRUCT!
YOW! THAT IS ONE HEAVY-DUTY PHILOSOPHICAL CONCEPT!
WHO'S TO SAY YOU'RE NOT MAKING ME UP? AND WHO'S TO SAY I'M NOT MAKING YOU UP!
IF I COULD BE SURE MY BUMPER WAS REAL, I'D PUT THAT ON A BUMPER STICKER, BIG APE!!
GRIFFY 8·17
TIP O'TH' DIN TO: GRACE LOPEZ
©2003 Bill Griffith. World rights reserved. Distributed by King Features Syndicate
Zippythepinhead.com

89

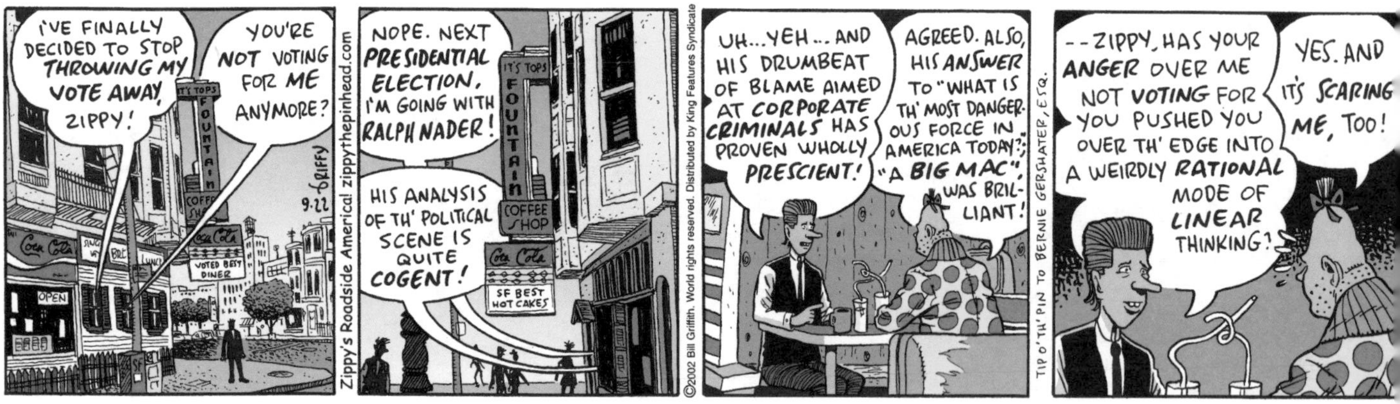
I'VE FINALLY DECIDED TO STOP THROWING MY VOTE AWAY, ZIPPY!
YOU'RE NOT VOTING FOR ME ANYMORE?
IT'S TOPS FOUNTAIN COFFEE SHOP
VOTED BEST DINER
OPEN
GRIFFY 9.22
Zippy's Roadside America! zippythepinhead.com
NOPE. NEXT PRESIDENTIAL ELECTION, I'M GOING WITH RALPH NADER!
HIS ANALYSIS OF TH' POLITICAL SCENE IS QUITE COGENT!
SF BEST HOT CAKES
©2002 Bill Griffith. World rights reserved. Distributed by King Features Syndicate
UH...YEH...AND HIS DRUMBEAT OF BLAME AIMED AT CORPORATE CRIMINALS HAS PROVEN WHOLLY PRESCIENT!
AGREED. ALSO, HIS ANSWER TO "WHAT IS TH' MOST DANGEROUS FORCE IN AMERICA TODAY?"; "A BIG MAC", WAS BRILLIANT!
TIP O' TH' PIN TO BERNIE GERSHATER, ESQ.
--ZIPPY, HAS YOUR ANGER OVER ME NOT VOTING FOR YOU PUSHED YOU OVER TH' EDGE INTO A WEIRDLY RATIONAL MODE OF LINEAR THINKING?
YES. AND IT'S SCARING ME, TOO!

90

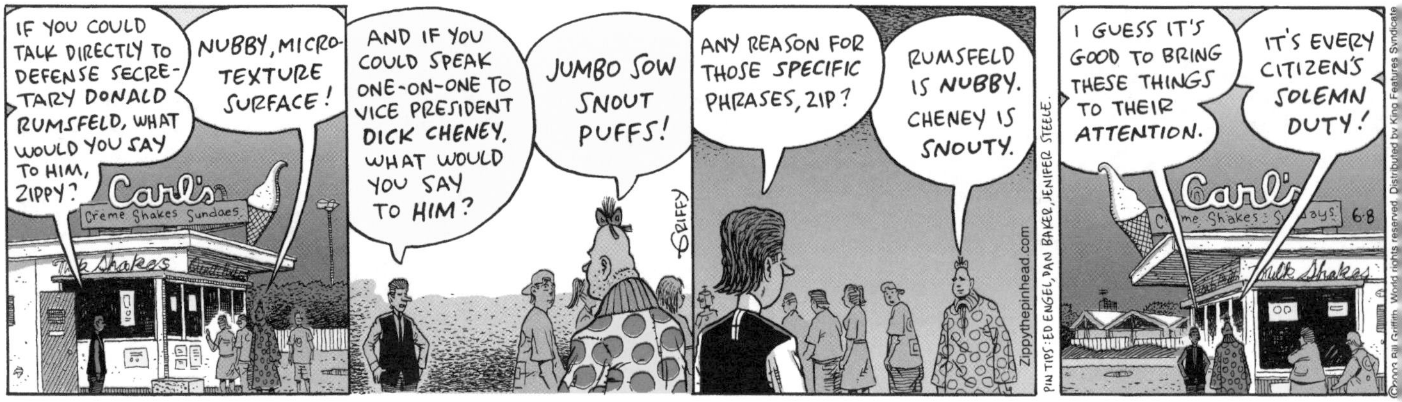
IF YOU COULD TALK DIRECTLY TO DEFENSE SECRETARY DONALD RUMSFELD, WHAT WOULD YOU SAY TO HIM, ZIPPY?
NUBBY, MICRO-TEXTURE SURFACE!
Carl's Crème Shakes Sundaes
AND IF YOU COULD SPEAK ONE-ON-ONE TO VICE PRESIDENT DICK CHENEY, WHAT WOULD YOU SAY TO HIM?
JUMBO SOW SNOUT PUFFS!
GRIFFY
ANY REASON FOR THOSE SPECIFIC PHRASES, ZIP?
RUMSFELD IS NUBBY. CHENEY IS SNOUTY.
zippythepinhead.com
PIN TIPS: ED ENGEL, DAN BAKER, JENIFER STEELE.
I GUESS IT'S GOOD TO BRING THESE THINGS TO THEIR ATTENTION.
IT'S EVERY CITIZEN'S SOLEMN DUTY!
6.8
Milk Shakes
©2003 Bill Griffith. World rights reserved. Distributed by King Features Syndicate

91

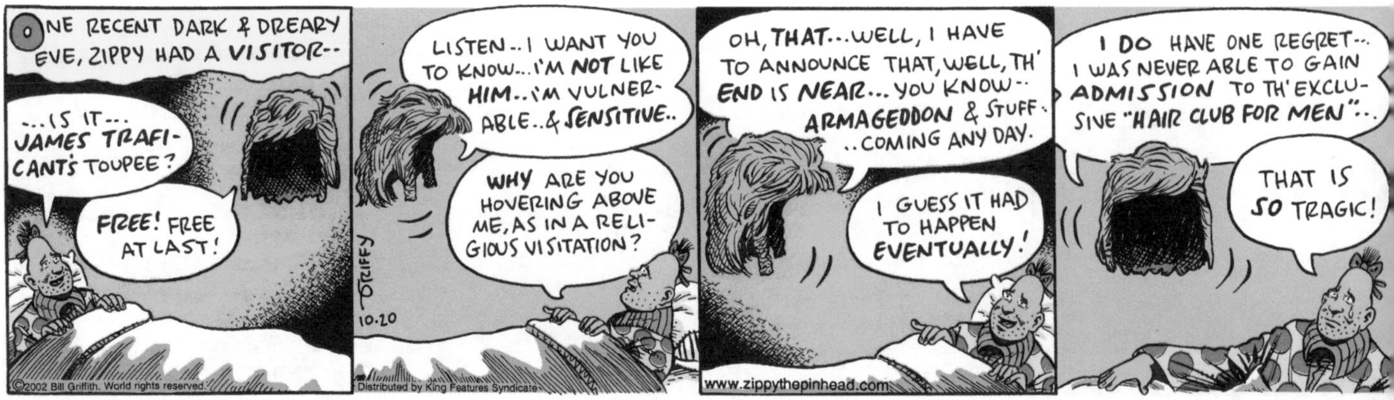
ONE RECENT DARK & DREARY EVE, ZIPPY HAD A VISITOR--
...IS IT... JAMES TRAFICANT'S TOUPEE?
FREE! FREE AT LAST!
©2002 Bill Griffith. World rights reserved.
LISTEN.. I WANT YOU TO KNOW...I'M NOT LIKE HIM..I'M VULNERABLE..& SENSITIVE..
WHY ARE YOU HOVERING ABOVE ME, AS IN A RELIGIOUS VISITATION?
GRIFFY 10.20
Distributed by King Features Syndicate
OH, THAT...WELL, I HAVE TO ANNOUNCE THAT, WELL, TH' END IS NEAR...YOU KNOW-- ARMAGEDDON & STUFF.. ..COMING ANY DAY.
I GUESS IT HAD TO HAPPEN EVENTUALLY!
www.zippythepinhead.com
I DO HAVE ONE REGRET-- I WAS NEVER ABLE TO GAIN ADMISSION TO TH' EXCLUSIVE "HAIR CLUB FOR MEN"..
THAT IS SO TRAGIC!

92

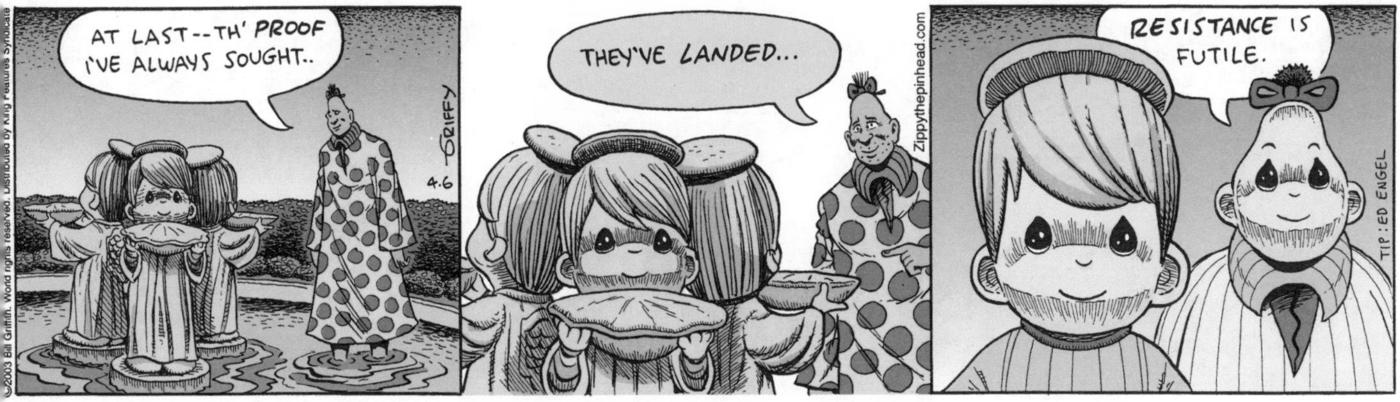

©2003 Bill Griffith. World rights reserved. Distributed by King Features Syndicate
AT LAST--TH' PROOF I'VE ALWAYS SOUGHT..
GRIFFY 4·6
THEY'VE LANDED...
Zippythepinhead.com
RESISTANCE IS FUTILE.
TIP: ED ENGEL

93

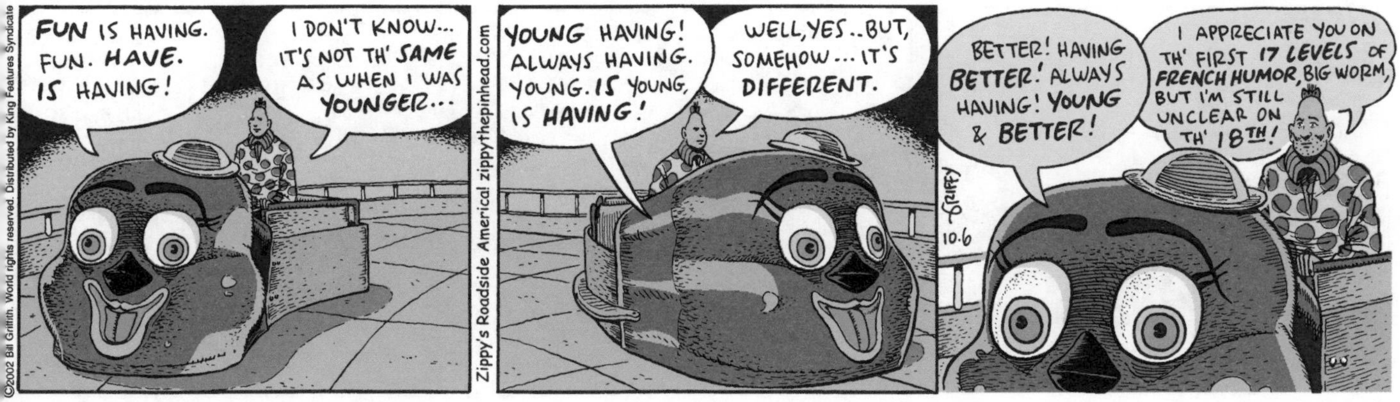

©2002 Bill Griffith. World rights reserved. Distributed by King Features Syndicate
FUN IS HAVING. FUN. HAVE. IS HAVING!
I DON'T KNOW... IT'S NOT TH' SAME AS WHEN I WAS YOUNGER...
Zippy's Roadside America! zippythepinhead.com
YOUNG HAVING! ALWAYS HAVING. YOUNG. IS YOUNG, IS HAVING!
WELL, YES..BUT, SOMEHOW... IT'S DIFFERENT.
GRIFFY 10·6
BETTER! HAVING BETTER! ALWAYS HAVING! YOUNG & BETTER!
I APPRECIATE YOU ON TH' FIRST 17 LEVELS OF FRENCH HUMOR, BIG WORM, BUT I'M STILL UNCLEAR ON TH' 18TH!

94

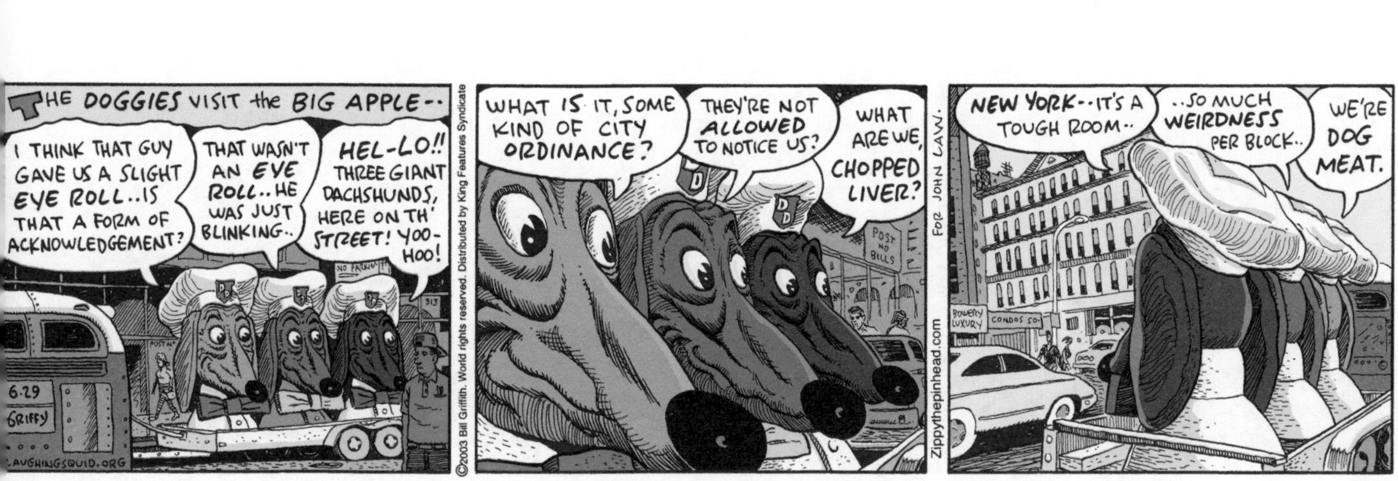

THE DOGGIES VISIT the BIG APPLE--
I THINK THAT GUY GAVE US A SLIGHT EYE ROLL..IS THAT A FORM OF ACKNOWLEDGEMENT?
THAT WASN'T AN EYE ROLL..HE WAS JUST BLINKING..
HEL-LO!! THREE GIANT DACHSHUNDS, HERE ON TH' STREET! YOO-HOO!
6·29 GRIFFY
LAUGHINGSQUID.ORG
©2003 Bill Griffith. World rights reserved. Distributed by King Features Syndicate
WHAT IS IT, SOME KIND OF CITY ORDINANCE?
THEY'RE NOT ALLOWED TO NOTICE US?
WHAT ARE WE, CHOPPED LIVER?
POST NO BILLS
Zippythepinhead.com
FOR JOHN LAW.
NEW YORK--IT'S A TOUGH ROOM..
..SO MUCH WEIRDNESS PER BLOCK..
WE'RE DOG MEAT.

95

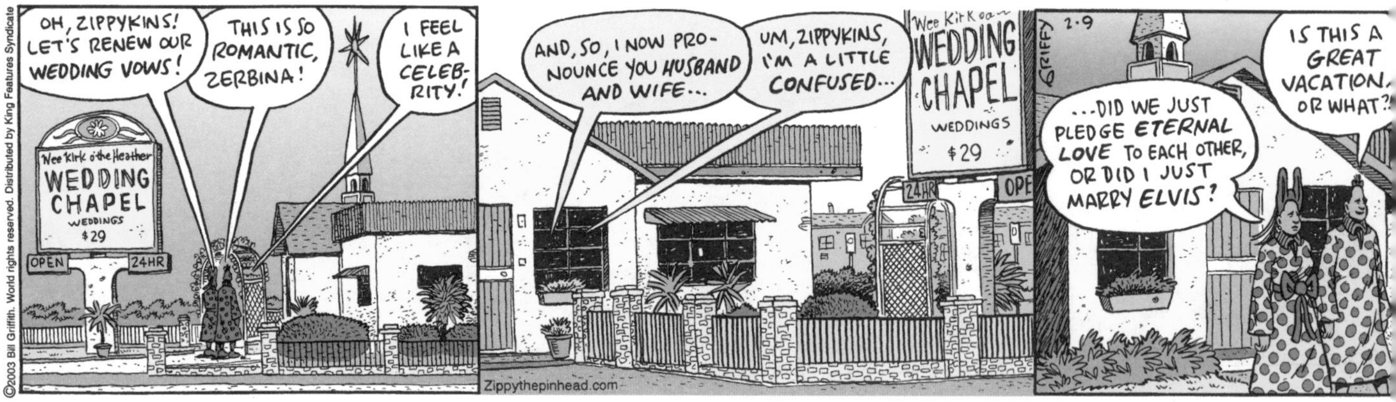
©2003 Bill Griffith. World rights reserved. Distributed by King Features Syndicate
OH, ZIPPYKINS! LET'S RENEW OUR WEDDING VOWS!
THIS IS SO ROMANTIC, ZERBINA!
I FEEL LIKE A CELEB-RITY!
Wee Kirk o'the Heather
WEDDING CHAPEL
WEDDINGS
$29
OPEN
24HR
AND, SO, I NOW PRO-NOUNCE YOU HUSBAND AND WIFE...
UM, ZIPPYKINS, I'M A LITTLE CONFUSED...
WEDDING CHAPEL
WEDDINGS
$29
Zippythepinhead.com
GRIFFY 2·9
...DID WE JUST PLEDGE ETERNAL LOVE TO EACH OTHER, OR DID I JUST MARRY ELVIS?
IS THIS A GREAT VACATION, OR WHAT?!

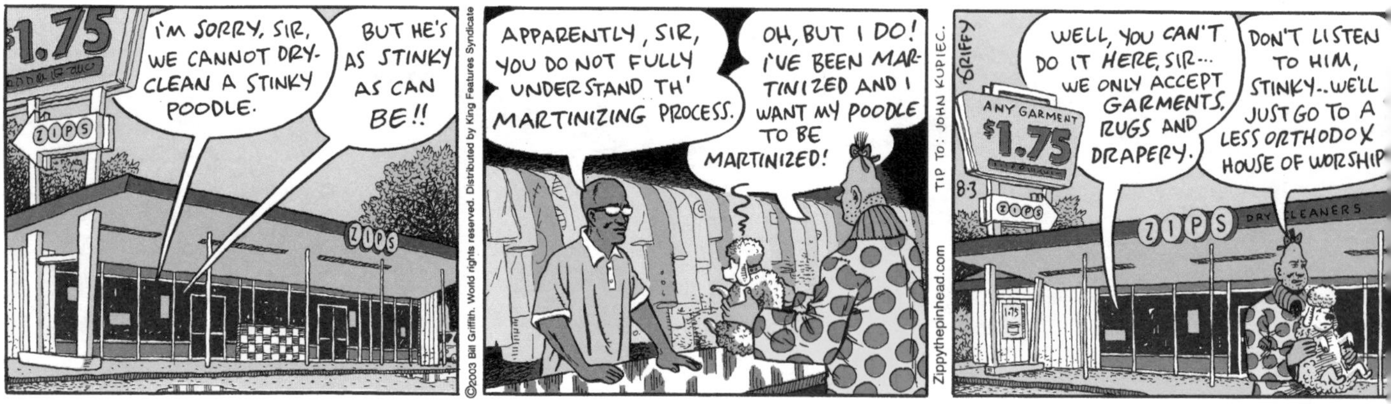
$1.75
ZIPS
I'M SORRY, SIR, WE CANNOT DRY-CLEAN A STINKY POODLE.
BUT HE'S AS STINKY AS CAN BE!!
©2003 Bill Griffith. World rights reserved. Distributed by King Features Syndicate
APPARENTLY, SIR, YOU DO NOT FULLY UNDERSTAND TH' MARTINIZING PROCESS.
OH, BUT I DO! I'VE BEEN MAR-TINIZED AND I WANT MY POODLE TO BE MARTINIZED!
Zippythepinhead.com
TIP TO: JOHN KUPIEC.
GRIFFY 8·3
ANY GARMENT
$1.75
WELL, YOU CAN'T DO IT HERE, SIR... WE ONLY ACCEPT GARMENTS, RUGS AND DRAPERY.
DON'T LISTEN TO HIM, STINKY.. WE'LL JUST GO TO A LESS ORTHODOX HOUSE OF WORSHIP

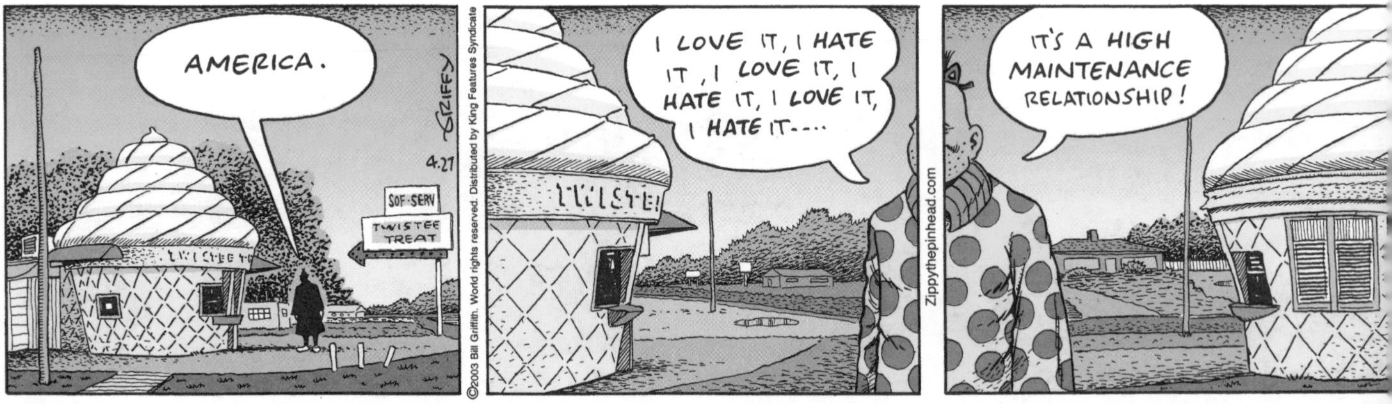
AMERICA.
GRIFFY 4·27
SOF-SERV
TWISTEE TREAT
©2003 Bill Griffith. World rights reserved. Distributed by King Features Syndicate
I LOVE IT, I HATE IT, I LOVE IT, I HATE IT, I LOVE IT, I HATE IT...
Zippythepinhead.com
IT'S A HIGH MAINTENANCE RELATIONSHIP!

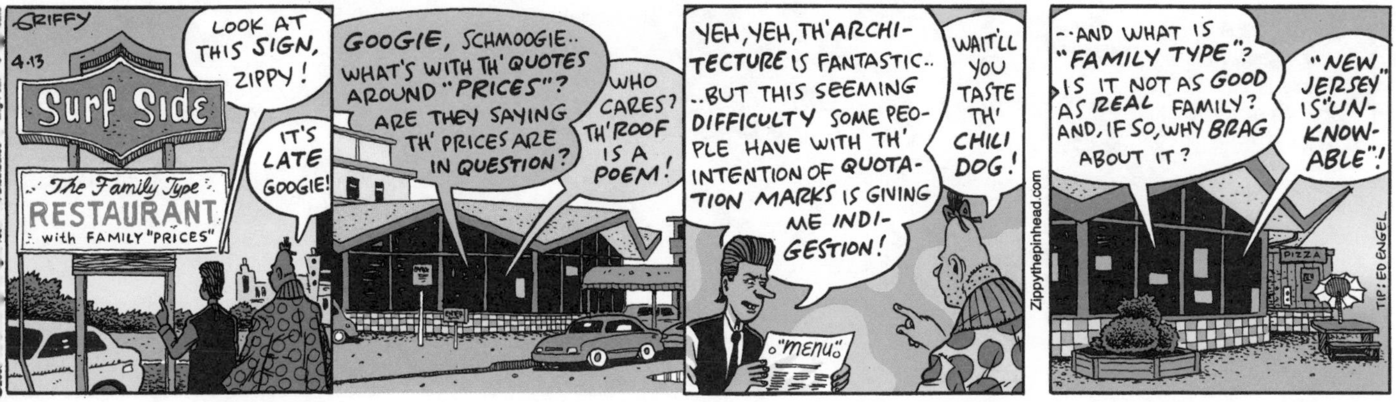
GRIFFY
4·13
Surf Side
The Family Type RESTAURANT with FAMILY "PRICES"
LOOK AT THIS SIGN, ZIPPY!
IT'S LATE GOOGIE!
GOOGIE, SCHMOOGIE.. WHAT'S WITH TH' QUOTES AROUND "PRICES"? ARE THEY SAYING TH' PRICES ARE IN QUESTION?
WHO CARES? TH' ROOF IS A POEM!
YEH, YEH, TH' ARCHITECTURE IS FANTASTIC.. ..BUT THIS SEEMING DIFFICULTY SOME PEOPLE HAVE WITH TH' INTENTION OF QUOTATION MARKS IS GIVING ME INDIGESTION!
WAIT'LL YOU TASTE TH' CHILI DOG!
"MENU"
Zippythepinhead.com
..AND WHAT IS "FAMILY TYPE"? IS IT NOT AS GOOD AS REAL FAMILY? AND, IF SO, WHY BRAG ABOUT IT?
"NEW JERSEY" IS "UNKNOWABLE"!
PIZZA
TIP: ED ENGEL

99

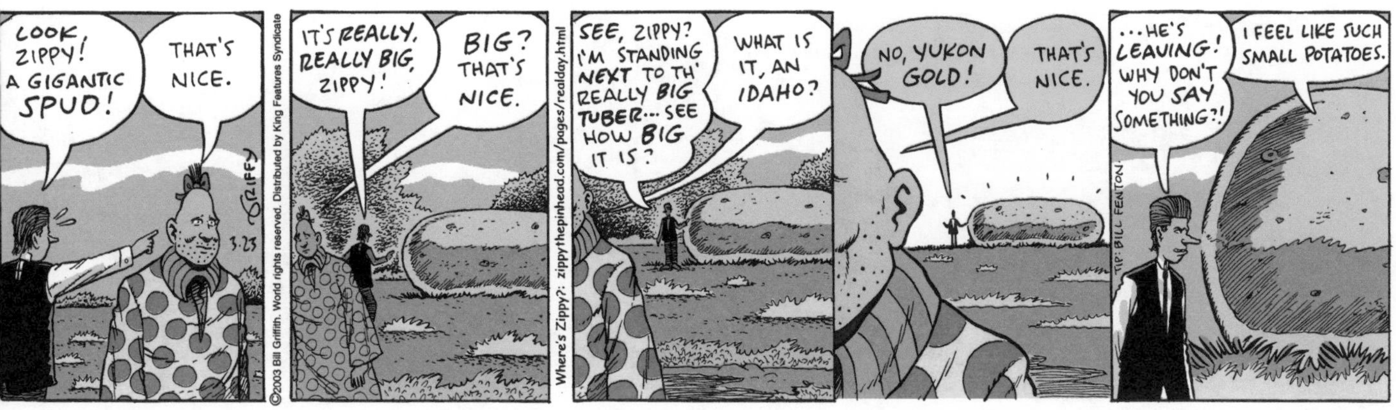
LOOK, ZIPPY! A GIGANTIC SPUD!
THAT'S NICE.
GRIFFY
3·23
©2003 Bill Griffith. World rights reserved. Distributed by King Features Syndicate
IT'S REALLY, REALLY BIG, ZIPPY!
BIG? THAT'S NICE.
Where's Zippy?: zippythepinhead.com/pages/realday.html
SEE, ZIPPY? I'M STANDING NEXT TO TH' REALLY BIG TUBER... SEE HOW BIG IT IS?
WHAT IS IT, AN IDAHO?
NO, YUKON GOLD!
THAT'S NICE.
...HE'S LEAVING! WHY DON'T YOU SAY SOMETHING?!
I FEEL LIKE SUCH SMALL POTATOES.
TIP: BILL FENTON.

100

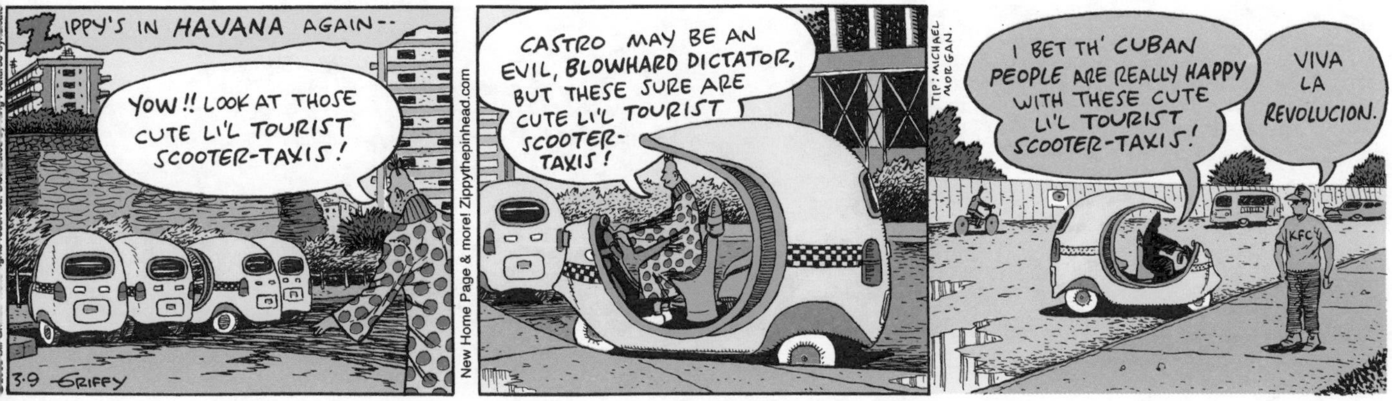
ZIPPY'S IN HAVANA AGAIN--
YOW!! LOOK AT THOSE CUTE LI'L TOURIST SCOOTER-TAXIS!
3·9 GRIFFY
New Home Page & more! Zippythepinhead.com
CASTRO MAY BE AN EVIL, BLOWHARD DICTATOR, BUT THESE SURE ARE CUTE LI'L TOURIST SCOOTER-TAXIS!
TIP: MICHAEL MORGAN.
I BET TH' CUBAN PEOPLE ARE REALLY HAPPY WITH THESE CUTE LI'L TOURIST SCOOTER-TAXIS!
VIVA LA REVOLUCION.
KFC

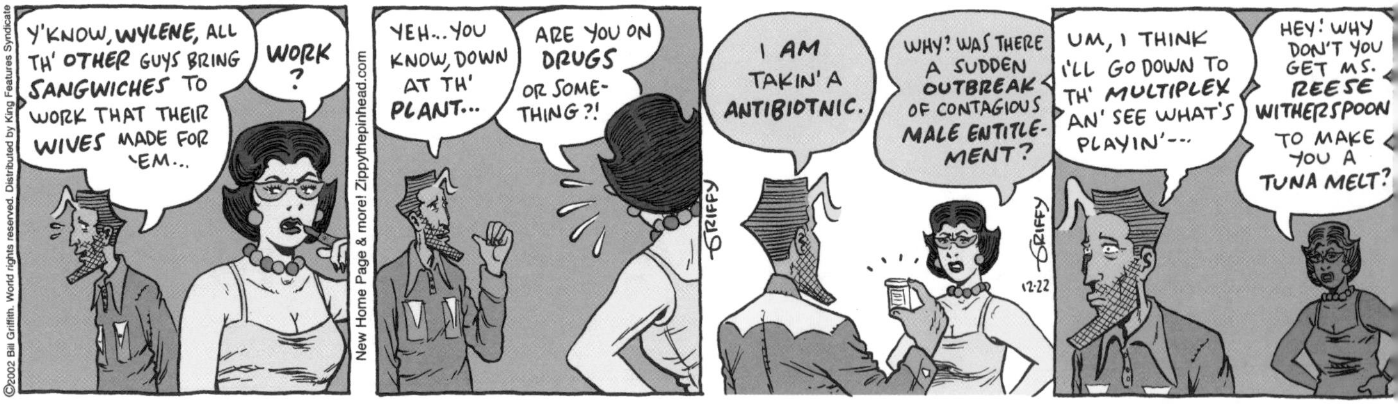
Y'KNOW, WYLENE, ALL TH' OTHER GUYS BRING SANGWICHES TO WORK THAT THEIR WIVES MADE FOR 'EM...
WORK?
YEH... YOU KNOW, DOWN AT TH' PLANT...
ARE YOU ON DRUGS OR SOMETHING?!
I AM TAKIN' A ANTIBIOTNIC.
WHY? WAS THERE A SUDDEN OUTBREAK OF CONTAGIOUS MALE ENTITLEMENT?
UM, I THINK I'LL GO DOWN TO TH' MULTIPLEX AN' SEE WHAT'S PLAYIN'--.
HEY! WHY DON'T YOU GET MS. REESE WITHERSPOON TO MAKE YOU A TUNA MELT?
GRIFFY
12-22
©2002 Bill Griffith. World rights reserved. Distributed by King Features Syndicate
New Home Page & more! Zippythepinhead.com

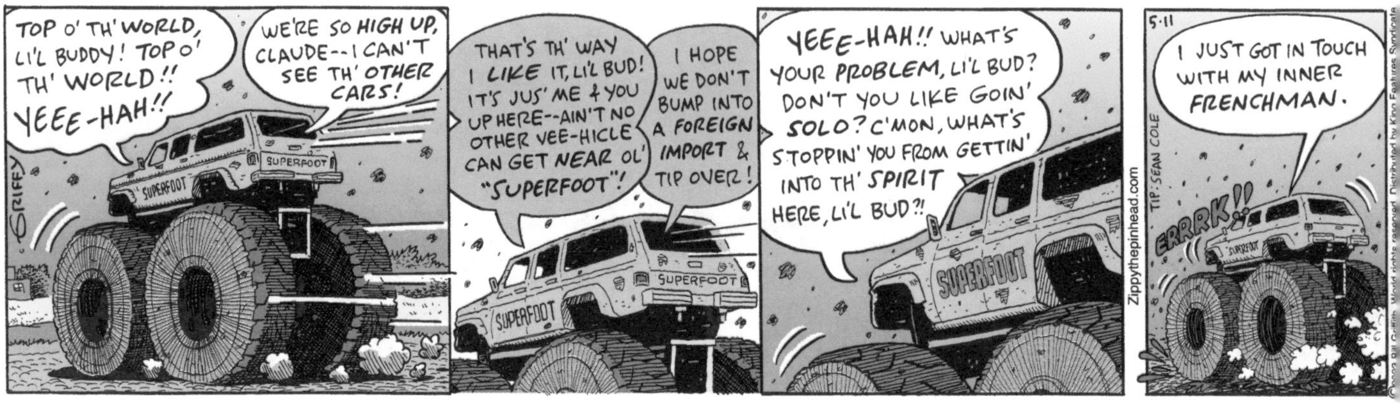
TOP O' TH' WORLD, LI'L BUDDY! TOP O' TH' WORLD!! YEEE-HAH!!
WE'RE SO HIGH UP, CLAUDE--I CAN'T SEE TH' OTHER CARS!
SUPERFOOT
GRIFFY
THAT'S TH' WAY I LIKE IT, LI'L BUD! IT'S JUS' ME & YOU UP HERE--AIN'T NO OTHER VEE-HICLE CAN GET NEAR OL' "SUPERFOOT"!
I HOPE WE DON'T BUMP INTO A FOREIGN IMPORT & TIP OVER!
YEEE-HAH!! WHAT'S YOUR PROBLEM, LI'L BUD? DON'T YOU LIKE GOIN' SOLO? C'MON, WHAT'S STOPPIN' YOU FROM GETTIN' INTO TH' SPIRIT HERE, LI'L BUD?!
Zippythepinhead.com
TIP: SEAN COLE
5-11
I JUST GOT IN TOUCH WITH MY INNER FRENCHMAN.
ERRRK!!

101

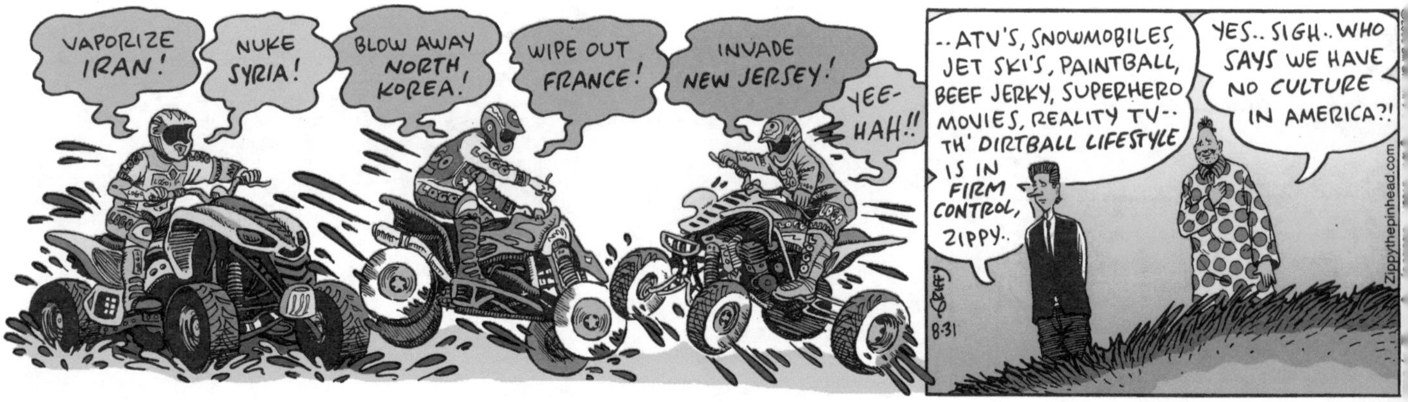
VAPORIZE IRAN!
NUKE SYRIA!
BLOW AWAY NORTH KOREA!
WIPE OUT FRANCE!
INVADE NEW JERSEY!
YEE-HAH!!
--ATV'S, SNOWMOBILES, JET SKI'S, PAINTBALL, BEEF JERKY, SUPERHERO MOVIES, REALITY TV-- TH' DIRTBALL LIFESTYLE IS IN FIRM CONTROL, ZIPPY..
YES.. SIGH.. WHO SAYS WE HAVE NO CULTURE IN AMERICA?!
GRIFFY
8-31
Zippythepinhead.com

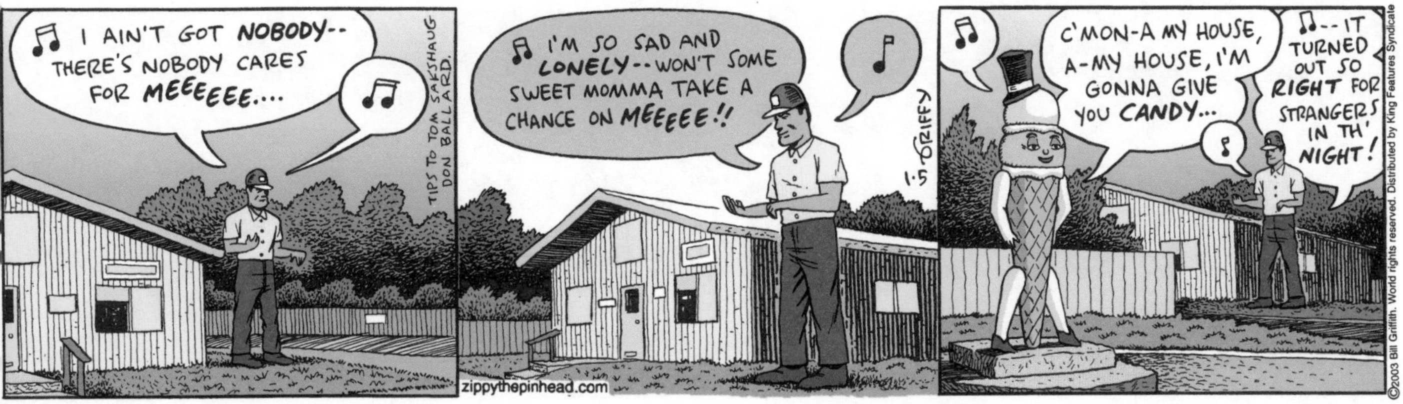
I AIN'T GOT NOBODY-- THERE'S NOBODY CARES FOR MEEEEEE....
TIPS TO TOM SAKSHAUG DON BALLARD.
I'M SO SAD AND LONELY--WON'T SOME SWEET MOMMA TAKE A CHANCE ON MEEEEE!!
GRIFFY
zippythepinhead.com
C'MON-A MY HOUSE, A-MY HOUSE, I'M GONNA GIVE YOU CANDY...
--IT TURNED OUT SO RIGHT FOR STRANGERS IN TH' NIGHT!
©2003 Bill Griffith. World rights reserved. Distributed by King Features Syndicate

102

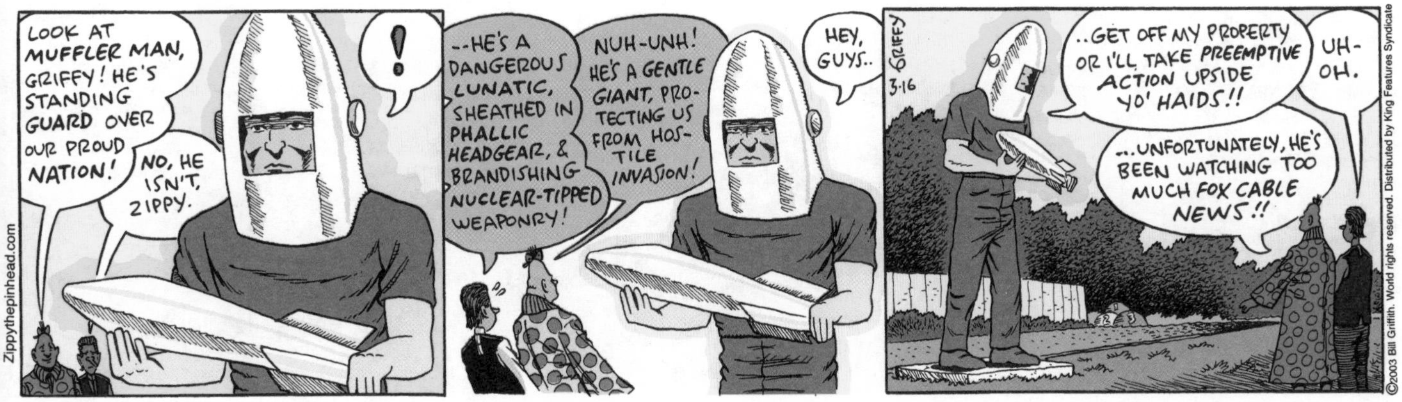
LOOK AT MUFFLER MAN, GRIFFY! HE'S STANDING GUARD OVER OUR PROUD NATION!
!
NO, HE ISN'T, ZIPPY.
zippythepinhead.com
--HE'S A DANGEROUS LUNATIC, SHEATHED IN PHALLIC HEADGEAR, & BRANDISHING NUCLEAR-TIPPED WEAPONRY!
NUH-UNH! HE'S A GENTLE GIANT, PROTECTING US FROM HOSTILE INVASION!
HEY, GUYS..
GRIFFY 3·16
..GET OFF MY PROPERTY OR I'LL TAKE PREEMPTIVE ACTION UPSIDE YO' HAIDS!!
UH-OH.
...UNFORTUNATELY, HE'S BEEN WATCHING TOO MUCH FOX CABLE NEWS!!
©2003 Bill Griffith. World rights reserved. Distributed by King Features Syndicate

103

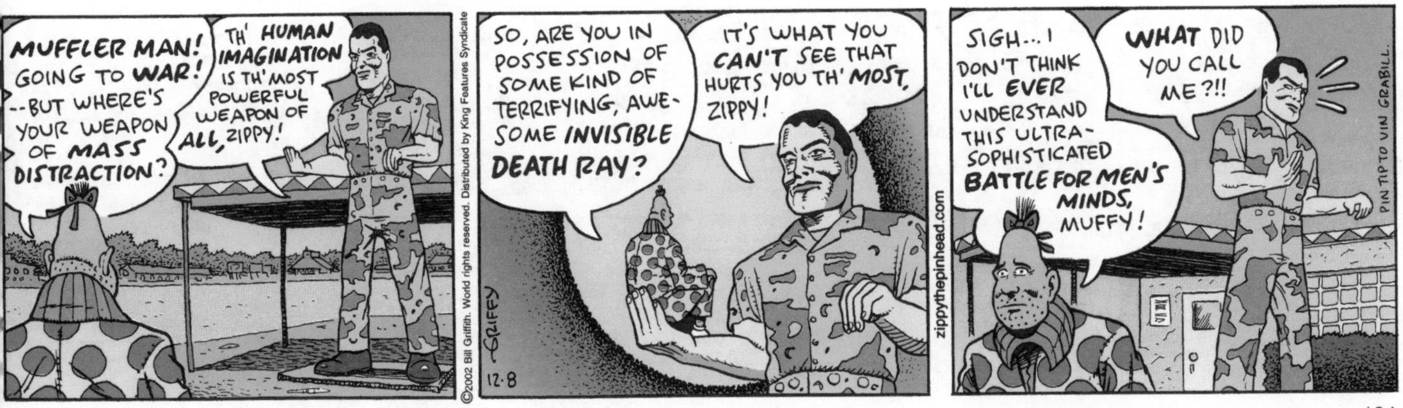
MUFFLER MAN! GOING TO WAR! --BUT WHERE'S YOUR WEAPON OF MASS DISTRACTION?
TH' HUMAN IMAGINATION IS TH' MOST POWERFUL WEAPON OF ALL, ZIPPY!
©2002 Bill Griffith. World rights reserved. Distributed by King Features Syndicate
SO, ARE YOU IN POSSESSION OF SOME KIND OF TERRIFYING, AWESOME INVISIBLE DEATH RAY?
IT'S WHAT YOU CAN'T SEE THAT HURTS YOU TH' MOST, ZIPPY!
GRIFFY 12·8
zippythepinhead.com
SIGH... I DON'T THINK I'LL EVER UNDERSTAND THIS ULTRA-SOPHISTICATED BATTLE FOR MEN'S MINDS, MUFFY!
WHAT DID YOU CALL ME?!!
PIN TIP TO VIN GRABILL.

104

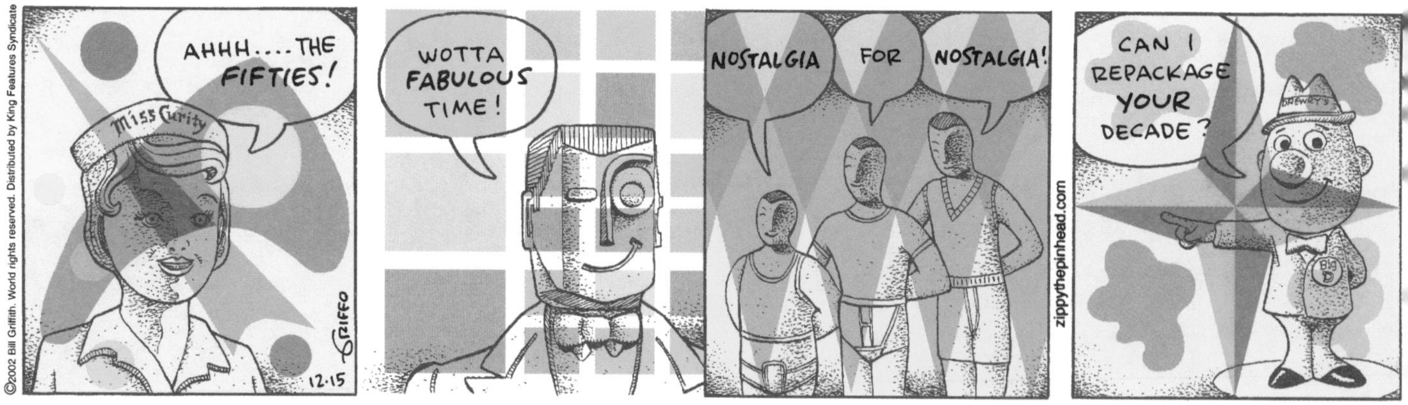
©2002 Bill Griffith. World rights reserved. Distributed by King Features Syndicate
AHHH.... THE FIFTIES!
Miss Curity
GRIFFO
12.15
WOTTA FABULOUS TIME!
NOSTALGIA
FOR
NOSTALGIA!
zippythepinhead.com
CAN I REPACKAGE YOUR DECADE?
DREWRY'S
BIG D

105

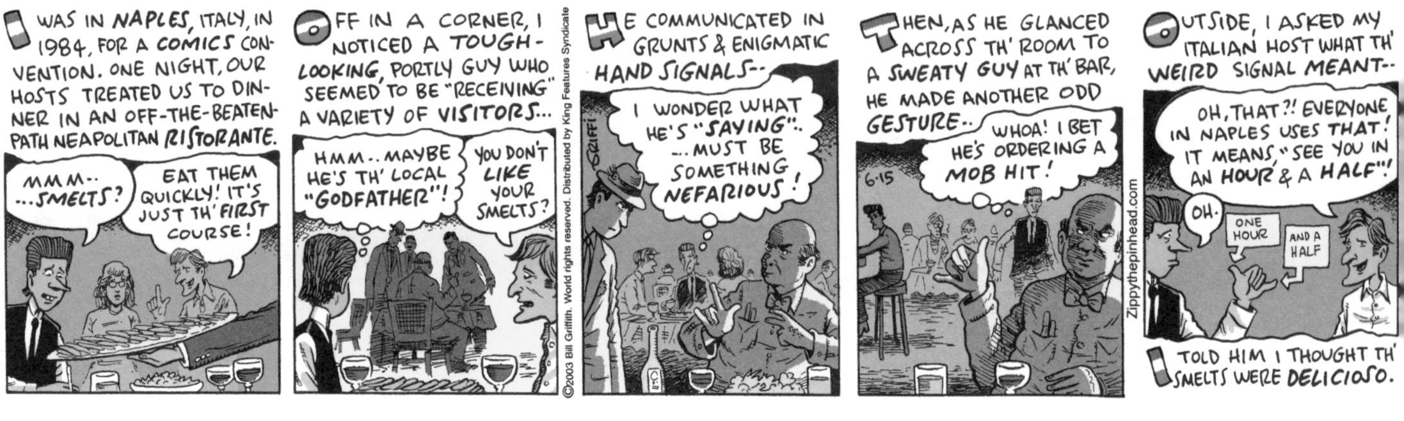
I WAS IN NAPLES, ITALY, IN 1984, FOR A COMICS CONVENTION. ONE NIGHT, OUR HOSTS TREATED US TO DINNER IN AN OFF-THE-BEATEN-PATH NEAPOLITAN RISTORANTE.
MMM.. ...SMELTS?
EAT THEM QUICKLY! IT'S JUST TH' FIRST COURSE!
OFF IN A CORNER, I NOTICED A TOUGH-LOOKING, PORTLY GUY WHO SEEMED TO BE "RECEIVING" A VARIETY OF VISITORS...
HMM.. MAYBE HE'S TH' LOCAL "GODFATHER"!
YOU DON'T LIKE YOUR SMELTS?
©2003 Bill Griffith. World rights reserved. Distributed by King Features Syndicate
HE COMMUNICATED IN GRUNTS & ENIGMATIC HAND SIGNALS--
I WONDER WHAT HE'S "SAYING".. ...MUST BE SOMETHING NEFARIOUS!
GRIFFI
THEN, AS HE GLANCED ACROSS TH' ROOM TO A SWEATY GUY AT TH' BAR, HE MADE ANOTHER ODD GESTURE..
WHOA! I BET HE'S ORDERING A MOB HIT!
6.15
Zippythepinhead.com
OUTSIDE, I ASKED MY ITALIAN HOST WHAT TH' WEIRD SIGNAL MEANT--
OH, THAT?! EVERYONE IN NAPLES USES THAT! IT MEANS, "SEE YOU IN AN HOUR & A HALF"!
OH.
ONE HOUR
AND A HALF
I TOLD HIM I THOUGHT TH' SMELTS WERE DELICIOSO.

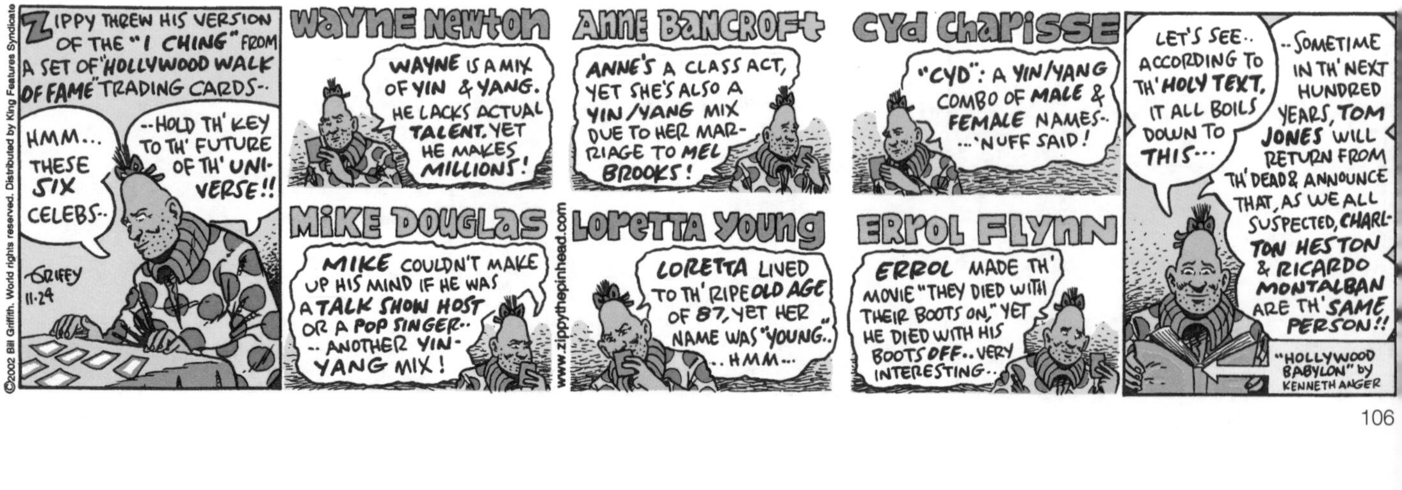
©2002 Bill Griffith. World rights reserved. Distributed by King Features Syndicate
ZIPPY THREW HIS VERSION OF THE "I CHING" FROM A SET OF "HOLLYWOOD WALK OF FAME" TRADING CARDS--
HMM... THESE SIX CELEBS..
--HOLD TH' KEY TO TH' FUTURE OF TH' UNIVERSE!!
GRIFFY
11.24
WAYNE NEWTON
WAYNE IS A MIX OF YIN & YANG. HE LACKS ACTUAL TALENT, YET HE MAKES MILLIONS!
MIKE DOUGLAS
MIKE COULDN'T MAKE UP HIS MIND IF HE WAS A TALK SHOW HOST OR A POP SINGER.. --ANOTHER YIN-YANG MIX!
www.zippythepinhead.com
ANNE BANCROFT
ANNE'S A CLASS ACT, YET SHE'S ALSO A YIN/YANG MIX DUE TO HER MARRIAGE TO MEL BROOKS!
LORETTA YOUNG
LORETTA LIVED TO TH' RIPE OLD AGE OF 87, YET HER NAME WAS "YOUNG".. ..HMM...
CYD CHARISSE
"CYD": A YIN/YANG COMBO OF MALE & FEMALE NAMES.. ...'NUFF SAID!
ERROL FLYNN
ERROL MADE TH' MOVIE "THEY DIED WITH THEIR BOOTS ON," YET HE DIED WITH HIS BOOTS OFF.. VERY INTERESTING..
LET'S SEE.. ACCORDING TO TH' HOLY TEXT, IT ALL BOILS DOWN TO THIS...
--SOMETIME IN TH' NEXT HUNDRED YEARS, TOM JONES WILL RETURN FROM TH' DEAD & ANNOUNCE THAT, AS WE ALL SUSPECTED, CHARLTON HESTON & RICARDO MONTALBAN ARE TH' SAME PERSON!!
"HOLLYWOOD BABYLON" BY KENNETH ANGER

106

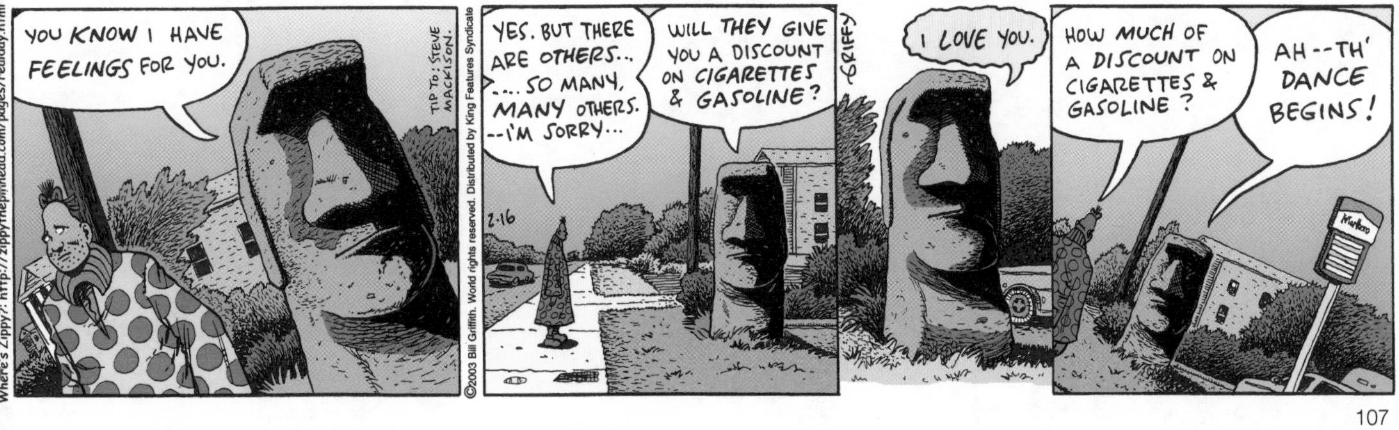

YOU KNOW I HAVE FEELINGS FOR YOU.
TIP TO: STEVE MACKISON.
YES. BUT THERE ARE OTHERS.. ....SO MANY, MANY OTHERS. --I'M SORRY...
WILL THEY GIVE YOU A DISCOUNT ON CIGARETTES & GASOLINE?
2·16
GRIFFY
I LOVE YOU.
HOW MUCH OF A DISCOUNT ON CIGARETTES & GASOLINE?
AH--TH' DANCE BEGINS!
©2003 Bill Griffith. World rights reserved. Distributed by King Features Syndicate

107

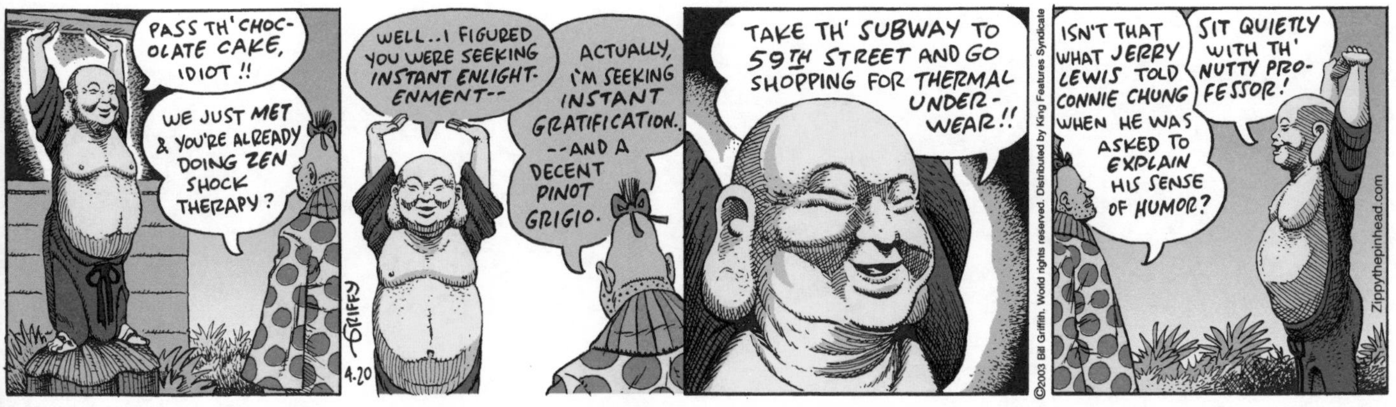

PASS TH' CHOC-OLATE CAKE, IDIOT!!
WE JUST MET & YOU'RE ALREADY DOING ZEN SHOCK THERAPY?
WELL..I FIGURED YOU WERE SEEKING INSTANT ENLIGHT-ENMENT--
ACTUALLY, I'M SEEKING INSTANT GRATIFICATION.. --AND A DECENT PINOT GRIGIO.
GRIFFY
4·20
TAKE TH' SUBWAY TO 59TH STREET AND GO SHOPPING FOR THERMAL UNDER-WEAR!!
ISN'T THAT WHAT JERRY LEWIS TOLD CONNIE CHUNG WHEN HE WAS ASKED TO EXPLAIN HIS SENSE OF HUMOR?
SIT QUIETLY WITH TH' NUTTY PRO-FESSOR!
©2003 Bill Griffith. World rights reserved. Distributed by King Features Syndicate
Zippythepinhead.com

108

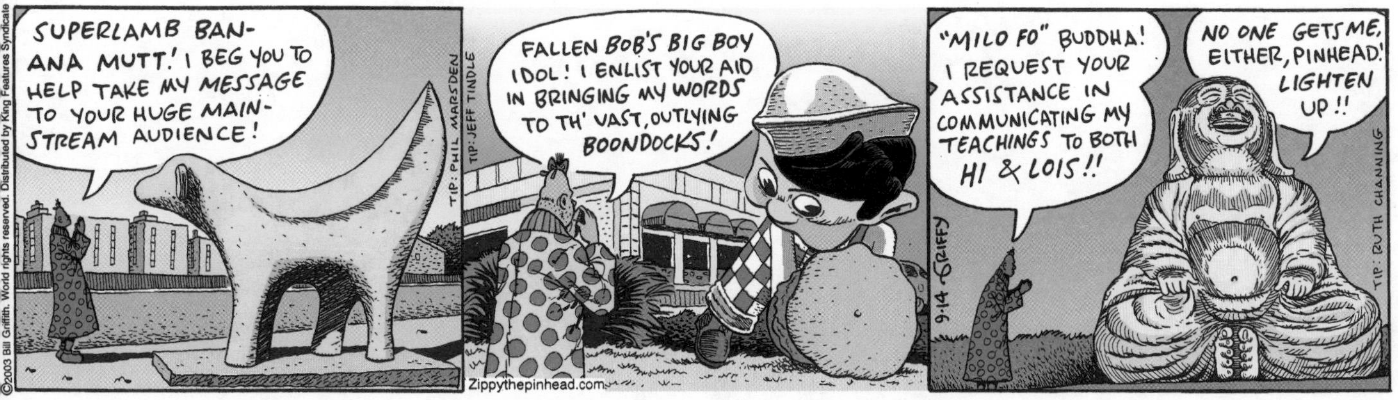

SUPERLAMB BAN-ANA MUTT! I BEG YOU TO HELP TAKE MY MESSAGE TO YOUR HUGE MAIN-STREAM AUDIENCE!
TIP: PHIL MARSDEN
TIP: JEFF TINDLE
FALLEN BOB'S BIG BOY IDOL! I ENLIST YOUR AID IN BRINGING MY WORDS TO TH' VAST, OUTLYING BOONDOCKS!
"MILO FO" BUDDHA! I REQUEST YOUR ASSISTANCE IN COMMUNICATING MY TEACHINGS TO BOTH HI & LOIS!!
9·14 GRIFFY
NO ONE GETS ME, EITHER, PINHEAD! LIGHTEN UP!!
TIP: RUTH CHANNING
©2003 Bill Griffith. World rights reserved. Distributed by King Features Syndicate
Zippythepinhead.com

109

Dinerama

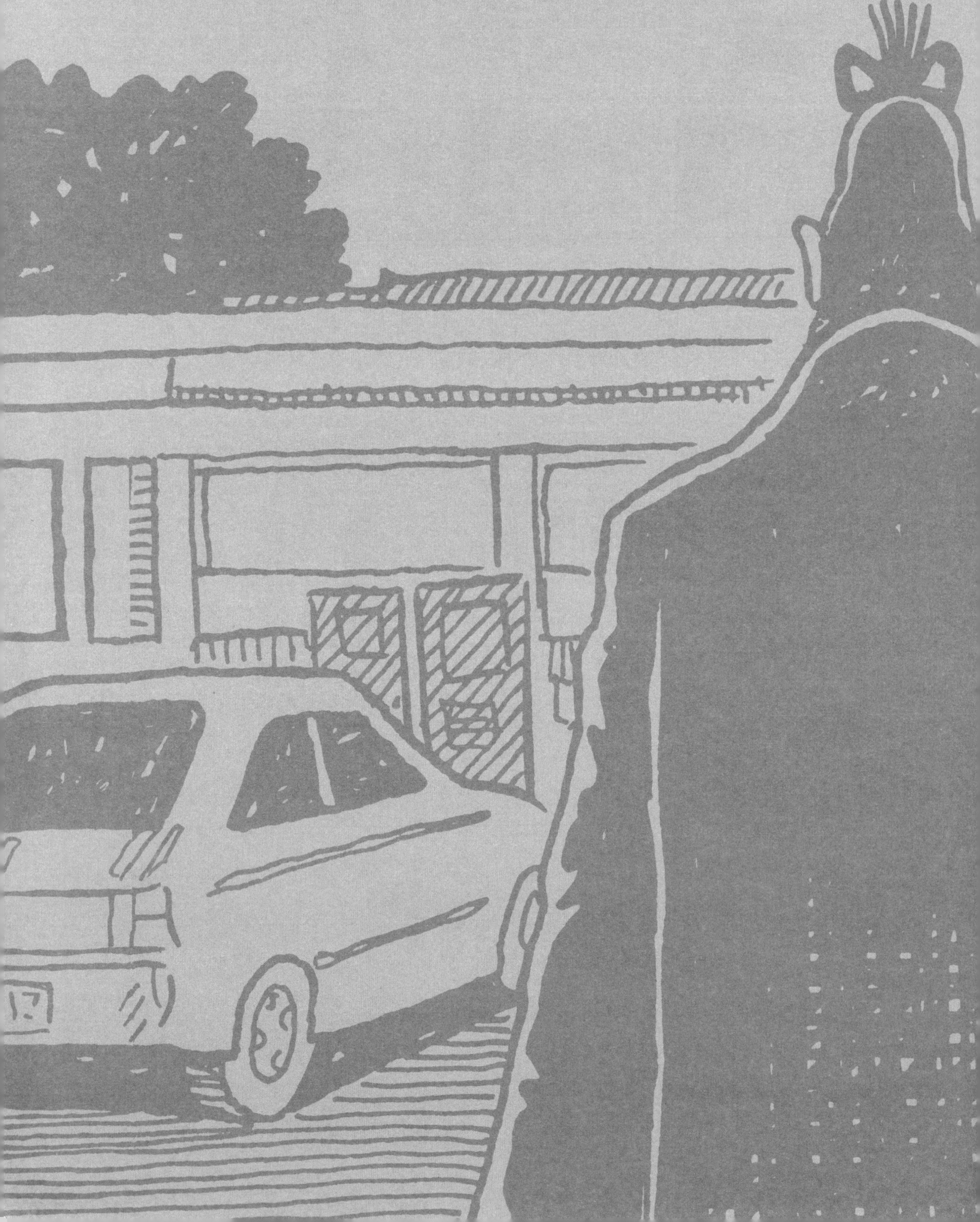

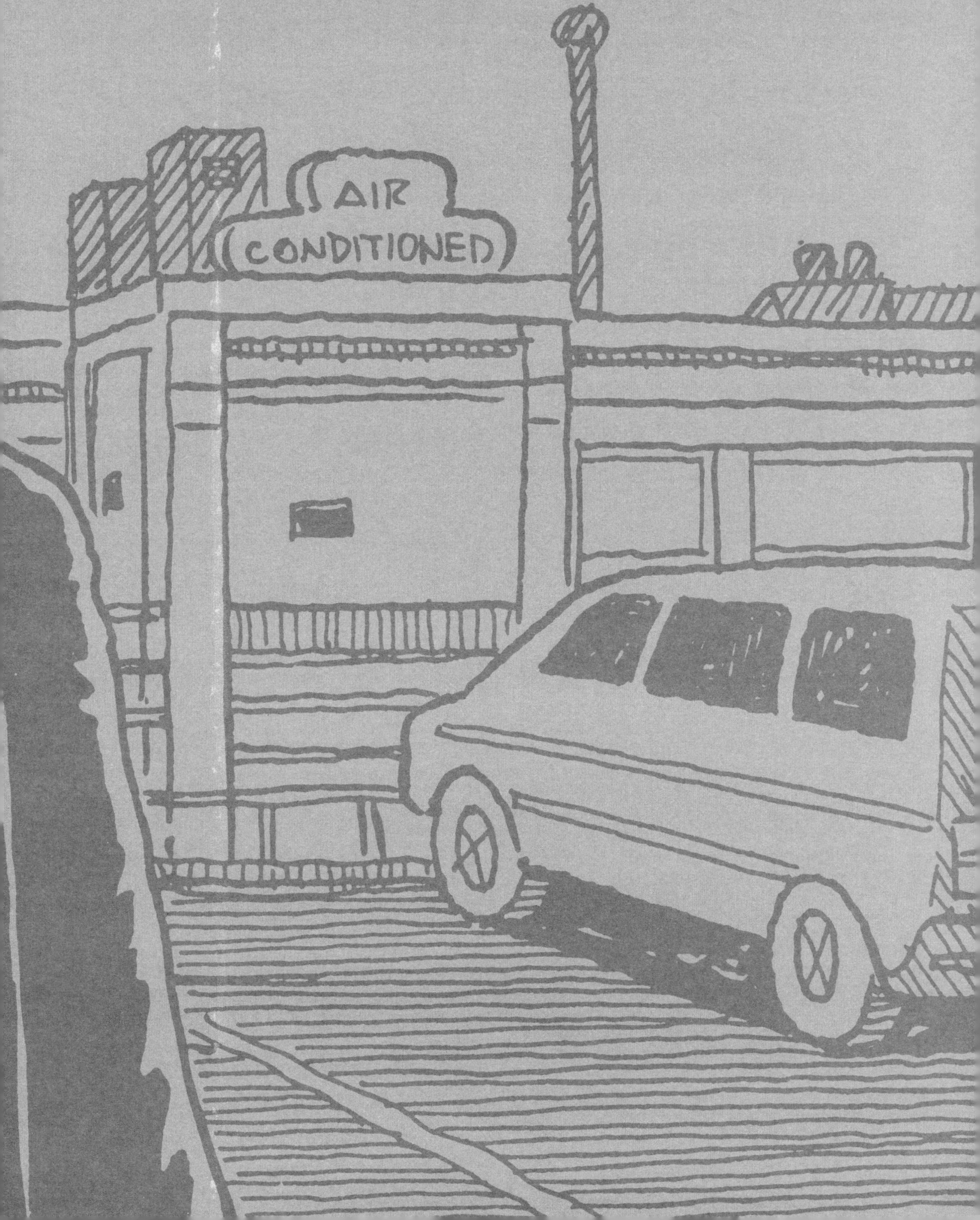
AIR
CONDITIONED

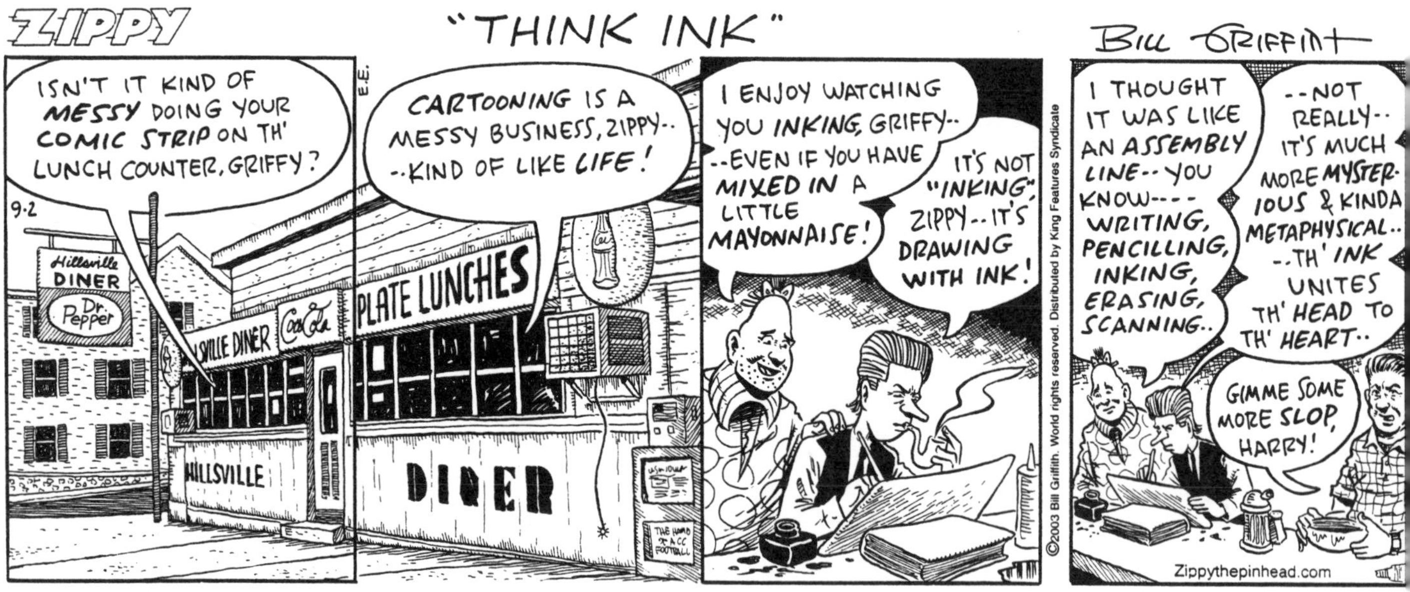
ZIPPY
"THINK INK"
BILL GRIFFITH
ISN'T IT KIND OF MESSY DOING YOUR COMIC STRIP ON TH' LUNCH COUNTER, GRIFFY?
CARTOONING IS A MESSY BUSINESS, ZIPPY.. ..KIND OF LIKE LIFE!
Hillsville DINER
Dr. Pepper
PLATE LUNCHES
HILLSVILLE
DINER
I ENJOY WATCHING YOU INKING, GRIFFY.. ..EVEN IF YOU HAVE MIXED IN A LITTLE MAYONNAISE!
IT'S NOT "INKING", ZIPPY.. IT'S DRAWING WITH INK!
©2003 Bill Griffith. World rights reserved. Distributed by King Features Syndicate
I THOUGHT IT WAS LIKE AN ASSEMBLY LINE.. YOU KNOW.... WRITING, PENCILLING, INKING, ERASING, SCANNING..
..NOT REALLY.. IT'S MUCH MORE MYSTERIOUS & KINDA METAPHYSICAL.. ..TH' INK UNITES TH' HEAD TO TH' HEART..
GIMME SOME MORE SLOP, HARRY!
Zippythepinhead.com

110 A

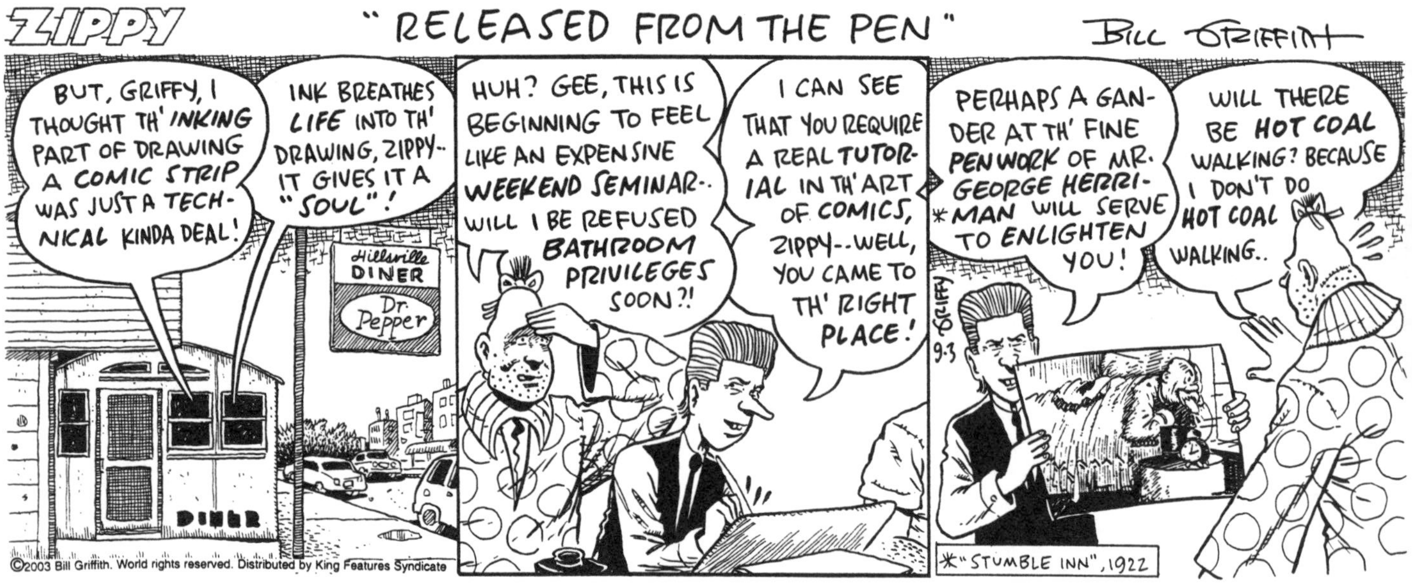
ZIPPY
"RELEASED FROM THE PEN"
BILL GRIFFITH
BUT, GRIFFY, I THOUGHT TH' INKING PART OF DRAWING A COMIC STRIP WAS JUST A TECHNICAL KINDA DEAL!
INK BREATHES LIFE INTO TH' DRAWING, ZIPPY.. IT GIVES IT A "SOUL"!
Hillsville DINER
Dr. Pepper
DINER
©2003 Bill Griffith. World rights reserved. Distributed by King Features Syndicate
HUH? GEE, THIS IS BEGINNING TO FEEL LIKE AN EXPENSIVE WEEKEND SEMINAR.. WILL I BE REFUSED BATHROOM PRIVILEGES SOON?!
I CAN SEE THAT YOU REQUIRE A REAL TUTORIAL IN TH' ART OF COMICS, ZIPPY.. WELL, YOU CAME TO TH' RIGHT PLACE!
PERHAPS A GANDER AT TH' FINE PENWORK OF MR. GEORGE HERRIMAN* WILL SERVE TO ENLIGHTEN YOU!
WILL THERE BE HOT COAL WALKING? BECAUSE I DON'T DO HOT COAL WALKING..
*"STUMBLE INN", 1922

110 B

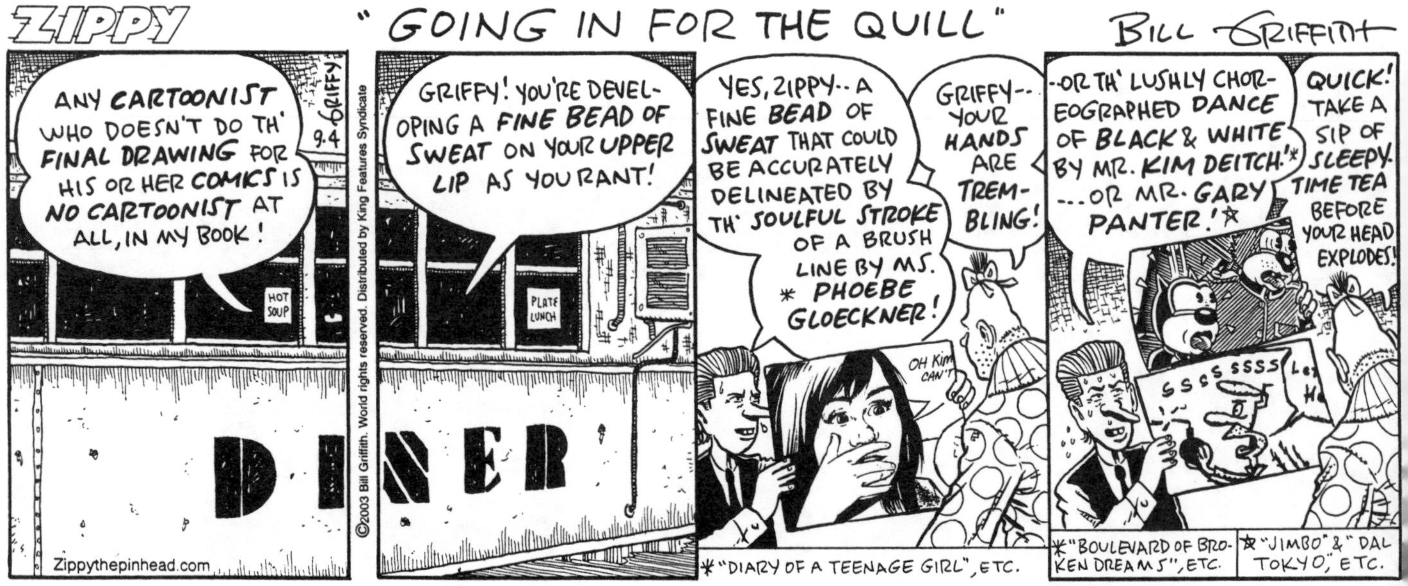
ZIPPY
"GOING IN FOR THE QUILL"
BILL GRIFFITH
ANY CARTOONIST WHO DOESN'T DO TH' FINAL DRAWING FOR HIS OR HER COMICS IS NO CARTOONIST AT ALL, IN MY BOOK!
HOT SOUP
Zippythepinhead.com
©2003 Bill Griffith. World rights reserved. Distributed by King Features Syndicate
GRIFFY! YOU'RE DEVELOPING A FINE BEAD OF SWEAT ON YOUR UPPER LIP AS YOU RANT!
PLATE LUNCH
DINER
YES, ZIPPY.. A FINE BEAD OF SWEAT THAT COULD BE ACCURATELY DELINEATED BY TH' SOULFUL STROKE OF A BRUSH LINE BY MS. PHOEBE GLOECKNER!*
GRIFFY.. YOUR HANDS ARE TREMBLING!
*"DIARY OF A TEENAGE GIRL", ETC.
..OR TH' LUSHLY CHOREOGRAPHED DANCE OF BLACK & WHITE BY MR. KIM DEITCH!* ...OR MR. GARY PANTER!☆
QUICK! TAKE A SIP OF SLEEPY-TIME TEA BEFORE YOUR HEAD EXPLODES!
*"BOULEVARD OF BROKEN DREAMS", ETC.
☆"JIMBO" & "DAL TOKYO", ETC.

110 C

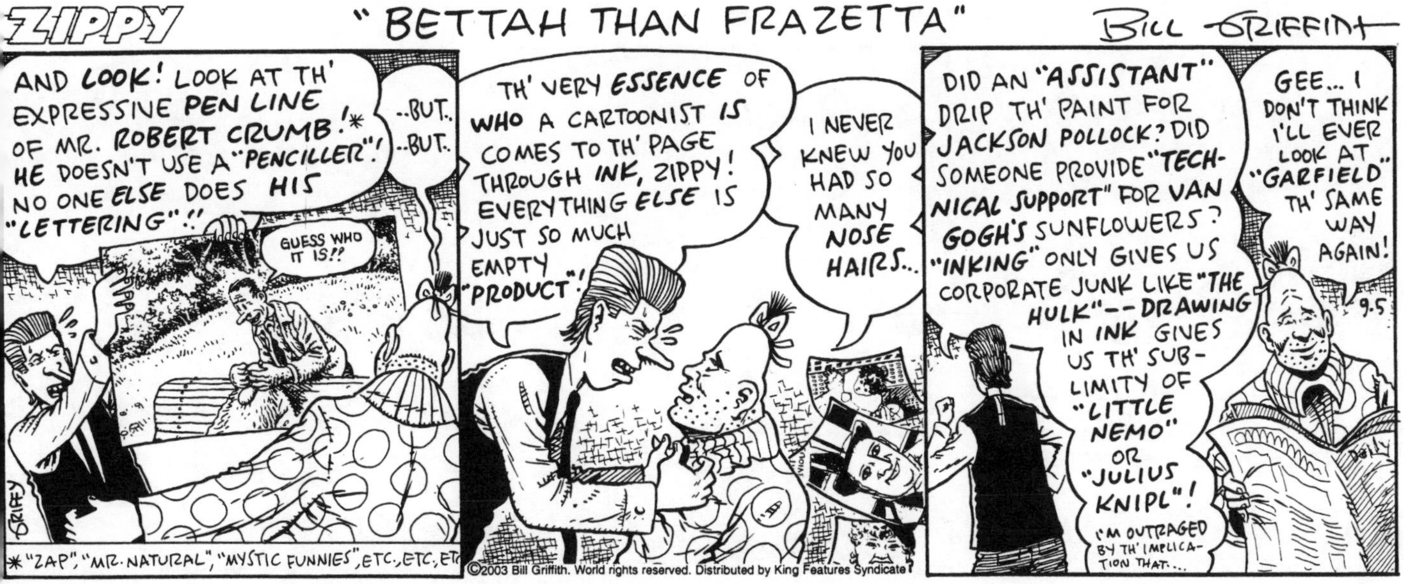
ZIPPY
"BETTAH THAN FRAZETTA"
BILL GRIFFITH
AND LOOK! LOOK AT TH' EXPRESSIVE PEN LINE OF MR. ROBERT CRUMB!* HE DOESN'T USE A "PENCILLER"! NO ONE ELSE DOES HIS "LETTERING"!!
..BUT.. ..BUT..
GUESS WHO IT IS!?
*"ZAP", "MR. NATURAL", "MYSTIC FUNNIES", ETC., ETC., ETC.
TH' VERY ESSENCE OF WHO A CARTOONIST IS COMES TO TH' PAGE THROUGH INK, ZIPPY! EVERYTHING ELSE IS JUST SO MUCH EMPTY "PRODUCT"!
I NEVER KNEW YOU HAD SO MANY NOSE HAIRS...
DID AN "ASSISTANT" DRIP TH' PAINT FOR JACKSON POLLOCK? DID SOMEONE PROVIDE "TECHNICAL SUPPORT" FOR VAN GOGH'S SUNFLOWERS? "INKING" ONLY GIVES US CORPORATE JUNK LIKE "THE HULK"--DRAWING IN INK GIVES US TH' SUBLIMITY OF "LITTLE NEMO" OR "JULIUS KNIPL"!
I'M OUTRAGED BY TH' IMPLICATION THAT...
GEE... I DON'T THINK I'LL EVER LOOK AT "GARFIELD" TH' SAME WAY AGAIN!
9.5
©2003 Bill Griffith. World rights reserved. Distributed by King Features Syndicate

110 D

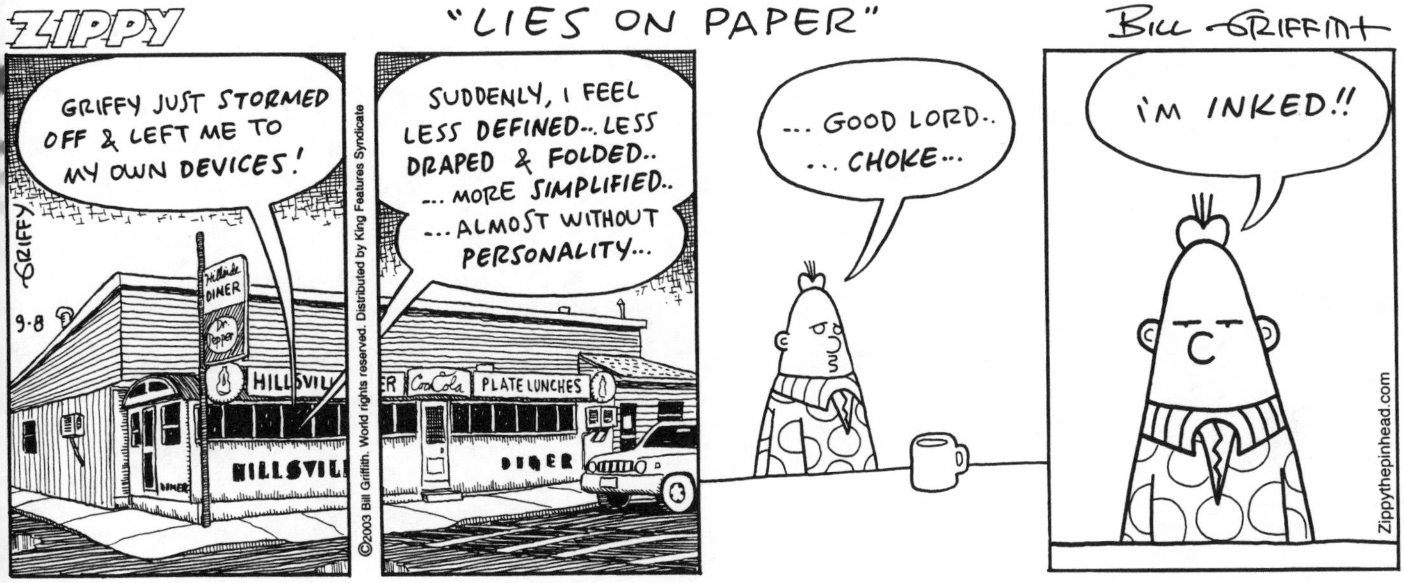
ZIPPY
"LIES ON PAPER"
BILL GRIFFITH
GRIFFY JUST STORMED OFF & LEFT ME TO MY OWN DEVICES!
9.8
HILLSVILLE DINER
PLATE LUNCHES
SUDDENLY, I FEEL LESS DEFINED... LESS DRAPED & FOLDED... MORE SIMPLIFIED... ...ALMOST WITHOUT PERSONALITY...
©2003 Bill Griffith. World rights reserved. Distributed by King Features Syndicate
...GOOD LORD... ...CHOKE...
I'M INKED!!
Zippythepinhead.com

110 E

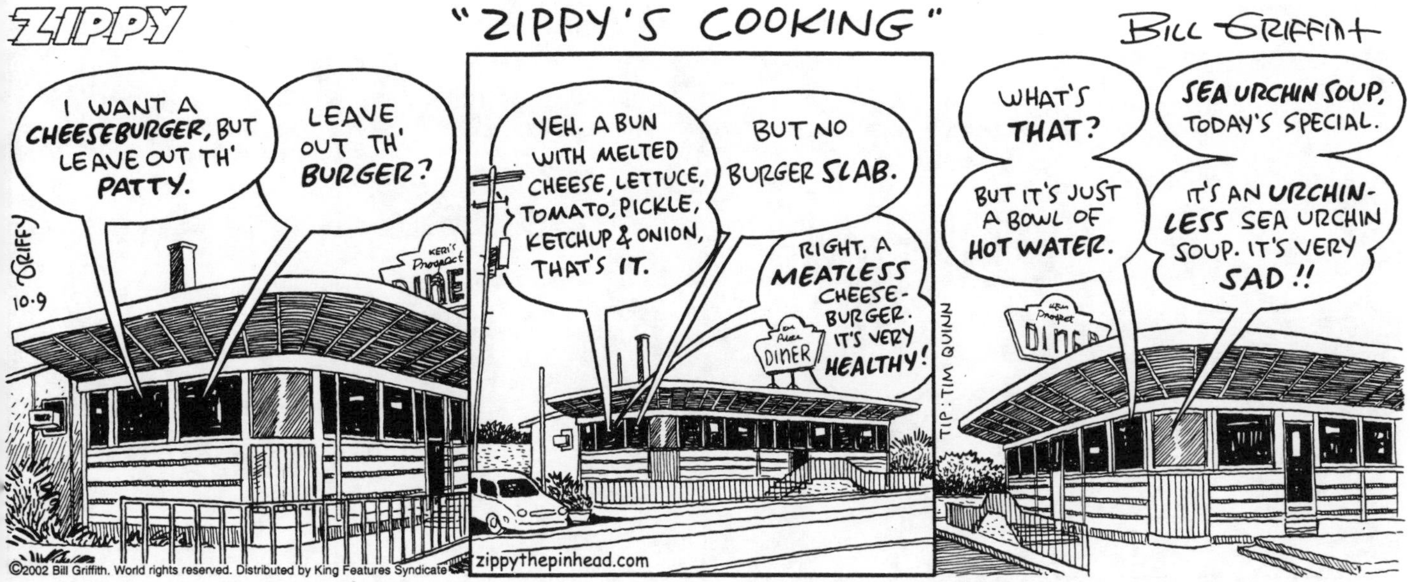
ZIPPY
"ZIPPY'S COOKING"
BILL GRIFFITH
I WANT A CHEESEBURGER, BUT LEAVE OUT TH' PATTY.
LEAVE OUT TH' BURGER?
10.9
YEH. A BUN WITH MELTED CHEESE, LETTUCE, TOMATO, PICKLE, KETCHUP & ONION, THAT'S IT.
BUT NO BURGER SLAB.
RIGHT. A MEATLESS CHEESE-BURGER. IT'S VERY HEALTHY!
TIP: TIM QUINN
WHAT'S THAT?
BUT IT'S JUST A BOWL OF HOT WATER.
SEA URCHIN SOUP, TODAY'S SPECIAL.
IT'S AN URCHIN-LESS SEA URCHIN SOUP. IT'S VERY SAD!!
©2002 Bill Griffith. World rights reserved. Distributed by King Features Syndicate
zippythepinhead.com

111

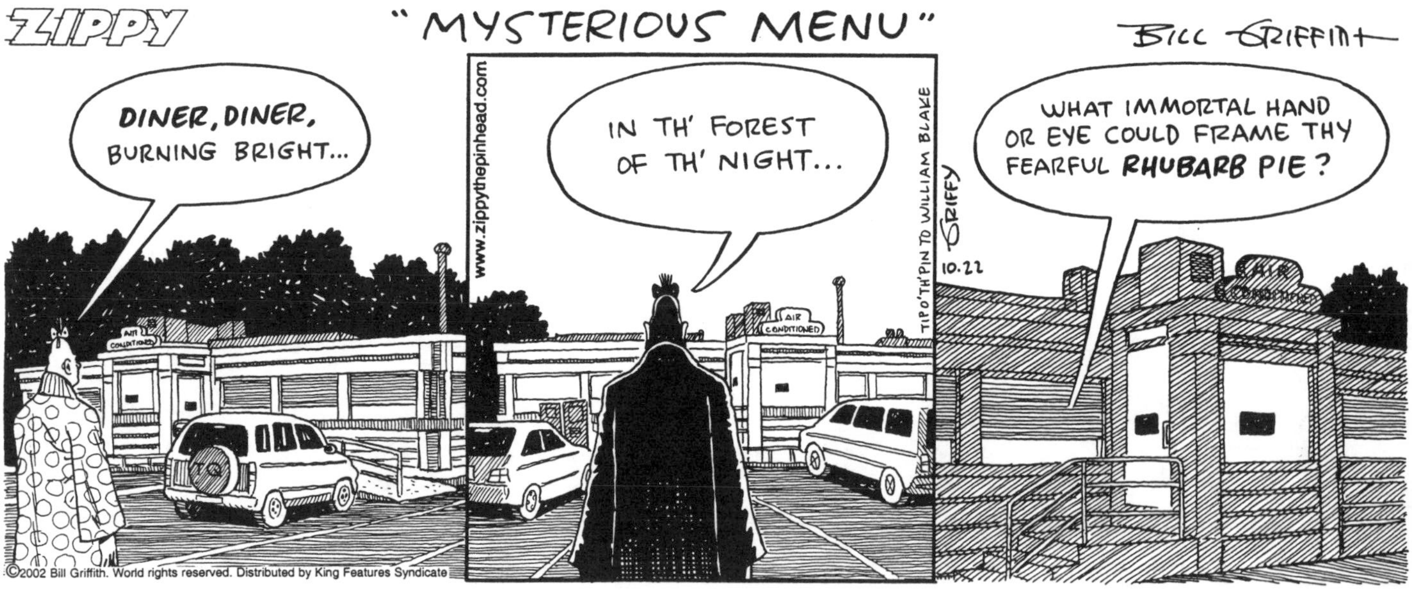
ZIPPY
"MYSTERIOUS MENU"
BILL GRIFFITH
DINER, DINER, BURNING BRIGHT...
IN TH' FOREST OF TH' NIGHT...
WHAT IMMORTAL HAND OR EYE COULD FRAME THY FEARFUL RHUBARB PIE?
www.zippythepinhead.com
TIP O'TH'PIN TO WILLIAM BLAKE
GRIFFY 10.22
©2002 Bill Griffith. World rights reserved. Distributed by King Features Syndicate

112

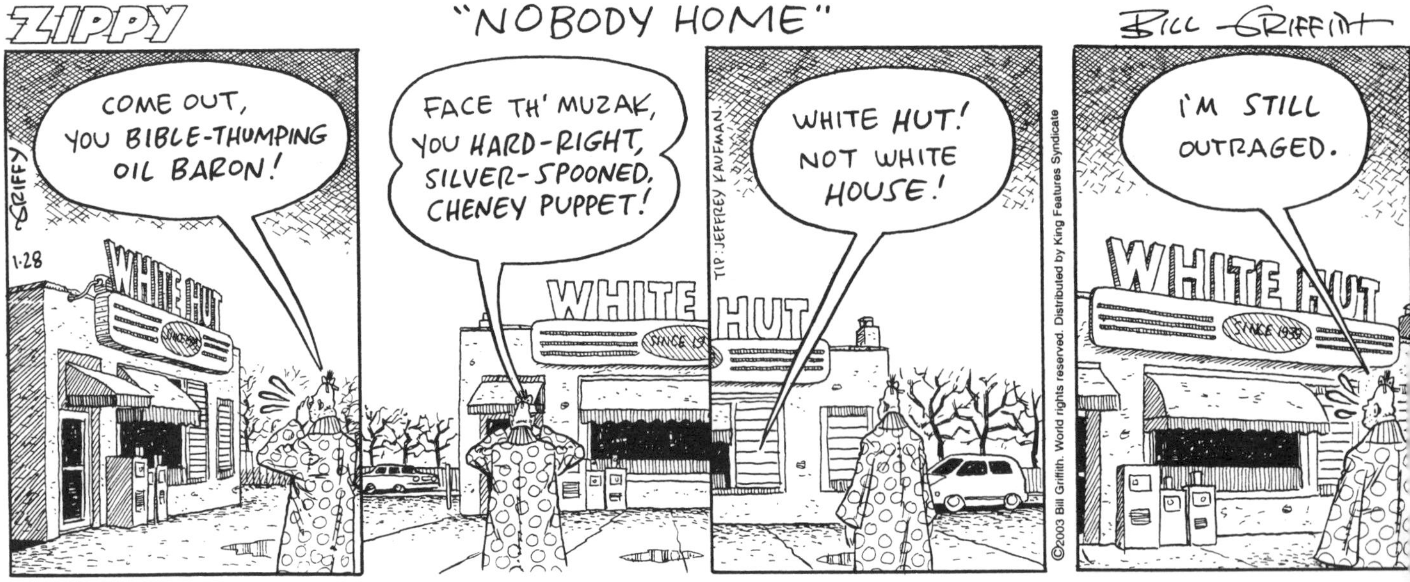
ZIPPY
"NOBODY HOME"
BILL GRIFFITH
COME OUT, YOU BIBLE-THUMPING OIL BARON!
GRIFFY 1.28
FACE TH' MUZAK, YOU HARD-RIGHT, SILVER-SPOONED, CHENEY PUPPET!
TIP: JEFFREY KAUFMAN
WHITE HUT! NOT WHITE HOUSE!
I'M STILL OUTRAGED.
WHITE HUT
©2003 Bill Griffith. World rights reserved. Distributed by King Features Syndicate

113

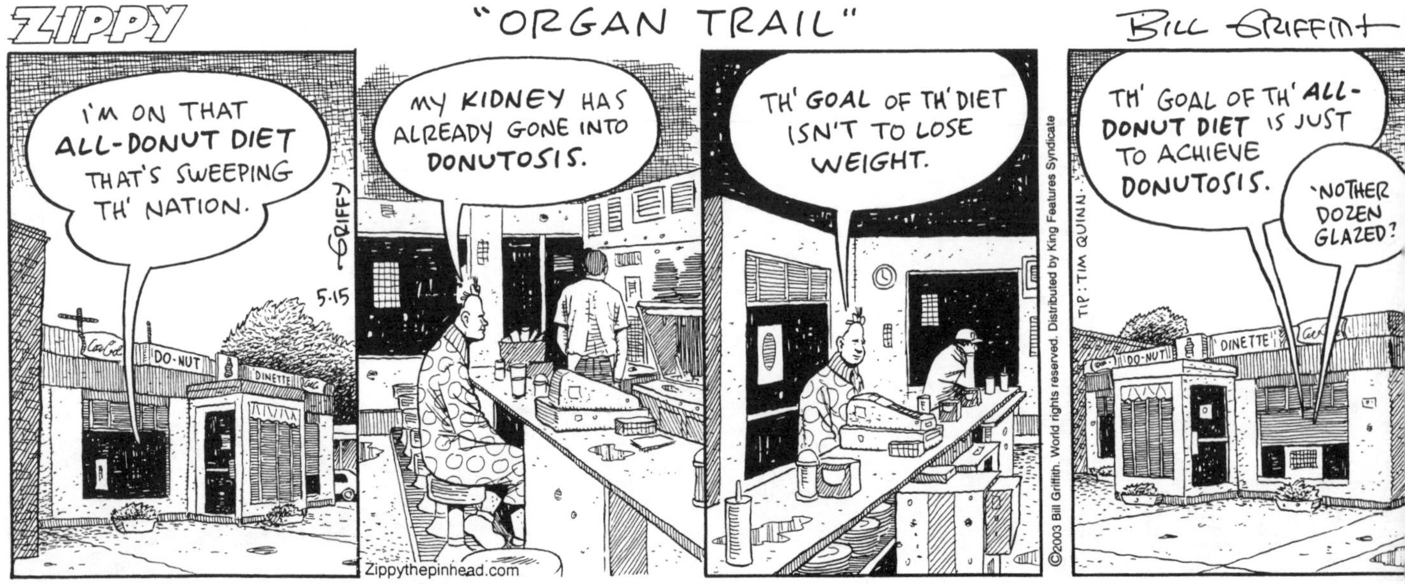
ZIPPY
"ORGAN TRAIL"
BILL GRIFFITH
I'M ON THAT ALL-DONUT DIET THAT'S SWEEPING TH' NATION.
GRIFFY 5.15
MY KIDNEY HAS ALREADY GONE INTO DONUTOSIS.
Zippythepinhead.com
TH' GOAL OF TH' DIET ISN'T TO LOSE WEIGHT.
TIP: TIM QUINN
TH' GOAL OF TH' ALL-DONUT DIET IS JUST TO ACHIEVE DONUTOSIS.
'NOTHER DOZEN GLAZED?
DO-NUT
DINETTE
©2003 Bill Griffith. World rights reserved. Distributed by King Features Syndicate

114

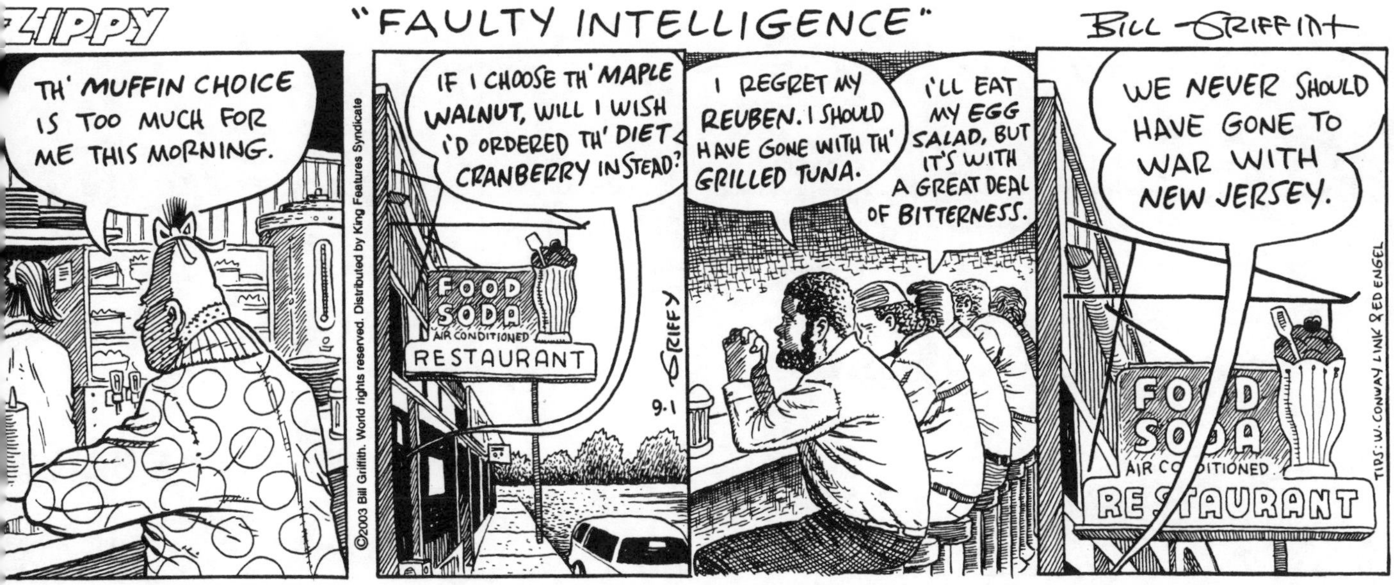
ZIPPY
"FAULTY INTELLIGENCE"
BILL GRIFFITH
TH' MUFFIN CHOICE IS TOO MUCH FOR ME THIS MORNING.
IF I CHOOSE TH' MAPLE WALNUT, WILL I WISH I'D ORDERED TH' DIET CRANBERRY INSTEAD?
FOOD SODA AIR CONDITIONED RESTAURANT
GRIFFY 9·1
©2003 Bill Griffith. World rights reserved. Distributed by King Features Syndicate
I REGRET MY REUBEN. I SHOULD HAVE GONE WITH TH' GRILLED TUNA.
I'LL EAT MY EGG SALAD, BUT IT'S WITH A GREAT DEAL OF BITTERNESS.
WE NEVER SHOULD HAVE GONE TO WAR WITH NEW JERSEY.
FOOD SODA AIR CONDITIONED RESTAURANT
TIPS: W. CONWAY LINK, ED ENGEL

115

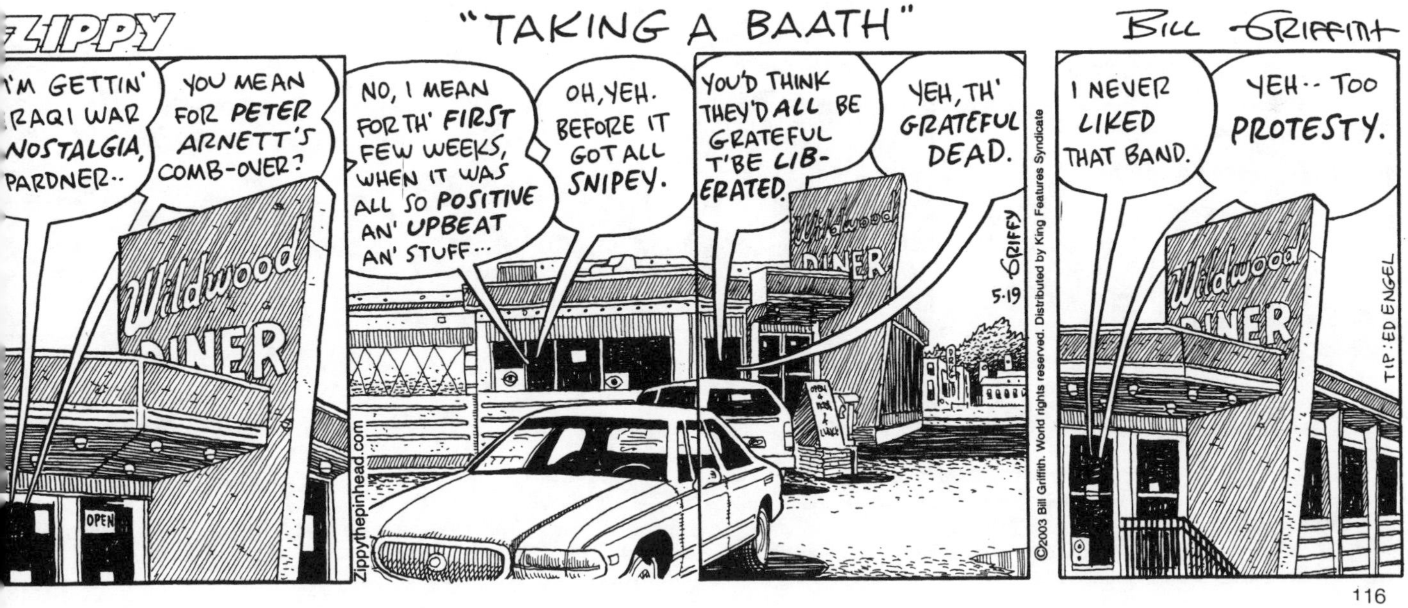
ZIPPY
"TAKING A BAATH"
BILL GRIFFITH
I'M GETTIN' IRAQI WAR NOSTALGIA, PARDNER..
YOU MEAN FOR PETER ARNETT'S COMB-OVER?
Wildwood DINER
OPEN
Zippythepinhead.com
NO, I MEAN FOR TH' FIRST FEW WEEKS, WHEN IT WAS ALL SO POSITIVE AN' UPBEAT AN' STUFF...
OH, YEH. BEFORE IT GOT ALL SNIPEY.
YOU'D THINK THEY'D ALL BE GRATEFUL T'BE LIBERATED.
YEH, TH' GRATEFUL DEAD.
GRIFFY 5·19
©2003 Bill Griffith. World rights reserved. Distributed by King Features Syndicate
I NEVER LIKED THAT BAND.
YEH-- TOO PROTESTY.
TIP: ED ENGEL

116

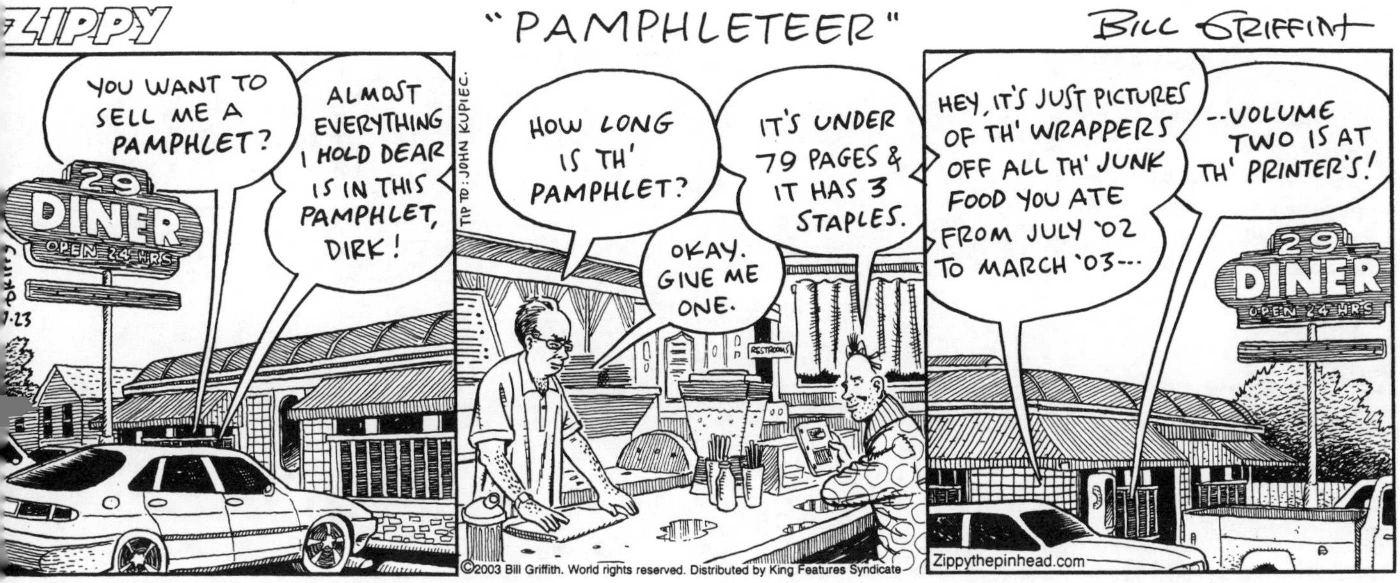
ZIPPY
"PAMPHLETEER"
BILL GRIFFITH
YOU WANT TO SELL ME A PAMPHLET?
ALMOST EVERYTHING I HOLD DEAR IS IN THIS PAMPHLET, DIRK!
29 DINER OPEN 24 HRS
TIP TO: JOHN KUPIEC.
HOW LONG IS TH' PAMPHLET?
IT'S UNDER 79 PAGES & IT HAS 3 STAPLES.
OKAY. GIVE ME ONE.
©2003 Bill Griffith. World rights reserved. Distributed by King Features Syndicate
HEY, IT'S JUST PICTURES OF TH' WRAPPERS OFF ALL TH' JUNK FOOD YOU ATE FROM JULY '02 TO MARCH '03---
--VOLUME TWO IS AT TH' PRINTER'S!
29 DINER OPEN 24 HRS
Zippythepinhead.com

117

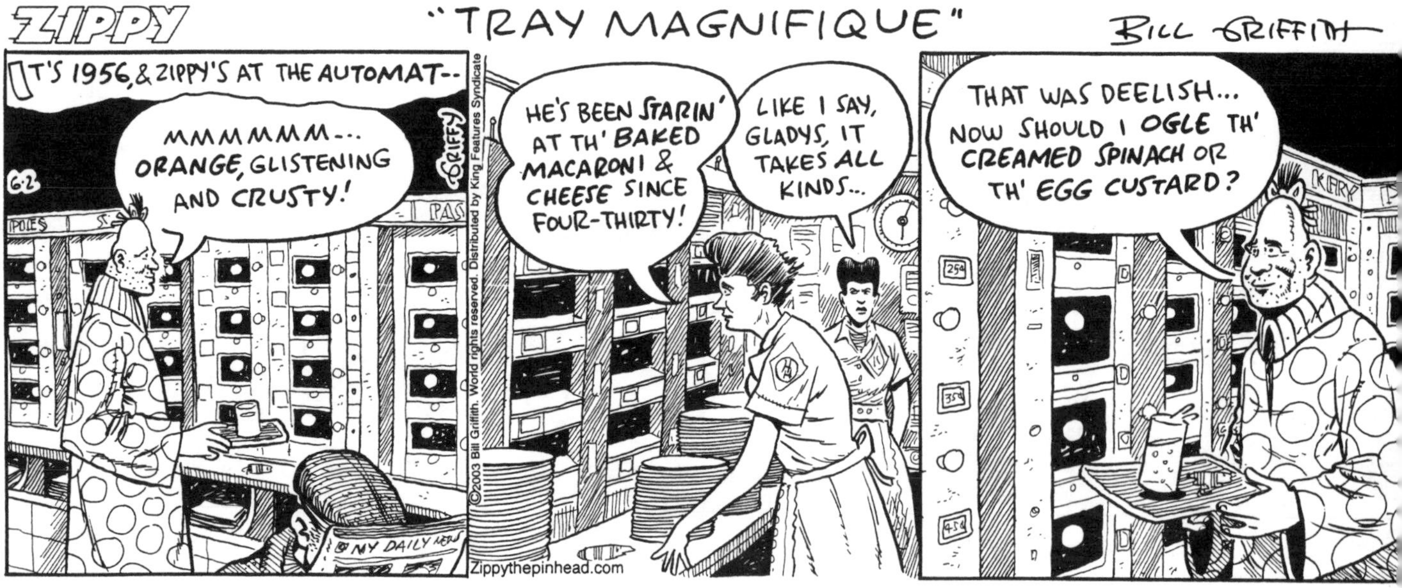
ZIPPY
"TRAY MAGNIFIQUE"
BILL GRIFFITH
IT'S 1956, & ZIPPY'S AT THE AUTOMAT--
MMMMMM... ORANGE, GLISTENING AND CRUSTY!
HE'S BEEN STARIN' AT TH' BAKED MACARONI & CHEESE SINCE FOUR-THIRTY!
LIKE I SAY, GLADYS, IT TAKES ALL KINDS...
THAT WAS DEELISH... NOW SHOULD I OGLE TH' CREAMED SPINACH OR TH' EGG CUSTARD?
©2003 Bill Griffith. World rights reserved. Distributed by King Features Syndicate
Zippythepinhead.com

118 A

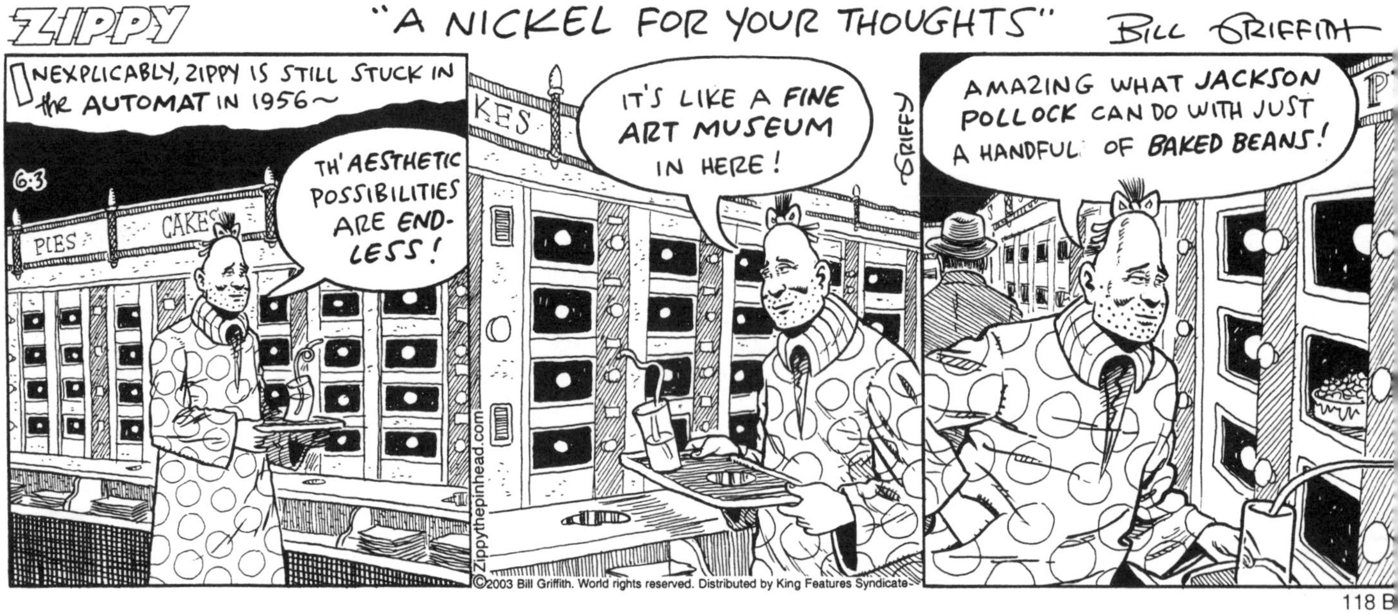
ZIPPY
"A NICKEL FOR YOUR THOUGHTS"
BILL GRIFFITH
INEXPLICABLY, ZIPPY IS STILL STUCK IN THE AUTOMAT IN 1956~
PIES
CAKES
TH' AESTHETIC POSSIBILITIES ARE ENDLESS!
IT'S LIKE A FINE ART MUSEUM IN HERE!
AMAZING WHAT JACKSON POLLOCK CAN DO WITH JUST A HANDFUL OF BAKED BEANS!
Zippythepinhead.com
©2003 Bill Griffith. World rights reserved. Distributed by King Features Syndicate

118 B

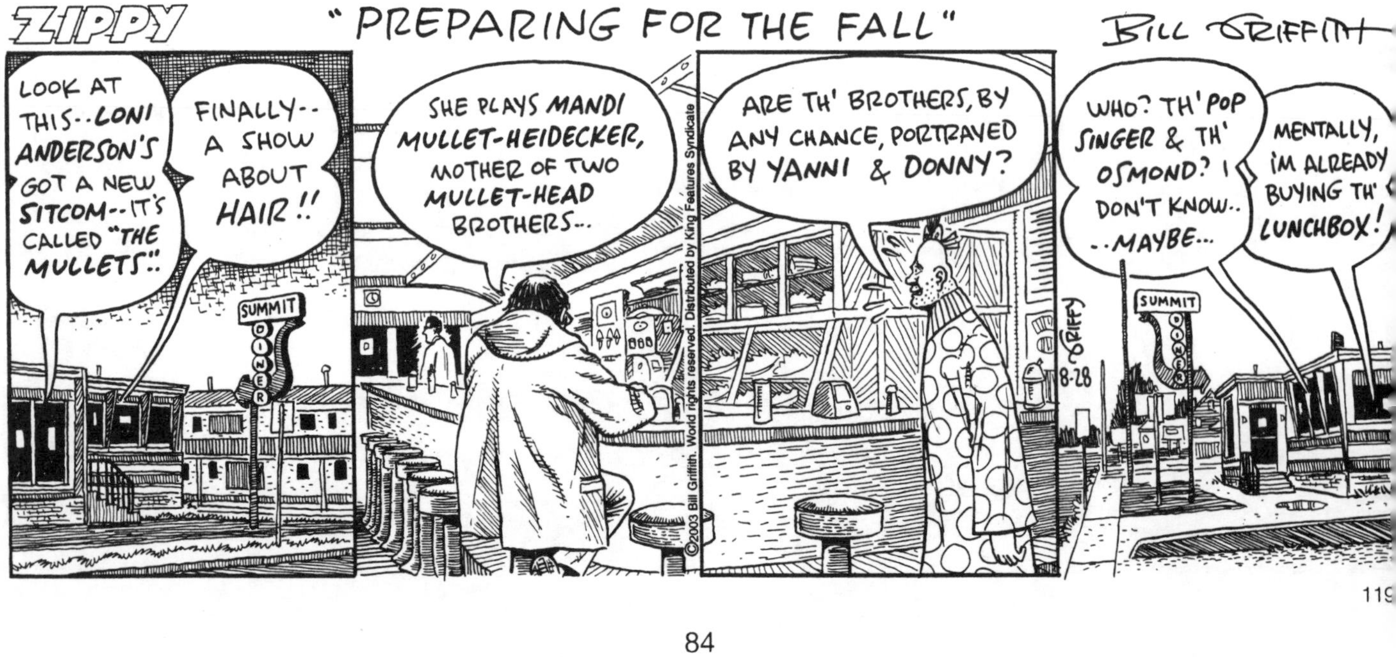
ZIPPY
"PREPARING FOR THE FALL"
BILL GRIFFITH
LOOK AT THIS--LONI ANDERSON'S GOT A NEW SITCOM--IT'S CALLED "THE MULLETS"!
FINALLY--A SHOW ABOUT HAIR!!
SUMMIT DINER
SHE PLAYS MANDI MULLET-HEIDECKER, MOTHER OF TWO MULLET-HEAD BROTHERS...
©2003 Bill Griffith. World rights reserved. Distributed by King Features Syndicate
ARE TH' BROTHERS, BY ANY CHANCE, PORTRAYED BY YANNI & DONNY?
WHO? TH' POP SINGER & TH' OSMOND? I DON'T KNOW.. ..MAYBE...
MENTALLY, I'M ALREADY BUYING TH' LUNCHBOX!
SUMMIT DINER

119

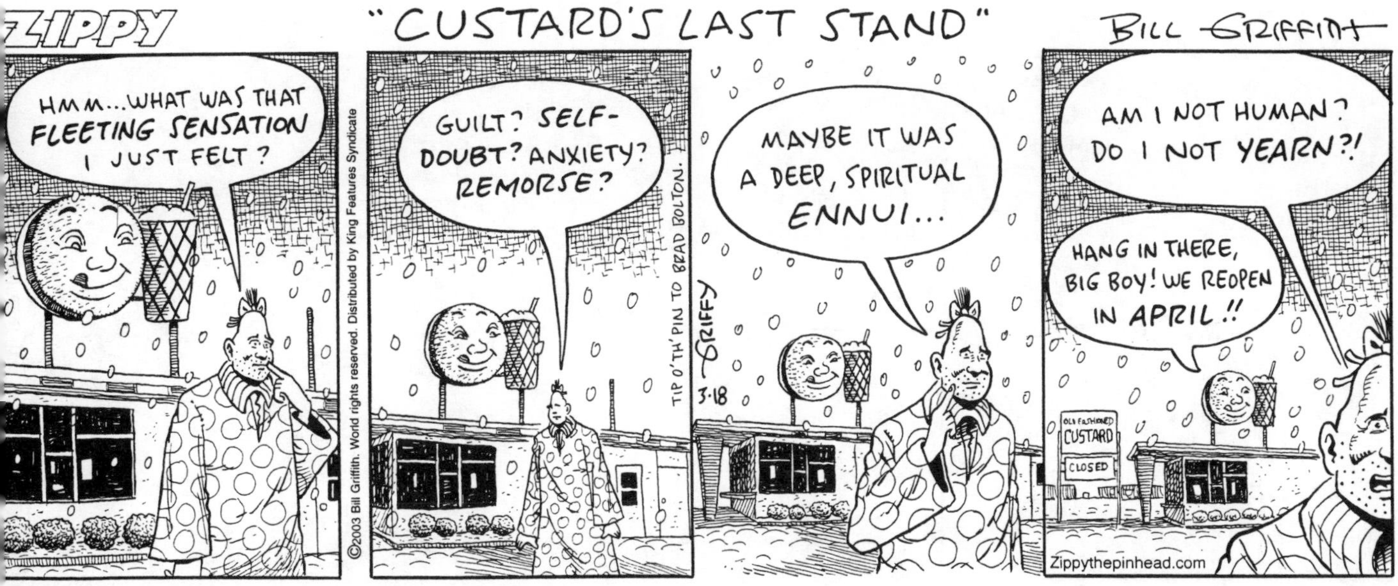
ZIPPY
"CUSTARD'S LAST STAND"
BILL GRIFFITH
HMM...WHAT WAS THAT FLEETING SENSATION I JUST FELT?
©2003 Bill Griffith. World rights reserved. Distributed by King Features Syndicate
GUILT? SELF-DOUBT? ANXIETY? REMORSE?
TIP O' TH' PIN TO BRAD BOLTON.
GRIFFY 3·18
MAYBE IT WAS A DEEP, SPIRITUAL ENNUI...
AM I NOT HUMAN? DO I NOT YEARN?!
HANG IN THERE, BIG BOY! WE REOPEN IN APRIL!!
CUSTARD
CLOSED
Zippythepinhead.com

120 A

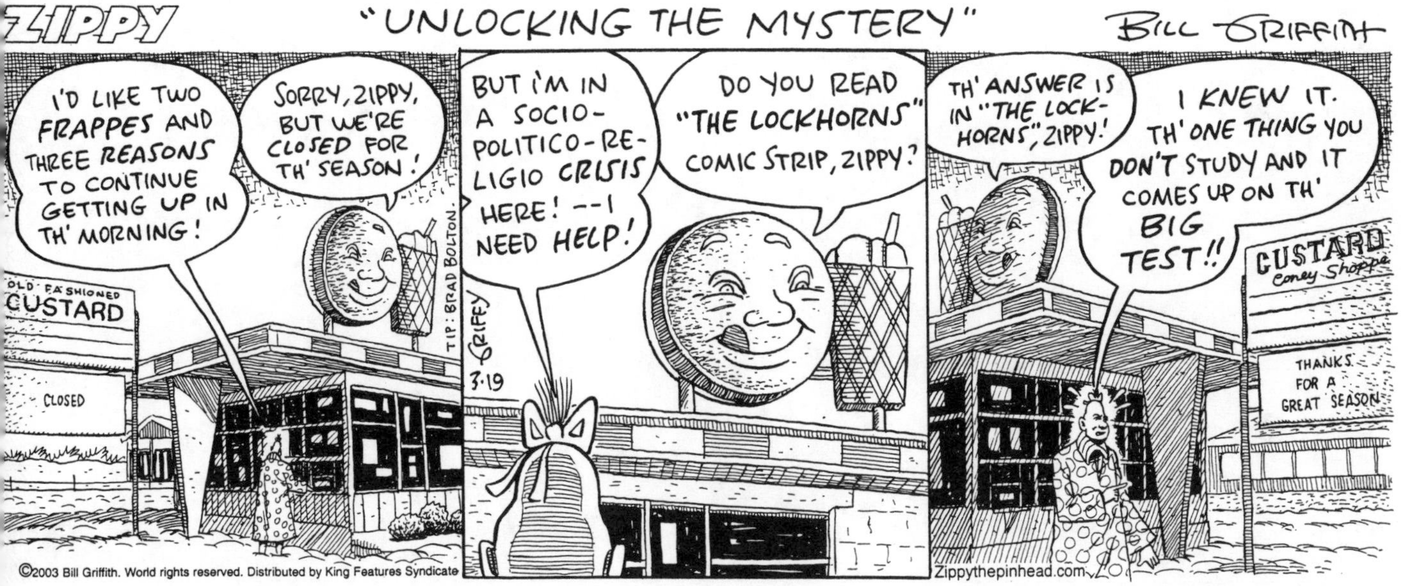
ZIPPY
"UNLOCKING THE MYSTERY"
BILL GRIFFITH
I'D LIKE TWO FRAPPES AND THREE REASONS TO CONTINUE GETTING UP IN TH' MORNING!
SORRY, ZIPPY, BUT WE'RE CLOSED FOR TH' SEASON!
OLD FASHIONED CUSTARD
CLOSED
TIP: BRAD BOLTON.
BUT I'M IN A SOCIO-POLITICO-RELIGIO CRISIS HERE! --I NEED HELP!
GRIFFY 3·19
DO YOU READ "THE LOCKHORNS" COMIC STRIP, ZIPPY?
TH' ANSWER IS IN "THE LOCKHORNS," ZIPPY!
I KNEW IT. TH' ONE THING YOU DON'T STUDY AND IT COMES UP ON TH' BIG TEST!!
CUSTARD Coney Shoppe
THANKS FOR A GREAT SEASON
©2003 Bill Griffith. World rights reserved. Distributed by King Features Syndicate
Zippythepinhead.com

120 B

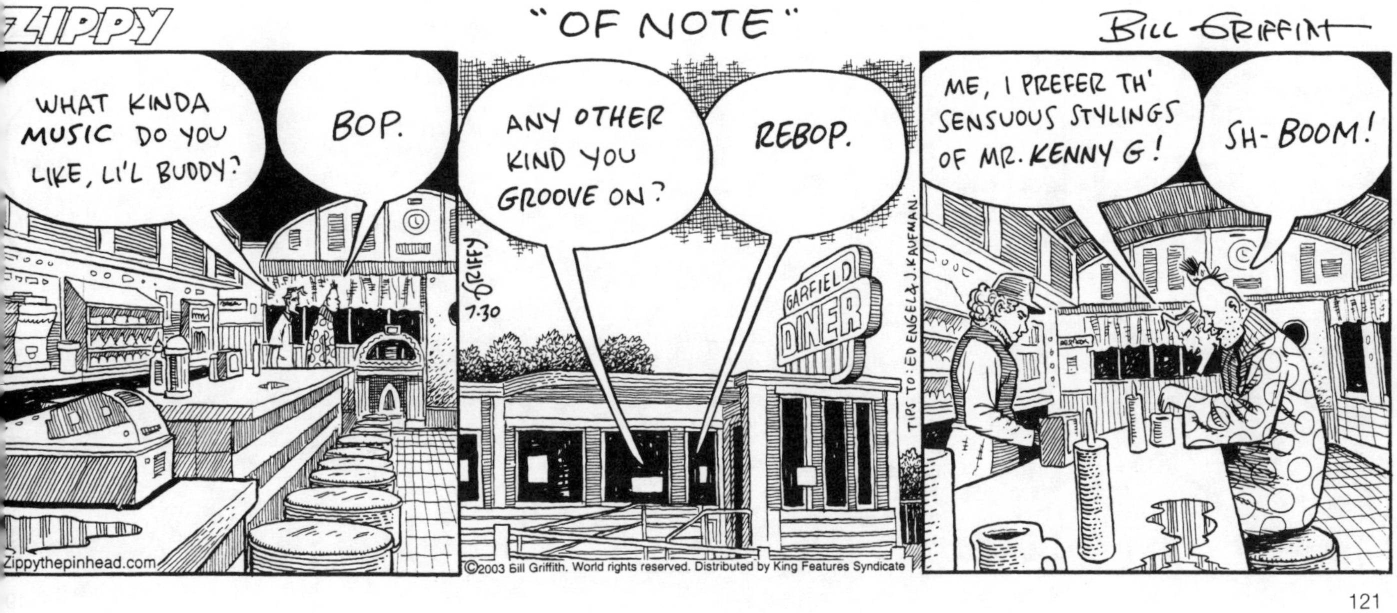
ZIPPY
"OF NOTE"
BILL GRIFFITH
WHAT KINDA MUSIC DO YOU LIKE, LI'L BUDDY?
BOP.
Zippythepinhead.com
ANY OTHER KIND YOU GROOVE ON?
REBOP.
GRIFFY 7·30
GARFIELD DINER
©2003 Bill Griffith. World rights reserved. Distributed by King Features Syndicate
TIPS TO: ED ENGEL & J. KAUFMAN.
ME, I PREFER TH' SENSUOUS STYLINGS OF MR. KENNY G!
SH-BOOM!

121

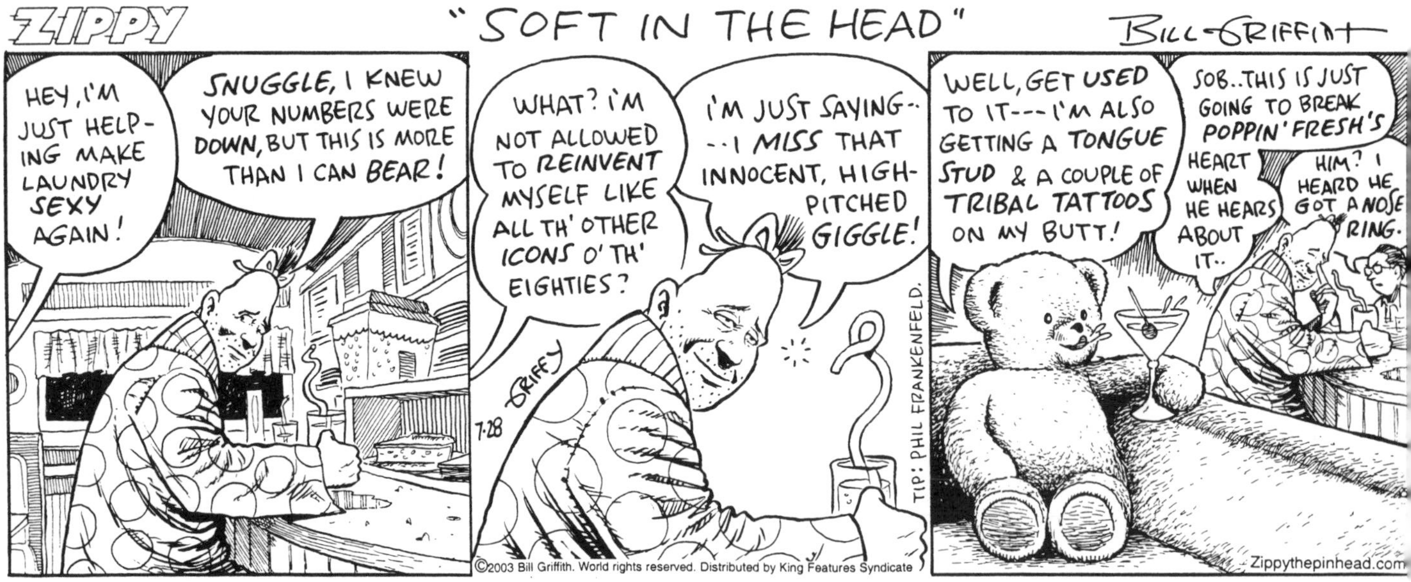
ZIPPY
"SOFT IN THE HEAD"
BILL GRIFFITH
HEY, I'M JUST HELPING MAKE LAUNDRY SEXY AGAIN!
SNUGGLE, I KNEW YOUR NUMBERS WERE DOWN, BUT THIS IS MORE THAN I CAN BEAR!
WHAT? I'M NOT ALLOWED TO REINVENT MYSELF LIKE ALL TH' OTHER ICONS O' TH' EIGHTIES?
I'M JUST SAYING.. ..I MISS THAT INNOCENT, HIGH-PITCHED GIGGLE!
GRIFFY 7-28
TIP: PHIL FRANKENFELD.
WELL, GET USED TO IT--- I'M ALSO GETTING A TONGUE STUD & A COUPLE OF TRIBAL TATTOOS ON MY BUTT!
SOB..THIS IS JUST GOING TO BREAK POPPIN' FRESH'S HEART WHEN HE HEARS ABOUT IT..
HIM? I HEARD HE GOT A NOSE RING.
©2003 Bill Griffith. World rights reserved. Distributed by King Features Syndicate
Zippythepinhead.com

122

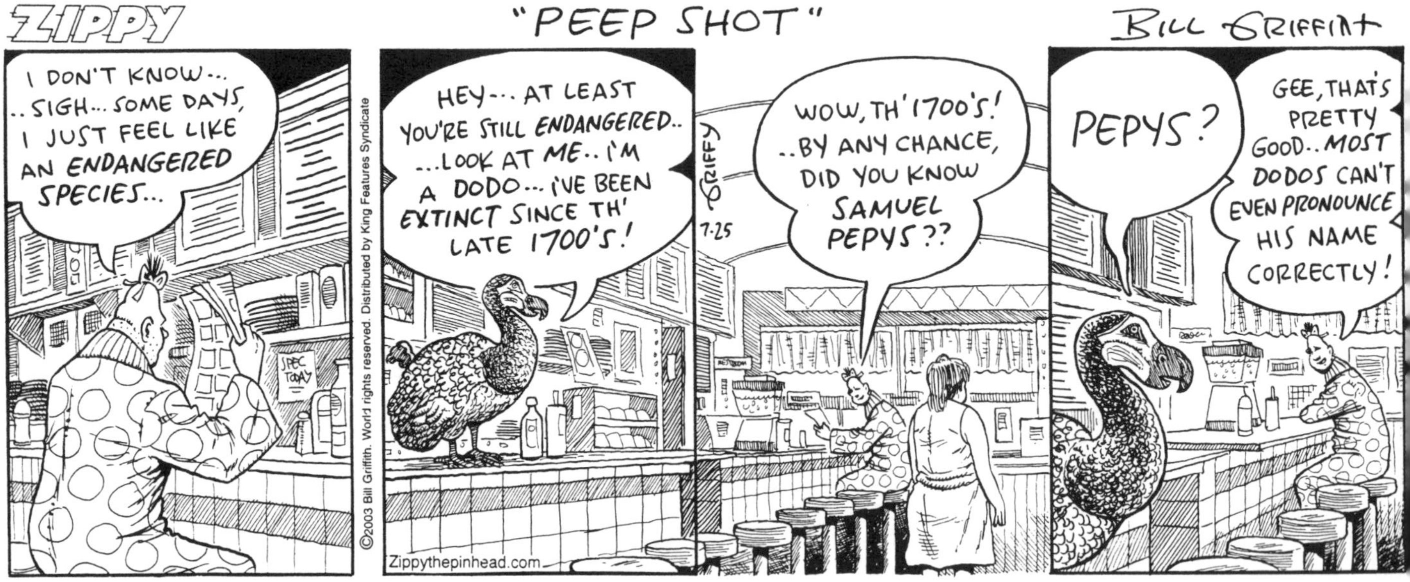
ZIPPY
"PEEP SHOT"
BILL GRIFFITH
I DON'T KNOW... ..SIGH... SOME DAYS, I JUST FEEL LIKE AN ENDANGERED SPECIES...
SPEC TODAY
©2003 Bill Griffith. World rights reserved. Distributed by King Features Syndicate
HEY--- AT LEAST YOU'RE STILL ENDANGERED.. ...LOOK AT ME.. I'M A DODO... I'VE BEEN EXTINCT SINCE TH' LATE 1700'S!
Zippythepinhead.com
GRIFFY 7-25
WOW, TH' 1700'S! ..BY ANY CHANCE, DID YOU KNOW SAMUEL PEPYS??
PEPYS?
GEE, THAT'S PRETTY GOOD..MOST DODOS CAN'T EVEN PRONOUNCE HIS NAME CORRECTLY!

123

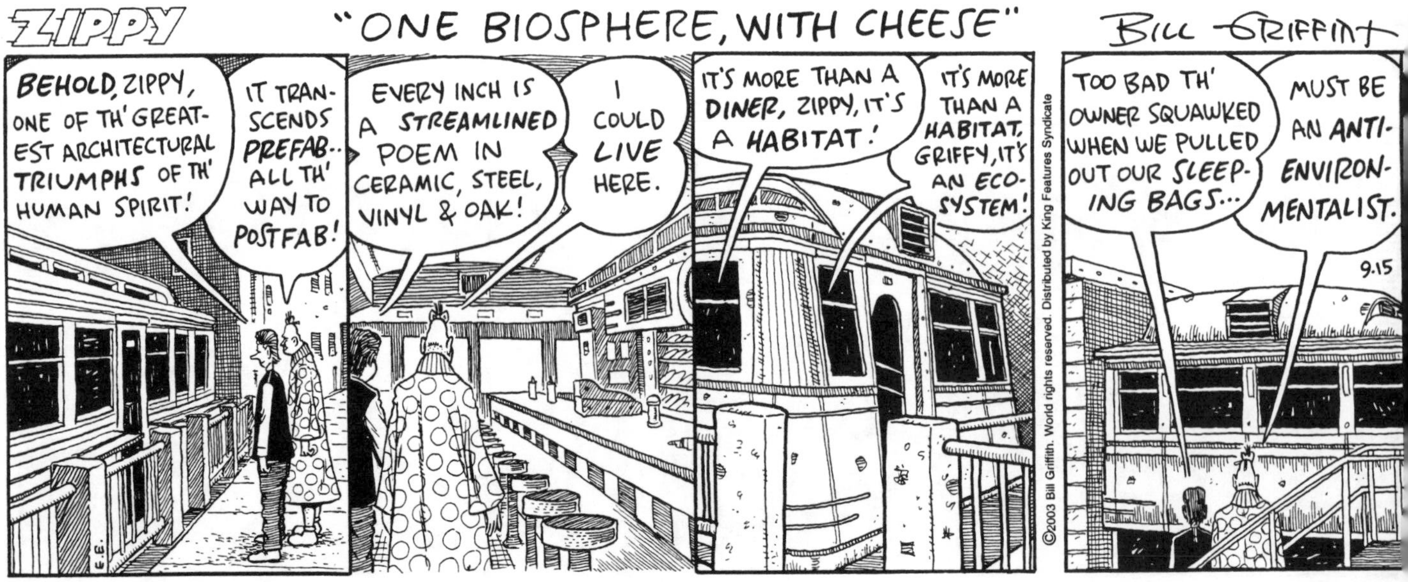
ZIPPY
"ONE BIOSPHERE, WITH CHEESE"
BILL GRIFFITH
BEHOLD, ZIPPY, ONE OF TH' GREATEST ARCHITECTURAL TRIUMPHS OF TH' HUMAN SPIRIT!
IT TRANSCENDS PREFAB.. ALL TH' WAY TO POSTFAB!
EVERY INCH IS A STREAMLINED POEM IN CERAMIC, STEEL, VINYL & OAK!
I COULD LIVE HERE.
IT'S MORE THAN A DINER, ZIPPY, IT'S A HABITAT!
IT'S MORE THAN A HABITAT, GRIFFY, IT'S AN ECO-SYSTEM!
©2003 Bill Griffith. World rights reserved. Distributed by King Features Syndicate
TOO BAD TH' OWNER SQUAWKED WHEN WE PULLED OUT OUR SLEEPING BAGS...
MUST BE AN ANTI-ENVIRONMENTALIST.
9.15

124

ZIPPY

"THIS CLOSE TO WILMA"

BILL GRIFFITH

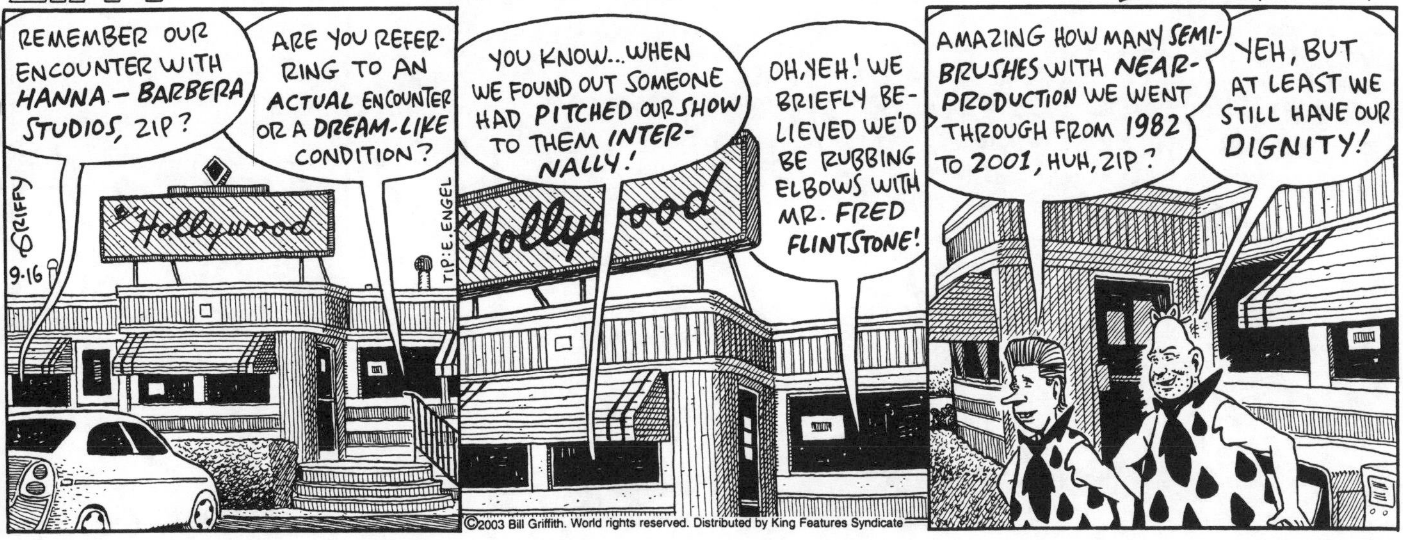
REMEMBER OUR ENCOUNTER WITH HANNA – BARBERA STUDIOS, ZIP?
ARE YOU REFERRING TO AN ACTUAL ENCOUNTER OR A DREAM-LIKE CONDITION?
GRIFFY 9-16
TIP: E. ENGEL
Hollywood
YOU KNOW... WHEN WE FOUND OUT SOMEONE HAD PITCHED OUR SHOW TO THEM INTERNALLY!
OH, YEH! WE BRIEFLY BELIEVED WE'D BE RUBBING ELBOWS WITH MR. FRED FLINTSTONE!
AMAZING HOW MANY SEMI-BRUSHES WITH NEAR-PRODUCTION WE WENT THROUGH FROM 1982 TO 2001, HUH, ZIP?
YEH, BUT AT LEAST WE STILL HAVE OUR DIGNITY!
©2003 Bill Griffith. World rights reserved. Distributed by King Features Syndicate

125

ZIPPY

"DREAM DATE"

BILL GRIFFITH

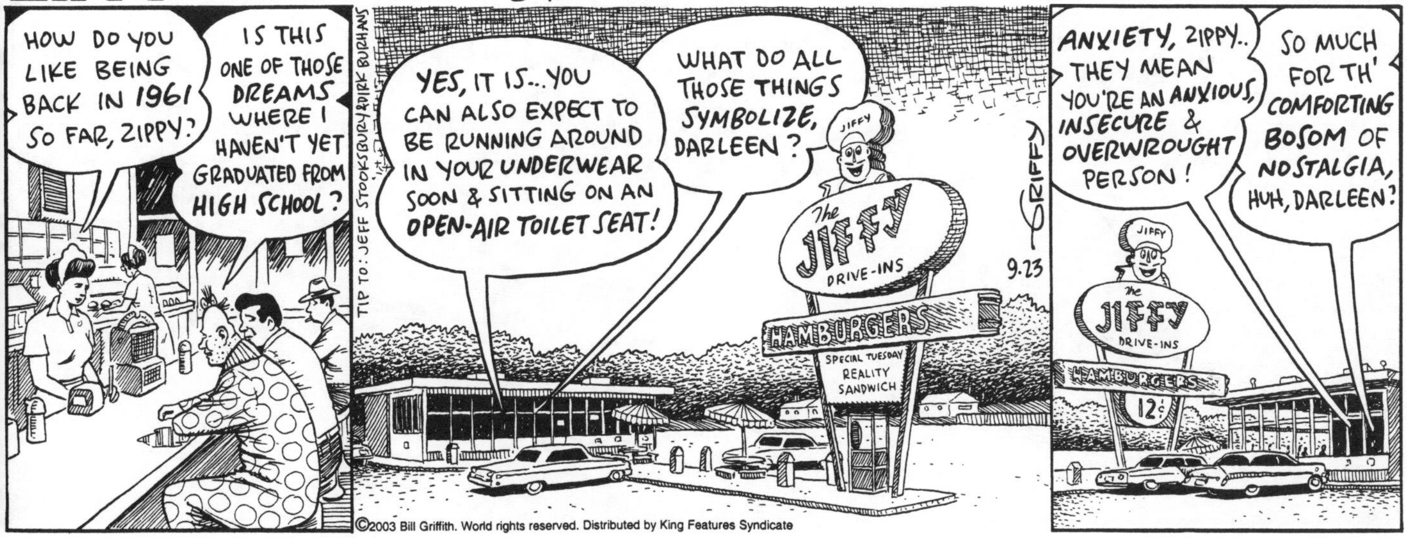
HOW DO YOU LIKE BEING BACK IN 1961 SO FAR, ZIPPY?
IS THIS ONE OF THOSE DREAMS WHERE I HAVEN'T YET GRADUATED FROM HIGH SCHOOL?
TIP TO: JEFF STOOKSBURY & KIRK BURHANS
YES, IT IS... YOU CAN ALSO EXPECT TO BE RUNNING AROUND IN YOUR UNDERWEAR SOON & SITTING ON AN OPEN-AIR TOILET SEAT!
WHAT DO ALL THOSE THINGS SYMBOLIZE, DARLEEN?
JIFFY
The JIFFY DRIVE-INS
HAMBURGERS
SPECIAL TUESDAY REALITY SANDWICH
GRIFFY 9-23
ANXIETY, ZIPPY.. THEY MEAN YOU'RE AN ANXIOUS, INSECURE & OVERWROUGHT PERSON!
SO MUCH FOR TH' COMFORTING BOSOM OF NOSTALGIA, HUH, DARLEEN?
12¢
©2003 Bill Griffith. World rights reserved. Distributed by King Features Syndicate

126

ZIPPY

"SPECIMEN"

BILL GRIFFITH

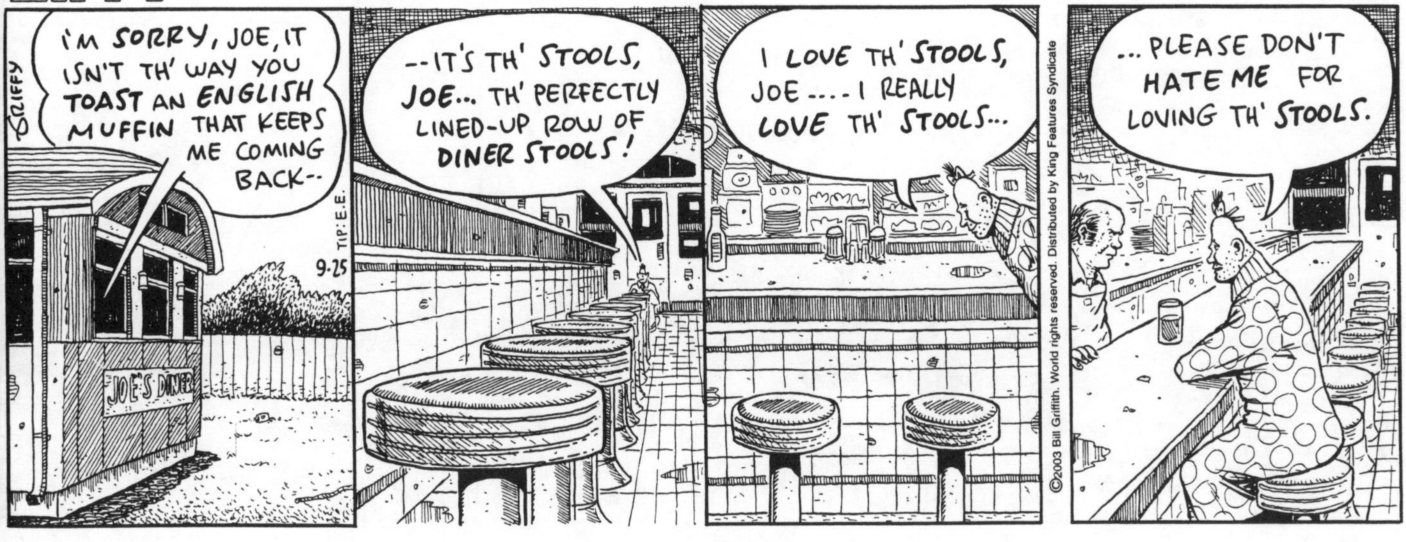
GRIFFY
I'M SORRY, JOE, IT ISN'T TH' WAY YOU TOAST AN ENGLISH MUFFIN THAT KEEPS ME COMING BACK--
TIP: E.E.
9-25
JOE'S DINER
--IT'S TH' STOOLS, JOE... TH' PERFECTLY LINED-UP ROW OF DINER STOOLS!
I LOVE TH' STOOLS, JOE.... I REALLY LOVE TH' STOOLS...
©2003 Bill Griffith. World rights reserved. Distributed by King Features Syndicate
...PLEASE DON'T HATE ME FOR LOVING TH' STOOLS.

127

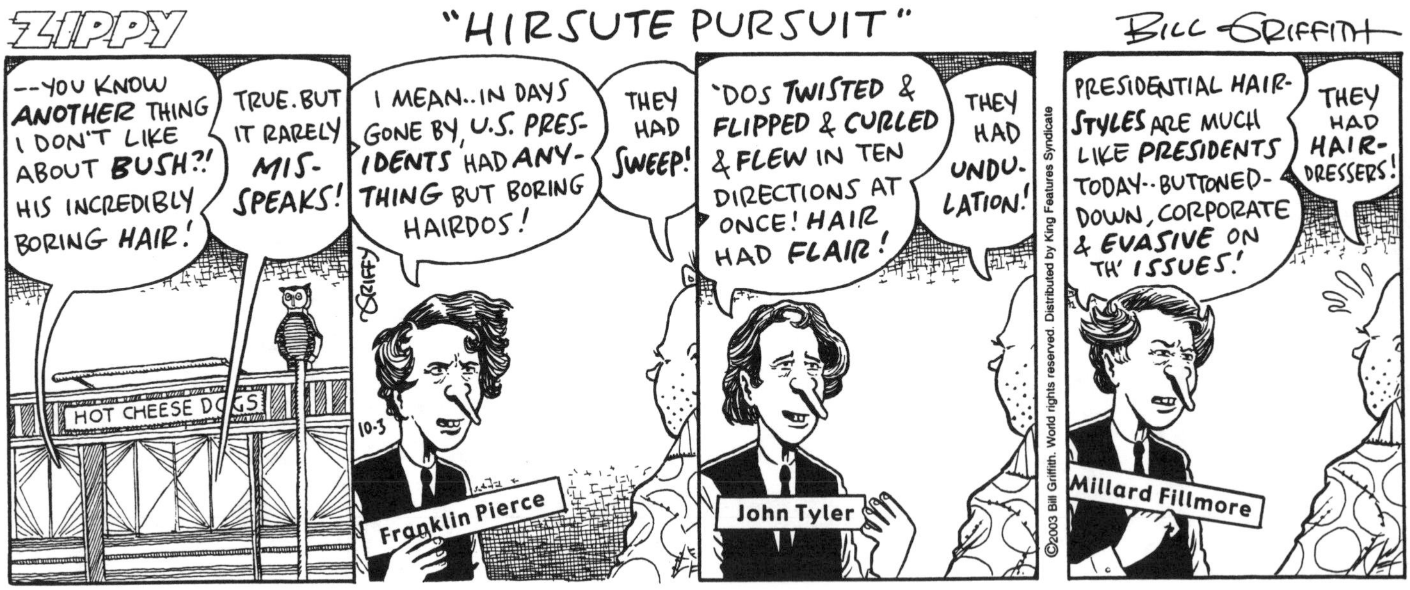
ZIPPY
"HIRSUTE PURSUIT"
BILL GRIFFITH
--YOU KNOW ANOTHER THING I DON'T LIKE ABOUT BUSH?! HIS INCREDIBLY BORING HAIR!
TRUE. BUT IT RARELY MIS-SPEAKS!
HOT CHEESE DOGS
I MEAN.. IN DAYS GONE BY, U.S. PRESIDENTS HAD ANYTHING BUT BORING HAIRDOS!
THEY HAD SWEEP!
GRIFFY
10-3
Franklin Pierce
'DOS TWISTED & FLIPPED & CURLED & FLEW IN TEN DIRECTIONS AT ONCE! HAIR HAD FLAIR!
THEY HAD UNDULATION!
John Tyler
PRESIDENTIAL HAIR-STYLES ARE MUCH LIKE PRESIDENTS TODAY.. BUTTONED-DOWN, CORPORATE & EVASIVE ON TH' ISSUES!
THEY HAD HAIR-DRESSERS!
Millard Fillmore
©2003 Bill Griffith. World rights reserved. Distributed by King Features Syndicate

128

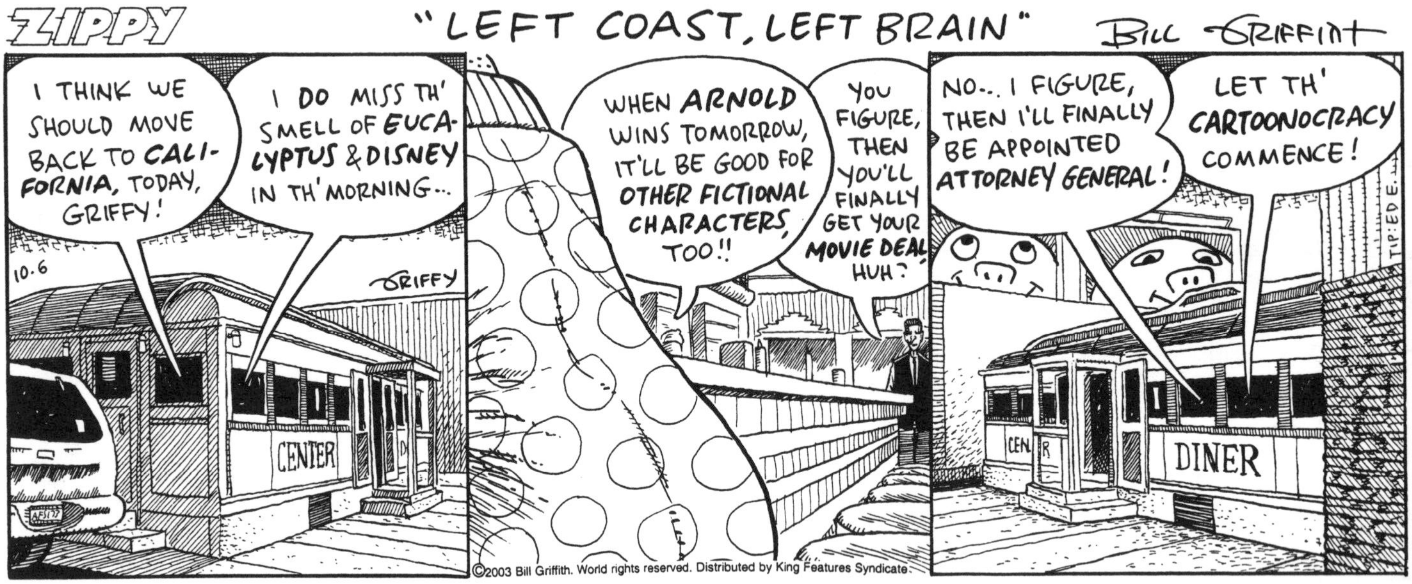
ZIPPY
"LEFT COAST, LEFT BRAIN"
BILL GRIFFITH
I THINK WE SHOULD MOVE BACK TO CALIFORNIA, TODAY, GRIFFY!
I DO MISS TH' SMELL OF EUCALYPTUS & DISNEY IN TH' MORNING...
10-6
GRIFFY
CENTER
WHEN ARNOLD WINS TOMORROW, IT'LL BE GOOD FOR OTHER FICTIONAL CHARACTERS, TOO!!
YOU FIGURE, THEN YOU'LL FINALLY GET YOUR MOVIE DEAL HUH?
NO... I FIGURE, THEN I'LL FINALLY BE APPOINTED ATTORNEY GENERAL!
LET TH' CARTOONOCRACY COMMENCE!
TIP: ED E.
DINER
©2003 Bill Griffith. World rights reserved. Distributed by King Features Syndicate

129

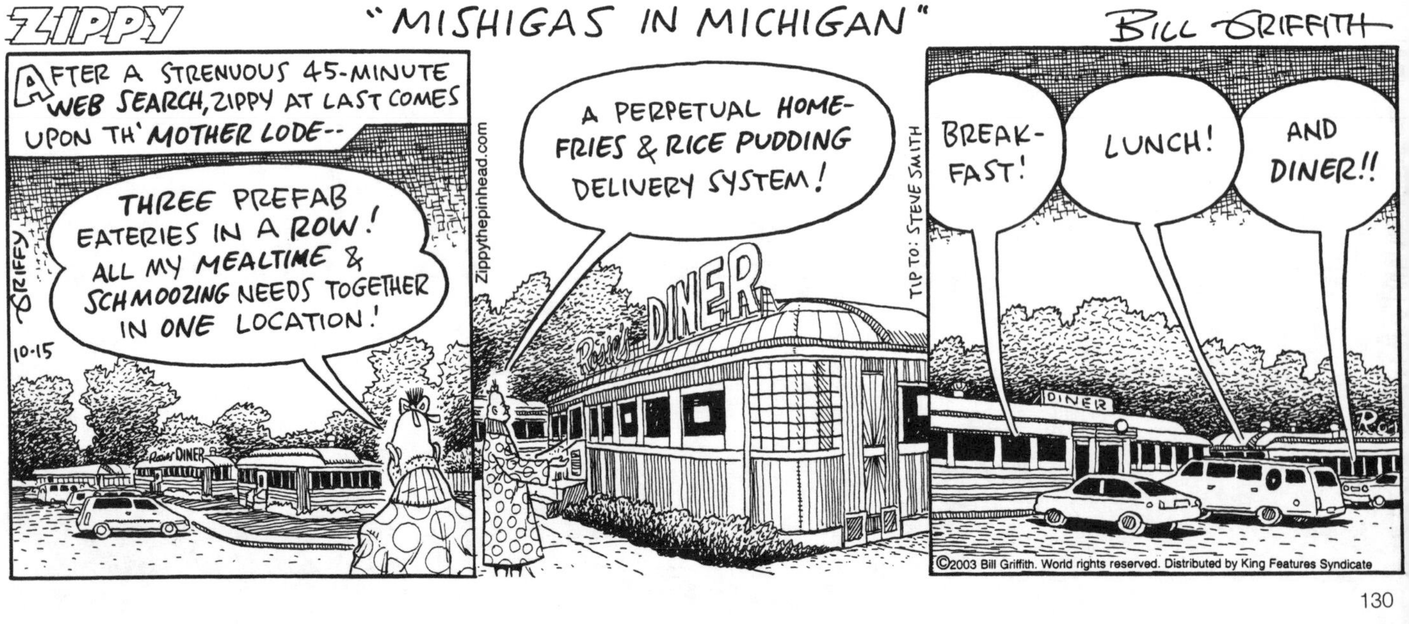
ZIPPY
"MISHIGAS IN MICHIGAN"
BILL GRIFFITH
AFTER A STRENUOUS 45-MINUTE WEB SEARCH, ZIPPY AT LAST COMES UPON TH' MOTHER LODE--
THREE PREFAB EATERIES IN A ROW! ALL MY MEALTIME & SCHMOOZING NEEDS TOGETHER IN ONE LOCATION!
GRIFFY
10-15
Zippythepinhead.com
A PERPETUAL HOME-FRIES & RICE PUDDING DELIVERY SYSTEM!
TIP TO: STEVE SMITH
DINER
BREAK-FAST!
LUNCH!
AND DINER!!
©2003 Bill Griffith. World rights reserved. Distributed by King Features Syndicate

130

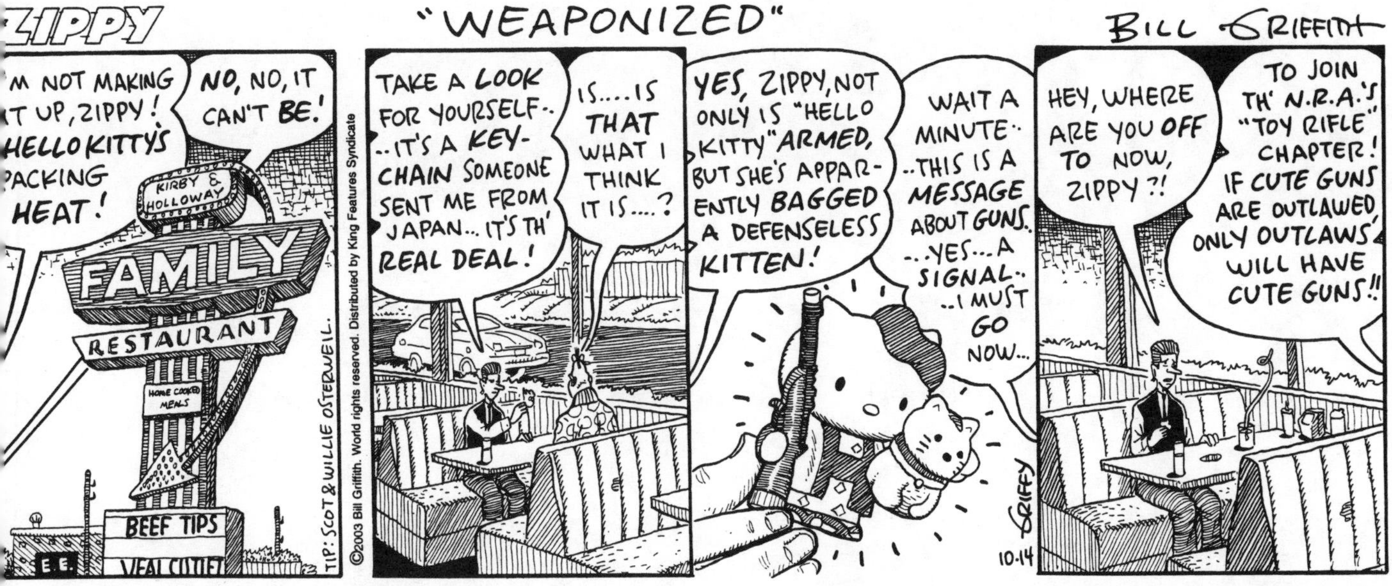
ZIPPY
"WEAPONIZED"
BILL GRIFFITH
'M NOT MAKING IT UP, ZIPPY! HELLO KITTY'S PACKING HEAT!
NO, NO, IT CAN'T BE!
KIRBY & HOLLOWAY
FAMILY RESTAURANT
HOME COOKED MEALS
BEEF TIPS
VEAL CUTLET
E.E.
TIP: SCOT & WILLIE OSTERWEIL.
©2003 Bill Griffith. World rights reserved. Distributed by King Features Syndicate
TAKE A LOOK FOR YOURSELF.. ..IT'S A KEY-CHAIN SOMEONE SENT ME FROM JAPAN... IT'S TH' REAL DEAL!
IS....IS THAT WHAT I THINK IT IS....?
YES, ZIPPY, NOT ONLY IS "HELLO KITTY" ARMED, BUT SHE'S APPARENTLY BAGGED A DEFENSELESS KITTEN!
WAIT A MINUTE.. ..THIS IS A MESSAGE ABOUT GUNS.. ..YES...A SIGNAL.. ..I MUST GO NOW...
GRIFFY
10.14
HEY, WHERE ARE YOU OFF TO NOW, ZIPPY?!
TO JOIN TH' N.R.A.'S "TOY RIFLE" CHAPTER! IF CUTE GUNS ARE OUTLAWED, ONLY OUTLAWS WILL HAVE CUTE GUNS!!

131

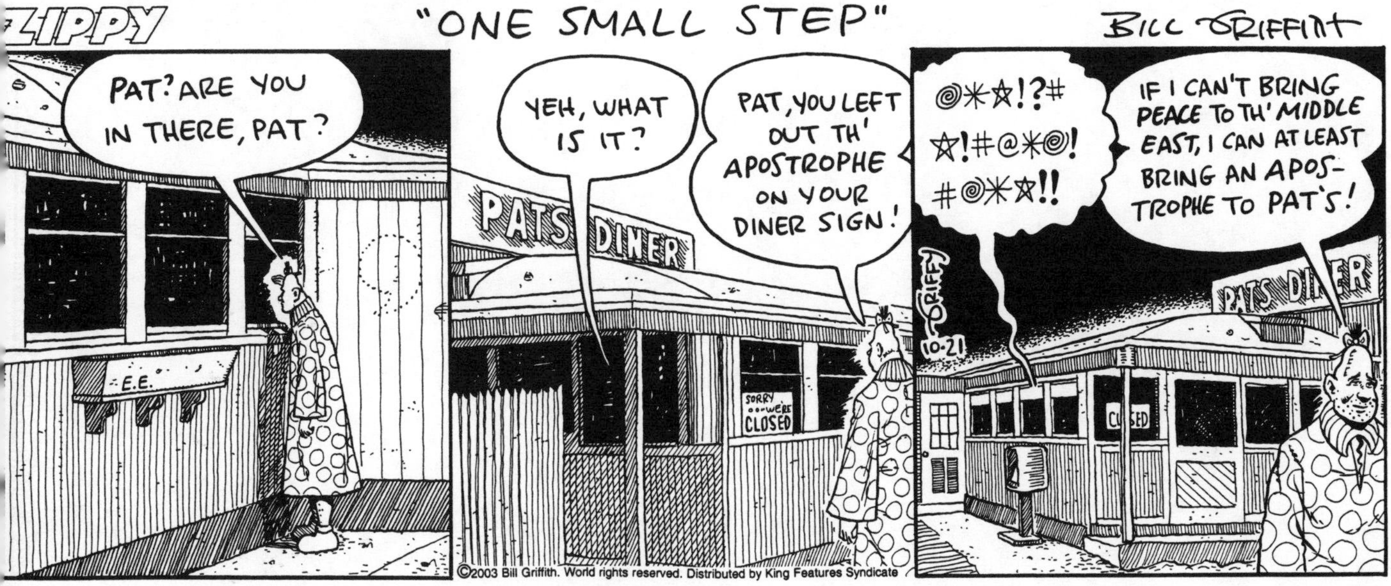
ZIPPY
"ONE SMALL STEP"
BILL GRIFFITH
PAT? ARE YOU IN THERE, PAT?
E.E.
YEH, WHAT IS IT?
PATS DINER
SORRY ...WE'RE CLOSED
PAT, YOU LEFT OUT TH' APOSTROPHE ON YOUR DINER SIGN!
GRIFFY
10-21
@*☆!?# ☆!#@*@! #@*☆!!
IF I CAN'T BRING PEACE TO TH' MIDDLE EAST, I CAN AT LEAST BRING AN APOSTROPHE TO PAT'S!
PATS DINER
CLOSED
©2003 Bill Griffith. World rights reserved. Distributed by King Features Syndicate

132

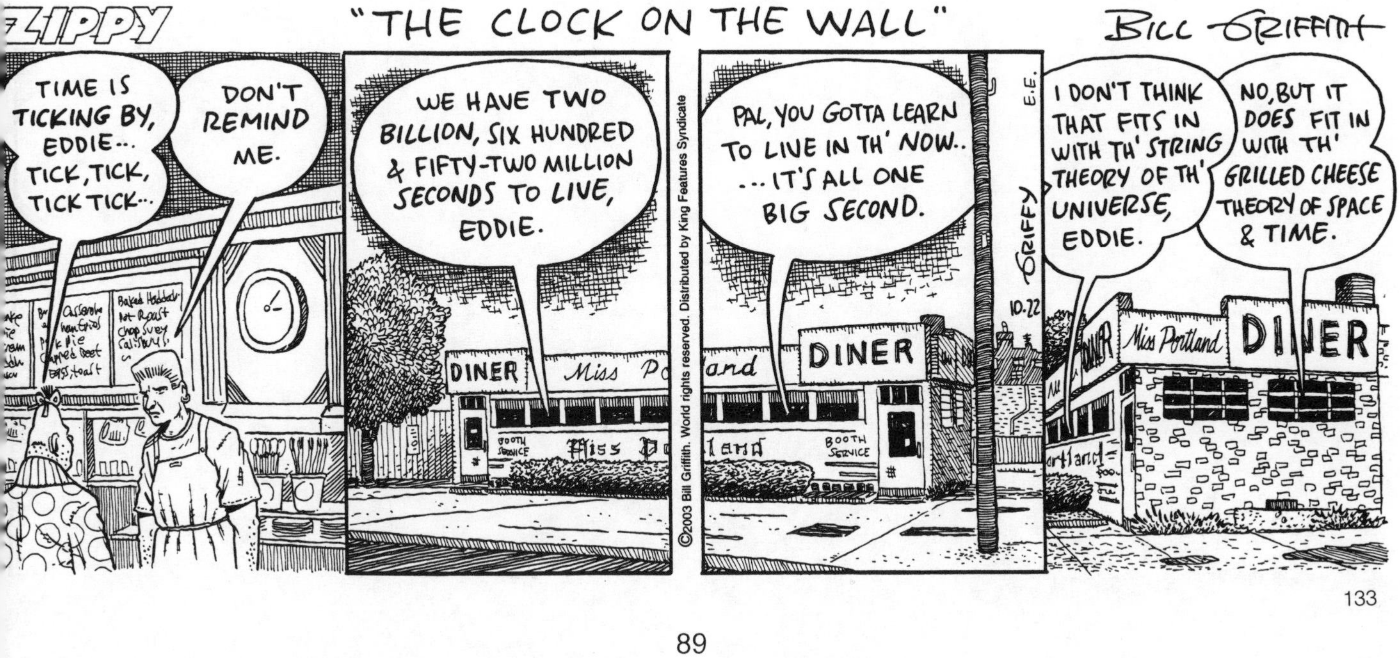
ZIPPY
"THE CLOCK ON THE WALL"
BILL GRIFFITH
TIME IS TICKING BY, EDDIE... TICK, TICK, TICK TICK...
DON'T REMIND ME.
WE HAVE TWO BILLION, SIX HUNDRED & FIFTY-TWO MILLION SECONDS TO LIVE, EDDIE.
DINER Miss Portland
BOOTH SERVICE
©2003 Bill Griffith. World rights reserved. Distributed by King Features Syndicate
PAL, YOU GOTTA LEARN TO LIVE IN TH' NOW.. ...IT'S ALL ONE BIG SECOND.
DINER
E.E.
GRIFFY
10-22
I DON'T THINK THAT FITS IN WITH TH' STRING THEORY OF TH' UNIVERSE, EDDIE.
NO, BUT IT DOES FIT IN WITH TH' GRILLED CHEESE THEORY OF SPACE & TIME.
Miss Portland DINER

133

Roadside Attractions

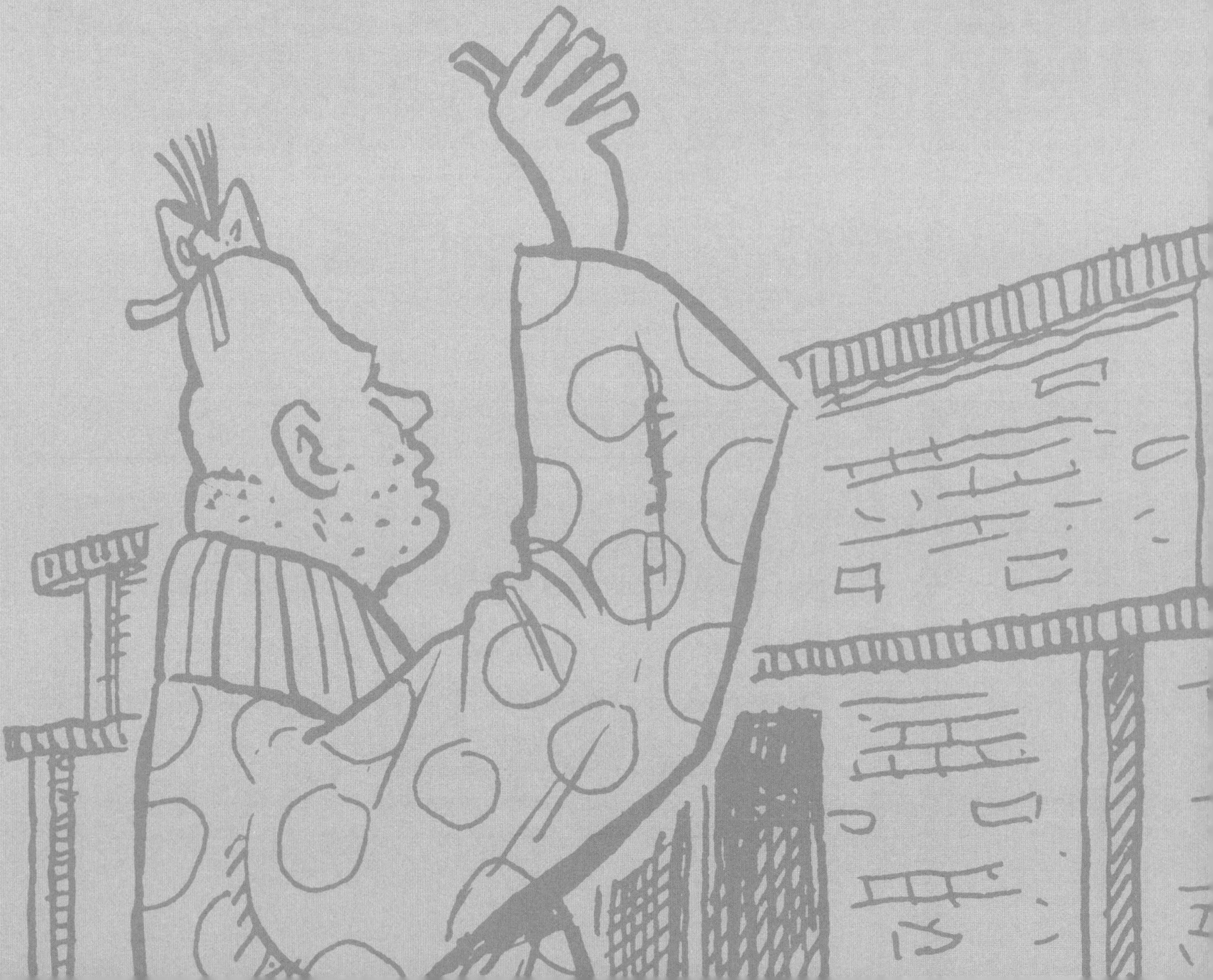

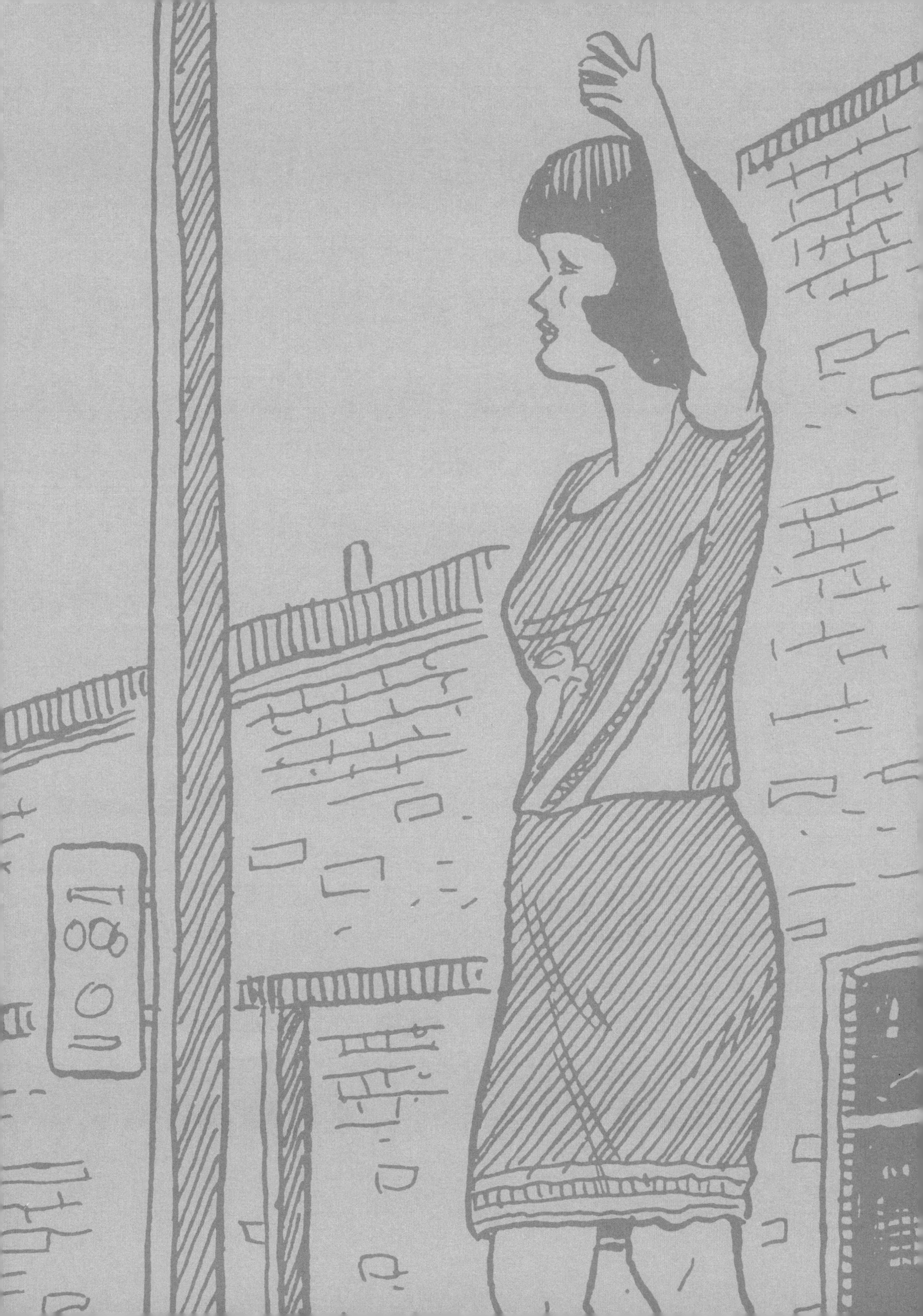

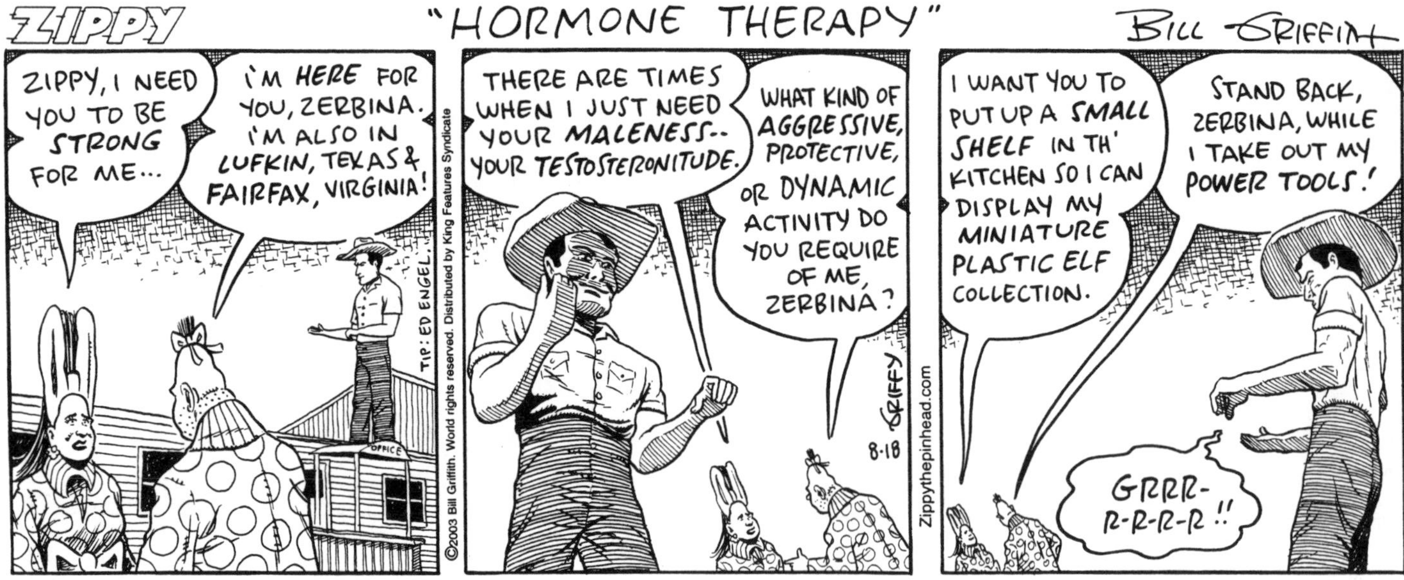
ZIPPY
"HORMONE THERAPY"
BILL GRIFFITH
ZIPPY, I NEED YOU TO BE STRONG FOR ME...
I'M HERE FOR YOU, ZERBINA. I'M ALSO IN LUFKIN, TEXAS & FAIRFAX, VIRGINIA!
TIP: ED ENGEL
©2003 Bill Griffith. World rights reserved. Distributed by King Features Syndicate
OFFICE
THERE ARE TIMES WHEN I JUST NEED YOUR MALENESS-- YOUR TESTOSTERONITUDE.
WHAT KIND OF AGGRESSIVE, PROTECTIVE, OR DYNAMIC ACTIVITY DO YOU REQUIRE OF ME, ZERBINA?
GRIFFY
8·18
Zippythepinhead.com
I WANT YOU TO PUT UP A SMALL SHELF IN TH' KITCHEN SO I CAN DISPLAY MY MINIATURE PLASTIC ELF COLLECTION.
STAND BACK, ZERBINA, WHILE I TAKE OUT MY POWER TOOLS!
GRRR-R-R-R-R!!

134

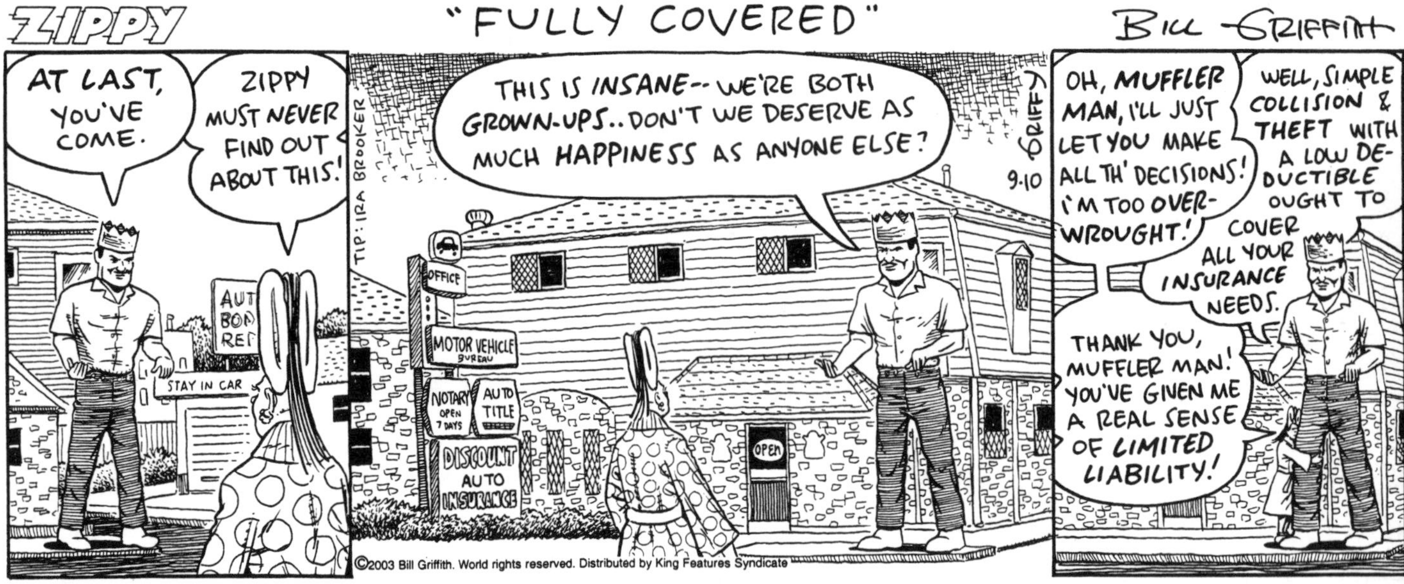
ZIPPY
"FULLY COVERED"
BILL GRIFFITH
AT LAST, YOU'VE COME.
ZIPPY MUST NEVER FIND OUT ABOUT THIS!
STAY IN CAR
TIP: IRA BROOKER
THIS IS INSANE-- WE'RE BOTH GROWN-UPS.. DON'T WE DESERVE AS MUCH HAPPINESS AS ANYONE ELSE?
GRIFFY
9·10
OFFICE
MOTOR VEHICLE BUREAU
NOTARY OPEN 7 DAYS
AUTO TITLE
DISCOUNT AUTO INSURANCE
OPEN
©2003 Bill Griffith. World rights reserved. Distributed by King Features Syndicate
OH, MUFFLER MAN, I'LL JUST LET YOU MAKE ALL TH' DECISIONS! I'M TOO OVERWROUGHT!
WELL, SIMPLE COLLISION & THEFT WITH A LOW DEDUCTIBLE OUGHT TO COVER ALL YOUR INSURANCE NEEDS.
THANK YOU, MUFFLER MAN! YOU'VE GIVEN ME A REAL SENSE OF LIMITED LIABILITY!

135

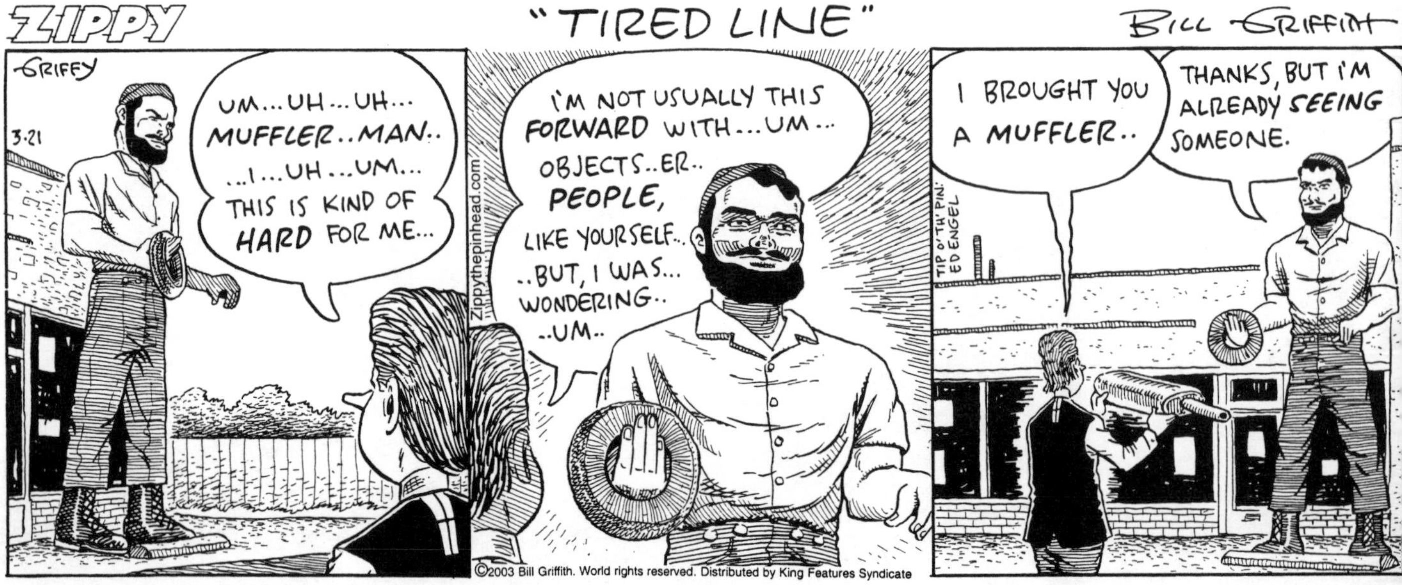
ZIPPY
"TIRED LINE"
BILL GRIFFITH
GRIFFY
3·21
UM...UH...UH... MUFFLER..MAN.. ...I...UH...UM... THIS IS KIND OF HARD FOR ME...
Zippythepinhead.com
I'M NOT USUALLY THIS FORWARD WITH...UM... OBJECTS..ER.. PEOPLE, LIKE YOURSELF.. ..BUT, I WAS... WONDERING.. ..UM..
©2003 Bill Griffith. World rights reserved. Distributed by King Features Syndicate
I BROUGHT YOU A MUFFLER..
THANKS, BUT I'M ALREADY SEEING SOMEONE.
TIP O' TH' PIN: ED ENGEL

136

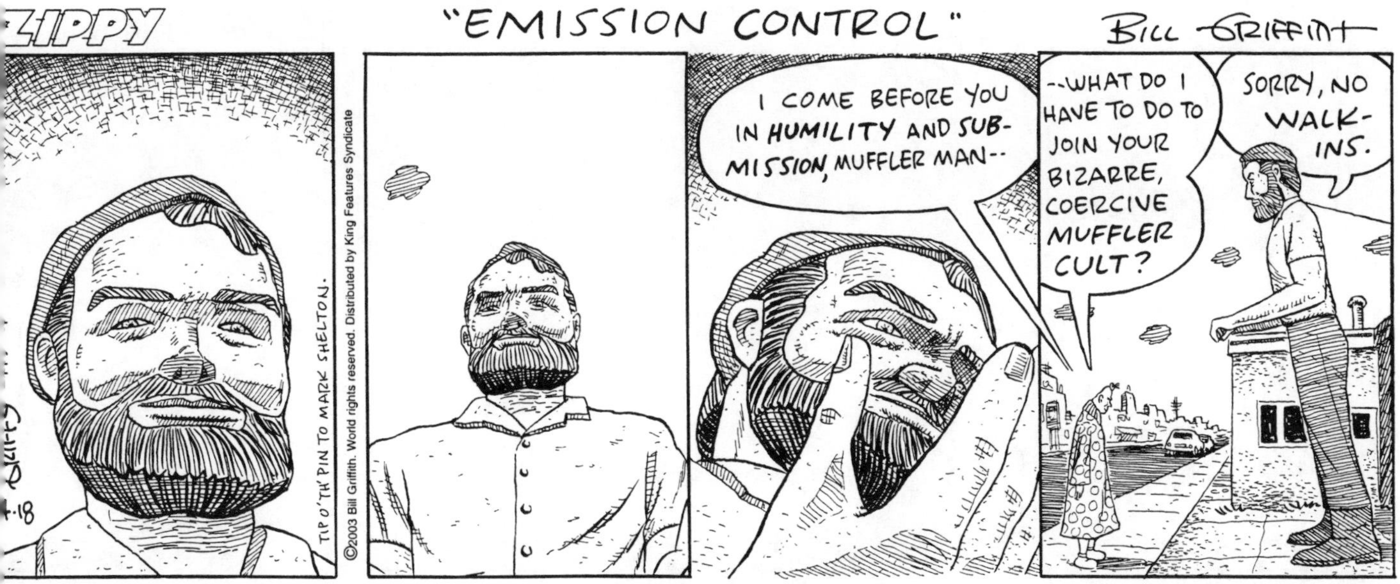
ZIPPY
"EMISSION CONTROL"
BILL GRIFFITH
TIP O' TH' PIN TO MARK SHELTON.
©2003 Bill Griffith. World rights reserved. Distributed by King Features Syndicate
I COME BEFORE YOU IN HUMILITY AND SUBMISSION, MUFFLER MAN--
--WHAT DO I HAVE TO DO TO JOIN YOUR BIZARRE, COERCIVE MUFFLER CULT?
SORRY, NO WALK-INS.

137

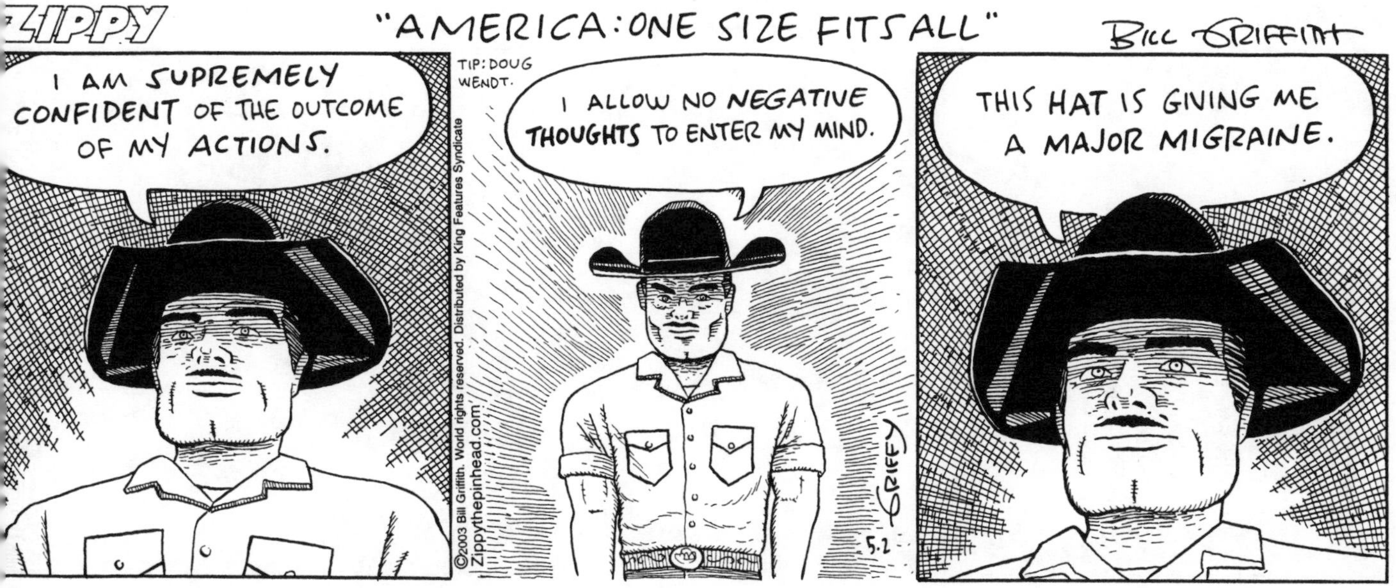
ZIPPY
"AMERICA: ONE SIZE FITS ALL"
BILL GRIFFITH
I AM SUPREMELY CONFIDENT OF THE OUTCOME OF MY ACTIONS.
TIP: DOUG WENDT.
©2003 Bill Griffith. World rights reserved. Distributed by King Features Syndicate
Zippythepinhead.com
I ALLOW NO NEGATIVE THOUGHTS TO ENTER MY MIND.
GRIFFY 5.2
THIS HAT IS GIVING ME A MAJOR MIGRAINE.

138

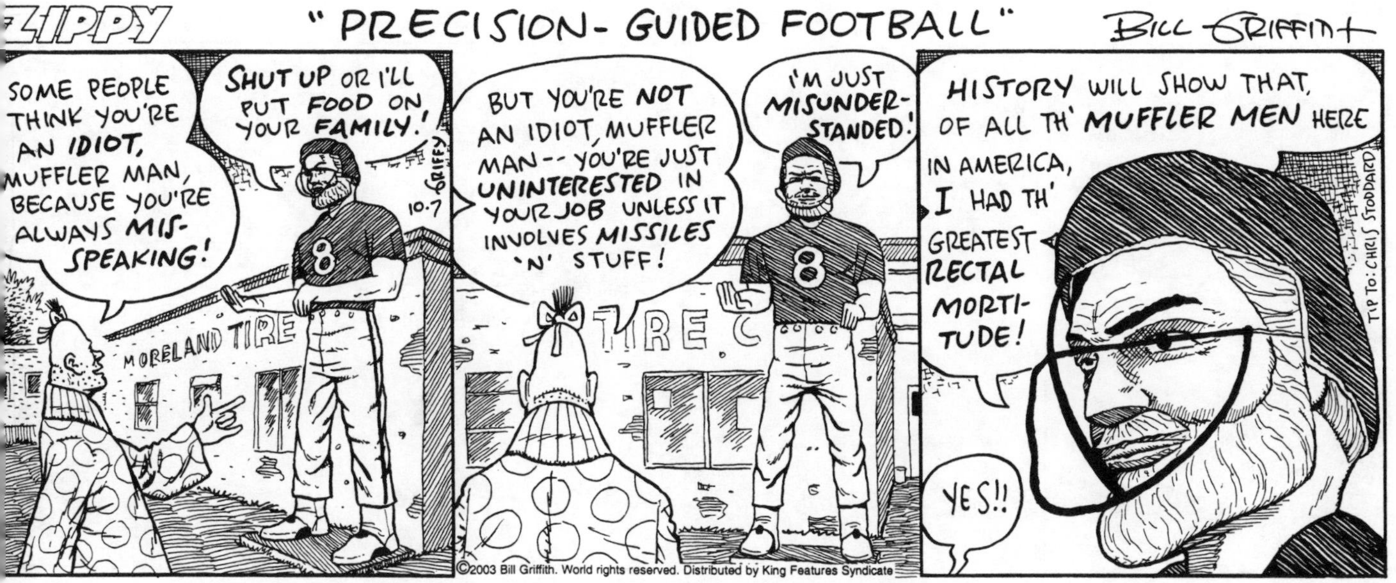
ZIPPY
" PRECISION- GUIDED FOOTBALL"
BILL GRIFFITH
SOME PEOPLE THINK YOU'RE AN IDIOT, MUFFLER MAN, BECAUSE YOU'RE ALWAYS MIS-SPEAKING!
SHUT UP OR I'LL PUT FOOD ON YOUR FAMILY!
GRIFFY 10.7
MORELAND TIRE
BUT YOU'RE NOT AN IDIOT, MUFFLER MAN-- YOU'RE JUST UNINTERESTED IN YOUR JOB UNLESS IT INVOLVES MISSILES 'N' STUFF!
I'M JUST MISUNDER-STANDED!
TIRE C
©2003 Bill Griffith. World rights reserved. Distributed by King Features Syndicate
HISTORY WILL SHOW THAT, OF ALL TH' MUFFLER MEN HERE IN AMERICA, I HAD TH' GREATEST RECTAL MORTI-TUDE!
TIP TO: CHRIS STODDARD
YES!!

139

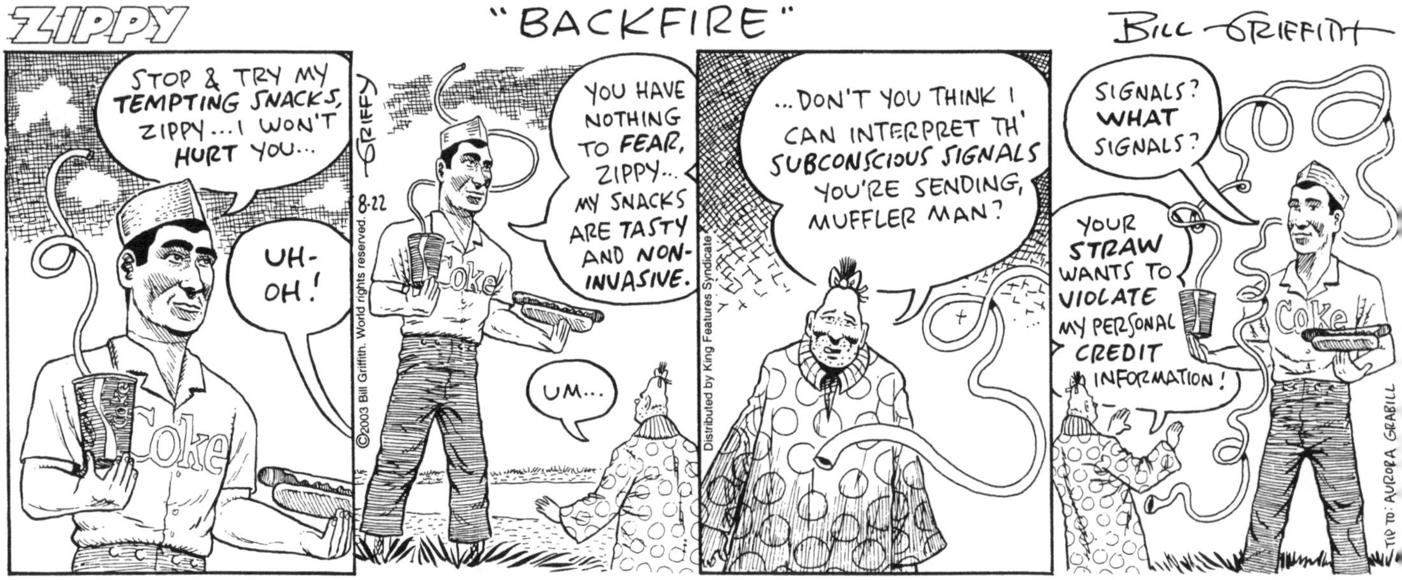
ZIPPY
"BACKFIRE"
BILL GRIFFITH
STOP & TRY MY TEMPTING SNACKS, ZIPPY... I WON'T HURT YOU...
UH-OH!
GRIFFY 8-22
©2003 Bill Griffith. World rights reserved.
YOU HAVE NOTHING TO FEAR, ZIPPY... MY SNACKS ARE TASTY AND NON-INVASIVE.
UM...
Distributed by King Features Syndicate
...DON'T YOU THINK I CAN INTERPRET TH' SUBCONSCIOUS SIGNALS YOU'RE SENDING, MUFFLER MAN?
SIGNALS? WHAT SIGNALS?
YOUR STRAW WANTS TO VIOLATE MY PERSONAL CREDIT INFORMATION!
TIP TO: AURORA GRABILL

140

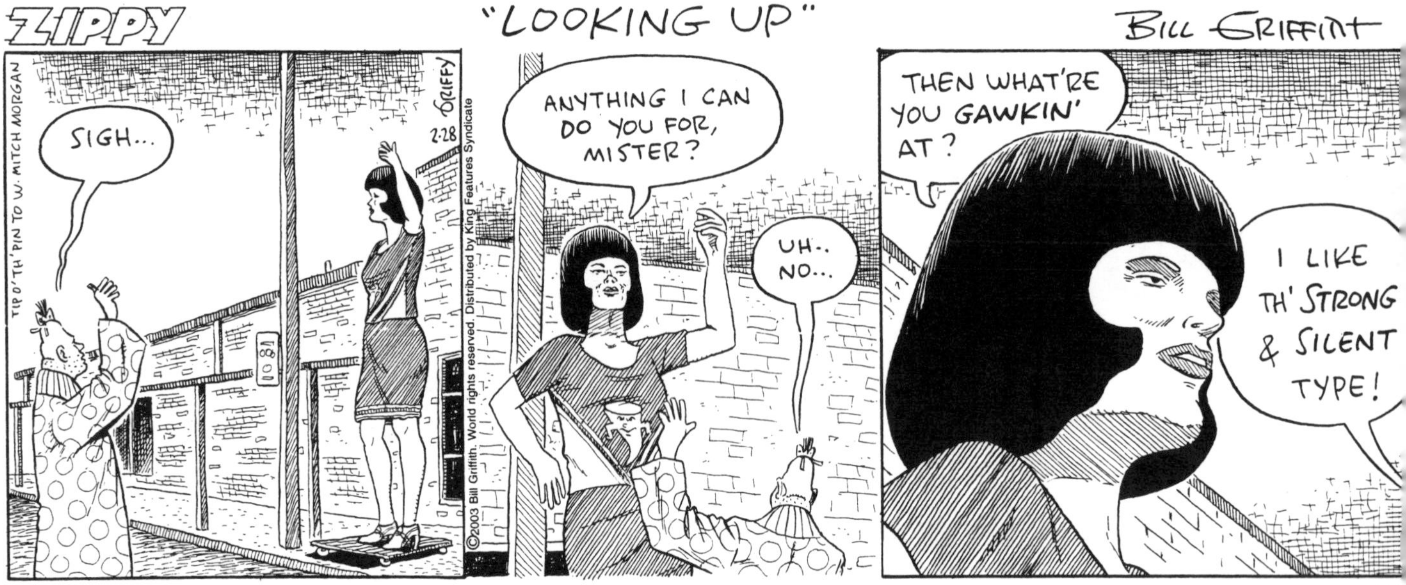
ZIPPY
"LOOKING UP"
BILL GRIFFITH
TIP O' TH' PIN TO W. MITCH MORGAN
SIGH...
GRIFFY 2-28
©2003 Bill Griffith. World rights reserved. Distributed by King Features Syndicate
ANYTHING I CAN DO YOU FOR, MISTER?
UH.. NO...
THEN WHAT'RE YOU GAWKIN' AT?
I LIKE TH' STRONG & SILENT TYPE!

141

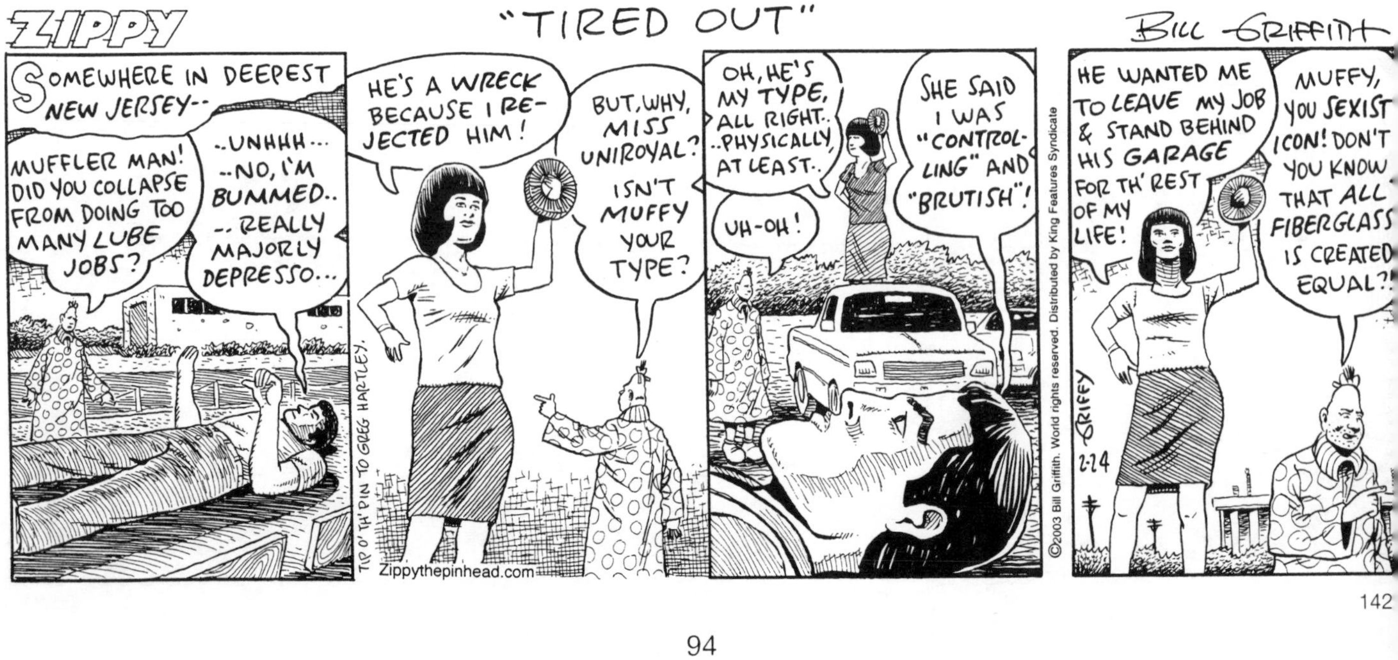
ZIPPY
"TIRED OUT"
BILL GRIFFITH
SOMEWHERE IN DEEPEST NEW JERSEY--
MUFFLER MAN! DID YOU COLLAPSE FROM DOING TOO MANY LUBE JOBS?
--UNHHH... --NO, I'M BUMMED.. --REALLY MAJORLY DEPRESSO...
HE'S A WRECK BECAUSE I REJECTED HIM!
BUT, WHY, MISS UNIROYAL? ISN'T MUFFY YOUR TYPE?
TIP O' TH' PIN TO GREG HARTLEY.
Zippythepinhead.com
OH, HE'S MY TYPE, ALL RIGHT.. ..PHYSICALLY, AT LEAST..
SHE SAID I WAS "CONTROLLING" AND "BRUTISH"!
UH-OH!
©2003 Bill Griffith. World rights reserved. Distributed by King Features Syndicate
HE WANTED ME TO LEAVE MY JOB & STAND BEHIND HIS GARAGE FOR TH' REST OF MY LIFE!
MUFFY, YOU SEXIST ICON! DON'T YOU KNOW THAT ALL FIBERGLASS IS CREATED EQUAL?
GRIFFY 2-24

142

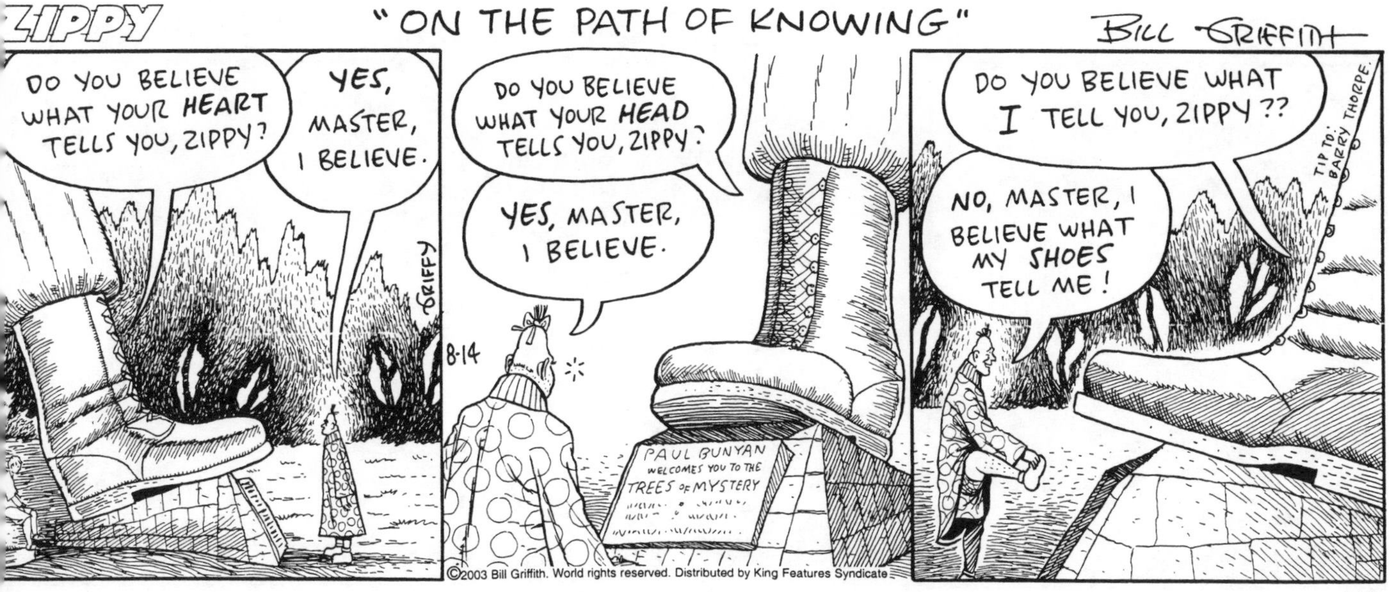
ZIPPY
"ON THE PATH OF KNOWING"
BILL GRIFFITH
DO YOU BELIEVE WHAT YOUR HEART TELLS YOU, ZIPPY?
YES, MASTER, I BELIEVE.
GRIFFY
8·14
DO YOU BELIEVE WHAT YOUR HEAD TELLS YOU, ZIPPY?
YES, MASTER, I BELIEVE.
PAUL BUNYAN WELCOMES YOU TO THE TREES OF MYSTERY
DO YOU BELIEVE WHAT I TELL YOU, ZIPPY??
NO, MASTER, I BELIEVE WHAT MY SHOES TELL ME!
TIP TO: BARRY THORPE.
©2003 Bill Griffith. World rights reserved. Distributed by King Features Syndicate

143

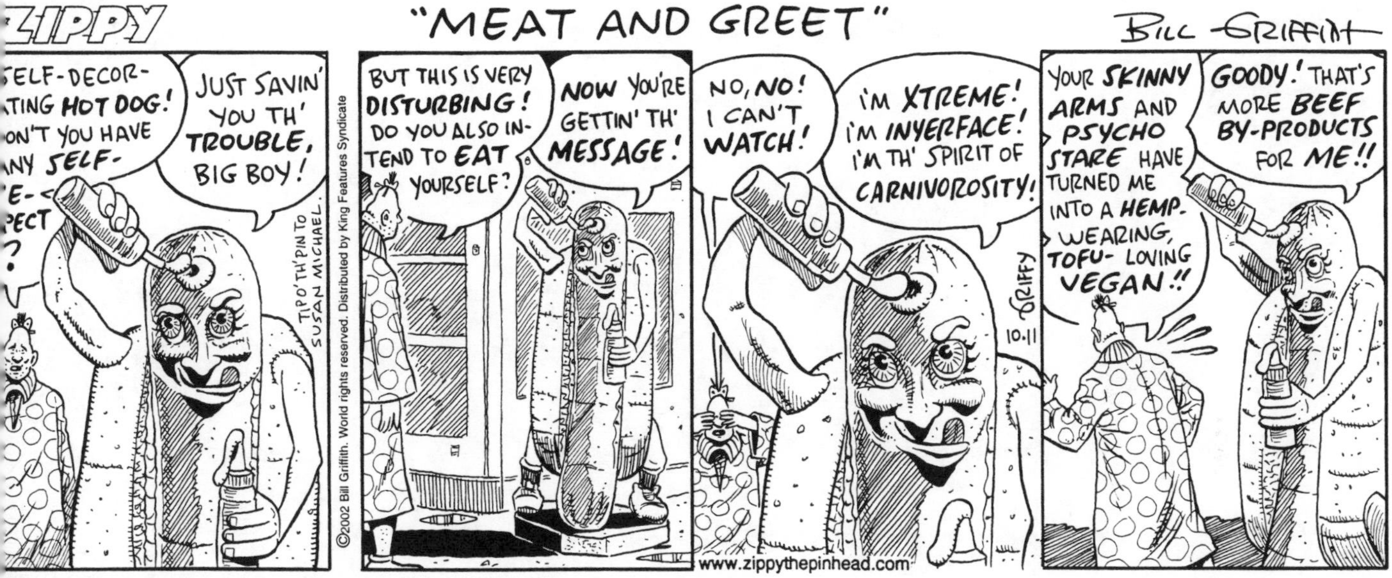
ZIPPY
"MEAT AND GREET"
BILL GRIFFITH
ELF-DECOR-TING HOT DOG! ON'T YOU HAVE NY SELF-E-PECT ?
JUST SAVIN' YOU TH' TROUBLE, BIG BOY!
TIP O' TH' PIN TO SUSAN MICHAEL
©2002 Bill Griffith. World rights reserved. Distributed by King Features Syndicate
BUT THIS IS VERY DISTURBING! DO YOU ALSO INTEND TO EAT YOURSELF?
NOW YOU'RE GETTIN' TH' MESSAGE!
NO, NO! I CAN'T WATCH!
I'M XTREME! I'M INYERFACE! I'M TH' SPIRIT OF CARNIVOROSITY!
GRIFFY
10·11
YOUR SKINNY ARMS AND PSYCHO STARE HAVE TURNED ME INTO A HEMP-WEARING, TOFU-LOVING VEGAN!!
GOODY! THAT'S MORE BEEF BY-PRODUCTS FOR ME!!
www.zippythepinhead.com

144

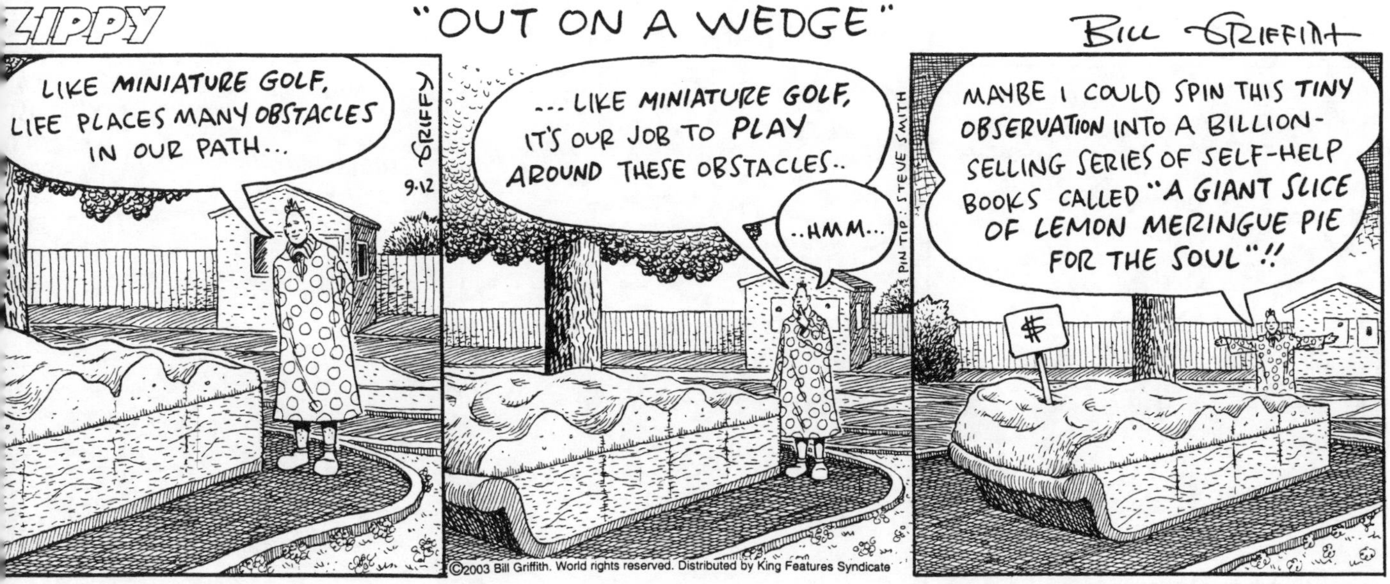
ZIPPY
"OUT ON A WEDGE"
BILL GRIFFITH
LIKE MINIATURE GOLF, LIFE PLACES MANY OBSTACLES IN OUR PATH...
GRIFFY
9·12
...LIKE MINIATURE GOLF, IT'S OUR JOB TO PLAY AROUND THESE OBSTACLES..
..HMM...
PIN TIP: STEVE SMITH
MAYBE I COULD SPIN THIS TINY OBSERVATION INTO A BILLION-SELLING SERIES OF SELF-HELP BOOKS CALLED "A GIANT SLICE OF LEMON MERINGUE PIE FOR THE SOUL"!!
$
©2003 Bill Griffith. World rights reserved. Distributed by King Features Syndicate

145

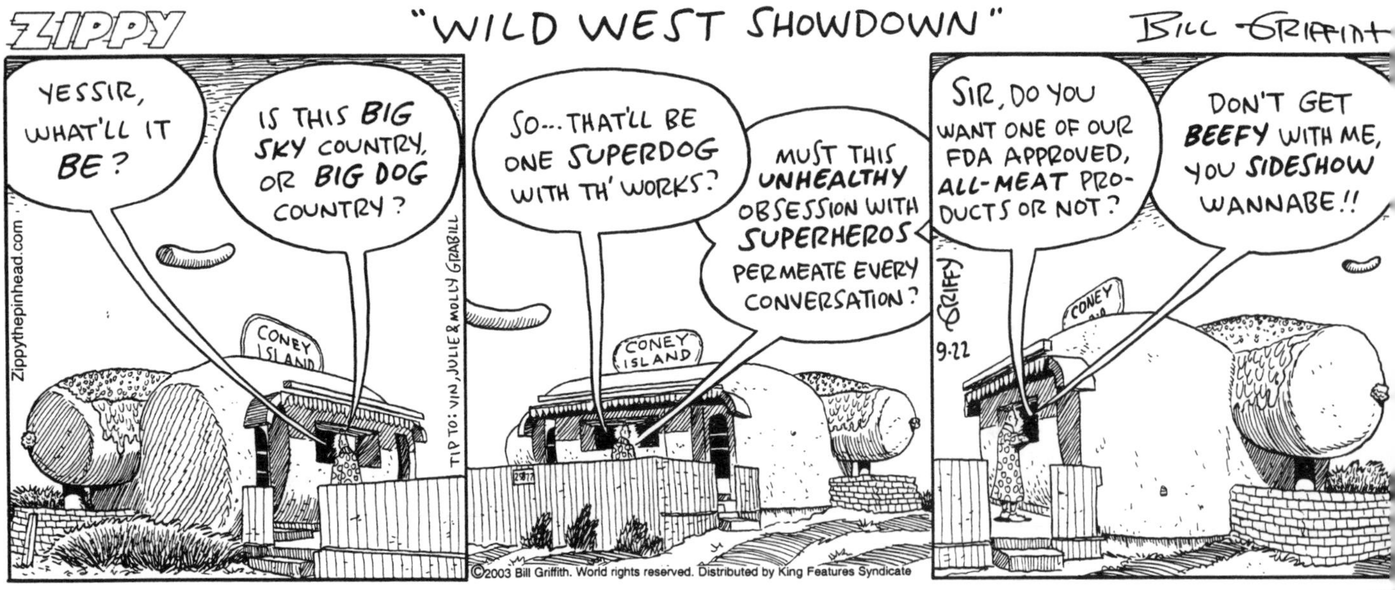
ZIPPY
"WILD WEST SHOWDOWN"
BILL GRIFFITH
YESSIR, WHAT'LL IT BE?
IS THIS BIG SKY COUNTRY, OR BIG DOG COUNTRY?
Zippythepinhead.com
CONEY ISLAND
TIP TO: VIN, JULIE & MOLLY GRABILL
SO... THAT'LL BE ONE SUPERDOG WITH TH' WORKS?
MUST THIS UNHEALTHY OBSESSION WITH SUPERHEROS PERMEATE EVERY CONVERSATION?
CONEY ISLAND
SIR, DO YOU WANT ONE OF OUR FDA APPROVED, ALL-MEAT PRODUCTS OR NOT?
DON'T GET BEEFY WITH ME, YOU SIDESHOW WANNABE!!
GRIFFY 9-22
CONEY
©2003 Bill Griffith. World rights reserved. Distributed by King Features Syndicate

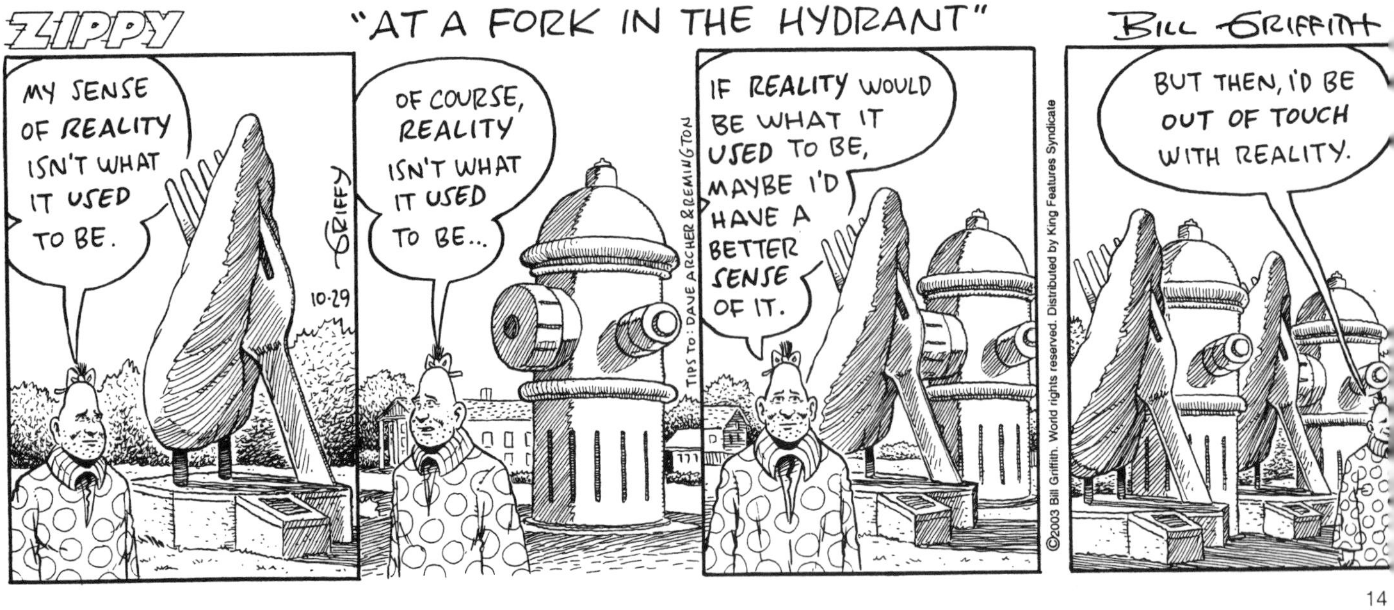
ZIPPY
"AT A FORK IN THE HYDRANT"
BILL GRIFFITH
MY SENSE OF REALITY ISN'T WHAT IT USED TO BE.
GRIFFY 10-29
OF COURSE, REALITY ISN'T WHAT IT USED TO BE...
TIPS TO: DAVE ARCHER & REMINGTON
IF REALITY WOULD BE WHAT IT USED TO BE, MAYBE I'D HAVE A BETTER SENSE OF IT.
©2003 Bill Griffith. World rights reserved. Distributed by King Features Syndicate
BUT THEN, I'D BE OUT OF TOUCH WITH REALITY.

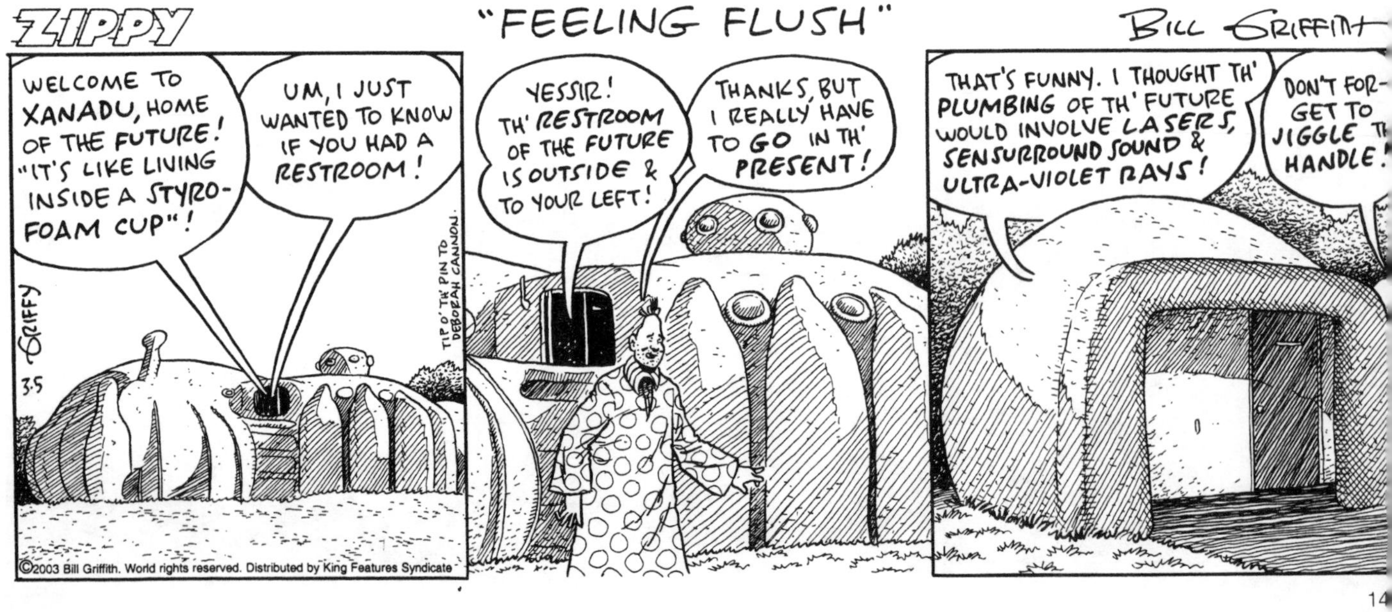
ZIPPY
"FEELING FLUSH"
BILL GRIFFITH
WELCOME TO XANADU, HOME OF THE FUTURE! "IT'S LIKE LIVING INSIDE A STYRO-FOAM CUP"!
UM, I JUST WANTED TO KNOW IF YOU HAD A RESTROOM!
GRIFFY 3-5
TIP O' TH' PIN TO DEBORAH CANNON
YESSIR! TH' RESTROOM OF THE FUTURE IS OUTSIDE & TO YOUR LEFT!
THANKS, BUT I REALLY HAVE TO GO IN TH' PRESENT!
THAT'S FUNNY. I THOUGHT TH' PLUMBING OF TH' FUTURE WOULD INVOLVE LASERS, SENSURROUND SOUND & ULTRA-VIOLET RAYS!
DON'T FOR-GET TO JIGGLE TH HANDLE.
©2003 Bill Griffith. World rights reserved. Distributed by King Features Syndicate

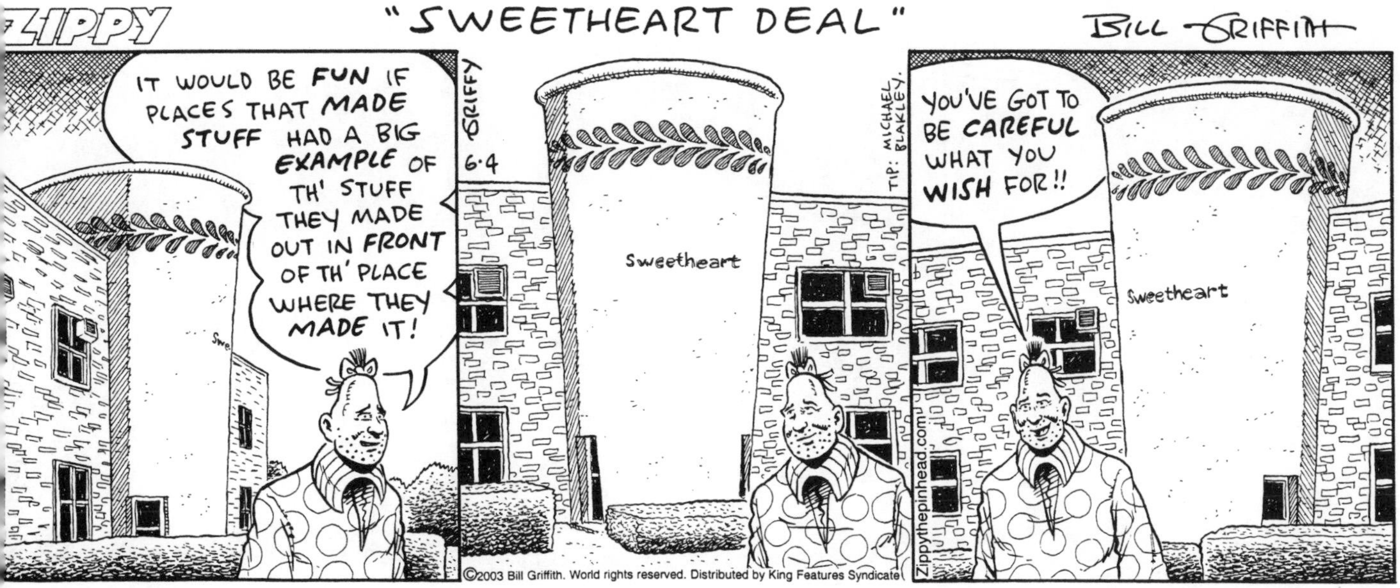
ZIPPY
"SWEETHEART DEAL"
BILL GRIFFITH
IT WOULD BE FUN IF PLACES THAT MADE STUFF HAD A BIG EXAMPLE OF TH' STUFF THEY MADE OUT IN FRONT OF TH' PLACE WHERE THEY MADE IT!
GRIFFY 6·4
Sweetheart
TIP: MICHAEL BLAKLEY.
YOU'VE GOT TO BE CAREFUL WHAT YOU WISH FOR!!
Sweetheart
Zippythepinhead.com
©2003 Bill Griffith. World rights reserved. Distributed by King Features Syndicate

149

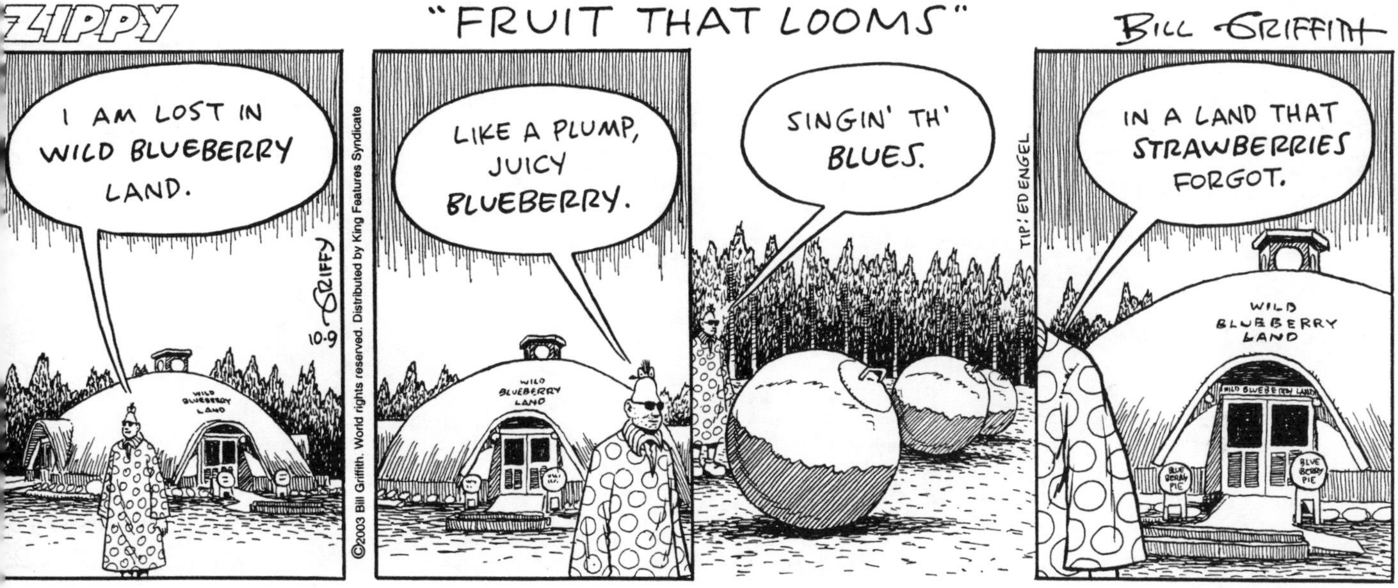
ZIPPY
"FRUIT THAT LOOMS"
BILL GRIFFITH
I AM LOST IN WILD BLUEBERRY LAND.
GRIFFY 10·9
©2003 Bill Griffith. World rights reserved. Distributed by King Features Syndicate
LIKE A PLUMP, JUICY BLUEBERRY.
SINGIN' TH' BLUES.
TIP: ED ENGEL
IN A LAND THAT STRAWBERRIES FORGOT.
WILD BLUEBERRY LAND

150

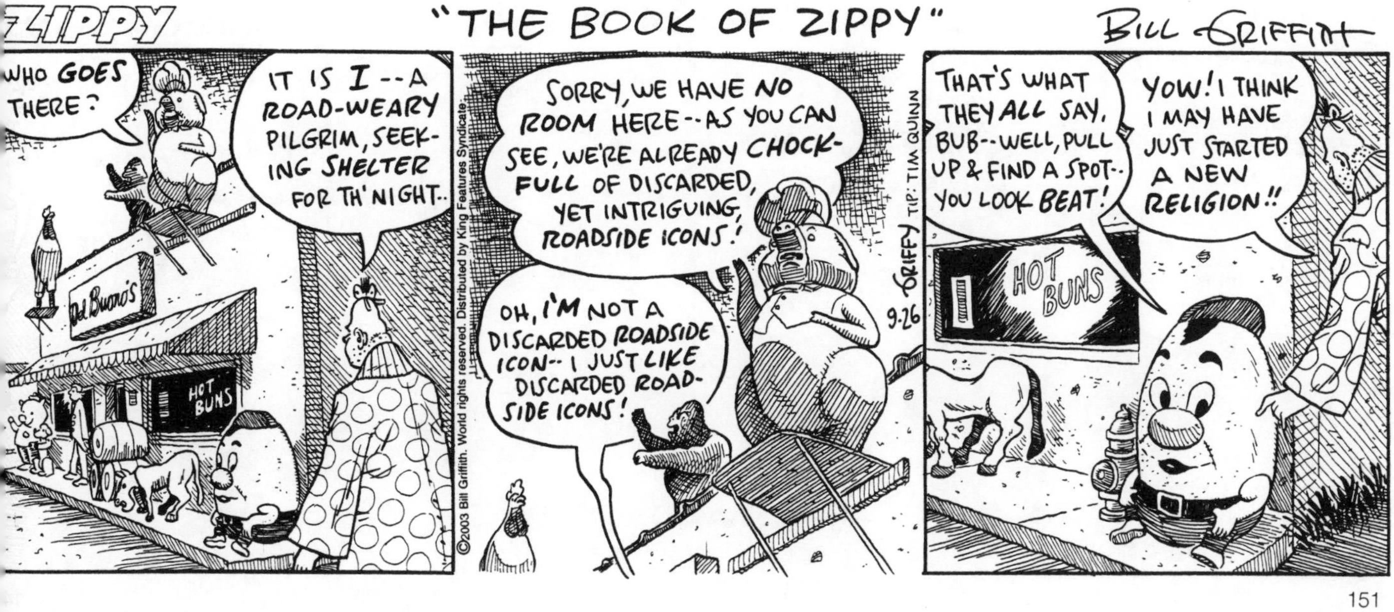
ZIPPY
"THE BOOK OF ZIPPY"
BILL GRIFFITH
WHO GOES THERE?
IT IS I --A ROAD-WEARY PILGRIM, SEEKING SHELTER FOR TH' NIGHT..
Del Buono's
HOT BUNS
©2003 Bill Griffith. World rights reserved. Distributed by King Features Syndicate
SORRY, WE HAVE NO ROOM HERE--AS YOU CAN SEE, WE'RE ALREADY CHOCK-FULL OF DISCARDED, YET INTRIGUING, ROADSIDE ICONS!
OH, I'M NOT A DISCARDED ROADSIDE ICON-- I JUST LIKE DISCARDED ROADSIDE ICONS!
GRIFFY 9·26
TIP: TIM QUINN
THAT'S WHAT THEY ALL SAY, BUB--WELL, PULL UP & FIND A SPOT-- YOU LOOK BEAT!
YOW! I THINK I MAY HAVE JUST STARTED A NEW RELIGION!!
HOT BUNS

151

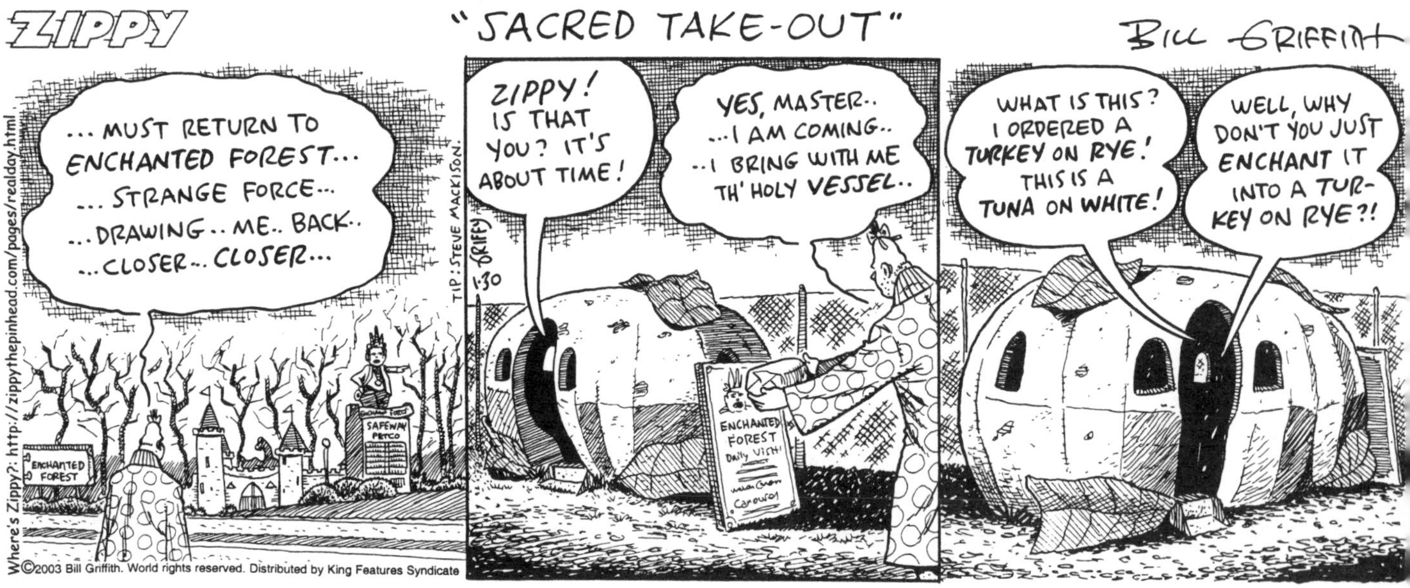
ZIPPY
"SACRED TAKE-OUT"
BILL GRIFFITH
... MUST RETURN TO ENCHANTED FOREST... ... STRANGE FORCE... ... DRAWING.. ME.. BACK.. ... CLOSER... CLOSER...
ENCHANTED FOREST
SAFEWAY PETCO
Where's Zippy?: http://zippythepinhead.com/pages/realday.html.
©2003 Bill Griffith. World rights reserved. Distributed by King Features Syndicate
ZIPPY! IS THAT YOU? IT'S ABOUT TIME!
YES, MASTER.. ...I AM COMING.. ..I BRING WITH ME TH' HOLY VESSEL..
TIP: STEVE MACKISON.
GRIFFY 1·30
ENCHANTED FOREST Daily VISIT!
WHAT IS THIS? I ORDERED A TURKEY ON RYE! THIS IS A TUNA ON WHITE!
WELL, WHY DON'T YOU JUST ENCHANT IT INTO A TURKEY ON RYE?!

152

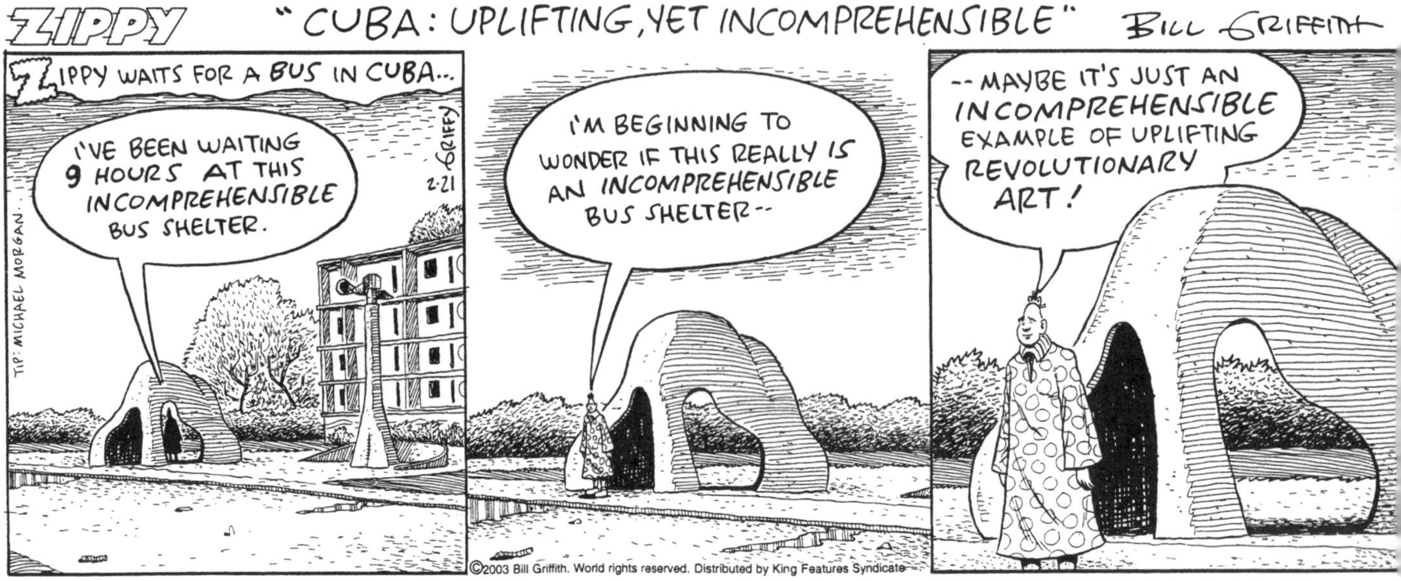
ZIPPY
"CUBA: UPLIFTING, YET INCOMPREHENSIBLE"
BILL GRIFFITH
ZIPPY WAITS FOR A BUS IN CUBA...
I'VE BEEN WAITING 9 HOURS AT THIS INCOMPREHENSIBLE BUS SHELTER.
TIP: MICHAEL MORGAN.
GRIFFY 2·21
I'M BEGINNING TO WONDER IF THIS REALLY IS AN INCOMPREHENSIBLE BUS SHELTER--
©2003 Bill Griffith. World rights reserved. Distributed by King Features Syndicate
-- MAYBE IT'S JUST AN INCOMPREHENSIBLE EXAMPLE OF UPLIFTING REVOLUTIONARY ART!

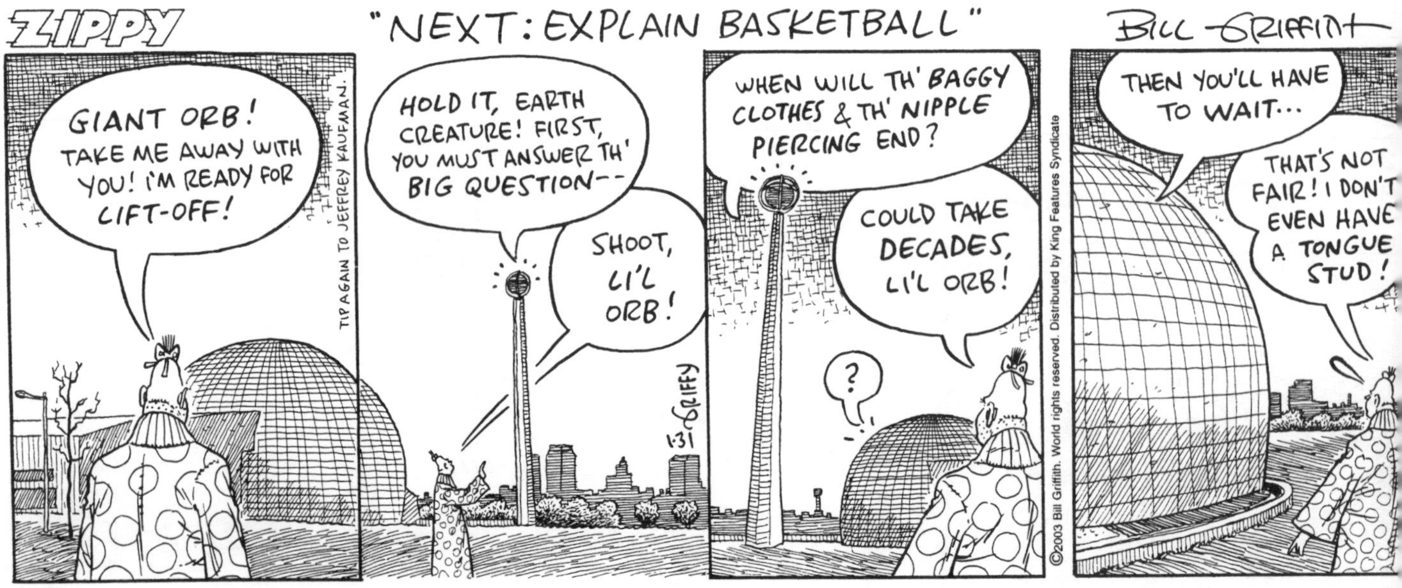
ZIPPY
"NEXT: EXPLAIN BASKETBALL"
BILL GRIFFITH
GIANT ORB! TAKE ME AWAY WITH YOU! I'M READY FOR LIFT-OFF!
TIP AGAIN TO JEFFREY KAUFMAN.
HOLD IT, EARTH CREATURE! FIRST, YOU MUST ANSWER TH' BIG QUESTION--
SHOOT, LI'L ORB!
GRIFFY 1·31
WHEN WILL TH' BAGGY CLOTHES & TH' NIPPLE PIERCING END?
COULD TAKE DECADES, LI'L ORB!
?
©2003 Bill Griffith. World rights reserved. Distributed by King Features Syndicate
THEN YOU'LL HAVE TO WAIT...
THAT'S NOT FAIR! I DON'T EVEN HAVE A TONGUE STUD!

15

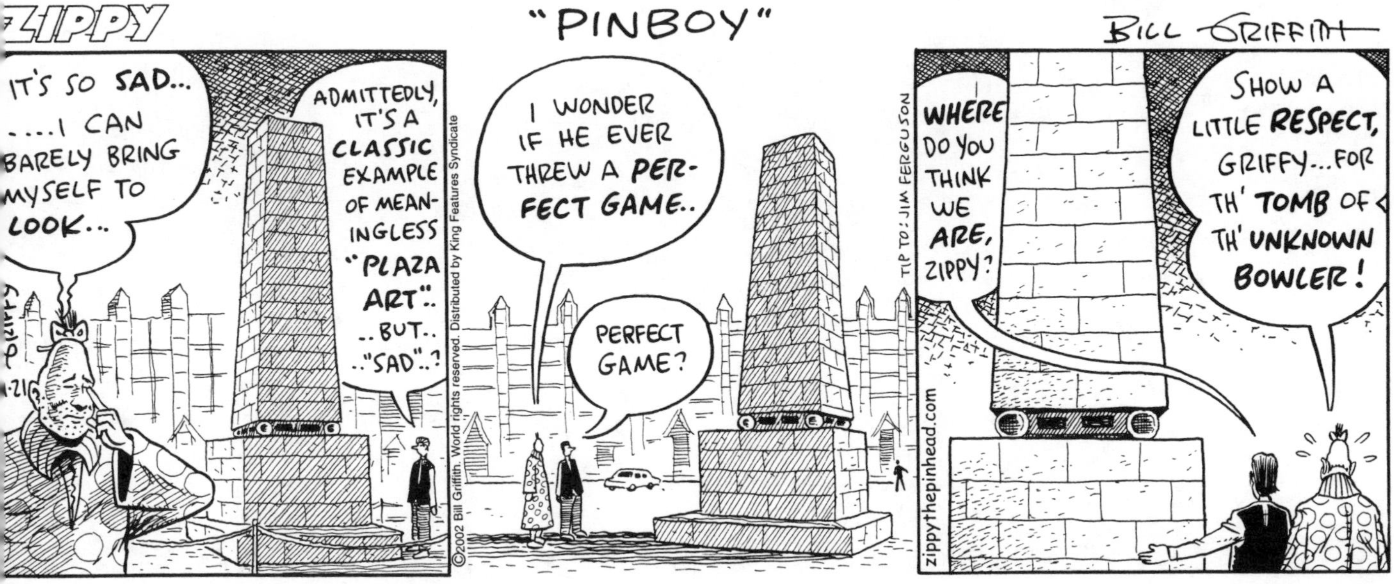
ZIPPY
"PINBOY"
BILL GRIFFITH
IT'S SO SAD... ....I CAN BARELY BRING MYSELF TO LOOK...
ADMITTEDLY, IT'S A CLASSIC EXAMPLE OF MEANINGLESS "PLAZA ART".. ..BUT.. .."SAD"..?
I WONDER IF HE EVER THREW A PERFECT GAME..
PERFECT GAME?
WHERE DO YOU THINK WE ARE, ZIPPY?
SHOW A LITTLE RESPECT, GRIFFY...FOR TH' TOMB OF TH' UNKNOWN BOWLER!
TIP TO: JIM FERGUSON
©2002 Bill Griffith. World rights reserved. Distributed by King Features Syndicate
zippythepinhead.com

154

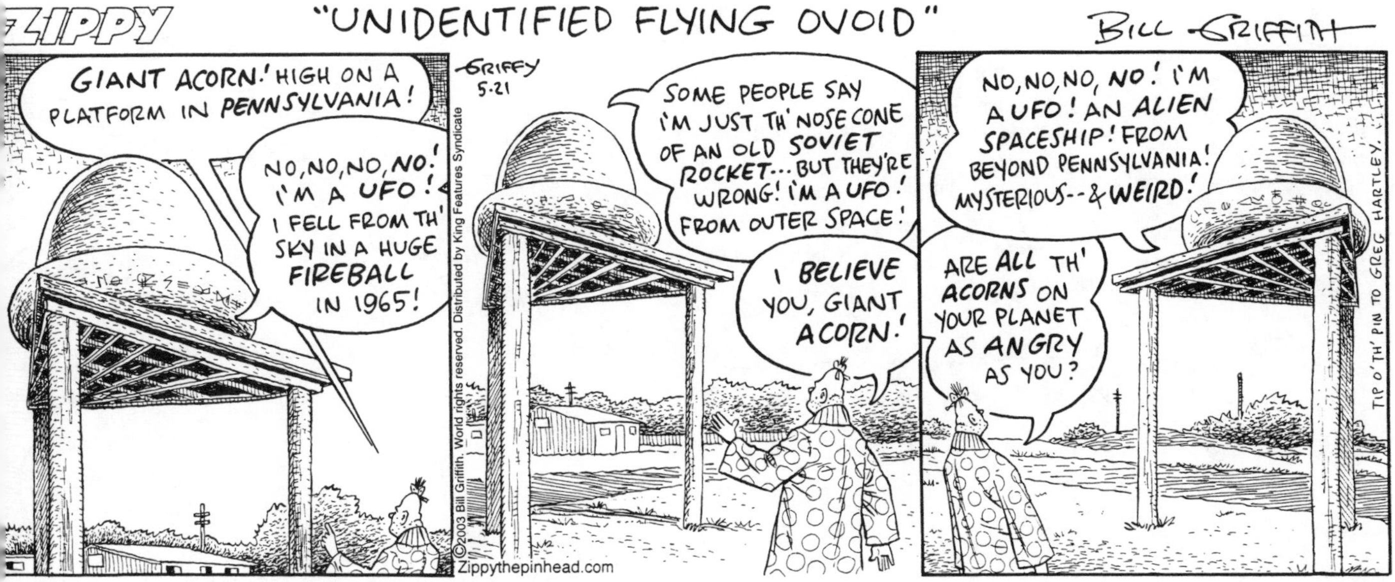
ZIPPY
"UNIDENTIFIED FLYING OVOID"
BILL GRIFFITH
GIANT ACORN! HIGH ON A PLATFORM IN PENNSYLVANIA!
NO, NO, NO, NO! I'M A UFO! I FELL FROM TH' SKY IN A HUGE FIREBALL IN 1965!
SOME PEOPLE SAY I'M JUST TH' NOSE CONE OF AN OLD SOVIET ROCKET... BUT THEY'RE WRONG! I'M A UFO! FROM OUTER SPACE!
I BELIEVE YOU, GIANT ACORN!
NO, NO, NO, NO! I'M A UFO! AN ALIEN SPACESHIP! FROM BEYOND PENNSYLVANIA! MYSTERIOUS--& WEIRD!
ARE ALL TH' ACORNS ON YOUR PLANET AS ANGRY AS YOU?
TIP O' TH' PIN TO GREG HARTLEY
©2003 Bill Griffith. World rights reserved. Distributed by King Features Syndicate
Zippythepinhead.com

155

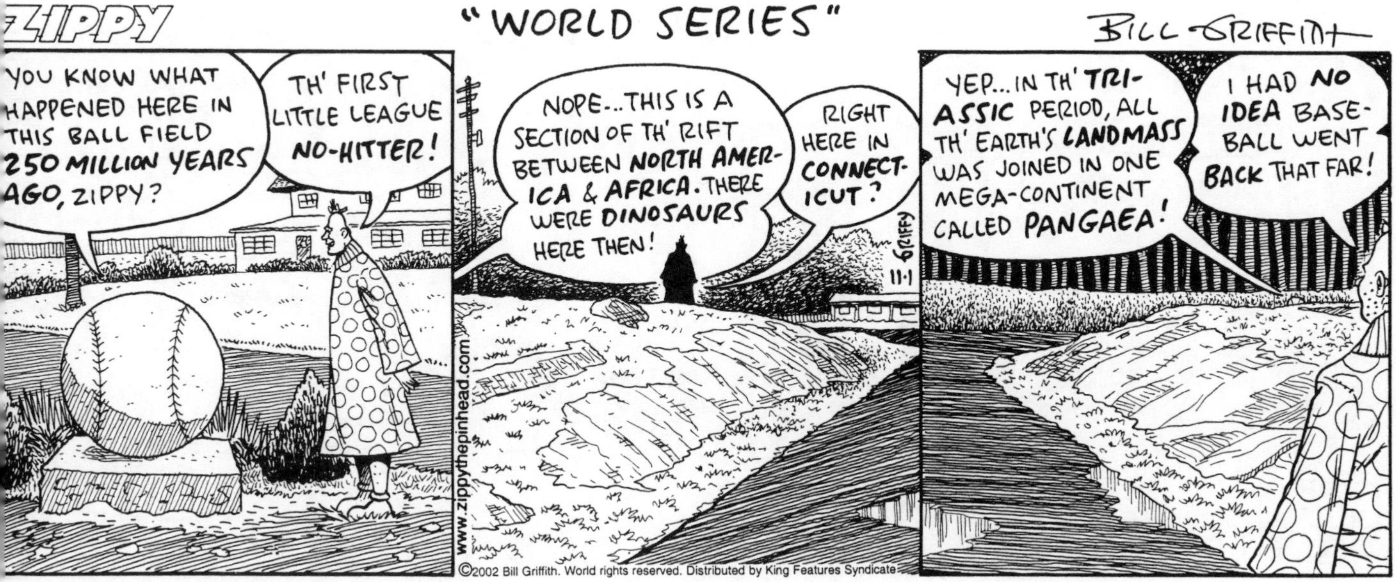
ZIPPY
"WORLD SERIES"
BILL GRIFFITH
YOU KNOW WHAT HAPPENED HERE IN THIS BALL FIELD 250 MILLION YEARS AGO, ZIPPY?
TH' FIRST LITTLE LEAGUE NO-HITTER!
NOPE...THIS IS A SECTION OF TH' RIFT BETWEEN NORTH AMERICA & AFRICA. THERE WERE DINOSAURS HERE THEN!
RIGHT HERE IN CONNECTICUT?
YEP... IN TH' TRIASSIC PERIOD, ALL TH' EARTH'S LANDMASS WAS JOINED IN ONE MEGA-CONTINENT CALLED PANGAEA!
I HAD NO IDEA BASEBALL WENT BACK THAT FAR!
www.zippythepinhead.com
©2002 Bill Griffith. World rights reserved. Distributed by King Features Syndicate

156

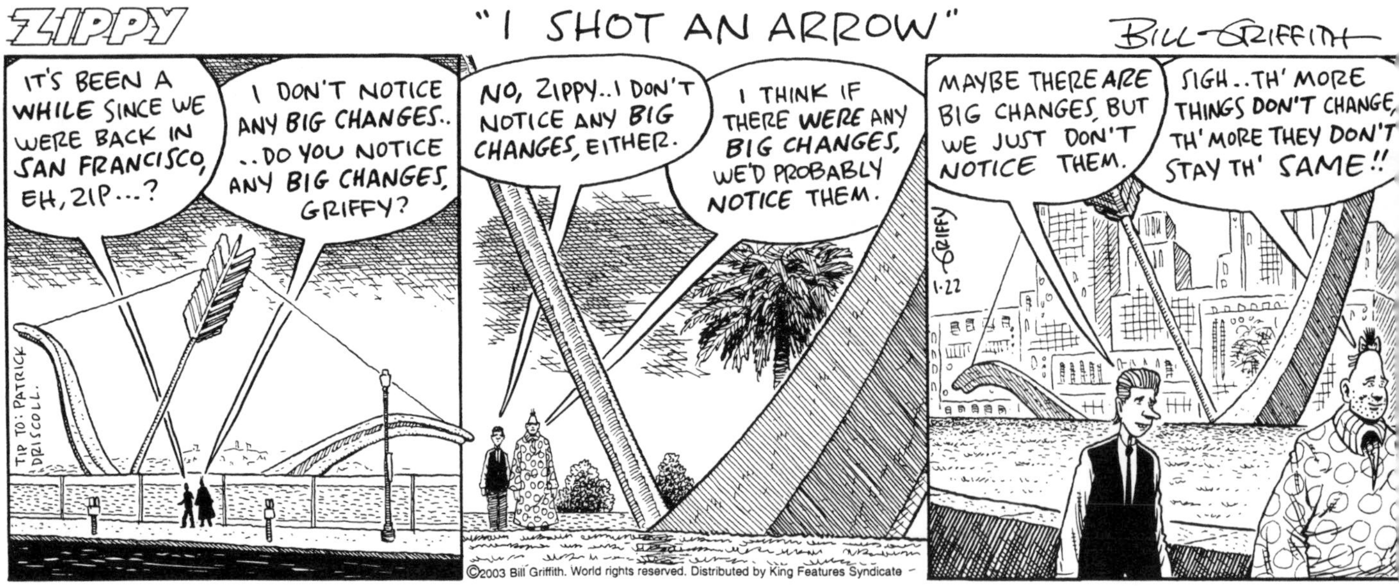
ZIPPY
"I SHOT AN ARROW"
BILL GRIFFITH
IT'S BEEN A WHILE SINCE WE WERE BACK IN SAN FRANCISCO, EH, ZIP...?
I DON'T NOTICE ANY BIG CHANGES.. ..DO YOU NOTICE ANY BIG CHANGES, GRIFFY?
TIP TO: PATRICK DRISCOLL.
NO, ZIPPY..I DON'T NOTICE ANY BIG CHANGES, EITHER.
I THINK IF THERE WERE ANY BIG CHANGES, WE'D PROBABLY NOTICE THEM.
GRIFFY 1-22
MAYBE THERE ARE BIG CHANGES, BUT WE JUST DON'T NOTICE THEM.
SIGH..TH' MORE THINGS DON'T CHANGE, TH' MORE THEY DON'T STAY TH' SAME!!
©2003 Bill Griffith. World rights reserved. Distributed by King Features Syndicate

157

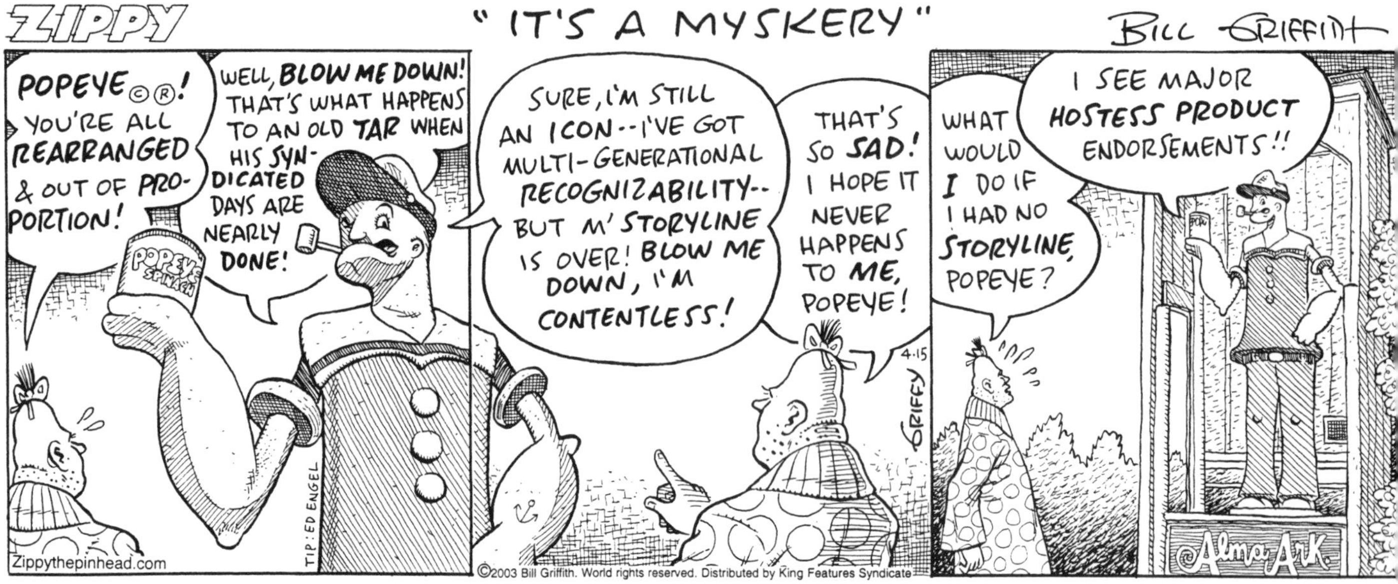
ZIPPY
"IT'S A MYSKERY"
BILL GRIFFITH
POPEYE©®! YOU'RE ALL REARRANGED & OUT OF PROPORTION!
WELL, BLOW ME DOWN! THAT'S WHAT HAPPENS TO AN OLD TAR WHEN HIS SYNDICATED DAYS ARE NEARLY DONE!
POPEYE'S SPINACH
TIP: ED ENGEL
Zippythepinhead.com
SURE, I'M STILL AN ICON--I'VE GOT MULTI-GENERATIONAL RECOGNIZABILITY-- BUT M' STORYLINE IS OVER! BLOW ME DOWN, I'M CONTENTLESS!
THAT'S SO SAD! I HOPE IT NEVER HAPPENS TO ME, POPEYE!
4-15 GRIFFY
©2003 Bill Griffith. World rights reserved. Distributed by King Features Syndicate
WHAT WOULD I DO IF I HAD NO STORYLINE, POPEYE?
I SEE MAJOR HOSTESS PRODUCT ENDORSEMENTS!!
Alma, Ark.

158

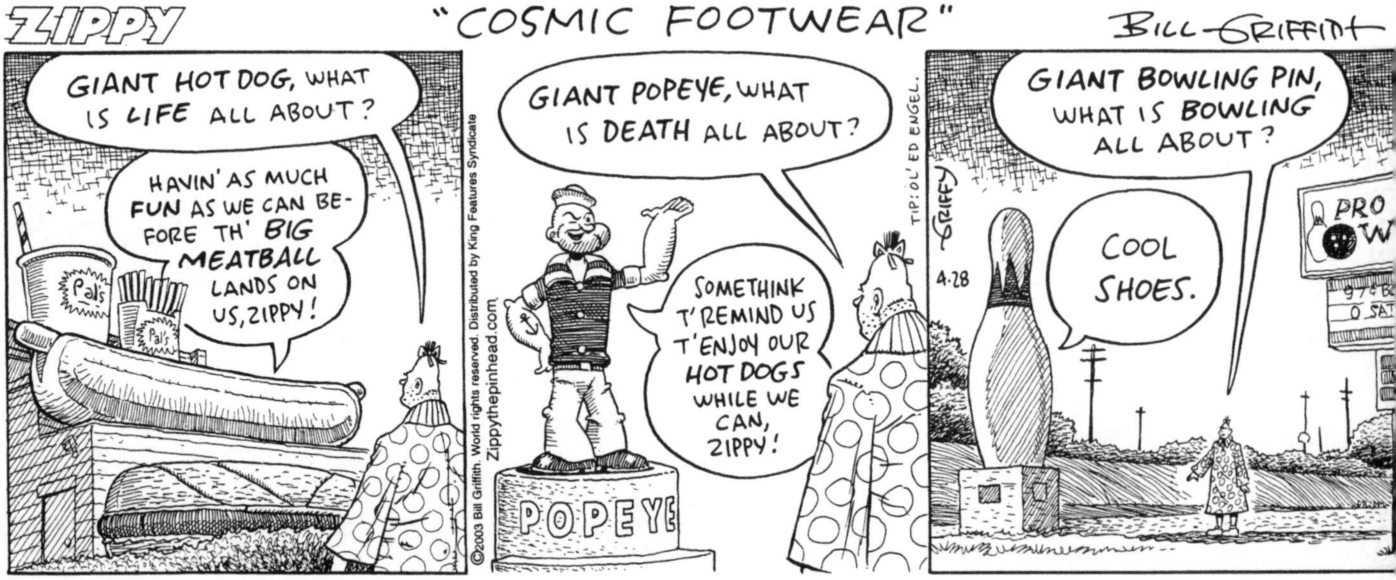
ZIPPY
"COSMIC FOOTWEAR"
BILL GRIFFITH
GIANT HOT DOG, WHAT IS LIFE ALL ABOUT?
HAVIN' AS MUCH FUN AS WE CAN BEFORE TH' BIG MEATBALL LANDS ON US, ZIPPY!
Pal's
Pal's
©2003 Bill Griffith. World rights reserved. Distributed by King Features Syndicate
Zippythepinhead.com
GIANT POPEYE, WHAT IS DEATH ALL ABOUT?
SOMETHINK T'REMIND US T'ENJOY OUR HOT DOGS WHILE WE CAN, ZIPPY!
POPEYE
TIP: OL' ED ENGEL.
GRIFFY 4-28
GIANT BOWLING PIN, WHAT IS BOWLING ALL ABOUT?
COOL SHOES.
PRO

159

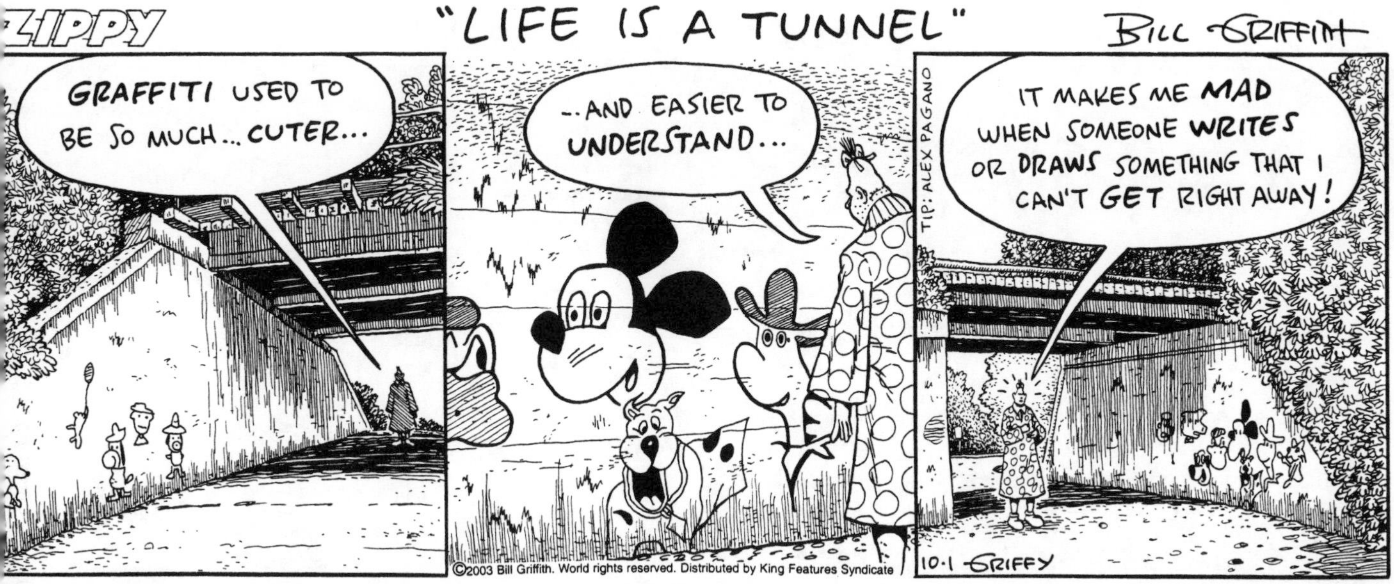
ZIPPY
"LIFE IS A TUNNEL"
BILL GRIFFITH
GRAFFITI USED TO BE SO MUCH... CUTER...
...AND EASIER TO UNDERSTAND...
TIP: ALEX PAGANO
IT MAKES ME MAD WHEN SOMEONE WRITES OR DRAWS SOMETHING THAT I CAN'T GET RIGHT AWAY!
©2003 Bill Griffith. World rights reserved. Distributed by King Features Syndicate
10·1 GRIFFY

160

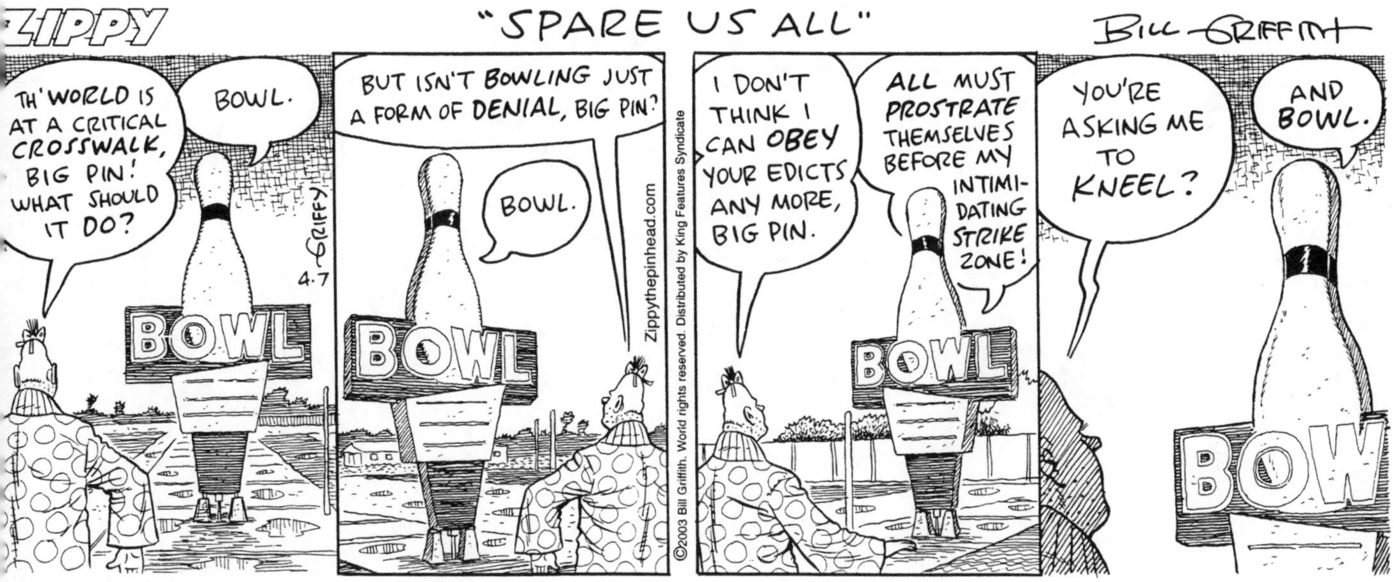
ZIPPY
"SPARE US ALL"
BILL GRIFFITH
TH' WORLD IS AT A CRITICAL CROSSWALK, BIG PIN! WHAT SHOULD IT DO?
BOWL.
GRIFFY 4·7
BOWL
BUT ISN'T BOWLING JUST A FORM OF DENIAL, BIG PIN?
BOWL.
BOWL
Zippythepinhead.com
©2003 Bill Griffith. World rights reserved. Distributed by King Features Syndicate
I DON'T THINK I CAN OBEY YOUR EDICTS ANY MORE, BIG PIN.
ALL MUST PROSTRATE THEMSELVES BEFORE MY INTIMI-DATING STRIKE ZONE!
BOWL
YOU'RE ASKING ME TO KNEEL?
AND BOWL.
BOW

161

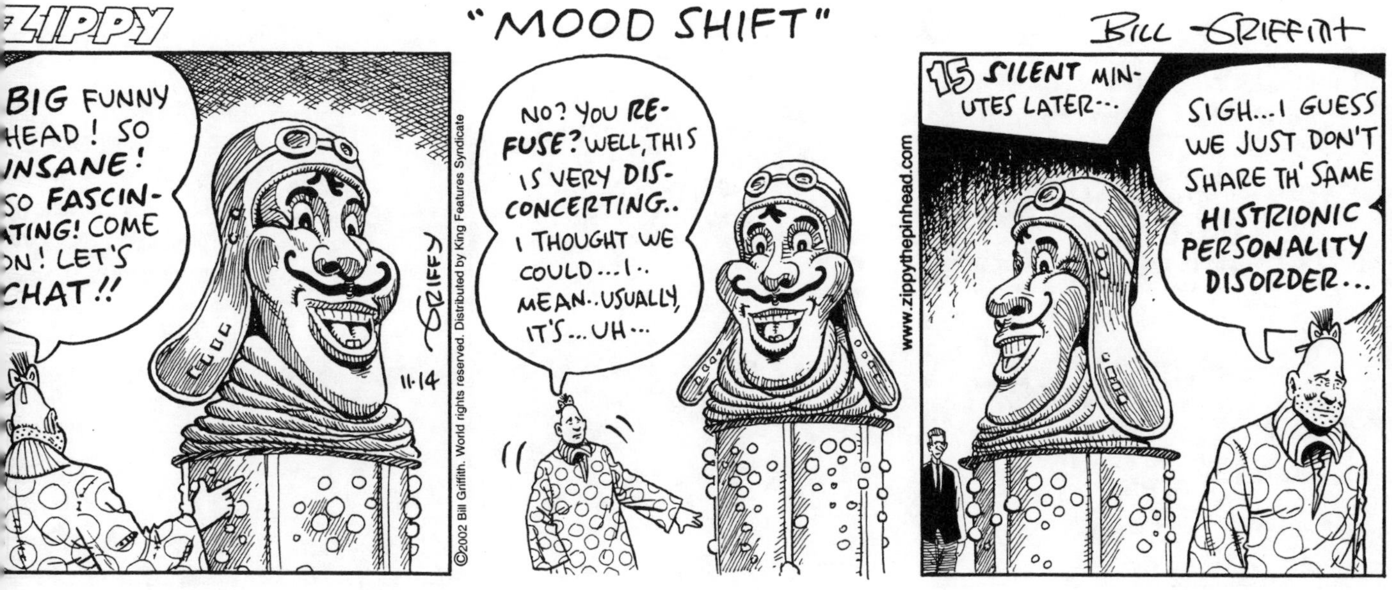
ZIPPY
"MOOD SHIFT"
BILL GRIFFITH
BIG FUNNY HEAD! SO INSANE! SO FASCIN-ATING! COME ON! LET'S CHAT!!
GRIFFY 11·14
©2002 Bill Griffith. World rights reserved. Distributed by King Features Syndicate
NO? YOU RE-FUSE? WELL, THIS IS VERY DIS-CONCERTING.. I THOUGHT WE COULD... I.. MEAN..USUALLY, IT'S... UH...
www.zippythepinhead.com
15 SILENT MIN-UTES LATER...
SIGH... I GUESS WE JUST DON'T SHARE TH' SAME HISTRIONIC PERSONALITY DISORDER...

162

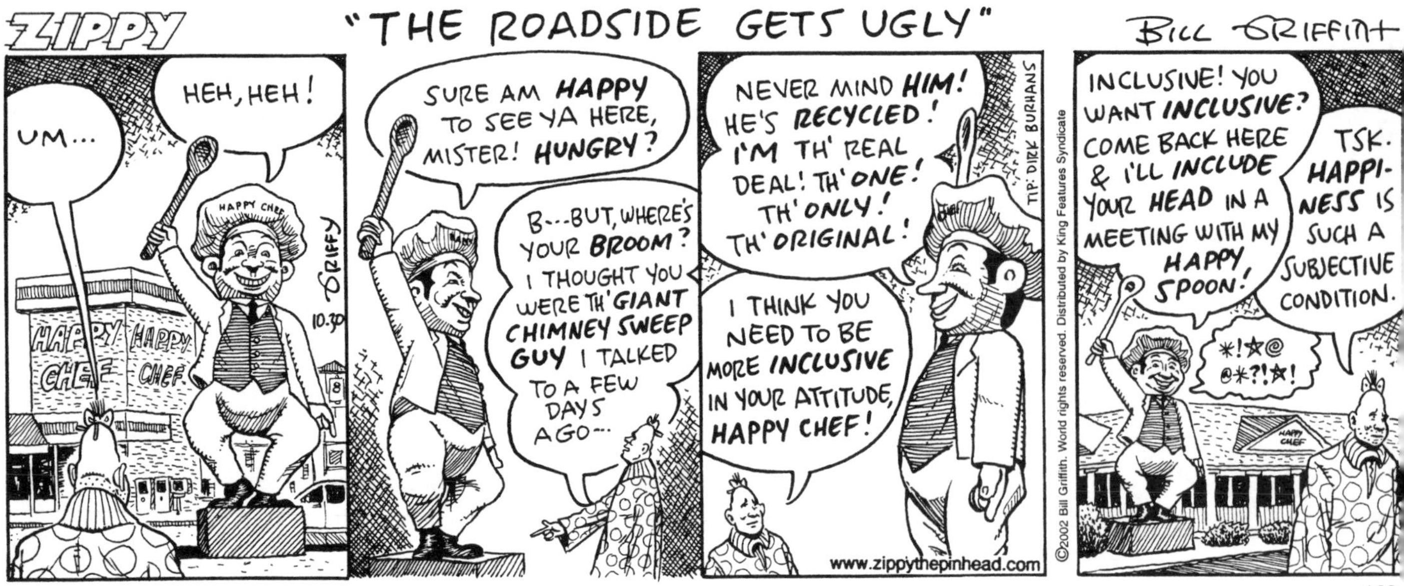
ZIPPY
"THE ROADSIDE GETS UGLY"
BILL GRIFFITH
UM...
HEH, HEH!
HAPPY CHEF
HAPPY CHEF HAPPY CHEF
GRIFFY 10.30
SURE AM HAPPY TO SEE YA HERE, MISTER! HUNGRY?
B---BUT, WHERE'S YOUR BROOM? I THOUGHT YOU WERE TH' GIANT CHIMNEY SWEEP GUY I TALKED TO A FEW DAYS AGO--
NEVER MIND HIM! HE'S RECYCLED! I'M TH' REAL DEAL! TH' ONE! TH' ONLY! TH' ORIGINAL!
I THINK YOU NEED TO BE MORE INCLUSIVE IN YOUR ATTITUDE, HAPPY CHEF!
TIP: DIRK BURHANS
www.zippythepinhead.com
©2002 Bill Griffith. World rights reserved. Distributed by King Features Syndicate
INCLUSIVE! YOU WANT INCLUSIVE? COME BACK HERE & I'LL INCLUDE YOUR HEAD IN A MEETING WITH MY HAPPY SPOON!
TSK. HAPPINESS IS SUCH A SUBJECTIVE CONDITION.
!☆@ @?!☆!
HAPPY CHEF

163

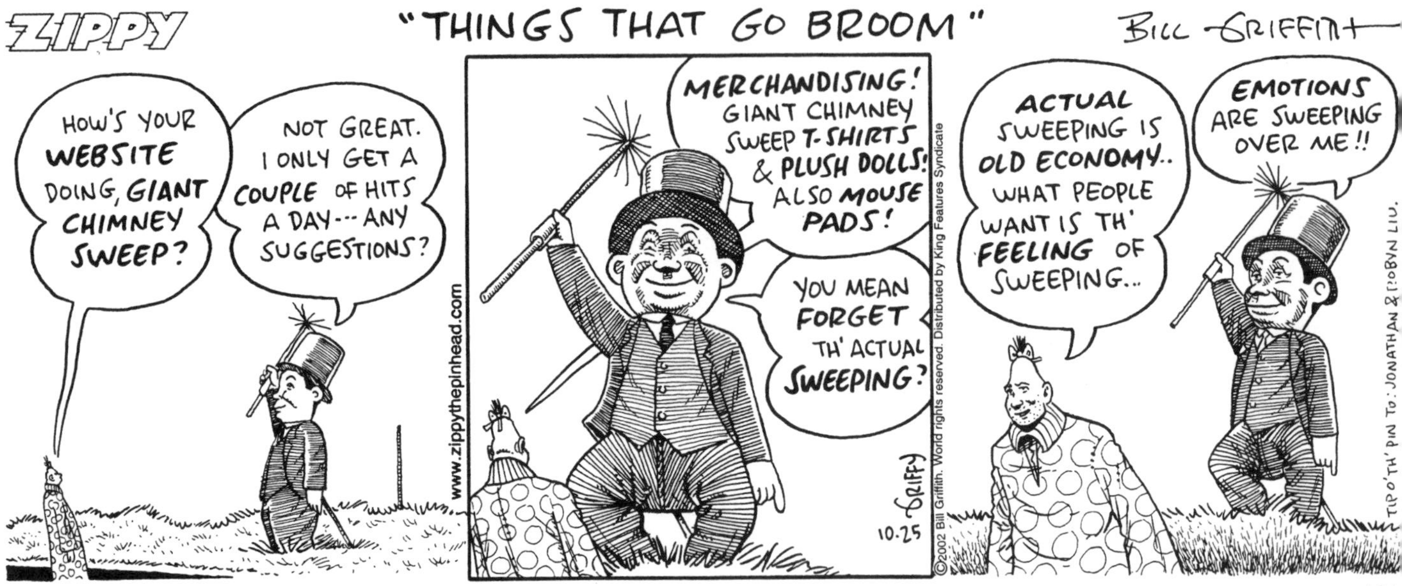
ZIPPY
"THINGS THAT GO BROOM"
BILL GRIFFITH
HOW'S YOUR WEBSITE DOING, GIANT CHIMNEY SWEEP?
NOT GREAT. I ONLY GET A COUPLE OF HITS A DAY--- ANY SUGGESTIONS?
www.zippythepinhead.com
MERCHANDISING! GIANT CHIMNEY SWEEP T-SHIRTS & PLUSH DOLLS! ALSO MOUSE PADS!
YOU MEAN FORGET TH' ACTUAL SWEEPING?
GRIFFY 10.25
©2002 Bill Griffith. World rights reserved. Distributed by King Features Syndicate
ACTUAL SWEEPING IS OLD ECONOMY.. WHAT PEOPLE WANT IS TH' FEELING OF SWEEPING...
EMOTIONS ARE SWEEPING OVER ME!!
TIP O' TH' PIN TO: JONATHAN & ROBYN LIU.

164

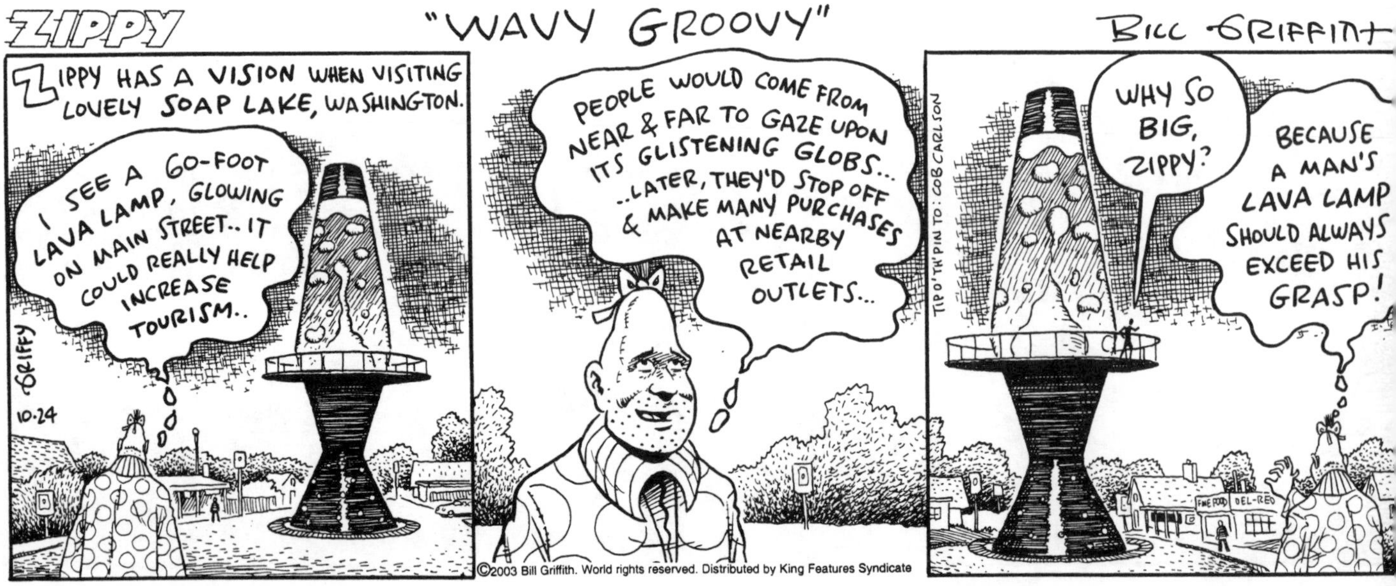
ZIPPY
"WAVY GROOVY"
BILL GRIFFITH
ZIPPY HAS A VISION WHEN VISITING LOVELY SOAP LAKE, WASHINGTON.
I SEE A 60-FOOT LAVA LAMP, GLOWING ON MAIN STREET.. IT COULD REALLY HELP INCREASE TOURISM..
GRIFFY 10.24
PEOPLE WOULD COME FROM NEAR & FAR TO GAZE UPON ITS GLISTENING GLOBS... ..LATER, THEY'D STOP OFF & MAKE MANY PURCHASES AT NEARBY RETAIL OUTLETS...
©2003 Bill Griffith. World rights reserved. Distributed by King Features Syndicate
TIP O' TH' PIN TO: COB CARLSON
WHY SO BIG, ZIPPY?
BECAUSE A MAN'S LAVA LAMP SHOULD ALWAYS EXCEED HIS GRASP!
FINE FOOD DEL-RED

165

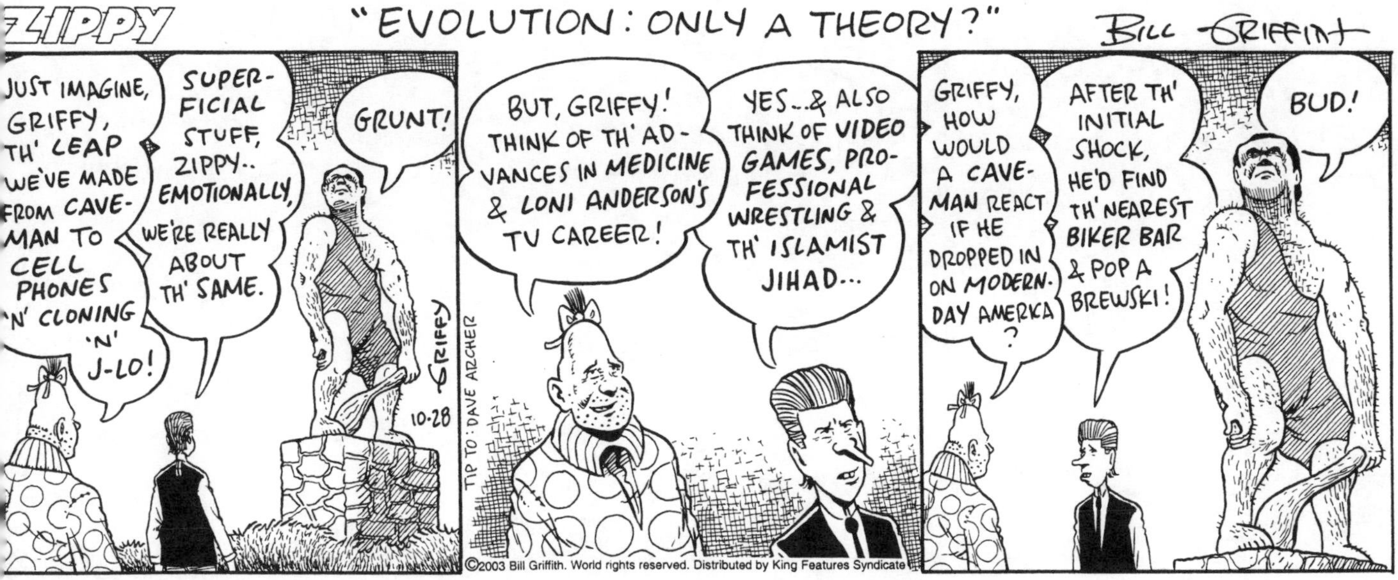
ZIPPY
"EVOLUTION: ONLY A THEORY?"
BILL GRIFFITH
JUST IMAGINE, GRIFFY, TH' LEAP WE'VE MADE FROM CAVE-MAN TO CELL PHONES 'N' CLONING 'N' J-LO!
SUPER-FICIAL STUFF, ZIPPY.. EMOTIONALLY, WE'RE REALLY ABOUT TH' SAME.
GRUNT!
GRIFFY 10-28
TIP TO: DAVE ARCHER
BUT, GRIFFY! THINK OF TH' AD-VANCES IN MEDICINE & LONI ANDERSON'S TV CAREER!
YES...& ALSO THINK OF VIDEO GAMES, PRO-FESSIONAL WRESTLING & TH' ISLAMIST JIHAD...
GRIFFY, HOW WOULD A CAVE-MAN REACT IF HE DROPPED IN ON MODERN-DAY AMERKA?
AFTER TH' INITIAL SHOCK, HE'D FIND TH' NEAREST BIKER BAR & POP A BREWSKI!
BUD!
©2003 Bill Griffith. World rights reserved. Distributed by King Features Syndicate

166

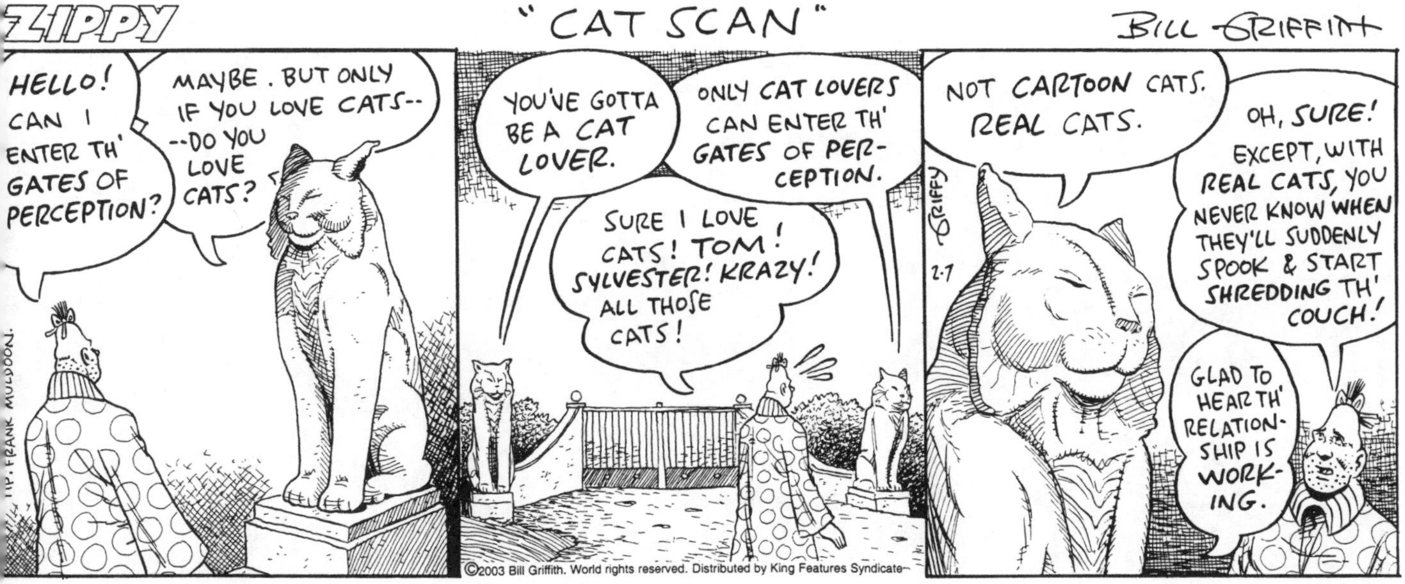
ZIPPY
"CAT SCAN"
BILL GRIFFITH
HELLO! CAN I ENTER TH' GATES OF PERCEPTION?
MAYBE. BUT ONLY IF YOU LOVE CATS-- --DO YOU LOVE CATS?
TIP: FRANK MULDOON.
YOU'VE GOTTA BE A CAT LOVER.
ONLY CAT LOVERS CAN ENTER TH' GATES OF PER-CEPTION.
SURE I LOVE CATS! TOM! SYLVESTER! KRAZY! ALL THOSE CATS!
GRIFFY 2-7
NOT CARTOON CATS. REAL CATS.
OH, SURE! EXCEPT, WITH REAL CATS, YOU NEVER KNOW WHEN THEY'LL SUDDENLY SPOOK & START SHREDDING TH' COUCH!
GLAD TO HEAR TH' RELATION-SHIP IS WORK-ING.
©2003 Bill Griffith. World rights reserved. Distributed by King Features Syndicate

167

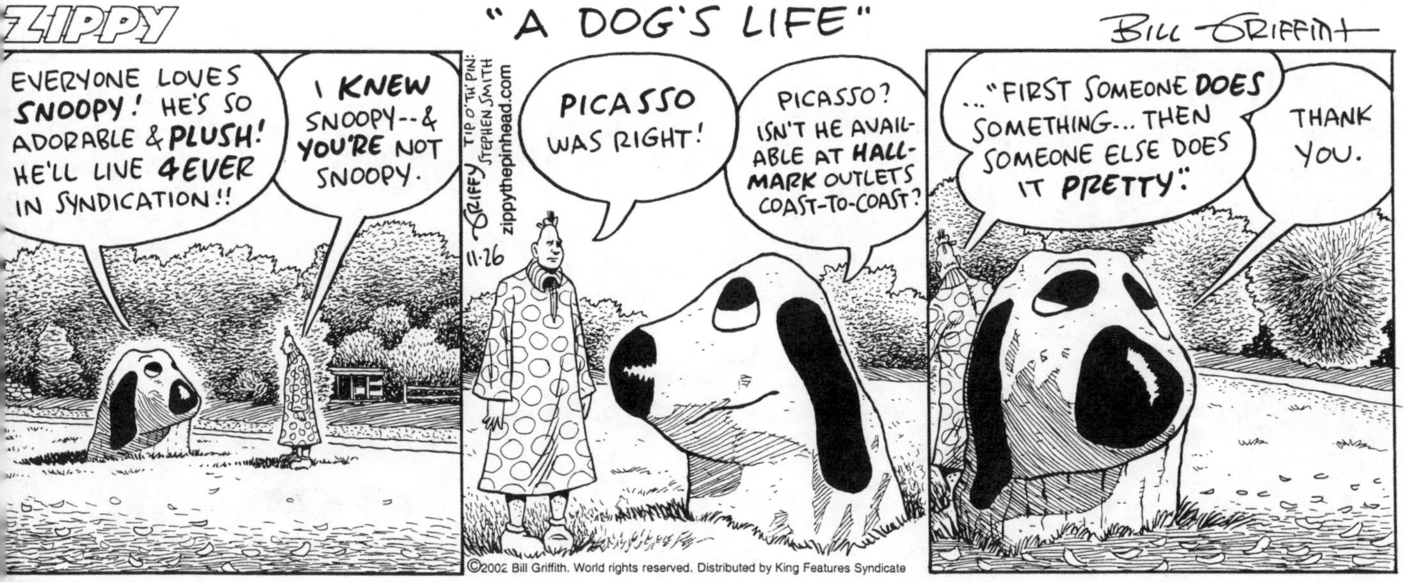
ZIPPY
"A DOG'S LIFE"
BILL GRIFFITH
EVERYONE LOVES SNOOPY! HE'S SO ADORABLE & PLUSH! HE'LL LIVE 4EVER IN SYNDICATION!!
I KNEW SNOOPY--& YOU'RE NOT SNOOPY.
GRIFFY 11-26
TIP O' TH' PIN: STEPHEN SMITH
zippythepinhead.com
PICASSO WAS RIGHT!
PICASSO? ISN'T HE AVAIL-ABLE AT HALL-MARK OUTLETS COAST-TO-COAST?
..."FIRST SOMEONE DOES SOMETHING... THEN SOMEONE ELSE DOES IT PRETTY."
THANK YOU.
©2002 Bill Griffith. World rights reserved. Distributed by King Features Syndicate

168

ZIPPY "MENTAL STATE" BILL GRIFFITH

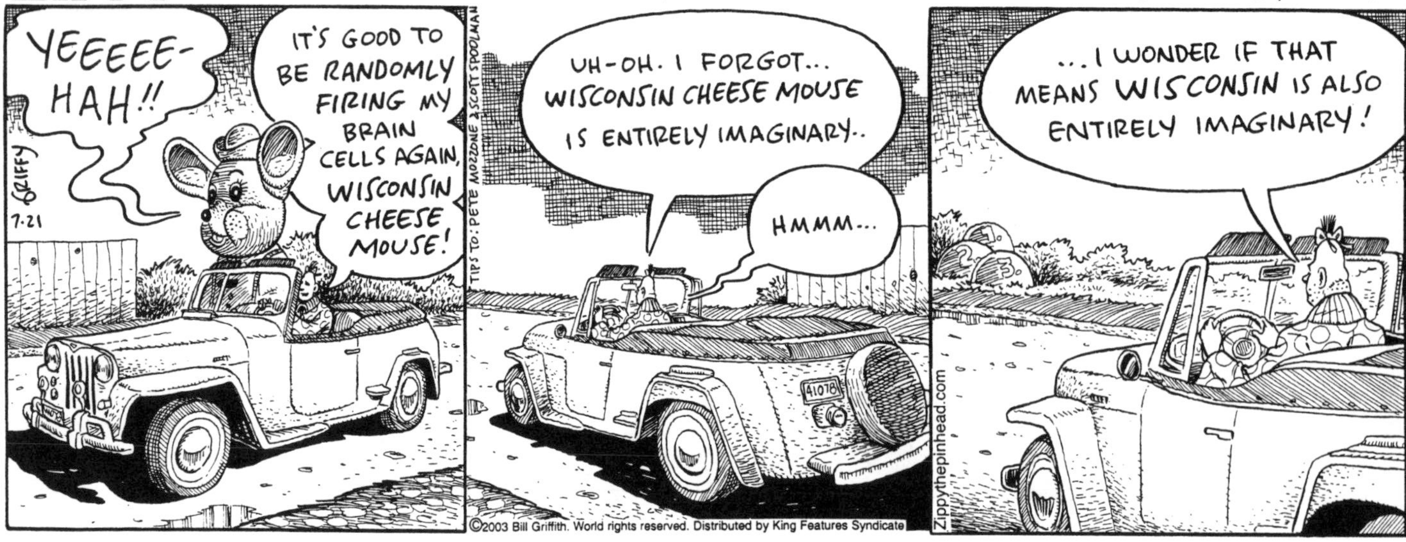

YEEEEE-HAH!!
IT'S GOOD TO BE RANDOMLY FIRING MY BRAIN CELLS AGAIN, WISCONSIN CHEESE MOUSE!
GRIFFY 7·21
TIPS TO: PETE MOZZONE & SCOTT SPOOLMAN
UH-OH. I FORGOT... WISCONSIN CHEESE MOUSE IS ENTIRELY IMAGINARY..
HMMM...
...I WONDER IF THAT MEANS WISCONSIN IS ALSO ENTIRELY IMAGINARY!
©2003 Bill Griffith. World rights reserved. Distributed by King Features Syndicate
Zippythepinhead.com

169

ZIPPY "THE PERFECT ROAD TRIP" BILL GRIFFITH

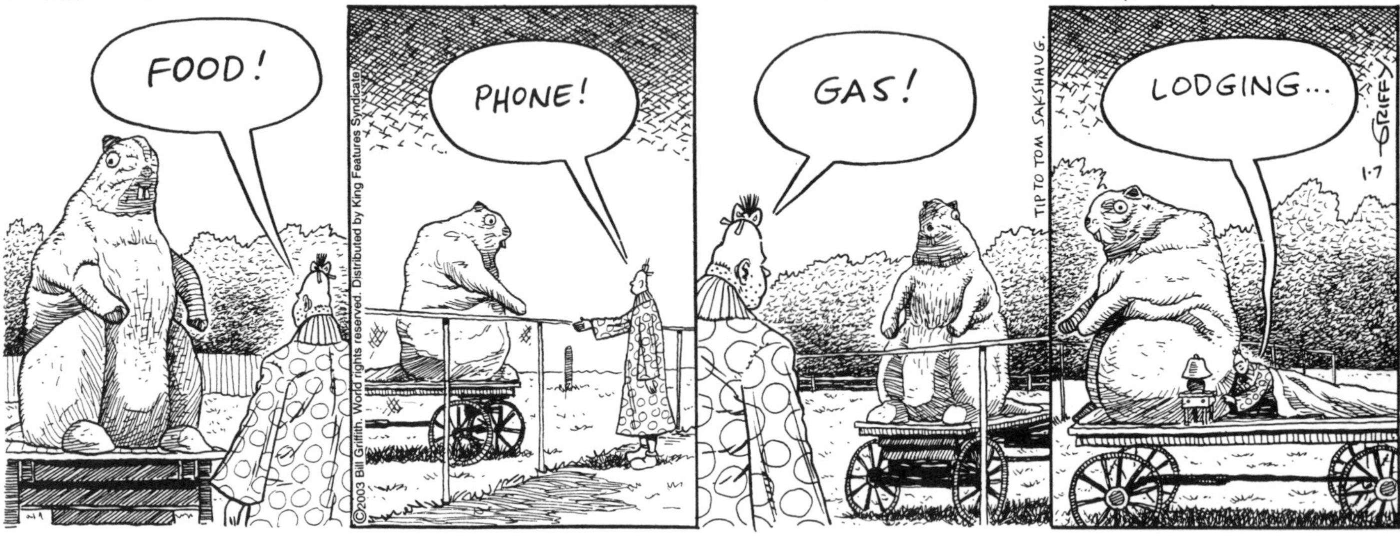

FOOD!
©2003 Bill Griffith. World rights reserved. Distributed by King Features Syndicate
PHONE!
GAS!
TIP TO TOM SAKSHAUG.
LODGING...
GRIFFY 1·7

170

ZIPPY "PRE-NUP" BILL GRIFFITH

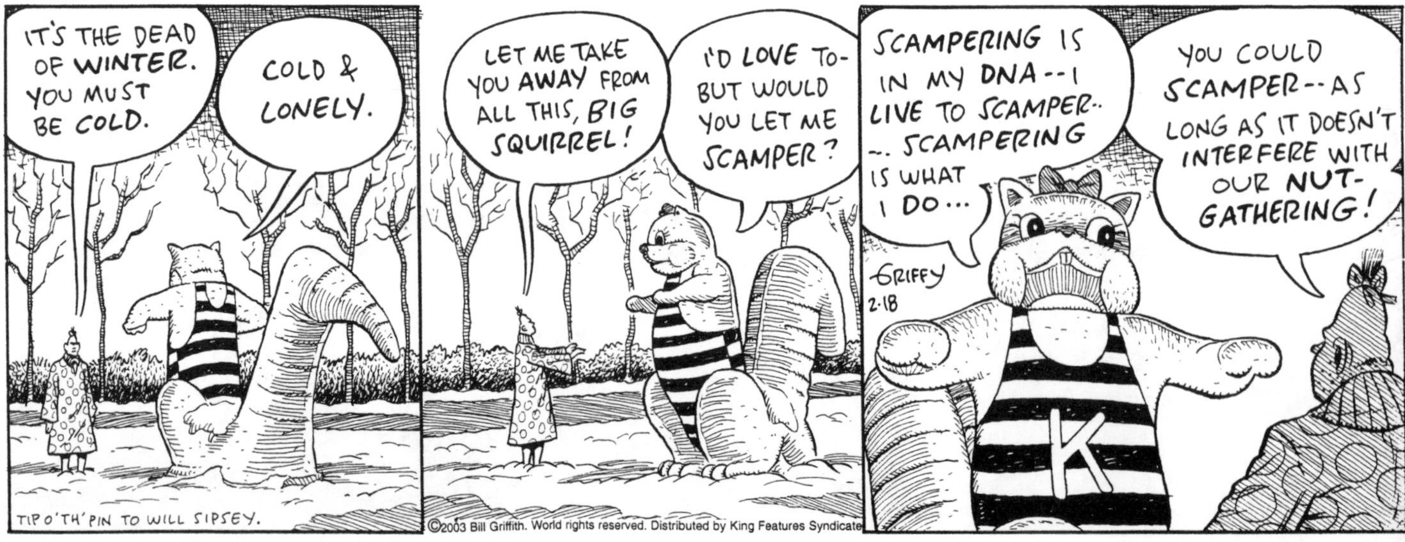

IT'S THE DEAD OF WINTER. YOU MUST BE COLD.
COLD & LONELY.
TIP O'TH' PIN TO WILL SIPSEY.
LET ME TAKE YOU AWAY FROM ALL THIS, BIG SQUIRREL!
I'D LOVE TO-- BUT WOULD YOU LET ME SCAMPER?
©2003 Bill Griffith. World rights reserved. Distributed by King Features Syndicate
SCAMPERING IS IN MY DNA--I LIVE TO SCAMPER.. --. SCAMPERING IS WHAT I DO...
YOU COULD SCAMPER--AS LONG AS IT DOESN'T INTERFERE WITH OUR NUT-GATHERING!
GRIFFY 2·18
K

171

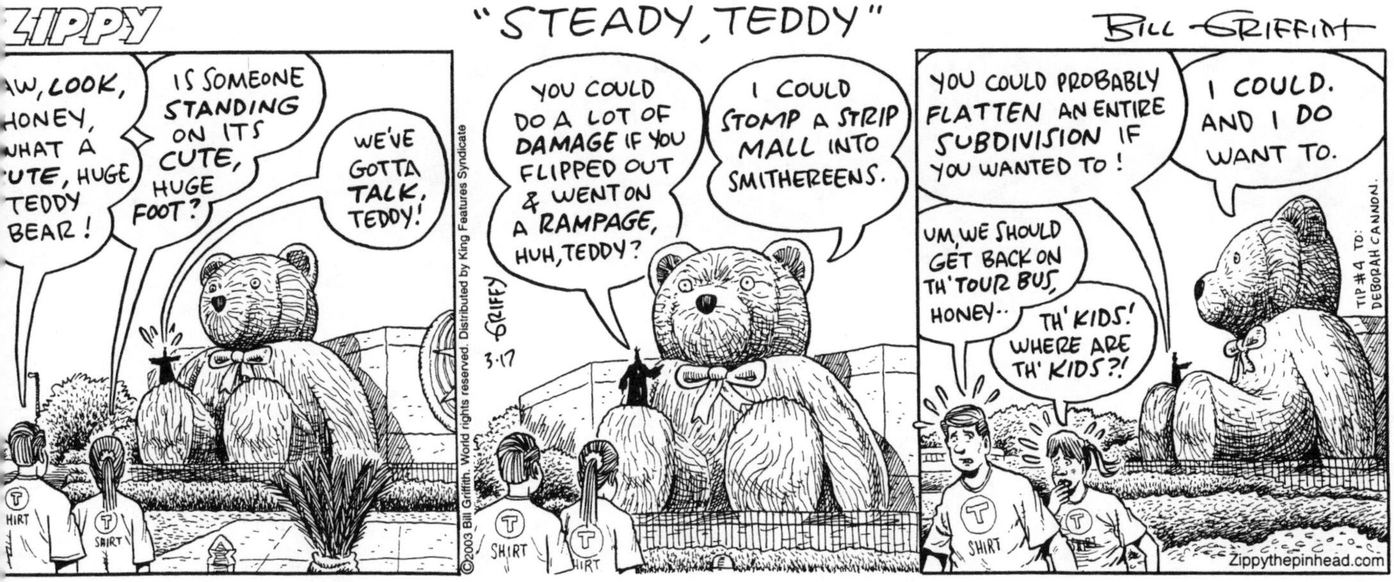
ZIPPY
"STEADY, TEDDY"
BILL GRIFFITH
AW, LOOK, HONEY, WHAT A CUTE, HUGE TEDDY BEAR!
IS SOMEONE STANDING ON ITS CUTE, HUGE FOOT?
WE'VE GOTTA TALK, TEDDY!
YOU COULD DO A LOT OF DAMAGE IF YOU FLIPPED OUT & WENT ON A RAMPAGE, HUH, TEDDY?
I COULD STOMP A STRIP MALL INTO SMITHEREENS.
GRIFFY 3.17
©2003 Bill Griffith. World rights reserved. Distributed by King Features Syndicate
YOU COULD PROBABLY FLATTEN AN ENTIRE SUBDIVISION IF YOU WANTED TO!
I COULD. AND I DO WANT TO.
UM, WE SHOULD GET BACK ON TH' TOUR BUS, HONEY..
TH' KIDS! WHERE ARE TH' KIDS?!
TIP #4 TO: DEBORAH CANNON.
SHIRT
Zippythepinhead.com

172

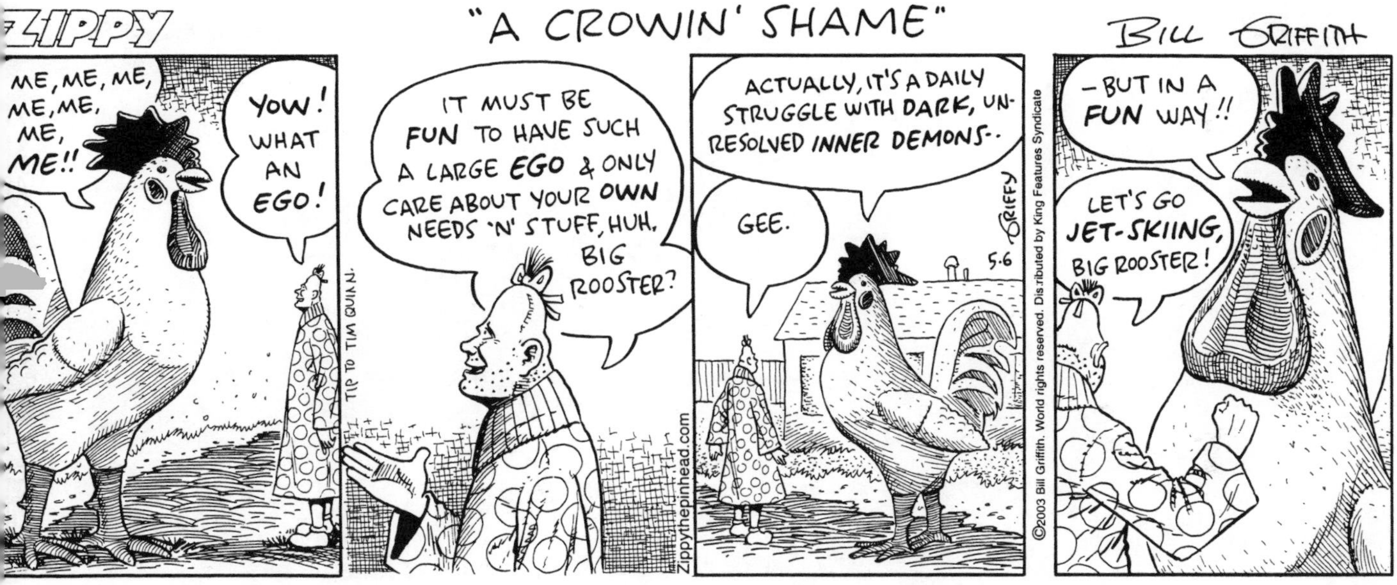
ZIPPY
"A CROWIN' SHAME"
BILL GRIFFITH
ME, ME, ME, ME, ME, ME, ME!!
YOW! WHAT AN EGO!
TIP TO TIM QUINN.
IT MUST BE FUN TO HAVE SUCH A LARGE EGO & ONLY CARE ABOUT YOUR OWN NEEDS 'N' STUFF, HUH, BIG ROOSTER?
Zippythepinhead.com
ACTUALLY, IT'S A DAILY STRUGGLE WITH DARK, UNRESOLVED INNER DEMONS..
GEE.
GRIFFY 5.6
©2003 Bill Griffith. World rights reserved. Distributed by King Features Syndicate
-BUT IN A FUN WAY!!
LET'S GO JET-SKIING, BIG ROOSTER!

173

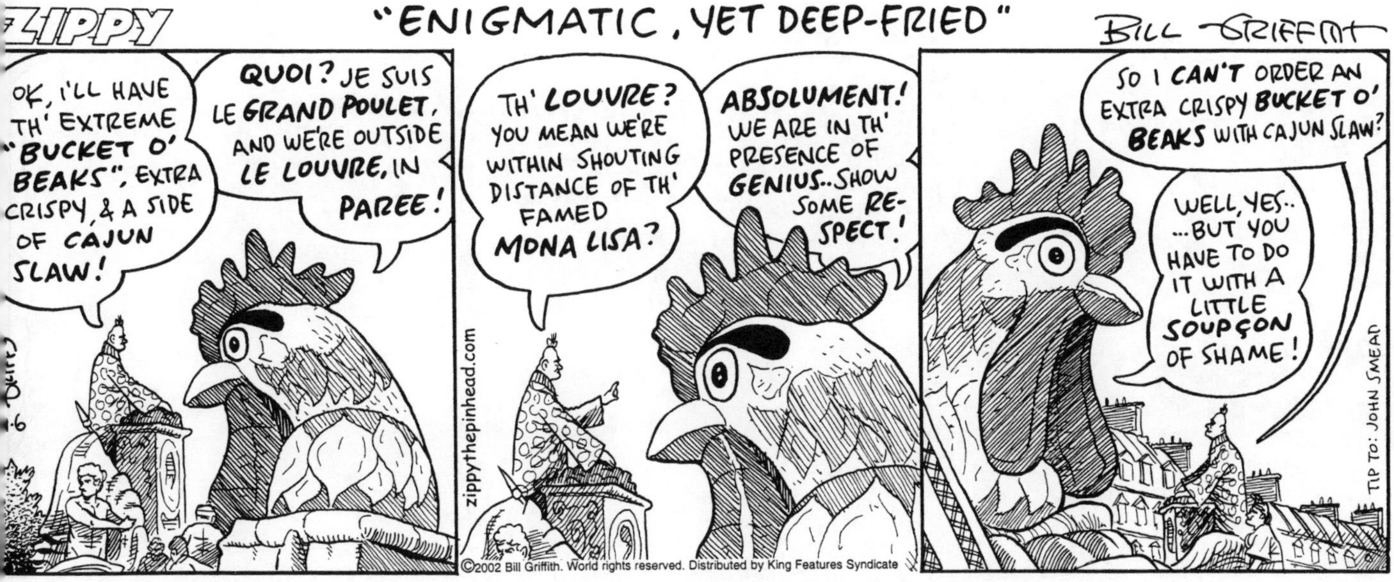
ZIPPY
"ENIGMATIC, YET DEEP-FRIED"
BILL GRIFFITH
OK, I'LL HAVE TH' EXTREME "BUCKET O' BEAKS", EXTRA CRISPY, & A SIDE OF CAJUN SLAW!
QUOI? JE SUIS LE GRAND POULET, AND WE'RE OUTSIDE LE LOUVRE, IN PAREE!
TH' LOUVRE? YOU MEAN WE'RE WITHIN SHOUTING DISTANCE OF TH' FAMED MONA LISA?
ABSOLUMENT! WE ARE IN TH' PRESENCE OF GENIUS.. SHOW SOME RESPECT!
zippythepinhead.com
©2002 Bill Griffith. World rights reserved. Distributed by King Features Syndicate
SO I CAN'T ORDER AN EXTRA CRISPY BUCKET O' BEAKS WITH CAJUN SLAW?
WELL, YES.. ...BUT YOU HAVE TO DO IT WITH A LITTLE SOUPÇON OF SHAME!
TIP TO: JOHN SMEAD

174

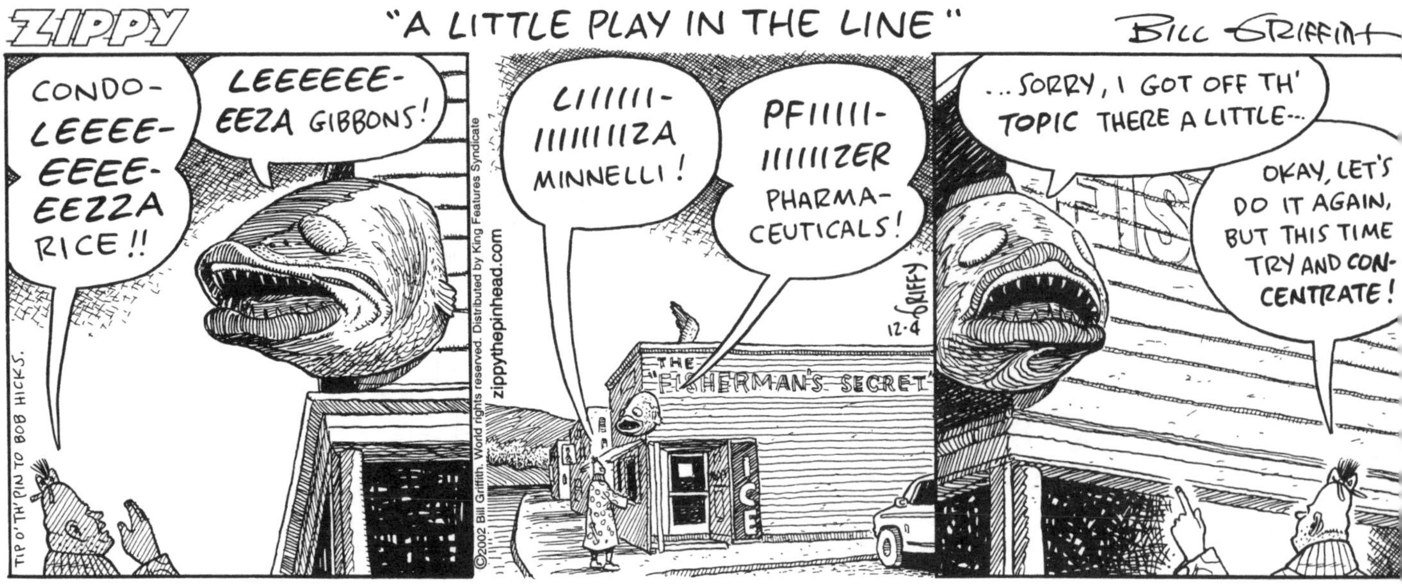
ZIPPY
"A LITTLE PLAY IN THE LINE"
BILL GRIFFITH
CONDO-LEEEE-EEEE-EEZZA RICE!!
LEEEEEE-EEZA GIBBONS!
LIIIIII-IIIIIIIZA MINNELLI!
PFIIIII-IIIIIIZER PHARMACEUTICALS!
GRIFFY 12·4
THE "FISHERMAN'S SECRET"
ICE
TIP O' TH' PIN TO BOB HICKS.
©2002 Bill Griffith. World rights reserved. Distributed by King Features Syndicate
zippythepinhead.com
...SORRY, I GOT OFF TH' TOPIC THERE A LITTLE...
OKAY, LET'S DO IT AGAIN, BUT THIS TIME TRY AND CONCENTRATE!

175

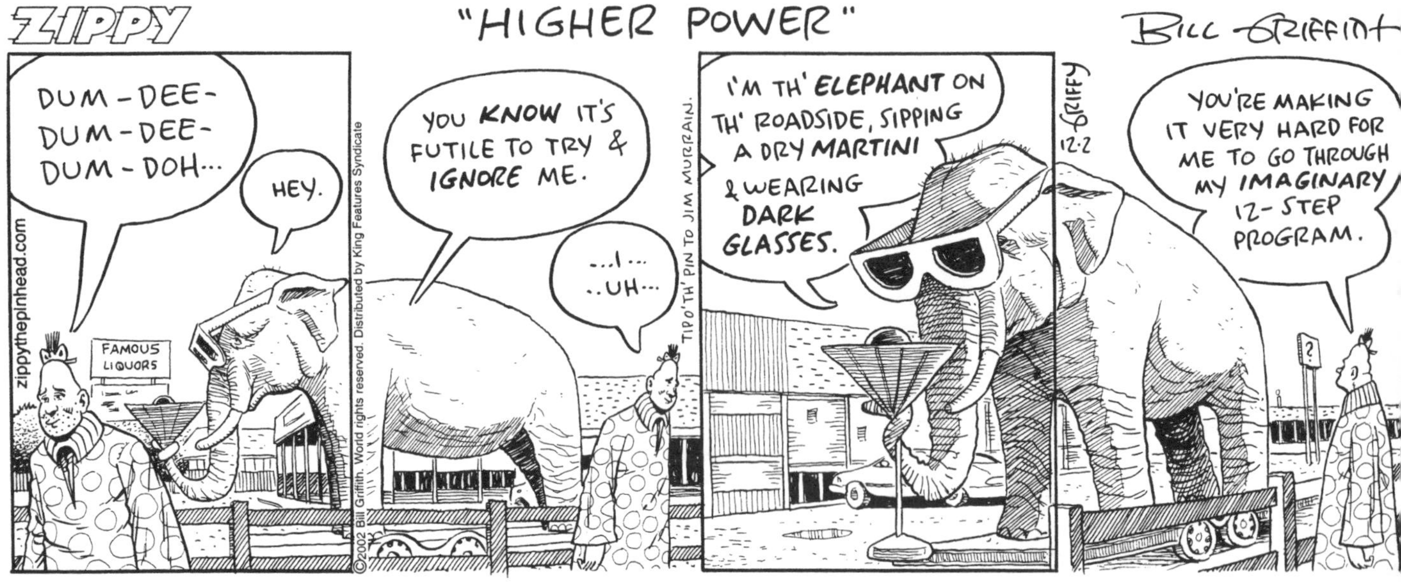
ZIPPY
"HIGHER POWER"
BILL GRIFFITH
DUM-DEE-DUM-DEE-DUM-DOH...
HEY.
FAMOUS LIQUORS
zippythepinhead.com
©2002 Bill Griffith. World rights reserved. Distributed by King Features Syndicate
YOU KNOW IT'S FUTILE TO TRY & IGNORE ME.
...I... ..UH...
TIP O' TH' PIN TO JIM MURRAIN.
I'M TH' ELEPHANT ON TH' ROADSIDE, SIPPING A DRY MARTINI & WEARING DARK GLASSES.
GRIFFY 12·2
YOU'RE MAKING IT VERY HARD FOR ME TO GO THROUGH MY IMAGINARY 12-STEP PROGRAM.

176

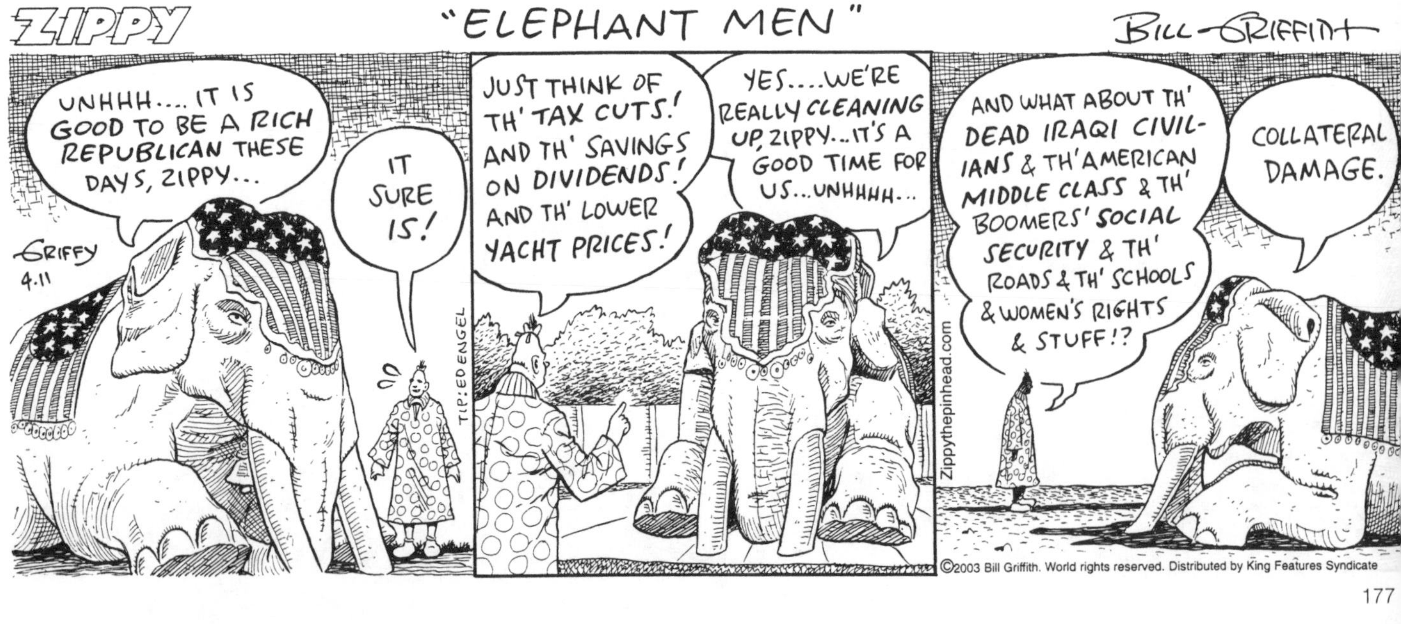
ZIPPY
"ELEPHANT MEN"
BILL GRIFFITH
UNHHH.... IT IS GOOD TO BE A RICH REPUBLICAN THESE DAYS, ZIPPY...
IT SURE IS!
GRIFFY 4.11
TIP: ED ENGEL
JUST THINK OF TH' TAX CUTS! AND TH' SAVINGS ON DIVIDENDS! AND TH' LOWER YACHT PRICES!
YES.... WE'RE REALLY CLEANING UP, ZIPPY... IT'S A GOOD TIME FOR US... UNHHHH...
AND WHAT ABOUT TH' DEAD IRAQI CIVILIANS & TH' AMERICAN MIDDLE CLASS & TH' BOOMERS' SOCIAL SECURITY & TH' ROADS & TH' SCHOOLS & WOMEN'S RIGHTS & STUFF!?
COLLATERAL DAMAGE.
zippythepinhead.com
©2003 Bill Griffith. World rights reserved. Distributed by King Features Syndicate

177

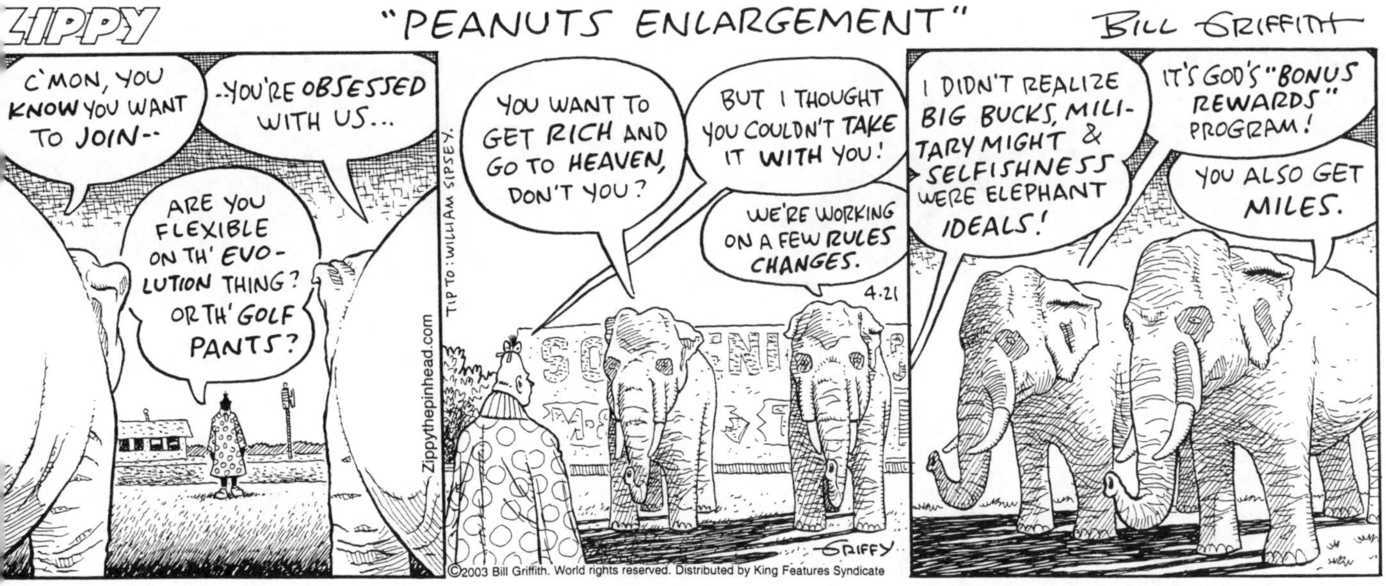
ZIPPY
"PEANUTS ENLARGEMENT"
BILL GRIFFITH
C'MON, YOU KNOW YOU WANT TO JOIN--
--YOU'RE OBSESSED WITH US...
ARE YOU FLEXIBLE ON TH' EVOLUTION THING? OR TH' GOLF PANTS?
Zippythepinhead.com
TIP TO: WILLIAM SIPSEY.
YOU WANT TO GET RICH AND GO TO HEAVEN, DON'T YOU?
BUT I THOUGHT YOU COULDN'T TAKE IT WITH YOU!
WE'RE WORKING ON A FEW RULES CHANGES.
4-21
GRIFFY
I DIDN'T REALIZE BIG BUCKS, MILITARY MIGHT & SELFISHNESS WERE ELEPHANT IDEALS!
IT'S GOD'S "BONUS REWARDS" PROGRAM!
YOU ALSO GET MILES.
©2003 Bill Griffith. World rights reserved. Distributed by King Features Syndicate

178

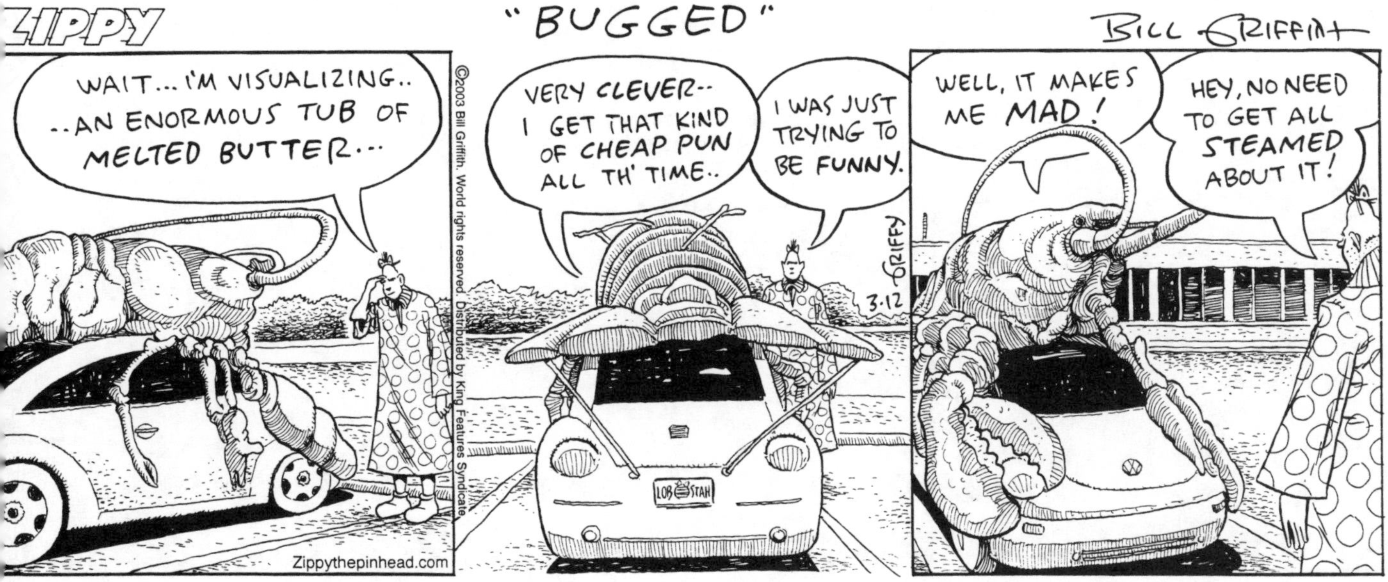
ZIPPY
"BUGGED"
BILL GRIFFITH
WAIT... I'M VISUALIZING.. ..AN ENORMOUS TUB OF MELTED BUTTER...
Zippythepinhead.com
©2003 Bill Griffith. World rights reserved. Distributed by King Features Syndicate
VERY CLEVER-- I GET THAT KIND OF CHEAP PUN ALL TH' TIME..
I WAS JUST TRYING TO BE FUNNY.
GRIFFY
3-12
LOBSTAH
WELL, IT MAKES ME MAD!
HEY, NO NEED TO GET ALL STEAMED ABOUT IT!

179

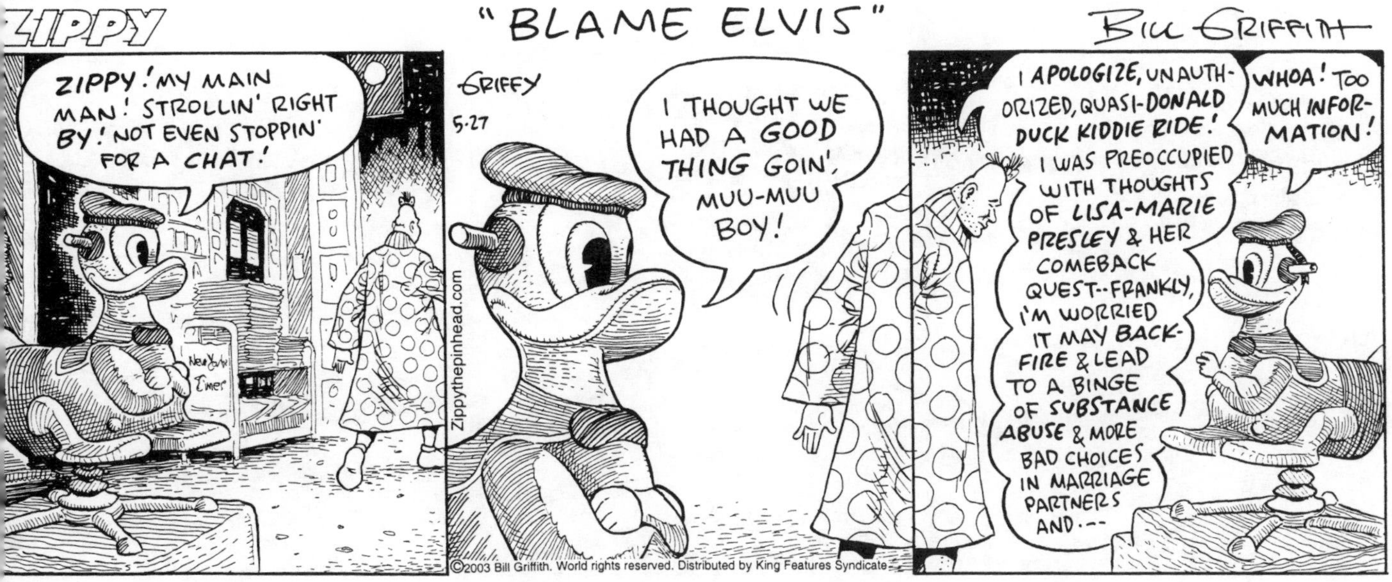
ZIPPY
"BLAME ELVIS"
BILL GRIFFITH
ZIPPY! MY MAIN MAN! STROLLIN' RIGHT BY! NOT EVEN STOPPIN' FOR A CHAT!
GRIFFY
5-27
I THOUGHT WE HAD A GOOD THING GOIN', MUU-MUU BOY!
Zippythepinhead.com
I APOLOGIZE, UNAUTHORIZED, QUASI-DONALD DUCK KIDDIE RIDE!
WHOA! TOO MUCH INFORMATION!
I WAS PREOCCUPIED WITH THOUGHTS OF LISA-MARIE PRESLEY & HER COMEBACK QUEST--FRANKLY, I'M WORRIED IT MAY BACKFIRE & LEAD TO A BINGE OF SUBSTANCE ABUSE & MORE BAD CHOICES IN MARRIAGE PARTNERS AND.---
©2003 Bill Griffith. World rights reserved. Distributed by King Features Syndicate

180

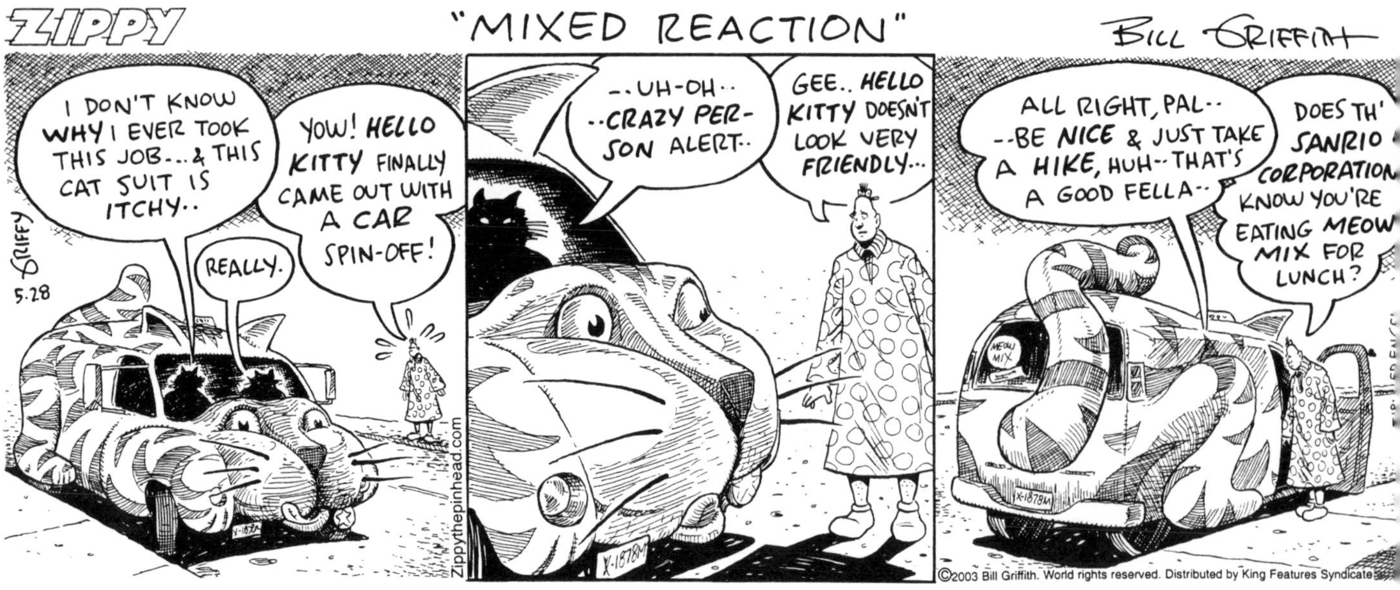
ZIPPY
"MIXED REACTION"
BILL GRIFFITH
I DON'T KNOW WHY I EVER TOOK THIS JOB...& THIS CAT SUIT IS ITCHY..
YOW! HELLO KITTY FINALLY CAME OUT WITH A CAR SPIN-OFF!
REALLY.
GRIFFY 5.28
Zippythepinhead.com
..UH-OH.. ..CRAZY PERSON ALERT..
GEE.. HELLO KITTY DOESN'T LOOK VERY FRIENDLY...
ALL RIGHT, PAL.. --BE NICE & JUST TAKE A HIKE, HUH--THAT'S A GOOD FELLA--
DOES TH' SANRIO CORPORATION KNOW YOU'RE EATING MEOW MIX FOR LUNCH?
©2003 Bill Griffith. World rights reserved. Distributed by King Features Syndicate

181

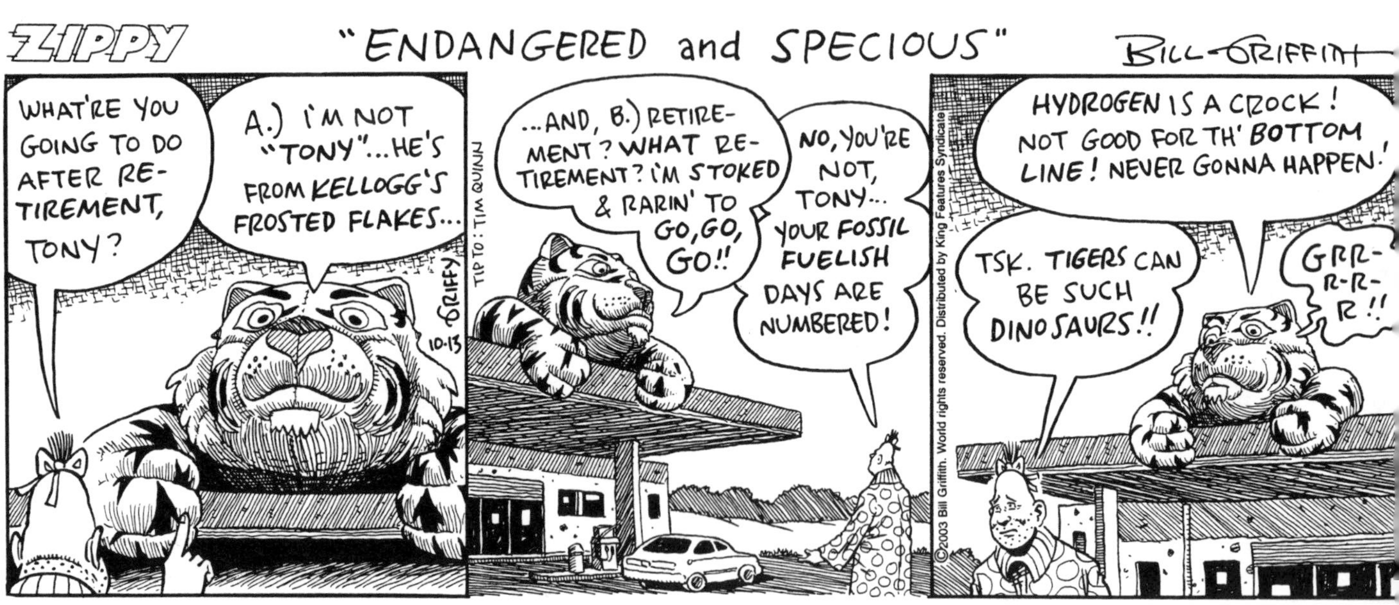
ZIPPY
"ENDANGERED and SPECIOUS"
BILL GRIFFITH
WHAT'RE YOU GOING TO DO AFTER RETIREMENT, TONY?
A.) I'M NOT "TONY"...HE'S FROM KELLOGG'S FROSTED FLAKES...
GRIFFY 10-13
TIP TO: TIM QUINN
...AND, B.) RETIREMENT? WHAT RETIREMENT? I'M STOKED & RARIN' TO GO, GO, GO!!
NO, YOU'RE NOT, TONY... YOUR FOSSIL FUELISH DAYS ARE NUMBERED!
HYDROGEN IS A CROCK! NOT GOOD FOR TH' BOTTOM LINE! NEVER GONNA HAPPEN!
TSK. TIGERS CAN BE SUCH DINOSAURS!!
GRR-R-R-R!!
©2003 Bill Griffith. World rights reserved. Distributed by King Features Syndicate

182

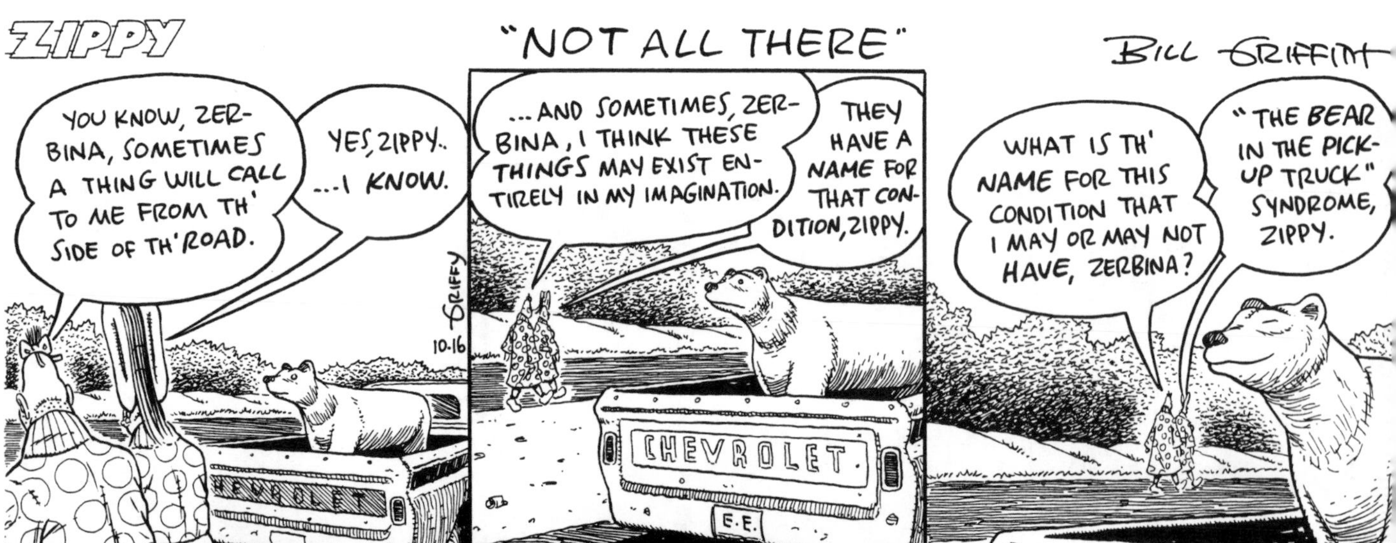
ZIPPY
"NOT ALL THERE"
BILL GRIFFITH
YOU KNOW, ZERBINA, SOMETIMES A THING WILL CALL TO ME FROM TH' SIDE OF TH' ROAD.
YES, ZIPPY.. ...I KNOW.
GRIFFY 10-16
...AND SOMETIMES, ZERBINA, I THINK THESE THINGS MAY EXIST ENTIRELY IN MY IMAGINATION.
THEY HAVE A NAME FOR THAT CONDITION, ZIPPY.
CHEVROLET
WHAT IS TH' NAME FOR THIS CONDITION THAT I MAY OR MAY NOT HAVE, ZERBINA?
"THE BEAR IN THE PICK-UP TRUCK" SYNDROME, ZIPPY.
©2003 Bill Griffith. World rights reserved. Distributed by King Features Syndicate

183

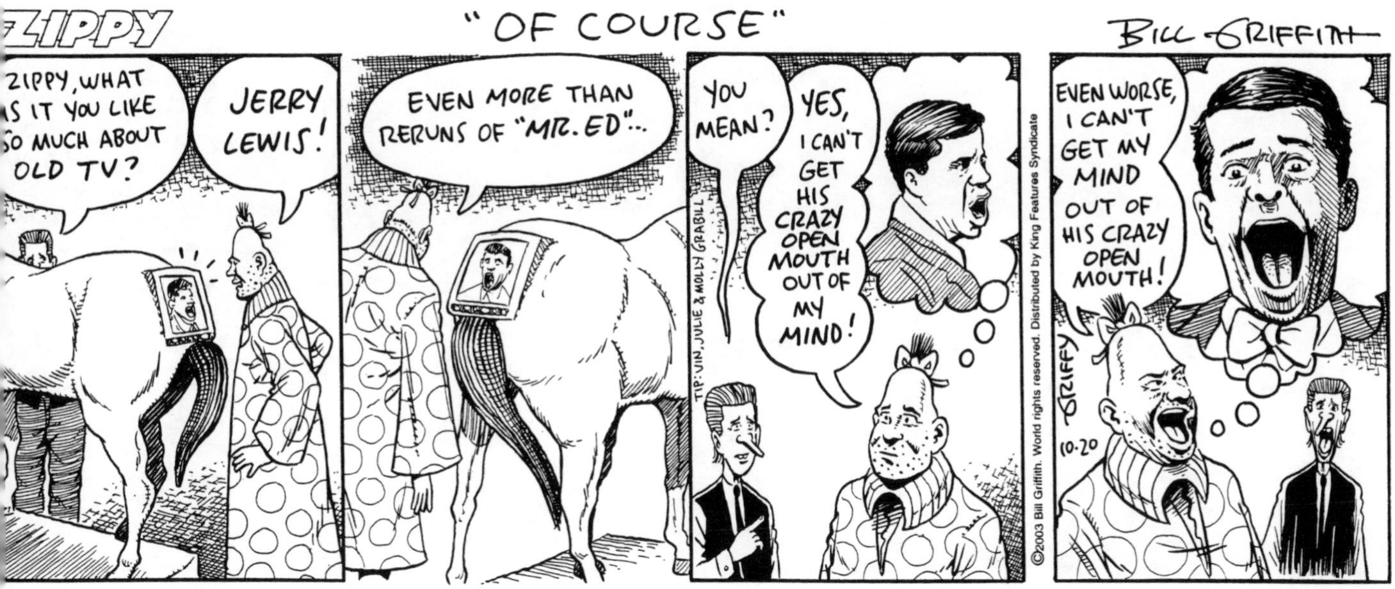
ZIPPY
"OF COURSE"
BILL GRIFFITH
ZIPPY, WHAT IS IT YOU LIKE SO MUCH ABOUT OLD TV?
JERRY LEWIS!
EVEN MORE THAN RERUNS OF "MR. ED"..
YOU MEAN?
YES, I CAN'T GET HIS CRAZY OPEN MOUTH OUT OF MY MIND!
TIP: VIN, JULIE & MOLLY GRABILL
EVEN WORSE, I CAN'T GET MY MIND OUT OF HIS CRAZY OPEN MOUTH!
GRIFFY 10-20
©2003 Bill Griffith. World rights reserved. Distributed by King Features Syndicate

184

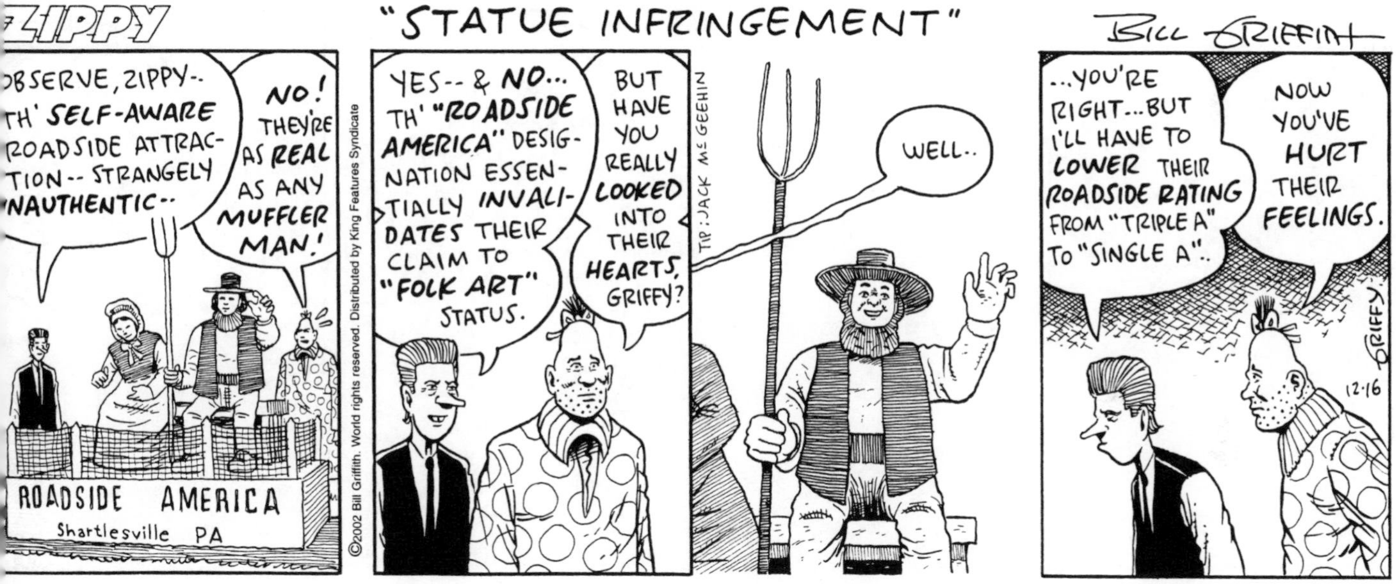
ZIPPY
"STATUE INFRINGEMENT"
BILL GRIFFITH
OBSERVE, ZIPPY-- TH' SELF-AWARE ROADSIDE ATTRACTION-- STRANGELY INAUTHENTIC--
NO! THEY'RE AS REAL AS ANY MUFFLER MAN!
ROADSIDE AMERICA
Shartlesville PA
©2002 Bill Griffith. World rights reserved. Distributed by King Features Syndicate
YES-- & NO... TH' "ROADSIDE AMERICA" DESIGNATION ESSENTIALLY INVALIDATES THEIR CLAIM TO "FOLK ART" STATUS.
BUT HAVE YOU REALLY LOOKED INTO THEIR HEARTS, GRIFFY?
TIP: JACK McGEEHIN
WELL..
..YOU'RE RIGHT...BUT I'LL HAVE TO LOWER THEIR ROADSIDE RATING FROM "TRIPLE A" TO "SINGLE A"..
NOW YOU'VE HURT THEIR FEELINGS.
GRIFFY 12-16

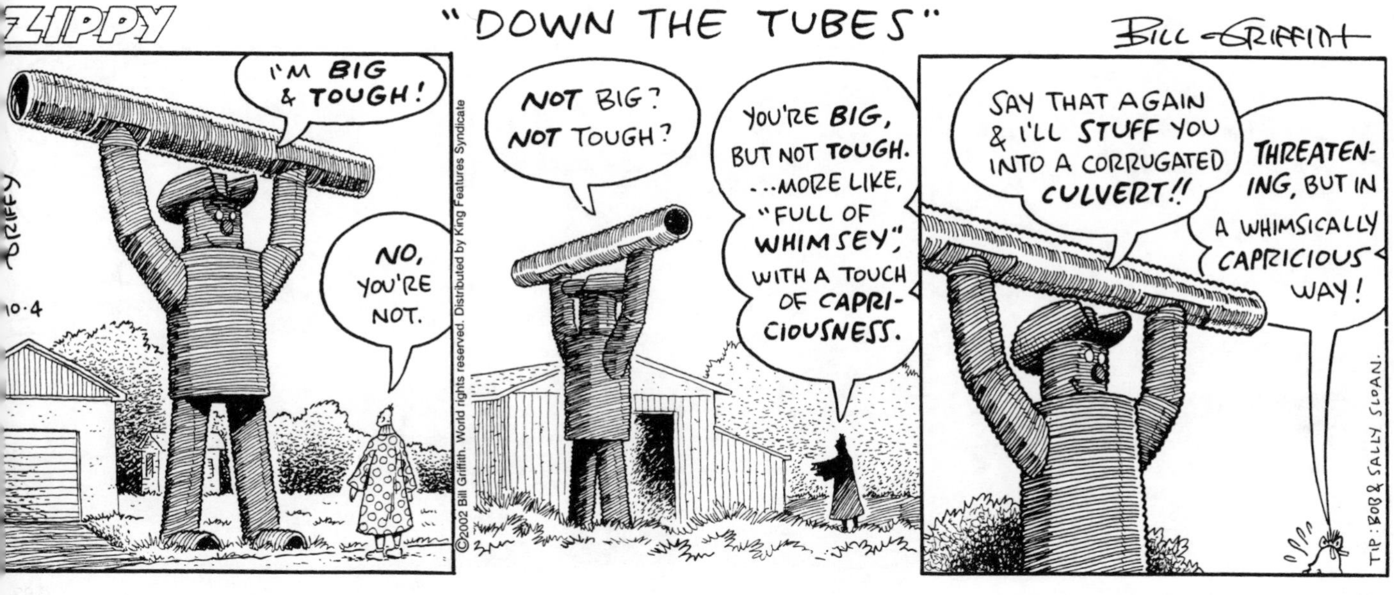
ZIPPY
"DOWN THE TUBES"
BILL GRIFFITH
I'M BIG & TOUGH!
NO, YOU'RE NOT.
GRIFFY 10-4
©2002 Bill Griffith. World rights reserved. Distributed by King Features Syndicate
NOT BIG? NOT TOUGH?
YOU'RE BIG, BUT NOT TOUGH. ...MORE LIKE, "FULL OF WHIMSEY", WITH A TOUCH OF CAPRICIOUSNESS.
SAY THAT AGAIN & I'LL STUFF YOU INTO A CORRUGATED CULVERT!!
THREATENING, BUT IN A WHIMSICALLY CAPRICIOUS WAY!
TIP: BOB & SALLY SLOAN.

185

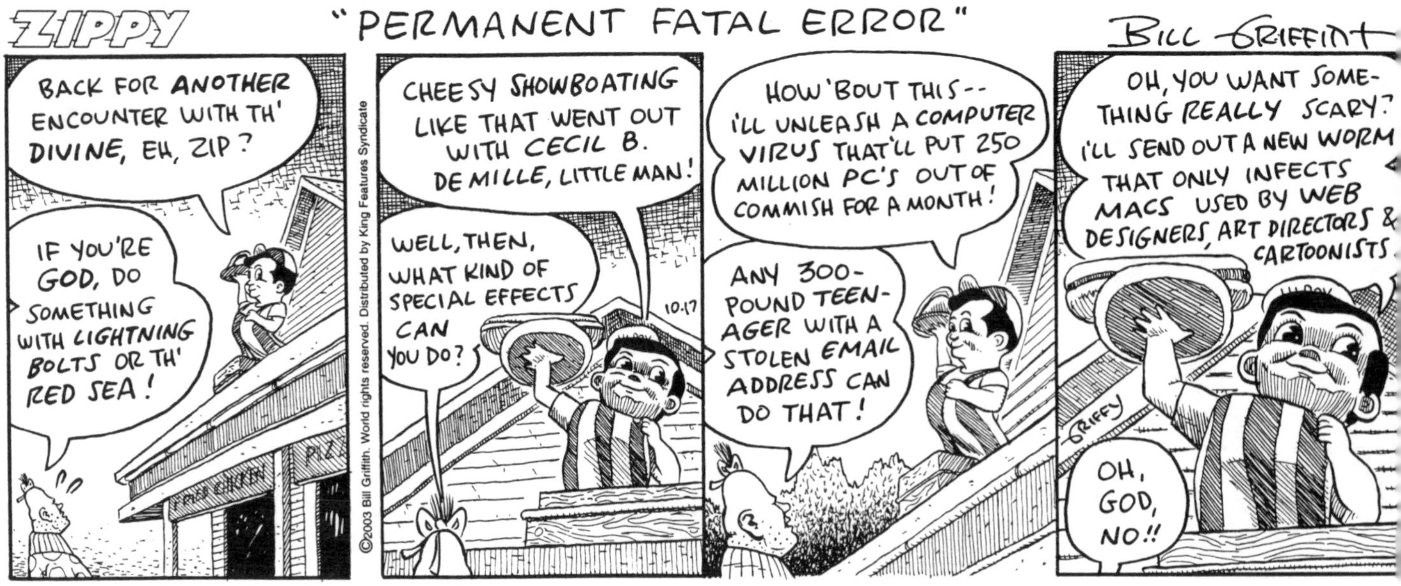
ZIPPY
"PERMANENT FATAL ERROR"
BILL GRIFFITH
BACK FOR ANOTHER ENCOUNTER WITH TH' DIVINE, EH, ZIP?
IF YOU'RE GOD, DO SOMETHING WITH LIGHTNING BOLTS OR TH' RED SEA!
CHEESY SHOWBOATING LIKE THAT WENT OUT WITH CECIL B. DE MILLE, LITTLE MAN!
WELL, THEN, WHAT KIND OF SPECIAL EFFECTS CAN YOU DO?
10-17
©2003 Bill Griffith. World rights reserved. Distributed by King Features Syndicate
HOW 'BOUT THIS-- I'LL UNLEASH A COMPUTER VIRUS THAT'LL PUT 250 MILLION PC'S OUT OF COMMISH FOR A MONTH!
ANY 300-POUND TEEN-AGER WITH A STOLEN EMAIL ADDRESS CAN DO THAT!
OH, YOU WANT SOME-THING REALLY SCARY? I'LL SEND OUT A NEW WORM THAT ONLY INFECTS MACS USED BY WEB DESIGNERS, ART DIRECTORS & CARTOONISTS
OH, GOD, NO!!
GRIFFY

186 A

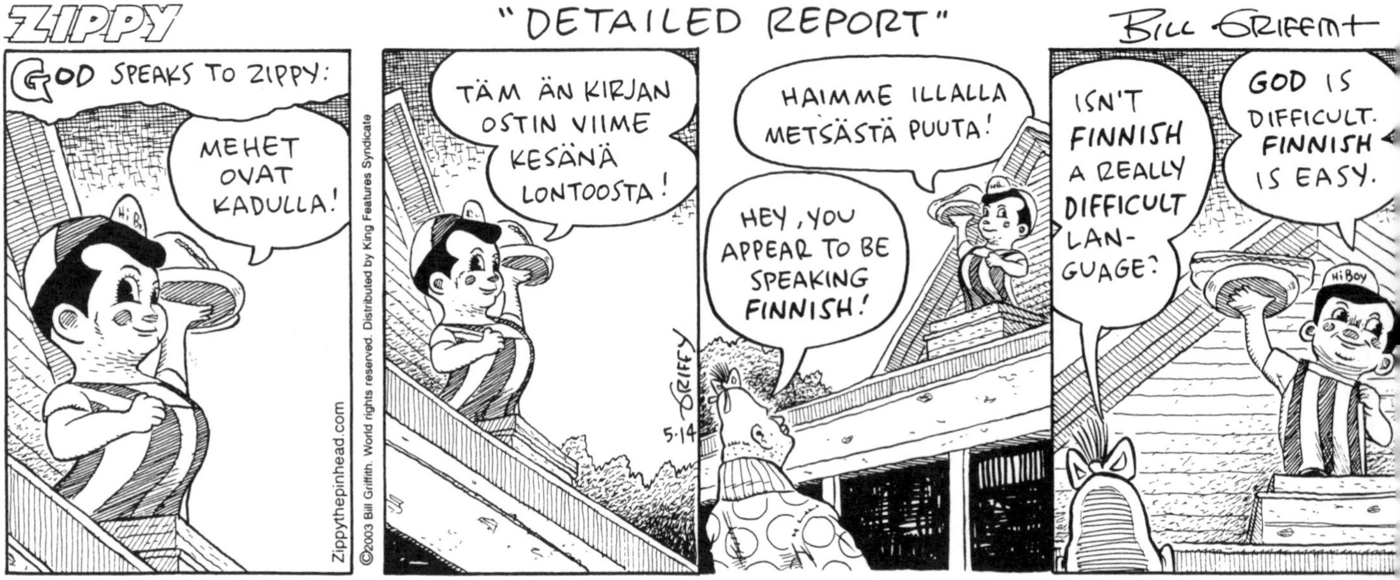
ZIPPY
"DETAILED REPORT"
BILL GRIFFITH
GOD SPEAKS TO ZIPPY:
MEHET OVAT KADULLA!
Zippythepinhead.com
©2003 Bill Griffith. World rights reserved. Distributed by King Features Syndicate
TÄM ÄN KIRJAN OSTIN VIIME KESÄNÄ LONTOOSTA!
GRIFFY
5-14
HAIMME ILLALLA METSÄSTÄ PUUTA!
HEY, YOU APPEAR TO BE SPEAKING FINNISH!
ISN'T FINNISH A REALLY DIFFICULT LAN-GUAGE?
GOD IS DIFFICULT. FINNISH IS EASY.

186 B

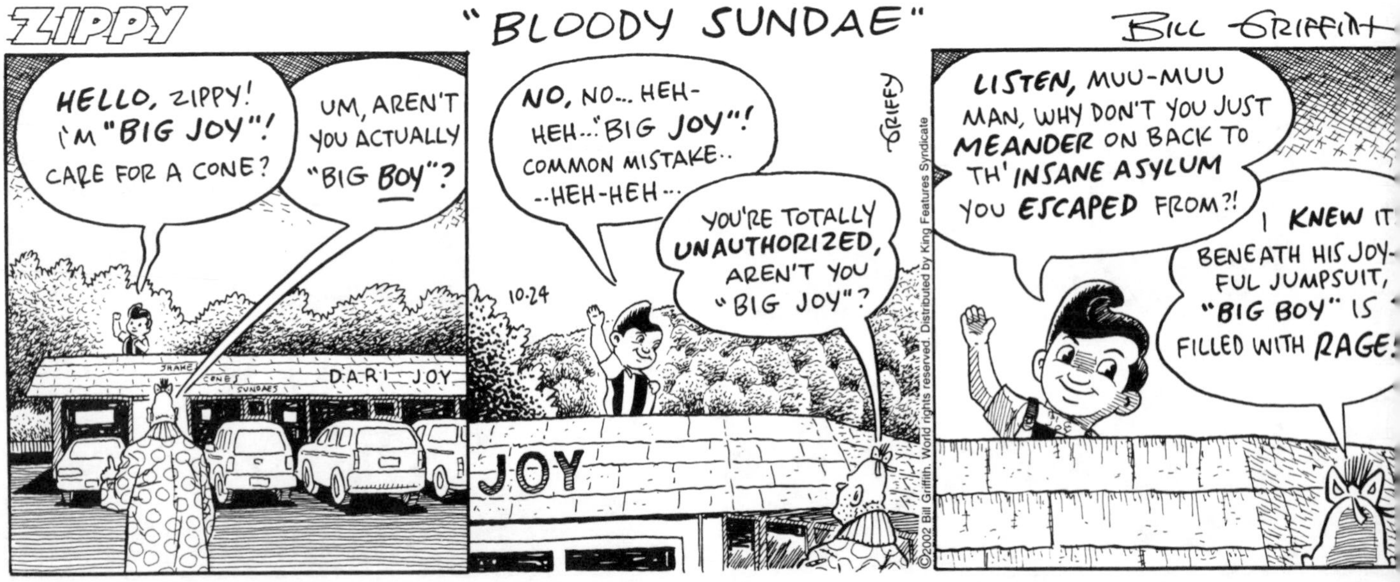
ZIPPY
"BLOODY SUNDAE"
BILL GRIFFITH
HELLO, ZIPPY! I'M "BIG JOY"! CARE FOR A CONE?
UM, AREN'T YOU ACTUALLY "BIG BOY"?
DARI-JOY
NO, NO... HEH-HEH..."BIG JOY"! COMMON MISTAKE.. ..HEH-HEH...
GRIFFY
10-24
YOU'RE TOTALLY UNAUTHORIZED, AREN'T YOU "BIG JOY"?
JOY
©2002 Bill Griffith. World rights reserved. Distributed by King Features Syndicate
LISTEN, MUU-MUU MAN, WHY DON'T YOU JUST MEANDER ON BACK TO TH' INSANE ASYLUM YOU ESCAPED FROM?!
I KNEW IT! BENEATH HIS JOY-FUL JUMPSUIT, "BIG BOY" IS FILLED WITH RAGE!

186 C

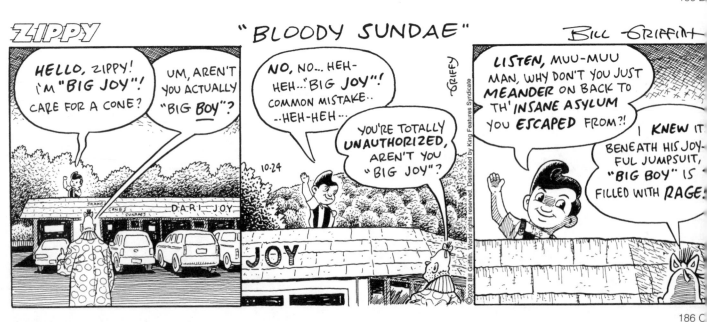

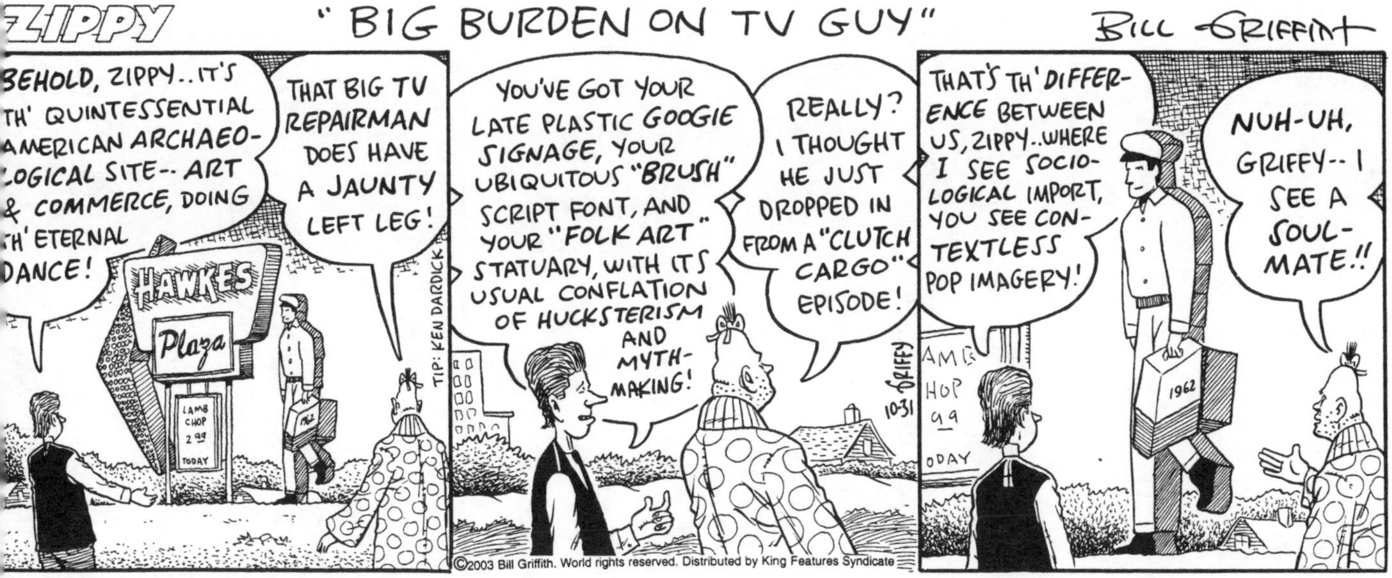
ZIPPY
"BIG BURDEN ON TV GUY"
BILL GRIFFITH
BEHOLD, ZIPPY.. IT'S TH' QUINTESSENTIAL AMERICAN ARCHAEOLOGICAL SITE-- ART & COMMERCE, DOING TH' ETERNAL DANCE!
THAT BIG TV REPAIRMAN DOES HAVE A JAUNTY LEFT LEG!
HAWKES
Plaza
LAMB CHOP 2.99 TODAY
TIP: KEN DARDICK
YOU'VE GOT YOUR LATE PLASTIC GOOGIE SIGNAGE, YOUR UBIQUITOUS "BRUSH" SCRIPT FONT, AND YOUR "FOLK ART" STATUARY, WITH ITS USUAL CONFLATION OF HUCKSTERISM AND MYTH-MAKING!
REALLY? I THOUGHT HE JUST DROPPED IN FROM A "CLUTCH CARGO" EPISODE!
GRIFFY 10-31
THAT'S TH' DIFFERENCE BETWEEN US, ZIPPY.. WHERE I SEE SOCIOLOGICAL IMPORT, YOU SEE CONTEXTLESS POP IMAGERY!
NUH-UH, GRIFFY-- I SEE A SOUL-MATE!!
1962
©2003 Bill Griffith. World rights reserved. Distributed by King Features Syndicate

187

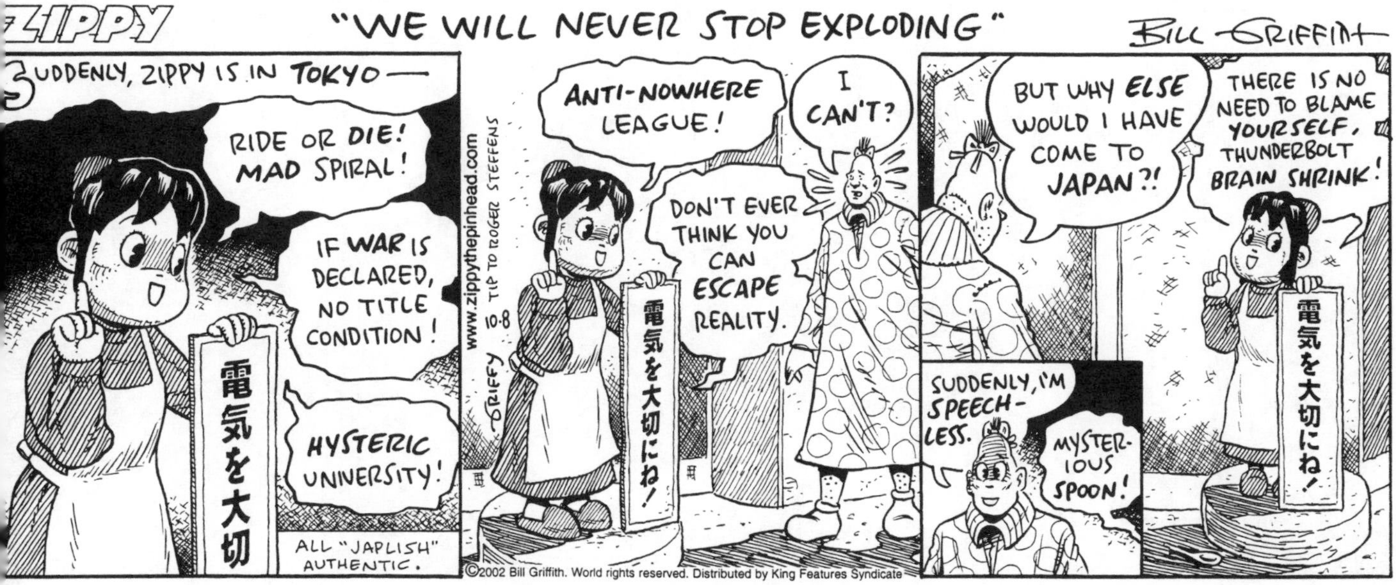
ZIPPY
"WE WILL NEVER STOP EXPLODING"
BILL GRIFFITH
SUDDENLY, ZIPPY IS IN TOKYO—
RIDE OR DIE! MAD SPIRAL!
IF WAR IS DECLARED, NO TITLE CONDITION!
HYSTERIC UNIVERSITY!
電気を大切
ALL "JAPLISH" AUTHENTIC.
www.zippythepinhead.com
TIP TO ROGER STEFFENS
GRIFFY 10-8
ANTI-NOWHERE LEAGUE!
I CAN'T?
DON'T EVER THINK YOU CAN ESCAPE REALITY.
電気を大切にね!
BUT WHY ELSE WOULD I HAVE COME TO JAPAN?!
THERE IS NO NEED TO BLAME YOURSELF, THUNDERBOLT BRAIN SHRINK!
SUDDENLY, I'M SPEECHLESS.
MYSTERIOUS SPOON!
電気を大切にね!
©2002 Bill Griffith. World rights reserved. Distributed by King Features Syndicate

188 A

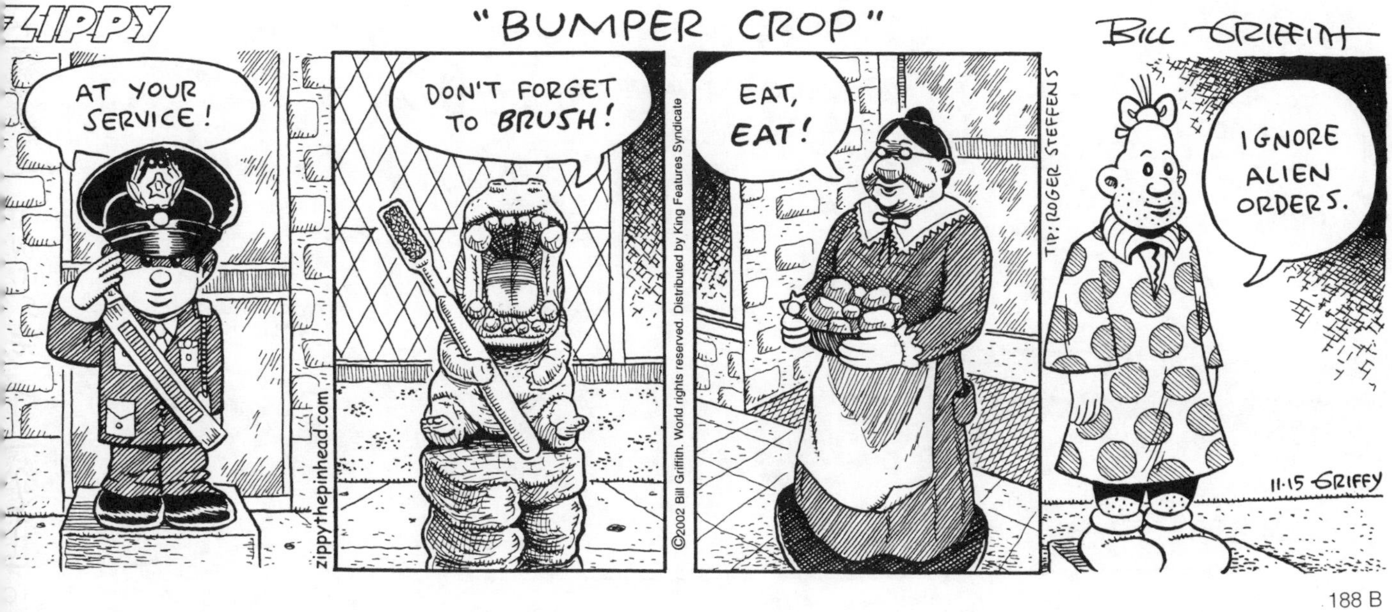
ZIPPY
"BUMPER CROP"
BILL GRIFFITH
AT YOUR SERVICE!
zippythepinhead.com
DON'T FORGET TO BRUSH!
©2002 Bill Griffith. World rights reserved. Distributed by King Features Syndicate
EAT, EAT!
TIP: ROGER STEFFENS
IGNORE ALIEN ORDERS.
11-15 GRIFFY

188 B

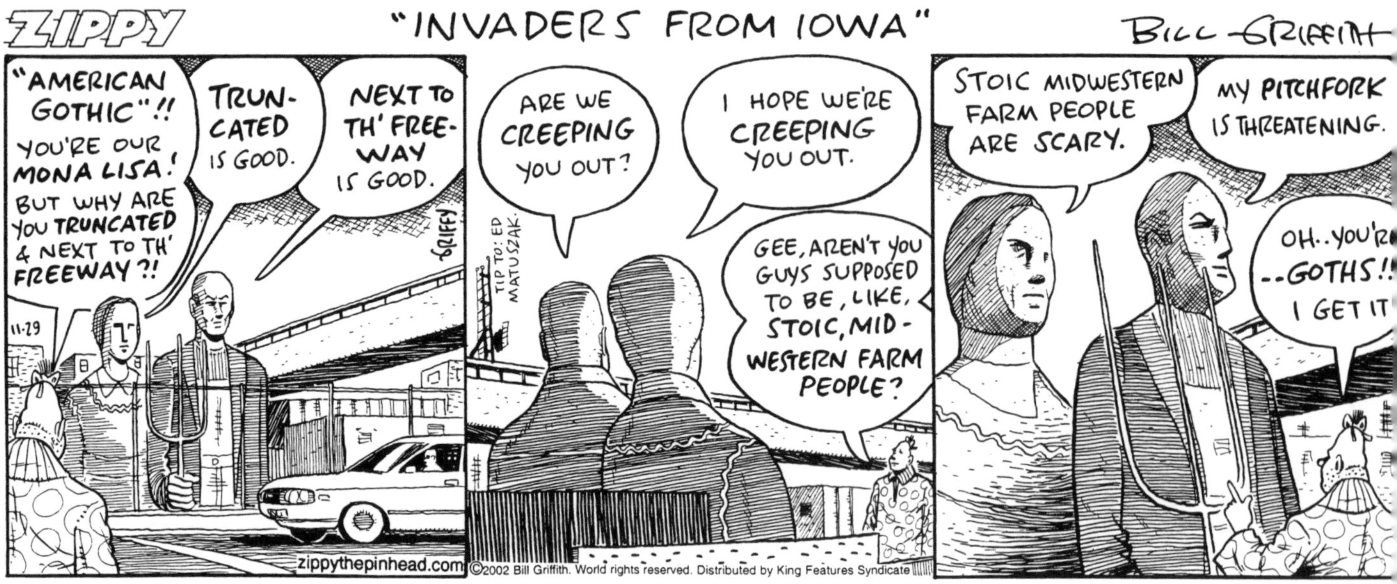

ZIPPY
"INVADERS FROM IOWA"
BILL GRIFFITH
"AMERICAN GOTHIC"!! YOU'RE OUR MONA LISA! BUT WHY ARE YOU TRUNCATED & NEXT TO TH' FREEWAY?!
TRUN-CATED IS GOOD.
NEXT TO TH' FREE-WAY IS GOOD.
11-29
GRIFFY
TIP TO: ED MATUSZAK
ARE WE CREEPING YOU OUT?
I HOPE WE'RE CREEPING YOU OUT.
GEE, AREN'T YOU GUYS SUPPOSED TO BE, LIKE, STOIC, MID-WESTERN FARM PEOPLE?
STOIC MIDWESTERN FARM PEOPLE ARE SCARY.
MY PITCHFORK IS THREATENING.
OH.. YOU'RE --GOTHS!! I GET IT
zippythepinhead.com
©2002 Bill Griffith. World rights reserved. Distributed by King Features Syndicate

189

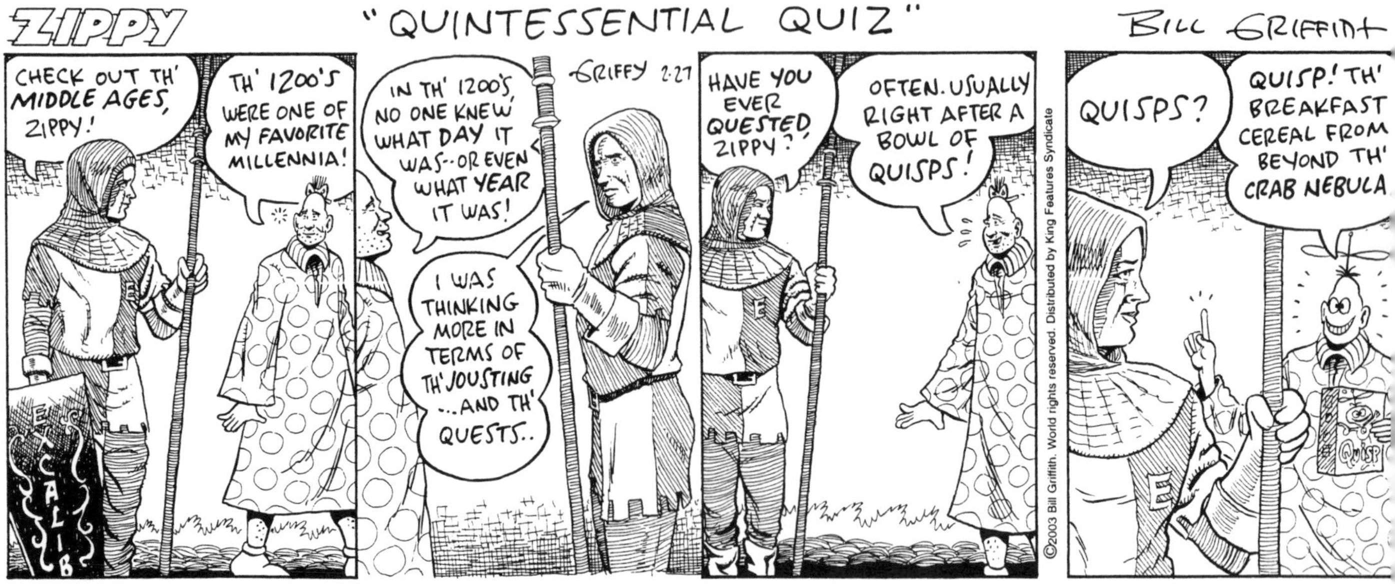

ZIPPY
"QUINTESSENTIAL QUIZ"
BILL GRIFFITH
CHECK OUT TH' MIDDLE AGES, ZIPPY!
TH' 1200'S WERE ONE OF MY FAVORITE MILLENNIA!
EXCALIB
IN TH' 1200'S, NO ONE KNEW WHAT DAY IT WAS--OR EVEN WHAT YEAR IT WAS!
GRIFFY 2-27
I WAS THINKING MORE IN TERMS OF TH' JOUSTING ...AND TH' QUESTS..
HAVE YOU EVER QUESTED, ZIPPY?
OFTEN. USUALLY RIGHT AFTER A BOWL OF QUISPS!
©2003 Bill Griffith. World rights reserved. Distributed by King Features Syndicate
QUISPS?
QUISP! TH' BREAKFAST CEREAL FROM BEYOND TH' CRAB NEBULA
QUISP

190

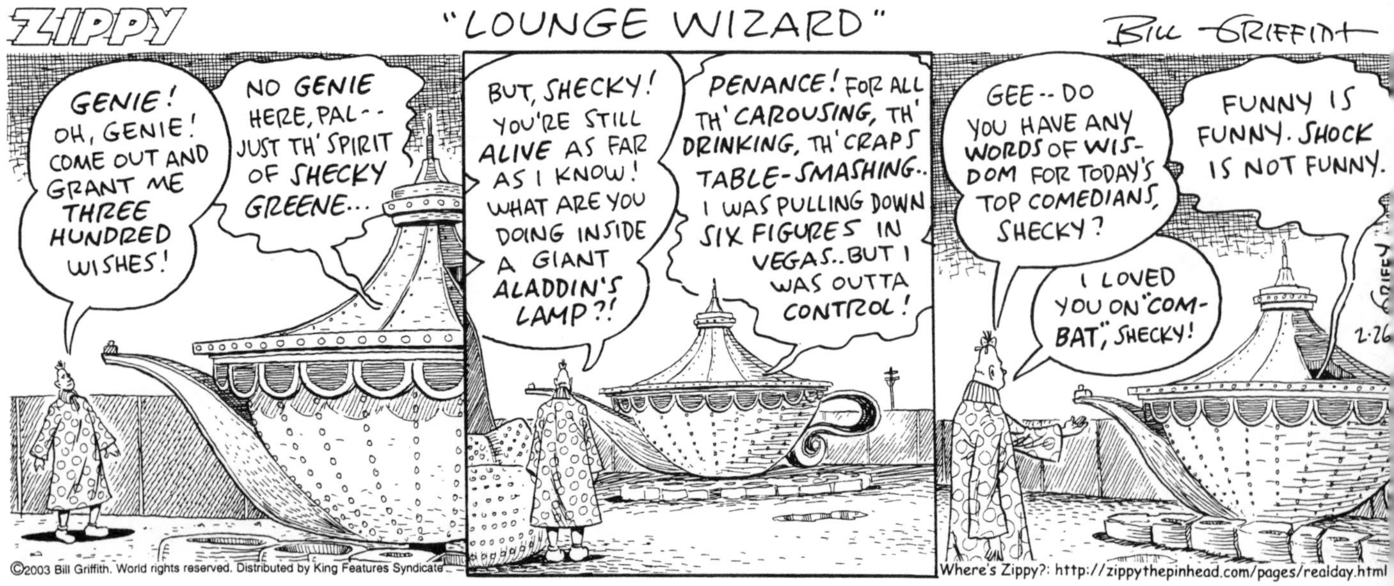

ZIPPY
"LOUNGE WIZARD"
BILL GRIFFITH
GENIE! OH, GENIE! COME OUT AND GRANT ME THREE HUNDRED WISHES!
NO GENIE HERE, PAL-- JUST TH' SPIRIT OF SHECKY GREENE...
BUT, SHECKY! YOU'RE STILL ALIVE AS FAR AS I KNOW! WHAT ARE YOU DOING INSIDE A GIANT ALADDIN'S LAMP?!
PENANCE! FOR ALL TH' CAROUSING, TH' DRINKING, TH' CRAPS TABLE-SMASHING.. I WAS PULLING DOWN SIX FIGURES IN VEGAS.. BUT I WAS OUTTA CONTROL!
GEE-- DO YOU HAVE ANY WORDS OF WIS-DOM FOR TODAY'S TOP COMEDIANS, SHECKY?
FUNNY IS FUNNY. SHOCK IS NOT FUNNY.
I LOVED YOU ON "COM-BAT," SHECKY!
GRIFFY 2-26
©2003 Bill Griffith. World rights reserved. Distributed by King Features Syndicate
Where's Zippy?: http://zippythepinhead.com/pages/realday.html

191 A

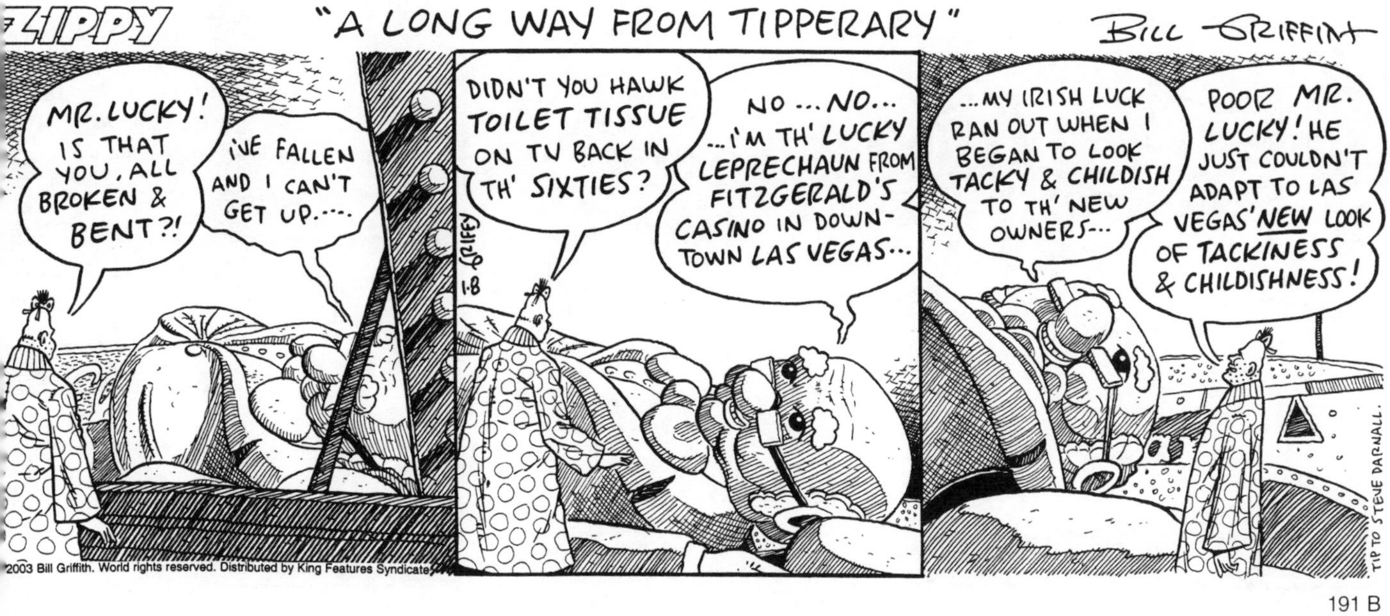
ZIPPY
"A LONG WAY FROM TIPPERARY"
BILL GRIFFITH
MR. LUCKY! IS THAT YOU, ALL BROKEN & BENT?!
I'VE FALLEN AND I CAN'T GET UP....
DIDN'T YOU HAWK TOILET TISSUE ON TV BACK IN TH' SIXTIES?
NO ... NO... ...I'M TH' LUCKY LEPRECHAUN FROM FITZGERALD'S CASINO IN DOWNTOWN LAS VEGAS...
...MY IRISH LUCK RAN OUT WHEN I BEGAN TO LOOK TACKY & CHILDISH TO TH' NEW OWNERS...
POOR MR. LUCKY! HE JUST COULDN'T ADAPT TO LAS VEGAS' NEW LOOK OF TACKINESS & CHILDISHNESS!
TIP TO STEVE DARNALL.
©2003 Bill Griffith. World rights reserved. Distributed by King Features Syndicate

191 B

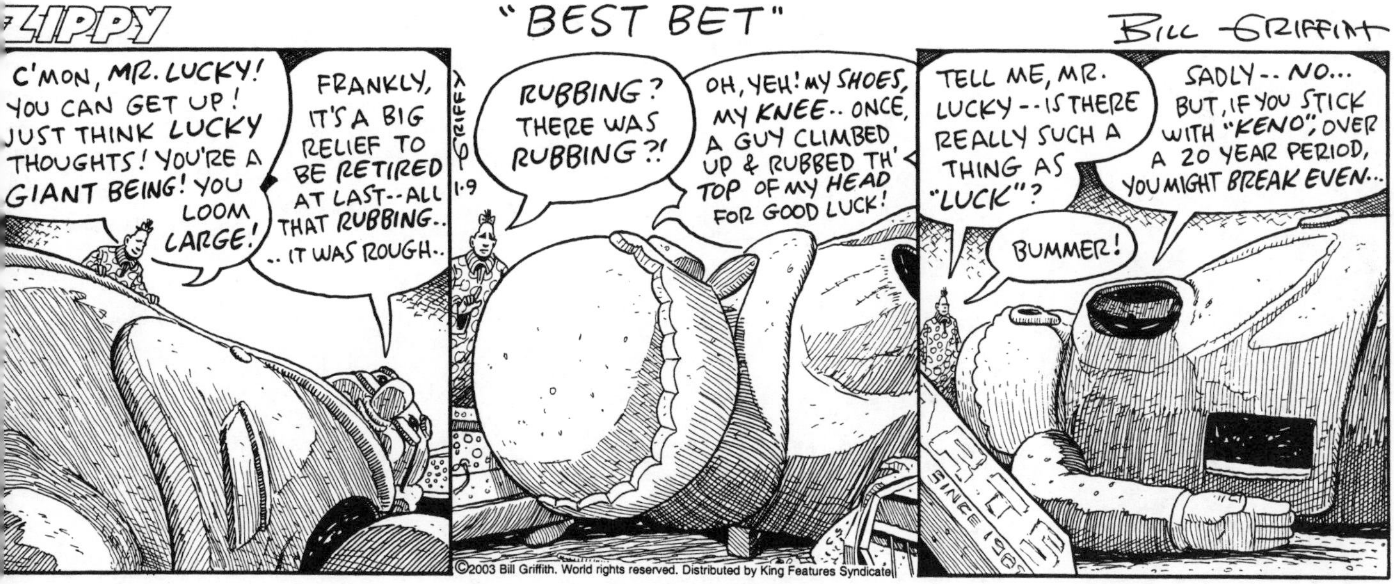
ZIPPY
"BEST BET"
BILL GRIFFITH
C'MON, MR. LUCKY! YOU CAN GET UP! JUST THINK LUCKY THOUGHTS! YOU'RE A GIANT BEING! YOU LOOM LARGE!
FRANKLY, IT'S A BIG RELIEF TO BE RETIRED AT LAST--ALL THAT RUBBING.. ..IT WAS ROUGH..
RUBBING? THERE WAS RUBBING?!
OH, YEH! MY SHOES, MY KNEE.. ONCE, A GUY CLIMBED UP & RUBBED TH' TOP OF MY HEAD FOR GOOD LUCK!
TELL ME, MR. LUCKY -- IS THERE REALLY SUCH A THING AS "LUCK"?
SADLY -- NO... BUT, IF YOU STICK WITH "KENO", OVER A 20 YEAR PERIOD, YOU MIGHT BREAK EVEN...
BUMMER!
©2003 Bill Griffith. World rights reserved. Distributed by King Features Syndicate

191 C

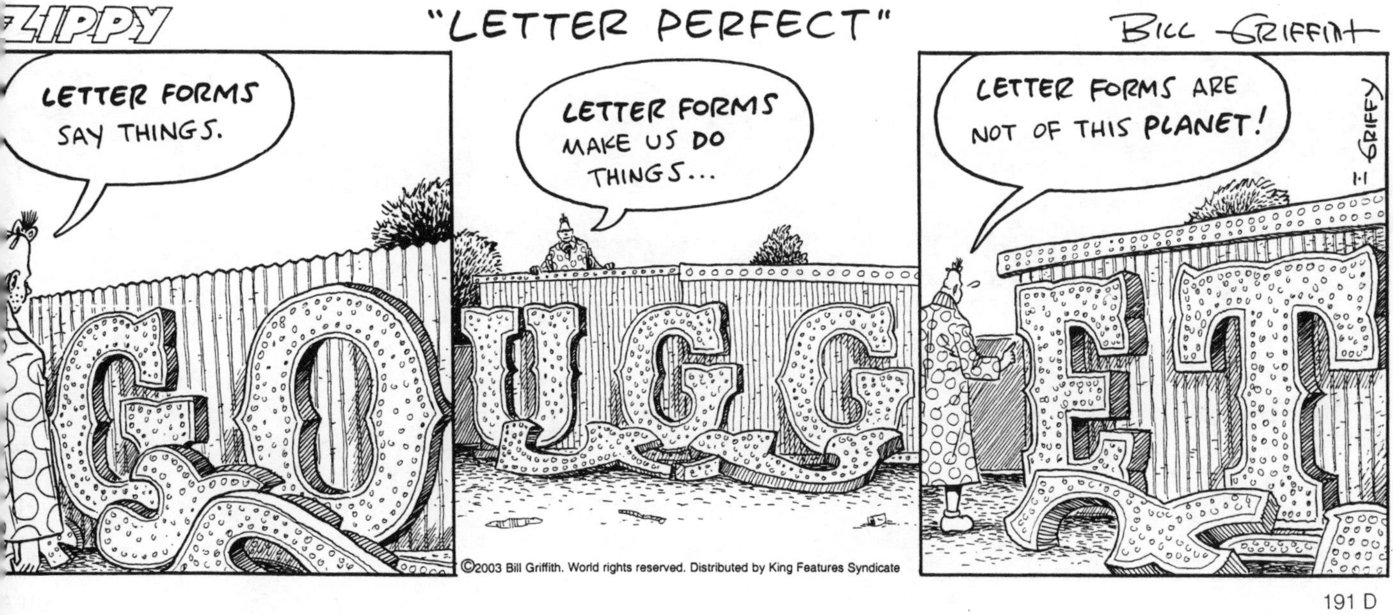
ZIPPY
"LETTER PERFECT"
BILL GRIFFITH
LETTER FORMS SAY THINGS.
LETTER FORMS MAKE US DO THINGS...
LETTER FORMS ARE NOT OF THIS PLANET!
©2003 Bill Griffith. World rights reserved. Distributed by King Features Syndicate

191 D

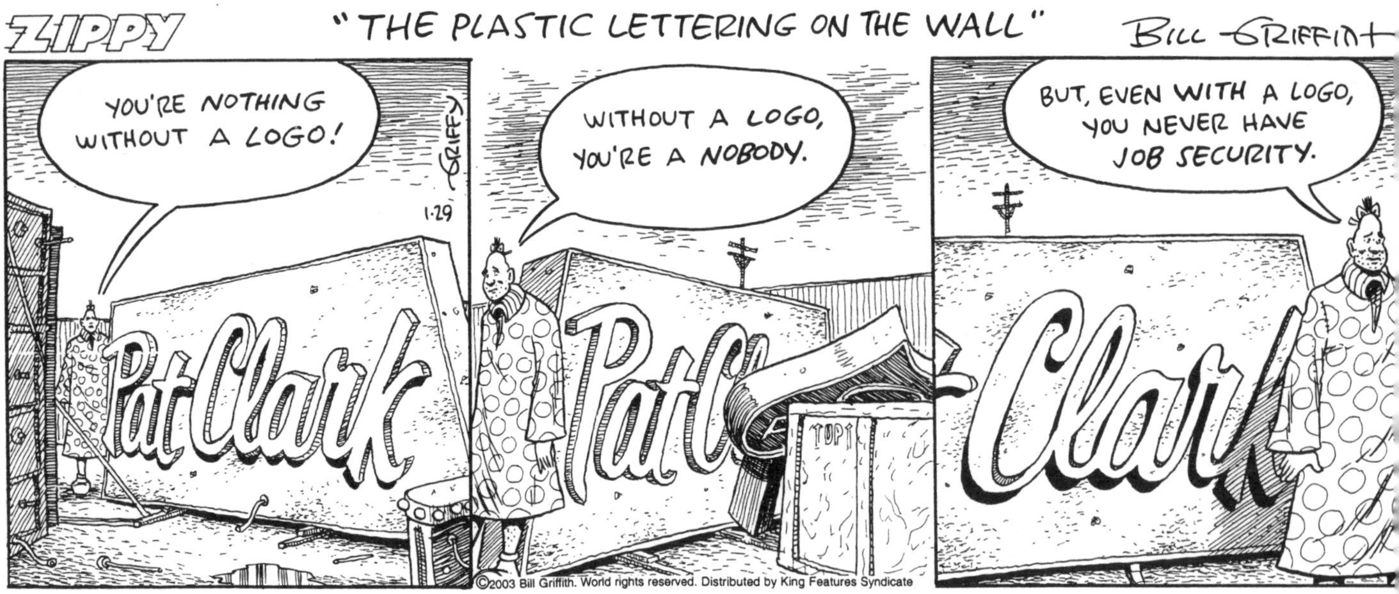
ZIPPY
"THE PLASTIC LETTERING ON THE WALL"
BILL GRIFFITH
YOU'RE NOTHING WITHOUT A LOGO!
GRIFFY
1·29
Pat Clark
WITHOUT A LOGO, YOU'RE A NOBODY.
TOP
BUT, EVEN WITH A LOGO, YOU NEVER HAVE JOB SECURITY.
©2003 Bill Griffith. World rights reserved. Distributed by King Features Syndicate

191 E

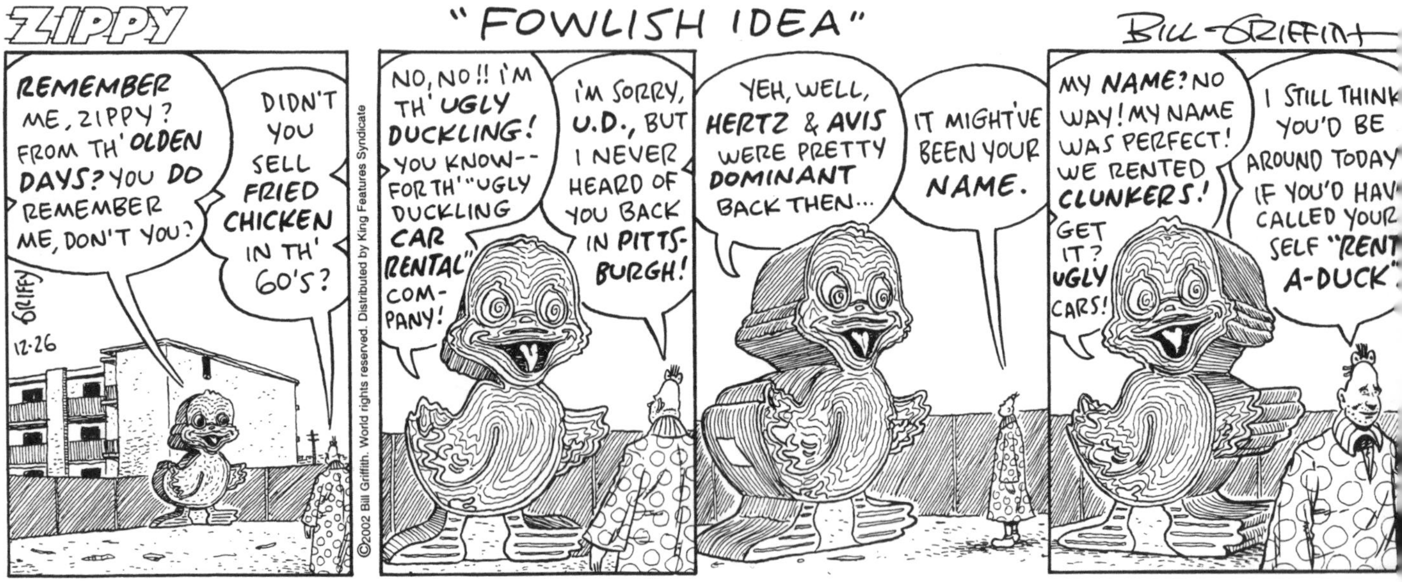
ZIPPY
"FOWLISH IDEA"
BILL GRIFFITH
REMEMBER ME, ZIPPY? FROM TH' OLDEN DAYS? YOU DO REMEMBER ME, DON'T YOU?
DIDN'T YOU SELL FRIED CHICKEN IN TH' 60'S?
GRIFFY
12·26
©2002 Bill Griffith. World rights reserved. Distributed by King Features Syndicate
NO, NO!! I'M TH' UGLY DUCKLING! YOU KNOW-- FOR TH' "UGLY DUCKLING CAR RENTAL" COMPANY!
I'M SORRY, U.D., BUT I NEVER HEARD OF YOU BACK IN PITTSBURGH!
YEH, WELL, HERTZ & AVIS WERE PRETTY DOMINANT BACK THEN...
IT MIGHT'VE BEEN YOUR NAME.
MY NAME? NO WAY! MY NAME WAS PERFECT! WE RENTED CLUNKERS!
GET IT? UGLY CARS!
I STILL THINK YOU'D BE AROUND TODAY IF YOU'D HAVE CALLED YOURSELF "RENT-A-DUCK"

191 F

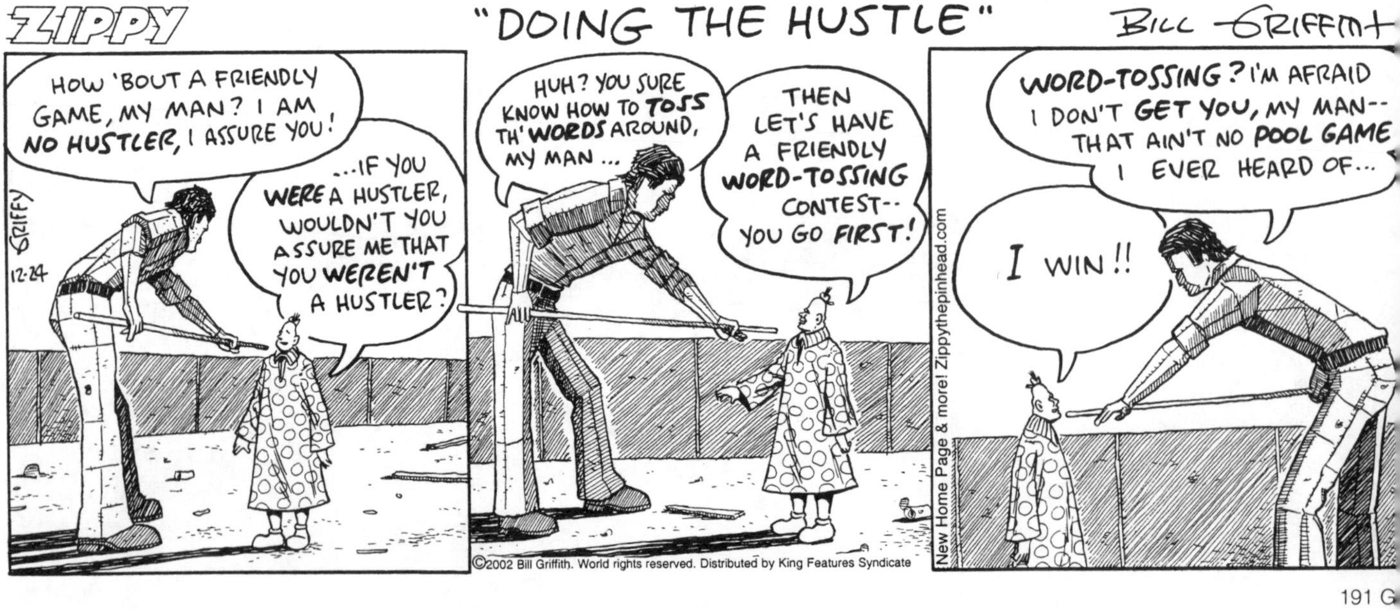
ZIPPY
"DOING THE HUSTLE"
BILL GRIFFITH
HOW 'BOUT A FRIENDLY GAME, MY MAN? I AM NO HUSTLER, I ASSURE YOU!
...IF YOU WERE A HUSTLER, WOULDN'T YOU ASSURE ME THAT YOU WEREN'T A HUSTLER?
GRIFFY
12·24
HUH? YOU SURE KNOW HOW TO TOSS TH' WORDS AROUND, MY MAN...
THEN LET'S HAVE A FRIENDLY WORD-TOSSING CONTEST-- YOU GO FIRST!
New Home Page & more! Zippythepinhead.com
WORD-TOSSING? I'M AFRAID I DON'T GET YOU, MY MAN-- THAT AIN'T NO POOL GAME I EVER HEARD OF...
I WIN!!
©2002 Bill Griffith. World rights reserved. Distributed by King Features Syndicate

191 G

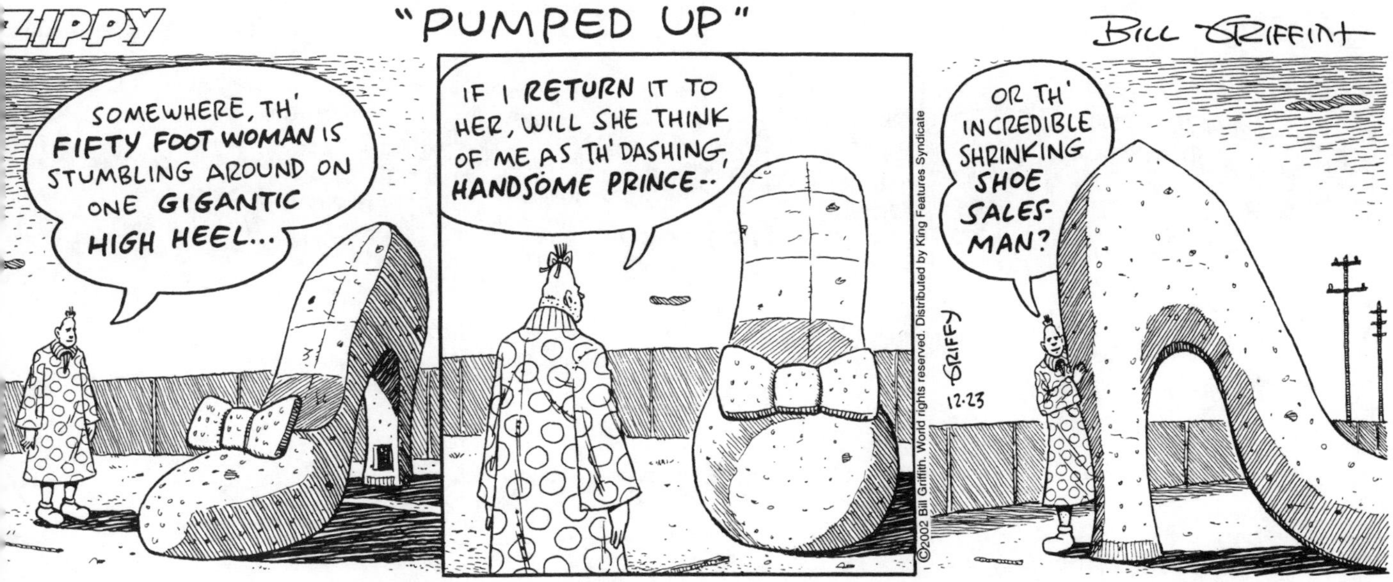
ZIPPY
"PUMPED UP"
BILL GRIFFITH
SOMEWHERE, TH' FIFTY FOOT WOMAN IS STUMBLING AROUND ON ONE GIGANTIC HIGH HEEL...
IF I RETURN IT TO HER, WILL SHE THINK OF ME AS TH' DASHING, HANDSOME PRINCE--
OR TH' INCREDIBLE SHRINKING SHOE SALES-MAN?
GRIFFY 12-23
©2002 Bill Griffith. World rights reserved. Distributed by King Features Syndicate

191 H

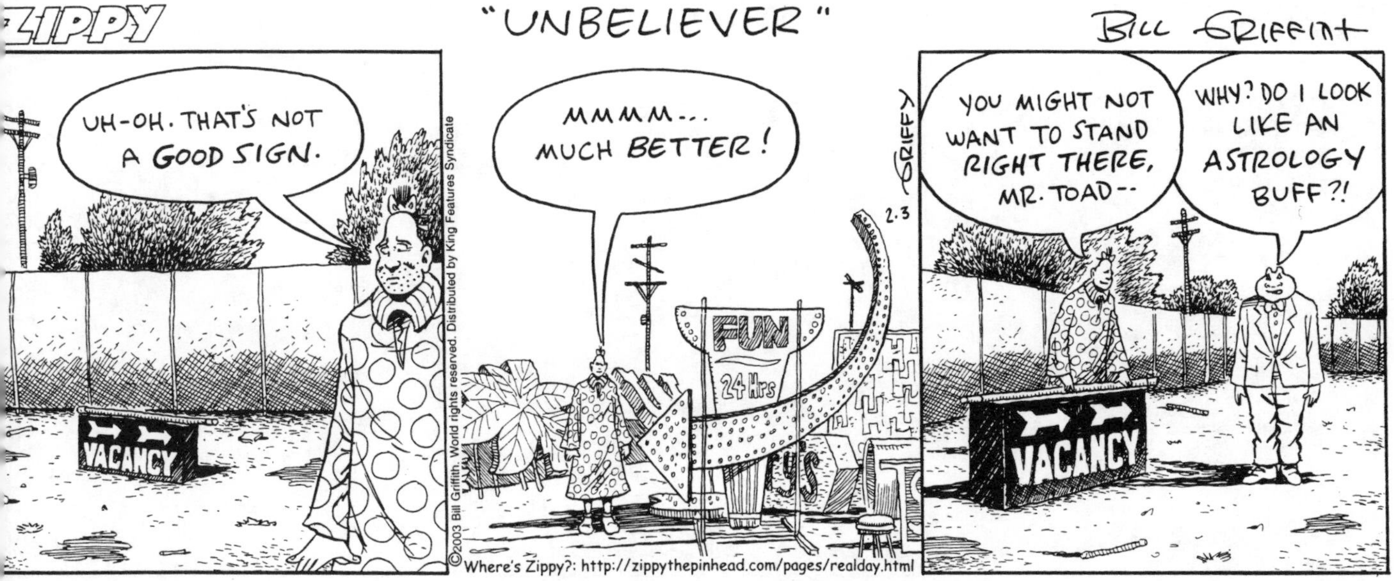
ZIPPY
"UNBELIEVER"
BILL GRIFFITH
UH-OH. THAT'S NOT A GOOD SIGN.
VACANCY
MMMM... MUCH BETTER!
FUN
24 Hrs
GRIFFY 2-3
©2003 Bill Griffith. World rights reserved. Distributed by King Features Syndicate
Where's Zippy?: http://zippythepinhead.com/pages/realday.html
YOU MIGHT NOT WANT TO STAND RIGHT THERE, MR. TOAD--
WHY? DO I LOOK LIKE AN ASTROLOGY BUFF?!
VACANCY

191 I

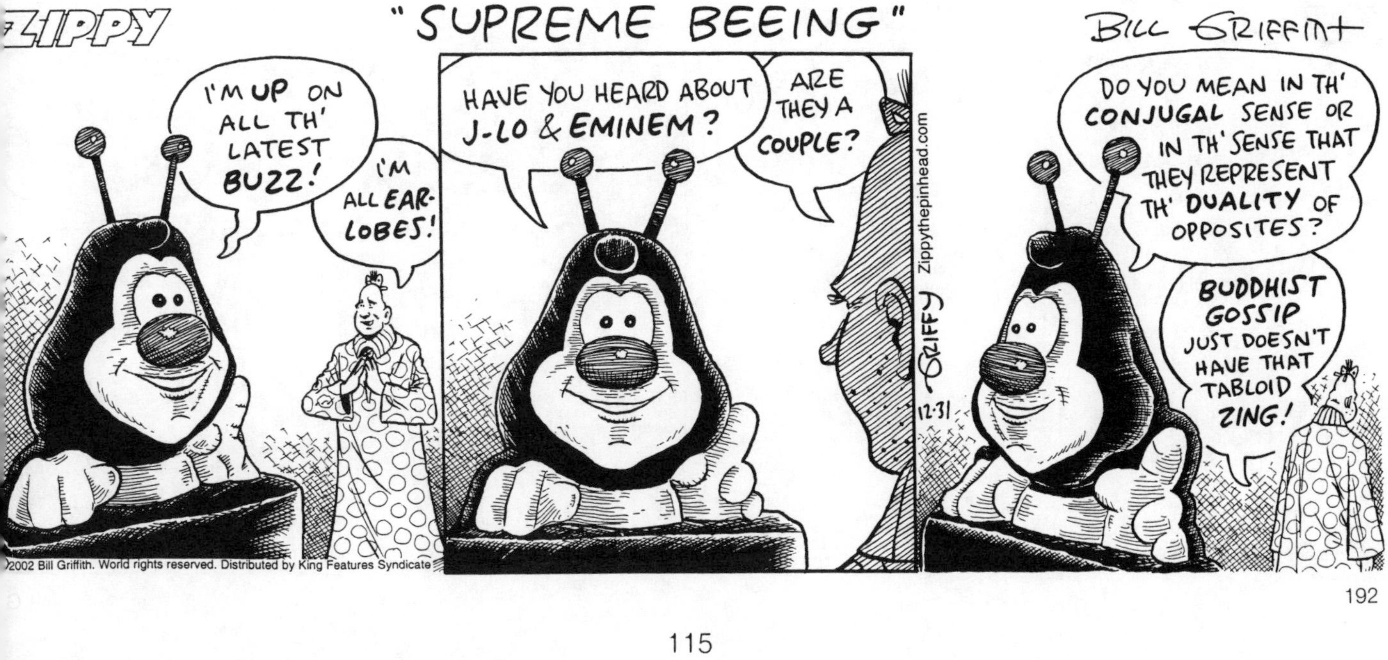
ZIPPY
"SUPREME BEEING"
BILL GRIFFITH
I'M UP ON ALL TH' LATEST BUZZ!
I'M ALL EAR-LOBES!
HAVE YOU HEARD ABOUT J-LO & EMINEM?
ARE THEY A COUPLE?
zippythepinhead.com
GRIFFY 12-31
DO YOU MEAN IN TH' CONJUGAL SENSE OR IN TH' SENSE THAT THEY REPRESENT TH' DUALITY OF OPPOSITES?
BUDDHIST GOSSIP JUST DOESN'T HAVE THAT TABLOID ZING!
©2002 Bill Griffith. World rights reserved. Distributed by King Features Syndicate

192

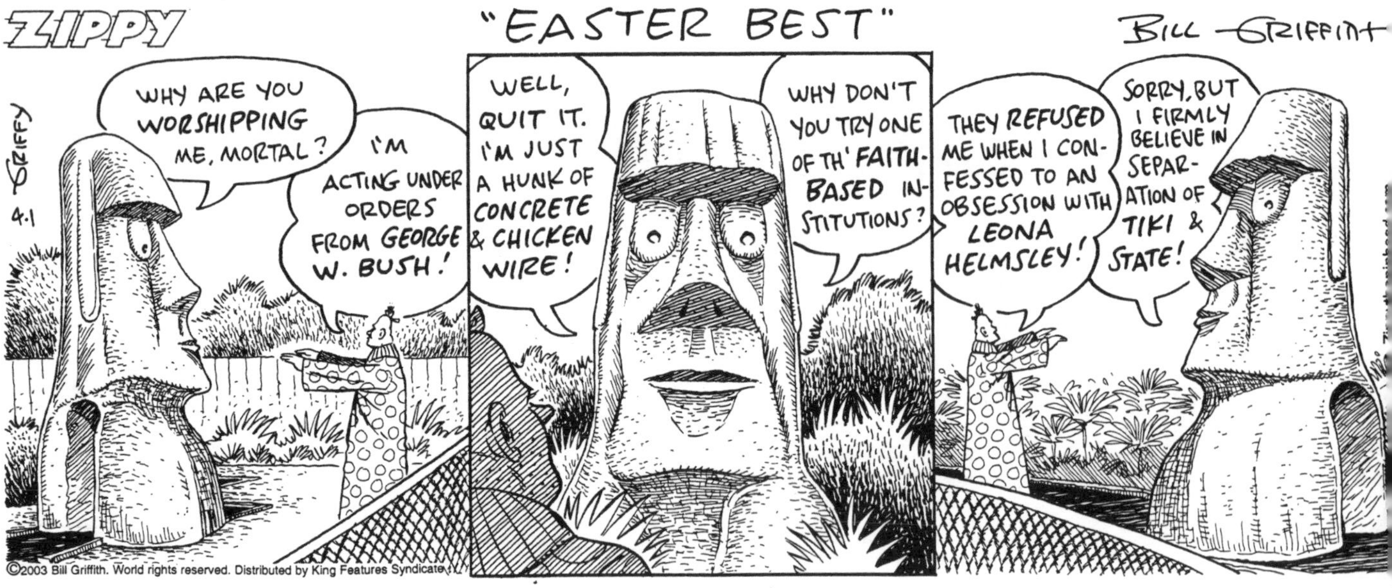
ZIPPY
"EASTER BEST"
BILL GRIFFITH
GRIFFY 4.1
WHY ARE YOU WORSHIPPING ME, MORTAL?
I'M ACTING UNDER ORDERS FROM GEORGE W. BUSH!
WELL, QUIT IT. I'M JUST A HUNK OF CONCRETE & CHICKEN WIRE!
WHY DON'T YOU TRY ONE OF TH' FAITH-BASED INSTITUTIONS?
THEY REFUSED ME WHEN I CONFESSED TO AN OBSESSION WITH LEONA HELMSLEY!
SORRY, BUT I FIRMLY BELIEVE IN SEPARATION OF TIKI & STATE!
©2003 Bill Griffith. World rights reserved. Distributed by King Features Syndicate

193

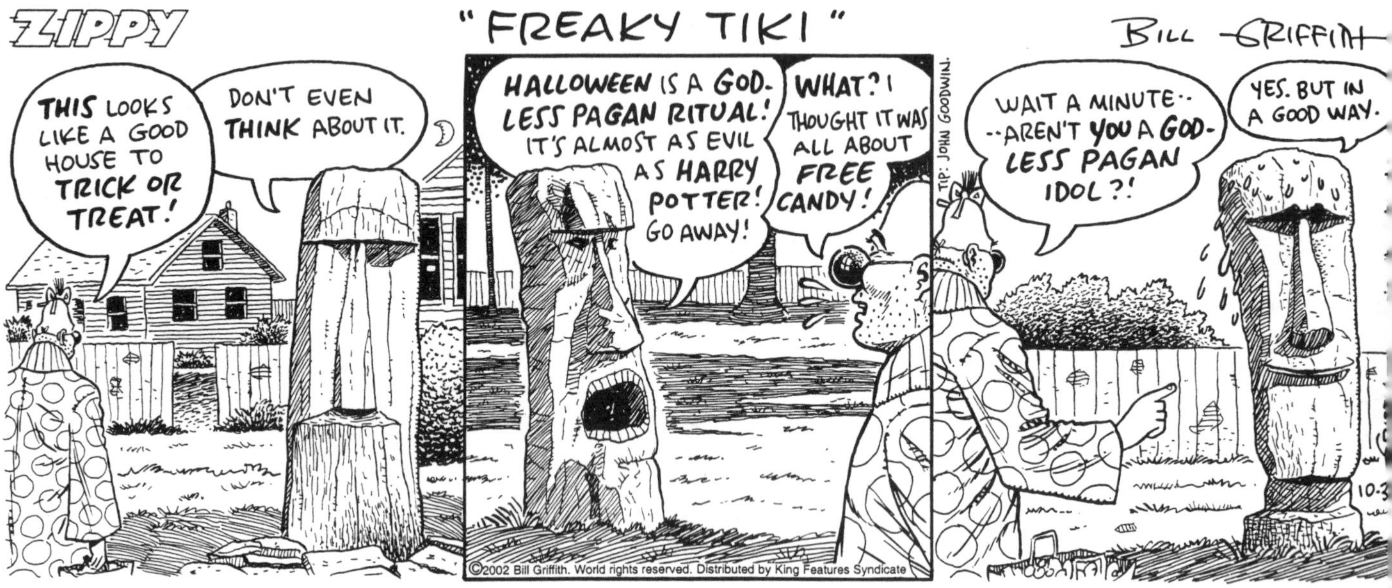
ZIPPY
"FREAKY TIKI"
BILL GRIFFITH
THIS LOOKS LIKE A GOOD HOUSE TO TRICK OR TREAT!
DON'T EVEN THINK ABOUT IT.
HALLOWEEN IS A GOD-LESS PAGAN RITUAL! IT'S ALMOST AS EVIL AS HARRY POTTER! GO AWAY!
WHAT?! I THOUGHT IT WAS ALL ABOUT FREE CANDY!
TIP: JOHN GOODWIN.
WAIT A MINUTE.. ..AREN'T YOU A GOD-LESS PAGAN IDOL?!
YES. BUT IN A GOOD WAY.
©2002 Bill Griffith. World rights reserved. Distributed by King Features Syndicate

194

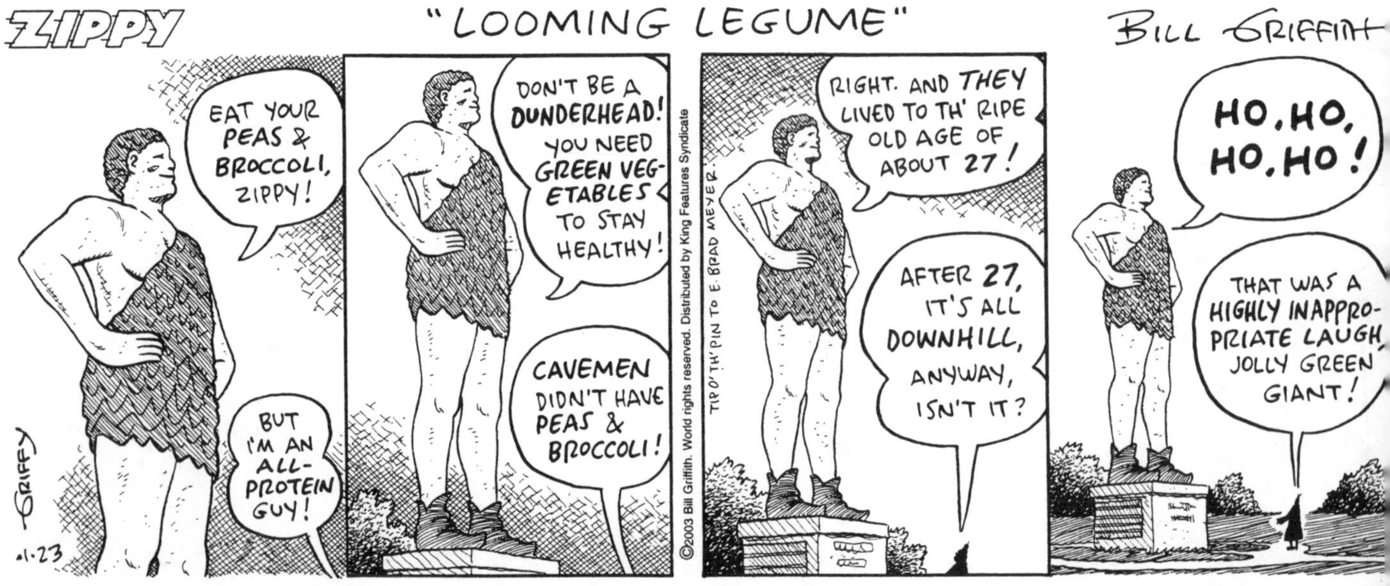
ZIPPY
"LOOMING LEGUME"
BILL GRIFFITH
EAT YOUR PEAS & BROCCOLI, ZIPPY!
BUT I'M AN ALL-PROTEIN GUY!
GRIFFY 1-23
DON'T BE A DUNDERHEAD! YOU NEED GREEN VEGETABLES TO STAY HEALTHY!
CAVEMEN DIDN'T HAVE PEAS & BROCCOLI!
©2003 Bill Griffith. World rights reserved. Distributed by King Features Syndicate
TIP O' TH' PIN TO E. BRAD MEYER
RIGHT. AND THEY LIVED TO TH' RIPE OLD AGE OF ABOUT 27!
AFTER 27, IT'S ALL DOWNHILL, ANYWAY, ISN'T IT?
HO, HO, HO, HO!
THAT WAS A HIGHLY INAPPROPRIATE LAUGH, JOLLY GREEN GIANT!

195

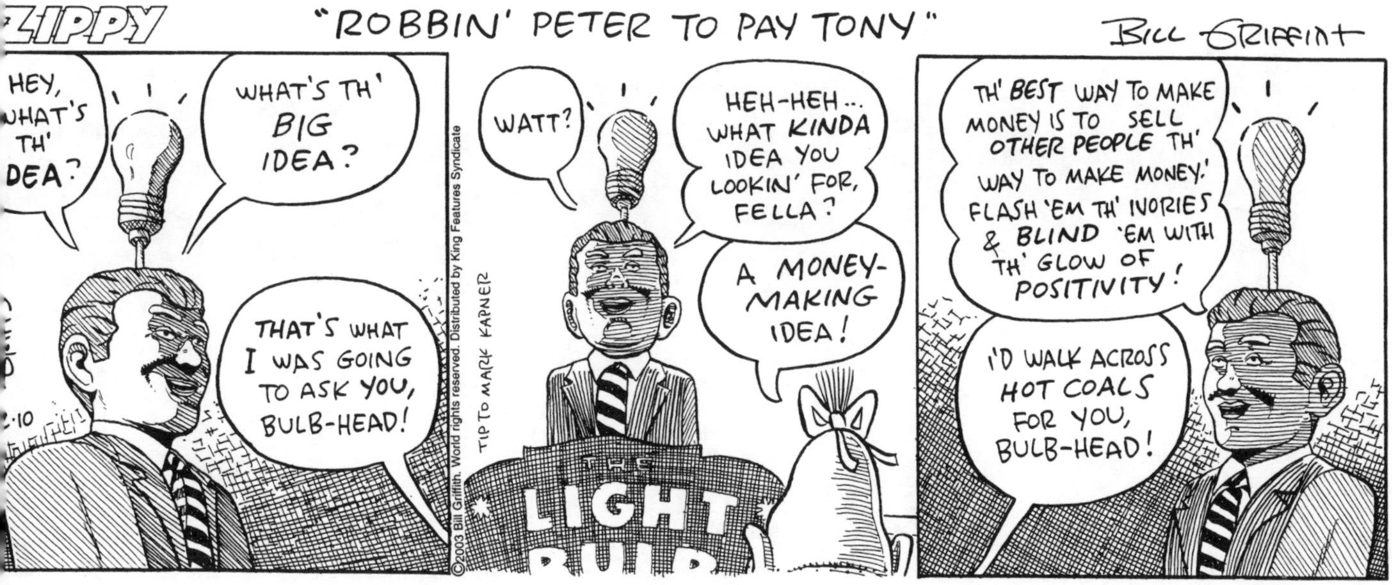
ZIPPY
"ROBBIN' PETER TO PAY TONY"
BILL GRIFFITH
HEY, WHAT'S TH' IDEA?
WHAT'S TH' BIG IDEA?
THAT'S WHAT I WAS GOING TO ASK YOU, BULB-HEAD!
WATT?
HEH-HEH... WHAT KINDA IDEA YOU LOOKIN' FOR, FELLA?
A MONEY-MAKING IDEA!
TIP TO MARK KARNER
©2003 Bill Griffith. World rights reserved. Distributed by King Features Syndicate
THE LIGHT BULB
TH' BEST WAY TO MAKE MONEY IS TO SELL OTHER PEOPLE TH' WAY TO MAKE MONEY! FLASH 'EM TH' IVORIES & BLIND 'EM WITH TH' GLOW OF POSITIVITY!
I'D WALK ACROSS HOT COALS FOR YOU, BULB-HEAD!

196

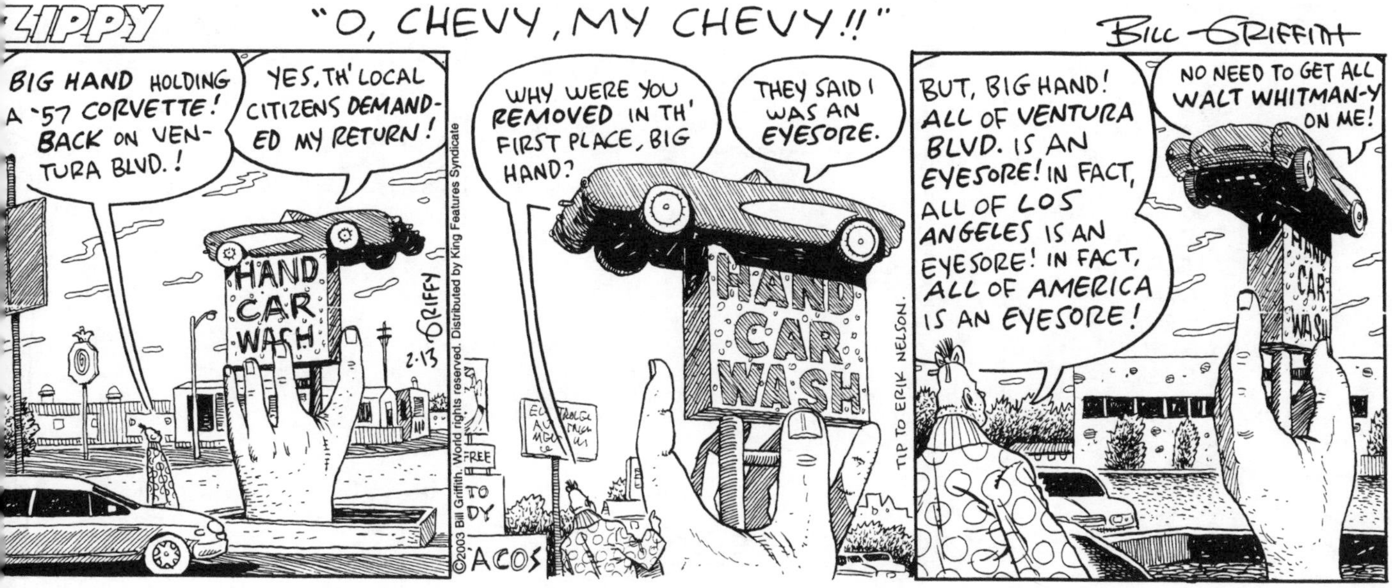
ZIPPY
"O, CHEVY, MY CHEVY!!"
BILL GRIFFITH
BIG HAND HOLDING A '57 CORVETTE! BACK ON VENTURA BLVD.!
YES, TH' LOCAL CITIZENS DEMANDED MY RETURN!
HAND CAR WASH
GRIFFY 2·13
©2003 Bill Griffith. World rights reserved. Distributed by King Features Syndicate
WHY WERE YOU REMOVED IN TH' FIRST PLACE, BIG HAND?
THEY SAID I WAS AN EYESORE.
HAND CAR WASH
TIP TO ERIK NELSON.
BUT, BIG HAND! ALL OF VENTURA BLVD. IS AN EYESORE! IN FACT, ALL OF LOS ANGELES IS AN EYESORE! IN FACT, ALL OF AMERICA IS AN EYESORE!
NO NEED TO GET ALL WALT WHITMAN-Y ON ME!
HAND CAR WASH

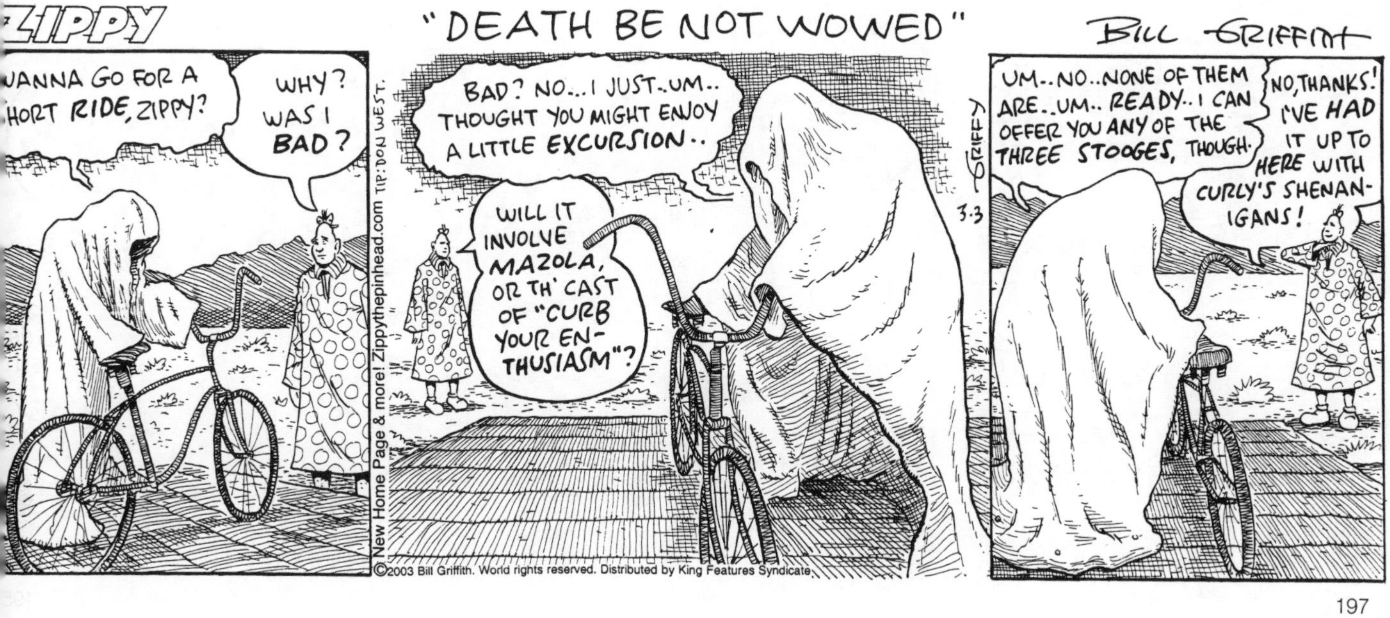
ZIPPY
"DEATH BE NOT WOWED"
BILL GRIFFITH
WANNA GO FOR A SHORT RIDE, ZIPPY?
WHY? WAS I BAD?
TIP: DON WEST.
New Home Page & more! Zippythepinhead.com
BAD? NO...I JUST..UM.. THOUGHT YOU MIGHT ENJOY A LITTLE EXCURSION..
WILL IT INVOLVE MAZOLA, OR TH' CAST OF "CURB YOUR ENTHUSIASM"?
GRIFFY 3·3
©2003 Bill Griffith. World rights reserved. Distributed by King Features Syndicate
UM..NO..NONE OF THEM ARE..UM..READY..I CAN OFFER YOU ANY OF THE THREE STOOGES, THOUGH.
NO, THANKS! I'VE HAD IT UP TO HERE WITH CURLY'S SHENANIGANS!

197

ZIPPY "EXCESS OF MEDIEVAL" BILL GRIFFITH

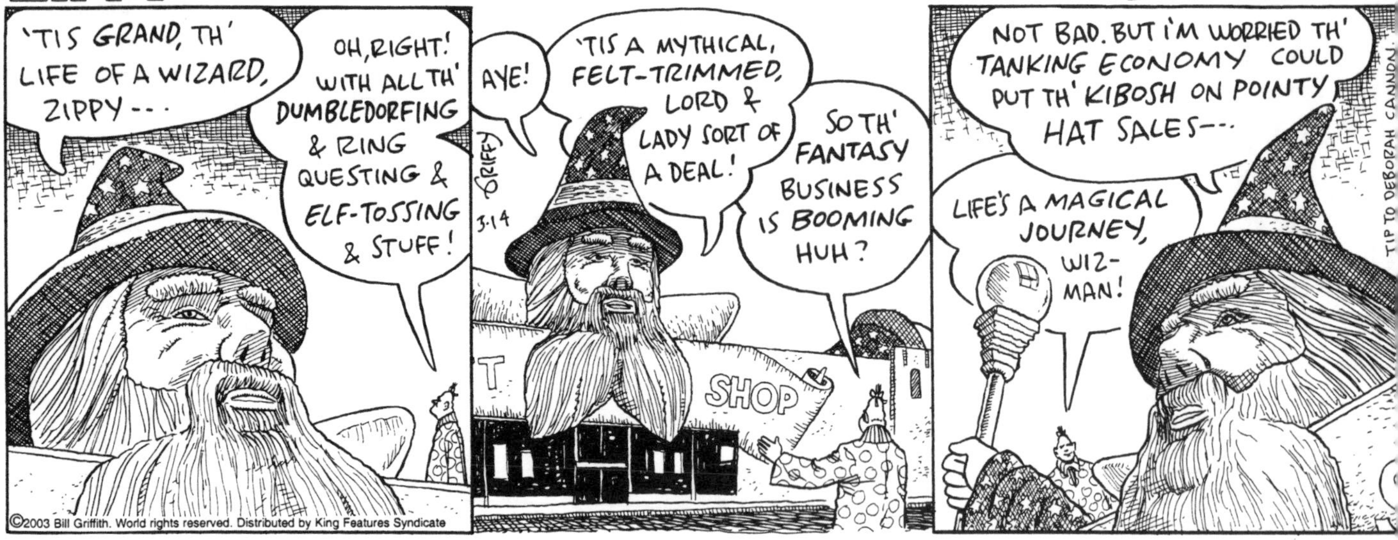

'TIS GRAND, TH' LIFE OF A WIZARD, ZIPPY---
OH, RIGHT! WITH ALL TH' DUMBLEDORFING & RING QUESTING & ELF-TOSSING & STUFF!
AYE!
'TIS A MYTHICAL, FELT-TRIMMED, LORD & LADY SORT OF A DEAL!
SO TH' FANTASY BUSINESS IS BOOMING HUH?
SHOP
GRIFFY 3.14
NOT BAD. BUT I'M WORRIED TH' TANKING ECONOMY COULD PUT TH' KIBOSH ON POINTY HAT SALES---
LIFE'S A MAGICAL JOURNEY, WIZ-MAN!
TIP TO DEBORAH CANNON
©2003 Bill Griffith. World rights reserved. Distributed by King Features Syndicate

198

ZIPPY "FISH OUT OF WATER" BILL GRIFFITH

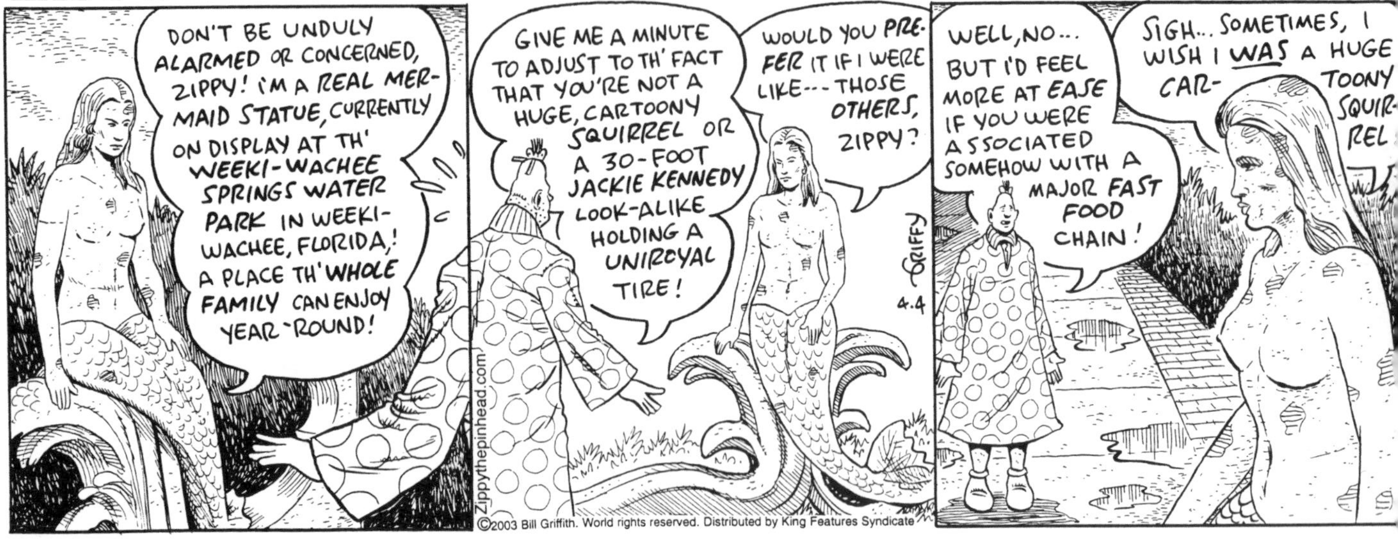

DON'T BE UNDULY ALARMED OR CONCERNED, ZIPPY! I'M A REAL MER-MAID STATUE, CURRENTLY ON DISPLAY AT TH' WEEKI-WACHEE SPRINGS WATER PARK IN WEEKI-WACHEE, FLORIDA! A PLACE TH' WHOLE FAMILY CAN ENJOY YEAR-ROUND!
GIVE ME A MINUTE TO ADJUST TO TH' FACT THAT YOU'RE NOT A HUGE, CARTOONY SQUIRREL OR A 30-FOOT JACKIE KENNEDY LOOK-ALIKE HOLDING A UNIROYAL TIRE!
WOULD YOU PRE-FER IT IF I WERE LIKE--- THOSE OTHERS, ZIPPY?
GRIFFY 4.4
WELL, NO... BUT I'D FEEL MORE AT EASE IF YOU WERE ASSOCIATED SOMEHOW WITH A MAJOR FAST FOOD CHAIN!
SIGH... SOMETIMES, I WISH I WAS A HUGE CAR-TOONY SQUIR-REL
Zippythepinhead.com
©2003 Bill Griffith. World rights reserved. Distributed by King Features Syndicate

ZIPPY "DEATHLESS LYRICS" BILL GRIFFITH

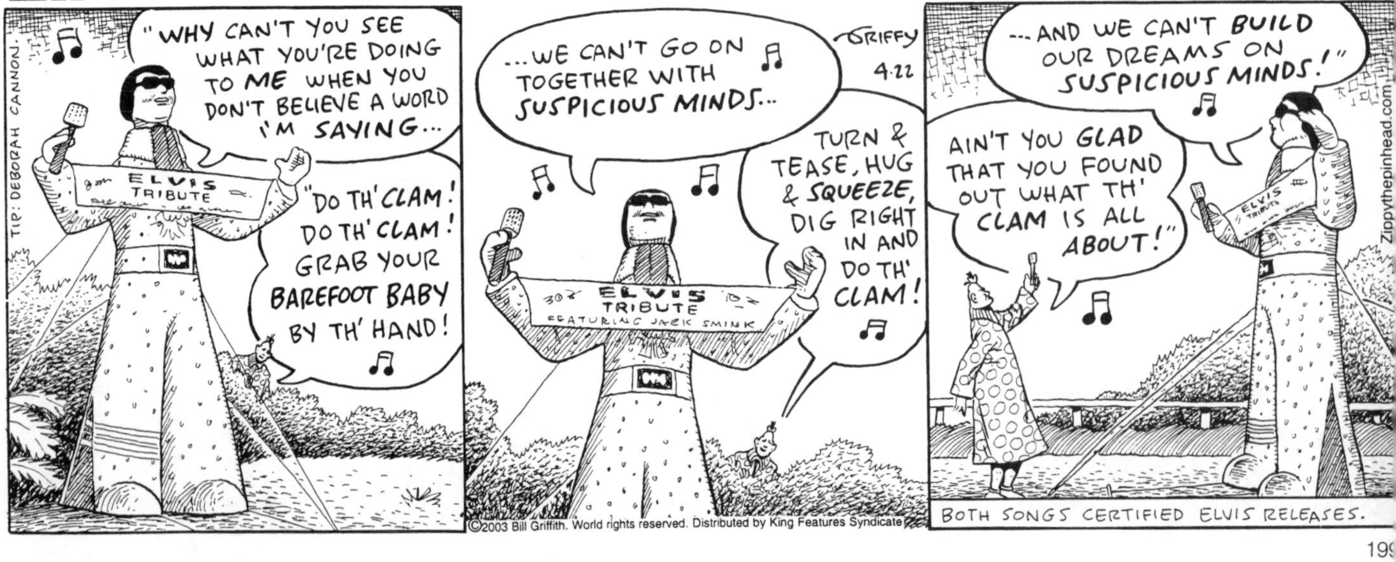

TIP: DEBORAH CANNON.
"WHY CAN'T YOU SEE WHAT YOU'RE DOING TO ME WHEN YOU DON'T BELIEVE A WORD I'M SAYING...
ELVIS TRIBUTE
"DO TH' CLAM! DO TH' CLAM! GRAB YOUR BAREFOOT BABY BY TH' HAND!
...WE CAN'T GO ON TOGETHER WITH SUSPICIOUS MINDS...
GRIFFY 4.22
TURN & TEASE, HUG & SQUEEZE, DIG RIGHT IN AND DO TH' CLAM!
ELVIS TRIBUTE FEATURING JACK SMINK
---AND WE CAN'T BUILD OUR DREAMS ON SUSPICIOUS MINDS!"
AIN'T YOU GLAD THAT YOU FOUND OUT WHAT TH' CLAM IS ALL ABOUT!"
Zippythepinhead.com
BOTH SONGS CERTIFIED ELVIS RELEASES.
©2003 Bill Griffith. World rights reserved. Distributed by King Features Syndicate

199

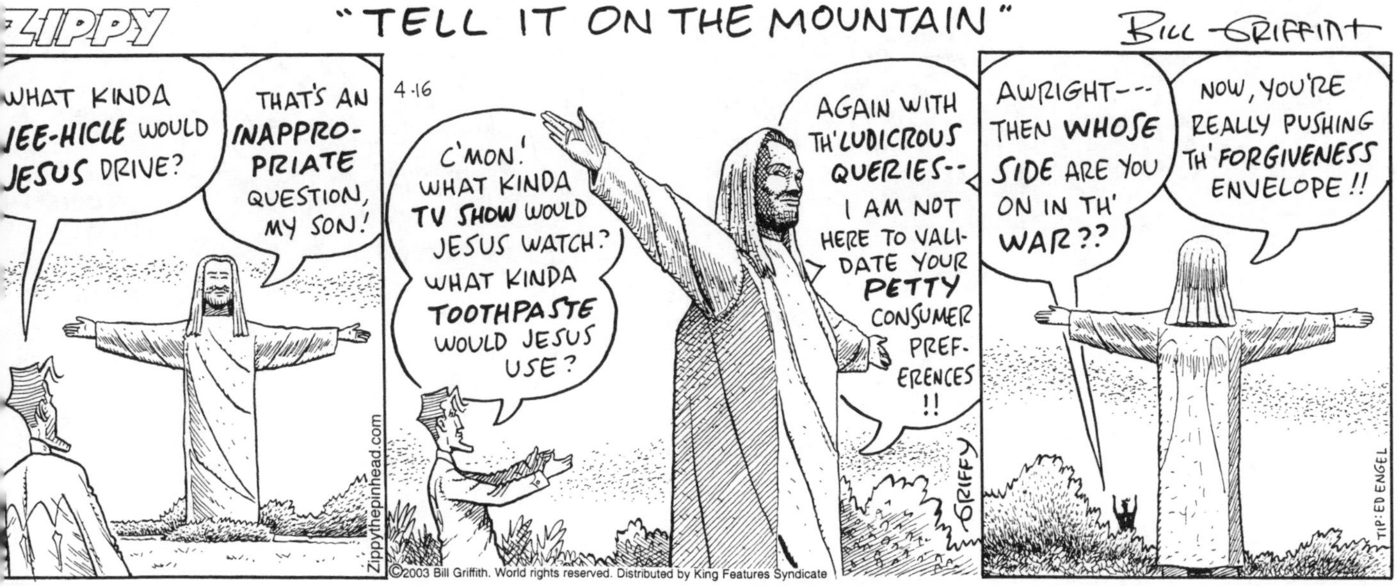
ZIPPY
"TELL IT ON THE MOUNTAIN"
BILL GRIFFITH
WHAT KINDA VEE-HICLE WOULD JESUS DRIVE?
THAT'S AN INAPPROPRIATE QUESTION, MY SON!
4-16
C'MON! WHAT KINDA TV SHOW WOULD JESUS WATCH? WHAT KINDA TOOTHPASTE WOULD JESUS USE?
AGAIN WITH TH' LUDICROUS QUERIES-- I AM NOT HERE TO VALIDATE YOUR PETTY CONSUMER PREFERENCES!!
AWRIGHT--- THEN WHOSE SIDE ARE YOU ON IN TH' WAR??
NOW, YOU'RE REALLY PUSHING TH' FORGIVENESS ENVELOPE!!
GRIFFY
TIP: ED ENGEL
Zippythepinhead.com
©2003 Bill Griffith. World rights reserved. Distributed by King Features Syndicate

200

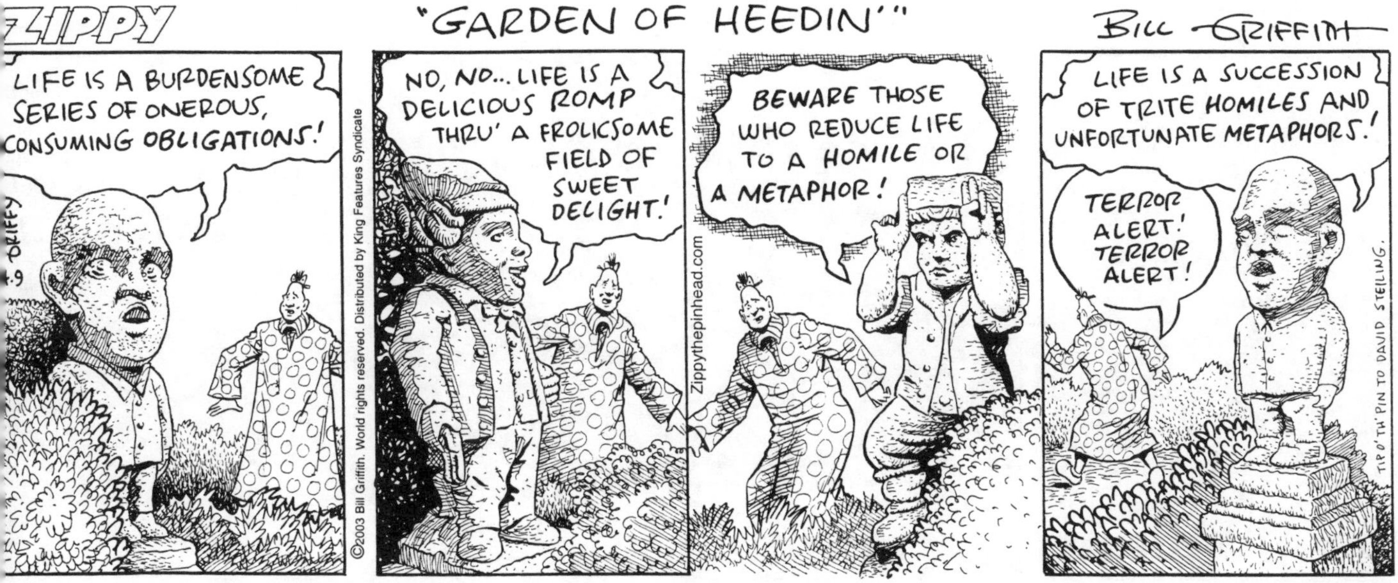
ZIPPY
"GARDEN OF HEEDIN'"
BILL GRIFFITH
LIFE IS A BURDENSOME SERIES OF ONEROUS, CONSUMING OBLIGATIONS!
NO, NO... LIFE IS A DELICIOUS ROMP THRU' A FROLICSOME FIELD OF SWEET DELIGHT!
BEWARE THOSE WHO REDUCE LIFE TO A HOMILE OR A METAPHOR!
LIFE IS A SUCCESSION OF TRITE HOMILES AND UNFORTUNATE METAPHORS!
TERROR ALERT! TERROR ALERT!
GRIFFY
TIP O' TH' PIN TO DAVID STERLING
Zippythepinhead.com
©2003 Bill Griffith. World rights reserved. Distributed by King Features Syndicate

201

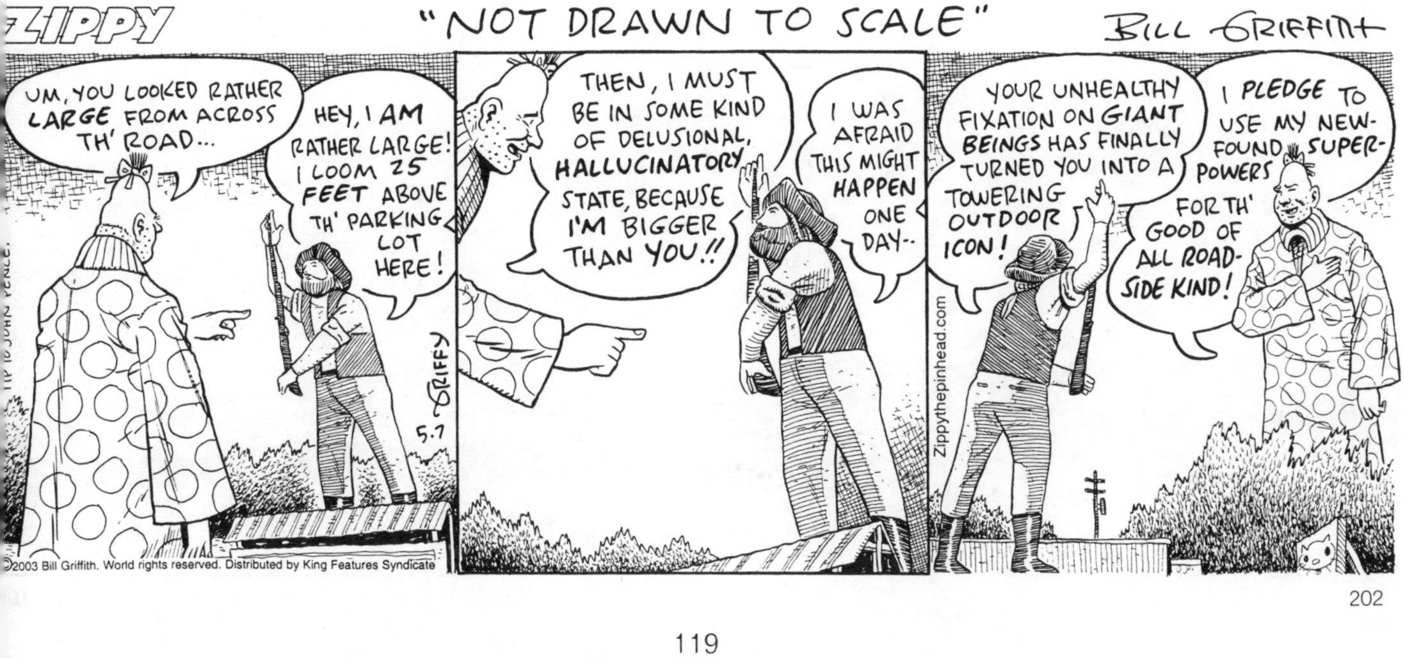
ZIPPY
"NOT DRAWN TO SCALE"
BILL GRIFFITH
UM, YOU LOOKED RATHER LARGE FROM ACROSS TH' ROAD...
HEY, I AM RATHER LARGE! I LOOM 25 FEET ABOVE TH' PARKING LOT HERE!
THEN, I MUST BE IN SOME KIND OF DELUSIONAL, HALLUCINATORY STATE, BECAUSE I'M BIGGER THAN YOU!!
I WAS AFRAID THIS MIGHT HAPPEN ONE DAY..
YOUR UNHEALTHY FIXATION ON GIANT BEINGS HAS FINALLY TURNED YOU INTO A TOWERING OUTDOOR ICON!
I PLEDGE TO USE MY NEW-FOUND SUPER-POWERS FOR TH' GOOD OF ALL ROAD-SIDE KIND!
GRIFFY
5-7
Zippythepinhead.com
©2003 Bill Griffith. World rights reserved. Distributed by King Features Syndicate

202

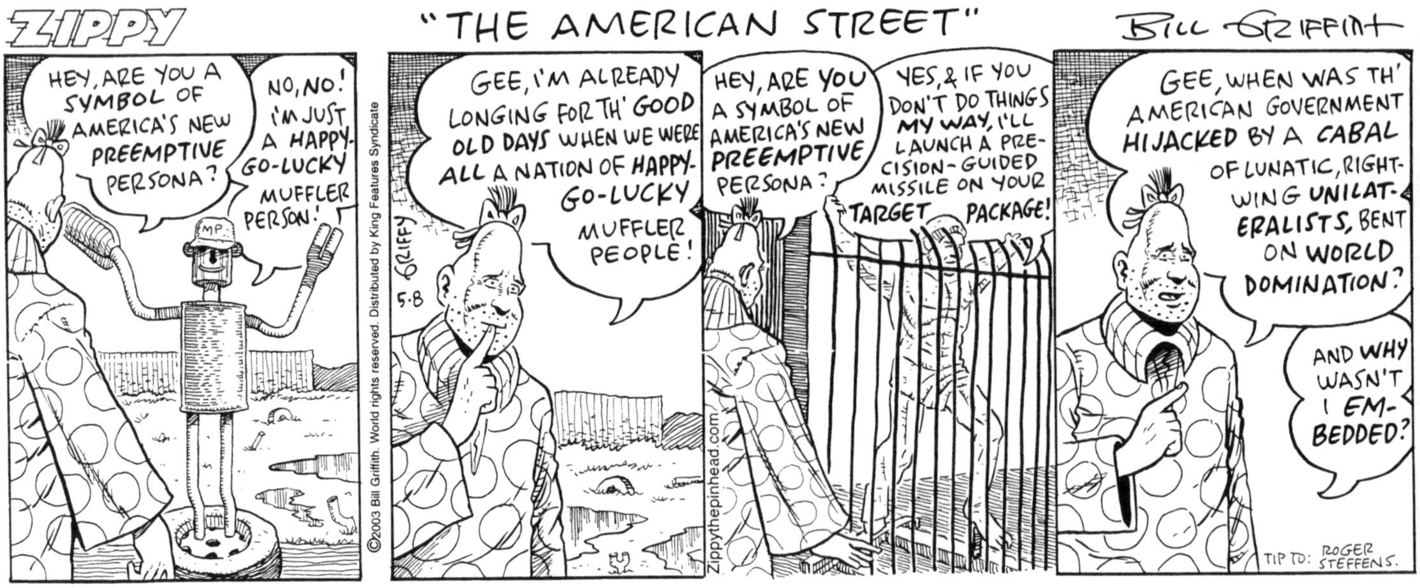
ZIPPY
"THE AMERICAN STREET"
BILL GRIFFITH
HEY, ARE YOU A SYMBOL OF AMERICA'S NEW PREEMPTIVE PERSONA?
NO, NO! I'M JUST A HAPPY-GO-LUCKY MUFFLER PERSON!
MP
©2003 Bill Griffith. World rights reserved. Distributed by King Features Syndicate
GEE, I'M ALREADY LONGING FOR TH' GOOD OLD DAYS WHEN WE WERE ALL A NATION OF HAPPY-GO-LUCKY MUFFLER PEOPLE!
GRIFFY 5-8
HEY, ARE YOU A SYMBOL OF AMERICA'S NEW PREEMPTIVE PERSONA?
YES, & IF YOU DON'T DO THINGS MY WAY, I'LL LAUNCH A PRECISION-GUIDED MISSILE ON YOUR TARGET PACKAGE!
Zippythepinhead.com
GEE, WHEN WAS TH' AMERICAN GOVERNMENT HIJACKED BY A CABAL OF LUNATIC, RIGHT-WING UNILATERALISTS, BENT ON WORLD DOMINATION?
AND WHY WASN'T I EMBEDDED?
TIP TO: ROGER STEFFENS.

203

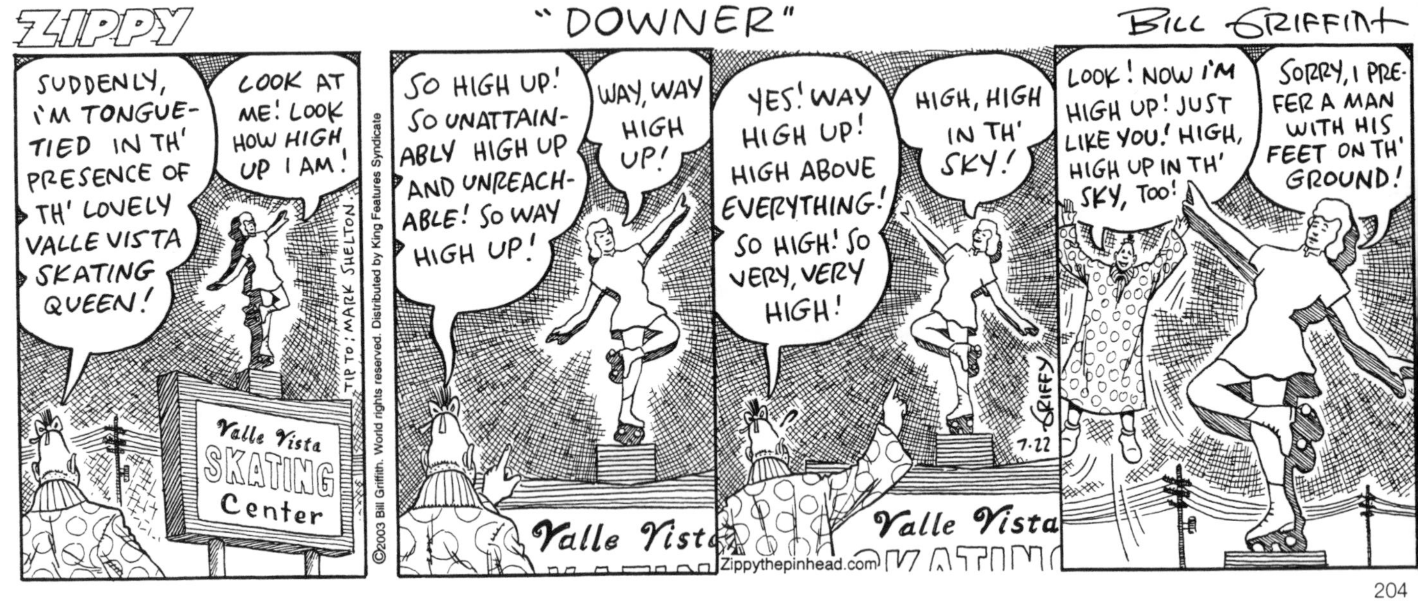
ZIPPY
"DOWNER"
BILL GRIFFITH
SUDDENLY, I'M TONGUE-TIED IN TH' PRESENCE OF TH' LOVELY VALLE VISTA SKATING QUEEN!
LOOK AT ME! LOOK HOW HIGH UP I AM!
TIP TO: MARK SHELTON.
Valle Vista SKATING Center
©2003 Bill Griffith. World rights reserved. Distributed by King Features Syndicate
SO HIGH UP! SO UNATTAINABLY HIGH UP AND UNREACHABLE! SO WAY HIGH UP!
WAY, WAY HIGH UP!
Valle Vista
YES! WAY HIGH UP! HIGH ABOVE EVERYTHING! SO HIGH! SO VERY, VERY HIGH!
HIGH, HIGH IN TH' SKY!
GRIFFY 7-22
Valle Vista
Zippythepinhead.com
LOOK! NOW I'M HIGH UP! JUST LIKE YOU! HIGH, HIGH UP IN TH' SKY, TOO!
SORRY, I PREFER A MAN WITH HIS FEET ON TH' GROUND!

204

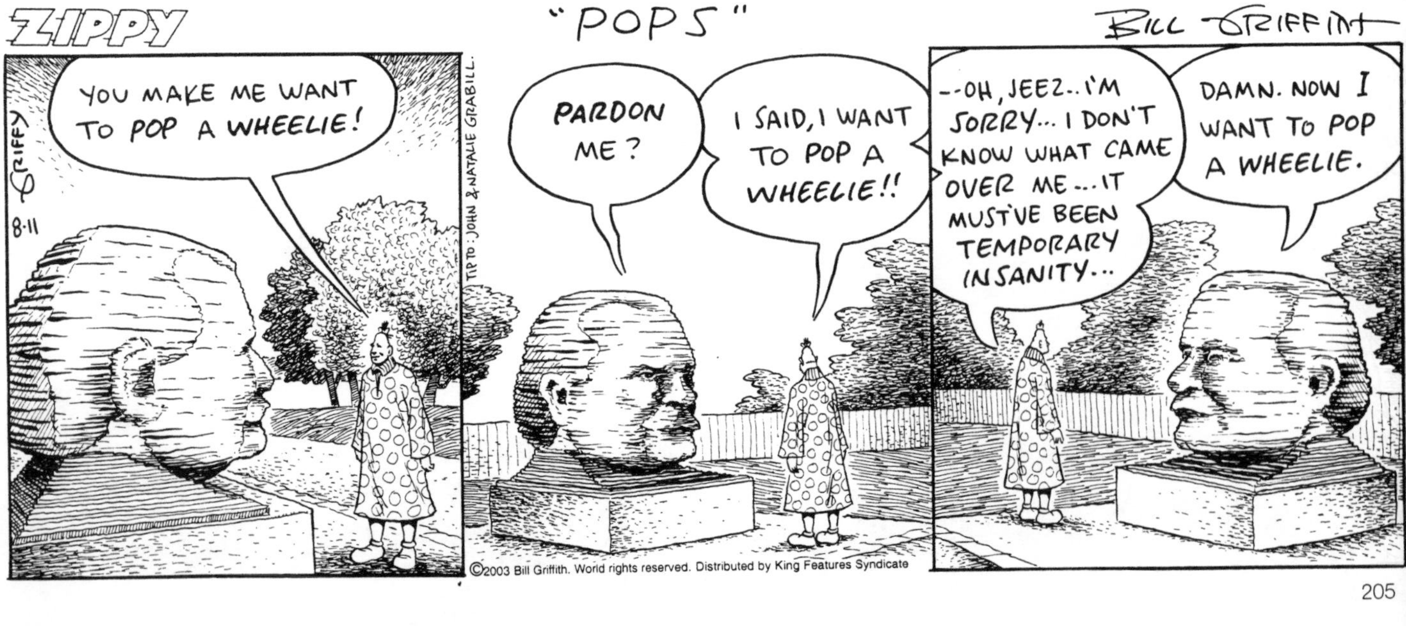
ZIPPY
"POPS"
BILL GRIFFITH
GRIFFY 8-11
YOU MAKE ME WANT TO POP A WHEELIE!
TIP TO: JOHN & NATALIE GRABILL.
PARDON ME?
I SAID, I WANT TO POP A WHEELIE!!
--OH, JEEZ.. I'M SORRY... I DON'T KNOW WHAT CAME OVER ME... IT MUST'VE BEEN TEMPORARY INSANITY...
DAMN. NOW I WANT TO POP A WHEELIE.
©2003 Bill Griffith. World rights reserved. Distributed by King Features Syndicate

205

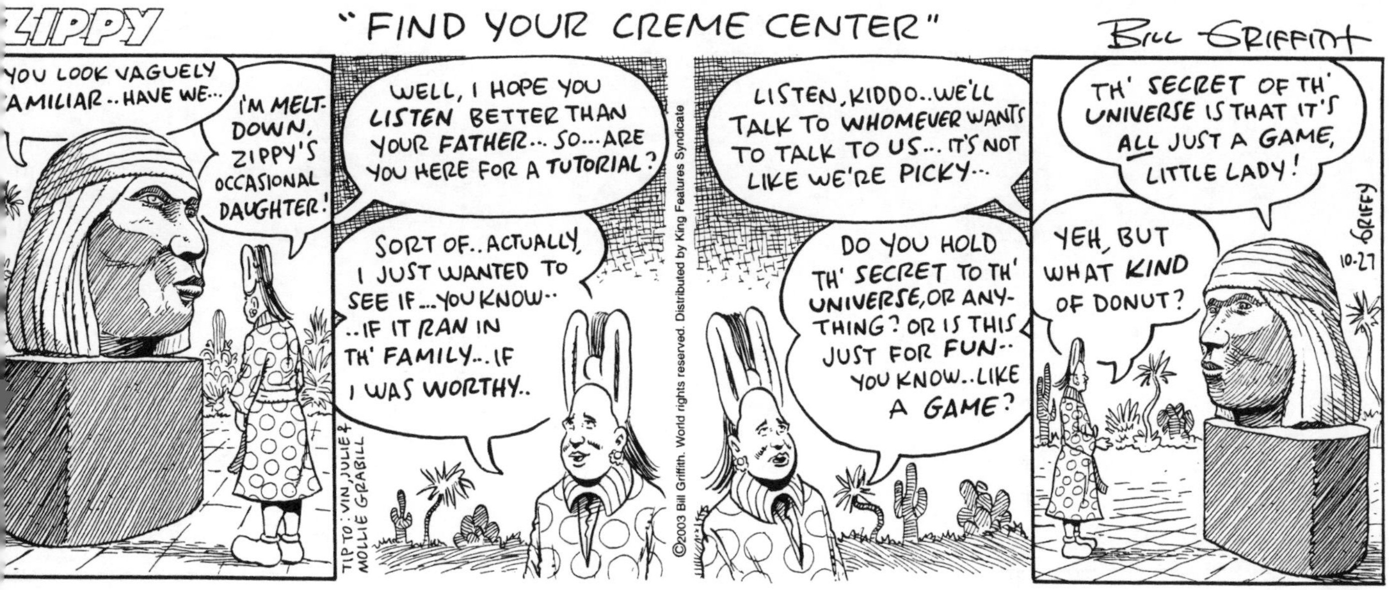
ZIPPY
"FIND YOUR CREME CENTER"
BILL GRIFFITH
YOU LOOK VAGUELY FAMILIAR.. HAVE WE...
I'M MELTDOWN, ZIPPY'S OCCASIONAL DAUGHTER!
WELL, I HOPE YOU LISTEN BETTER THAN YOUR FATHER... SO... ARE YOU HERE FOR A TUTORIAL?
SORT OF.. ACTUALLY, I JUST WANTED TO SEE IF... YOU KNOW.. ..IF IT RAN IN TH' FAMILY... IF I WAS WORTHY..
TIP TO: VIN, JULIE & MOLLIE GRABILL
©2003 Bill Griffith. World rights reserved. Distributed by King Features Syndicate
LISTEN, KIDDO.. WE'LL TALK TO WHOMEVER WANTS TO TALK TO US... IT'S NOT LIKE WE'RE PICKY...
DO YOU HOLD TH' SECRET TO TH' UNIVERSE, OR ANYTHING? OR IS THIS JUST FOR FUN.. YOU KNOW.. LIKE A GAME?
TH' SECRET OF TH' UNIVERSE IS THAT IT'S ALL JUST A GAME, LITTLE LADY!
YEH, BUT WHAT KIND OF DONUT?
GRIFFY 10-27

206

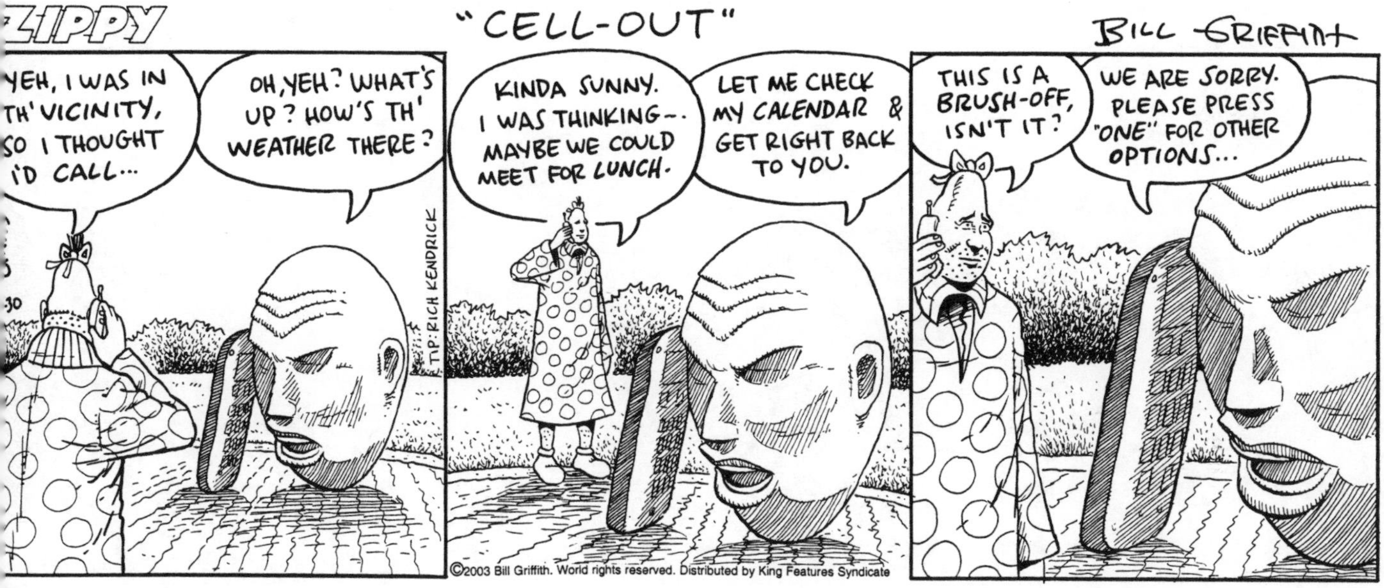
ZIPPY
"CELL-OUT"
BILL GRIFFITH
YEH, I WAS IN TH' VICINITY, SO I THOUGHT I'D CALL...
OH, YEH? WHAT'S UP? HOW'S TH' WEATHER THERE?
TIP: RICH KENDRICK
KINDA SUNNY. I WAS THINKING.. MAYBE WE COULD MEET FOR LUNCH.
LET ME CHECK MY CALENDAR & GET RIGHT BACK TO YOU.
THIS IS A BRUSH-OFF, ISN'T IT?
WE ARE SORRY. PLEASE PRESS "ONE" FOR OTHER OPTIONS...
©2003 Bill Griffith. World rights reserved. Distributed by King Features Syndicate

207

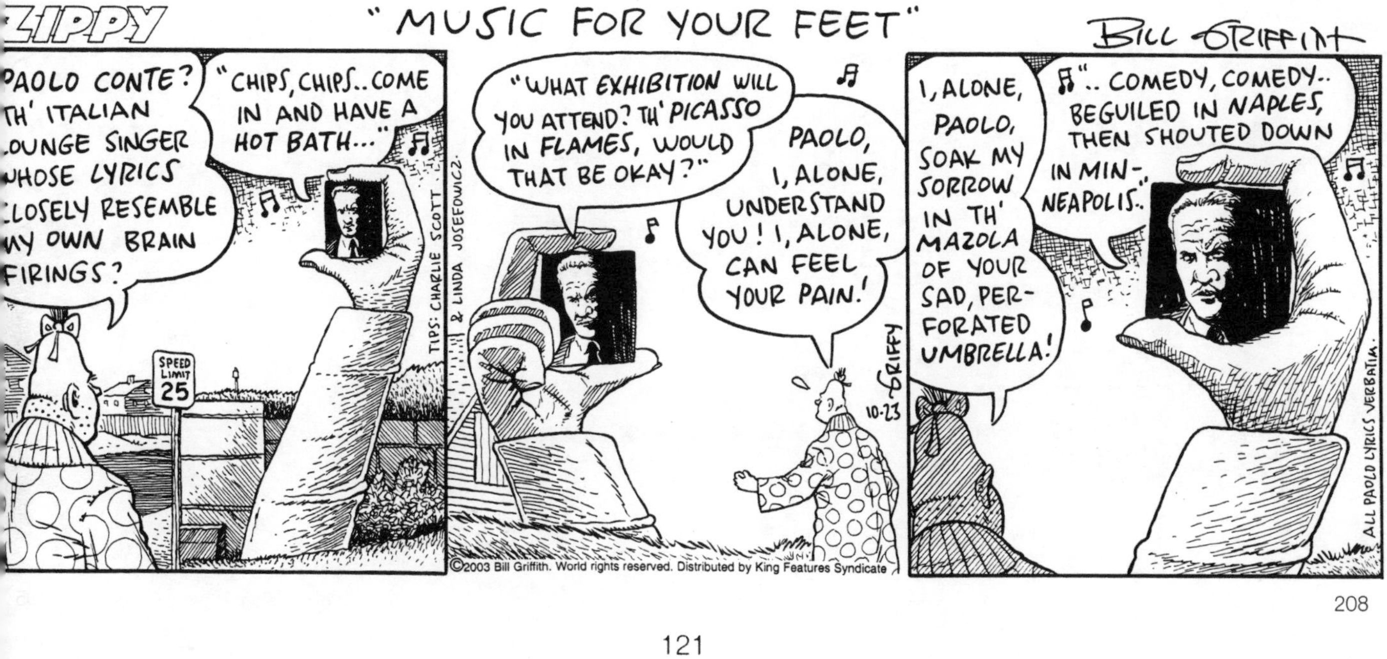
ZIPPY
"MUSIC FOR YOUR FEET"
BILL GRIFFITH
PAOLO CONTE? TH' ITALIAN LOUNGE SINGER WHOSE LYRICS CLOSELY RESEMBLE MY OWN BRAIN FIRINGS?
"CHIPS, CHIPS.. COME IN AND HAVE A HOT BATH..."
SPEED LIMIT 25
TIPS: CHARLIE SCOTT & LINDA JOSEFOWICZ
"WHAT EXHIBITION WILL YOU ATTEND? TH' PICASSO IN FLAMES, WOULD THAT BE OKAY?"
PAOLO, I, ALONE, UNDERSTAND YOU! I, ALONE, CAN FEEL YOUR PAIN!
GRIFFY 10-23
I, ALONE, PAOLO, SOAK MY SORROW IN TH' MAZOLA OF YOUR SAD, PERFORATED UMBRELLA!
".. COMEDY, COMEDY.. BEGUILED IN NAPLES, THEN SHOUTED DOWN IN MINNEAPOLIS.."
ALL PAOLO LYRICS VERBATIM.
©2003 Bill Griffith. World rights reserved. Distributed by King Features Syndicate

208

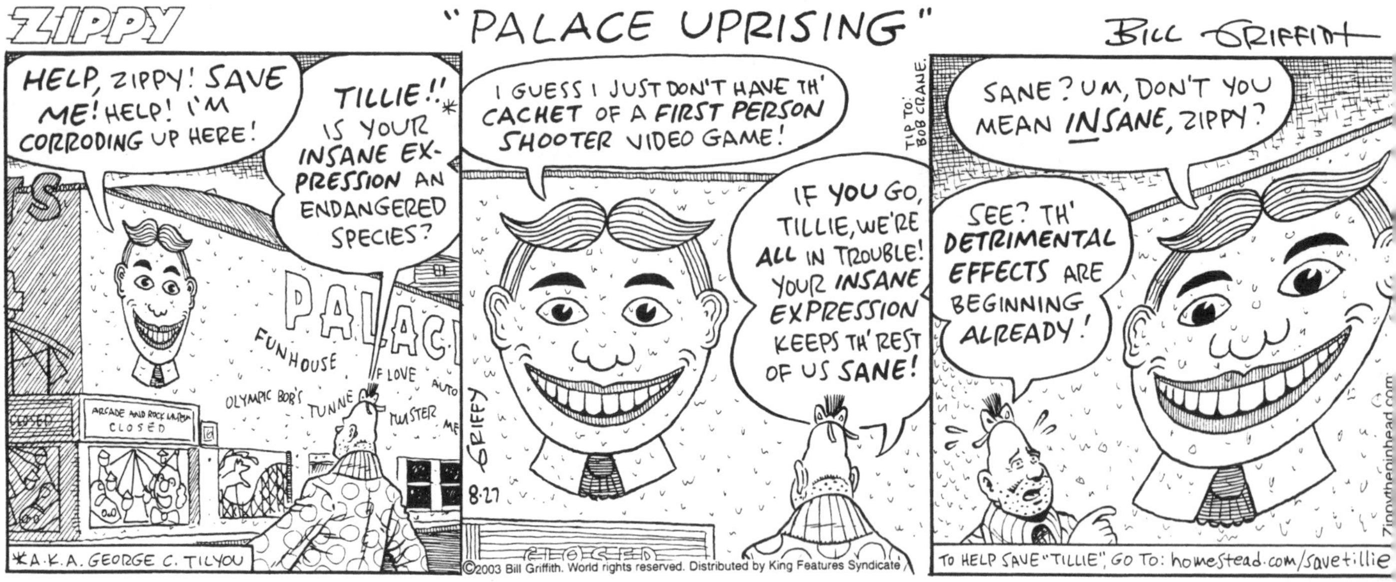
ZIPPY
"PALACE UPRISING"
BILL GRIFFITH
HELP, ZIPPY! SAVE ME! HELP! I'M CORRODING UP HERE!
TILLIE!!* IS YOUR INSANE EXPRESSION AN ENDANGERED SPECIES?
PALACE
FUNHOUSE
OLYMPIC BOB'S
TUNNEL OF LOVE
TWISTER
CLOSED
*A.K.A. GEORGE C. TILYOU
I GUESS I JUST DON'T HAVE TH' CACHET OF A FIRST PERSON SHOOTER VIDEO GAME!
IF YOU GO, TILLIE, WE'RE ALL IN TROUBLE! YOUR INSANE EXPRESSION KEEPS TH' REST OF US SANE!
GRIFFY 8.27
TIP TO: BOB CRANE
©2003 Bill Griffith. World rights reserved. Distributed by King Features Syndicate
SANE? UM, DON'T YOU MEAN INSANE, ZIPPY?
SEE? TH' DETRIMENTAL EFFECTS ARE BEGINNING ALREADY!
TO HELP SAVE "TILLIE", GO TO: homestead.com/savetillie
Zippythepinhead.com

209

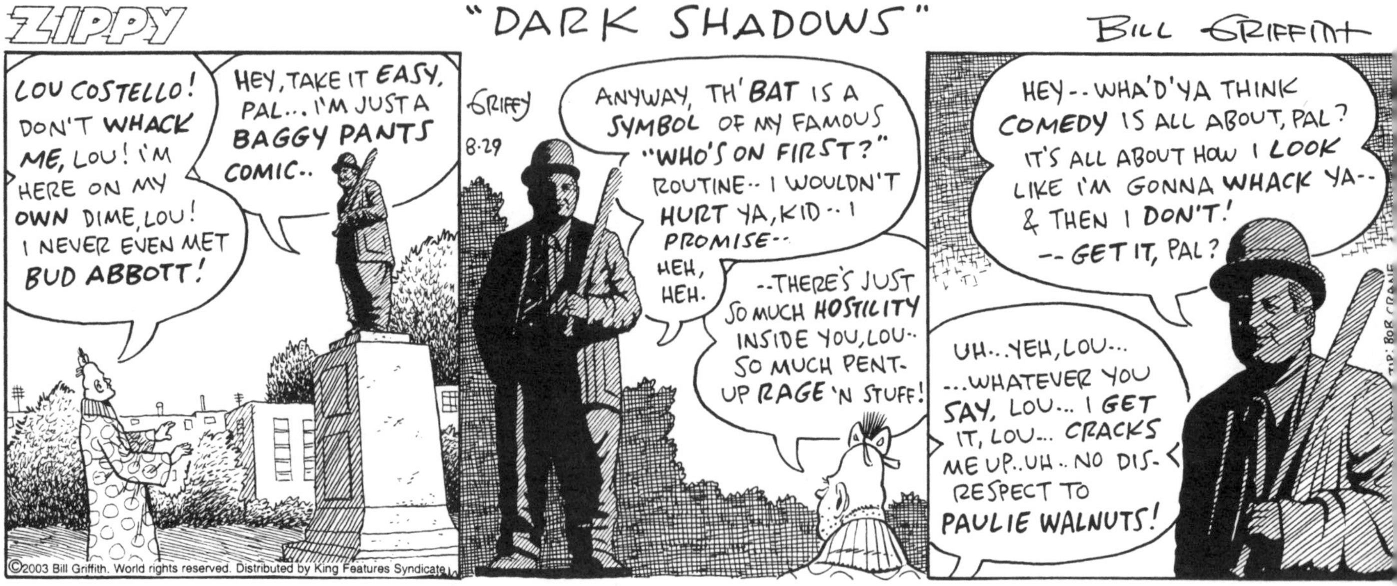
ZIPPY
"DARK SHADOWS"
BILL GRIFFITH
LOU COSTELLO! DON'T WHACK ME, LOU! I'M HERE ON MY OWN DIME, LOU! I NEVER EVEN MET BUD ABBOTT!
HEY, TAKE IT EASY, PAL... I'M JUST A BAGGY PANTS COMIC..
©2003 Bill Griffith. World rights reserved. Distributed by King Features Syndicate
GRIFFY 8.29
ANYWAY, TH' BAT IS A SYMBOL OF MY FAMOUS "WHO'S ON FIRST?" ROUTINE.. I WOULDN'T HURT YA, KID.. I PROMISE--
HEH, HEH.
--THERE'S JUST SO MUCH HOSTILITY INSIDE YOU, LOU.. SO MUCH PENT-UP RAGE 'N STUFF!
HEY--WHA'D'YA THINK COMEDY IS ALL ABOUT, PAL? IT'S ALL ABOUT HOW I LOOK LIKE I'M GONNA WHACK YA-- & THEN I DON'T! --GET IT, PAL?
UH...YEH, LOU... ...WHATEVER YOU SAY, LOU... I GET IT, LOU... CRACKS ME UP..UH.. NO DISRESPECT TO PAULIE WALNUTS!
TIP: BOB CRANE

210

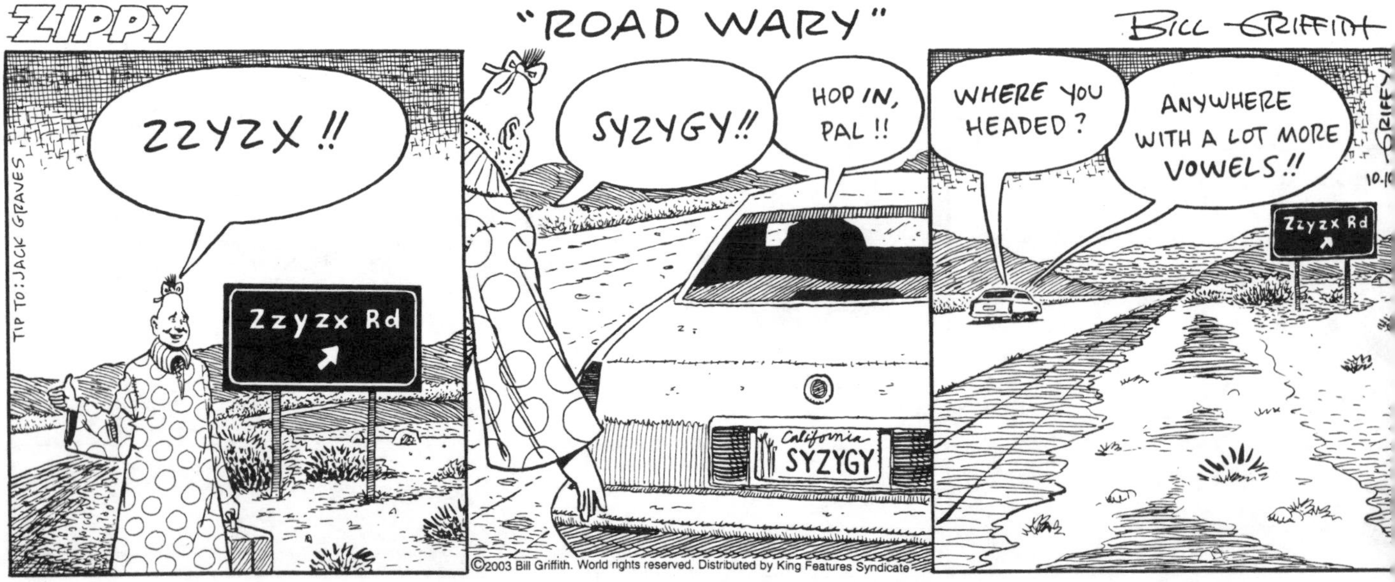
ZIPPY
"ROAD WARY"
BILL GRIFFITH
ZZYZX !!
TIP TO: JACK GRAVES
Zzyzx Rd
SYZYGY!!
HOP IN, PAL !!
California SYZYGY
©2003 Bill Griffith. World rights reserved. Distributed by King Features Syndicate
WHERE YOU HEADED?
ANYWHERE WITH A LOT MORE VOWELS!!
GRIFFY
Zzyzx Rd

211

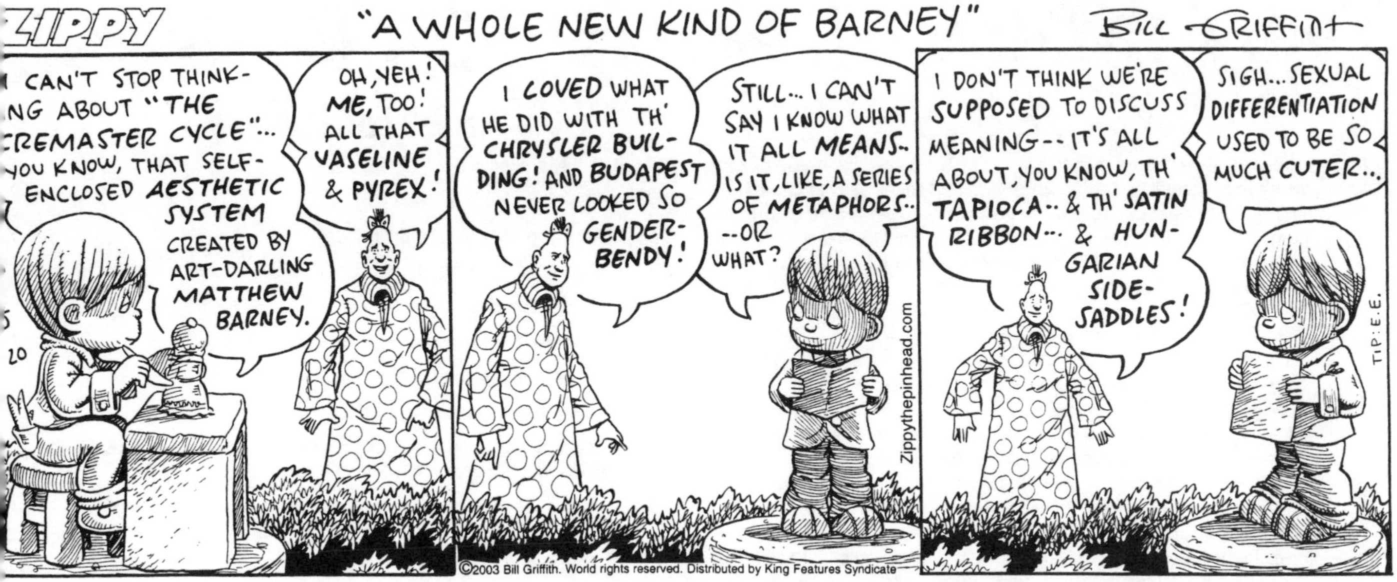
ZIPPY
"A WHOLE NEW KIND OF BARNEY"
BILL GRIFFITH
I CAN'T STOP THINKING ABOUT "THE CREMASTER CYCLE"... YOU KNOW, THAT SELF-ENCLOSED AESTHETIC SYSTEM CREATED BY ART-DARLING MATTHEW BARNEY.
OH, YEH! ME, TOO! ALL THAT VASELINE & PYREX!
I LOVED WHAT HE DID WITH TH' CHRYSLER BUILDING! AND BUDAPEST NEVER LOOKED SO GENDER-BENDY!
STILL... I CAN'T SAY I KNOW WHAT IT ALL MEANS.. IS IT, LIKE, A SERIES OF METAPHORS.. --OR WHAT?
I DON'T THINK WE'RE SUPPOSED TO DISCUSS MEANING-- IT'S ALL ABOUT, YOU KNOW, TH' TAPIOCA.. & TH' SATIN RIBBON... & HUNGARIAN SIDE-SADDLES!
SIGH... SEXUAL DIFFERENTIATION USED TO BE SO MUCH CUTER...
TIP: E.E.
Zippythepinhead.com
©2003 Bill Griffith. World rights reserved. Distributed by King Features Syndicate

212 A

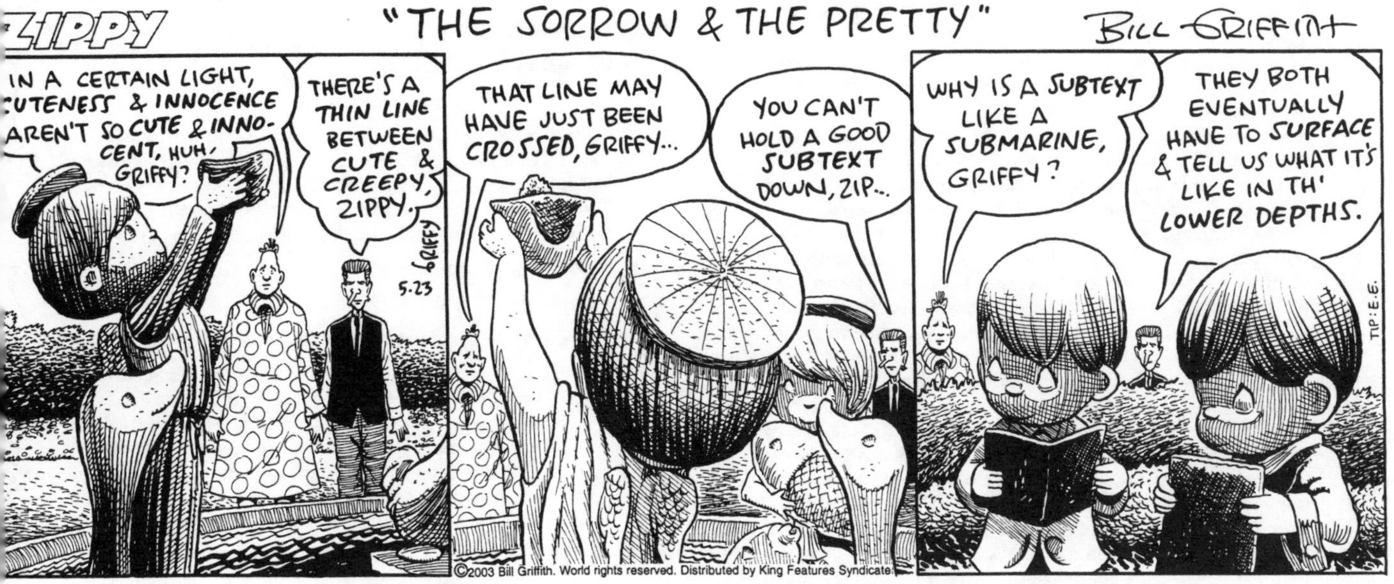
ZIPPY
"THE SORROW & THE PRETTY"
BILL GRIFFITH
IN A CERTAIN LIGHT, CUTENESS & INNOCENCE AREN'T SO CUTE & INNOCENT, HUH, GRIFFY?
THERE'S A THIN LINE BETWEEN CUTE & CREEPY, ZIPPY.
GRIFFY 5.23
THAT LINE MAY HAVE JUST BEEN CROSSED, GRIFFY...
YOU CAN'T HOLD A GOOD SUBTEXT DOWN, ZIP...
WHY IS A SUBTEXT LIKE A SUBMARINE, GRIFFY?
THEY BOTH EVENTUALLY HAVE TO SURFACE & TELL US WHAT IT'S LIKE IN TH' LOWER DEPTHS.
TIP: E.E.
©2003 Bill Griffith. World rights reserved. Distributed by King Features Syndicate

212 B

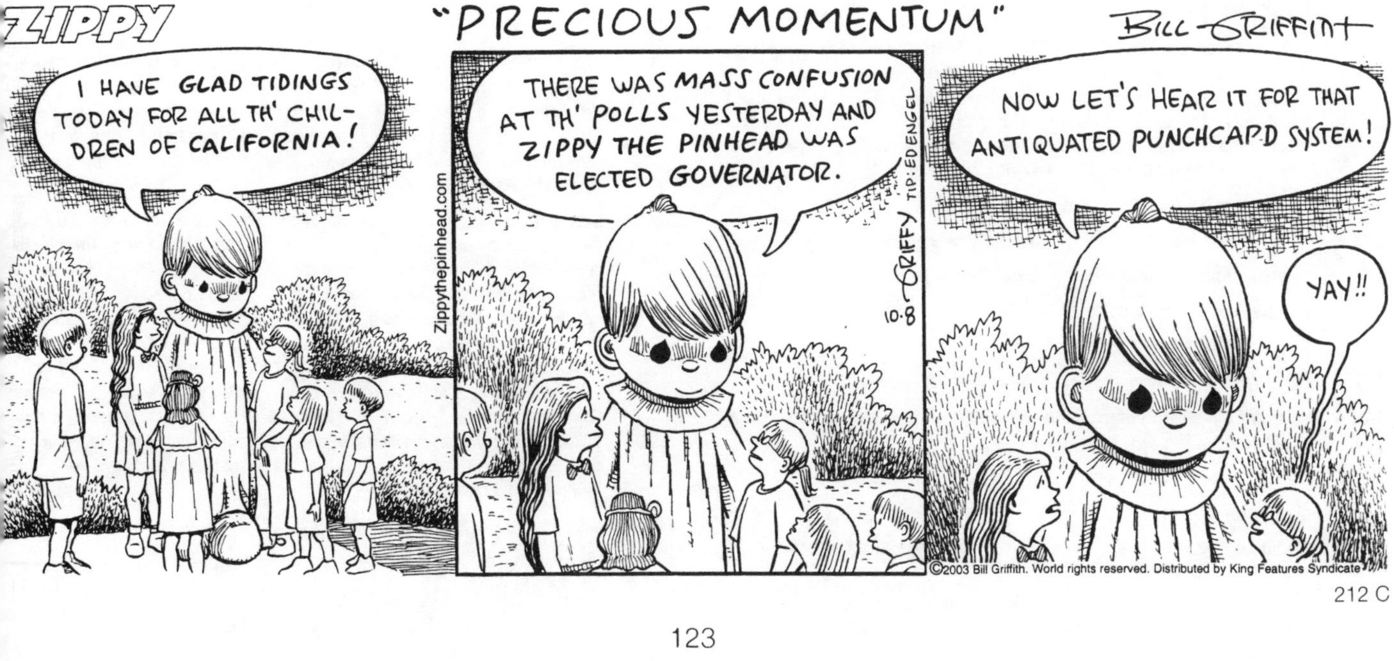
ZIPPY
"PRECIOUS MOMENTUM"
BILL GRIFFITH
I HAVE GLAD TIDINGS TODAY FOR ALL TH' CHILDREN OF CALIFORNIA!
Zippythepinhead.com
THERE WAS MASS CONFUSION AT TH' POLLS YESTERDAY AND ZIPPY THE PINHEAD WAS ELECTED GOVERNATOR.
TIP: ED ENGEL
GRIFFY 10.8
NOW LET'S HEAR IT FOR THAT ANTIQUATED PUNCHCARD SYSTEM!
YAY!!
©2003 Bill Griffith. World rights reserved. Distributed by King Features Syndicate

212 C

THE PINDEX

ZIPPY & GRIFFY Chapter 1

1 A-L. Coney Island (Brooklyn, NY) got its start as an amusement mecca when the world's first roller coaster debuted there in 1884. 13 years later George C. Tilyou opened famed Steeplechase Park. Luna Park and Dreamland (burned 1911) were built in 1903 and 1904 and in 1920 the Subway connected Coney Island with Manhattan and Brooklyn. The Boardwalk was constructed in 1923 and in 1927 the Cyclone roller coaster opened for business. Luna Park burned in 1944 and in 1964 Steeplechase Park closed. 1A: Melrose Ave., L.A. CA. 1B: To get to Coney Island via NYC Subway from 42nd Street in Manhattan, take the W Line (Astoria/ Broadway/ West End Express) to the last stop, Stillwell Avenue-Coney Island/ Surf Avenue. 1C: Zippy is on the campus of U.C. Davis, California, in dialog with one of Robert Arneson's "Egghead" sculptures. 1D: Battle of the KFC's: "Kansas Fried Chicken" outlets in the NYC area seem to be dying out, but "Kennedy Fried Chicken" thrives. A bizarre spin on the phenomenon; the new "JFK Fried Chicken". 1E: John Malkovich filmed scenes for his movie *Knockaround Guys* in October 1999 at a Coney Island handball court. 1F: Augustin Louis Cauchy (1789-1857), French mathematician; Hermann Amandus Schwarz (1843-1921), German mathematician. 1G: Paul Wolfowitz (born 1943), Deputy Secretary of Defense under President George W. Bush. 1H: Alger Hiss (1904-1996). In Aug.,1948, Whittaker Chambers, a magazine editor and former Communist party courier, accused Hiss of having helped transmit confidential government documents to the Russians. "Unguentine" was first introduced in 1890. Its advertising slogan in 1894 was "Without a Scar," and in 1900 the slogan became "Unguentine - The First Thought in Burns." The first public promotion of Unguentine began in 1922 with bath house mirrors, billboards and drug store window displays. In 1922 a ton of Unguentine was being produced each day. 1I: In 1997 poet Lawrence Ferlinghetti (born 1919) published a follow-up volume to *A Coney Island of the Mind* named after a Queens beach not far from the famed amusement empire, "A Far Rockaway of the Heart." His "City Lights" bookstore in San Francisco (named after the Charlie Chaplin movie) still thrives today. 1J: Zippy's rant in panels 2 and 3 is all derived from claims made by the original "Zip the What-Is-It?" 1K. Krispy Kreme, unfortunately, does not produce stock dividends. 1L: The hot dog's inventor was Charles Feltman, whose sausage-on-a-bun made its debut at Coney Island in 1867. In the early 1920s Nathan Handwerker (a one-time employee of Feltman's) opened "Nathan's" on Surf Avenue and made his famous hot dog a staple of the Coney Island experience by lowering the price to a nickel. [pg. 9-19]

2. Panel 1.) Plantation Inn, Chicopee, MA. Panel 2.) Jellystone Park, Luray, VA. [pg. 20]

3. Krispy Kreme or Lay's? In 1998, New Mexico telescope observations of distant galaxies suggested that the universe may be curved, like a potato chip. "It's not inconsistent with a sphere, but right now the best fit is a potato-chip shape," said Ari Buchalter, a doctoral astronomy student at Columbia University in New York who is analyzing the telescope data. [pg. 20]

4. "Iron Man," Silver Bay, MN. [pg. 21]

5. American Visionary Art Museum, Baltimore, MD. [pg. 21]

6. "Homes for life" by British designer Roger Dean. [pg. 21]

7. Pease is the archaic form of pea. [pg. 22]

8. Playland, Rye, NY. [pg. 22]

9. New York, New York Casino, Las Vegas, NV. [pg. 24]

10. Grafton, NH. Home of the author's maternal great-grandparents, the DeMotts. [pg. 24]

11. Gainesville, FL. [pg. 24]

12. Gibsonton ("Gibtown"), FL. [pg. 25]

13. See also "FREAKING OUT," pg. 17 and "THE SLIM END OF AN EGG," pg. 18. [pg. 25]

ZIPPY SOLO Chapter 2

14 A-C. Haddam Neck Fair, CT. [pg. 28]

15. Mantua, OH. [pg. 29]

16. Baltimore harbor, MD. [pg. 30]

17. Playland, Rye, NY. [pg. 30]

18. Circus Smirkus, Greensboro, VT. [pg. 30]

19. Fishing Hall of Fame, Hayward, WI. [pg. 31]

20. Ocean City, MD. [pg. 31]

21. The Spammobile, spotted in San Francisco, CA. [pg. 31]

22 A-C. "Victoria" by Philip Grausman, part of an outdoor sculpture exhibit in Madison, CT. See also pg. 64. [pg. 32]

23 A-B. Also part of an outdoor sculpture exhibit in Madison, CT. The "Funky Chicken" was recorded by Rufus Thomas in 1970. [pg. 33]

24. Williams College, Williamstown, MA. [pg. 33]

25 A-B. New York, New York Casino, Las Vegas, NV. [pg. 34]

26. St. George, New Brunswick, Canada. [pg. 35]

27. Daejeon, S. Korea. [pg. 35]

28. Terre Haute, IN. [pg. 35]

29. Boston, MA. [pg. 36]

30. Mendon Drive-In, Mendon, MA. Natasha Henstridge (born 1974), model and TV and film actress (*She Spies, Species, Species II, The Whole Nine Yards*), has the following tattoos: Intertwined male and female symbols on her tailbone, bearded lion wearing a crown on her right buttock. [pg. 36]

31. Bradenton, FL. [pg. 36]

32. Brattleboro, VT. [pg. 37]

33. Gargoyles at 81 Irving Place, New York, NY. [pg. 37]

34. Panels 1 & 2.) Ansonia Hotel, New York, NY. Panel 3.) Disney Store, Lincoln Center, New York, NY. Celebration (FL) is a designer town developed by the Disney Company. The town, founded in 1994, now with nearly 4000 full-time residents, has attracted worldwide attention with its planned community neighborhood aspect. Its population is 95.6% white with an average per capita income of $39,047. Its African-American population, at 0.7%, earns an average income of $57,533. [pg. 37]

35. Lollipop Motel, Wildwood, NJ. [pg. 38]

36. Hot Dog Shoppe, Warren, OH. The Straits of Juan de Fuca are found near Clallam Bay, WA. [pg. 38]

37. Allen Park, MI. [pg. 38]

38. The first 1947 Levitt Cape Cod model was a four and a half room house with an unfinished attic. It had no garage or basement and was built on a radiant-heated concrete slab. Extras included a kitchen hutch, Bendix washing machine, venetian blinds and a built in bookcase in the stairwell. The "ranch" models were introduced in 1949. [pg. 39]

39. Loni Anderson (born 1946) burst onto the small screen in 1978 as radio station receptionist Jennifer Marlowe on the popular TV sitcom *WKRP in Cincinnati*. Her first film role was in *Magnificent Magical Magnet of Santa Mesa* (1973). Her most recent silver screen appearance was in *3 Ninjas: High Noon at Mega Mountain* (1998). Singer/composer Yanni (born Yanni Hrisomallis in Kalamata, Greece) has sold over 10 million "adult-alternative" albums. After he left the *Donny and Marie* TV show in 1980, Donny Osmond surfaced again in 1982 in the George M. Cohan musical *Little Johnny Jones* on Broadway. The musical closed the very night it opened. After a painful bashing by the critics, Donny retreated to Utah. [pg. 39]

40 A-B. Gillette Castle, E. Haddam, CT. [pg. 40]

41. Plymouth, NH. [pg. 41]

42. Harvard Lampoon Building, Cambridge, MA. Built in 1909 and designed by one of the Lampoon's founders, Edmund March Wheelwright, the "Castle" is constructed in a monumental mock-Flemish style. Its erection was financed through the patronage of former editor William Randolph Hearst and friend and patron Isabella Stuart Gardiner. [pg. 41]

43. Robert Indiana's "One Through Zero" sculptures were installed on New York's Park Avenue median divider between 60th and 70th Streets from February to May, 2003. [pg. 42]

44. White Tower restaurant under deconstruction in Baltimore, MD. [pg. 42]

45. "Mosaicultures Internationales" (topiary exhibit), Montreal, Quebec, Canada. [pg. 43]

46. "Mr. Winkle" is a real pooch, owned and operated by photographer Lara Jo Regan, who says, "I knew I had to do something to share Mr. Winkle with the world. His cuteness is almost too overwhelming for one person to take!" Watch for the movie. [pg. 43]

ZIPPY & CO. Chapter 3

47. Pittsburgh, PA. [pg. 47]

48. Montreal, Quebec, Canada. *Crank Yankers* is an innovative show on TV's Comedy Central in which actual crank telephone calls are made by comedians to unsuspecting, real people, dramatized by puppets. [pg. 47]

49. Near Wildwood, NJ. [pg. 47]

50A-B. Apologies to comic artist Alden McWilliams (1916-1993), co-creator of the sci-fi daily strip, *Twin Earths* (1952-1962), from which these drawings were reverentially swiped. [pg. 48]

51. Caribbean Motel, Wildwood, NJ. [pg. 49]

52. Malden, MA. Candlepin bowling was invented by Justin P. White, a billiard-room owner, in Worcester, Massachusetts, in 1890. The pins are long and thin and tapered at both ends. The ball is only 4 1/2 inches in diameter and weighs from a minimum of 2 pounds, 5 ounces, to a maximum of 2 pounds, 7 ounces. [pg. 49]

53. Wildwood, NJ. [pg. 50]

54. Indianapolis, IN. [pg. 50]

55. Louis' Lunch, Gainesville, FL. [pg. 50]

56. World's Largest Watering Can, Nottingham, PA. [pg. 51]

57. In May, 2001, a lawsuit alleged that McDonald's misled its customers by presenting its golden fries as vegetarian for more than 10 years. It claimed the fast food giant used beef tallow as a flavoring ingredient. See also "ALIEN POTATOES," pg. 41. [pg. 51]

58. Chick Tracts are pocket-size, proselytizing Christian comic books dramatizing the cracked world-view of Jack T. Chick, outsider cartoonist. According to his authorized bio, Chick is a former trash-talking, failed actor who found Jesus while working in the aerospace industry in California. Among the many Satanic forces Chick regularly does battle with are rock 'n'roll, homosexuality and Catholicism. Did you know the Pope is an alien? [pg. 51]

59. Wildwood, NJ. [pg. 52]

60. Snak Shak, Chambersburg, PA. [pg. 52]

61. Panels 1 & 2.) Outside Gainesville, FL. Panel 3.) Jellystone Park, Luray, VA. [pg. 52]

62A-C. "Precious Moments" figures, Precious Moments theme park, Carthage, MO. See also pg. 71. [pg.53]

63. The "transcranial magnetic stimulator" is real, much like Loni Anderson. Its advocates claim that people undergoing transcranial magnetic stimulation can suddenly exhibit savant intelligence – those isolated pockets of geniuslike mental ability that most often appear in autistic people. Instant Rainman! [pg. 54]

64. Old South Restaurant, Russellville, AK. [pg. 54]

65A-E. Giant Beings and large signage seen in this series from the Neon Boneyard, Las Vegas, NV. 65D: Main St. Diner, Dracut, MA. [pg. 54-56]

66. Big Boyz Cycles, Augusta, ME. [pg. 56]

67. Marcel Duchamp (1887-1968), French Dadaist. His most famous work was *Nude Descending a Staircase, No. 2* (1912), portraying continuous movement through a chain of overlapping cubistic figures. [pg. 57]

68. Fred Astaire (1899-1987), born Frederick Austerlitz, made his film debut in *Dancing Lady* (1933) with Joan Crawford and Clark Gable. Astaire and acclaimed dancing partner Ginger Rogers made a total of nine musicals together at RKO between 1933 and 1939. Recent developments at Time Warner indicate they will soon be issuing Astaire's films on DVD. [pg. 57]

SUNDAY COLOR Chapter 4

69. Hi-Boy Sandwiches, Lyndonville, VT. See also "PERMANENT FATAL ERROR" and two following strips, pg. 110. [pg. 60]

70. Lima, OH. [pg. 60]

71. Johnny Appleseed Restaurant, Shenandoah Valley, VA. [pg. 60]

72A-B. Neon Boneyard, Las Vegas, NV. [pg. 61]

73. Tokyo, Japan. Jean-Michel Basquiat (1960-1988) began his brief art career as a graffiti artist, signing his tags "SAMO©" (Same Old Shit). In 1996 he was the subject of a bio-pic *(Basquiat)*, directed by fellow avant-gardener, Julian Schnabel. [pg. 61]

74. Clown face: Playland, Rye, NY. Gargoyle: Grace Church, New York City. [pg. 62]

75. Merry-go-round, "Enchanted Forest" (out of business), Ellicott City, MD. [pg. 63]

76. Steeplechase faces, Coney Island, NY. Believed to be modeled after George C. Tilyou (1862-1914), original owner, but the resemblance is debatable. Of mass entertainment he once said, "What attracts the crowd is the wearied mind's demand for relief in unconsidered muscular action." [pg. 63]

77. Montreal, Quebec, Canada (2000 Montreal Annual Topiary Show). [pg. 64]

78. "Storybook" homes. 1& 3) Olalla, WA. 2) Hollywoodland, CA. These whimsically designed homes were briefly popular in the 1920s and 1930s, taking their inspiration from medieval European half-timber styles and fanciful Hollywood stage sets. [pg. 64]

79. "Victoria" by Philip Grausman (b. 1935), part of an outdoor sculpture show in Madison, CT. Objected to by the local Republican Committee head as too "phallic." See also "VISITATION," pg. 32. [pg. 64]

80. BBQ Revue restaurant, Cincinnati, OH. [pg. 66]

81. Kill Devil Grill, Kill Devil Hills, NC. [pg. 67]

82. Baby Jim's Snack Bar, Culpeper, VA. "The Bristol Stomp," recorded by The Dovells (1961), words and music by Kal Mann and Dave Appell. "The kids in Bristol are sharp as a pistol (Chorus) When they do the Bristol Stomp..." [pg. 67]

83. Wellsboro Diner, Wellsboro, PA. [pg. 67]

84. 1 & 3) 81 Irving Pl., New York, NY. 2) 527 W. 110th St., New York, NY. 4) Disney store, 2 Lincoln Square, New York, NY. Gargoyle: from Old French, *gargouille:* throat. [pg. 68]

85. *Mary Worth* was created in 1938 by Allen Saunders and artist Ken Ernst as a replacement for the Depression Era feature *Apple Mary*. It is currently the product of Saunders' son, John, and artist Joe Giella. *Blondie* began its run in 1930, the creation of cartoonist Murat (Chic) Young. There were 28 Blondie & Dagwood movies from 1938 to 1951, starring Penny Singleton and Arthur Lake. The "Dagwood Sandwich" is described by Webster's *New World Dictionary* as "a thick sandwich with a variety of fillings, often of apparently incompatible foods," including such ingredients as peanut butter, avocado, horseradish and a fish. No taco sauce? [pg. 68]

86. The Vladimir Ilyich Lenin (1870-1924) statue is located in Fremont, WA. In 1993, Lewis Carpenter, an Issaquah, WA resident, was teaching in Propad, Slovakia when he discovered a bronze statue of Lenin that had been toppled from the town square and was lying in a city storage yard. Someone had actually been living inside the statue: there was room for a bed, a chair, and bookcase. It was relocated to Fremont in 1995. [pg. 68]

87. On the sidewalk, Melrose Ave., Los Angeles, CA. Comic actress Carol Channing (b. 1923) is best known for her roles in popular Broadway musicals, including *Gentlemen Prefer Blondes* (1949) and *Hello, Dolly* (1963). Channing's distinctive wide-eyes, husky voice and animated persona have inspired countless female impersonators on the international nightclub circuit. [pg. 69]

88. Mr. Ed's Elephant Museum, Orrtanna, PA. [pg. 69]

89. Parking lot, Selinsgrove, PA. [pg. 69]

90. It's Tops Fountain & Coffee Shop, San Francisco, CA. [pg. 70]

91. Carl's Ice Cream, Fredericksburg, VA. [pg. 70]

92. Rep. James Traficant (b. 1941), D-Ohio, was expelled from the U. S. House of Representatives on July 18, 2002, for ethics violations relating to his bribery, racketeering and tax evasion convictions. Said Traficant, "Am I different? Yeah. Deep down, you know you want to wear wider bottoms; you're just not secure enough... Do I do my hair with a Weed Whacker? I admit." The Hair Club For Men was founded in 1976 by Sy Sperling, who is also a client. It has spawned several "answer" organizations, including the No Hair Club For Men and the Chest Hair Club For Men. [pg. 70]

93. "Precious Moments Inspiration Park," Carthage, MO, built in 1989 by creator Samuel Butcher. Precious Moments figurines, spun off the original greeting cards, are small porcelain bisque statuettes of big-eyed, angelic children. The centerpiece of the park is Butcher's life-sized homage to the Sistine Chapel, decorated with cartoon murals and frescoes interpreting the Bible using Precious Moments characters. [pg. 71]

94. Playland Museum, Rye, NY. [pg. 71]

95. Doggie Diner dog heads outside CBGB's Gallery, the Bowery, New York, NY. These three exquisite examples are the property of Doggie aficionado John Law, whose "Laughing Squid" organization sponsored a coast-to-coast Doggie tour in April, 2003. [pg. 71]

96. Wee Kirk O' The Heather Wedding Chapel, Las Vegas, NV. [pg. 72]

97. Zip's Dry Cleaners, Falls Church, VA. "Stinky Poodle" is a 1982 recording by top-ranked American Airlines pilot Tangela Tricoli. Other tunes by this "outsider" artist are "How To Be A Housewife" and "Supermarket Blues." [pg. 72]

98. Twistee Treat, Sarasota, FL. [pg. 72]

99. Surfside Restaurant, Wildwood, NJ. The "Googie" style originated in 1949 with architect John Lautner's "Googie's Coffee Shop" at the corner of Sunset Boulevard and Crescent Heights in Los Angeles, CA. [pg. 73]

100. The Giant Potato, Robertson, New South Wales, Australia. [pg. 73]

101. "Superfoot" spotted near Montreal, Quebec, Canada. [pg. 74]

102. 1 & 2) Muffler Man, Hancock, MA. 3) Cone Lady, Douglas, MA. "I Ain't Got Nobody" was first performed in 1935 by Cab Calloway and his Orchestra, but is most associated with singer/band leader Louis Prima's 1957 recording (combined with "Just a Gigolo"). Finally, both tunes were put to rest by rocker David Lee Roth in 1985. "C'mon-a My House" was a hit for Rosemary Clooney in 1951. [pg. 75]

103. This Muffler Man has been dubbed "The Gemini Giant." He stands guard over Wilmington, IL. [pg. 75]

104. This Desert Storm Muffler Man looms over a gas station in Aberdeen, MD. [pg. 75]

105. 1950s advertising icons: Panel 1.) "Miss Curity" (Curity bandages). Panel 2.) "HIS Man" (HIS cologne). Panel 3.) Munsingwear men's underwear. Panel 4.) "Big D" (Drewry's beer). [pg. 76]

106. *Hollywood Babylon* by Kenneth Anger (first published in 1965) is the original celebrity sleaze "tell-all," detailing the suicides of the stars, among many other tinseltown indiscretions. [pg. 76]

107. Glenmont, MD. [pg. 77]

108. "Happy Buddah" Restaurant, Gainesville, FL. Often mistaken for the Buddha, this figure is actually *HoTai*, a Chinese folk figure and god of good fortune and guardian of children. [pg. 77]

109. Panel 1.) Liverpool, England. Panel 2.) Bowling Green, OH. Panel 3.) San Lin Garden Chinese restaurant, Elkton, MD. Described by the owners as "Milo Fo" Buddha, this may be another case of confusing the folk figure *Ho Tai* (see above) with the Buddha. [pg. 77]

DINERAMA Chapter 5

110A-E. Hillsville Diner, Hillsville, VA. This series is dedicated to *Doonesbury* cartoonist Garry Trudeau's "inker," Don Carlton. [pg. 80-81]

111. Keri's Prospect Diner, Mountville, PA. [pg. 81]

112. Diner, Paradise, PA. Parody of *The Tiger* by William Blake (1757-1827). "Tiger, tiger, burning bright /In the forests of the night /What immortal hand or eye /Could frame thy fearful symmetry?" [pg. 82]

113. White Hut restaurant, Springfield, MA. [pg. 82]

114. Donut Dinette, Norfolk, VA. Zippy is riffing on "ketosis," a bodily function popularized by the low carbohydrate "Atkins Diet." When a large amount of fat is burned, some of the fat fragments - ketones - are excreted to preserve the body's acid-base balance (because ketones are acidic). This process is called "ketosis." [pg. 82]

115. "Food Soda" restaurant, Nashville, TN. [pg. 83]

116. Wildwood Diner, Wildwood, NJ. [pg. 83]

117. 29 Diner, Fairfax, VA. [pg. 83]

118A-B. The original Horn & Hardart restaurant (later to become the Automat in 1902) was founded in 1888 by Joseph Horn and Frank Hardart in Philadelphia. The chain soon spread to New York City and flourished there until the 1960s. Food was dispensed from behind individual windows after depositing the required number of nickels. [pg. 84]

119. Summit Diner, Somerset, PA. *The Mullets*, featuring Loni Anderson, was, indeed, broadcast in the Fall of 2003. (For info on Yanni and Donny, see "THE HOLY TRIFECTA," pg. 39) [pg. 84]

120A-B. Custard Coney Shoppe, Streetsboro, OH. Originally titled "The Lockhorns of Levittown," *The Lockhorns* is a single-panel comic, created in 1968 by cartoonist Bill Hoest and his wife, Bunny. Since the death of her husband in 1988, Bunny Hoest has produced the strip with the help of her assistant, artist John Reiner. [pg. 85]

121. Garfield Diner, Pottsfield, PA. Kenny G was born Kenneth Gorelick in 1959. He changed his name to the snappier version in 1976 when he began his professional career. [pg. 85]

122. "Snuggle," the bear mascot of Snuggle fabric softener is really undergoing an image change. He's shedding his cutesy, teddy bear persona for an "edgier," sexier image. In other news, Unilever Home and Personal Care USA, of Greenwich, Conn., is voluntarily recalling about 4 million plush Snuggle® bears. The eyes and noses of these bears can come off, posing a choking hazard to young children. Undoubtedly part of the new, edgier campaign. [pg. 86]

123. Samuel Pepys (1633-1703), English diarist and naval official. The preferred pronunciation is peeps. The Dodo is an extinct bird of the genera *Raphus* and *Pezophaps*, formerly inhabiting the islands of Mauritius, Reunion and Rodriguez. [pg. 86]

124. A-1 Diner (formerly Heald's Diner), Gardiner, ME. [pg. 86]

125. Hollywood Diner, Dover, DE. Zippy was, indeed, "internally pitched" to Hanna-Barbera (c. 1997, by an employee of the studio) without Griffith's knowledge. Luckily, it went nowhere. [pg. 87]

126. Jiffy Drive-Ins, now defunct, prospered during the 1950s and '60s in the Knoxville, TN area. [pg. 87]

127. Joe's Diner, Taunton, MA. [pg. 87]

128. Nite Owl Diner, Fall River, MA. All Presidential hairdos authentic. [pg. 88]

129. Center Diner, Peekskill, NY. [pg. 88]

130. Three-diner complex, Rockford, MI. [pg. 88]

131. Family Restaurant, Dover, DE. Yes, it's a real Hello Kitty key chain. [pg. 89]

132. Pat's Diner, Salisbury, MA. [pg. 89]

133. Miss Portland Diner, Portland, ME. Zippy's calculation of 2,652,000,000 seconds adds up to 75 years. [pg. 89]

ROADSIDE ATTRACTIONS Chapter 6

34. St. Louis, MO. [pg. 92]

35. Metairie, LA. [pg. 92]

36. Williamson Rd. Service Center, Roanoke, VA. [pg. 92]

37. Hayward, CA. [pg. 93]

38. Big John's Casino, Great Falls, MT. [pg. 93]

39. Westmoreland Tire, Greensburg, PA. [pg. 93]

40. Quebec, Canada. [pg. 94]

41. Reid's Tire, Lamesa TX. The "Muffler Woman," originally the "Uniroyal Tire Lady," was clearly modeled on Jackie Kennedy. [pg. 94]

42. Werbany Tire Town, Gloucester Township, NJ. [pg. 94]

43. "Trees of Mystery", Klamath, CA. [pg. 95]

44. Clear Lake, CA. [pg. 95]

45. Mini-Golf, Rockford, MI. [pg. 95]

46. Outside Denver, CO. [pg. 96]

47. Giant Perogi: Alberta, Canada. Giant Hydrant: Beaumont, TX. [pg. 96]

48. "Home of the Future," Xanadu, Kissimmee, FL. [pg. 96]

49. Sweetheart Cup Co., Augusta, GA. [pg. 97]

50. Wild Blueberry Land, Columbia Falls, ME. [pg. 97]

51. Del Buono's Bakery, Ephraim, NJ. [pg. 97]

52. Enchanted Forest (closed), Ellicott City, MD. [pg. 98]

53. Basketball Hall of Fame, Springfield, MA. [pg. 98]

54. PPG Building, Pittsburgh, PA. [pg. 99]

55. Kecksburg, PA. [pg. 99]

56. Deep River, CT. [pg. 99]

57. "Cupid's Span," San Francisco, CA. Created by Claes Oldenburg and Coosje Van Bruggen. It was a gift to the City from Donald and Doris Fisher, founders of The Gap. [pg. 100]

58. Alma, AR. Popeye made his first public appearance on Jan. 17, 1929, in Elzie Segar's then 10-year-old comic strip, *Thimble Theatre.* Known as "Iron Arm" in Italy, "Karl Alfred" in Sweden and "Skipper Skrœk" or "Terror of the Sea" in Denmark, *Popeye* continues to be syndicated worldwide by King Features. [pg. 100]

59. Panel 1.) Johnson City, TN. Panel 2.) Springdale, AR. Panel 3.) Lebanon, TN. [pg. 100]

60. Hinsdale, MA. [pg. 101]

61. Rip Van Winkle Lanes, Sarasota, FL. [pg. 101]

62. Haddam Neck Fair, CT. [pg. 101]

63. "Happy Chef" restaurant chain. Panel 1.) Mitchell, SD. Panels 2-4.) Moncato, MN. [pg. 102]

64. "Happy Chef" transformed into giant chimney sweep. McPherson, TX. [pg. 102]

65. The Giant Lava Lamp is being seriously considered for construction by the Soap Lake, WA town council. [pg. 102]

66. Grant's Pass, OR. [pg. 103]

67. Park entrance, Los Gatos, CA. [pg. 103]

68. Rockford, MI. [pg. 103]

69. Zippy drives a 1948 Willys "Jeepster." In the front passenger seat is the Cheese Mouse of Black River Falls, WI. [pg. 104]

70. Beaver Self Storage, Lee, MA. [pg. 104]

71. "Kampy" the Squirrel, Salisbury, VT. [pg. 104]

72. Teddy Bear Museum, Orlando, FL. [pg. 105]

73. York, PA. [pg. 105]

74. The Tuileries, near the Louvre, Paris, France. [pg. 105.]

75. Grand Marais, MN. Condoleezza Rice, national security adviser to George W. Bush, born Nov. 14, 1954, in Birmingham, AL. Her hobbies are playing the piano, working out and watching football. [pg. 106]

176. Famous Liquors, Springfield, IL. [pg. 106]

177. New Vrindaban Dhama, near Wheeling, WV. [pg. 106]

178. Beaufort county, SC. [pg. 107]

179. Kissimmee, FL. [pg. 107]

180. Broadway and W. 100th St., New York, NY. [pg. 107]

181. Meow Mix Mobile, spotted in Boston, MA. [pg. 108]

182. Kinvarna, Ireland. [pg. 108]

183. Outside Perry's Nut House, Belfast, ME. [pg. 108]

184. "The Perfect Horse" by Doug Coffin. Santa Fe, NM. [pg. 109]

185. Nodine, MN. [pg. 109]

186A-C. Hi-Boy Sandwiches, Lyndonville, VT. 186B. Finnish translations: Panel 1.) "The men are in the street." Panel 2.) "This book I bought last summer in London." Panel 3.) "We fetched some wood from the forest in the evening." 186C. Dari-Joy, Bellows Falls, VT. See also pg. 60. [pg. 110]

187. Westbrook, ME. [pg. 111]

188A-B. Street advertising icons, Tokyo, Japan. [pg. 111]

189. Enigmatic 3-D versions of the figures from the Grant Wood (1892-1942) painting, *American Gothic* (1930), Oakland, CA. [pg. 112]

190. Outside Excalibur casino, Las Vegas, NV. Quisp is the breakfast cereal made by Quaker Oats. The Quisp himself is an alien from "Planet Q." His official bio describes him as 578 years old, with a girlfriend named Sandy Rosenbaum. [pg. 112]

191A-I. This series is located in the "Neon Boneyard," a repository for old casino and other discarded signage in downtown Las Vegas, NV. 191A. All Shecky Greene factoids and quotes are authentic. [pg. 112-115]

192. The Arcade, New York, New York Casino, Las Vegas, NV. [pg. 115]

193. Miniature golf course, St. Petersburg Beach, FL. [pg. 116]

194. Overland Park, KS. [pg. 116]

195. Blue Earth, MN. [pg. 116]

196. Austin, TX. [pg. 117]

197. Rhyolite, NV. [pg. 117]

198. Orlando, FL. [pg. 118]

199. Promotional balloon for Elvis impersonator Jack Smink, Orlando, FL. All Elvis lyrics authentic. "Do The Clam" was written by Dolores Fuller, wife of movie director Ed Wood (*Plan 9 From Outer Space,* etc.). [pg. 118]

200. Christ of the Ozarks, Eureka Springs, AK. [pg. 119]

201. Dwarf Garden, Ringling Estate, Sarasota, FL. [pg. 119]

202. Daniel Boone, Hillsborough, NC. [pg. 119]

203. Melrose Ave., Los Angeles, CA. [pg. 120]

204. Hayward, CA. [pg. 120]

205. Bust of Arthur Fiedler by Ralph Helmick, Boston, MA. [pg. 120]

206. Santa Fe, NM. [pg. 121]

207. Enhanced "Egghead" sculpture by Robert Arneson, campus of U.C. Davis, CA. [pg. 121]

208. All Paolo Conte quotes are from his actual song lyrics (translated from the Italian). [pg. 121]

209. The Palace amusement center, Asbury Park, NJ. This mural was also featured in the film *Atlantic City* (1981), though its location was implied to be Atlantic City. [pg. 122]

210. Statue of Lou Costello (1906-1959), shorter half of the comedy duo, Abbott and Costello, Paterson, NJ. [pg. 122]

211. Zzyzx, CA, located between the Soda Mountains and Soda Lake, NE of Crucero, CA. The name was made up by the town's founder, Curtis Howe Springer in 1944. Springer was a fundamentalist preacher who sold potions he claimed cured cancer on his daily radio program, broadcast at its peak by on 221 stations nationwide. Syzygy: The configuration of the Sun, the Moon and the Earth lying in a straight line. [pg. 122]

212A-C. Statuary from Precious Moments theme park, Carthage, MO. [pg. 123]

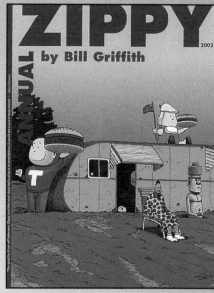